THE CAMBRIDGE COMPANION TO

THE AGE OF ATTILA

Edited by

MICHAEL MAAS

Rice University

CAMBRIDGE
UNIVERSITY PRESS

CAMBRIDGE
UNIVERSITY PRESS

32 Avenue of the Americas, New York NY 10013-2473, USA

Cambridge University Press is part of the University of Cambridge.

It furthers the University's mission by disseminating knowledge in the pursuit of education, learning and research at the highest international levels of excellence.

www.cambridge.org
Information on this title: www.cambridge.org/9781107633889

© Cambridge University Press 2015

First published 2015

A catalogue record for this publication is available from the British Library

Library of Congress Cataloguing in Publication data
The Cambridge companion to the Age of Attila / Michael Maas, Rice University.
pages cm. – (Cambridge companions to the ancient world)
Includes bibliographical references and index.
ISBN 978-1-107-02175-4 (hardcover) – ISBN 978-1-107-63388-9 (pbk.)
1. Attila, –453.   2. Huns – History.   3. Rome – History – Empire, 284–476.   I. Maas,
Michael, 1951– editor, author.   II. Title: Age of Attila.
D141.C36   2014
937'.09–dc23   2014009752

ISBN 978-1-107-02175-4 Hardback

THE CAMBRIDGE COMPANION TO

THE AGE OF ATTILA

This book examines the Age of Attila, roughly the fifth century CE, an era in which western Eurasia experienced significant geopolitical and cultural changes. The Roman Empire collapsed in western Europe, replaced by new "barbarian" kingdoms, but it continued in Christian Byzantine guise in the eastern Mediterranean. New states and peoples changed the face of northern Europe where Rome had never ruled, while in Iran, the Sasanian Empire developed new theories of power and government. At the same time, the great Eurasian steppe became increasingly important in European affairs. This book treats Attila, the notorious king of the Huns, as both an agent of change and a symbol of the wreck of the old world order.

Michael Maas is Professor of History and Classical Studies at Rice University. The focus of his research is late antiquity. His publications include *The Cambridge Companion to the Age of Justinian* (2005); *Exegesis and Empire in the Early Byzantine Mediterranean* (2003); and *Readings in Late Antiquity: A Sourcebook*, second edition (2010).

IN MEMORIAM

THOMAS SIZGORICH

1970–2011

CONTENTS

TEXT FIGURES

List of Maps

CONTRIBUTORS

RA'ANAN BOUSTAN is Associate Professor of History, University of California, Los Angeles.

JONATHAN P. CONANT is Assistant Professor of History, Brown University.

BRIAN CROKE is Adjunct Professor of History, Macquarie University, and Honorary Associate, University of Sydney.

SUSANNA ELM is Professor of History and Classics, University of California, Berkeley.

HUGH ELTON is Professor of Ancient History and Classics, Trent University.

GEOFFREY GREATREX is Professor, Department of Classics and Religious Studies, University of Ottawa.

PETER J. HEATHER is Professor of Medieval European History, King's College, London.

KENNETH G. HOLUM is Professor of History, University of Maryland, College Park.

CAROLINE HUMFRESS is Professor of History, Birkbeck College, University of London.

SCOTT F. JOHNSON is Dumbarton Oaks Teaching Fellow in Byzantine Greek, Georgetown University.

CHRISTOPHER KELLY is a Fellow of Corpus Christi College, Cambridge.

ÉTIENNE DE LA VAISSIÈRE is Professor of Central Asian Medieval History, École des Hautes Études en Sciences Sociales, Paris.

NOEL LENSKI is Associate Professor of Classics, University of Colorado.

MICHAEL MAAS is Professor of History and Classical Studies, Rice University.

MAYA MASKARINEC is a Ph.D. candidate in the History Department, University of California, Los Angeles, and a Fellow in Mediaeval Studies at the American Academy in Rome.

ANDY MERRILLS is Senior Lecturer in Ancient History, University of Leicester.

RICHARD PAYNE is Assistant Professor of Ancient Near Eastern History, The Oriental Institute, University of Chicago.

WALTER POHL is Professor of Medieval History, University of Vienna, and Director of the Institute of Medieval Research at the Austrian Academy of Sciences.

MICHELE RENEE SALZMAN is Professor of History, University of California, Riverside.

JOSEPH E. SANZO is a Postdoctoral Research Fellow in Comparative Religion, Hebrew University of Jerusalem.

PETER SARRIS is Reader in Late Roman, Medieval, and Byzantine History and Fellow of Trinity College, University of Cambridge.

RAYMOND VAN DAM is Professor of History, University of Michigan.

EDWARD WATTS is Professor of History, University of California, San Diego.

SUSAN WESSEL is Associate Professor of Theology and Religious Studies, Catholic University of America.

PREFACE AND
ACKNOWLEDGMENTS

The Age of Attila, which lasted from the late fourth through the early sixth century CE, witnessed manifold changes in western Eurasia. During this transformative era, the peoples and polities of the greater Roman Mediterranean world, northern Europe, the Iranian realm, and the Eurasian steppe itself took new forms and found new voices. Alterations in the geopolitical map across this broad horizon were more than matched by profound internal changes in cultural, religious, economic, and political life. Attila, the king of the Huns who terrified Europe in the middle of the fifth century, stands as an emblem of this turbulent period and gives this volume its title. Although Attila was indisputably a significant figure, this book is not about him or even about the kingdom of the Huns, though their presence is felt throughout the pages that follow. Instead, this volume provides a provocative new overview of the long fifth century, largely from a Roman perspective, by introducing many different vectors of change.

The Cambridge Companion to the Age of Attila is intended for an Anglophone university audience, students and specialists alike. The contributors strove to make their discussions accessible to a more general readership as well. Consequently, English translations of most ancient sources will be found in the bibliography, and secondary sources in other languages have been kept to an essential minimum. At all times, interested readers will be guided to further reading. A chronology of important events mentioned in the volume is found at the beginning of the volume in the Chronology, and thumbnail sketches of the main ancient authors, and modern translations of their works into English, are provided in Selected Ancient Sources.

It is a most pleasant duty to thank colleagues and friends whose encouragement and assistance contributed greatly to the making of this book. Beatrice Rehl, now Director of Publishing, Humanities, at Cambridge University Press deserves pride of place for commissioning the volume as a partner to *The Cambridge Companion to the Age of Constantine* and *The Cambridge Companion to the Age of Justinian*, which are its bookends. She was also a source of limitless calm and practical advice, especially at a time of transition at the Press, as was Asya Graf, Editor, Archaeology and Renaissance Studies, who expertly saw the manuscript through submission and production. I am happy to thank James W. Dunn, Senior Production Editor and Designer at the Press, for bringing the volume to light. I am also most grateful to Maura High, of High Editorial LLC, for editing the manuscript prior to its final submission; to Kate Mertes, of Kate Mertes Editorial Services, for preparing the index; to Ross Twele and the staff at the Ancient World Mapping Center in Chapel Hill, North Carolina, for preparing the maps; and to Lora Wildenthal, Chair of the History Department at Rice University, for granting a subvention for the preparation of the maps from the departmental faculty research fund. Several students at Rice were of great assistance, for which I am most appreciative. Michael Domeracki and Kara van Schilfgaarde helped with a variety of editorial tasks, and Meghan Doherty and Zachary Kingston assisted in the preparation of materials for the maps. Corisande Fenwick, a Postdoctoral Fellow at Brown University, kindly provided a photograph. Maya Maskarinec, a graduate student at the University of California, Los Angeles, and currently a Fellow of the American Academy in Rome, prepared the chronology and the thumbnail sketches of ancient authors and assisted with a variety of other matters as well. Nicola Di Cosmo advised on Central Asian questions. Paula Sanders provided a voice of encouragement throughout. To all of these friends I am most grateful. I owe special thanks to the contributors to this volume for their advice on different matters and for their patience in the preparation of the manuscript, completed in 2013. *The Cambridge Companion to the Age of Attila* is dedicated to the memory of Tom Sizgorich, a fine scholar and wonderful friend, who discussed the book with me in its early stages and was to have contributed a chapter. Tom is greatly missed.

CHRONOLOGY

312	Battle of the Milvian Bridge; conversion of Constantine
325	Council of Nicaea
363	Death of Julian, the last pagan emperor
ca. 370	Huns appear in western steppe
376	Goths cross the Danube into Roman Empire
378	Battle of Adrianople; death of Emperor Valens
382	Settlement of Goths south of the Danube
388	Peace treaty between Persian and Roman Empires
402	Ravenna becomes an imperial residence
405	Radagaisus invades Italy
406	Vandals, Alans, and Sueves cross the Rhine into Roman Empire
410	Sack of Rome by Alaric's Visigoths; end of Roman rule in Britain
412	Theodosian Walls built in Constantinople
418	Settlement of Visigoths in southwestern Gaul
429	End of Jewish Patriarchate; Vandals enter North Africa
431	Council of Ephesus
434	Attila becomes ruler of Huns
438	*Theodosian Code* issued
439	Vandals conquer Carthage
441	Persians invade Roman Empire
441–447	Attila's Huns raid Balkans
451	Council of Chalcedon; Attila invades Gaul and is defeated at the Battle of the Catalaunian Plains
452	Attila invades Italy
453	Death of Attila
455	Vandals sack Rome
468	Expedition from Constantinople against Vandals fails
474	Persian king Peroz captured by Hephthalite Huns
476	Deposition of last western emperor, Romulus Augustulus

476–493	Odovacar rules Italy
481	Clovis becomes king of Franks
484	Hephthalite Huns seize Bactria from Persians
493	Theodoric becomes ruler of Italy
507	Battle of Vouillé; Franks defeat the Visigoths
ca. 507–511	Clovis promulgates Salic Law for the Franks
517	Promulgation of the Burgundian Law Code
527	Justinian becomes Roman emperor

LIST OF ABBREVIATIONS

AB	*Analecta Bollandiana*
ABull	*Art Bulletin*
AHB	*Ancient History Bulletin*
AHR	*American Historical Review*
AJA	*American Journal of Archaeology*
AJAH	*American Journal of Ancient History*
AJN	*American Journal of Numismatics*
AJP	*American Journal of Philology*
AM	*Archéologie Médiévale*
Amm. *Res gest.*	Ammianus Marcellinus, *Res gestae*
AN	*The American Neptune*
An Tard	*Antiquité Tardive*
Anth. Lat.	Anthologia Latina
Anth. Pal.	Anthologia Palatina
Aug. *Ep.*	Augustine, *Epistulae*
AugStud	*Augustinian Studies*
AWE	*Ancient West and East*
BAI	*Bulletin of the Asia Institute*
BEFEO	*Bulletin de l'École Française d'Extrême-Orient*
BICS	*Bulletin of the Institute of Classical Studies*
Blockley	Roger C. Blockley (see *FCH*)
BMGS	*Byzantine and Modern Greek Studies*
BSOAS	*Bulletin of the School of Oriental and African Studies*
ByzSlav	*Byzantinoslavica*
ByzZ	*Byzantinische Zeitschrift*
C&M	*Classica et Mediaevalia*
CAH	*Cambridge Ancient History*
CAJ	*Central Asiatic Journal*
Cass. *Inst.*	Cassiodorus, *Institutiones/Institutes*
CCSL	Corpus Christianorum Series Latina
CFHB	Corpus Fontium Historiae Byzantinae

CH	*Church History*
CIL	Corpus Inscriptionum Latinarum
CJ	*Classical Journal*
Cod. Just.	Codex Justinianus
CPh	*Classical Philology*
CQ	*Classical Quarterly*
CRAI	*Comptes rendus de l'Académie des Inscriptions et Belles-Lettres*
CSCO SS	Corpus Scriptorum Christianorum Orientalium Scriptores Syri
CSEL	Corpus Scriptorum Ecclesiasticorum Latinorum
CSHB	Corpus Scriptorum Historiae Byzantinae
CTh	*Codex Theodosianus*
DA	*Les Dossiers d'archéologie*
Damasc. *Vit. Isid.*	Damascius, *Vita Isidorii*
Dio Cass.	Dio Cassius
DOP	*Dumbarton Oaks Papers*
EHR	*English Historical Review*
EMedE	*Early Medieval Europe*
ETL	*Ephemerides Theologicae Lovanienses*
Eunap. *Hist.*	Eunapius, *Fragmenta* (*FCH*)
Eunap. *Vit. Soph.*	Eunapius, *Vitae Sophistarum*
Evagr. *HE*	Evagrius, *Historia ecclesiastica*
FCH	*The Fragmentary Classicising Historians of the Later Roman Empire: Eunapius, Olympiodorus, Priscus and Malchus*, by Roger C. Blockley, 2 vols. (Liverpool, 1981–1983)
Ferrandus, *Vit. Fulg.*	Ferrandus, *Vita S. Fulgentii episcopi Ruspensi*
GCS	Griechischen christlichen Schriftsteller der ersten drei Jahrhunderte
GRBS	*Greek, Roman, and Byzantine Studies*
Greg. Mag.	Gregorius Magnus, Gregory the Great
HR	*History of Religions*
HTR	*Harvard Theological Review*
Hyd.	Hydatius Lemicensis, *Chronicon*
IG	*Inscriptiones Graecae*
IJNA	*International Journal of Nautical Archaeology*
IM	*Imago Mundi*
JAAR	*Journal of the American Academy of Religion*
JAC	*Journal of Agrarian Change*
JAJ	*Journal of Ancient Judaism*

JAOS	*Journal of the American Oriental Society*
JEA	*Journal of Egyptian Archaeology*
JECS	*Journal of Early Christian Studies*
JEH	*Journal of Ecclesiastical History*
Jer. *Adv. Jud.*	Jerome, *Adversus Judaeos*
Jer. *Ep.*	Jerome, *Epistulae*
JIAA	*Journal of Inner Asian Art and Archaeology*
JLA	*Journal of Late Antiquity*
Joh. Ant., fr.	John of Antioch, *Fragmenta*
Jord. *Get.*	Jordanes, *Getica/History of the Goths*
JRS	*Journal of Roman Studies*
JTS	*Journal of Theological Studies*
Just. *Const. omnem*	Justinian, *Constitutio omnem*
Just. *Inst.*	Justinian, *Institutiones*
Just. *Nov.*	Justinian, *Novellae*
Leo *Ep.*	Leo, *Epistles*
Leo *Serm.*	Leo, *Sermons*
Liban. *Ep.*	Libanius, *Epistolae*
Liban. *Or.*	Libanius, *Orationes*
LRE	*The Later Roman Empire, 284–602: A Social, Economic and Administrative Survey*, by A. H. M. Jones (Oxford, 1964) 3 vols.
Malch. fr.	Malchus, *Fragmenta (FCH)*
Marc. Com.	Marcellinus Comes
Marin. *Vit. Proc.*	Marinus, *Vita Procli*
MedArch	*Mediterranean Archaeology*
MGH AA	Monumenta Germaniae Historica Auctores Antiquissimi
MGH LNG	Monumenta Germaniae Historica Leges Nationum Germanicarum
MGH SRM	Monumenta Germaniae Historica Scriptores Rerum Merovingicarum
MHR	*Mediterranean Historical Review*
MRDTB	*Memoirs of the Research Department of the Toyo Bunko*
Nov. Theod.	Theodosius II, *Novellae*
Nov. Val.	Valentinian III, *Novellae*
NPNF	Select Library of Nicene and Post-Nicene Fathers of the Christian Church
Olymp. fr.	Olympiodorus of Thebes, *Fragmenta (FCH)*

Olymp. *In Alc.*	Olympiodorus of Alexandria, *In Platonis Alcibiadem*
Oros.	Orosius
P&P	*Past and Present*
Par. Gr.	Codex Parisinus Graecus
PBSR	*Papers of the British School at Rome*
PFlor	Papyrus, Florence
PG	Patrologia Graeca
PGiess	Papyrus, Giessen
Philostorg. *Hist. eccl.*	Philostorgius, *Historia Ecclesiastica*
Philostrat. *VS*	Philostratus, *Vitae Sophistarum*
PL	Patrologia Latina
PLips.	Papyrus, Leipzig
PLRE	*The Prosopography of the Later Roman Empire, 260–395*, ed. A. H. M. Jones, John R. Martindale, and John Morris, 3 vols. (Cambridge, 1971–1992)
PO	Patrologia Orientalis
POxy	Papyrus Oxyrhynchus
Prisc. fr. (Blockley)	Priscus of Panium, *Fragmenta (FCH)*
Proc. *BV*	Procopius, *De bello vandalico*
Prosp.	Prosper of Aquitaine
REArm	*Revue des Études Arméniennes*
RSO	*Rivista degli Studi Orientali*
Sal. *Ad eccl.*	Salvian of Marseille, *Ad ecclesiam*
Sal. *De gub. Dei*	Salvian of Marseille, *De gubernatione Dei*
SC	Sources Chrétiennes
SemClas	*Semitica et Classica*
Sid. Ap. *Ep.*	Sidonius Apollinarus, *Epistulae*
Soc. *Hist. eccl.*	Socrates Scholasticus, *Historia ecclesiastica*
Soz. *Hist. eccl.*	Sozomen, *Historia ecclesiastica*
SP	*Studia Patristica*
StIr	*Studia Iranica*
Syn. *Ep.*	Synesius of Cyrene, *Epistulae*
T&MBYZ	*Travaux et Mémoires du Centre de recherches d'hist. et civil. byzantines*
TAPhA	*Transactions of the American Philological Association*
Theod. *Ep.*	Theodoret, *Epistulae*
Theophan.	Theophanes
TRHS	*Transactions of the Royal Historical Society*
VChr	*Vigiliae Christianae*
Vict. Vit.	Victor of Vita

YClS	*Yale Classical Studies*
ZAC	*Zeitschrift für Antikes Christentum*
Zach. *Ammon.*	Zacharias Scholasticus, *Ammonius*
Zach. *Vit. Sev.*	Zacharias Scholasticus, *Vita Severi Antiocheni*
ZDMG	*Zeitschrift der deutschen morgenländischen Gesellschaft*
Zos.	Zosimus
ZRGG	*Zeitschrift für Religions und Geistesgeschichte*

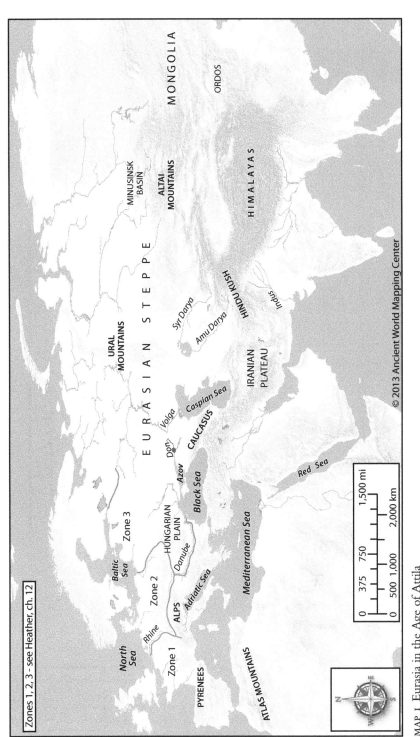

Zones 1, 2, 3 - see Heather, ch. 12

MAP 1 Eurasia in the Age of Attila

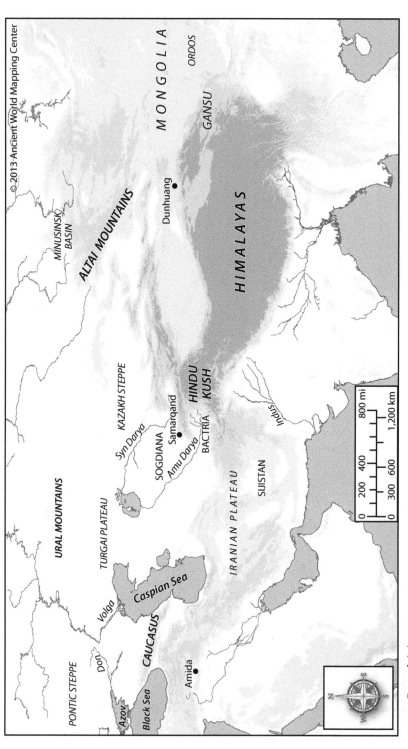

MAP 2 Central Asia

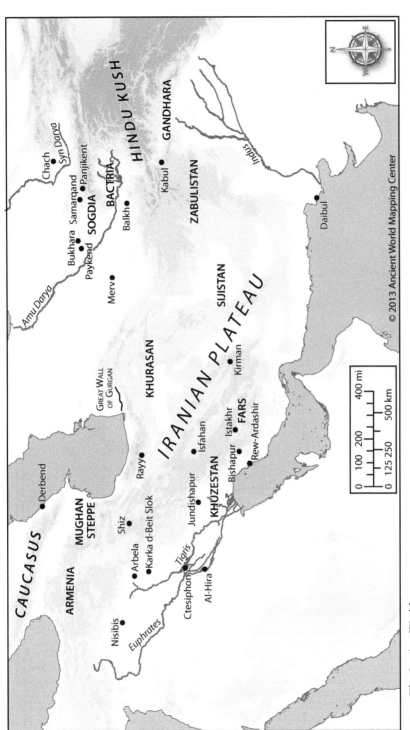

MAP 3 The Iranian World

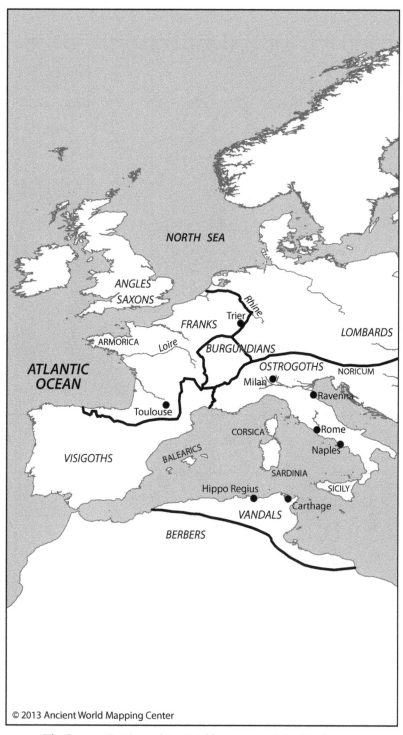

NORTH SEA

ANGLES
SAXONS

FRANKS

Rhine

Trier

ARMORICA

Loire

BURGUNDIANS

LOMBARDS

ATLANTIC
OCEAN

OSTROGOTHS

NORICUM

Milan

Ravenna

Toulouse

CORSICA

Rome

VISIGOTHS

BALEARICS

Naples

SARDINIA

SICILY

Hippo Regius

VANDALS

Carthage

BERBERS

© 2013 Ancient World Mapping Center

MAP 4a The Roman Empire and Its Neighbors ca. 510 (The West)

MAP 4b The Roman Empire and Its Neighbors ca. 510 (The East)

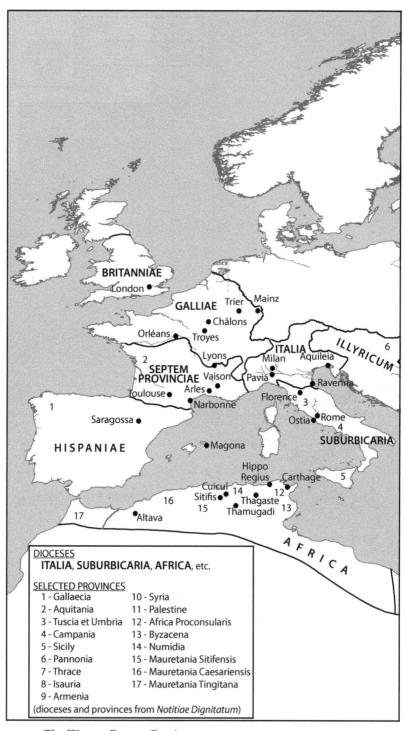

BRITANNIAE
London

GALLIAE Trier Mainz
Châlons
Orléans Troyes
Lyons ITALIA ILLYRICUM
SEPTEM Milan Aquileia
PROVINCIAE Vaison Pavia
Toulouse Arles Ravenna
Narbonne Florence 3
Saragossa Ostia Rome
4
HISPANIAE Magona SUBURBICARIA

Hippo
Regius Carthage 5
Cuicul 14
Sitifis Thagaste 12
15 Thamugadi 13
Altava 16
17

AFRICA

DIOCESES
ITALIA, SUBURBICARIA, AFRICA, etc.

SELECTED PROVINCES
1 - Gallaecia   10 - Syria
2 - Aquitania   11 - Palestine
3 - Tuscia et Umbria 12 - Africa Proconsularis
4 - Campania   13 - Byzacena
5 - Sicily   14 - Numidia
6 - Pannonia   15 - Mauretania Sitifensis
7 - Thrace   16 - Mauretania Caesariensis
8 - Isauria   17 - Mauretania Tingitana
9 - Armenia
(dioceses and provinces from *Notitiae Dignitatum*)

MAP 5a The Western Roman Empire ca. 400

MAP 5b The Eastern Roman Empire ca. 400

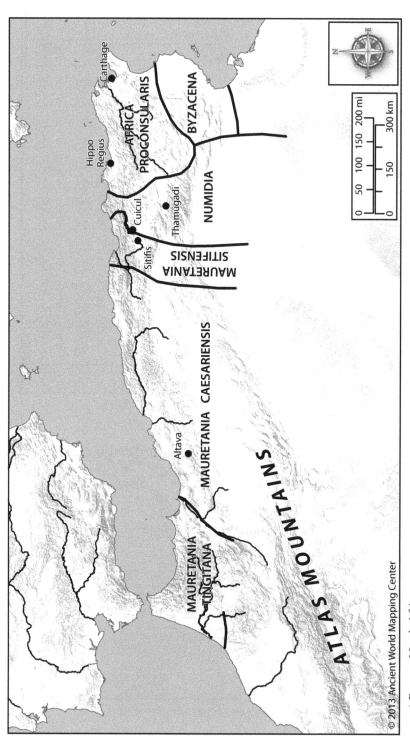

MAP 6 Roman North Africa ca. 400

© 2013 Ancient World Mapping Center

PART I

THE ROMAN EMPIRE

1: Reversals of Fortune: An Overview of the Age of Attila

Michael Maas

Attila's Painting

A story was told in antiquity that when Attila the Hun captured Milan in 452, he noticed a painting – perhaps decorating a public building – that showed the eastern and western Roman emperors on golden thrones with steppe nomads lying dead at their feet. The infuriated Hun king immediately summoned an artist to render a counterimage: in the new painting *he* would be the man on the throne while servile Roman emperors poured gold coins before him from leather money bags. In a triumphant mood, Attila was rejecting old stereotypes of nomad inferiority and boasting of the enormous treasure he had extorted from the Roman government.[1] Attila's painting, if it ever existed, would have been a scandalous outrage to a Roman viewer, and that is precisely what the Roman writer who described this episode wanted to convey.[2] He meant to shock his readers with an intimation of a world in which Roman claims of universal victory were successfully challenged and mocked by an uncivilized Hun.

Attila and the Huns left a deep stamp on European history. From 434 until his death in 453, the "Scourge of God" controlled a vast domain in central Europe and the western Eurasian steppe, from which the Huns had entered the European consciousness nearly a century

---

[1] The annual payment reached 2,100 pounds of gold per year. See Christopher Kelly, chapter 11 in this volume.

[2] *Suidae Lexicon*, ed. Ada Adler (1928, repr. Leipzig, 2001–2004); Suda On Line: http://www.stoa.org/sol/. The entry is κ 2123, for "kôrukos," leather sack. The source of the entry is not named. It could be from Priscus of Panium.

earlier. For a generation, his army of Huns and subject peoples assaulted the eastern Roman Empire, alternately coercing huge sums of cash and causing enormous destruction. During the last three years of his life, Attila campaigned in western Europe. When his momentum stopped after a great battle in Gaul in 451, he pulled back to Italy, where he fought with mixed results until his death. Attila's name came to resonate grandly in medieval legend,[3] and today he and his Hunnic armies still stand for violence and aggression. They were, however, only part of a much bigger and even more colorful story.

This book uses Attila to represent a world that was changing far more profoundly than the author of the anecdote above could have imagined. The *Companion to the Age of Attila* introduces readers to a long period stretching from the latter half of the fourth century, when Huns first appeared in the west Eurasian steppe and the Roman Empire still stretched from the Atlantic Ocean to the Black Sea, to the beginning of the sixth century, by which time Attila was yesterday's news and the Roman state based at Constantinople had become a regional power in the eastern Mediterranean, though it was still the strongest kingdom in Europe. Attila gives his name to the age, not because he was its prime mover or even because of the terrifying legacy he left in the European imagination, but because of the deep-seated transformations that he represents and that this book explores.

To help visualize the scope of the complex story of the Age of Attila, it is helpful to think of four interlocking geopolitical zones, each a composite with its own long history of local traditions, economies, political communities, and varieties of religious expression. These zones were (1) the Eurasian Steppe, a corridor of grasslands and desert that stretched from the Hungarian Plain to the Gobi Desert,[4] impeded only in part by the arc of the Carpathian Mountains;[5] (2) Sasanian Persia, which controlled the Iranian plateau, shared the Near Eastern culture area with Rome and reached the fringes of the Eurasian steppe north of the Caucasus range; (3) the lands of northern Europe that had never been included in the Roman state, bounded roughly

---

[3] Franz H. Bäuml and Marianna D. Birnbaum, eds., *Attila: The Man and His Image* (Budapest, 1993).

[4] Mark Whittow, "Geographical Survey," in *The Oxford Handbook of Byzantine Studies*, ed. Elizabeth Jeffreys, with John Haldon and Robin Cormack (Oxford, 2008) 219–231; Étienne de la Vaissière, "Central Asia and the Silk Road," in *The Oxford Handbook of Late Antiquity*, ed. Scott F. Johnson (Oxford, 2012) 142–169, here 142–144.

[5] Roger Batty, *Rome and the Nomads: The Pontic and Danubian Realm in Antiquity* (Oxford, 2007) 89–94.

by the Atlantic Ocean, the Rhine and Danube Rivers, and the great forests beyond eastern Europe;[6] and (4) the Roman Empire, based in the Mediterranean but controlling lands from Britain to the Red Sea. Rome receives the lion's share of attention in the chapters ahead. (map 1).

During the Age of Attila, the inhabitants of these zones came to interact differently with one another, while internally they experienced radical discontinuities as well as transmutations of far older cultural and political practices. This developmental aspect of the Age of Attila should be stressed. Despite all its violence and destruction, the period under discussion here, the "long" fifth century, should be seen as a time of unexpected growth, a threshold era that was as much witness to the emergence of the medieval world as it was to the end of so much of the classical age. This introductory chapter considers the four zones in turn, beginning with the Eurasian Steppe that produced the Huns.

ZONE I: THE EURASIAN STEPPE

For Roman writers of the imperial period, the Eurasian steppe was synonymous with frostbite and savagery, but historians today understand the steppe quite differently. Its populations were more than able to generate their own quite sophisticated political and social formations without dependence on outlying empires, and they were not at all stuck in a rut of primitive life as was once believed. Although quite diverse culturally and linguistically, they shared certain traits of herding, trading, and fighting across the steppe's enormous expanse.[7] The nomads often lived in peaceful, complex synergy with nearby agricultural and commercial communities,[8] and they also benefited from long-distance trade.[9] In addition to caring for their herds, raiding the settled lands to acquire loot and livestock became regular practice among them.[10] Mounted warrior elites noted for their ferocity and high degree of mobility across the steppe directed affairs through elaborate networks of authority and dependence.

---

[6] See Peter J. Heather, chapter 12 in this volume.

[7] Nicola Di Cosmo, *Ancient China and Its Enemies* (Cambridge, 2002) 42–43; Peter B. Golden, *Central Asia in World History* (Oxford, 2011) 9–20, for introductory survey.

[8] Golden, *Central Asia*, 11.

[9] Xinriu Liu, *The Silk Road in World History* (Oxford, 2010) 63; Golden, *Central Asia*, 16–17.

[10] Golden, *Central Asia*, 16.

The Age of Attila marked an important phase in the long history of the steppe and the great empires surrounding it.[11] Although peoples originating in the Eurasian Steppe had fought ferociously with Rome on the Danube frontier in earlier centuries, it was only with the arrival of the Huns that the steppe as the seat of nomad empires became a permanent presence in Roman political calculations, especially for the eastern Roman Empire that confronted steppe peoples on the Danube frontier.[12] The steppe would remain a point of departure for Avars, Turks, and many other implacable enemies in the centuries to come.

The canvas gets even larger. Rome's greatest rival, Sasanian Persia, endured profound internal readjustments in response to the kingdoms of the Hephthalite, Chionite, and Kidarite Huns (not connected to Attila's domain) on their northeastern frontier.[13] Much farther afield, the Gupta empire in northern India became deeply preoccupied with the Hephthalites,[14] while China, temporarily in a state of political disunion, fought with other groups from the steppe as well.[15] This volume focuses on the kaleidoscopic alterations in the political, religious, and social landscape "only" from the Atlantic to the western steppe. Nevertheless, we can say that over an even greater area, the Age of Attila inaugurated a new order in world affairs.

The Arrival of the Huns

Bands of Huns reached the western Eurasian steppe in the second half of the fourth century, around 370, perhaps driven in part by climate

---

[11] The steppe has been inhabited by modern humans for nearly fifty thousand years, but pastoral nomadism only emerged after a long and piecemeal development about 1200 BCE; Di Cosmo, *Ancient China and Its Enemies*, 13–42, surveys theories.

[12] Dennis Sinor, "The Hun period," in *The Cambridge History of Early Inner Asia*, ed. Dennis Sinor (Cambridge, 1990) 177–205; Roger Batty, *Rome and the Nomads*, 347–456.

[13] Frantz Grenet, "Regional Interaction in Central Asia and Northwest India in the Kidarite and Hephthalite periods," in *Indo-Iranian Languages and Peoples*, ed. Nicholas Sims-Williams, *Proceedings of the British Academy* 116 (Oxford, 2002) 203–224; on divisions of the Huns, Mark Ščukin, Michel Kazanski, and Oleg Sharev, *Des les Goths aux Huns: Le nord de la Mer Noire au Bas-empire et a l'epoque des grandes migrations*, British Archaeological Reports International Series 1535 (Oxford, 2006) 111.

[14] Richard N. Frye, *The Heritage of Central Asia: From Antiquity to the Turkish Expansion* (Princeton, 1998) 177–178.

[15] Mark E. Lewis, *China between Empires: The Northern and Southern Dynasties* (Cambridge, Mass., 2009) 144–151.

changes in their Central Asian homelands.[16] Their arrival on the western side of the Volga River changed the political landscape of the western steppe in a dramatic fashion. Some scholars believe that to some extent they brought with them political and cultural attachments to the defunct Xiongnu empire (ca. 200 BCE to 100 CE) on the northwest Chinese frontier, credited as being the first nomad empire [LA VAISSIÈRE].[17] As they crossed the steppe, their ranks were increased by defeated tribes and other groups that willingly joined them, as regularly happened on the steppe.[18]

Initially, Huns came in separate groups, with different names and leadership traditions, and they settled over a very wide area.[19] Within a century, however, their elites controlled all of the steppe and its indigenous peoples between Hungary and the Urals, although they were never unified under one ruler (maps 1 and 2).[20] Kidarites, Chionites, and Hephthalites in turn established their kingdoms northeast of Iran, while "European" Huns moved further west, basing themselves first in the Pontic-Danubian region[21] and then on the Hungarian Plain. Their arrival was a calamity for the western steppe's other nomadic peoples as well as for its settled populations, most importantly Gothic kingdoms that had been established between the Danube Basin and the Black Sea for several generations.[22] Much of the Gothic population fled west from the Huns and sought refuge across the Danube in the Roman Empire, instigating a cascade of events that led to the disastrous battle of Adrianople in 378 (see below) and the eventual settlement of Goths

---

[16] La Vaissière, "Central Asia and the Silk Road," 144–147.

[17] Nicola Di Cosmo, "Ethnogenesis, Coevolution and Political Morphology of the Earliest Steppe Empire: The Xiongnu Question Revisited," in *Xiongnu Archaeology: Multidisciplinary Perspectives of the First Steppe Empire in Inner Asia*, ed. Ursula Brosseder and Bryan K. Miller (Bonn, 2011) 35–48.

[18] Golden, *Central Asia*, 15–17.

[19] Étienne de la Vaissière, chapter 10 in this volume; Frye, *The Heritage of Central Asia*, 169–170.

[20] See Richard Payne, chapter 16 in this volume; Ščukin, Kazanski, and Sharev, *Des les Goths aux Huns*, 111.

[21] Batty, *Rome and the Nomads*, 2, calls this region "a zone of interaction" rather than a place with strict territorial boundaries.

[22] Peter J. Heather, "The Huns and the End of the Roman Empire in Western Europe," *English Historical Review* 110 (1995) 4–41; Peter J. Heather, *The Goths* (Oxford, 1996); Marina G. Moshkova, "A Brief Review of the History of the Sauromatian and Sarmatian Tribes," in *Nomads of the Eurasian Steppes in the Early Iron Age*, ed. Jeannine Davis-Kimball, Vladimir A. Bashilov, and Leonid T. Yablonsky (Berkeley, 1995) 87.

within the empire.[23] Some Alans, who were a nomadic people in the region, also fled further west, but many of them, as well as Goths and others, remained under Hun dominance.[24]

Huns based in the Pontic Steppe soon attacked the Middle East. In 395–396, war bands, perhaps driven by famine, crossed the Caucasus Mountains and raided in force into Armenia, Syria, Palestine, and northern Mesopotamia. They took slaves, cattle, and other movable goods back to the steppe.[25] At the same time, Huns in Europe hired out as armies in the service of Rome on various occasions, sometimes in considerable number.[26] In this way they played a significant role in Roman political affairs. An indication of scale (probably the high end) is given by the perhaps sixty thousand Huns employed as auxiliaries by the western general Aetius in 425 for service in a revolt against emperor Theodosius II.[27]

By the early years of the fifth century, the western Huns coalesced into a more unified confederation under the leadership of Rua.[28] He invaded Thrace in 422 from his base on the Hungarian Plain (the westernmost extension of the Eurasian Steppe) and extorted from the Roman government an annual payment of 350 pounds of gold, setting a precedent for relations with Constantinople. After his death in 433, his nephews Bleda and Attila assumed leadership of the Huns of the west.[29] They began a more aggressive policy toward Rome, and in 435, they negotiated a new treaty which doubled their annual subsidy from Constantinople. This brought five years of peace, but in 441, Attila attacked again. Negotiation, extortion, and extreme levels of violence marked his interactions with Roman authorities as well as with his own subjects [KELLY]. He forbade any movement of people out of his empire and insisted that Romans return all fugitives to be punished [POHL].[30]

---

[23] Ammianus Marcellinus, *Res gestae*, ed. and trans. John C. Rolfe (Cambridge, Mass., 1935) book 31.

[24] Roger Batty, *Rome and the Nomads*, 368–374; Moshkova, "Brief Review," 88–89; on Alans: Agustí Alemany, *Sources on the Alans: A Critical Compilation* (Leiden, 2000), and Bernard S. Bachrach, *A History of the Alans in the West: From Their First Appearance in the Sources of Classical Antiquity through the Early Middle Ages* (Minneapolis, 1973).

[25] Dennis Sinor, "The Hun Period," in Sinor, *The Cambridge History of Early Inner Asia*, 177–205, here 182–184.

[26] Hyun Jin Kim, *The Huns, Rome, and the Birth of Europe* (Cambridge, 2013).

[27] Aetius changed sides at the last minute and sent the Huns home after paying them.

[28] Heather, "Huns and the End of the Roman Empire," 14–17.

[29] Attila ruled with his brother Bleda from 434 to 445, and alone from 445 to 453.

[30] Andreas Schwarcz, "Relations between Ostrogoths and Visigoths in the Fifth and Sixth Centuries and the Question of Visigothic Settlement in Aquitaine and Spain,"

At its greatest extent, Attila's realm stretched from the Volga to central Gaul. Hun influence may have reached as far north as the Baltic Sea as well.[31] This was the first steppe-based empire of such a size to have an impact on European events.

Attila's rule and his influence on the Roman Empire and neighboring lands are evaluated in detail in various chapters within this book. Some paradoxes may be pointed out here. On the one hand, Attila never established a state on Roman territory or even won a major battle against Roman forces [KELLY, HEATHER]. On the other hand, the indirect effects of the Huns on the Roman Empire were quite significant. As the following chapters describe, the destabilizing presence of the Huns contributed to imperial economic weakness and inability to retake lost western territories for financial and strategic reasons. Huns played a role, although scholars debate the extent, in pushing various barbarian groups into the empire [KELLY, HEATHER]. They had considerable influence on other zones as well. In northern Europe, they helped create an environment that contributed to the rise of the Slavs [HEATHER]. Further to the east, Iran's Hunnic neighbors forced changes in Sasanian political ideology and cosmology [PAYNE].

How did the steppe itself change during the Age of Attila? Several points may be made. First of all, Huns brought new ethnic elements with them when they crossed the Volga and entered European history.[32] The doors to populations from further east would remain open, most immediately for Avars and Turks who would dominate the western steppe from the late sixth century.[33] Through their conflicts with Rome and Persia, and the accompanying financial extortion and diplomatic interaction, these peoples of the steppe gained experience – and heightened expectations – of dealing with the rich settled empires. Perhaps most significant were the consequences for trade and economy.

in *Integration and Authority in the Early Middle Ages*, ed. Walter Pohl and Max Diesenberger (Vienna, 2002) 217–226, here, 223.

[31] Priscus, fr. 8, ed. Roger C. Blockley, in *The Fragmentary Classicising Historians of the Later Roman Empire: Eunapius, Olympiodorus, Priscus and Malchus*, 2 vols. (Liverpool, 1981–1983); Priscus Panita, *Excerpta et Fragmenta*, ed. Pia Carolla (Berlin, 2008) 51. Some influences were seen in Sweden: Ščukin, Kazanski, and Sharev, *Des les Goths aux Huns*, 116 on extent of the empire, and 111 for Roman sources.

[32] Peter B. Golden, "The Peoples of the South Russian Steppes," in Sinor, *The Cambridge History of Early Inner Asia*, 256–284, here 256–258.

[33] Samuel Szádeczky-Kardoss, "The Avars," in Sinor, *The Cambridge History of Early Inner Asia*, 206–228, here 206–207, Walter Pohl, *Die Awaren: Ein Steppenvolk in Mitteleuropa* (Munich, 1988) 567–822.

The once-rich kingdom of Bactria suffered terribly in the wars between the Hunnic nomads and the forces of Sasanian Persia, remaining largely depopulated until the sixth century. As a result, trade routes – collectively known as the Silk Road – shifted north into Sogdia, which prospered greatly. Nomadic elites made Sogdian towns centers of wealth in Central Asia that would dominate trade across Central Asia until the rise of the Muslim Caliphate in the mid-eighth century.[34] [LA VAISSIÈRE]. It was along these trading networks that Christian missionaries traveled east from the late fifth century, bringing their Nestorian beliefs to Central Asia and China. At the same time Buddhists journeyed west from China but did not reach Europe.[35]

ZONE 2: SASANIAN PERSIA

The Sasanian dynasty, which rose to power in Iran in 224 and created an empire that lasted until the Arab conquest in 651, had many borders to defend during the Age of Attila (map 3). On its western flank it confronted Rome's eastern provinces across the Mesopotamian Plain, and it struggled with Rome for the Caucasus region, particularly for Armenia.[36] On its southwest border lay northern Arabia, the Persian Gulf, and a portion of the Indian Ocean. Control of these regions enabled seaborne trade with India. To the east lay the Gupta Empire, with which Sasanian Iran maintained diplomatic relations and conducted extensive trade.

The most perilous frontier for Persia, however, was the one shared with the steppe. Passes through the Caucasus Mountains provided an avenue for nomad raiders. More significant was the border north and east of the Caspian Sea, where Iran abutted Central Asia and the disputed lands of Transoxiana. In the late fourth century, Sasanian monarchs fought wars on this frontier with Chionite Huns and in the first half of the fifth century with Kidarite Huns. The rise of the Hephthalite kingdom and its seizure of the rich trading kingdom of Sogdia after the middle of the century put Sasanian monarchs on the defensive. Caught in a Hephthalite trap while campaigning on the steppe, the Persian monarch Peroz died in battle in 484. Subsequently, Hephthalite rulers

---

[34] La Vaissière, "Central Asia and the Silk Road," 146–148; Étienne de la Vaissière, *Sogdian Traders: A History*, trans. James Ward (Leiden, 2005) 95–107.
[35] Joel Walker, "From Nisibis to Xi'an: The Church of the East in Late Antique Eurasia," in Johnson, *The Oxford Handbook of Late Antiquity*, 994–1052.
[36] This disputed region rebelled against Persia in 451 and 482.

interfered in royal Sasanian dynastic politics, and they helped Kavad, who had married into the Hephthalite royal family, regain the Persian throne in 498.[37]

Interacting with these Hunnic kingdoms profoundly affected the Sasanian political system. In the face of defeat, humiliation, and loss of territory, the Sasanian regime reinvented itself, creating a new ideology of empire based on historical legends and Zoroastrian teachings. (The emergence of this new conceptual system roughly parallels the transformation of Rome into a Christian-Roman polity.) The Sasanian monarch held paramount authority, but his power depended on finding consensus among the great aristocratic clans of Iran. Aristocratic involvement in the new imperial ideology proved critical for its success [PAYNE].

Rome and Persia enjoyed peaceful relations through most of the Age of Attila, but they fought a cold war in North Arabia and southern Iraq through their Arab proxies. The Ghassanid federation led by the Jafnid clan fought for Rome, while the Lakhmid tribes led by the Nasrids took the Persian side. At stake in this competition was control of the highly lucrative trade coming from farther east.[38]

ZONE 3: NORTHERN EUROPE (BARBARICUM)

Romans designated all of the lands in northern Europe that they had not conquered as "Barbaricum." This derogatory term suggested a clear distinction between their own civilized realm and the lands beyond. Reality offered no such obvious absolute differences. Roman defensive fortifications and system of alliances and accommodations with client kings on the other side were intended to protect the Roman provinces by keeping out invaders, but the border had never been impermeable. Traders, slavers, and artisans went back and forth quite often, as did settlers who had imperial permission to enter Roman territory. For centuries, recruits from the north had joined Roman armies in different capacities, and when their enlistment ended, many returned to their homes across the highly militarized frontier.

---

[37] Michael Maas, "The Equality of Empires: Procopius on Adoption and Guardianship across Imperial Borders," in *Motions of Late Antiquity: Religion, Politics and Society from Constantine to Charlemagne. Essays in Honour of Peter Brown*, ed. Jamie Kreiner and Helmut Reimitz (Turnhout, 2015); Frye, *Heritage of Central Asia*, 177–179.

[38] Irfan Shahîd, *Byzantium and the Arabs in the Fifth Century* (Washington, D.C., 1989) esp. 22–24.

In his chapter, Peter Heather describes barbarian Europe as comprising three parallel regions. The westernmost part, consisting of Gaul and some lands just east of the Rhine, had largely been absorbed by Rome and was the most developed. The second region, which included Central Europe as far as the Vistula in modern Poland, was home to large-scale and powerful political units, known to Romans as warlike tribes and confederacies. Large numbers of people emigrated into the Roman Empire from this region, the notorious "barbarian invaders" of the fifth century, and, after the Huns left the scene, various small kingdoms emerged there, created by groups that had been components of the Hunnic empire. In the third region, which was the least developed materially, the Slavic inhabitants began to emerge in new political configurations once older Germanic power elites, and the Huns themselves, were dispersed [HEATHER]. The archaeologist Simon Esmonde Cleary has noted many changes in the western region and suggested that 500 CE may represent an archaeological threshold.[39] Heather also points out significant changes in the central and easternmost regions of barbarian Europe by the same approximate date, linking these developments to the presence of the Huns. By the end of the Age of Attila, a new era had begun for Northern Europe.[40]

ZONE 4: THE ROMAN EMPIRE

Until the Age of Attila, the Roman Empire for the most part remained strong and intact, generally able to maintain the loyalty of its military and administrative cadres, keep its peasants and slaves under control, repel attackers, absorb newcomers, and when necessary adjust its internal government structures to meet compelling circumstances. Just as brutal as any enemy but far better organized, the Roman state could marshal unmatchable resources of manpower and supplies to keep its population of perhaps fifty million people secure – most of the time. This resilience became evident in the third century when the empire faltered due to civil war, invasion, and economic crisis. In response, the emperor Diocletian (r. 284–305), building on the work of his immediate

---

[39] Simon Esmonde Cleary, *The Roman West, AD 200–500: An Archaeological Study* (Cambridge, 2013) 466–482.
[40] For an overview, Walter Pohl, "Rome and the Barbarians in the Fifth Century," *Antiquité Tardive* 16 (2008) 93–101.

predecessors, enacted far-reaching military, economic, and administrative reforms that enabled the following century to be a time of security and prosperity.[41] From 324 Constantinople (the "New Rome") and Ravenna from 402 served as the hubs from which power flowed to all the empire's lesser cities with their dependent agricultural territories. Networks of aristocratic power and patronage anchored in the cities extended throughout imperial territories. These great imperial capitals generated sufficient centripetal power to hold the disparate elements of the empire together under firm administrative control. Above all, no one could ever forget that Rome's great armies, and the terrible force they could wield, provided the tightest bonds of all.

During the course of the Age of Attila, however, the entire empire endured tremendous shocks. The ties that for centuries had drawn its varied populations together yielded to centrifugal forces of political, cultural, and religious fragmentation, most notably in the western European provinces that spun off from Roman control. The eastern portion of the empire weathered the storm, but for the western empire there would be no recovery.

In the West. In the western part of the Roman Empire, centuries-old political bands dissolved, and all of the provinces, from Britain to North Africa, including the Italian homeland, with their manpower and revenues, gradually fell from imperial control.[42] Under a cascade of invasions, usurpations, and vicious civil war, imperial authority caved in, although its supporters put up a vigorous fight. While Roman authority diminished, smaller, more distinct regions split from its core, each deploying its Roman inheritance somewhat differently.[43] Thus, what had been a coherent Roman Empire in the fourth century underwent a process of re-regionalization in which new political structures, new formulations of self-interest, new forms of cultural and religious expression, and new identities emerged, all of them displaying both continuity and innovation.[44]

New kingdoms eventually took shape in Rome's old western territories, sometimes through conquest (as with the Angles and Saxons in

---

[41] Averil Cameron, *The Later Roman Empire* (Cambridge, Mass., 1993) 30–46.

[42] Peter Brown calls it a "return to normal in the long term history of western Europe," in Peter Brown, *The Rise of Western Christendom: Triumph and Diversity*, A.D. 200–1000, 2nd ed. (Oxford, 2003) 96.

[43] Chris Wickham, *Framing the Middle Ages: Europe and the Mediterranean, 400–800* (Oxford, 2005) 10.

[44] Michael Kulikowski, "The Western Kingdoms," in Johnson, *The Oxford Handbook of Late Antiquity*, 31–59.

Britain after 410) or negotiation with the government (as with the Visigoths in Aquitania in 417). Except in Britain, all the nascent states built extensively on Roman foundations and with heavy Roman involvement. Provincial Romans had to learn to live without the empire. While adjusting to new management they had to make choices about what aspects of Roman life to hang on to and what it even meant to be Roman. Solutions differed, but throughout the century being Roman provided a widespread sense of unity [CONANT].

By 500, the western provinces were entirely lost to the empire (map 4a and b). A look at the map in the early sixth century shows the kingdom of the Franks dominant north of the Alps, the Visigoths masters of Spain, Vandals controlling North Africa, Britain in the hands of Angles and Saxons, and Italy ruled by an Ostrogothic monarch. We should not imagine, however, as many historians of earlier times have done, that an unstoppable wave of distinct barbarian tribes systematically pried the provinces from Roman control simply by brute force. That would be a great oversimplification. Although all of these "tribal" groups bore ethnic names that reflected some shared ideas about their collective identity, they also included hardened soldiers drawn from many backgrounds. The chapters that follow explore a very complex political and social environment in the west, of which the movement of militarized barbarian groups into the empire was only one vector of change.

No single cause for the disintegration of the empire in the west can be isolated, though we can watch five linchpins of empire corrode and snap in the course of our period. In previous centuries, they had held the wheels on the imperial wagon; without them the imperial enterprise skidded and crashed.

Control of the army. During the fifth century, imperial authorities gradually lost control of the armed forces, a process that left the borders permeable and internal government precarious.

The tax system. The tax system that could support the state's military and administrative apparatus fell apart. The destruction caused by invasions, chronic civil war, and the rupture of links between the imperial administration and local aristocrats caused its breakdown. In some of the successor kingdoms, however, the new rulers made attempts to keep the tax system running, but of course kept the revenues for themselves.[45]

---

[45] Peter Brown, *Through the Eye of a Needle. Wealth: The Fall of Rome, and the Making of Christianity in the West, 350–550 AD* (Princeton, 2012) 389.

Recruitment. Owing in part to the steady loss of revenues and to the reluctance of great landowners in the West to release their tenants for military service, the Roman system of internal military recruitment broke down, and Roman authorities found it increasingly difficult to find Roman soldiers to fill the ranks. Military commanders increasingly relied on bands of fighters from outside the empire. For the most part, these were small bands of mixed origin under their own commander, though sometimes they bore a specific ethnic identification.[46] They received land, not coin, in payment for military service, which contributed to further economic decline [SARRIS]. By the middle of the century, no distinct Roman military identity remained.[47] [ELTON].

Loyalty. A fourth casualty of the Age of Attila was the loyalty of western provincial elites to the imperial order. Forced to make hard choices to protect their lands and authority, provincial aristocrats found ever fewer reasons to participate in imperial administrative structures. More often than not, landed aristocrats turned to barbarian leaders for protection.

Assimilation. For centuries, Roman officials had stage-managed the entry of settlers into the empire through negotiation. By rewarding the newcomers with land and citizenship, Rome gained military benefit.[48] In the Age of Attila, the Roman Empire still remained an attractive goal for outsiders who sought loot and land, but their leaders additionally hoped for recognition by imperial authorities and a place in the imperial system. The soldiers did not wish for the empire's destruction, as demonstrated especially by the Goths, whose leader Alaric jockeyed for a position in the Roman military establishment even while causing mayhem and destruction, and by the Huns, who depended on the empire as a source of gold and slaves [LENSKI]. In the course of the century, however, the process of assimilation into Roman culture lost force. Newcomers to the empire, whether invaders or entrants by treaty, gradually found it impractical, undesirable, or impossible to participate in the ever-weakening imperial power structures. When the dust settled, their leaders began to construct new power relations with the local provincial populations and with the imperial government.[49] In Vandal

---

[46] Walter Pohl, chapter 14 in this volume; Heather, *Kingdoms of the Empire*.

[47] Esmonde Cleary, *The Roman West*, 467.

[48] See the various chapters in Hans-Werner Goetz, Jörg Jarnut, and Walter Pohl, eds., *Regna and Gentes: The Relationship between Late Antique and Early Medieval Peoples and Kingdoms in the Transformation of the Roman World* (Leiden, 2003), esp. the "Introduction," by Hans-Werner Goetz, 1–11.

[49] Brown, *Through the Eye of a Needle*, 393–394.

Africa, for example, the first step in the creation of the Vandal regime after the conquest of Carthage was appropriation and redistribution of land among the supporters of the king and the rank and file of the Vandal army [MERRILLS]. A treaty with the government in Constantinople followed two years later, in 442. Other start-up kingdoms made different arrangements with local aristocrats and the imperial government, but all of them involved seizure and distribution of the best lands for the new settlers [SARRIS].

For readers unfamiliar with the history of the fifth-century collapse of the Roman Empire, it is useful to describe some signal events, which occurred in three phases.

First Phase: Summer 378 to Midwinter 405–406

In 378, a force of Goths crossed the Danube and destroyed two thirds of the eastern army led by the emperor Valens at the battle of Adrianople in Thrace, a terrible disaster but by no means a lethal blow to the empire. The new eastern emperor, Theodosius I, who ruled in the east from 379 to 392 and was sole ruler of the entire empire from 392 to 395, managed to contain the Gothic incursion, which dealt great damage in the Balkans. Usurpers in the West who often had the support of provincial aristocrats, proved to be greater threats to his authority.[50] When the last was overcome in 394, Theodosius once again divided the empire into two discrete parts with separate administrative and military establishments. After his death in 395, his two sons ruled the different halves of the empire, Arcadius in Constantinople and Honorius in Ravenna [GREATREX].

Second Phase: From the Rhine Crossings to Attila, 405–406

In midwinter 405–406 the Rhine boundary broke irremediably. Large bands of Sueves, Vandals, Alans, and Burgundians, with their allies and their dependents crossed the upper Rhine near Mainz. These groups originated in different places in central Europe [HEATHER]. Temporarily halted by an army of Frankish settlers, and further restrained for two years by a usurper from Britain who had brought the last Roman troops from the island with him, the invaders finally penetrated deep into Gaul and beyond, taking advantage of civil strife that prevented

---

[50] Matthew Innes, *Introduction to Early Medieval Europe, 300–900: The Sword, the Plough and the Book* (Milton Park, U.K., 2007) 83.

adequate defense. The invading groups were too large to be defeated by Roman forces or to be absorbed readily into the imperial fabric, and at the same time they were too small to deal a lethal blow to the empire. Consequently, for three or four decades, they moved through the western provinces seeking land from the authorities. They took part in civil war and caused great damage and suffering while enduring many misfortunes themselves.[51] The image before us should be of capable, armed war bands of mixed origin, not helpless refugees.

In the West. Roman defenses of the West came under the control of military strongmen who advanced the cause of the imperial house, for principles of dynasty remained a compelling force [CROKE]. These strongmen pitted the invaders against one another, against claimants to the throne, and against rebellious provincial populations with great effect. Two names stand out. Stilicho, whose father was a Vandal and who was married to Theodosius's niece, served as regent to the child-emperor Honorius from 394 to 408. Notable for sparring with the Gothic general Alaric in the Balkans and Italy and for halting a separate Gothic invasion of Italy in 406, he was executed in 410 following the sack of Rome by Alaric. Another highly effective general, Flavius Aetius, dominated military affairs in the West from 433 to 454. His policy was to work closely with the Huns, who by this time were expanding into western Europe from their base on the Hungarian Plain, while he established control within the western imperial realm. When Attila invaded Gaul in 451, however, Aetius organized the defense against him, creating a coalition of Visigoths, Franks, Romans, and others. After Attila's defeat at the Catalaunian Fields (somewhere near Chalons in France) and his death in Italy in 453, Aetius's policy fell apart, and he was soon murdered. For the rest of the century, other competing warlords and emperors dominated affairs, causing imperial politics in the West to become ever more convoluted and treacherous.[52]

Sometimes imperial forces went on the offensive. The emperor Majorian (r. 457–461) campaigned successfully against the Visigothic and Burgundian kingdoms, forcing them to accept subordinate federate status. He reasserted control over much of Spain, but was unable to mount a successful expedition against the Vandals, by this time securely established in North Africa. Ricimer, a barbarian commander with whom he had been collaborating in the management of the empire

---

[51] Bryan Ward-Perkins, *The Fall of Rome and the End of Civilization* (Oxford, 2005).
[52] Penny MacGeorge, *Late Roman Warlords* (Oxford, 2002).

had him murdered A series of barbarian generals began to compete for the western throne by backing other Roman politicians. One of these military strongmen, Odoacer, put an end to the charade by deposing the last emperor in the West, Romulus Augustulus, in 476 and openly holding power as king of Italy. Odoacer cleverly demonstrated his deference to the emperor Zeno in Constantinople by returning all the imperial regalia that remained in Italy. Odoacer in turn was murdered by the Goth Theoderic, who had moved west with his army from the Balkans with Emperor Zeno's encouragement. He absorbed Odoacer's troops and established a highly successful kingdom in Italy that lasted until Emperor Justinian's armies destroyed it in the middle of the next century.[53]

In the midst of the century's political developments, various Roman Christian groups fiercely struggled for doctrinal preeminence in western Europe, as they did in the eastern empire (see below), and the church establishment grew rich as new Christian aristocracies emerged after the empire's collapse.[54] A problem of doctrinal affiliation developed in the West due to the fact that unlike the mostly Catholic Romans, the majority of the newcomers to the empire followed Arian Christianity. The post-imperial kingdoms responded in different ways. For the Vandals, Arianism seemed a good way to reinforce their identity in the ocean of North African Catholics whom they ruled [MERRILLS]. Ostrogoths in Italy likewise found it sensible to maintain separate church establishments for themselves and their Catholic subjects. The situation was complicated, however, by the fact that there was an active Arian community in Italy before their arrival. Clovis, the Frankish king, found it convenient to convert to Catholicism with his followers in 496, which had the effect of making assimilation of the Gallo-Romans and the Franks much easier. Salvian of Marseilles, a Gallic cleric painfully aware of the suffering of his fellow provincials at the hands of both Roman landlords and barbarian invaders, developed a new interpretation of events. He explained that the Arian Vandals and Goths had brought God's punishment upon the Romans. Because of their Arianism, the barbarians could not follow God's law properly. Catholic Romans, on the other hand, should have known better and so had earned divine anger. For Salvian, knowledge of God's law – that is, doctrinal correctness – determined the character of communities

---

[53] John Morehead, *Theoderic in Italy* (Oxford, 1992); Innes, *Introduction to Early Medieval Western Europe*, 142–155.

[54] Brown, *Through the Eye of a Needle*, esp. 369–384.

more than anything else. The time-honored distinction of Roman and barbarian meant little to him.[55]

In the East. Unlike its western counterpart, the eastern half of the Roman Empire held firmly together. Constantinople doubled in size to about 600,000 inhabitants, replacing Rome (which dramatically shrank in population) as the greatest consumer capital in the empire [VAN DAM]. The imperial house, the bureaucracy, and the army maintained their integrity and effectiveness.[56] [GREATREX]. Nevertheless, the eastern empire's character changed substantially, due to the influence of Christianity on government and society. The result was a state Roman in administration, law, and other traditions; Greek in language and cultural heritage; and now deeply Christian. We call this realm Byzantium, although the inhabitants of the eastern empire always understood themselves to be Romans.

As the masters of a vastly shrunken empire, the eastern Romans had to rethink their priorities. After Adrianople in 378, the Goths in the Balkans posed the most immediate threat. When Hunnic raids began in the first decades of the fifth century, military and diplomatic attention focused on the Danube frontier, the interface with the steppe.[57] Roman authorities maintained this border, although it remained permeable to devastating Hunnic raids when negotiations and the payment of subsidies stopped.[58]

The eastern empire suffered economically when taxes had to be raised to pay for Attila's extortionate demands.[59] His incursions had a catastrophic effect on the Balkans: roughly 150,000 people were taken into captivity, only some of whom were ransomed [LENSKI]. At the same time, Sasanian leaders felt enormous pressure from the steppe along their northeastern border. Because they did not wish to fight on two fronts they cultivated peaceful relations with Rome. During the fifth

---

[55] Michael Maas, "Ethnicity, Orthodoxy, and Community in Salvian of Marseilles," in *Fifth-Century Gaul: A Crisis of Identity?*, ed. John F. Drinkwater and Hugh Elton (Cambridge, 1992) 275–284; Brown, *Through the Eye of a Needle*, 444–446.

[56] Michael Whitby, "The Army, c. 420–603," in *The Cambridge Ancient History*, vol. 14: *Late Antiquity: Empire and Successors, A.D. 425–600*, ed. Averil Cameron, Bryan Ward-Perkins, and Michael Whitby (Cambridge, 2001) 288–314, here 300–301.

[57] A. D. Lee, "The Eastern Empire: Theodosius to Anastasius," in *The Cambridge Ancient History* 14, 33–62.

[58] Lee, "Eastern Empire," 40–42. For diplomacy: Ekaterina Nechaeva, *Embassies, Negotiations, Gifts: Systems of East Roman Diplomacy in Late Antiquity* (Stuttgart, 2014); Roger C. Blockley, *East Roman Foreign Policy: Formation and Conduct from Diocletian to Anastasius* (Leeds, 1992).

[59] Lee, "Eastern Empire," 41.

century the empires fought only two brief wars, and sometimes they actively cooperated with one another, an enormous benefit to both.[60] These relations, however, would not survive in the sixth century.[61]

Attila's death in 453 and the rapid dissolution of his empire brought new and perhaps more complicated problems to the government in Constantinople. Some of Attila's sons continued to cause trouble in the Danube region into the 460s, but more dangerous were the large populations of Goths, Heruls, Gepids, Rugi, Sciri, and others who had been subjected to Hunnic rule for decades and now began to create new kingdoms. They developed independent relations with the regime at Constantinople. Roman officials sought to control these peoples through diplomacy, bribes, and occasional warfare. Whenever possible they tried to set the barbarians at each other's throats and encourage them to move westward. As seen above, the Goths freed from Attila's rule, now referred to as Ostrogoths, found a place in Italy under Theoderic's leadership after defeating Odoacer and his mixed barbarian forces.

Eastern rulers did not forget the West. Perpetuating dynastic ties remained a compelling force drawing the two halves of the empire as well as Romans and non-Romans toward one another [CROKE]. The idea of regaining lost territory died hard. Occasionally, eastern expeditionary forces attempted to help the regime in Ravenna, but defending the Balkans always came first. In 441, for example, Theodosius II canceled preparations for an attack on the Vandals because of Huns rampaging in the Balkans [ELTON]. After several costly, failed attempts at seizing North Africa from Vandal control,[62] many members of the governing elite concluded that Roman fleets could no longer keep the Mediterranean a Roman lake. After the Vandal sack of Rome in 457, Constantinopolitans hurried to build great defensive walls around their city.[63] Contrary to expectations, however, in the first half of the sixth

---

[60] Geoffrey Greatrex, "The Two Fifth-Century Wars between Rome and Persia," *Florilegium* 12 (1993) 1–14; Michael Maas, "The Equality of Empires."

[61] Geoffrey Greatrex, "Byzantium and the East in the Sixth Century," in Michael Maas, ed., *The Cambridge Companion to the Age of Justinian* (Cambridge, 2005) 477–509.

[62] In the years 441, 460, and 468; Andy Merrills and Richard Miles, *The Vandals* (Chichester, 2010) 109–113.

[63] For a later date: Cyril Mango, "The Shoreline of Constantinople in the Fourth Century," in *Byzantine Constantinople: Monuments, Topography and Everyday Life*, ed. Nevra Necipoğlu (Leiden, 2001) 17–28, here 24–25; Neslihan Asutay-Effenberger, *Die Landmauer von Konstantinopel-Istanbul: Historisch-topographische und baugeschichtliche Untersuchungen* (Berlin, 2007) 2 with note 7.

century, the emperor Justinian accomplished what fifth-century emperors could not, seizing back the lost territories of North Africa in 534 as well as Italy, and some coastal areas in Spain by 552.

On the empire's southern flank, various Arab tribal configurations developed, but remained malleable to Roman influence.[64] Muhammad would not be born for another century, and the teachings of Islam were still unknown.

Paradoxically, Christian belief proved to be as much a divisive as a unifying force in the East, where the most visible internal changes resulted from bitter debate about theological doctrine. Three church councils at the time of Theodosius II (r. 408–450) shaped Christian discussion about doctrine for centuries to come. Bishops at these meetings dealt especially with the question of the human and divine natures of Christ. These were the First and Second Councils of Ephesus (in 431 and 449, respectively), and of greatest importance the Council of Chalcedon, in 451.[65] Intended to bring unity of faith to believers, in their establishment of formulas of "correct" doctrine, they intensified divisions among the religious communities of the empire, thereby helping to fragment the entire Roman world in a new way. The theological intricacies and their political ramifications cannot be traced here, but three observations should be made.

First, after the Council of Chalcedon in 451, emperors and church leaders at Constantinople supported its interpretation of Christianity, which they wished to be the universally accepted statement of the faith.[66] Individuals and communities that objected most strongly on doctrinal grounds were viewed as heretical.[67] Second, the Church of the East rose to prominence in the Syriac-speaking East. This church is also known as the Nestorian Church because its teachings about the

---

[64] Irfan Shahîd, *Byzantium and the Arabs in the Fifth Century*; Fred M. Donner, "The Background to Islam," in Maas, *The Cambridge Companion to the Age of Justinian*, 510–533.

[65] Fergus Millar, *A Greek Roman Empire: Power and Belief under Theodosius II, 408–450* (Berkeley, 2006) app. A, "The Acta of the Fifth-Century Councils: A Brief Guide for Historians," 235–247, is an invaluable introduction; Patrick T. R. Gray, "The Legacy of Chalcedon: Christological Problems and Their Significance," in Maas, *The Cambridge Companion to the Age of Justinian*, 215–238.

[66] The council established that Christ has both human and divine natures, separate but unified in one person and one subsistence.

[67] On the growth and significance of heresiological discourse in identity formation, see Eduard Iricinschi and Holger M. Zellentin, eds., *Heresy and Identity in Late Antiquity* (Tübingen, 2008).

distinct human and divine natures of Christ were put forward by Nestorius (386–451). The first Council of Ephesus condemned him and his teachings, producing the Nestorian Schism. Nestorius's followers fled to Persia, where they worshiped safely. From there they carried their beliefs through Central Asia as far as China,[68] an important instance of linkage of the steppe to European concerns. Third, new cultural-religious realms defined by these variants of Christian belief gained a sharp profile in the course of the fifth century, making use of holy writings, including the Bible and the New Testament, in the languages of the region: Coptic in Egypt, Syriac in many parts of the Middle East, and Armenian and Georgian in the Caucasus. In consequence, self-identity in the eastern empire increasingly reflected Christian doctrinal affiliation rather than much older civic or provincial formulations, all of which nevertheless remained in play. Rivalry among the great bishops over authority and precedence further contributed to internal divisions.[69]

In light of these developments and in reaction to the suffering of the general population that he saw all about him, Leo, the bishop of Rome and a man of broad vision, attempted to extend his influence into North Africa, Gaul, Spain, Constantinople, Egypt, and Syria by pursuing an ideal of unity that recognized both Christ's divinity and human suffering. The regional churches were ambivalent about their ties to Rome, however, and in the end Syria, Egypt, and much of Spain were unable to share his doctrinal and political vision [WESSEL].

Doctrinal arguments also found expression in monasticism and asceticism, which had become basic parts of Christian life in the fourth century and taken on a highly political charge. Monastic and ascetic interaction with imperial and church authorities – and reaction to barbarian invasions – contributed to regional differences in East and West [ELM].

Christianity powerfully influenced the character of urban life in the eastern empire. Under the Theodosians, Constantinople became imbued with Christian piety.[70] Other cities followed suit. This ensured

---

[68] Joel Walker, "From Nisibis to Xi'an: The Church of the East in Late Antique Eurasia," in Johnson, *The Oxford Handbook of Late Antiquity*, 994–1052.

[69] David M. Gwynne, "Episcopal Leadership" in Johnson, *The Oxford Handbook of Late Antiquity*, 876–915.

[70] Brian Croke, "Reinventing Constantinople: Theodosius I's imprint on the imperial city," in *From the Tetrarchs to the Theodosians: Later Roman History and Culture, 284–450 CE*, ed. Scott McGill, Cristiana Sogno, and Edward Watts (Cambridge, 2010) 241–264.

the eventual death of pagan practices of every sort; sacrifice was forbidden by law, temples were destroyed, and participants in traditional cults were cruelly punished.[71] This is not to say that the entire population immediately embraced Christianity. Very large pockets of traditional practice lasted well in to the next century, especially in the countryside, and various elements of nonsacrificial practices remained deeply ingrained in social life, to the dismay of bishops, who railed against them [SALZMAN].

With new criteria for inclusion within (and exclusion from) authoritative communities of faith enforced by both church and state, violence could be targeted against dissident groups, Christian and non-Christian alike. Jewish communities found themselves caught at the intersection of church and empire [SANZO AND BOUSTAN]. Imperial law protected Jewish communities but also limited their public presence, while zealous bishops often spurred their followers to attack them.

In fifth-century cities, conversion to Christianity often happened as a top-down process. Councilmen, the political and social elite in the empire's cities, sometimes converted in order to maintain their high position and to compete with bishops for local influence. This led in turn to broader acceptance of Christianity at lower levels of society [HOLUM]. In a parallel development, the urban educational system changed. Because of heightened imperial interest in controlling education a rather more centralized system developed, but it faded by the end of the fifth century [WATTS]. Nevertheless, traditional Hellenistic education became integrated with Christianity in new ways, and survived to become a basic element of Byzantine culture.[72] In the course of the century new Christian interpretations of the cosmos displaced older forms of geographical knowledge across the Mediterranean and Middle East [JOHNSON]. For example, the peoples of the steppe took a permanent place in the Christian imagination as Gog and Magog, mentioned in the Bible and developed in the New Testament as hordes of demons prophesied to play a monstrous role in world affairs before the Last Judgment.[73] This became a topic of discussion not limited to the East. While Ambrose of Milan identified the Goths as Gog following

---

[71] Jaclyn Maxwell, "Paganism and Christianization," in Johnson, *The Oxford Handbook of Late Antiquity*, 849–875.

[72] Yannis Papadogiannakis, *Christianity and Hellenism in the Fifth-Century Greek East. Theodoret's Apologetics against the Greeks in Context* (Washington, D.C., 2012).

[73] Revelation 20:7–8.

Adrianople,[74] Augustine warned in *The City of God* against identifying these prophetic names with any contemporary peoples.[75] Despite Augustine's reservations, however, Gog and Magog continued to be linked to Goths, Huns, and other peoples from the steppe throughout the late antique period in the Latin, Greek, and Syriac realms, doing much to shape how the steppe was viewed for centuries to come.

Only a few other signs of internal changes in the East can be noted here. Old local languages were dying out in many places where they were not used in church or administrative contexts. Even comprehension of Latin, the language of law and government, could not be taken for granted among the educated elite. Although the Roman tongue remained the language of law and official documents, the east was governed in Greek. The *Acta* of the Council of Chalcedon, at which leading clergy from the East were present, shows that they could not understand Latin. It was a "Greek Roman Empire."[76] Laws, however, continued to be issued in Latin. The Theodosian Code, a codification of the laws of Christian emperors since Constantine in 312, was published in the East in 438 and in the West in the following year. Rulers of the successor kingdoms in the West started to issue law codes on the Roman model at the close of the century [HUMFRESS].

When the Age of Attila ended about 500, the Roman Empire in the East was transformed, differently but no less thoroughly than its old territories in western Europe. The state was now conceived of as one unified community that shared the Orthodox faith. All were subject to the will of the Christian emperor, and no room remained for people holding alternate doctrinal positions. Jews walked a tightrope, and pagan worship was absolutely forbidden. Constantinople, the New Rome, stood at the center of this imperial Christian polity, which in

---

[74] Ambrose, *De fide ad Gratianum*, II.16.137, in Ambrosius von Mailand, *De fide [ad Gratianum]*, text with translation and commentary by Christoph Markschies (Turnholt, 2005); *On Faith to Gratian*, ii.16; Edward Runni Anderson, *Alexander's Gate, Gog and Magog, and the Inclosed Nations* (Cambridge, Mass., 1932) 9; Emeri van Donzel and Andrea Schmidt, *Gog and Magog in Early Eastern Christian and Islamic Sources: L Sallam's Quest for Alexander's Wall* (Leiden, 2010) 12–13; Mark Humphries, "'Gog Is the Goth': Biblical Barbarians in Ambrose of Milan's *De fide*," in *Unclassical Traditions*, vol. 1: *Alternatives to the Classical Past in Late Antiquity*, ed. Christopher Kelly, Richard Flower, and Michael Stuart Williams, *Proceedings of the Cambridge Philological Society*, suppl. vol. 34 (2010) 44–57.

[75] *City of God*, 20.11, trans. David Knowles, *City of God* (London, 1971) 917–918: book 20 is about the Last Judgment.

[76] Millar, *Greek Roman Empire*, 1–38. Knowledge of Greek had similarly diminished in the West.

theory existed as the image of heaven on earth. The political idiom of expression for much of this remained imperial and Roman, but a new, total view of the cosmos and its communities in Christian terms had started to take shape [JOHNSON].[77] At century's end, the stage was set for the genuinely reactionary Age of Justinian.

CONCLUSION

The chapters that follow will explain in greater detail the realignments of culture and power that characterize the Age of Attila. They will show how the Roman world shifted gears in the course of the fifth century, falling apart in the West but refashioned with a new Christian face in the East. We will see that equally important shifts also occurred in northern Europe and Iran, as well as on the western Eurasian steppe, which took a permanent place as one of the major building blocks of the West. As much as the Age of Attila stands as an era of destructive change, it was also a time of fresh growth as a new international order emerged from the Pillars of Hercules to the Volga.

---

[77] Michael Maas, "*Mores et Moenia*: Ethnography and the Decline in Urban Constitutional Autonomy in Late Antiquity," in *Integration and Authority in the Early Middle Ages*, ed. Walter Pohl and Max Diesenberger (Vienna, 2001) 25–35.

2: GOVERNMENT AND MECHANISMS OF CONTROL, EAST AND WEST

Geoffrey Greatrex

As Aetius was explaining the finances and calculating the tax revenues, with a shout Valentinian suddenly leaped up from his throne and cried out that he would no longer endure to be abused by such treacheries. He alleged that, by blaming him for the troubles, Aetius wished to deprive him of power in the West, as he had done in the Eastern Empire, insinuating that it was only because of Aetius that he did not go and remove Marcian from his throne. While Aetius was stunned by this unexpected rage and was attempting to calm his irrational outburst, Valentinian drew his sword from its scabbard and, together with Heraclius, who was holding a cleaver ready under his cloak (for he was *primicerius sacri cubiculi*), fell upon him. They both rained blows on his head and killed him, a man who had performed many brave actions against enemies both internal and foreign.[1]

The dramatic death in September 454 of the man who had dominated the western empire for twenty years and defeated Attila only three years earlier vividly illustrates the precarious

[1] Priscus, fr. 30.1.13–27 = John of Antioch, fr. 224.2, trans. (revised) in Sergei Mariev, ed., *Ioannis Antiocheni fragmenta quae supersunt omnia*, Corpus Fontium Historiae Byzantinae, Series Berolinensis 47 (Berlin, 2008), and Roger C. Blockley, *The Fragmentary Classicising Historians of the Later Roman Empire: Eunapius, Olympiodorus, Priscus and Malchus*, vol. 2 (Liverpool, 1983). A more detailed version of this chapter was published in Esperanto in the *Aktoj de la IKU, 66a sesio*, ed. A. Wandel and R. McCoy (Rotterdam, 2013) and is available on-line.

nature of court politics in the fifth century. Beyond that, however, the episode highlights several issues that are critical to the focus of this chapter. We observe the *magister militum* and *patricius* Aetius, the supreme commander in the West since 433, discussing finances at the imperial court in Rome with the emperor: as will emerge, Valentinian III and his advisers were only too aware of their dwindling resources and the need to raise revenue to defend the empire. It is significant too that Aetius, although his responsibilities were essentially military, was heavily involved in this domain. Such was his grip on the administration, indeed, that the only senior office holder that Valentinian took into his confidence was a eunuch; when the eastern emperor Leo eliminated the general Aspar in 471, on the other hand, he could count on much more extensive support.[2] The intense rivalries and competition for influence at court thus clearly emerge, along with the spectacular consequences of failure.[3] The personal involvement of the emperor is also striking, as is his demeanor. Whereas his father-in-law Theodosius II was renowned for his placid nature, Valentinian's fury at his minister was evident and, perhaps, comprehensible: the emperor cannot have been unaware of the fate of his predecessor Valentinian II, who died under suspicious circumstances in 392 after having failed to dismiss his *magister militum* Arbogast.[4] Lastly, the poor relations between the two halves of the empire (see map 5a and b), now distinct entities, are evident: Valentinian, as the senior Augustus, should have been consulted about the succession after the death of Theodosius II in July 450, but the eastern court had defied protocol and unilaterally raised Marcian to the throne.[5]

At the start of the fifth century, the Roman Empire still stretched from Britain to the Euphrates. It was ruled by two brothers, Honorius in the West and Arcadius in the East, the two young sons of Theodosius I, who had come to the throne upon his death in 395. There was nothing unprecedented in such a division, since (for instance) the three sons

---

[2] See Briggs L. Twyman, "Aetius and the Aristocracy," *Historia* 19 (1970) 480–503, esp. 483–484. Cf. Timo Stickler, *Aëtius* (Munich, 2002) 70–75, 294–295; Peter Heather, *The Fall of the Roman Empire: A New History* (Oxford, 2005) 371–373; Averil Cameron, *The Mediterranean World in Late Antiquity, AD 395–700* (Abingdon, U.K., 2012) 37.

[3] Cf. John Matthews, *Western Aristocracies and Imperial Court, A.D. 364–425* (Oxford, 1975) 302.

[4] Socrates Scholasticus, *Historia ecclesiastica*, 7.22; cf. John of Antioch, fr. 219. On Theodosius's nature, see Matthews, *Western Aristocracies*, 238–239.

[5] Richard Burgess, "The Accession of Marcian in the Light of Chalcedonian Apologetic and Monophysite Polemic," *Byzantinische Zeitschrift* 86–87 (1993–1994) 49.

of Constantine had likewise succeeded their father in 337. In this case, however, the split turned out to be definitive. The increasing external pressures on the empire, most obviously the army of the Gothic leader Alaric in the Balkans, sharpened rivalries between the two imperial courts and their leading ministers – Stilicho in the West and Rufinus, then Eutropius, in the East. Although, like Valentinian in 450, Honorius had wanted to intervene personally in the East upon the death of his brother in 408, the two courts were never reunited, thus solidifying regional divisions. Nevertheless, in the first half of the century, Theodosius II struggled consistently to stabilise the situation in the West, for example by installing Valentinian III on the western throne in 425, by marrying his daughter Eudoxia to his western colleague in October 437, or by attempting to regain control of North Africa from the Vandals (in 435 and in 439–440). The sending of a copy of the Theodosian Code to Rome in 438 was a potent symbol of the ties that still bound the two parts of the empire.[6] As the work itself shows, laws continued to be issued in the name of both emperors, even if communications between the two courts over the following years were limited.[7] With the death of both Theodosius II and Valentinian III in the 450s, however, the dynastic ties were broken and the West was forced to fall back on its own dwindling resources. Theodosius's successor, Marcian (450–457), whose election had so vexed Valentinian, broke abruptly with previous policies by refusing payments to Attila and by renouncing any effort to retake North Africa.[8] Leo I (457–474) was the last eastern emperor to try to save the West, but neither his ambitious naval expedition against the Vandals (in 468) nor his nominee to the western throne, Anthemius (467–472), was able to redress the situation.[9] By the end of the century, western Europe was governed by a patchwork of barbarian kingdoms, many of which, especially Theoderic the Ostrogoth's Italy, continued to be administered to a significant degree by the same élites that had

---

[6] Heather, *The Fall*, 285–286, 290–292; John Matthews, *Laying Down the Law* (New Haven, 2000) chap. 1 on the marriage, chap. 3 on the arrival of the code in Rome. Cf. Fergus Millar, *A Greek Roman Empire* (Berkeley, 2006) 51, 56–58; and Walter Kaegi, *Byzantium and the Decline of Rome* (Princeton, 1968) 16–29.

[7] *Novellae Theodosii* 2 (447), cf. Eunapius, fr. 66.2; Millar, *Greek Roman Empire*, 1–2.

[8] Edward A. Thompson, "The Foreign Policies of Theodosius II and Marcian," *Hermathena* 76 (1950) 58–75; Robert Hohlfelder, "Marcian's Gamble: A Reassessment of Eastern Imperial Policy toward Attila," *American Journal of Ancient History* 9 (1984) 54–69.

[9] Heather, *The Fall*, 390–407; Guy Halsall, *Barbarian Migrations and the Roman West, 376–568* (Cambridge, 2007) 272–277; Kaegi, *Byzantium*, 226.

already long been prominent. The date 476 for the "end" of the western empire, the moment at which the boy emperor Romulus "Augustulus" was pensioned off by King Odoacer (476–493), should therefore be given short shrift. Not only had there already been periods without any occupant of the western throne, but, more significantly, so little had things apparently changed under Theoderic (493–526) that one inscription could declare the king to be "the propagator of the Roman name, the tamer of peoples," while his minister Cassiodorus could even refer to the kingdom as the *res publica Romana* (the Roman state).[10]

In what follows, my aim is to analyse the means by which the imperial government, in both East and West, sought to maintain its authority, in relation both to external peoples and to competing groups within the empire – with varying degrees of success. As will emerge, it is a topic that involves consideration not only of obvious political levers of power, but also of more indirect factors (such as the image of the emperor) that might serve to reinforce imperial authority. I shall begin by considering the figure of the emperor himself and his entourage before turning to the bureaucracy and administrative structures that had become the hallmark of the late Roman state. I shall then examine the role of the aristocracy, traditionally a bulwark of Roman power, as well as that of the church and of the people of the empire, some of whom voted with their feet and opted for barbarian rule. I shall leave the military aspect to one side, to be dealt with in chapter 7.

THE EMPEROR AND HIS ADVISERS

The emperor was ubiquitous in the fifth-century empire. His image was to be found on coins, on statues set up throughout the empire, on monuments, and on silver plates; on the Monza diptych of Stilicho and his wife Serena, the young emperors Honorius and Arcadius are both depicted on his shield. Wherever the people assembled for games or for protest, his name – and those of his ministers – would be on everyone's lips; indeed, the Theodosian Code specifies that the acclamations of the

---

[10] *Corpus Inscriptionum Latinarum* 10.6850, for the inscription; cf. Michael McCormick, *Eternal Victory* (Cambridge, 1986) 270–275 for other Roman parallels. Cassiodorus, *Variae*, 1.20.1, 3.18.2, noted by Patrick Amory, *People and Identity in Ostrogothic Italy, 489–554* (Cambridge, 1997) 53. See also Halsall, *Barbarian Migrations*, 332–333; T. E. Kitchen, "Contemporary Perceptions of the Roman Empire in the Later Fifth and Sixth Centuries," Ph.D. diss., Cambridge University, 2008, chap. 5.

people should be recorded and brought to his attention. Soldiers would swear loyalty to the emperor and shout out his name as they launched an assault, just as they did when storming the rebel stronghold at Cherris in Isauria in 488.[11] Even after the "fall" of the West, Theoderic presented a thoroughly imperial style of rulership, sponsoring repairs to buildings in Rome, Ravenna, and elsewhere, triumphantly entering the city of Rome in 500 to celebrate thirty years of rule, holding games in the circus, and distributing largesse to the people.[12]

Such prominence might seem surprising, given the young age of the emperors who held sway in the first half of the fifth century: Theodosius II, already Augustus before his first birthday in 402, inherited the throne just after turning seven in 408, while Valentinian III was installed on the western throne in 425 at the age of six. These two emperors, and Theodosius in particular, have often been regarded as mere figureheads, the playthings of ambitious politicians at court, such as Theodosius's sister Pulcheria or the eunuch Chrysaphius.[13] Although in their minority leading courtiers, such as the praetorian prefect Anthemius or Valentinian's mother, Galla Placidia, undoubtedly wielded great power, it would be a mistake to underestimate the personal role played by the emperor himself. From the very start of the empire under Augustus, the emperor's power had been highly personalised, and he was the object of an unceasing flow of petitions and requests from the entire empire. Even with the considerable bureaucratic apparatus that had grown up over the fourth century, decision-making remained highly personal and depended ultimately on the will of the emperor. Leading ministers, such as the *magister officiorum* (the master of offices, who prepared the agenda

---

[11] Ramón Teja, "Il cerimoniale imperiale," in *Storia di Roma*, vol. 3.1: *L'età tardoantico*, eds. A. Carandini et al. (Turin, 1993) 629–633; Jochen Martin, "Das Kaisertum in der Spätantike," in *Usurpationen in der Spätantike*, eds. François Paschoud and Joachim Szidat (Stuttgart, 1997) 59, citing, e.g., *Codex Theodosianus*, 1.16.6; Millar, *Greek Roman Empire*, 198; Joh. Ant. fr. 237.10 on Cherris.

[12] John Moorhead, *Theoderic in Italy* (Oxford, 1992) 42–43, 60–63; cf. McCormick, *Eternal Victory*, 273.

[13] So Prisc. fr. 3.1–2; Joh. Ant. frs. 220, 222. Cf. Arnold H. M. Jones, *The Later Roman Empire, 284–602: A Social, Economic and Administrative Survey* (Oxford, 1964) 173, 341; and Michael McCormick, "Emperor and Court," *Cambridge Ancient History*, vol. 14: *Late Antiquity: Empire and Successors, A.D. 425–600*, ed. Averil Cameron, Bryan Ward-Perkins, and Michael Whitby (Cambridge, 2000) 143. But see Hugh Elton, "Imperial Politics at the Court of Theodosius II," in *The Power of Religion in Late Antiquity*, ed. Andrew Cain and Noel Lenski (Aldershot, 2009) 134–137; Millar, *Greek Roman Empire*, 206–207; cf. Tony Honoré, *Law in the Crisis of Empire, 379–455 AD* (Oxford, 1998) 259 (on Valentinian).

for meetings), the praetorian prefect (responsible for finances and for supplying the army), the *quaestor sacri palatii* (the quaestor of the sacred palace, responsible for framing laws) and the *praepositus sacri cubiculi* (the head of the sacred bedchamber, typically a eunuch, who controlled access to the imperial apartments), as well as *magistri militum* (masters of soldiers, i.e., generals), would convene with the emperor in a gathering known as the *consistorium*, so called because, while the monarch would be seated, they would be standing (*consisto*). It was no doubt at one of these that Aetius was assassinated.[14] In the eastern empire, meetings of this select group would take place in the imperial palace at Constantinople. Ministers would be lobbied by nobles and leading churchmen; gifts might provide further inducements, something that Cyril, the patriarch of Alexandria, took into account in his dealings with members of the court. Proposals would then be put forward and debated, but it was the emperor who took the final decision, arbitrating between the competing and often overlapping branches of the administration; this in turn might result in the issuing of an edict that would be incorporated into the Theodosian Code (or, later, issued separately as a *Novel*, i.e., a new law). Sudden shifts in policy and falls from power were not unusual, such as Theodosius's withdrawal of support from the patriarch Nestorius in 431, the abrupt dismissal of the city prefect Cyrus in 441, or the usurper Basiliscus's *volte-face* in 476, rescinding the *Encyclicon* he had issued only months earlier. These dramatic breaks not only allowed the emperor to respond to popular pressure, notably in the last case, but also afforded him the opportunity of ridding himself of a minister whose influence or power threatened to eclipse his own (as in the second case).[15]

The emperor takes centre stage in the fifth century not only symbolically, but also, as we have seen, in practical terms. His rule was regarded moreover as divinely sanctioned, his household was referred to as *sacer* (sacred), and in the East he was (at least from the mid-fifth century) blessed by the patriarch of Constantinople.[16] Unlike his martial

[14] Jones, *LRE* 333–341; Stephen Mitchell, *A History of the Later Roman Empire* (Oxford, 2007) 173–180; McCormick, "Emperor and Court," 140.

[15] Sam Barnish, A. Doug Lee, and Michael Whitby, "Government and Administration," in *CAH* 14: 200; Henry Chadwick, *The Church in Ancient Society* (Oxford, 2003) 530–536, 593. On sudden falls, see Elton, "Imperial Politics," 137–140; cf. Christopher Kelly, *Ruling the Later Roman Empire* (Cambridge, Mass., 2004) chap. 5.

[16] Kaegi, *Byzantium*, 199–203, 233; Sabine MacCormack, *Art and Ceremony in Late Antiquity* (Berkeley, 1981) 240–256; cf. Frank Kolb, *Herrscherideologie in der Spätantike* (Berlin, 2001) 97–102; Teja, "Il cerimoniale," 624–629.

predecessors of earlier centuries, he tended to reside in his capital, be it Constantinople, Ravenna or Rome, yet he was capable of defeating his enemies even from within the palace: Theodosius II's prayers, it was believed, had contributed to the defeat of the Persians in 421. Victory remained essential to imperial rule, and a ceremonial procession into a city, known as an *adventus*, allowed the ruler to appropriate for himself any successes that his generals had won.[17] Ceremonies helped to reinforce the image of imperial power, such as official audiences in the palace or processions in Constantinople, whether for church services, the reception of saints' relics, the inspection of granaries, or a victory celebration. In the hippodrome or on the streets the emperor might be met by loyal acclamations or, on occasion, by abuse and rioting.[18] It is striking, however, that the people generally retained a fundamental loyalty to the emperor, at least to one who was well established or whose dynastic right to rule was unimpeachable. Thus Honorius was narrowly able to quell a serious mutiny among his troops in Ticinum in 408, in the course of which many of his senior ministers had been murdered, by appearing before them in humble clothes rather than his purple imperial robes; in the same way, a century later, Anastasius regained control of the streets of Constantinople by presenting himself in the hippodrome without his crown.[19]

The position of emperor was thus paramount yet vulnerable. As we shall see, many people had high expectations of him which were often mutually exclusive. Generosity was an important attribute of an emperor, as Theodosius II acknowledged: "We almost believe that We have received a favour whenever the occasion is presented to Us to grant a favour, and without any doubt We suspect that We have lost a day if it is not illuminated by the munificence of Our Divinity."[20] Such an approach, while popular, put in jeopardy revenues vital to the empire's survival, as will emerge in what follows. Moreover, despite the manifold difficulties that beset them, emperors became increasingly

---

[17] Kenneth Holum, *Theodosian Empresses* (Berkeley, 1982) 102–110, 121–122; cf. (more generally) McCormick, *Eternal Victory*, 109–111; Millar, *Greek Roman Empire*, 73–74; Kolb, *Herrscherideologie*, 123–124.

[18] McCormick, "Emperor and Court," 141–143, 156–160; Brian Croke, *Count Marcellinus and His Chronicle* (Oxford, 2001) 116–124. See further below.

[19] Zosimus, 5.32.5; Fiona Haarer, *Anastasius I* (Cambridge, 2006) 157.

[20] *Nov. Theod.* 5.1 (438), tr. C. Pharr; cf. *Novellae Valentiniani*, 1.1 (440–441) with Giovanni A. Cecconi, "Conscience de la crise, groupements de pression, idéologie du *beneficium*: L'état impérial tardif pouvait-il se réformer?," *Antiquité Tardive* 13 (2005) 297.

concerned to promote an ambitious vision of their role. As (again) Theodosius II makes clear, it was his duty to display benevolence and "to understand how the race of men may be unharmed as far as possible and to protect them from all injustice, since We recognise that We have been chosen [by God] for this purpose."[21] But at the same time as Theodosius and Valentinian were putting forth such high-minded statements, their efforts were all too frequently being undermined by their own administration and by the opposition of a powerful nobility.[22] It is to these that we must now turn.

THE IMPERIAL BUREAUCRACY

One of the features that distinguished the later Roman Empire from its earlier self was its extensive bureaucracy. Some thirty thousand functionaries were employed by the government, whether in bureaux in the imperial capitals or in the provinces. Service in the administration – known as *militia* on account of its military origins – was popular, offering not only salaries and immunities from various duties, but also the possibility of further enrichment by charging the public for carrying out one's duties.[23] Despite such peculation, the bureaucracy remained a powerful tool whose object was to ensure the regular flow of taxes to the emperor, so that in turn the armies could be paid. It was an instrument, however, that threatened to escape the emperor's control. Over time, the ministries had naturally developed their own practices and cultures, and they were capable of continuing their administrative tasks no matter who occupied the throne. Promotions were made according to seniority, but in some cases it was possible for an outsider to buy a post – honorific or actual – and seek to recoup his expenses by

---

[21] *Nov. Theod.* 17.2. pr. (444), tr. C. Pharr; cf. *Codex Justinianus*, 1.48.1, 3 (479, with Mitchell, *History*, 178); *Novellae Marciani*, 2. pr. (450), *Novellae Maioriani*, 1.1 (458), and *Nov. Just.* 149.2 (569).

[22] Cf. Cecconi, "Conscience," 303; Honoré, *Law*, 258–262 (on Valentinian's frustration).

[23] Cecconi, "Conscience," 297 n. 93; Kelly, *Ruling*, 111; on numbers, cf. Peter J. Heather, "Senators and Senates," *The Cambridge Ancient History*, vol. 13: *The Late Empire, A.D. 337–425*, ed. Averil Cameron and Peter Garnsey (Cambridge, 1998) 204–205; Bernhard Palme, "The Imperial Presence: Government and Army," in *Egypt in the Byzantine World, 300–700*, ed. Roger Bagnall (Cambridge, 2007) 251 (for Egypt); these naturally decreased in the West over the century: see Matthews, *Western Aristocracies*, 347. Cecconi, "Conscience," 289 on fees, 300 on advantages; cf. Kelly, *Ruling*, 64–68, chap. 4.

exploiting the power it brought. Although the sale of offices may have helped to diversify the bureaucracy, ensuring that it was not entirely self-contained, the danger lay in the fact that the emperor's control shrank as the autonomy of his administration grew and appointments slipped from his grasp. Successive rulers adopted different solutions to this issue, sometimes permitting the purchase of office (*suffragium*) and taking part of the proceeds, sometimes forbidding it altogether.[24] It was a constant battle for emperors to maintain their grip, but the stakes were high. On the one hand, their agents were responsible for the financial well-being of the empire, although it is clear particularly from the *Novels* of Valentinian III that they did not hesitate to collect more money than they were entitled to and to keep much for themselves; sometimes fraudsters might even collect taxes for themselves by impersonating imperial agents. The state thus not only lost revenue vital for its security, but alienated its own population, which might then seek refuge in the protection either of local aristocrats or of barbarians.[25] On the other hand, the sale and purchase of office to some degree privatised the imperial bureaucracy: someone who had bought their position, not unnaturally, considered the post to be his own, to do with as he pleased. This could only encourage further corruption and the siphoning off of revenue destined for the state.[26]

Whatever the moral failings in this system, it also clearly brought with it grave dangers. The *Novels* of Valentinian III testify both to the awareness of the emperor and his ministers of this problem as also to the difficulty of implementing any change. As Giovanni Cecconi has eloquently demonstrated, the fifth-century empire, in the West at any rate, was caught in a vicious circle from which it proved unable to escape. The emperor might issue laws to curtail the power of one ministry or another, but soon afterwards found himself obliged to reverse his measure: he could not afford to lose the support of his civil servants, without whose services his administration could not survive.[27] Worse still, because of the numerous vested interests of various groups, notably of the bureaucracy itself, but also of the aristocracy and the

---

[24] Cecconi, "Conscience," 290–291; Kelly, *Ruling*, 152–158.

[25] See *Nov. Val.* 1.3 (450) for a vivid description of bogus tax-collectors; see also *Codex Theodosianus*, 6.29, 10–12 (412–415), *Nov. Maj.* 2.2 (458) and Salvian, *De gubernatione Dei*, 5.24, with Cecconi, "Conscience," 293, and n. 28 in this chapter.

[26] Cecconi, "Conscience," 289; cf. Barnish et al., "Government and Administration," 170–171; and Sal. *De gub. Dei* 5.17.

[27] *Nov. Val.* 7.1–2 (440–442) for such a reverse, with Cecconi, "Conscience," 299; cf. Paul S. Barnwell, *Emperors, Prefects and Kings* (London, 1992) 28–29.

army, it proved impossible to reverse the many generous tax immunities and concessions that had been granted earlier. Consequently the tax burden fell increasingly on those least able to pay it, reinforcing the alienation of the ordinary provincials.[28] Diocletian's bureaucratic system may have helped to restore the fortunes of the empire after the turbulent third century, but as time progressed, its increasingly entrenched powers threatened to overshadow those of the emperor, at least in a situation like that in the West, where countervailing forces could not be brought to bear.

THE SENATORIAL ARISTOCRACY

One such force might have been found in the landed nobility of the empire, who were certainly known to express criticisms of the growing bureaucracy. In the West, however, a limited group of wealthy aristocratic families succeeded in maintaining a dominant role, often by actually integrating themselves with the imperial administration, in particular by occupying the bureaux concerned with tax collection. It was under pressure from them above all that Valentinian was forced to back down from his attempts to eradicate the over-generous exemptions and privileges accorded by his predecessors.[29] In the East, on the other hand, there had grown up an "aristocracy of service," composed chiefly of those recruited over the fourth century as members of the new senate in Constantinople. This group was hence linked closely to the bureaucracy but did not possess the long entrenched power and influence of the noble families of the West. As we shall see, moreover, there were other groups in the East, such as the people of Constantinople and the church, that were capable of exerting influence over the emperor to balance that of imperial ministers.[30]

In fact, the late Roman aristocracy can be perceived as an element that contributed significantly to the unravelling of imperial power, to

---

[28] Cecconi, "Conscience," 292–293, 300–303; Charles R. Whittaker and Peter Garnsey, "Rural Life in the Later Roman Empire," *CAH* 13: 281, 287–311; Peter Sarris, *Empires of Faith* (Oxford, 2011) 37–38, with *Nov. Val.* 10. pr. (441); Sal. *De gub. Dei* 5.28–31; see also Peter Bell, *Social Conflict in the Age of Justinian* (Oxford, 2013) chap. 3; and n. 33 below.

[29] *Nov. Val.* 4 (440), 10 (441), with Cecconi, "Conscience," 293, 299–300; cf. Matthews, *Western Aristocracies*, 387–388; and Stickler, *Aetius*, 276–277.

[30] Heather, "Senators and Senates," 184–197; Peter Sarris, *Economy and Society in the Age of Justinian* (Cambridge, 2006) 181–183.

the extent that Valentinian in particular seems to have had to resort to appeals to Roman patriotism to bring its members into line. But eastern emperors also had difficulties in maintaining their grip on an increasingly entrenched nobility: Justinian himself, in the sixth century, could barely contain his anger at the effrontery of the magnates of Cappadocia, for instance.[31] As in the case of the bureaucracy, past emperors had proved unsustainably generous. Landowners had been allowed to take over tax collection from the government with responsibility for those working on their land or leasing parcels of it: it was an easy short-term solution for the government, which was reversed only with great difficulty in the eastern empire.[32] Furthermore, whereas in the past there had been a clear division between those administering a province and the élite of that province, now the two began to merge. In the fifth century, it was possible for the native of a province to become its governor; in the sixth century, it became the norm. The intertwining of state officials and provincial élites led to an increasing regionalization and to the tightening of the grip of these regional notables. Some even employed soldiers on their lands, despite laws to the contrary; others offered their patronage to peasants fleeing oppression from the tax-collectors: once on land for which the nobles had obtained *autopragia,* the right to collect taxes themselves, they had some degree of protection. The draining of manpower from taxable lands to the estates of the wealthy inevitably had a serious impact on imperial revenues.[33] Although some scholars characterise these tendencies as a sort of co-option of the aristocracy by the emperors, so that these large estates might be termed "semi-public," it is more plausible, as others have argued, that the state was fighting a rearguard action to protect its interests, conceding only what it had to. In the West, of course, it lost its battle. In Italy, even as Alaric was threatening Rome itself, senators continued to insist on, and receive, tax concessions and to refuse to contribute to the defence

---

[31] *Nov. Val.* 6.2.2 (443); cf. *Nov. Theod.* 7.3.1 (440); Sarris, *Economy*, 2–3; Sarris, *Empires of Faith*, 130.

[32] Cameron, *Mediterranean World*, 96.

[33] On governors, see Avshalom Laniado, *Recherches sur les notables municipaux dans l'empire protobyzantin* (Paris, 2002) chap. 10; cf. David S. Potter, "The Unity of the Roman Empire," in *From the Tetrarchs to the Theodosians*, ed. Christiana Sogno et al. (Cambridge, 2010) 25–27; Jones, *LRE* 774–780. On the West, see Stickler, *Aetius*, 283–290; and Matthews, *Western Aristocracies*, 28–31, 331–334, 359–361; cf. Heather, "Senators and Senates," 201–204. On *autopragia*, see Barnish et al., "Government and Administration," 187; and Sarris, *Economy*, 103–114, 151–152.

of Italy. In Gaul, local magnates, who already enjoyed considerable autonomy, did not hesitate to abandon their allegiance to the emperor if it no longer suited their interests: the praetorian prefect of Gaul, Arvandus, was condemned for giving his support to the Visigothic king Euric in 469.[34] In the East, as Peter Sarris has documented, successive emperors made efforts to restrain the growth in the power of land-holding families, such as that of the Apiones in Egypt. Even if these efforts were never entirely successful, it is a measure of the East's underlying strength that the government was able to tighten up on tax payments under Theodosius II, even from the senatorial nobility.[35]

In this context, it is worth remembering that our main literary sources on the fifth century, as for other periods, are associated with this milieu. Historians such as Priscus, Olympiodorus, or Socrates, while themselves not members of the senatorial aristocracy, served as officials on the staff of generals or as lawyers (or both) and wrote for patrons who belonged to this group. Their works therefore reflect the interests of the wealthiest classes of the empire. As a result, the emperor Marcian, for instance, enjoyed a remarkably good press from posterity – save among opponents of the Council of Chalcedon – while the verdict on Theodosius II has been rather less positive. The former, whose claim to the throne was justifiably disputed by Valentinian, secured his position by generous tax breaks to the senators, who had been increasingly squeezed by Theodosius to fund his expensive payments to Attila.[36]

THE PEOPLE OF THE CAPITALS AND OF THE PROVINCES

As we have seen, the emperors of the fifth century well knew that they were expected to look after the welfare of their subjects and in particular to ensure that justice prevailed. It is clear from various sources that their

[34] Sarris, *Economy*, 137–148, 161–176, 183–193, cf. Sarris, *Empires*, 55–68, 129–131, for a broader view; Barnwell, *Emperors*, 60–62, 126–127. See Kitchen, "Contemporary Perceptions," 107–112, on Arvandus.

[35] Jairus Banaji, *Agrarian Change in Late Antiquity* (Oxford, 2001) chap. 6; Sarris, *Economy*, chap. 9–10; Palme, "The Imperial Presence," 250–255 (at various levels); Jones, *LRE* 205–207, 467.

[36] See Thompson, "The Foreign Policies of Theodosius II and Marcian," 72–75; Edward A. Thompson, *The Huns* (Oxford, 1996) 210–218. See also Bell, *Social Conflict*, 226–229.

efforts were unsuccessful: the dialogue reported between Priscus and a Roman merchant who professed to find life preferable at Attila's court is the most famous instance of disaffection with the administration of justice, but in the West, the poet Salvian alludes to similar problems.[37] This inability to see that justice was done is linked to the proliferation of the imperial bureaucracy, the layers of government that separated the emperor from the people. News filtered through only slowly to the ruler, who was, thus to a large extent, at the mercy of his advisers and agents.[38] But the emperor was also more physically removed from the populace than any of his predecessors had been: closeted most of the time in the imperial palace, he only rarely came forth for ceremonial occasions or a visit to a nearby city. Few emperors ventured to take the field: while Marcian and Majorian did lead armies, Valentinian III's attempt to take command after the assassination of Aetius was swiftly followed by his assassination, and Zeno had to abandon a proposed campaign in Thrace because of the unreliability of his troops.[39]

At a more basic level, the retreat of Roman power reduced the emperor's room for manoeuvre, leading in turn to a more brutal approach to government. To ensure the payment of taxes or to regain control of a region that had lapsed from imperial rule for a time, federate forces could be employed, leading to further oppression of the provincials; a plausible explanation for the uprisings of Bacaudae in Gaul in the fifth century links them to efforts by local people to resist being subjected to imperial rule and taxes after a period of relative autonomy.[40] Worse still, these very federates might be granted land in a province, such as the Alans, who in 442 were settled by Aetius in Gaul, probably near Orléans; Aetius did not hesitate to expel local landowners and to use force against other opponents. This phenomenon was not confined to the West: in 479 the inhabitants of Thessalonica, convinced that Zeno

---

[37] Prisc. fr. 11.2, with Michael Maas, "Fugitives and Ethnography in Priscus of Panium," *Byzantine and Modern Greek Studies* 19 (1995) 149–154, cf. Sal. *De gub. Dei* 5.25; Orosius, *Historia adversus paganos*, 7.41.7; Arnaldo Marcone, "Late Roman Social Relations," *CAH* 13: 357, 366; Barnish et al., "Government and Administration," 181; Sarris, *Economy*, 230–234.

[38] So Kelly, *Ruling*, chap. 5, esp. 224–225.

[39] Heather, *Fall*, 341 (Marcian; cf. Hohlfelder, "Marcian's Gamble," 61), 373–374 (Valentinian), 398–399 (Majorian); Malchus, fr. 18.3 (Zeno).

[40] So John F. Drinkwater, "Bacaudae of Fifth-Century Gaul," in John F. Drinkwater and Hugh Elton, eds., *Fifth-Century Gaul: A Crisis of Identity?* (Cambridge, 1992) 216–217.

intended to hand their city over to Theoderic the Ostrogoth, then in the vicinity, set about destroying statues of the emperor and attacking the praetorian prefect of Illyricum in protest. The situation was only brought under control by the city's clergy.[41] Similarly, in 447 Theodosius II insisted that the garrison of Asemus, close to the Danube, restore to Attila Roman prisoners that it had succeeded in freeing from his army.[42] Paradoxically, on the other hand, the government found itself obliged on occasion to arm the civilian populace against the barbarians, as in the case of Italy when faced by Vandal raids in the 440s.[43] The frequent collaboration between the imperial government and foreign peoples, to the detriment of the provincials, led, not unnaturally, to local resistance and to confusion as to what constituted loyalty to Rome: a leader such as Aegidius in Gaul, for instance, is referred to both as a Roman general and as *rex Romanorum* (king of the Romans) but, while once loyal to Majorian, opposed the policies of his successor Libius Severus, whose minister Agrippinus seems to have collaborated with the Visigoths.[44]

The people of the imperial capitals, on the other hand, could exercise significant influence on the government, to the point even of threatening the emperor's position. This is more obvious in the East, where the population of Constantinople on more than one occasion showed its readiness to resort to violence in pursuit of its interests, for example in attacking the Gothic troops of Gaïnas in 399 or in burning the headquarters of the city prefect during a bread shortage in 412.[45] The Roman population too, however, was well-known for its fractiousness: when Valentinian's short-lived successor, Petronius Maximus, proved incapable of defending the city against the Vandals, he was killed by the people as he fled.[46] Rome remained the centre of power in Italy, despite the frequent absences of the imperial court in Milan and Ravenna, and it is significant that after Valentinian's death (in Rome) his successors chose to establish themselves there definitively,

---

[41] Malch. fr. 20 on Thessalonica; Matthews, *Western Aristocracies*, 330–331, 337–338, on Gaul.

[42] Prisc. fr. 9.3.

[43] *Nov. Val.* 9 (440); Andy Merrills and Richard Miles, *The Vandals* (Oxford, 2010) 111–112.

[44] See Kitchen, "Contemporary Perceptions," 133–137; Penny MacGeorge, *Late Roman Warlords* (Oxford, 2002) chap. 6.

[45] J. H. W. G. Liebeschuetz, *Barbarians and Bishops* (Oxford, 1990) chap. 10; *Chronicon Paschale*, 571.

[46] Joh. Ant. fr. 224.4; cf. Heather, *Fall*, 378–379.

among the powerful aristocracy and the urban populace.[47] In the eastern empire, another element in relations between emperor and people of the capital became ever more important over the fifth century – that of doctrinal orthodoxy and piety. The emperor Marcian, for instance, even towards the end of his life, took part in religious processions outside the city on foot, inspiring the patriarch to follow his example. Such manifestations of piety offered a crucial means for binding the people of the city, and much of the empire, to the emperor. But although this theological element could bolster imperial authority, for instance in preventing Arian barbarian leaders such as Aspar or his sons from gaining the throne in 470, it could also limit the emperor's scope for resolving the Christological disputes that racked the empire: Basiliscus's regime was effectively brought down in 476 by pressure from the patriarch Acacius, the holy man Daniel the Stylite, and the population of Constantinople. Likewise, Anastasius's anti-Chalcedonian policies met with increasingly violent resistance.[48]

CHURCH AND STATE

The importance of ecclesiastical affairs and the numerous servants of the church across the empire cannot be underestimated (see chapters 17 and 18). The conduct of secular and religious politics went hand in hand; high-ranking generals and courtiers exchanged letters with bishops on issues from taxation to doctrine. Over the fifth century, bishops came to wield great influence and could hope to obtain tangible benefits for their sees from the government. Theodoret of Cyrrhus, for instance, sought tax relief for his see, and a certain bishop Appion of Syene petitioned Theodosius to defend his flock. In the West, Bishop Germanus of Auxerre travelled to Ravenna in order to obtain protection for the Armoricans in the north of Gaul from an attack by the Alans, who were to be settled in the region by Aetius.[49]

---

[47] See Andrew Gillett, "Rome, Ravenna and the Last Roman Emperors," *Papers of the British School at Rome* 69 (2001) esp. 162–165.

[48] Theophanes, *Chronicle*, 109 (A.M. 5949) on Marcian. See Martin, "Das Kaisertum," 54, 60–61; Elton, "Imperial Politics," 139–140; Millar, *Greek Roman Empire*, 155–156.

[49] On Theodoret, see Millar, *Greek Roman Empire*, 29, 146–147; on Appion, see Millar, *Greek Roman Empire*, 22–23; cf. 59–61 on Synesius; on Germanus, Constantius, see *V Germani*, 28, with Matthews, *Western Aristocracies*, 337; and Halsall, *Barbarian Migrations*, 244.

Just as ecclesiastical figures were drawn into the secular domain, so generals and courtiers came to be involved in church matters: the *comes domesticorum* Candidianus presided over the Council of Ephesus in 431, while his colleague, the *comes sacrarum largitionum* John, helped deal with the aftermath. Troops might be required to enforce decisions that had been taken at church councils: Marcian was obliged to despatch soldiers to Alexandria in the wake of the Council of Chalcedon, when the local population vigorously opposed the pro-Chalcedonian patriarch Proterius.[50] In this context, it is worth stressing the remarkable resources available to church leaders: the wealth that Patriarch Cyril of Alexandria was able to channel to leading figures at Theodosius's court is well attested, but he could also call on several hundred *parabalani*, stretcher-bearers that functioned, in effect, as a paramilitary force, often in opposition to the secular authorities. The church of Constantinople, for its part, counted some fifteen hundred functionaries of various types. The figures emerge, moreover, from efforts by the imperial government to limit these numbers – an uphill struggle, to judge by the sequence of rescripts.[51]

Thus the success of the Christian faith in rooting itself in the empire's population was far from an unmixed blessing for the imperial government. On the one hand, Christianity, and in particular Nicene Christianity, might act as a rallying force, especially on the eastern frontier, where it was used on several occasions to recruit Arab allies; in the West, it provided a focus for resistance to the Arian (i.e., non-Nicene) Vandal occupiers of North Africa.[52] On the other hand, the complexity and ambiguity of its doctrines, coupled with its inherently intolerant tendencies, tended to give rise to bitter disputes, then persecutions. In the West, moreover, the church increasingly eluded the grasp of the emperor. Some fifty years after Ambrose had obliged Theodosius I to do penance for the massacre at Thessalonica, Valentinian III granted the force of law to the decisions of the bishop of Rome (or pope). By the end of the century, Pope Gelasius I (492–496) was affirming the precedence of church over state, a doctrine with a long future.[53]

---

[50] Elton, "Imperial Politics," 140–141; cf. Chadwick, *The Church*, 535–536; Evagrius, *Historia ecclesiastica*, 2.5; Chadwick, *The Church*, 588.

[51] Millar, *Greek Roman Empire*, 141, 220–221; cf. Elton, "Imperial Politics," 140.

[52] Malch. fr. 1, with Greg Fisher, *Between Empires* (Oxford, 2011) 34–39; Sarris, *Empires*, 91–93.

[53] *Nov. Val.* 17 (445); Chadwick, *Church in Ancient Society*, 603–604.

CONCLUSION

The Roman state – or rather, the Roman states – remained a powerful force in the fifth century. For although eastern and western empires emphasised their unity, for example, in the presentation of the Theodosian Code to the West and in continuing to issue laws in the name of both reigning emperors, there were frequent sources of friction. Roman government was perhaps more complex than it ever had been before, a factor that contributed to emperors' difficulties in implementing change. The eastern emperor continued to be able to mobilise sufficient troops not only to defend his empire, but even to intervene in the West on numerous occasions. Had one of the eastern expeditions to North Africa succeeded, it is conceivable that the shrinking of the western empire could have been halted and imperial power maintained.[54] Yet both empires were faced with significant structural problems. In essence, as Cecconi has demonstrated, the imperial authorities (in the West) could not carry through the measures needed to restore imperial fortunes because this would rupture the consensus needed to govern, that is, the collaboration of officials and nobles. In the end, however, these elements failed to assist the government, while others, such as the provincials, found themselves squeezed for taxes and even abandoned to foreign powers. The Roman army gradually faded from view, as emperors and generalissimos such as Stilicho and Aetius sought to preserve "Roman" power through ever greater use of non-Roman elements – a case of subcontracting run riot. In some respects, however, these forces proved more dependable than the landed nobility, which battled doggedly to further its own interests rather than those of the state. Moreover, in a situation where non-Roman leaders might create their own emperors, as Alaric and Athaulf did with Priscus Attalus, or Ricimer and his numerous nominees in Italy, contemporaries no longer could distinguish among emperors, usurpers, and kings even before the dismissal of the last "emperor."[55] Regional networks of nobles and of patronage, secular and ecclesiastic, came to supplant the levers of government: senate and bishops could survive without an emperor. In the East, on the other hand, despite some blurring of identity in the Balkans between Roman and barbarian leaders, the multiple attempts

---

[54] Cf. Heather, *Fall*, 396–397.

[55] Sarris, *Empires*, 55; John Mann, "Power, Force and the Frontiers of Empire," *JRS* 69 (1979) 183; Cecconi, "Conscience," 300–304; Kitchen, "Contemporary Perceptions," 284–289.

for the throne that marked the reign of Zeno testify to the enduring importance of the emperor, rather than to "a crisis of authority at the heart of the imperial office."[56] Indeed, it had become unimaginable that the eastern empire should be governed by anyone other than a pious, orthodox emperor, and therein lay the key to its survival.

[56] On the Balkans, see Kitchen, "Contemporary Perceptions," 167; quotation from Sarris, *Empires*, 128.

3: Urban and Rural Economies in the Age of Attila

Peter Sarris

The fifth century would set in motion a fundamental recasting of social and economic conditions in many of the northern and western territories of the Roman world.[1] This transformation would culminate in the sixth and seventh centuries, which would witness the fading away of many vestigial traces of the old Roman order.[2] But it was in the fifth century that the transformation began, driven on by the objective military and political circumstances associated with the era of Hunnic ascendancy and the entering into Roman territory of the various barbarian peoples. In order to understand the genesis of this process, however, we must first come to terms with the nature of the urban and rural economies of the Roman Empire in the fourth century.

CITIES, TAXES, AND EMPIRE

The Roman Empire on the eve of the Hunnic ascendancy remained what it had always been: an empire of cities.[3] That is not to claim that the empire was urban in the modern sense of the word: in Rome, as in all pre-industrial societies, the overwhelming proportion of the emperors' subjects lived and worked in the countryside, and it was

---

[1] See Chris Wickham, *Framing the Early Middle Ages* (Oxford, 2005).
[2] See Peter Sarris, *Empires of Faith: The Fall of Rome to the Rise of Islam* (Oxford, 2011).
[3] The best guide (on which I draw for much that follows) remains Bryan Ward-Perkins, "The Cities," in *The Cambridge Ancient History*, vol. 13: *The Late Empire, A.D. 337–425*, ed. Averil Cameron and Peter Garnsey (Cambridge, 1998) 371–410.

agricultural land and those who worked it that were the main source of the taxes upon which the Roman state depended.[4] Hence although, in the early fourth century, the Emperor Constantine had introduced a tax on mercantile profits (the so-called *collatio lustralis* or *chrysargyron*), in the late fifth century, the eastern emperor Anastasius felt free to abolish that tax without seemingly having to worry too much about the financial implications of his largesse.[5] Moreover, in economic terms, the dividing line between city and countryside was not nearly as clear-cut as is sometimes supposed. The great imperial capital of Constantinople, for example, maintained extensive stretches of agricultural land within the embrace of its formidable walls, and in the economically most developed regions – such as Egypt (where perhaps up to a third or so of the population lived in what were formally termed cities) – the levels of artisanal production and commercialised exchange in the countryside rendered any economically functional distinction between the countryside as a zone of primary production, and the city as a centre for secondary and tertiary economic activities largely superfluous.[6]

Rather, the Roman Empire was quintessentially urban in terms of ideology and political culture, in that those settlements that were formally and legally recognised as cities served as the key nodal points of imperial administration and control. It was in the city (known in Latin as the *civitas* or in Greek as the *polis*) that the local governor resided with his officers and staff. Importantly, there he was joined by members of the locally dominant landowning families (drawn from the surrounding area known as the *territorium* or *chôra*), who were enrolled onto the city councils (*curiae* or *boulai*) of the empire, to which many administrative and fiscal responsibilities had traditionally been delegated, effectively rendering the Roman Empire of the first and second centuries what has been depicted as a "patchwork quilt" of self-governing communities.[7]

---

[4] Bryan Ward-Perkins, "Land, Labour and Settlement," in *The Cambridge Ancient History*, vol. 14: *Late Antiquity: Empire and Successors, A.D. 425–600*, ed. Averil Cameron, Bryan Ward-Perkins, and Michael Whitby (Cambridge, 2000) 315–345.

[5] A. H. M. Jones, *The Later Roman Empire, 284–602: A Social, Economic and Administrative Survey*, 2 vols. (Oxford, 1964) 1: 237.

[6] Cyril Mango, *Le développement urbain de Constantinople* (Paris, 1985); Peter Sarris, "The Early Byzantine Economy in Context: Aristocratic Property and Economic Growth Reconsidered," *Early Medieval Europe* 19.3 (2011) 255–284.

[7] Peter Brown, *The World of Late Antiquity* (London, 1971) 63–69. On the ideology of urbanism, see Geoffrey E. M. de Ste Croix, *The Class Struggle in the Ancient Greek World* (London, 1983).

By the end of the fourth century, cities had lost some of their autonomy, but the basic model still held true.[8]

Indeed, in Rome's northern and western provinces, where cities had been largely introduced as a direct product of Roman imperialism, the drawing in of regional elites to the local city, the enrollment of their members into the ranks of the council, their co-option into the imperial system, and their associated acquisition of Greco-Roman cultural values and political identity, had been central to how Rome as an empire had become provincially embedded by the start of the fourth century.[9] To the east, an urban infrastructure had been inherited from the world of the Greeks and the Hellenistic kingdoms, from whom the Romans themselves had acquired their city-focused culture.[10] Hundreds of years earlier, the Greek philosopher Aristotle had declared that man was by nature "a political animal" (*politikon zôon*), meaning that it was the city or *polis* that was a person's natural habitat and most fulfilling abode.[11] By the fourth century, this position had become a deeply entrenched assumption in the minds of members of the Roman regional elites from the furthest reaches of Britain to the banks of the Euphrates.

The city was, therefore, the seat of government, the focus for elite ambitions, and a *locus* for the transmission and reproduction of high culture. In that sense, it was differentiated from other "dense" settlements (as human geographers would call them) both administratively and socially. As a corollary to this, they were also differentiated from other settlements in terms of their monumental architecture and appearance, in that they were expected to possess the great public monuments which, to the classical mind, characterised the city: processional paved roads, a properly ordered *agora* or *forum* to serve as a public marketplace, bath houses, places of worship, perhaps an acropolis, and (increasingly from the third century) impressive city walls. The city provided, in short, a specific type of monumentalised public space in which the Roman elite male could deport himself after the extrovert manner of the gentleman of antiquity, living his life in the constant gaze of his peers, his equals, and his rivals.[12]

---

[8] John H. W. G. Liebeschuetz, *The Decline and Fall of the Roman City* (Oxford, 2001).
[9] Greg Woolf, *Becoming Roman* (Cambridge, 1999).
[10] A. H. M. Jones, *The Greek City from Alexander to Justinian* (Oxford, 1940).
[11] Aristotle, *Politics*, 1.2.
[12] Ward-Perkins, "The Cities."

The cities of the Roman Empire necessarily varied enormously in size and scale. This diversity in terms of size was particularly marked in the fourth and fifth centuries. Some cities, such as the great *megalopoleis* of the East, comprising Antioch, Alexandria, and Constantinople, covered areas substantially over one hundred hectares and possessed populations of perhaps up to half a million. Others, particularly in the more underdeveloped West, could be tiny in comparison, with populations of perhaps only a few hundred. Nevertheless, to contemporaries, all these were cities, and were to be differentiated as such from towns or villages that lacked their defining characteristics and official designation, even if these towns or villages were actually larger than the cities concerned. Broadly speaking, the largest cities tended to be those at which emperors and their courts resided: most obviously Rome and Constantinople, or those cities closer to the frontiers that were turned into imperial capitals in the third and fourth centuries to face down burgeoning military threats from beyond imperial territory (such as Trier, Ravenna, or Vienne [in Gaul]).[13] So, for example, the anonymous author of the fourth-century gazetteer of the empire known as the *Expositio totius mundi et gentium* (Account of the Whole World and Its Peoples) wrote of the occasional imperial residence and capital of Antioch thus: "Take the city of Antioch, in which all delights are plentiful, especially those of the circus. Why, you ask, all delights? Because this is the seat of the emperor, and everything is necessary on his account."[14]

Many of the cities of the Roman Empire of the fourth century, however, were clearly substantial institutions and – crucially – ones which were not, typically, an organic part of the surrounding landscape in which they stood. As a result, they could only maintain their population levels, their monumental character, and their prosperity by means of the tightest possible control over the agrarian resources of the surrounding countryside, and by means of the active support and the active subvention of the Roman state. Many of these cities, as we have seen, were the product of Roman imperial will and were only maintained in an alien landscape by imperial *fiat*.

This was most evident with respect to Rome and Constantinople, the inhabitants of which were critically dependant on the imperial shipment of vast quantities of grain, at enormous difficulty and expense,

---

[13] Ibid.
[14] Jean Rougé, ed., *Expositio totius mundi et gentium* (Paris, 1969).

from North Africa and Egypt respectively.[15] Without such long-distance grain supplies, these great imperial cities would have found it impossible to feed themselves and would have been obliged to contract dramatically (as each would do, in the sixth and seventh centuries respectively). But such arrangements, encountered in their most spectacular form in the cases of Rome and Constantinople, would also appear to have been repeated hundreds of times over (albeit at a reduced level) in relation to the other cities of the empire.[16] Thus, writing in the sixth century, the Greek historian Procopius informs us that the annual shipment of grain from Egypt, via Alexandria, to Constantinople was meant not only to meet the needs of Constantinople, but also that such grain left over after the needs of the imperial city had been met was automatically assigned to what he simply describes as "the cities of the East."[17] He does not describe this process in any detail, as to him it was a perfectly standard feature of imperial life.

At the same time, all cities were fundamentally reliant on the fiscal infrastructure of the Roman state in a secondary sense, in that the role of cities as functioning centres of commercialised production and exchange, and their status as centres of elite residence, were critically dependent on the existence of a highly monetised economy, created and supported by the monetised fiscal demands of the Roman state. The state demanded that its subjects pay tax in coin to support the army and bureaucracy, and minted vast quantities of coin accordingly.[18] This in turn enabled farmers and landowners to sell their goods at market to pay their taxes.[19] At the same time, however, it allowed landowners, by selling the produce of their estates in return for coin, to escape the narrow confines of rural life and instead, by living at some remove from the physical source of their wealth, to maintain the quintessentially urban existence that Roman elite culture demanded. Cities, taxes, and empire thus went hand in hand, and, as we shall see, both the fiscal and urban infrastructures that Rome had generated and sustained would have difficulty surviving when the empire itself began to fragment under barbarian pressure.

---

[15] Adriaan J. B. Sirks, *Food for Rome: The Legal Structures of the Transportation and Processing of Supplies for the Imperial Distribution in Rome and Constantinople* (Amsterdam, 1991).

[16] Jean Durliat, *De la ville antique à la ville byzantine* (Rome, 1990).

[17] Procopius, *Anecdota*, 22.14–17.

[18] Michael Hendy, *Studies in the Byzantine Monetary Economy* (Cambridge, 1985).

[19] Keith Hopkins, "Taxes and Trade in the Roman Empire, 200 B.C.–A.D. 400," *Journal of Roman Studies* 70 (1980) 101–125.

TRANSFORMING THE COUNTRYSIDE

As already indicated, there were, of course, regional differences in the urban economies and cultures of the Roman Empire of the fourth century. Urbanism was most firmly rooted in the Greek-speaking East. In Rome's northern and western provinces, by contrast, although landowners everywhere aspired to an urban existence, they appear to have spent more time in their rural villas than elsewhere. In certain of Rome's frontier territories, moreover, such as north-western Gaul, there are indications that the chronic military insecurity of the third century had dealt a blow to urban life from which some cities were never to recover.[20] This stands in marked contrast to the rest of the empire, where the fourth century would witness rising population levels and urban growth. In general terms, the fourth and fifth centuries would witness urban expansion to the south and east, and growing evidence of stagnation and decline to the north and west.[21] These regional trajectories were driven above all by objective military circumstances, to which cities and their populations were highly sensitive.

Likewise, there were significant regional differences in the underlying structure of the agrarian economy, beyond those dictated by variations in climate, soil and crop. Again, in broad terms, distinctions are commonly drawn between east and west. To the east, where the urban focus of elite culture was most pronounced, rural society was characterised to a high degree by the existence of nucleated village settlements notable (in parts of Syria, for example) for their institutional cohesion and strong sense of identity. To the west, patterns of settlement tended to be much more dispersed, and were increasingly given coherence primarily by local networks of villas.[22] Both east and west, however, the interests and needs of the countryside were subordinated to those of the city. In the context of a world that was often perched on a knife edge between sufficiency and famine, this could have devastating implications for the lives of countryfolk.[23] This emerges with horrific clarity from the writings of the Roman medical author Galen. In his treatise "On Wholesome and Unwholesome Foods," written in the second century, Galen draws a distinction between the effects of bad harvests on the rich and the poor, and on city dwellers and the inhabitants of

---

[20] Ward-Perkins, "The Cities."
[21] Ibid.
[22] Wickham, *Framing the Early Middle Ages*, 442–481.
[23] Peter Garnsey, *Famine and Food Supply in the Graeco-Roman World* (Cambridge, 1989).

the countryside. Describing one particular year of bad yields in Asia Minor, Galen wrote of how:

> Immediately after Summer was over, those who live in the cities, in accordance with their universal practice of collecting a sufficient supply of corn to last a whole year, took from the fields all the wheat. . . . So the people in the countryside, after consuming during the winter what had been left, were compelled to use unhealthy forms of nourishment. Through the Spring they ate twigs and shoots of trees, bulbs and roots of unwholesome plants. . . . I myself in person saw some of them at the end of Spring, and almost all at the beginning of Summer were afflicted with numerous ulcers covering their skin, not of the same kind in every case . . . some from inflamed tumours, others from spreading boils, others had an eruption resembling lichen and scabs and leprosy.[24]

Galen goes on to describe how, predictably, many of these wretches soon died. The lives of the empire's rural subjects were also framed and determined by the ambitions of those same city dwellers in the sense that, as noted earlier, the countryside was the main source of elite wealth: the city councillors and senators of the late Roman world may chiefly have been men of the city, but they were also landowners who were constantly on the lookout to increase the extent and productivity of their rural estates.

There is every indication that the fourth century was a period when such estates (worked by both slave and "free" labour) were on the rise. The ever more widespread dissemination from the reign of the Emperor Constantine onwards of a new gold currency – the *solidus* – greatly facilitated the monetisation of the Roman economy, and with it the opportunities for commercialised production and exchange from which large estates (with the advantages they offered in terms of economies of scale and the more rational organisation of labour) were well placed to profit.[25] In particular, feeding the expanding urban populations of the fourth century could be highly lucrative for the owners of large estates, not least given the fact that, as members of the local

---

[24] Galen, *On Wholesome and Unwholesome Foods*, 1.1–7. Translation from de Ste Croix, *The Class Struggle*.

[25] Jairus Banaji, *Agrarian Change in Late Antiquity: Gold, Labour and Aristocratic Dominance*, 2nd ed. (Oxford, 2007).

city council to whom the organisation of civic food supplies was traditionally delegated, such men could effectively rig the market to line
their own pockets. In the city of Antioch, for example, members of the
council – in cahoots with local merchants – are reported to have deliberately withheld grain at a time of famine in order to send its market
price skyrocketing. As ever, the poor man's hunger was the rich man's
opportunity.[26]

Above all, the fourth century witnessed a dramatic increase in
the size of the imperial bureaucracy. In response to a "crisis of under-
governance" that had bedevilled emperors amid the military crisis of
the third century, rulers from Diocletian (284–305) onwards had considerably expanded the numbers of those provincial administrators and
officials (both military and civilian) directly employed by the Roman
state. These new posts were primarily recruited for from amongst the
ranks of the leading families of the cities of the provinces, whose members were increasingly enrolled into the senatorial order both east and
west, and thus came to enter into a new and more direct relationship with imperial power that served to bolster their own resources
of authority, wealth, and prestige. The holders of these new governmental posts, in short, formed the kernel of what would become a
new imperial aristocracy of service, whose members exercised authority and intermarried at a transregional level, thus allowing their power
to expand beyond the territorial confines of their home towns.[27] As
the social and economic clout of members of this newly transregional
elite snowballed, so too did they increasingly invest their authority
and wealth in land, leading to a growing concentration of landownership across the Roman world, which in turn resulted in the creation
of what has been vividly described as "an increasingly proletarianised
peasantry."[28] It should also be noted that some of the best evidence we
have for rural slavery in the Roman world comes from precisely this
period.[29]

This concentration of landownership necessarily took different
forms in different regions, but everywhere a fundamental restructuring

---

[26] Peter Sarris, *Economy and Society in the Age of Justinian* (Cambridge, 2006) 127.

[27] Banaji, *Agrarian Change in Late Antiquity*; Peter Heather "New Men for New
Constantines? Creating an Imperial Elite in the Eastern Mediterranean," in *New
Constantines*, ed. Paul Magdalino (Aldershot, 1994) 11–44; John Matthews, *Western
Aristocracies and Imperial Court, AD 364–425* (Oxford, 1975).

[28] Jairus Banaji "Aristocracies, Peasantries and the Framing of the Early Middle Ages,"
Journal of Agrarian Change 9 (2009) 59–91.

[29] Kyle Harper, *Slavery in the Late Roman World, AD 275–425* (Cambridge, 2011).

of agrarian social relations is evident across the fourth and early fifth centuries (one which the imperial authorities would effectively set in legal stone through the development of the institution of the "adscript colonate," which served to bind agricultural labourers and their families to the expanding large estates).[30] In Egypt, the documentary papyri reveal a proliferation and expansion of directly managed properties, which would culminate in the sixth century in the crystallization of extensive landed enterprises such as that of the Apion family recorded around the Middle Egyptian city of Oxyrhynchus, from which a rich cache of documentary texts survives. These texts reveal the Apion estates (which first become visible in the early fifth century) to have been highly commercialised, with agriculture carefully managed and geared towards maximising the family's income in gold. The estates combined landholdings in and around villages (*kômai*) and urban property in the city of Oxyrhynchus, with entirely estate-owned labour settlements (*epoikia*), to which local labourers and their families were drawn. There, these agricultural workers were rewarded with wages in the form of cash, credit, share of crop, or access to plots of land in return for their commodified labour. These estates formed only one part of the Apion property portfolio, and we have evidence for the existence of higher levels of estate management beyond the Oxyrhynchite in both Alexandria and Constantinople, where members of the family held high office.[31]

The spread of similarly structured estates is recorded in the epigraphic evidence for Palestine at around the same time, which again attests to a proliferation of estate-owned *epoikia*.[32] Likewise, inscriptions from the rich coastal zone of western Asia Minor reveal a wave of fourth-century estate expansion, with landowners extending their control over both individual parcels of land (*agroi*) and entire villages (*chôria*) worked by a combination of resident labourers (*paroikoi*) and slaves.[33] A similar pattern appears to have pertained in Syria, where the

---

[30] Peter Sarris, "Aristocrats, Peasants and the State in the Later Roman Empire," in *Der wiederkehrende Leviathan: Staatlichkeit und Staatswerdung in Spätantike und Früher Neuzeit*, ed. Peter Eich, Sebastian Schmidt-Hofner, and Christian Wieland (Heidelberg, 2011) 377–394.

[31] Sarris, *Economy and Society*, 21–95.

[32] Yitzhak Hirschfeld, "Farms and Villages in Byzantine Palestine," *Dumbarton Oaks Papers* 51 (1997) 31–71, here 36.

[33] Peter Thonemann, *The Maeander Valley: A Historical Geography from Antiquity to Byzantium* (Cambridge, 2011) 251–259; Kyle Harper, "The Greek Census Inscriptions of Late Antiquity," *Journal of Roman Studies* 98 (2008) 83–119.

churchman (and future patriarch of Constantinople) John Chrysostom denounced the exploitation of peasants drawn onto the estates of the powerful.[34]

At the same time, entire villages (*kômai*) were passing into the private ownership of such men: the Antiochene *rhetor* Libanius, for example, contrasted those "large villages" (*kômai megalai*) in the vicinity of his native city belonging to many masters, to others which belonged to a single lord. Local military "bigwigs," he complained, were attempting to extend their patronage and control over both.[35] Certainly, by the sixth century, we know of entire villages – from Palestine to Armenia – that were being purchased outright by the wealthy, or which were being awarded by the imperial government to its favoured clients.[36]

In the village-dominated world of the East, the rise of the great estate thus combined the creation of estate labour settlements with the extension of aristocratic control over what were often deeply rooted and long-standing village communities. In the West, by contrast, where settlement patterns were more dispersed, the process of aristocratic enrichment took a slightly different form, and is most visible archaeologically in what has been termed a fourth-century "villa boom" discernible from Britain to Sicily, whereby villa complexes simultaneously proliferated and expanded, becoming at once both more sophisticated and highly capitalised.[37]

Indeed, by the late fourth century, members of the western senatorial order (now dominated by members of the new service aristocracy) had become proverbial for the productivity and extent of their estates. The contemporary historian Ammianus Marcellinus, for example, related how they would "hold forth unasked on the immense extent of their family property, multiplying in the imagination the annual produce of their fertile lands which extend, they boastfully declare, from farthest east to farthest west."[38] For the early fifth century, the Greek account of the life of Saint Melania records that she and her husband owned property throughout the western provinces: in Italy, Spain, Sicily, Africa, Mauretania, Britain, and, the hagiographer adds, "the other regions."[39]

---

[34] John Chrysostom, *Homily in Matthew*, 61.3.
[35] Libanius, *On Protection Systems* (= oration 47) 4 and 11.
[36] Procopius, *Anecdota*, 18–20; Procopius, *Wars*, 2.3.1–2.
[37] Peter Sarris, "The Origins of the Manorial Economy: New Insights from Late Antiquity," *English Historical Review* 99 (2004) 279–311, here 304–305.
[38] Ammianus Marcellinus, *Res gestae*, 14.6.10.
[39] Denys Gorce, ed., *Vie de Ste Mélanie* (Paris, 1962) 2: 146.

It is sometimes suggested that, perhaps in contrast to the forms of direct management encountered in the East, members of the late Roman aristocracy in the West tended simply to lease out their land to tenant farmers in return for economically static rental incomes. The evidence for this claim, however, is meagre. Rather, both eastern and western sources indicate (at least with respect to the best quality land) a marked aristocratic preference for the direct management of estates, such as we encounter in the documentary papyri from Egypt. Regimes of direct management, for example, are taken entirely for granted in the agronomic texts that survive from Late Antiquity in both Latin and Greek.[40] Likewise, the fifth-century Gallic landowner Paulinus of Pella (who also inherited property in Greece) recorded how, as a young *dominus*, he had personally driven on his estate workers.[41] Both east and west, such landowners were also characterised by their commercial drive and their lust for gold. The fifth-century historian Olympiodorus of Thebes, for example, provides estimates for the annual incomes of the leading western senatorial families which reveal a marked preference for hard cash, whilst an eastern law contained in the *Theodosian Code* exempted from the tax on mercantile profits those landowners who marketed the produce of their estates (with or without the help of intermediaries): such men, the emperor declared, "should be thought of not so much as merchants, but rather as skilled and zealous masters."[42] Again, such economic strategies would come under pressure in the West in the fifth century as objective military and political conditions combined to curtail opportunities for commercialised agriculture and monetised exchange. Before attempting to understand that process, however, we must first turn to the world beyond Rome, beginning with social and economic conditions to the East.

THE WORLD BEYOND ROME

The Roman-Persian frontier in the fourth and fifth centuries bisected a Mesopotamian world that essentially formed a linguistic, cultural, social,

---

[40] See discussion in Banaji, "Aristocracies, Peasantries."
[41] Paulinus of Pella, *Eucharisticon*, lines 191–193.
[42] At 41.2, in Roger C. Blockley, ed., *The Fragmentary Classicising Historians of the Later Roman Empire: Eunapius, Olympiodorus, Priscus and Malchus* (Liverpool, 1983) 2: 204–205; *Codex Theodosianus*, 13.1.6.

and economic whole. As a result, it should not surprise us that social and economic conditions on the Persian side of the frontier should have broadly mirrored those encountered in Roman territory. Like Roman Syria, Sasanian Assyria (Iraq) was highly urbanised. Moreover, like the Roman Empire, the Sasanian Empire in general was a highly ranked society characterised by stark disparities of wealth.[43] Indeed, it is possible to argue that over the course of the fourth and fifth centuries, East Roman and Sasanian social relations were drawing closer together. The outright ownership of villages and control of their inhabitants that aristocrats in Syria, Palestine, and Egypt were aspiring to in this period, for example, would appear to have been something that members of the great Iranian noble families had long been able to take for granted. If peasantries in the East were becoming increasingly vulnerable and insecure over the course of the fourth and fifth centuries, it was perhaps in the core territories of the Sasanian Empire that their state of dependence and subjugation was at its most complete. The Roman historian Ammianus Marcellinus (who saw active military service in Persia) claimed that members of the Sasanian nobility enjoyed rights of life and death not only over their slaves, but also over what he termed the "undifferentiated masses" (*plebs obscura*).[44]

The societies to Rome's immediate north, by contrast, although also ranked societies, dominated by an archaeologically visible military elite, were characterised by much shallower social hierarchies than those encountered in either the Roman or Sasanian Empires. Both in the realm of the West Germanic peoples beyond the Rhine and also in the territory occupied by the Goths and other East Germanic and Slavonic peoples between the Danube and Crimea, the evidence points to a landscape primarily inhabited by sedentary agriculturalists, whose first instinct was to remain wedded to the land that they worked unless obliged to migrate by objective military or climatic conditions.[45] Although, at the level of village society, domestic slavery clearly existed, this was a world dominated by free peasant producers to an extent that was inconceivable in much of the territory ruled by Rome.[46]

This comes across very clearly with respect to the Goths. Warlords and their retinues played an important role in fourth-century Gothic society. The most successful or forceful of these men were capable

---

[43] Banaji, "Aristocracies, Peasantries."
[44] Amm. *Res gest.* 23.6.80.
[45] For a different approach, see Walter Goffart, *Barbarian Tides* (Philadelphia, 2006).
[46] Wickham, *Framing the Early Middle Ages*, 53–55 and 384–558.

of projecting their authority over extensive areas. Military kingship itself, however, which would become so important to the Goths once settled in Roman territory, appears to have been a relatively embryonic social institution even in the years immediately following the crossing of the Danube in 376, and the "weapon-bearing free" embraced a much broader swathe of society than those who clustered around such characters as aspired to it.[47]

Thus whilst we do have archaeological evidence for sites of elite residence in Gothic-settled territory for the period before the 370s (some of it revealing signs of Roman architectural influence), and there are indications that disparities of wealth and power were widening by virtue of economic and cultural contact with Rome, what is most striking about the archaeology of Gothic settlement between the Danube and Crimea from the late third to mid-fourth centuries is the extent to which it bears witness to the existence of a vibrant peasant society rooted in an economy devoted largely to subsistence agriculture (although there are considerable indications of craft specialisation and the possible use of Roman coinage as a medium of exchange).[48]

This impression is reinforced by a fourth-century text, the *Passion of Saint Saba*, recording the sufferings of a Gothic convert to Christianity, who was martyred on Gothic territory beyond the Danube in 372. The account is laced with vignettes concerning the nature of village society and the relationship between the villagers and the locally dominant warlord, who is depicted as living beyond the village, and the interventions of whose followers are depicted as unwelcome, destabilising, and – from the perspective of the locals – best ignored or, if not ignored, subverted.[49] Thus when the holy Saba is commanded to publicly abjure his faith by eating the flesh of pagan sacrificial victims, the villagers offer to get him out of a tricky situation by secretly swapping the polluted meat with something more innocuous (a suggestion he inevitably refuses). There are incidental references to the existence of a village council and of gatherings of a broader body of villagers. The accoutrements of village life make fleeting appearances: wagons, wooden roof-beams, a woman preparing dinner. Only when the holy

---

[47] Sarris, *Empires of Faith*, 87 and 107–108.

[48] Michael Kulikowski, *Rome's Gothic Wars from the Third Century to Alaric* (Cambridge, 2007) 34–42 and 100–122; Peter Heather and John Matthews, *The Goths in the Fourth Century*, 2nd ed. (Liverpool, 2004) 47–95.

[49] Heather and Matthews, *Goths in the Fourth Century*, 102–110, on which I rely for what follows.

man insults the Gothic lord in the presence of his retainers was his fate sealed and his martyrdom secured.

HUNS, GOTHS, ROMANS, AND THE DEMISE OF THE IMPERIAL ECONOMY

Naturally, those Goths who had settled on the Pontic steppe in southern Russia, were obliged to adapt to ecological and cultural conditions very different to those encountered to the immediate north of the Roman Empire's Danubian frontier. Here, many historical societies have found it useful to differentiate between those nomadic or transhumant groups inhabiting the open steppe, who tend to support themselves from the rearing of stock (primarily cattle and horses), and the sedentary agriculturalists of the woodland zone (hence the Slavonic *poljane* "field dwellers" and *drevljane* "wood dwellers").[50] As philologists have suggested, the Gothic division into *Greutungi* (derived from a Germanic root for "sandy soil") and *Tervingini* (from a root for "tree") that we find in the fourth century mirrors this distinction and thus would appear to have been a product of ecological realities.[51] From the world of the steppe, the Gothic language would also acquire the word for horses bred for warfare (Old Gothic *[h]ros*), and technical terms for warlords leading units made up of a hundred and a thousand men (*hundafaths* and *thusundithafs* respectively – words reflecting the organisation of nomadic military formations).[52]

As these loan words would suggest, the encounter between the Germanic peoples and the Huns would appear to have primarily affected the former at the level of military and elite culture. This is clear, for example, from the Hunnic tradition of skull-binding that the Gothic elite adopted under nomad influence; from their adoption of Hunnic names; and from the deportment on horseback of their leading men in battle, which echoed the martial traditions of the steppe.[53] Likewise,

---

[50] Dennis H. Green, "Linguistic Evidence for the Early Migrations of the Goths," in *The Visigoths from the Migration Period to the Seventh Century: An Ethnographic Perspective*, ed. Peter Heather (Woodbridge, U.K., 1999) 11–42, here 17–18.

[51] Ibid., 18.

[52] Ibid., 27–29.

[53] Ibid., 19; Bernard Bachrach, *A History of the Alans in the West: From Their First Appearance in the Sources of Classical Antiquity through the Early Middle Ages* (Minneapolis, 1973) 67–69; Doris Pany and Karin Wiltschke-Schrotta, "Artificial Cranial Deformation in a Migration Period Burial of Schwarzenbach, Lower Austria," *Viavias* 2

with respect to the West Germanic peoples, we should note the burial of horses encountered in conjunction with the gravesite of the late fifth-century Frankish king Childeric, a style of elite burial attested from the Rhine to Manchuria, which we can probably trace back to the era of Hunnic ascendancy.[54] In economic terms, the important point to note is that, in spite of nomadic overlordship, the Germanic peoples' preference for the lifestyle of the sedentary agriculturalist remained intact.

This fact would have major implications for the Roman Empire. As noted elsewhere in this volume, the Hunnic elite of the fourth and fifth centuries (like that of the Avars and Turks in the sixth and seventh centuries thereafter) brought with them from the world of China a taste for tribute and a predisposition to rule from cities.[55] As a result, theirs would be an essentially parasitic relationship with the Roman state, predicated upon the pumping out from imperial coffers of as much gold as possible. However devastating the military consequences of Hunnic aggression, therefore, Hunnic demands were ultimately dependent upon the smooth operation of the Roman fiscal economy. Like any hungry parasite, the Huns required a healthy host, and this meant preserving Roman fiscal, urban, and economic structures substantially intact (just as the Arabs would preserve and feed off Roman economic and fiscal structures in the Near East in the seventh century).[56]

Those Germanic warlords and their allies who crossed into Roman territory in the 370s and the early years of the fifth century, by contrast, primarily wanted good-quality agricultural land, and were determined to acquire it, by negotiation or force. The hard-line eastern bishop Synesius of Cyrene, for example, was highly critical of how, in the aftermath of the battle of Adrianople, the emperor Theodosius I bought peace with the Goths by "generously making them gifts of land."[57] Likewise, the *Chronicle of Hydatius* records how, around 411, the invading Alans, Vandals, and Sueves in Spain "apportioned to themselves by lot tracts of the provinces to inhabit" ("sorte ad inhabitandum sibi provinciarum dividunt regiones").[58] In Gaul, Italy, and Africa, the settlement of Goths, Franks, Burgundians, and Vandals would on every occasion ultimately be associated with the establishment

---

(2008) 18–23; Proc. *Wars* 8.31.18 (Baduila's horseback war dance, described here, bears close resemblance to that attested with respect to Turkic nomadic warriors).
[54] Sarris, *Empires of Faith*, 71–72.
[55] See Richard Payne, chapter 16 in this volume.
[56] Wickham, *Framing the Early Middle Ages*, 759–780.
[57] Sarris, *Empires of Faith*, 58.
[58] Hydatius Lemicensis, *Chronicon*, s.a. 411.

of these invaders as landowners. As the Burgundian evidence in particular makes clear, this meant the acquisition of land not only on the part
of the "barbarian" leadership, but also on the part of the military rank-
and-file.[59]

Good-quality land always has a master, and lands belonging to the
imperial government, or to absentee landowners, are likely to have been
confiscated outright. There are indications, for example, that the landed
wealth of the Merovingian dynasty, concentrated around the "Paris
basin" in northern Gaul, owed much to what had once been imperial
estates that had passed into Frankish control. In Vandal Africa too, much
land was confiscated from aristocrats resident in Italy. Alternatively, land
could be taken from those who were still present. The enrichment of
the Burgundian rank-and-file, for example, was evidently achieved at
the expense of local Roman landowners, who were obliged to cede
portions of their estates in return for protection and peace. A similar
division of estates occurred in southern Gaul, Italy, and Spain, to the
benefit of the Goths.[60]

An important ramification of the barbarian settlement of the fifth
century, therefore, was an undermining of the economic dominance
of members of the late Roman aristocracy in the West. By virtue of
the same phenomenon, the economic and social significance of small-
or medium-scale landowners, such as the Burgundian soldiery, was
bolstered (although directly managed large estates continued to exist).
But for the structures of the underlying fiscal economy in those regions
that passed out of direct Roman control, the consequences were to be
far more pronounced. For, as noted in the first section of this essay, the
highly monetised and highly urbanised economy of the Roman Empire
of the fourth century was primarily sustained and given cohesion by
the monetised fiscal demands of the Roman state. By minting and
circulating vast quantities of coinage with which to pay the army and
the civil service, and by demanding that taxes be paid in coin, the
Roman state had catalysed and facilitated a much broader and deeper
monetisation of the economy. At the same time, it had used its wealth
to support cities, and had rendered practicable the urban aspirations of
members of the provincial elite.

By virtue of the barbarian "land grabs" of the fifth century, however, local society in the West would become increasingly dependent
militarily not on a standing army primarily paid in coin, but rather

---

[59] Sarris, *Empires of Faith*, 58–68.
[60] Ibid., 58–68.

on bands of barbarian warriors, the majority of whom were rewarded with land in return for their military service. As a result, both the fiscal and monetary structures inherited from the Roman state began to fade away, as the collection of the land tax in coin became both less necessary and more politically problematic, and as post-Roman rulers responded by minting coin in significantly diminished volume. As coinage became scarcer, trade began to contract, and as trade contracted, so too did the urban lifestyle of surviving members of the Roman elite become increasingly difficult to maintain, leading in most regions to a final aristocratic flight from *civitas* to *villa* that would be complete by the seventh century. The ultimate effect of the barbarian settlement in the West, therefore, would be a dismantling of much of the sophisticated economic infrastructure that had come to characterise the Roman world.[61] If Attila and the Huns had wanted an ever-larger slice of the fiscal cake of the late Roman state, many of his erstwhile followers ended up effectively closing down the metaphorical bakery. This was not, however, so much the result of the greater destructiveness of the Germanic invaders as compared to the Huns, but rather, it was an expression of the differing priorities and contrasting economic cultures that they had brought with them into Roman territory.

[61] Ibid., 68–82.

4: MEDITERRANEAN CITIES IN THE FIFTH CENTURY: ELITES, CHRISTIANIZING, AND THE BARBARIAN INFLUX

Kenneth G. Holum

In the period roughly 350–450, urban communities of the classical Mediterranean type, as many as nine hundred of them,[1] endured momentous changes. Affected were the imperial capitals Rome and Constantinople, treated in a separate chapter, as well as regional metropolises such as Trier and Carthage in the West, Antioch and Alexandria in the East, with populations of perhaps 100,000 to 400,000, but also the far larger numbers of provincial capitals and average cities focused on here, with populations anywhere from a few thousand to more than 50,000. In the foreground are the elites. From Londinium in Britain to Petra in the Arabian desert, city elites experienced long-term economic stresses that precipitated changes in social relations and government. Studying elites will also clarify why cities adopted Christianity as the predominant religion, and why, in lands where barbarians settled, traditional urban patterns began to disintegrate.

First, a few words about concepts, to be illustrated in the immensely rich writings of Augustine of Hippo (354–430).[2] After the Gothic sack of Rome (410), beginning his great book *On the City of God*, Augustine conceived of a world populated by the traditional Mediterranean city, the *civitas*, or, as he defined it, "a large number of

---

[1] See A. H. M. Jones, *The Later Roman Empire, 284–602*, 2 vols. (Oxford, 1964) 2: 712–719 (hereafter *LRE*), for numbers and distribution; and, for cities in general, ibid., 712–766, and John H. W. G. Liebeschuetz, *The Decline and Fall of the Roman City* (Oxford, 2001).

[2] Peter Brown, *Augustine of Hippo: A Biography*, 2nd ed. (Berkeley, 2000) esp. 312–329.

men and women being of one mind" (1.15). Apparently, his point was the high level of social cohesion that ideally characterized a relatively small city like Hippo, where he was bishop, or his hometown Thagaste, both in Africa Proconsularis (Algeria). Nevertheless, the Gothic sack directed his thinking toward Rome, a far larger city, so he adopted a grandiose metaphor to explain God's operation in history. Augustine constructed Rome itself as the archetypal "earthly city" that had suffered in 410, while perceiving within this earthly city the presence, since the beginning of history, of a "city of God" composed of men and women whose "one mind" was to worship the Christian God. Of course, by Augustine's day most inhabitants of all the cities in the Roman Empire, *civitates* (sing. *civitas*) in the Latin-speaking West or *poleis* (sing. *polis*) in the Greek East, had come to share citizenship of Rome, a single, Mediterranean-style city, albeit a most powerful one, and they also claimed membership in their local communities, each also appropriately termed "city."[3] Augustine chose *civitas* for his two cities because it evoked belonging, loyalty, or the "being of one mind" characteristic of fellow citizens. On the other hand, he and his contemporaries lacked vocabulary to express what we would call today a comprehensive citizenship of one's "nation" or "country." That is precisely why Augustine chose to write of the *city* of God. In the fourth and fifth centuries it was primarily in the city that ancient Mediterranean people experienced "being of one mind." In modern terms, cities scattered across the terrain remained the social setting in which Mediterranean people worked out their personal and group identities.[4] For them civic identity was prime. Hence as Augustine, many years earlier, had matured and left Africa for Italy where he turned to asceticism, he had typically moved among a coterie of friends from Thagaste, who while abroad depended on one another for support, among them his wealthy patron Cornelius Romanianus, his son Licentius and their relative Alypius, and Evodius, who had retired from the secret police.[5]

Comprehending identity is fundamental to understanding cities, but we need to explore further the concept of *civitas* in Augustine's time

---

[3] See esp. Claude Lepelley, *Les cités de l'Afrique romaine au Bas-Empire*, 2 vols. (Paris, 1981) 2: 113–125 (Hippo), 175–184 (Thagaste).

[4] Guy Halsall, "Social Identities and Social Relationships in Early Merovingian Gaul," in *Franks and Alamanni in the Merovingian Period: An Ethnographic Perspective*, ed. Ian Wood (Woodbridge, U.K., 1998) 141–175.

[5] Augustine, *Confessions*, 6.7, 14, 9.8.17; cf. Lepelley, *Les cités de l'Afrique romain*, 2: 178–183, and Brown, *Augustine of Hippo*, 498, on Romanianus and his family.

and of related terms in Latin and Greek. *Civitas*, from *civis*, "citizen," meant not a "city" of buildings and streets but either a specific group of citizens living in one continuous space, or else the concept of citizenship itself. Writing of Rome or any other Mediterranean city as a physical place Augustine employed other words (*urbs, oppidum*) for a densely occupied urban center. *Polis* in Greek served equally well for the physical city, or its inhabitants, or both. The point is important because either *civitas* or *polis*, as a group of citizens, therefore comprehended not just the urban center but also the surrounding territory, the fields, villages, and towns that belonged to the city.[6] The surrounding fields, gardens, groves, and pastures produced much of the city's wealth, and hence strong bonds existed between the countryside and the urban center. Elite landlords owned rural estates but generally chose residence in the urban center, and it was from the center that the elite collected both rents owed to the landlords and taxes due to the state. Thus Augustine wrote to Romulus, a wealthy Hippo landowner, urging him to rescind the order to his tenants that these "wretched and impoverished men pay to the agent placed over them twice what they actually owed" (*Epistles*, 247.1).

Of course, Augustine also had a clear concept of the city in a physical, visible sense with "dwelling quarters, streets, marketplaces, theaters, and temples" (*City of God*, 3.27), and he might have added public baths supplied by aqueducts, and of course fortification walls surrounding the urban center. Most characteristic were the theaters, along with amphitheaters, stadia, and circuses or hippodromes, all sites of spectacles organized at public expense or by wealthy benefactors, featuring mimes and musicians, beast-hunts, or chariot races. In the theatrical crowd, community members became visible to one another, seated in rank order and often arrayed by membership in craft or cultic associations.[7] For his part, Augustine recoiled instinctively at spectacles, not just because they offered sensuous and exciting performances,[8] but (one suspects) because he thought the theater's pull challenged the growth of the visible "city of God." In a Christian community, by contrast, it was in the churches that people saw one another: "the

---

[6] Augustine, *City of God*, 3.16, on Rome's territory in the regal period.

[7] Charlotte Roueché, *Performers and Partisans at Aphrodisias in the Roman and Late Roman Periods* (London, 1993) esp. 83–128.

[8] For Augustine theaters and spectacles were a main fixation; see, e.g. *Confessions*, 3.2, 6.7; *City of God*, 1.32–33, 2.4, 8, 14, 20, 27, 3.1, 19, 4.27, 8.13. Cf. Lepelley, *Les cités de l'Afrique romaine*, 1: 376–385.

people flock to the churches in pious celebration, the sexes properly segregated" (*City of God*, 2.28).

THE COUNCILMEN, "VISCERA OF THE CITIES"

Understanding the fifth-century city requires special attention to the city's landlord elite who owned income-producing property in the urban center and the city's territory. Prominent among them was a legally recognized order of councilmen, called *curiales* in Latin or *bouleutai* in Greek, who sat together in the city's *curia* or *boulē*, the city council.[9] In 458 Emperor Majorian issued an anxious law recalling councilmen to their duties because they were "sinews of the state, the viscera of the cities" (*Novels of Majorian*, 7 praef.). Such anxieties were well founded.

These city councilmen ranked below senators of Rome or of Constantinople, some of whom, although living in Rome or elsewhere, owned land in another city's territory.[10] The family of Melania the Younger, for example, of the Roman senatorial order, owned a huge estate in the territory of Thagaste, to which she fled after the sack of 410.[11] Ranking among a city's elite if they resided there, neither senators of Rome, nor "immune" higher clergy, nor imperial officials owning local estates numbered among the councilmen. Thus among a larger elite the councilmen themselves formed a critical group of a few dozen in the smallest city to several hundred in the largest. From Thamugadi (modern Timgad), located three hundred kilometers southwest of Thagaste and Hippo, the nearly complete text survives on stone of the roster (*album*) of the local elite, dated 363. Inscribed in rank order, the list of 233 elite men began with ten Roman senators, and then came the city's councilmen, first the current city magistrates (*curator, duumviri, aediles, quaestores*) and "perpetual priests," and then ordinary council members not currently in office.[12] Last were Christian priests and provincial officials who resided at Thamugadi or owned land there. Of 283 listed, as many as 188, not being Roman senators or otherwise

---

[9] *LRE* 2: 737–757; Avshalom Laniado, *Recherches sur les notables municipaux dans l'Empire protobyzantin* (Paris, 2002).

[10] Augustine knew of many senators of Rome who had never seen the imperial city (*City of God*, 5.17).

[11] Gerontius, *Life of Melania*, 21.

[12] *LRE* 2: 730–731; Laniado, *Recherches sur les notables municipaux*, 6; André Chastagnol, *L'Album municipal de Timgad* (Bonn, 1978) esp. 22–39, 89–90.

immune, were eligible for "honors," as contemporaries called the magistrates' positions,[13] and were likewise subject to the compulsory public "duties" (*munera, leitourgiai*) that the local elite performed for the city and the Roman state. These included ensuring security, maintenance of streets, public buildings, and the water supply, fuel for the baths, and stable market prices of grain as a hedge against famine.[14] Above all, councilmen administered finance in the city and surrounding territory, serving as collectors of current and back-due taxes. Performing functions essential to both the city and the Roman state, the councilmen came under intense pressure. In the past, income from city-owned land and other properties had financed many city services, but in the fourth century the Roman government, pressed for cash, had confiscated most of these resources,[15] so "honors" and "duties" became crushing financial burdens on many councilmen, especially on the less affluent.

In the average city the councilmen naturally occupied a spectrum of wealth and power. In the *City of God* Augustine envisions one councilman as "a poor man, or rather average," possessing a single estate sufficient for his needs, dear to his family, at peace with friends and neighbors, another as a man of "exceeding wealth" who is "inflamed with greed, never worry-free, always striving, panting from everlasting quarrels with his enemies, through such miseries expanding his patrimony beyond measure" (4.3). A man of the first type, Augustine's father Patricius possessed a landed estate, however modest it was, since the famous pear tree from which young Augustine and other rowdy boys stole fruit grew near the vineyard of his family.[16] Indeed, Augustine's companions from Thagaste all appear to have stemmed from curial families that were likewise landlords. In particular Romanianus's family was one of "exceeding wealth," occupying the very pinnacle of the steep social pyramid. Late in 386 Augustine addressed Romanianus in his treatise *Against the Academics* (1.2) urging him to turn away from the temporary felicities of a very rich man, one who owns several elegant mansions equipped with lavish private baths and reception halls, who much enjoys the hunt and banqueting on exotic dishes that appealed to

---

[13] On magistrates, see *LRE* 2: 725–731; Alan K. Bowman, *The Town Councils of Roman Egypt* (Toronto, 1971) 39–67.

[14] On "duties" see *LRE* 2: 734–737; Lepelley, *Les cités de l'Afrique romain*, 1: 206–216.

[15] *CTh* 15.1.18; *LRE* 2: 732–734.

[16] *Confessions*, 2.4.9; also *Epistles*, 126.7 for Augustine's paternal estate as "tiny fields." On Patricius, see *Confessions*, 2.3.5, where *municeps . . . tenuis* means a councilman of modest means, also Lepelley, *Les cités de l'Afrique romain*, 2: 175–177, citing Possidius, *Life of Augustine*, 1.1–2.

the most exquisite tastes. The vast fortune of Romanianus, drawn from faithfully managed estates, enabled him to finance entertainments for the citizens in the theater and amphitheater, even bear hunts and spectacles so unheard-of that the "foolish crowd" praised him to the skies. Hence bronze tablets designated him patron of Thagaste and neighboring cities. Statues were erected. Romanianus had already held all of the municipal offices or "honors" of Thagaste and received even higher positions from the governor and emperor. His was the paradigmatic career of a most successful member of the urban elite.

Hence society was distinctly top-down. Symptomatic was the mentality of Augustine himself, whose social gaze indeed did encompass the undifferentiated "poor," who crowded the city's colonnades, always starving, seeking shelter against the cold, in whom he saw the naked Christ.[17] Yet defining himself as "a poor man from a poor family" Augustine can only be comparing the house of Patricius to wealthiest families of Thagaste while ignoring the vast majority of the genuine poor.[18] Writing of the general Christian community, he has in mind substantial men of his own social level with families and established households and property, who live in harmony with one another, husbands and wives, fathers and sons, masters and slaves, and who strive to acquire worldly and temporal goods, surely not a prospect for most who populated the cities but within the reach of even modest men of the elite.[19] Similarly, when chastising his congregations Augustine enumerated sins more accessible to the wealthy and preeminent – avarice, sharp dealing, perjury, money lending, luxurious living, as well as drunkenness, fornication, and consulting a sorceress "every time you have a headache" – than to slaves, dependents, and the laboring man or woman.[20] Augustine's social gaze characterized city-based elites all over the empire.

From a quantitative perspective, we observe that 282 men listed on Thamugadi's roster meant perhaps 1,200–1,500 elite men, women, and children dominating an overall population of 75,000 or so in the city itself and the surrounding countryside. Perhaps 15,000 occupied

---

[17] Augustine, *Sermons*, 25.8, Peter Brown, *Poverty and Leadership in the Later Roman Empire* (Hanover, N.H., 2002) 65–66, esp. 74 on the "change in the social imagination" that rendered the poor visible.

[18] *Sermons*, 356.13; cf. Brown, *Augustine*, 413.

[19] *City of God*, 1.9.

[20] For Augustine's favorite sins, see *Sermons*, 88.25, 224.1; *Commentary on Psalms*, 127.11, cited by Brown, *Augustine*, 247, with n. 1.

the city center,[21] including landlords, as well as tradesmen and their families, slave and free, while in the countryside most lived in villages, some of them free peasants who owned their land, many, however, cultivators of landlords' land in return for rent. Papyrus land registers dated to the 350s indicate that at Hermopolis, on the west bank of the Nile in Upper Egypt, only about one in six or seven families who lived in the built-up city owned any land at all, while the top 10 percent of landlords held 78 percent of the land, most of it concentrated nearby but some located near more distant villages.[22] The Thamugadi elite would similarly have dominated landholding, as did Romanianus and others like him at Thagaste.

Ruling the Mediterranen city, therefore, was a narrow clique of like-minded men, themselves under the thumb of the provincial gover-nor and other officers of the Roman state. In the theaters and circuses the people of a Roman city, sometimes led by the professional cheer-leaders, still chanted rhythmic acclamations praising or blaming local or imperial leaders, assured that their "voices" would be made known to the emperor.[23] Otherwise no vestige remained of popular participation. In local affairs the councilmen were in charge, and even among this small group the game had always been "follow the leader." A modest councilman like Patricius or an exceptionally powerful one like Roma-nianus would sit on the city's *curia* or *boulē*. This group issued the bronze tablets that honored the city's patrons, assigned the "duties" to coun-cilmen and others qualified by wealth, and they appointed members to local offices or "honors." In the fourth and fifth centuries the old official titles of the Thamugadi roster rarely survived, and increasingly a chief magistrate was "curator of the city," responsible for finances, or "city defender," a judicial officer. Members of the local elite, chief magistrates received their offices by nomination in the council with approval of the provincial governor.

But those who counted had long been the elite of the elite. Like others the Thamugadi roster listed members in rank order. The leading

---

[21] Lepelley, *Les cités de l'Afrique romain*, 2: 445, gives Thamugaid's spatial extent as seventy hectares, while Chastagnol, *L'Album municipal de Timgad*, 89, proposes 10,000 inhabitants, considering too high Courtois's estimate of 15,000.

[22] The main papyri are *PFlor* 71 and *PGiess* 117; see Alan K. Bowman, "Landholding in the Hermopolite Nome in the Fourth Century A.D.," *Journal of Roman Studies* 75 (1985) 137–163; and Roger S. Bagnall, "Landholding in Late Roman Egypt: The Distribution of Wealth," *JRS* 82 (1992) 128–149.

[23] Charlotte Roueché, "Acclamations in the Later Roman Empire," *JRS* 74 (1984) 181–199.

member convoked the council, announced the agenda, and presided over discussion, and then the councilmen spoke and voted in rank order[24] so each would know how those who outranked him had voted and would be disinclined to break with the leadership. Actual minutes of a council meeting, preserved on papyrus, illuminate the procedures. In 370 the council of Oxyrhynchus in Egypt met to hear a complaint of Macrobius, an ordinary member.[25] The presiding officer had assigned to him the additional "duty" of administering soldiers' woolen clothing, although his name already appeared on the wax tablet that the governor had approved assigning duties to twenty-four councilmen. According to the minutes, Macrobius himself spoke first, registering his complaint, and at once all the councilmen "shouted together" that "what is on the tablet is valid." Even in the council the vote was by acclamation. Then spoke eleven senior members of the council who had held major magisterial positions in the city, all in support of Macrobius. Without delay the president agreed and relieved Macrobius of the additional duty. The papyrus records no mention of a tally, or whether any of perhaps a hundred or more ordinary councilmen, other than Macrobius himself, spoke during the session, or were even present. Such were the normal procedures of top-down city government. The only speakers whose views counted sufficiently to be written in the minutes were eleven senior members. For practical purposes, it was their words that constituted the "one mind" that Augustine considered to be the definition of a city.

The best evidence for the makeup and inner working of the average city council dates to the later fourth century but is also more or less valid for much of the fifth. For the greater cities we have the orations and correspondence of the sophist Libanius of Antioch (d. 393), who, like Augustine, identified himself with his native city, especially with the landholding elite of councilmen, whose social vision he shared.[26] Libanius also informs us in sharp words about the two major social movements of the period that affected the councilmen. First was the flight of many councilmen from their duties, as addressed in Majorian's 458 law, either by selling or abandoning their properties in order

---

[24] Justinian, Digest, 50.3.1 praef., 1.1–2 (Ulpian), in Corpus iuris civilis, ed. Paul Krueger, Theodor Mommsen et al. (1872), vol. 1; cf. Chastagnol, L'Album municipal de Timgad, 31, pointing out that the rule appears to have been followed at Thamugadi in 363.

[25] This is Papyrus Oxyrhynchus (POxy) 2110. For discussion, see esp. Bowman, Town Councils, passim.

[26] Isabella Sandwell, Religious Identity in Late Antiquity: Greeks, Jews, and Christians in Antioch (Cambridge, 2007) 161–169.

to escape curial obligations, or by securing immune positions as officials of the Roman governor and state.[27] Augustine's early ambition to become a teacher of rhetoric, an immune profession, constituted similar flight from duties, and his coterie of friends harbored similar hopes of immunity. Hence Libanius laments in two orations of the 380s a catastrophic drop in membership of the Antioch council, from six hundred to sixty.[28]

Libanius exaggerated, no doubt, in order to convey a sense of urgency, yet the converse of declining numbers was a second social development, the ascendancy of an upper circle of councilmen generally termed "first men" (*principales, prōteuontes*) because their names appeared first on the official rosters. These were men like Romanianus of Thagaste who had not attempted to avoid obligations because they found such functions to be profitable and exploited them to increase their wealth and power within community. Legislation in the Theodosian Code confirms that they practiced extortion (386), and, writing in Gaul in the 440s the priest Salvian declared "all councilmen [are] bullies," accusing them of converting tax obligations into personal profit.[29] The flight of the councilmen and the consequent prosperity and rise of "first men" represented a gradual steepening of the already precipitous social pyramid. Harried ordinary councilmen such as Augustine's father Patricius became a closed, tightly controlled caste of tax collectors, hoping to escape, but at the pinnacle Romanianus and others amassed wealth and power and by their benefactions preserved the traditional Mediterranean city.

"FLOWING TOGETHER TO THE CHURCH": THE CONVERSION OF CITIES

Since Constantine, emperors had issued numerous laws against paganism and sacrifice and had threatened dire penalties,[30] yet temples and their

---

[27] John H. W. G. Liebeschuetz, *Antioch: City and Imperial Administration in the Later Roman Empire* (Oxford, 1972) 174–186; also *LRE* 739–757; Laniado, *Recherches sur les notables municipaux*, 3–26.

[28] Libanius, *Orations*, 48.4, 49.8; cf. Liebeschuetz, *Antioch*, 181–182.

[29] *CTh* 12.6.22; Salvian, *On the Governance of God*, 5.4; cf. Liebeschuetz, *Antioch*, 184–186; Lepelley, *Les cités de l'Afrique romain*, 1: 214–215. On "first men" Liebeschuetz, *Antioch*,171–174; Laniado, *Recherches sur les notables municipaux*, 131–233.

[30] Many collected in *CTh* 16.10; cf. Frank R. Trombley, *Hellenic Religion and Christianization c. 370–529*, 2 vols. (Leiden, 1993) 1: 1–97.

cults still flourished in most cities toward the end of the fourth century. Looking back to his days in Carthage during the 380s, Augustine in the *City of God* recalled with horror the urban festival of the goddess Dea Caelestis. Her vast and ornate temple still dominated the city, surrounded by a broad paved esplanade and by smaller shrines of the city's other gods. The festivities Augustine described included public banqueting, contests honoring the goddess, and a procession in which priests carried the divine image on a litter before a multitude "of both sexes," enticed further to attend by choral hymns and by mimes and actresses in lewd performances.[31] Augustine does not mention sacrifice.

In most cities of the empire, pagan temples and cults represented populations still devoted to the ancient gods. In 395 virtually the entire population of Gaza in Palestine and its territory remained pagan, except for a tiny congregation of 280 Christian men, women, and children. Gaza's councilmen, likewise all pagans, refused to select Christians for offices that would admit them to the council and hence to the elite.[32] At Carthage "the impious superstition of a few polluted the whole city," it was said, on the eve of the Vandal conquest in 439, because "the wealthy and powerful families," that is, those of the councilmen and other resident grandees, "shaped the [views of] the undisciplined crowd."[33] Thus city elites across the empire remained bastions of paganism.

Around 400, though, the tide was turning.[34] Christianizing varied from one city to another, and the pace was slow until the reigns of Emperor Theodosius I and his descendants (379–455). Then bishops and monks more frequently undertook the hard labor of pulling down temples, often having secured the emperor's backing. In the West pagan shrines sometimes declined from neglect, including the great Caelestis temple at Carthage, by 421 already abandoned and invaded by brush and thorns. In Gaul a few decades earlier Martin, bishop of Tours, generally focused his destructive energy on village and country shrines, often meeting stiff resistance from the local people armed with swords and

---

[31] Augustine, *City of God*, 2.4, 26; cf. Lepelley, *Les cités de l'Afrique romain*, 2: 42–43, citing the eyewitness Quodvultdeus, *Book of the Promises and Prophecies of God*, 3.38.

[32] Mark the Deacon, *Life of Porphyry*, 19, 32, 40, 64; cf. Trombley, *Hellenic Religion and Christianization*, 1: 187–282.

[33] *On the Governance of God*, 8.3.14. On pagan majorities in councils also Augustine, *Epistles*, 50, 232, cf. Lepelley, *Les cités de l'Afrique romain*, 2: 136–137, 305–307.

[34] See generally Kenneth G. Holum, "In the Blinking of an Eye: The Christianizing of Classical Cities in the Levant," in *Religion and Politics in the Ancient Near East*, ed. Adele Berlin (Bethesda, Md., 1996) 131–150.

knives.[35] By contrast, Bishop Marcellus of Apamea in Syria destroyed his city's temple of Zeus in the 380s with the backing of one thousand imperial troops, and in 391 Bishop Theophilus of Alexandria directed a Christian mob that demolished the city's celebrated Serapeum and incinerated the wooden cult statue of Sarapis himself, from whose severed head a colony of mice beat a swift retreat.[36]

By far the best known of such episodes was Bishop Porphyrius's campaign in Gaza 395–402, recounted faithfully by his associate, Mark the Deacon. After years of tense pagan–Christian relations, Porphyrius took ship for Constantinople, where he secured the support of the emperor and empress, Arcadius and Eudoxia. In 402, an imperial count arrived, bringing troops, and with their support the Christian mob captured and burned the Marneion and other pagan temples. In terror the pagan councilmen had meanwhile abandoned the city for the safety of their country estates. Five years later, another officer arrived from Constantinople with specifications for building on the Marneion site, now cleansed of pagan impurities, a monumental church to be ornamented with Carystian marble columns that the empress herself had donated.[37]

Hailed as "trophies" of Christian triumph, as "banners of the victories of the Lord," the new churches did not themselves make the cities Christian, nor did evangelism turn the tide, or preaching the Christian Gospel.[38] Christianization meant all social levels adopting the new faith, and for that to happen, in a top-down society, the councilmen were the key. Giving words to Emperor Arcadius, Mark the Deacon assessed the actual situation around 400 succinctly: "Gaza cooperates by paying taxes and contributes much to the treasury, so if we use terror they will flee and we will lose revenues" (*Life of Porphyry*, 41). Arcadius had in mind those crucial tax collectors, councilmen still secure in their paganism because the emperors needed them. "So we will press them a little and will withhold their honors and offices," the emperor continued. Indeed, in this top-down world councilmen everywhere likewise required imperial favor if they wished to scale the ever-steeper social pinnacle. In this society, as elites embraced the new faith so did their families and dependents. In Gaza, for instance, a woman named

[35] Quodvultdeus, *Book of the Promises*, 3.38, cf. Lepelley, *Les cités de l'Afrique romain*, 2: 43 (Carthage); Sulpicius Severus, *Life of St. Martin*, 13–15.

[36] Theodoret, *Historia ecclesiastica*, 5.22; cf. Trombley, *Hellenic Religion and Christianization*, 1: 123–145.

[37] Mark the Deacon, *Life of Porphyry*, 33–84, 92–94; Trombley, *Hellenic Religion and Christianization*, 1: 187–245.

[38] Mark the Deacon, 2; Jerome, *Epistles*, 6.13.4; Holum, "In the Blinking of an Eye."

Ailia, pagan wife of a pagan councilman, giving birth after three days of severe labor, credited to Porphyrius and to Christ both her life and the life of her newborn son. Thus she accepted the "seal of Christ" and became a catechumen, together with her entire family, numbering sixty-four, probably including slaves and dependents.[39] In Africa, where the elite "shaped the views of the crowd," Augustine urged Christian landlords to impose uniformity of faith on their estates, and in 412 Emperor Honorius even required that they beat slaves and cultivators into conforming.[40]

We glimpse the social process of Christianizing cities most clearly in another contemporary text, the so-called *Letter of Severus*.[41] On Minorca, one of the Balearic Islands in the Mediterranean, an elite of Jewish landlords dominated the small *civitas* Magona on the eastern shore, chief among them Theodorus, who had already finished all of the duties that the council assigned, had held office as "defender," and now ranked as patron among the councilmen (6.1–3). In February 418 Severus, author of the *Letter* and bishop of the small Christian city Jamona on the west of Minorca, led a throng of the Christian faithful, inflamed by the arrival on the island of relics of Saint Stephen, against the Jews of Magona. Violence erupted, the Christians burned the synagogue down, and fearing more violence some Jews embraced Christ. Three days later, when Theodorus had returned from inspecting his estates, Jews and Christians confronted one another at the ruined synagogue, and voices were heard proclaiming (incorrectly) that "Theodorus has converted." At once the Jews of the elite lost heart and fled, as had the pagans of Gaza, fearing for their lives and property. Suddenly without a following and without power, Theodorus now acquiesced to changing his religion, and the rest of the Magona Jews "flowed together to the church" (21.4). Within eight days the number of those ready to accept baptism totaled 540, presumably the entire Jewish elite of Magona together with their families and dependents. The new Christians constructed a church where the synagogue had stood, carrying the stones on their own backs.

---

[39] Mark the Deacon, 29–31; Trombley, *Hellenic Religion and Christianization*, 1:198.

[40] Augustine, *Commentary on Psalms*, 54.13; also *Epistles*, 89.8, 112.3; *CTh* 16.5.52 addressing heresy (Donatism) not paganism, but the principle was the same; cf. Lepelley, *Les cités de l'Afrique romain*, 1: 326, 361.

[41] Severus of Minorca, *Letter on the Conversion of the Jews*, ed. and trans. Scott Bradbury (Oxford, 1996), whence the in-text references.

Severus's account, replete with miracle and prejudice, does resemble other evidence for city conversion, including Gaza, and thus merits credence. Here too a bishop organized violence, with Saint Stephen providing the needed muscle, and the intimidated non-Christian elite lost its confidence. The Jews all followed their leaders, as the pattern of top-down conversion repeated itself. Clearly evident here, though, as nowhere else, is that Theodorus and his fellow non-Christian councilmen suddenly lost their ability to lead. It was a crisis of group identity. The former social cohesion, the "being of one mind" essential to peace and security in a Mediterranean city, had disintegrated before the threat of force, and Theodorus clearly saw embracing Christianity as the surest route to restoring community integrity. Severus put revealing words in the mouth of the Jew Reuben, a fellow councilman, already converted (16.14–15, trans. Bradbury): "What do you fear, Lord Theodorus? If you truly wish to be safe and honoured and wealthy, believe in Christ, just as I too have believed. Right now you are standing, and I am seated with bishops; if you should believe, you will be seated, and I will be standing before you." In the Mediterranean city patrons sat while their clients and dependents stood in respect before them. Henceforth, on the island of Minorca, as elsewhere, the leading councilmen, more and more as the fifth century progressed, would find that identifying themselves as Christian would buttress their authority, and that henceforth they would share their power with the Christian bishops.

MEDITERRANEAN-STYLE URBAN CENTERS: EASTERN PROSPERITY, WESTERN REGRESSION

Augustine sheds little light on the physical environment of the Mediterranean city, but archaeology has demonstrated continued vitality and that in architecture and city planning builders adhered to ancient traditions. In the East this holds for Antioch and Alexandria, and for cities of second rank such as Ephesus in Asia and Apamea in Syria. Scythopolis (Beth Shean) in Palestine is a prime example, extensively and well excavated in the 1990s (fig. 4.1).[42] Between the fourth century and the mid-sixth, the population increased significantly, to perhaps thirty to

---

[42] Yoram Tsafrir and Gideon Foerster, "Urbanism at Scythopolis-Bet Shean in the Fourth to Seventh Centuries," *Dumbarton Oaks Papers* 51 (1997) 85–146; generally, Liebeschuetz, *Decline and Fall*, 30–74.

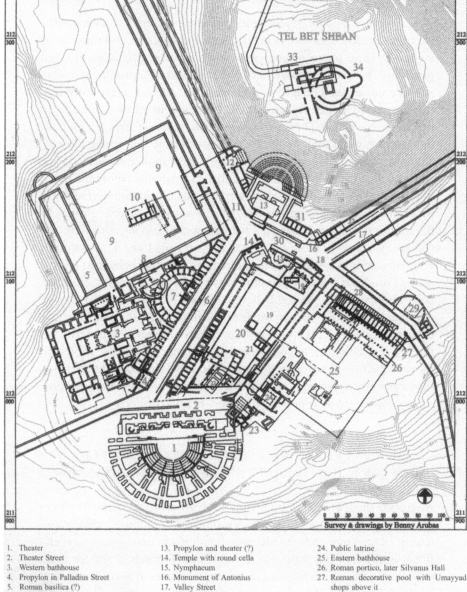

FIGURE 4.1 Scythopolis–Beth Shean, Israel, map of central area showing monumental construction or reconstruction of the later fourth through early sixth centuries: 3 western bathhouse, 6 Palladius street, 7 sigma building, 15 Nymphaeum, 20 Byzantine agora, 25 eastern bathhouse, 28 Silvanus street. Drawn by Benny Arubas, Courtesy of the Hebrew University Expedition at Beth Shean, Israel.

TEL BET SHEAN

Survey & drawings by Benny Arubas

1. Theater
2. Theater Street
3. Western bathhouse
4. Propylon in Palladius Street
5. Roman basilica (?)
6. Palladius Street
7. Semicircular Byzantine plaza (Sigma)
8. Odeon
9. Reconstructed Roman forum or temenos
10. Byzantine public building
11. Northwest Street
12. Propylon and stairway to acropolis
13. Propylon and theater (?)
14. Temple with round cella
15. Nymphaeum
16. Monument of Antonius
17. Valley Street
18. Central Monument
19. Early Roman basilica with Abbasid mosque above it
20. Byzantine agora
21. Umayyad pottery workshop
22. Temple
23. Roman cult structures
24. Public latrine
25. Eastern bathhouse
26. Roman portico, later Silvanus Hall
27. Roman decorative pool with Umayyad shops above it
28. Silvanus Street
29. Semicircular plaza (Sigma?)
30. Street of the Monuments
31. Shops of the Street of the Monuments
32. Abbasid quarter above Valley Street
33. Temple of Zeus Akraios
34. Round church

thirty-eight thousand persons densely contained within a new fortification wall built sometime in the fifth century. In our period, or a
bit later, new construction included two public baths, a marketplace in
the city center, and paved streets with water pipelines beneath them,
some flanked by marble columns in a high classical style. Performances
continued in the theater, and the authorities reconstituted the second-
century hippodrome in a new residential quarter to the south as an
amphitheater for beast fights and other spectacles. In Greek inscriptions
the provincial governors resident in Scythopolis took credit for new
construction and restoration of dilapidated monuments, but the funding
would have come from taxes the councilmen collected in Scythopolis
and its territory and delivered to the provincial treasury. At Scythopolis
as elsewhere, newly dominant Christians sometimes decapitated statues
of gods and goddesses in order to demobilize the demons thought to
inhabit them, but generally citizens remained proud of and identified
with the lavish sculptural ornaments of their city and long kept many
of them on public display.

Unless as in Gaza the destroyers had rooted out a pagan temple in
order to remove every trace of pollution, eastern bishops at first tended
to site churches elsewhere within the urban center. Desanctified temples survived as part of a city's ornamentation, like the marble columns
and the decapitated statues. For the churches architects adopted basil-
ical or central plans rooted in classical architecture, but they moved
the optically engaging exterior colonnades of classical temples to the
building's interior – including, for example, the thirty-two Carystian
columns that Empress Eudoxia had sent to Gaza, "glimmering like
emeralds" (Mark the Deacon, *Life of Porphyry*, 84). Hence beginning in
this period Christianity increasingly "refigured" the classical Mediterranean city.[43]

Another trend of the period evident everywhere was the fixation
of the councilmen and other elites on their urban mansions, to which
they devoted ever more personal wealth. Though much elite housing stock survived from the High Empire, new construction was not
rare, as, for example the House of Bacchus in Cuicul (Djemila, Algeria)
(fig. 4.2). Grand houses often occupied fifteen hundred meters square or
more, organized around one or two interior peristyles, accessed through
an imposing entrance. As the social pyramid steepened, some mansions succumbed to subdivision into three or more modest dwellings.

[43] Annabel J. Wharton, *Refiguring the Classical City: Dura Europos, Jerash, Jerusalem and Ravenna* (Cambridge, 1995) esp. 64–104.

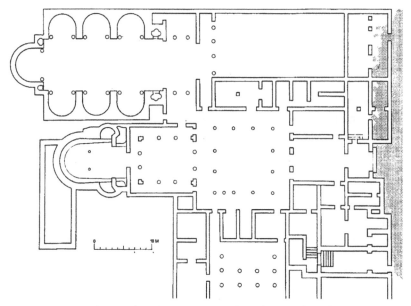

FIGURE 4.2 Cuicul/Djemila, Algeria, House of Bacchus, with multi-apsed dining room of the fourth–early fifth century. North is at upper right. Drawn by Jean Lenne (CNRS, IAM), reproduced by permission from J. Lassus, "La salle à sept apsides de Djemila-Cuicul," *Antiquités africaines* 5 (1971) 197, fig. 4.

Nevertheless, renovation and expansion also persisted, with emphasis on spacious vestibules and apsidal reception halls where patrons met their ordinary clients. Private baths proliferated. Distinct from reception rooms were the more exclusive dining rooms, richly decorated with figured mosaic pavements and sumptuous embroidered hangings, for higher-ranking guests only (fig. 4.3). These now reclined on the fashionable semicircular couches to dine on exotic fishes and meats served in vast quantities with quality wines by swarms of household slaves. Such were the dinners of Romanianus of Thagaste, who understood that sheer quality and quantities of food were a visible index of social preeminence. Frequently, the diners occupied a raised dais within a semidomed apse (or multiple apses), where the master of the house and his guests inhabited the architectural space of the enthroned emperor, or of the resurrected Christ ascending in glory. Dining culture displays vividly the dominance of the urban elites and the steepening of the social pyramid.[44]

[44] Yvon Thébert, "Private Life and Domestic Architecture in Roman Africa," in *A History of Private Life*, vol. 1: *From Pagan Rome to Byzantium*, ed. Paul Veyne,

FIGURE 4.3 Funerary banquet, mosaic pavement from a cemetery near Antioch, Syria, dated ca. 400. Represented are women reclining on a *stibadium* couch around a *sigma* table, evoking the luxury of elite banqueting in the later fourth and early fifth centuries. Worcester Art Museum, Worcester, Massachusetts, Excavation of Antioch and Vicinity funded by the bequests of the Reverend Dr. Austin S. Garver and Sarah C. Garver, 1936.26 Image ©Worcester Art Museum, all rights reserved.

When Augustine confessed that he "struggle[d] every day against concupiscence in eating and drinking" (*Confessions*, 10.31) – again focusing on a sin that only the well-off could afford – he likely had such dinners on his conscience, which like the spectacles competed as social practice with the efforts of the ascetic bishop to promote the City of God within the Mediterranean city. Indeed, as J. H. W. G. Liebeschuetz suggested,[45] it was when they gathered in the reception and dining rooms of the great houses that the elites most seriously

trans. Arthur Goldhammer (Cambridge, Mass., 1987) 313–410; Katherine M. D. Dunbabin, *The Roman Banquet: Images of Conviviality* (Cambridge, 2003) 141–202.

[45] Liebeschuetz, *Decline and Fall*, 107, 117, 121, esp. 405, writing of "a vaguely defined, self-appointed group of magnates, making decisions and nominating officials in the privacy of the audience hall of one of the great houses." My point is that, while true, this was nothing new.

sized one another up and talked about communal issues that mattered, such as conferring the honor of patron or "defender" on someone, or distributing the advantages and burdens of the "duties."

In summer 430, as Augustine lay dying in Hippo, Vandal invaders surrounded a city crowded with refugees, still protected by serviceable fortifications (Possidius, *Life of Augustine*, 28–31). After the invaders seized Carthage in 439, elite Vandals took over both the luxurious urban dwellings and the rural estates of the wealthiest councilmen (Procopius, *Vandal Wars*, 3.5.11–12), while others had no choice but to accommodate themselves to the new masters, performing for them the "duty" of tax collection, and still others fled to regions still under imperial rule – to Cuicul, for instance, where one of them may have occupied the House of Bacchus.[46] In other parts of the West the Mediterranean-style city had already regressed by 430, less so, it has been argued, in the Spanish provinces, Italy, and southern Gaul than in Britain, on the Rhine and its tributaries, and along the upper Danube. Fortified urban space contracted. Not just temples but public baths, basilicas, buildings for spectacles, and street colonnades tended to fall into ruin, while cheap housing invaded marketplaces and other public spaces. In the fifth century, Roman public building virtually ceased. Church building alone flourished, most often at peripheral sites within the walls or in the suburbs, and when barbarians raided cities the bishops often organized the defense.[47] The barbarian influx contributed to urban regression, but in several cases the physical decline appears to have preceded the storm. The cities of Britain decayed gradually throughout the fourth century, and the withdrawal of the imperial military presence early in the fifth left Londinium virtually deserted. In northern Gaul, Trier suffered horribly in 406–407, when barbarian tribal groups crossed the Rhine en masse, or so the priest Salvian alleges (*On the Governance of God*, 6.13–15). Yet the case of nearby Metz has proved ambiguous. Guy Halsall argued that Roman-style urbanism ended abruptly around 400, that the Vandals "sacked" Metz in 407, and that thereafter it became virtually a "ghost town"; but Bernard Bachrach has written a spirited refutation, asserting that when Attila's forces attacked Metz in 451, just before the battle of Chalons, the city remained in bloom, protected like Augustine's Hippo by serviceable

[46] Lepelley, *Les cités de l'Afrique romain*, 1: 409–414.
[47] Liebeschuetz, *Decline and Fall*, 74–103.

fortification walls that the Huns had to "break into" (Hydatius, *Chronography*, 150).[48]

This debate will no doubt continue, but less contestable is the centrality of the councilmen in the West, as in the East, to the well-being of Mediterranean-style cities. When Salvian wrote "all councilmen are bullies" in the 440s, he had in mind councilmen of Trier and the other *civitates* of northern Gaul who might now be called upon to organize collecting taxes for new rulers. Under these new rulers, whether breakaway emperors or barbarian kings, urban society would remain distinctly top-down, but henceforth elites would need the patronage of princes who did not hold the ancient Mediterranean city dear. Writing in the 390s, the historian Ammianus declared that barbarians "avoided actual towns as if they were tombs surrounded by nets" (16.2.12, trans. Rolfe). Eventually such an attitude would work itself out in the emergence of new, postclassical elites whose identities ceased to be civic. To put it succinctly, the fate of the councilmen and other elites would also be the doom of the ancient Mediterranean city.

[48] Guy Halsall, *Settlement and Social Organization: The Merovingian Region of Metz* (Cambridge, 1995) esp. 219–231; Bernard S. Bachrach, "Fifth-Century Metz: Late Roman Christian Urbs or Ghost Town?," *Antiquité Tardive* 10 (2002) 361–383.

5: BIG CITIES AND THE DYNAMICS OF THE MEDITERRANEAN DURING THE FIFTH CENTURY

Raymond Van Dam

The increasing size of Rome paralleled the expansion of the Roman Empire, and by the time the emperor Augustus finally ruled almost all of the Mediterranean Sea, Rome had become the first city in world history with one million residents. Three hundred years later during the Age of Constantine, it was still the largest city in the world. It had also become a capital city that was no longer an imperial residence. In fact, emperors hardly even visited Rome. During his long reign of over thirty years Constantine visited Rome only three times, for a total residence of five months.

In 330 Constantine presided over the inauguration of Constantinople as a new capital in the East. At the time Constantinople had only perhaps thirty thousand residents. A century later its population had increased tenfold; two centuries after its foundation, during the Age of Justinian, its population had perhaps doubled again. By then its population was also about ten times the population of Rome. The rising population of Constantinople and the declining population of Rome had intersected most likely in the mid-fifth century, sometime during the Age of Attila. While Constantinople was expanding into the largest city in the world, Rome was crumbling into a ghost town.

For four centuries the Roman Empire had been primarily a Mediterranean empire. The Roman Empire is still the only state to have governed all of the Mediterranean Sea. As a result, evaluating the transformation of the empire requires thinking about the changing dynamics of the Mediterranean. In the early empire the political unification of the entire Mediterranean had encouraged economic integration around the supply of Rome and other large cities. In addition to grain, other foodstuffs, and building supplies, big cities required a constant flow of immigrants to sustain their large populations. Big cities were the most important catalysts for the movement of both commodities and people.

During the fifth century the dynamics of big cities changed dramatically. Trier, an important imperial residence on the Rhine frontier, had been linked to the Mediterranean world through Arles; now the settlements of barbarian groups separated northern Europe from southern Mediterranean Europe. Rome had depended on shipments of grain from Carthage; now the establishment of the Vandals in North Africa isolated Rome and turned the western Mediterranean into a frontier zone. Constantinople depended on shipments of grain from Alexandria. Because that connection survived, emperors retained their authority in Egypt despite the theological controversies that seemed to splinter the eastern empire. Antioch and the surrounding region of Syria flourished in the eastern Roman Empire, but then faced invasions from the neighboring Persian Empire, whose capital was at Ctesiphon, in southern Mesopotamia. The changes in these intersections both reflected and determined the currents of the Mediterranean world.

Understanding the dynamics of big cities, the distribution of food, and the movements of people requires some quantification. For ancient societies reliable numbers are scarce. To be candid up front, the numbers deployed here are conjectures, based on modern scholars' impressions developed from reading late Roman texts and introducing comparative evidence derived from other premodern societies. Using actual numbers makes it easier to calculate comparisons and simulate intersections; but it is important to remember that the numbers are themselves metaphors with no certain warranty.[1]

BIG CITIES

In the Roman world there were approximately two thousand cities, divided about evenly between the western and eastern halves of the empire. Each of these cities included both an urban monumental center and a surrounding rural hinterland. For almost all cities the

---

[1] For "numerical metaphors," see Raymond Van Dam, "Bishops and Clerics: Numbers and Their Implications," in *Episcopal Elections in Late Antiquity*, ed. J. Leemans et al. (Berlin, 2011) 217–242.

biggest business was agriculture, and most people worked as farmers or herders. In this sort of underdeveloped agrarian society, working the land required at least 75 percent, and probably closer to 90 percent, of the labor force. As a result, most people who counted as citizens of cities nevertheless lived in the countryside on farms or in outlying villages, close to their fields and pastures. In the urban centers many of the residents worked as laborers, artisans, and merchants. They acquired their food through purchase, by cash or by exchange for their goods or services. The populations of cities also included aristocrats, who were typically large landowners. These local notables frequently deployed their wealth to fund the construction of municipal buildings and monuments, or to underwrite the acquisition and marketing of grain.

In the early Roman Empire the total population had peaked at over sixty million people. A severe outbreak of plague during the later second century had trimmed the population by perhaps 10 percent, and the appearance of another plague during the mid-third century, as well as political instability and frequent military campaigns, probably continued to depress the population. At the beginning of the fifth century the total population of the empire might be estimated at around fifty million people. Only a comparatively small percentage of this considerable total lived in the urban centers, and the urban population of most cities was typically fewer than ten thousand residents, often only a few thousand. The aggregate urban population was perhaps one-eighth or one-ninth of the total population of the empire. Urban consumers and rural producers were all citizens of cities, but the relative size of the two groups represented a delicate balance between the production and the consumption of food.[2]

One of the wonders of the Roman Empire is that the urban populations of some cities far transcended these limits. Supplying the one million residents of early imperial Rome and sustaining that supply for three centuries were spectacular accomplishments. Every year over one thousand shiploads of grain arrived for Rome, totaling hundreds of thousands of tons, primarily from Sicily, North Africa, and Egypt. Hundreds more ships brought olive oil and wine. Much of the grain was distributed at no cost. For purchases of additional food, clothing, and services many residents of Rome could earn wages as laborers for construction projects, the manufacture of bricks, or the transportation of supplies. The most important employers were emperors and, on a

---

[2] Walter Scheidel, "Demography," in *The Cambridge Economic History of the Greco-Roman World*, ed. Walter Scheidel et al. (Cambridge, 2007) 79.

lesser scale, wealthy senators. Because the emperors acquired their own resources as taxes paid by provincials and as rents from imperial estates, the residents of Rome lived off revenues paid by provincials as well as supplies imported from the provinces. Rome was hence a massively scaled-up version of provincial cities. Ordinary cities depended on the commodities from their own rural hinterlands and also some interregional exchange. In contrast, a city of one million residents such as Rome required the exploitation of a "hinterland" consisting of the entire Mediterranean basin and its surrounding regions.[3]

At Rome the prefects of the grain supply administered the unloading and storage of the grain at a harbor, its shipment up the Tiber and storage in Rome, and its final distribution to bakers. But only the emperors had the authority to guarantee the working of the supply network at this scale and for so long. During the fourth century the magistrates of Rome sometimes worried about emperors' commitment. During his tenure as prefect of the city in 384 Symmachus praised the emperor Theodosius for directing "the imperial fleet of ships to augment the maintenance of the loyal people [of Rome] with supplies of free grain." According to Symmachus, the emperor's divine power provided the "wind" for the sails of the grain ships.[4]

In the Mediterranean basin the provisioning of Rome defined the movement of bulk utilitarian commodities over long distances. The supply of this huge city created great demand, which pulled in commodities such as food and building supplies, and the extraction of these resources seems to have compelled an increase in production and labor productivity in the provinces. Rome was a consumer city, parasitic on the provinces, but also a stimulus for increasing production. Through the fourth century the supply of Rome was the most important factor contributing to the integration of the Mediterranean.

EUROPE: TRIER AND ARLES

During the fourth century Trier had become an important residence for emperors, and their patronage contributed to a boom in construction. "All of these buildings," one panegyrist announced to Constantine, "are the gifts of your presence." The population of Trier expanded,

---

[3] Raymond Van Dam, *Rome and Constantinople: Rewriting Roman History during Late Antiquity* (Waco, Tex., 2010) 16–24.
[4] Symmachus, *Relationes*, 9.7, 18.3.

perhaps fivefold, to perhaps fifty thousand residents. A Gallic teacher who held high office at the court thought that Trier had become an "Augustan city," the equivalent of Rome.[5]

Emperors resided at Trier in order to lead military campaigns. During the fourth century over one hundred thousand soldiers were stationed along the Rhine and in Britain. The supplies for both the imperial court and this large concentration of troops in the Rhineland came from various sources. Many supplies arrived, predictably, from nearby regions in central and northern Gaul and southern Britain. Other important regional sources for supplies were the adjacent districts on the other side of the nominal frontiers. The main items imported from beyond the frontier were cattle, horses, and sheep, either as tribute or in exchange for grain. Some supplies also came from the Mediterranean world, such as olive oil from North Africa and southern Spain. The gateway was Arles, at the mouth of the Rhone River. Even though the two cities were over four hundred miles apart, Arles was considered a port for Trier.[6]

Northern Europe was quite different from the Mediterranean world, with a different ecology and a different diet. People often substituted beer and butter for wine and olive oil. But over the centuries of Roman rule, the establishment of so many troops in Britain and northern Gaul and then the emergence of Trier as an imperial residence had led to the economic integration of northern Europe. The demands of the court and the army also provided a strong bond between northern Europe and the Mediterranean.

Then the Roman emperors withdrew from northern Europe and preferred to reside in northern Italy. By the early fifth century the seat of the prefect of Gaul had been transferred from Trier to Arles. The emperors also withdrew troops from the northern frontier. In the past the Roman state had recruited barbarians from across the frontier to serve as Roman soldiers, on average perhaps half of the total of about five thousand soldiers needed each year to replenish the troops in the Rhineland and Britain. After completing their service, these barbarian soldiers might receive allotments of land inside the empire. As a result, the army had long served as the most important institution for integrating barbarians into Gallic society. In the early fifth century this

---

[5] Ausonius, *Mosella*, 421, with Edith M. Wightman, *Gallia Belgica* (Berkeley, 1985) 98, 237, for the population of Trier.
[6] *Expositio totius mundi et gentium*, 58.

pipeline failed, and the controlled dripping of recruitment and discharge became a steady stream of immigrants and invaders. A Roman army was no longer available to moderate the inflow of barbarians. Now the people of Gaul and Britain had to deal with newcomers directly. In 410 when cities in Britain requested assistance from Honorius, the emperor replied that they should defend themselves. The emperor had outsourced public defense to private security forces.[7]

The withdrawal of Roman rule had important consequences for northern Europe. One was the appearance of warlords, both barbarian and Roman. The Vandals, the Visigoths, and the Franks expanded into Roman Gaul. Despite the sometimes hysterical comments of contemporaries, these groups of barbarians were small, with only thousands, most likely only a few thousands, of warriors. At the same time Roman aristocrats might organize their own private retinues of soldiers; one even earned the title of "king of the Romans." For much of the fifth century local warlords dominated in Gaul and Britain. Only toward the end of the fifth century did the Franks under King Clovis begin to consolidate their control over northern and central Gaul.[8]

A second consequence was the shrinking of economic integration. If the circulation of ceramics can be used as an indicator of the circulation of commodities, then goods such as wine, salt, livestock, slaves, and cloth were exchanged between neighboring city territories in localized networks that extended to a distance of only about sixty miles. The rents collected by great landowners largely replaced imperial taxes and the complementary demand of supplying artificially large cities and a standing army. Only limited quantities of goods from the Mediterranean arrived in northern Gaul. Economic regionalism now matched political fragmentation.[9]

A final consequence was the weakening of the connections between northern Europe and the Mediterranean. The development of Trier as an important imperial residence on the Rhine frontier had represented the culmination of the expansion of a Mediterranean lifestyle. That lifestyle had included familiarity with Latin classical culture and, eventually, the introduction of Christianity. During the fifth century,

---

[7] Zosimus, *Historia nova*, 6.10.2.
[8] Excellent discussion of warlords in Charles R. Whittaker, *Frontiers of the Roman Empire: A Social and Economic Study* (Baltimore, 1994) 243–278.
[9] Excellent survey in Chris Wickham, *Framing the Early Middle Ages: Europe and the Mediterranean 400–800* (Oxford, 2005) 794–805.

however, barbarians pillaged Trier no fewer than three times. Roman aristocrats at Trier once asked the emperors to return and celebrate games in the circus; instead, in 461 the emperor Majorian visited Gaul to preside over games at Arles. While southern Gaul might still be considered an extension of an "Italian" Roman Empire, northern Gaul had slipped out of Roman control.[10]

The interaction between Trier and Arles had represented the larger interaction between northern Europe and the Mediterranean world. For centuries the Rhone had been a primary connecting link. During the fifth century that link rusted away, and northern Europe began drifting away from Mediterranean Europe.

WESTERN MEDITERRANEAN: ROME AND CARTHAGE

At the beginning of the fifth century the facade of a unified and integrated Mediterranean empire was cracking. After the death of the emperor Theodosius in 395, separate courts were established, one in Constantinople, the other in northern Italy, usually at Ravenna. The population of Rome had already declined to perhaps about 500,000 residents, and the primary sources of its overseas grain were now North Africa and Sicily. In terms of political administration and fiscal policy, the Mediterranean was now divided, the West integrated around the supply of Rome, the East around the supply of Constantinople.

Rome was also, unexpectedly, under assault from barbarians. The most effective strategy was not a direct attack against the walls. Instead, it was to sever the supply of grain. Because Rome was vulnerable both at the sources of grain and during its transportation, its massive walls were no defense against interruptions in its food supply.

The Tiber River, as the primary connector between Rome and its coastal ports, had always been a bottleneck. In 409 a band of Visigoths were able to impose a puppet emperor at Rome after capturing the port granaries. In 410 the Visigoths ransacked the city for three days, before leaving with plunder and captives. Contemporaries were quite dismayed upon hearing the news, in part because the master narrative of Roman rule had never anticipated the sack of Rome as its culmination.

---

[10] Sidonius Apollinaris, *Epistulae*, 1.11.10, with Raymond Van Dam, *The Roman Revolution of Constantine* (Cambridge, 2007) 62–78.

Italy itself had seemingly become a frontier region, similar to northern Gaul, and Rome had become a frontier capital, similar to Trier, with barbarians at its walls. The sack of Rome upended Roman history and turned the geography of empire inside out.[11]

The Visigoths soon moved on to Gaul and Spain. The Vandals meanwhile moved through Gaul and Spain into North Africa. In 439 they captured Carthage, and subsequently Sicily too. Although the fall of Carthage was not as widely lamented as the sack of Rome, the outcome was much more devastating. The primary sources of overseas grain for Rome were now lost, and the people of the capital again had to cope with the vulnerabilities of great size.

The population of Rome declined dramatically. In antiquity large cities had reputations as death traps, and during the early empire simply maintaining the population of Rome at one million residents had required the immigration of about 10,000 new residents every year, that is, 1 percent of the total population. Even during the fourth century, when the population of Rome had declined by (we assume) 50 percent to 500,000 residents, there still had been a few thousand immigrants each year, in order to keep the annual decline at less than 1 percent. But between the mid-fifth century, when the population was still perhaps 350,000 residents, and the early sixth century, when it had fallen to perhaps 60,000 residents, the total decline was almost 85 percent. That decline, at an annual rate of over 2 percent, was steeper than can be accounted for by normal mortality rates alone. Now residents of Rome were leaving.[12]

Even the presence of emperors could no longer deal adequately with the concerns over the importation of food and the outward migration of residents. Rome again became a primary imperial residence under Valentinian III for much of the decade before his death in 455. The emperor thought that the Vandal king Geiseric was preparing a large fleet at Carthage. But he had little to offer Rome. He allowed Greek merchants to conduct business in the city, with the expectation that their activities would somehow restore both "abundance" and "a larger population" to Rome. His military resources were even more restricted. Valentinian promised that the eastern emperor would send an army; as the last line of security, he suggested that people protect themselves with their own weapons. Valentinian seems to have sensed

---

[11] Van Dam, *Rome and Constantinople*, 33–45.
[12] Ibid., 49–50.

that to survive as a large city, Rome needed the support of food supplies and soldiers from the East.[13]

Two months after Valentinian's death, the Vandals attacked Rome. In an ironic twist, their fleet may have included former grain ships, now arriving to loot Rome, not supply the city. This time the ships were filled with cargo sailing south, not north. In the past the western Mediterranean had been a highway servicing Rome; now it had become a battle zone between Rome and Carthage.

By the end of the fifth century, barbarian kingdoms encircled the western Mediterranean, including the Vandals in North Africa and the Ostrogoths in much of Italy. These barbarian states now interacted with one another just as the early Roman empire had interacted with barbarians across its frontiers, with an intriguing combination of confrontation and exchange.

In the past grain and olive oil from Roman North Africa, extracted as taxes, had supported the population of Rome. The Vandal kings retained the internal Roman system for collecting taxes. The primary difference, however, was that they had few expenses. They provided their Vandal soldiers with estates to support themselves. They continued to maintain Carthage. They sent grain overseas as gifts or through sales. They also accumulated a vast royal treasury. Under the Vandals, North Africa still produced surplus food; but by the end of the fifth century there were fewer overseas consumers.[14]

The internal agrarian economy of Italy itself slowly splintered into largely disconnected subregions. Ravenna became the preferred residence for the Ostrogothic kings, and subsequently for the officials representing the eastern Roman empire. As a result, northern continental Italy was disengaged from southern, peninsular Italy. The supply of Rome was still a concern, because even though noticeably diminished in size, it was still the largest city in Italy. The resources of Theodoric, king of the Ostrogoths, for assisting the food supply were constrained, primarily by topography. Districts of Italy could produce a surplus of grain, especially in the Po River valley in northern Italy, but transporting that food to Rome was difficult. Overland the mouth of the Po

---

[13] Valentinian III, *Novellae*, 5 (issued in March 440); with Mark Humphries, "Valentinian III and the City of Rome (425–55): Patronage, Politics, Power," in *Two Romes: Rome and Constantinople in Late Antiquity*, ed. Lucy Grig and Gavin Kelly (Oxford, 2012) 161–182.

[14] Procopius, *Bella*, 4.4.34, with Andy Merrills and Richard Miles, *The Vandals* (Chichester, 2010) 141–176.

was less than three hundred miles from Rome, but by ship about five times more distant. Instead, Theodoric looked for food from overseas. During the 520s the king ordered magistrates to arrange for supplies of grain to be shipped from Spain, supposedly justified as a continuation of the "ancient tribute" owed to Rome. The king may also have tried to acquire grain from North Africa, but now by purchase from the Vandals rather than as the payment of taxes.[15]

During the fifth century the western Mediterranean stopped being a Roman sea. In the early Roman empire the European frontier along the Rhine and Danube and the African frontier facing the Saharan desert had been distant from the Mediterranean. By the end of the fifth century the frontiers crisscrossed the western Mediterranean itself, most clearly between Italy and North Africa. The western Mediterranean had become a frontier zone, divided among rival barbarian kingdoms.

EASTERN MEDITERRANEAN: CONSTANTINOPLE AND ALEXANDRIA

On the surface the eastern empire was as roiled as the western empire during the fifth century. The primary instigators of these confrontations were not barbarians, but churchmen arguing over theology. Doctrinal disputes and sectarian violence seemed to have the potential to fragment the eastern empire from within.

The bishops of big cities typically led these disputes. In 381 an ecumenical council had characterized Constantinople as "New Rome" and attributed to the city's bishop a "seniority of honor" that was "second only to the bishop of Rome." Bishops at other great cities in the East were soon resentful about the increasing prominence of this upstart capital and its bishops. Because the eastern emperors resided at Constantinople and promoted its vast expansion in size, they too were participants in these rivalries. During the fourth century the population of Constantinople had increased at such a volatile rate, that one critic complained that other cities were being left as "widows."[16] During the fifth century the number of migrants increased, so that the population of Constantinople doubled to perhaps 600,000 residents by the

---

[15] Cassiodorus, *Variae*, 5.35, with Neil Christie, *From Constantine to Charlemagne: An Archaeology of Italy, AD 300–800* (Aldershot, 2006) 251, on the abandonment of granaries in Portus and in Rome.

[16] Eunapius, *Vitae sophistarum*, 462.

early sixth century. Given this huge increase in population and the high mortality rates associated with very large cities, during the long century from about 400,000 to about 530,000 of new residents moved to Constantinople every year, over 800,000 in total. Most of these immigrants were from eastern provinces.[17]

The dislocation of population was accompanied by a reallocation of imperial resources. The grain previously shipped to Rome from Egypt was now diverted to Constantinople; in fact, eventually more Egyptian grain was shipped to Constantinople than had previously been shipped to Rome. One observer thought that so many ships were now sailing between Egypt and Constantinople that the sea looked like dry land.[18]

This reliance on overseas imports might seem to have made the emperors, bishops, and residents of Constantinople quite vulnerable. Because the well-being of the capital rested on the provision of Egyptian grain, there was the possibility of shutting off that spigot of supplies. In fact, already immediately after the foundation of the new capital the bishops of Alexandria acquired a reputation for threatening the flow of grain. In 335 Bishop Athanasius was accused of having hinted at blocking the ships; Constantine exiled him to Gaul.[19] The bishops of Alexandria might even try to extend their direct influence to Constantinople through the support of the sailors working on the grain ships. When Bishop Theophilus of Alexandria visited Constantinople in 403, "sailors from Alexandria greeted him with acclamations." Theophilus had arrived to be judged for his treatment of monks; he left after engineering the exile of John Chrysostom, the bishop of Constantinople. The bishops of Alexandria had apparently acquired great leverage on events at the new capital through their influence on the supply of grain from Egypt.[20]

Often overlooked in discussions of the supply of Constantinople is the realization that Alexandria was also a very large city that faced its own problems of supply. Even though it was not an imperial residence and emperors rarely even visited, Alexandria remained an enormous city, with a population in the later empire of perhaps two hundred thousand or more residents. Enough grain was certainly produced in Egypt for feeding such a large concentration of people. In fact, because

[17] Van Dam, *Rome and Constantinople*, 53.
[18] Theopylact Simocatta, *Historiae*, 2.14.7.
[19] Athanasius, *Apologia contra Arianos*, 87.
[20] Socrates Scholasticus, *Historia ecclesiastica*, 6.15.11.

of the advantages of the Nile for transportation, Alexandria was the easiest big city to supply.[21]

For Alexandria grain was readily available; but the obvious question is: who paid for the food? Even if civic revenues from rents, endowments, tariffs, and local taxes were substantial, even if local notables were uncommonly generous, even if residents could earn wages as laborers on the docks, there were still the practical problems of organizing the transportation, storage, and distribution of grain and other foodstuffs, on a very large scale. Supplying a very large city such as Alexandria would have strained the capabilities of municipal magistrates and wealthy aristocrats.

Only emperors had the authority and resources. The supply of free grain seems to be attested already in the mid-third century, subsidized by the Roman state or by the city, and subsequent emperors enlarged these grants. By the early fifth century the annual grant of grain was enough to feed about sixty-five thousand people, perhaps even one hundred thousand people. This provision from the state granaries included both the distribution of free grain and the sale of grain at a steady price.[22]

As a result, emperors had great leverage over the bishops of Alexandria. In his own rivalry with Bishop Athanasius the emperor Constantius used the grain supply for Alexandria as a weapon. In 339 he promoted Gregorius as a replacement bishop. In order to strengthen the new bishop's authority, his supporters confiscated "the loaves of the clerics and the virgins." "They seized the loaves of some people so that they would ... accept Gregorius, who had been sent by the emperor Constantius." In 355 Constantius ordered that the grain supply was to be removed from Athanasius's supervision and given to his rivals. In the next year an imperial magistrate announced that the emperor would withhold their bread if the people did not comply with his intention of replacing Athanasius. Constantius hoped to turn the people of Alexandria against Athanasius by manipulating the city's food supply.[23]

An even more blatant example of such coercive tactics involved Bishop Dioscorus in the mid-fifth century. Dioscorus himself had apparently indulged in the politics of food within Egypt. At the Council

---

[21] For a population of 200,000, see Christopher Haas, *Alexandria in Late Antiquity: Topography and Social Conflict* (Baltimore, 1997) 340; up to 500,000, see Roger S. Bagnall and Bruce W. Frier, *The Demography of Roman Egypt* (Cambridge, 1994) 54.

[22] Jean Durliat, *De la ville antique à la ville byzantine: Le problème des subsistances* (Paris, 1990) 323–349; cf. *Codex Theodosianus*, 12.6.3, for a *praefectus annonae Alexandriae*, in 349.

[23] Athanasius, *Epistula encyclica*, 4.3, and *Historia Arianorum*, 10.1, 31.2, 54.1.

of Chalcedon in 451 he was accused of having confiscated the grain that emperors had given to the churches of Libya and instead selling it for a profit during a food shortage.[24] After the council a riot by the partisans of Bishop Dioscorus threatened the transport of grain from Egypt. This time the emperor Marcian terminated the allowance of grain for Alexandria and instead had Egyptian grain brought down the Nile to Pelusium, on the other side of the delta, for shipping to Constantinople. This redirection of the transportation of grain left the people of Alexandria starving, forced to petition the emperor for relief.[25]

The supply of grain had created a symbiotic relationship between Constantinople and Alexandria. By granting an allocation of grain to Alexandria, distant emperors could try to maintain control over the city. But because emperors needed to import so much grain from Egypt to feed Constantinople, riots in Alexandria could be disruptive. The leaders in each city – emperors at Constantinople, bishops at Alexandria – had leverage over the other. In a sense, Alexandria was an extension of Constantinople, an overseas suburb, an offshore pier. Supplying grain to support the large population of Alexandria was the price the emperors paid in order to procure grain to support the even larger population of Constantinople. Egypt produced the grain; but only emperors could both demand the export of grain to Constantinople and grant a supply of grain to Alexandria. The large size of each city seemed dependent on the other. Despite their arguments over theology, neither the emperors at Constantinople nor the bishops of Alexandria could afford to upset this relationship.

THE NEAR EAST: ANTIOCH AND CTESIPHON

During the fifth century the eastern end of the Mediterranean flourished. This prosperous region of Greater Syria extended from Cilicia, south of the Taurus Mountains in southern Asia Minor, to Palestine, on the edge of the Arabian desert. Roman rule had furthermore expanded east of Syria to include the upper reaches of the Euphrates and Tigris Rivers in northern Mesopotamia.

Much of the agricultural expansion was consumed by the state. Olive oil and wine were shipped from Cilicia, Syria, and Palestine to

---

[24] Richard Price and Michael Gaddis, *The Acts of the Council of Chalcedon* (Liverpool, 2005) 2: 54.
[25] Theophanes, *Chronographia*, AM 5945.

Constantinople as taxes. Within Syria Antioch was another big city, with perhaps 150,000 residents. To survive as a large city, Antioch too, like Constantinople and Alexandria, received supplies of grain from imperial subsidies. Greater Syria also supported a large encampment of over one hundred thousand Roman soldiers along the entire eastern frontier from Armenia to Arabia. Even after providing food for Constantinople, Antioch, and the army, the local residents had enough surplus wealth to invest in agricultural infrastructure and to fund the enlargement of their houses and the construction of churches.[26]

The increasing density of settlements in Syria and the upper Euphrates and Tigris river valleys during the later fourth and fifth centuries suggests an increase in population. In the early Roman empire before the outbreak of the Antonine plague the total population had most likely grown slowly. This increase had been a consequence in part of an internal annual growth rate of perhaps 0.15 percent. At the beginning of the fifth century Greater Syria had a population of perhaps 3.9 million people. This total was, of course, constantly shrinking, as migrants moved to big cities such as Constantinople. But on the assumption that the total population was, despite this slow attrition, growing at the same rate as in the early empire, then over one century the population of Greater Syria would have increased by about 16 percent to about 4.5 million people.[27]

One factor contributing to this prosperity during the fifth century was the relative calm along the eastern frontier facing the Sasanian Persian empire. By the standards of ancient empires, the Persian Empire of Late Antiquity was large. But in comparison with the Roman Empire, its resources were deficient. The total land surface of the Persian Empire was about one-half the land surface of the Roman Empire, and much of

---

[26] Georges Tate, *Les campagnes de la Syrie du Nord du IIe au VIIe siècle: Un exemple d'expansion démographique et économique à la fin de l'antiquité* (Paris, 1992), for the prosperity of Syria during the fourth and fifth centuries; Raymond Van Dam, "Imagining an Eastern Roman Empire: A Riot at Antioch in 387 C.E.," in *The Sculptural Environment of the Roman Near East: Reflections on Culture, Ideology, and Power*, ed. Yaron Z. Eliav, Elise A. Friedland, and Sharon C. Herbert (Leuven, Belgium, 2008) 451–481, for late Roman Antioch.

[27] Bruce W. Frier, "Demography," in *The Cambridge Ancient History*, vol. 11: *The High Empire, A.D. 70–192*, 2nd ed., ed. Alan K. Bowman, Peter Garnsey, and Domonic Rathbone (Cambridge, 2000) 813, for growth rate; and Van Dam, "Bishops and Clerics," 227, for population estimates. Tate, *Les campagnes*, 347, and Clive Foss, "Syria in Transition, A.D. 550–750: An Archaeological Approach," *Dumbarton Oaks Papers* 51 (1997) 189–269, suggest a population increase in the territory east of Antioch.

its territory was desert or mountains. Its total population was relatively small. In 400 the total population of the eastern empire was perhaps just under twenty million people, but would probably start rising during the fifth century. In contrast, the total population of the Persian Empire during the fifth century was, at best, about two-thirds of the population of the eastern empire, with up to nine million people in Mesopotamia (modern Iraq) and between four and five million in Iran. Much of the Persian Empire was empty space.[28]

The most fertile region in the Persian Empire was middle and lower Mesopotamia, whose ecology and agriculture were dominated by the Tigris, the Euphrates, and their tributary rivers. These rivers were a mixed blessing. They provided water for irrigation, and they offered transportation for the concentration of resources downriver. But their water was difficult to exploit, with uneven flows during the agrarian year. Effective farming required the construction and maintenance of a complex irrigation system of canals and dykes.

Because of these limits on the agrarian infrastructure, Persian kings were constrained in developing political and military institutions. There were few large cities. The largest was Ctesiphon, the capital, with a population of most likely over one hundred thousand residents. There was no large standing army, and many regions were under the control of powerful local aristocrats. To demonstrate their superior authority, Persian kings organized some substantial projects, such as improving the irrigation system. They also led occasional military campaigns against Roman armies.

In practical terms the important objective of military campaigns was acquiring control over more people. In both Roman upper Mesopotamia and Persian lower Mesopotamia the most important resource was people. Wet farming through irrigation required a lot of labor. One striking outcome of earlier military campaigns had been the capture and movement of people by both Persian kings and Roman emperors. In the mid-fourth century the emperor Constantius moved the inhabitants of a Persian city to Thrace; the emperor Julian sent the residents of a Persian city on the Euphrates back to Chalcis, east of Antioch. When the emperor Jovian had to surrender some important

---

[28] Van Dam, "Bishops and Clerics," 227–229. For the Persian Empire, Josiah C. Russell, *Late Ancient and Medieval Population* (Philadelphia, 1958) 89, suggests population figures at the moment of transition from the Sasanian Empire to the caliphate during the seventh century: 9.1 million people in Mesopotamia/Iraq and 4.6 million on the Iranian plateau.

cities in upper Mesopotamia, he was able to negotiate the removal of the Roman residents.[29] King Shapur II replaced them with new settlers from southern Iran.[30]

During the peaceful fifth century the Roman provinces in Greater Syria produced a surplus of the one commodity that was very attractive to the Persian empire: people. It is not surprising that the Persian kings initiated a new series of attacks on Roman provinces during the sixth century. In 540 King Khusro looted Antioch and deported captives, whom he settled in a new city founded near Ctesiphon. With its baths and a hippodrome, this new city was built as a replica of Antioch, and its name was both a glorification of the king and mockery of the residents' hometown: "Khusro's-Better-Antioch." In 573 one of Khusro's generals burned Apamea and deported more captives. In the eastern Roman empire the total population was large enough to accommodate the slow but steady annual migration of thousands of provincials to the new capital of Constantinople and to other big cities. In the Persian Empire, or rather, in southern Mesopotamia, the foundation of a new city required the appropriation of a new captive population, almost the importation of a complete Roman city. Khusro had wanted to shift Antioch, Apamea, and their populations from the Roman end of the Fertile Crescent to the Persian end.[31]

This movement of people has two interesting implications. One would highlight the size of the migrations. If the population of Antioch had been still high, perhaps one hundred and fifty thousand people, and if Khusro's army had been able to herd one-quarter or even one-fifth of those people back to Mesopotamia, then that horde of tens of thousands of captives was larger than most of the barbarian groups that had invaded the western provinces during the fifth century.

A second implication emphasizes again the interactions between the Roman Empire and the Persian Empire. During the fifth century Roman Syria had flourished. Following this extended period of peace, however, Persian kings attacked Roman cities. The first half of the sixth century marked the height of Persian authority and prosperity. Survey archaeology within the Persian Empire indicates an increase in the density of settlement in middle and lower Mesopotamia that peaked in

---

[29] Libanius, *Orationes*, 59.83–85; Ammianus Marcellinus, *Res gestae*, 24.1.9, 25.7.11, 9.1–6.

[30] Geoffrey Greatrex and Samuel N. C. Lieu, *The Roman Eastern Frontier and the Persian Wars, part 2: AD 363–630: A Narrative Sourcebook* (London, 2002) 9.

[31] Greatrex and Lieu, *The Roman Eastern Frontier*, 104–108, 146–147.

the early and mid-sixth century.[32] This increase in the number and size of cities and villages seems to imply an increase in the total population in Persian Mesopotamia. As in the Roman world, some of this increasing population was perhaps due to a small uptick in annual birth rates. Another source would have been Roman captives, who were settled in Persian cities and given land. In an ironic outcome, the prosperity of Roman Syria during the fifth century may have contributed to the prosperity of Persian Mesopotamia in the sixth century.

GRAND THEMES

During the fifth century the old Roman world fragmented, first between West and East, then within the West into several barbarian states. The split between northern Europe and southern Mediterranean Europe previewed an important dynamic of the medieval period (and even of the modern period, with our contemporary tension between wealthy northern nations in Europe and overleveraged southern nations). The western Mediterranean became a frontier zone, and the population of Rome was in free fall. Constantinople became more vulnerable as its population inflated. The Roman Near East was constantly being pulled toward the Persian Middle East.

Modern scholarship often fragments in the same way, with specialist studies focused on either the Greek East or the various barbarian kingdoms of the West. As a result, these modern studies typically start with contrasting interpretive perspectives about the Roman world during the fifth century: disintegration and collapse in the West, but survival and even revival in the East. This disjointed outlook also fails to include consideration of neighboring states, such as the Persian Empire. One way to overcome these focused perspectives is to consider instead grand themes such as big cities, food, and migrations.

In ancient society "bigness" was difficult to sustain. In practical terms very big cities offered no advantages of scale or agglomeration. Instead, they created large burdens for the rest of the empire. The residents of big cities were primarily consumers, not producers. Even

---

[32] Robert M. Adams, *Heartland of Cities: Surveys of Ancient Settlement and Land Use on the Central Floodplain of the Euphrates* (Chicago, 1981) 183; and James D. Howard-Johnston, "The Two Great Powers in Late Antiquity: A Comparison," in *The Byzantine and Early Islamic Near East*, vol. 3: *States, Resources and Armies*, ed. Averil Cameron (Princeton, 1995) 203.

though many of them were of modest means, even poor, they were nevertheless privileged, because most of them did not directly work the land. Big cities relied on the commitment of rulers to extract and concentrate resources. Their great size was a reflection of ideological imperatives, not of utilitarian benefits.

During the Age of Attila the migration of barbarian peoples was only one example of extensive mobility, and not necessarily the most significant or even the most sizeable. Instead, the largest overall transfers of population were the substantial relocation of Greek provincials to Constantinople, the outflow of residents from Rome, and the forcible exodus of Romans into Persian Mesopotamia.

Compared to the barbarian migrations, these migrations of Romans were practically invisible, even undocumented in literary texts. They nevertheless provide an important alternative perspective on the fate of the Roman Empire. Barbarian migrations imply the fragmentation and dissolution of the Roman state, while the migrations of Romans to Rome and subsequently to Constantinople imply the continued exercise of state power. For centuries the movement of people and food had provided the underpinning for the growth and durability of big cities in the Roman world. When those connections were broken in the post-Roman world, there could be no more big cities.

6: Dynasty and Aristocracy in the Fifth Century

Brian Croke

The fifth century is regularly characterised as a period of upheaval and breakdown of Roman government and society, especially in the western provinces. Yet that is to overlook or underestimate the traditional social and political forces for continuity. Emperors may come and go, provinces may fall in and out of imperial authority, armies may form and reform with non-Roman generals and new military leaders; but the traditional drivers of power and influence, the imperial dynasties and aristocracies of both East and West, remain. The enduring pull of the dynastic principle, the quest to formally link self and family to a centre of power and influence, still drove and shaped fifth-century Roman political life. The Roman aristocracy traditionally dominated the imperial court through tenure of the highest civilian and military offices, while the impulse to dynasty continued to link the eastern and western imperial families and courts. Even so, dynasty and aristocracy were themselves subject to changes in character and texture over the fifth century.

This chapter explores the essential dynastic politics of the fifth century and the mutating Roman aristocracies, focussing on their relation to military and political authority at the imperial court. As the fifth century progressed, the fluctuating balance of power between East and West, and between Roman and non-Roman, became key dichotomies, which were forever in tension but never resolved. In the wider context of Roman political and cultural life in the fifth century these particular themes provide key anchor points for analysing how control and influence were acquired and mediated, and how Roman government and society were developing. The actions and attitudes of the Hun king Attila in the 440s and early 450s illuminate these themes by showing that, unlike the leaders of Goths, Burgundians, and Vandals in particular, he remained a barbarian warlord who never appreciated, nor fully engaged with, the dynastic and aristocratic mainstays of contemporary Roman politics and society. Therein lies the key to his ultimate political failure.

DYNASTY

Throughout the fifth century, no less than in other periods of Roman and Byzantine history, the dynastic principle regulated the quest for achieving, maintaining, and participating in the exercise of military, political, and social power.[1] The imperial dynasties of East and West, often just a single family, channelled imperial authority and prestige. The dynastic urge was a binding force, forever shaping the court and aristocracy around it. Being or becoming part of the prevalent imperial family conferred particular access and influence. Often these advantages flowed from a civic or military appointment in the service of the emperor in Rome, Ravenna, or Constantinople. This new pattern of office holding and intermarriage also gave more prominence to women and especially to marrying into the imperial family. Hence the mothers, wives, sisters, and daughters of emperors became increasingly powerful themselves at this period. An imperial *Augusta* possessed the wealth and property, her own courtiers and household, and often her own coinage, to enable her to assert her own authority virtually independently. She may not have been able to rule in her own right but she could choose and install an emperor: Galla Placidia stimulated the elevation of her young son Valentinian III (425), Pulcheria played a role in the accession of Marcian (450), Verina sanctioned both Basiliscus (475) and Leontius (484), while her daughter Ariadne facilitated the accession of Anastasius (491).[2]

House of Theodosius I, 395–457

For what the Romans called "barbarians," most of whom emerged from the higher ranks of the Roman army, access to dynastic linkage was through imperial favour and patronage. Over the course of the

---

[1] Gilbert Dagron, *Emperor and Priest* (Cambridge, 2003) 23.
[2] Michael McCormick, "Emperor and Court," in *The Cambridge Ancient History,* vol. 14: *Late Antiquity: Empire and Successors,* A.D. *425–600,* ed. Averil Cameron, Bryan Ward-Perkins, and Michael Whitby (Cambridge, 2000) 146–148.

fifth century such generals were integrated into the Roman aristocracy and imperial court, even the imperial family. In the late fourth century the emperor Theodosius I (fig. 6.1) promoted several key generals of non-Roman blood: Bauto the Frank, for example, who died in 388 and whose daughter was brought up in Constantinople;[3] Fravitta the Goth, who took a Roman wife with the blessing of the emperor;[4] Stilicho the Vandal, who married the emperor's niece Serena.[5] On his death in 395 Theodosius was succeeded separately by his sons, with Arcadius (aged twenty-one) ruling the East until 408 and Honorius (aged eleven) the West until 423. They were succeeded in turn by Arcadius's son Theodosius II (aged six) until 450, Arcadius's and Honorius's nephew Valentinian III (aged five) until 455 and Marcian (aged fifty-eight), brother-in-law of Theodosius II, until 457. Thus the dynasty of Theodosius I directly prevailed in both East and West until the 450s with their imperial tenure consolidated by marriage alliances with leading generals.

. . . in the West

It was the daughter of Theodosius I's Frankish general Bauto who became Arcadius's wife, the empress Eudoxia, while the Vandal general Stilicho's two daughters were married successively to Emperor Honorius – first Maria (died 407–408) then Thermantia (died 415). In the end, neither marriage bore offspring, so if Stilicho dreamed of being an imperial grandparent he now needed to look elsewhere. Accordingly, at one stage Stilicho sought to marry his son Eucherius to the half-sister of Arcadius and Honorius, Galla Placidia (born 388), who then lived at Ravenna. Honorius resisted this pressure and had Eucherius killed following the demise of his father Stilicho in 408. As for Galla, the emperor Honorius's general Constantius was anxious to marry her but was chagrined to see her become the wife of a Gothic king, Athaulf, in 414, which also demonstrated that the dynastic imperative trumped creedal alignment (she orthodox, he Arian).[6] Had he not died in infancy, Theodosius (born 415), the son of Athaulf and Galla, may well have succeeded to the western imperial throne on the death of Honorius in

---

[3] A. H. M. Jones, John R. Martindale, and John Morris, eds., *Prosopography of the Later Roman Empire, 260–395*, 3 vols. (Cambridge, 1971) 1: 159–160, "Flavius Bauto."
[4] *PLRE* 1: 372–373, "Flavius Fravitta."
[5] *PLRE* 1: 853–858, "Flavius Stilicho"; 824, "Serena."
[6] Alexander Demandt, "Der spätrömische Militäradel," *Chiron* 10 (1980) 620–621.

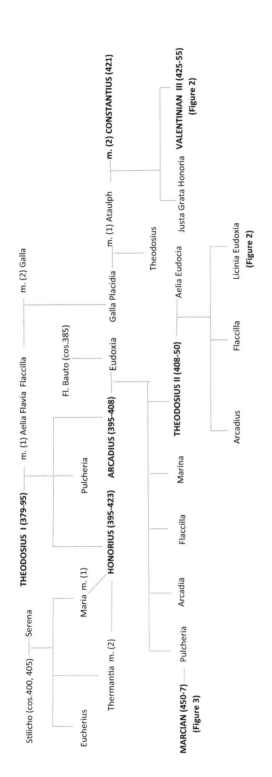

FIGURE 6.1 Family of Theodosius I

CAPITALS = Emperor

cos. = consulship

423 and proceeded to enjoy a long reign as the joint offspring of imperial and Gothic blood. Moreover, he may have unified or assimilated the Roman and Gothic realms.[7] Not long after the unexpected death of Athaulf, Constantius was finally able to wed Galla on his consular inauguration day in 417. It was their son Valentinian III (born 419) who ascended the throne as a young boy in 425, with their daughter Honoria (born 417) remaining a prize goal for all those aspiring to an imperial link. Constantius himself became a co-emperor to Honorius in 421 and ensured dynastic continuity in the West for the Theodosian house.[8]

. . . in the East

At Constantinople, meanwhile, Theodosius II (fig. 6.1), son of Arcadius and Eudoxia, enjoyed the longest imperial reign (408–450) of the fifth century. His elder sisters Flaccilla, Arcadia, and Pulcheria and his younger sister, Marina, frustrated all potential suitors by retarding the dynastic principle.[9] They preferred to turn their courtly life into a monastic routine of prayer, penance, study, and charity. Theodosius II, however, married a cultured young Athenian (Eudocia), who gave birth to a daughter Eudoxia, named after her Frankish grandmother, followed by a son, Arcadius, and another daughter, Flaccilla, both of whom died young.[10] In 437 the young Eudoxia married her western cousin Valentinian III, thereby reconnecting both eastern and western branches of the Theodosian clan. Soon after, around 441, Eudocia deserted her imperial husband, as well as the court and capital, for the spiritual delights of Jerusalem, where she lived until her death in 462.[11] Her husband Theodosius had died in 450 and it was only then that Pulcheria, his lone surviving sister and now well beyond child-bearing age herself, was persuaded to marry by providing an essential dynastic link for the Roman general Marcian. With her death in 453, followed by her husband Marcian's in 457, the eastern Theodosian dynasty expired.

---

[7] Stewart I. Oost, *Galla Placidia Augusta: A Biographical Essay* (Chicago, 1968) 133–134.

[8] Kenneth G. Holum, *Theodosian Empresses: Women and Imperial Dominion in Late Antiquity* (Berkeley, 1982) 128.

[9] Holum, *Theodosian Empresses*, 96–102.

[10] *PLRE* 2: 410–412, "Licinia Eudoxia"; 130, "Arcadius 1"; 473, "Flaccilla 2."

[11] *PLRE* 2: 407–408, "Eudocia 1." For date and context: Alan Cameron, "The Empress and the Poet: Paganism and Politics at the Court of Theodosius II," *Yale Classical Studies* 27 (1982) 258–263.

VALENTINIAN III AND FAMILY, 455–518

In the West, the Theodosian household (fig. 6.2) was carrying on through the daughters of Valentinian III and Eudoxia, namely Eudocia (born 438–489) and Placidia (born 440).[12] From a very young age both girls were at the centre of an intense competition among the most powerful Roman generals and barbarian kings. Marrying into the venerable house of Theodosius and Valentinian III bestowed not only the prestige of an imperial connection. It provided a possibility of future imperial parentage and the formation of new dynasties. No wonder it was so hard fought. By the early 450s the senior Roman general Aetius planned for his son Gaudentius one day to become the husband of young Placidia. but he failed. Her sister Eudocia, however, was espoused to the Vandal king Gaiseric's son Huneric, who had been sent as hostage to the court of Valentinian, probably as surety for the treaty negotiated between Romans and Vandals in 442. Huneric was already married to the daughter of the Visigothic king Theodoric, but at this point she was unceremoniously disfigured and sent back to her father. An imperial connection clearly offered more opportunity. Such bonds were not seen as unusual simply because they were between barbarians and Romans. Rather, they were traditional arrangements between two families striving to attain or retain power and influence. Court connections were the main reward.

. . . in the West

On Valentinian's death in 455 the political fortunes of the West would have been very different if the emperor had had a male heir to succeed him.[13] Instead, his wife Eudoxia and her daughters (fig. 6.2) were peremptorily coerced into new marriages by the new emperor, Petronius Maximus. Eudoxia herself was taken in marriage by Maximus, and her other daughter Placidia was betrothed to Maximus's son Palladius, instead of the general Majorian as her mother had evidently planned.[14] Eudoxia and Placidia provided dynastic legitimacy for Maximus and Palladius, as Pulcheria had done for Marcian in 450.[15] Aetius's imperial aspirations for his own son had perished with his murder the previous

---

[12] *PLRE* 2: 407–408, "Eudocia 1"; 887, "Placidia 1."
[13] Oost, *Galla Placidia Augusta*, 247.
[14] Stewart I. Oost, "Aetius and Majorian," *CPh* 59 (1964) 27–28.
[15] Alexander Demandt, *Die Spätantike*, 2nd ed. (Munich, 2007) 257.

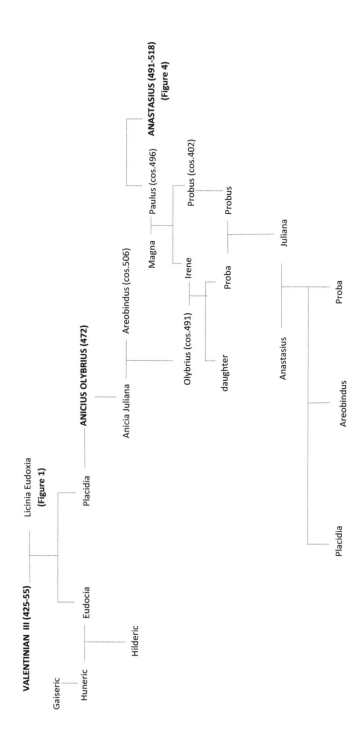

FIGURE 6.2 Family of Valentinian III

CAPITALS = Emperor

cos. = consulship

year (454) and may even have contributed to the imperial anger which resulted in his death. This sudden dynastic crisis in 455 was resolved when Gaiseric's Vandals mounted an expedition and took Rome, had the new emperor Petronius Maximus expelled, then escorted Eudoxia and both her daughters off to Carthage. The son of the Vandal king (Huneric) and the daughter of the Roman emperor (Eudocia) were now finally united. Their offspring Hilderic (born 456) could have become a Roman emperor and instantly reconciled and reunited Vandal Africa with the Roman empire. Instead, Vandal succession custom prevented him becoming king until late in life (523–530), by which time he was a "special friend" of the Roman emperor Justinian (527–565). Hilderic was never a serious imperial contender because, despite his imperial bond, he was born and raised in Carthage rather than in Rome or Ravenna.

. . . in the East

Some years later (462) Hilderic's sister-in-law Placidia and his mother-in-law Eudoxia, widow of Valentinian III since 455, left his Vandal court at Carthage for Constantinople, where they became the only Theodosians resident in the eastern capital. Indeed, until recently (457), the Theodosian dynasty was the only imperial family most of the living inhabitants of Constantinople had ever known. Their very presence once more revived and promoted their potent dynastic status. Meanwhile, following the earlier example of her grandmother and namesake, Eudocia left Africa for Jerusalem in 471 and died there shortly after. The dowager empress Eudoxia lived on at Constantinople into the 490s, while her other daughter, Placidia, was already married to a senator of distinguished lineage, Anicius Olybrius, thereby making him a potential emperor of either East or West.[16]

The first opportunity arose in 461 on the death of the western emperor Majorian, when the Vandal king Gaiseric strongly supported Olybrius's right to the throne. Gaiseric was now the father-in-law of

[16] PLRE 2: 796–798, "Anicius Olybrius 6," see also Frank M. Clover, "The Family and Early Career of Anicius Olybrius," *Historia* 27 (1978) 169–196, here 192–195. The proposal that Olybrius was the son of Petronius Maximus who organised the marriage with Placidia when Maximus was emperor in 455 (T. Stanford Mommaerts and David H. Kelley, "The Anicii of Gaul and Rome," in *Fifth-Century Gaul: A Crisis of Identity?*, ed. John F. Drinkwater and Hugh Elton [Cambridge, 1992] 119), has been convincingly rejected by Andrew Gillett, *Envoys and Political Communication in the Late Antique West, 411–533* (Cambridge, 2003) 88 n. 11.

Eudocia, sister of Olybrius's wife. Whether Gaiseric renewed Olybrius's claim on the death of the emperor Libius Severus in 467 is
not known. Instead, the eastern court appointed Anthemius (fig. 6.3),
husband of the only child of the late emperor Marcian and who
might have expected to succeed his father-in-law at Constantinople
ten years earlier.[17] The dynastic authority of Anthemius was further
cemented by marrying his daughter Alypia, who was daughter of one
emperor (Anthemius) and granddaughter of another (Marcian), to his
all-powerful barbarian general Ricimer.[18] Despite the new family bond,
before long relations between Anthemius and Ricimer deteriorated and
Ricimer revolted. So, in 471 Olybrius (fig. 6.3) was sent to Rome by
the eastern emperor Leo I to mediate the hostilities between them.
He failed to achieve that, but on Anthemius's death the following year
Olybrius unexpectedly found himself emperor at last, being proclaimed
such by Ricimer. At this point the Theodosian dynasty might have
been firmly restored in the West once more, had Olybrius not suddenly died six months later. Thereafter no real capacity for dynastic
continuity in the West was possible. The next few years saw a series
of brief and insecure reigns: Glycerius, sponsored by the Burgundian
general Gundobad in 473;[19] Nepos, husband of the empress Verina's
niece, who was sponsored by the eastern emperor Leo I in 474 to
reassert authority over the West;[20] and Romulus, sponsored in 475 by
his father Orestes, a Roman general and former secretary to the Hun
king Attila.[21] All three were deposed and exiled. After 476 Gothic kings
replaced emperors altogether at Rome and Ravenna.

THE HOUSE OF LEO, 457–518

Meanwhile at Constantinople, with the disruption to the Theodosian
household occasioned by the death of Marcian in 457, real power now
lay with the generals, and Aspar was foremost among them. He secured
the throne for a favoured military associate, Leo I (fig. 6.4), as he

---

[17] *PLRE* 2: 96–98, "Anthemius 3." This appointment was an overt symbol of reunifi-
cation of eastern and western courts: John M. O'Flynn, "A Greek on the Roman
Throne: The Fate of Anthemius," *Historia* 41 (1991) 125.

[18] *PLRE* 2: 942–945, "Fl. Ricimer 2"; see also Penny MacGeorge, *Late Roman Warlords*
(Oxford, 2002) 262–267.

[19] *PLRE* 2: 514, "Glycerius."

[20] *PLRE* 2: 777–778, "Iulius Nepos 3."

[21] *PLRE* 2: 949–950, "Romulus Augustus 4."

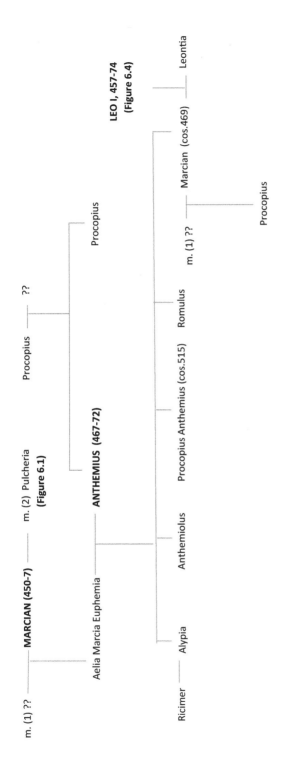

FIGURE 6.3 Family of Marcian

CAPITALS = Emperor

cos. = consulship

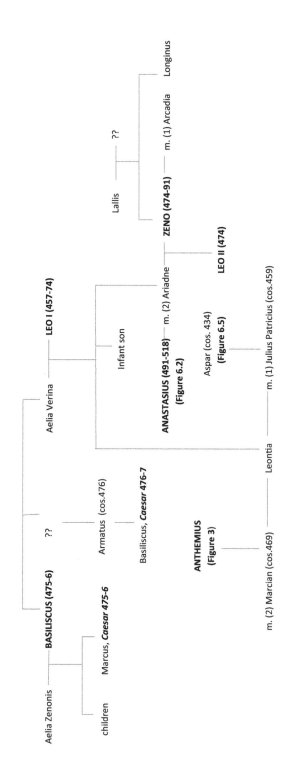

FIGURE 6.4 Families of Leo and Zeno

CAPITALS = Emperor

cos. = consulship

108

likely did for Marcian in 450.[22] As a barbarian, Aspar was ineligible to be emperor himself, but, like Bauto and Stilicho decades before, he could become an emperor's father-in-law thereby potentially securing his family's imperial connection for generations. In the early years of Leo I's reign, Aspar consolidated his influence by securing a marriage commitment for his son (Patricius) and Leo's daughter (Ariadne). Over time Leo's independent power grew, tension emerged with Aspar, and, when it was finally clear that Leo was intent on founding his own imperial dynasty, Aspar and his family were liquidated. As with the demise of Aetius in 454, the murder of Aspar and sons in 471 was triggered by the emperor's desire for greater dynastic autonomy.[23]

Leo had his own plans. The marriage in 467 of his younger daughter Leontia with Marcian, grandson of Emperor Marcian, and son of Anthemius, whom he soon sent as emperor to the West, was a deliberate act of dynastic continuity. It was Leo's elder daughter Ariadne, as the wife of successive emperors Zeno (474–491) and Anastasius (491–518), who represented the dynasty of Leo until her death in 515, having inhabited the imperial palace at Constantinople for nearly sixty years. If the venerable Ariadne had a rival, it would have been Anicia Juliana (fig. 6.3), daughter of Olybrius and the Theodosian Placidia, born in around 461–462. Her grandmother, the dowager empress Eudoxia, embodied her imperial power and image in the churches she constructed during her latter years at Constantinople, especially St. Polyeuktos, while her mother Placidia publicly consolidated the prestige of the imperial Theodosian family. Juliana's imperial lineage was proclaimed for all to see in the church of St. Polyeuktos as the "bright light of blessed parents sharing their royal blood in the fourth generation," that is from her great-grandmother Eudocia to Eudoxia to Placidia to Juliana.[24]

In 478 Leo I's son-in-law, the Isaurian emperor Zeno (fig. 6.4), saw an opportunity to associate his regime more closely with Roman imperial heritage by arranging a marriage between Anicia Juliana and the Goth Theodoric, then an eastern general, leader of his Gothic

---

[22] Richard W. Burgess "The Accession of Marcian in the Light of Chalcedonian Apologetic and Monophysite Polemic," *Byzantinische Zeitschrift* 86.7 (1993–1994) 47–68.

[23] Brian Croke, "Dynasty and Ethnicity: Emperor Leo I and the Eclipse of Aspar," *Chiron* 34 (2005) 147–203.

[24] *Anth. Pal.* 1.10.6–8; see also Mary Whitby, "The St Polyeuktos Epigram (*AP* 1.10): A Literary Perspective," in *Greek Literature in Late Antiquity*, ed. Scott F. Johnson (Aldershot, 2006) 159–188.

clan and later king of Italy (Malchus, fr. 18.3 [Blockley 432–433]). Again there would be potential to unite East and West within the authority of a single imperial family resonant with the Theodosian name. He failed, perhaps overruled by Ariadne. Instead, Juliana married into a more distinguished aristocratic family of barbarian lineage. Her husband Areobindus was the grandson of the generals and consuls of 434, the Alan Aspar and the Goth Areobindus (fig. 6.5). The emperor Zeno and his father-in-law Leo I had effectively seen off the dynastic aspirations of Aspar in 471, but they had now resurfaced in the marriage of Juliana and Areobindus. In the end it was not Aspar's son who formed a link with a woman of royal Roman blood, but his grandson. Juliana's husband himself became the distinguished consul of 506 but was preceded in the honour by their son Anicius Olybrius (consul 491), who married Irene, niece of the emperor Anastasius. Then, in 512, Areobindus was being promoted as a replacement emperor for the aged and unpopular Anastasius. By the early sixth century the combined dynasties of Theodosius (through Juliana) and Aspar (through Areobindus) had joined with the dynasty of Anastasius (through Irene).

In short, through the fifth-century East the ties of blood and office were woven more tightly and narrowly from generation to generation. The whole of the fifth century was dominated by two overarching imperial houses, those of Theodosius (379–457) and Leo (457–518), while in the West the Theodosian authority lasted until 455, followed by a series of unrelated emperors, mainly representing changing local power bases until 476. While unsuccessful, compared to the West, regular power struggles and threats of usurpation in the East are explained by the need to contest dynastic access. From the 430s nearly all imperial usurpers, both those who succeeded and those who failed, were related to the imperial family, principally Basiliscus (475), Marcian (479), Leontius (484), and Longinus (491), as well as the young Basiliscus (476), briefly recognised as Caesar by Zeno. He was the son of Armatus, who was the nephew of empress Verina and her brother Basiliscus.[25] In the fifth-century West, by contrast, Romans and barbarians occasionally intermarried but only rarely did kings and military leaders of other nations seek to form closer and more integrated relations with the Roman court. As Roman generals became more powerful they

---

[25] Brian Croke, "Basiliscus the Boy Emperor," *Greek, Roman, and Byzantine Studies* 24 (1983) 81–91, repr. in Brian Croke, *Christian Chronicles and Byzantine History, 5th–6th Centuries* (Aldershot, 1992).

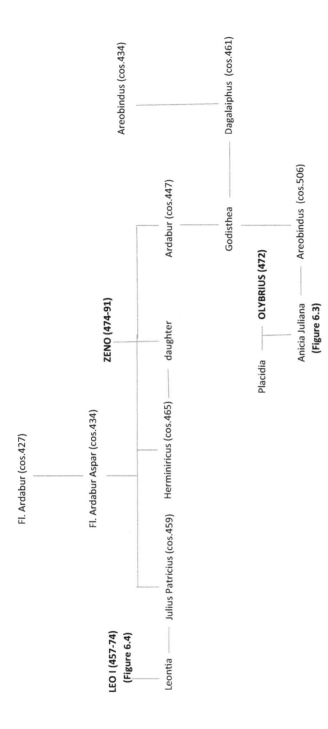

CAPITALS = Emperor

cos. = consulship

FIGURE 6.5 Family of Aspar

took the imperial throne: Avitus (455) and Majorian (457) in the West; Marcian (450), Leo (457), and Zeno (474) in the East. Those whose ethnic background barred their way to imperial authority became the power behind the throne instead: Areobindus, Ardaburius, and Aspar in the East; Ricimer and Gundobad in the West. Their goal was to link their family with that of the imperial dynasty.

More independent barbarian leaders such as Athaulf, Gaiseric, Theodoric I the Visigothic king in Gaul (418–451), and later Theodoric the Ostrogoth king in Italy (fig. 6.6), and the Burgundian Gundobad, generally preferred to avoid Roman aristocratic families by building their dynastic connections across nations. Only rarely (Athaulf in 414, Huneric in 442, Ricimer in 467) did they seek to join with the imperial household. Instead, Theodoric I the Visigoth married his daughter to the Suevic king Rechiarius in the 440s,[26] while a half-century later the Ostrogothic Theodoric, although virtually a Roman emperor and immersed in Roman court culture from a very young age, still looked outwards. He married his sister Amalfrida to the Vandal king Thrasamund, one daughter (Ostrogotho Areagni) to the Burgundian King Sigismund, another (Theodegotha) to the Visigothic king Alaric, and yet another (Amalasuintha) to Eutharic.[27]

HONORIA AND ATTILA: DYNASTY THWARTED

Of all the identifiable Roman-barbarian marriages across East and West, not one involved a Hun, male or female.[28] As Hun king in the 440s and early 450s Attila never showed any interest in seeking a marriage alliance with the Roman court for any of his sons. He never sought to compete for the daughters of Valentinian III with Roman generals such as Aetius and Majorian, distinguished aristocrats and imperial officials such as Petronius Maximus, or other kings such as the Vandal Gaiseric. Had he done so he may have been successful. Even so, at one time he suddenly found himself faced with the enticing prospect of an alliance with Honoria, the younger sister of Valentinian III. The exact roles of both Attila and Honoria in this affair are not entirely clear. By the time

---

[26] *PLRE* 2: 935, "Rechiarius."
[27] *PLRE* 2: 63–64, "Amalafrida"; 138–9, Areagni"; 1068, "Theodegotha"; 65, "Amalasuintha."
[28] Roger C. Blockley, "Roman-Barbarian Marriages in the Late Empire," *Florilegium* 4 (1982) 63–79.

FIGURE 6.6 Family of the Ostrogothic king Theodoric

Bold = tribal king

cos. = consul

Attila reached the height of his power Justa Grata Honoria (born 417) was an imperial princess in her early thirties with her own household and her own coinage, an *Augusta* of considerable standing, like her mother Galla Placidia.

In 449, so it would appear, Honoria was disenchanted by the prospect of a marriage organised by her brother to a distinguished Roman senator Flavius Bassus Herculanus. Consequently, she sought the help of Attila by sending a trusted eunuch from her household named Hyacinthus, who carried her signet ring as a symbol of good faith. Attila took her request as a marriage offer and insisted on it being finalised. After all, Attila was a Roman general, having been granted the title of *magister militum* by Theodosius II,[29] and it was not unusual for Roman imperial women such as Honoria to be betrothed to Roman generals. Apart from the example of Theodosius's niece Serena, wife of Stilicho, Honoria's own mother Galla had married the general Constantius. Before long (450) her aunt Pulcheria was to marry Marcian. Attila was also a tribal leader based outside the boundaries of the Roman empire but linked to it by imperial tribute and the routine channels of diplomacy. Again, Roman princesses were not beyond the expectation of leaders in Attila's position. Honoria's mother, Galla Placidia, had earlier married the Gothic leader Athaulf in 414, and her young niece Eudocia was already amicably betrothed to the son of the Vandal king Gaiseric.

Evidently, Theodosius II found nothing impossible or unprecedented about a union between Attila and Honoria, so he endorsed it, not least as a means of pacifying Attila, and he advised Valentinian III accordingly.[30] Attila's advisers will have known that Roman law also required a future wife to provide a dowry, which may have involved designated Roman territory and that Honoria had legal control over her own property.[31] Certainly that would have appealed to Attila. He probably had in mind, or was informed about, the recent precedent

---

[29] Priscus, fr. 11.2, ed. Roger C. Blockley, in *The Fragmentary Classicising Historians of the Later Roman Empire: Eunapius, Olympiodorus, Priscus and Malchus*, 2 vols. (Liverpool, 1983) 2: 278–279. Contra *PLRE* 2: 182, "Attila," he was appointed ca. 447 by Theodosius II (cf. Hrvoje Gracanin, "The Huns and South Pannonia," *Byzantinoslavica* 64 [2006] 51–52).

[30] John of Antioch, fr. 292.25–26, ed. Umberto Roberto, in *Ioannis Antiocheni Fragmenta ex Historia Chronica* (Berlin, 2005) 492; see also Christopher Kelly, *Attila the Hun: Barbarian Terror and the Fall of the Roman Empire* (London, 2008) 181.

[31] For legal details and documents: Judith Evans Grubbs, *Women and the Law in the Roman Empire* (London, 2002) 89–128.

of Theodosius II, who acquired sovereignty over some of the western provinces of Illyricum through the union of his daughter Eudoxia with the young Valentinian III in 424 (married 437). The territorial price paid to settle the pre-nuptial deal between the eastern and western courts, which had been negotiated by Galla Placidia, still rankled with the West a century later. At Ravenna in 533 Cassiodorus could explicitly claim that Galla had "purchased a daughter-in-law by the loss of Illyricum: rulers were united but the provinces lamentably divided,"[32] while shortly after, at Constantinople, the emperor Justinian could associate reorganising the administration of Illyricum with the "Age of Attila" (Just. *Nov.* 11.1). Attila's expectation, if not Honoria's offer, might have been for settlement of Huns in certain Illyrian provinces, similar to the current arrangements for Goths and Burgundians in Gaul, Sueves in Spain, and Vandals in Africa.

Nonetheless, notwithstanding Theodosius II's consent, when Honoria's brother Valentinian III discovered this overture to the Hun king, he was so enraged that he had the messenger Hyacinthus immediately killed and it took the pleading of their mother Galla for his sister Honoria herself to be spared. Attila persisted with his request for Honoria's hand, along with an imperial dowry consisting of "half the western empire," only to be rebuffed. Honoria was already married, so he was informed, and Valentinian flatly refused to permit any union with Attila. Attila then threatened to go to war with the Romans on her behalf, but events overtook him. The new eastern emperor Marcian supported Valentinian's opposition to the union, and by the time Attila invaded Italy in 452 the demand for Honoria and her dowry appears to have receded. Nothing more is heard of her, while Herculanus enjoyed the prominence of a consulship in that year, presumably highlighting his imperial connection. Whether Honoria saw herself as marrying Attila, as her mother had once married Athaulf, with a view to producing a male Theodosian heir, or whether she proposed that Attila would share imperial power in Gaul,[33] or whether Attila was seeking to replace Aetius as the chief imperial general at the western court through her, can only be speculation.

---

[32] Cassiodorus, *Variae*, 11.1.9, trans. Sam J. B. Barnish, *Cassiodorus: Variae* (Liverpool, 1992) 147; cf. Jordanes, *Romana*, 329, in *Iordanis Romana et Getica*, ed. Theodor Mommsen, MGH AA 6.1 (Berlin, 1882) 42 (the "whole of Illyricum"); Oost, *Galla Placidia*, 185, 244–245; Gracanin, "Huns and South Pannonia," 54–58.

[33] As proposed by John B. Bury, "Justa Grata Honoria," *Journal of Roman Studies* 9 (1919) 12.

In any event, it was an unplanned opportunity presented to Attila, but he was unable to take advantage of it. The potential power and prestige of a Roman dynastic link passed him by. As a result, Hun blood never ran in the veins of the extended imperial family and the command of Attila over his vast and destructive warrior confederation was lost in a single generation. A decade after Attila's death his hegemony and his military legacy had virtually disintegrated. Subject nations such as the Gepids and Goths soon began to muscle their way out of Hun submission as Attila's sons squabbled and forfeited authority when they divided up the various tribes between themselves.[34] The former subject nations now wanted what the Visigoths, Sueves, Burgundians, and Vandals already had: security of place and sustenance, and the ability to be part of the Roman Empire and imperial service. Some might even dare to dream of a link with the imperial dynasty or blending into the imperial aristocracy.

ARISTOCRACY

By the turn of the fifth century the aristocracy of the western part of the Roman empire was being formed and perpetuated by imperial and civic appointments, traditional wealth acquired principally but not always by land tenure, common cultural habits, and the routines of an elite life. At Rome, the particular political role of the senate defined aristocratic status and activity even more narrowly.[35] Even so, senators could be provincials and by now even military men. In the East, the imperial aristocracy was more recent and more diverse. Around the imperial court at Constantinople had emerged an aristocracy of office rather than one primarily of blood and heritage. There, more than in the West, a new governing and cultural elite was forged through wealthy local landowners and merchants, together with the notables of provincial towns who had acquired influence and office in the capital. Greek speakers from Syria and Palestine, Egypt, Greece, and Asia Minor, along with some Latin speakers from the Danubian and Balkan provinces, intermarried and progressively consolidated their hereditary position.

---

[34] See Jordanes, *Getica*, 259, in Mommsen, *Iordanis Romana et Getica*, 125, with Peter J. Heather, *The Fall of the Roman Empire: A New History* (London, 2005) 358–366.

[35] Michele R. Salzman, *The Making of a Christian Aristocracy: Social and Religious Change in the Western Roman Empire* (Cambridge, Mass., 2002) 19–68.

Generals of both Roman and non-Roman origin were also assimilated into the eastern aristocracy but political integration did not always mean cultural integration.[36] From the late fourth century the aristocratic households of both East and West became Christian, and their public and private religious practice became a new and important facet of aristocratic life.

Diversification

The period from 395 to about 440, which encompassed the reigns of the emperors Arcadius and Honorius (the sons of Theodosius I), and the childhood years of Theodosius II and Valentinian III, led to the formation of more socially and ethnically open aristocratic households, as well as a reformation in the authority of the imperial court and how it was presented both publicly and privately. Underpinning this transformation and expedited by the reign of child-emperors was the gradually entrenched influence of generals and bureaucrats.[37] For the rest of the fifth century these trends were solidified. Further, the rationale for aristocratic political contests and rivalry was not so much Christian against pagan, or Roman against barbarian, as so often described. Rather it was the traditional dynamic of Roman politics: shifting alliances based on sponsorship centred around the imperial court. In the West, emperors like Valentinian III promoted the long-established Roman senatorial aristocratic families,[38] while the urban elites from the affluent cites of the eastern provinces competed for imperial favour and patronage. In both East and West religious practice became an integral component of political life with the growth of episcopal power providing a new outlet for the local aristocracies from which most bishops now emerged.[39] By

---

[36] Chris Wickham, *Framing the Early Middle Ages* (Oxford, 2005), 155–168; Clemens Heucke, "Die Herrschaft des oströmischen Kaisers Zenon: Ein Beispiel für Integration?," in *Migration und Integration: Aufnahme und Eingliederung im historischen Wandel*, ed. Mathias Beer, Martin Kintzinger, and Marita Krauss (Stuttgart, 1997) 45–54.

[37] Meaghan McEvoy, "Rome and the Transformation of the Imperial Office in the Late Fourth–Mid-Fifth Centuries AD," *Papers of the British School at Rome* 78 (2010) 151–192.

[38] Mark Humphries, "Valentinian III and the City of Rome (AD 425–55): Patronage, Politics, and Power," in *Two Romes: Rome and Constantinople in Late Antiquity*, ed. Lucy Grig and Gavin Kelly (Oxford, 2012) 174–179.

[39] Claudia Rapp, *Holy Bishops in Late Antiquity: The Nature of Christian Leadership in an Age of Transition* (Berkeley, 2005) 188–195.

425 the broadly common Christian culture and way of life had seeped into the fabric of government and the civilian aristocracy.[40]

At Constantinople the notion of the populace as a single congregation explains the importance of aristocratic involvement in the public ritual and the newly liturgified ceremonial in the capital, which began with Theodosius I, then expanded over these decades.[41] It also explains the deep feeling aroused by threats to doctrinal orthodoxy and unity, especially after the councils of Ephesus in 431 and Chalcedon in 451, as well as the presence of senior officials and aristocrats at the church councils.[42] Securing the blessings of God's favour had become an essential part of imperial rhetoric and ideology, so aristocrats could be seen developing alliances with bishops but also vying for the patronage of holy men and women, as the former praetorian prefect Cyrus petitioned Daniel the Stylite (*Vita Dan. Styl.* 31). Most of the leading generals were also increasingly engaged at the intersection of political and ecclesiastical power. At the same time, in traditional Roman fashion the oligarchy provided a pathway into high office and status for a whole family. The empress Eudocia, for example, paved the way for her uncle Asclepiodotus to become consul in 423, while one of her brothers (Gessius) became praetorian prefect of Illyricum and another (Valerius) was vicar of Thrace.[43] This rapid transition in the character of the Roman aristocracy in both East and West collapsed the differences between Romans and others. Aristocracy and dynasty mainly subsumed ethnicity.[44]

---

[40] An illustrative example: Hugh Elton, "Imperial Politics at the Court of Theodosius II," in *The Power of Religion in Late Antiquity*, ed. Andrew Cain and Noel Lenski (Burlington, Vt., 2009) 133–142; Fergus Millar, *A Greek Roman Empire: Power and Belief under Theodosius II, 408–450* (Berkeley, 2006) 192–234.

[41] Brian Croke, "Reinventing Constantinople: Theodosius I's imprint on the Imperial City," in *From the Tetrarchs to the Theodosians*, ed. Scott McGill, Cristiana Sogno, and Edward Watts (New York, 2010) 241–264.

[42] Roland Delmaire, "Les dignitaires laïcs au Concile de Chalcédoine: Notes sur la hiérarchie et les préséances au milieu du Ve siècle," *Byzantion* 54 (1984) 141–175.

[43] *PLRE* 2: 160, "Ascelpiodotus 1"; 510–511, "Gessius 2"; 1144, "Valerius 4." It is also possible that Rufinus, the praetorian prefect of the East in 431 and recorded as a "relative" of Theodosius II, was a brother of Eudocia (*PLRE* 2: 953, "Rufinus 8").

[44] Croke, "Dynasty and Ethnicity," 147–203; Henning Börm, "Heerscher und Eliten," in *Commutatio et contentio: Studies in the Late Roman, Sasanian, and Early Islamic Near East*, ed. Henning Börm and Josef Wiesehöfer (Düsseldorf, 2010) 183. Likewise, the idea of hardened pro- and anti-Gothic factions during the revolt of the general Gaïnas in 400 has now evaporated (Alan Cameron, with Jacqueline Long and Lee Sherry, *Barbarians and Politics at the Court of Arcadius* [Berkeley, 1993]).

Consolidation

A barometer of these changes in the political and cultural expressions of elite power and prestige in the fifth century was the consulship and the annual holders of this routine symbol of imperial unity. For centuries already, and another century yet, each Roman year was officially labelled for posterity by the names of the two consuls whose period of office it covered. The annually appointed consuls were announced by each imperial court in Constantinople and Rome, or Ravenna. In the fifth century the consulship was still the pinnacle of any political career, with the honour monopolised by the emperor himself (eighteen times for Theodosius II, for instance), his relatives, and the most influential senators, courtiers, and generals.[45] Through marriage and family alignment in particular the civic and military leadership of the East grew closer together, less so in the West.[46] Now, however, it was increasingly likely that a consul could be a non-Roman who had risen to supreme military authority: Bauto (385), Stilicho (400, 405), Fravitta (401), Plinta (419), Areobindus (434), Ardaburius (427) and his son Aspar (434) and grandsons Ardaburius (447) and Ermanaric (465), Zeno (448), Ricimer (459), and Theodoric (484). Although the social and ethnic origins of consuls became more diverse during the fifth century, the diversity became less obvious. An increasingly common aristocratic ethos and style meant the way emperors presented themselves publicly as consuls became less distinguishable from the ways other consuls presented themselves in the same role. The demands of iconography and ceremonial suppressed such differences.

ATTILA AND ARISTOCRACY

As with dynasty, the way the Hun king Attila related to Roman officials and courtiers provides a useful insight into how the tension between Roman and non-Roman in the aristocratic ranks played out. Although endowed with the status of a Roman general by the emperor Theodosius II, Attila never sought a western or eastern consulship for himself or any of his family or his Roman associates. Yet he fully understood

---

[45] Richard Delbrueck, *Dittici consolari tardoantichi*, ed. Marilena Abbatepaolo (Bari, 2008); Elisabetta Ravegnani, *Consoli e dittici consolari nella tarda antichità* (Rome, 2006); Lorenzo Sguaitamatti, *Der spätantike Konsulat* (Fribourg, 2012).
[46] Demandt, "Militäradel," 622–627.

the significance of the consul's position and power. In 449 Attila insisted to the envoy Maximinus, and his companion the rhetor Priscus, who composed a famous account of the embassy,[47] that he would only deal with the most senior ex-consuls Nomus, Anatolius, or Senator (Priscus, fr. 13 [Blockley 282–283]).[48] In fact, the various representatives of the eastern and western Roman courts who met with Attila over the years are virtually all known and together they provide a clear insight into Attila's political style and character, as well as how power was brokered between Romans and Huns. They represent a narrow channel of engagement with the Roman government and imperial courts and aristocracy. Almost all these encounters occurred outside Roman territory.

. . . in the East

The first Roman envoy Attila encountered was likely Plinta, who was accompanied by the emperor's chief legal courtier, Epigenes.[49] Plinta was a Goth but for almost twenty years (419–438) was one of Theodosius's most senior generals.[50] He had been consul himself in 419. By now *quaestor*, Epigenes had enjoyed a distinguished legal career culminating in his recent appointment to the commission established to compile Theodosius's new legal code.[51] The next official occasion when Attila would have encountered imperial authority was in 441 when he and his brother Bleda negotiated a settlement with Aspar.[52] Like Plinta and Epigenes, Aspar was a powerful and experienced figure at court, as noted above. He had been a trusted general for a long time and by 447 was *magister militum* in Illyricum,[53] having been consul in 434. Here are two perfect examples of how a Goth and an Alan could now secure the highest imperial office through military service and the patronage that flowed from that. Following the Hun attacks through Roman Illyricum

---

[47] *PLRE* 2: 743, "Maximinus 11."

[48] Prisc. fr. 11.2 (Blockley 246–247). Theodosius was definitely consigning diplomatic relations with the Huns to a lower level than would be the case with Persia, for example; cf. Ralph Mathisen, "Patricians as Diplomats in Late Antiquity," *ByzZ* 79 (1986) 35–49, esp. 43–45.

[49] Prisc. fr. 2 (Blockley 224–227) following the chronology of C. Zuckerman, "L'empire d'orient et les Huns: Notes sur Priscus," *Travaux et Mémoires du Centre de recherches d'hist. et civil. byzantines* 12 (1994) 159–163.

[50] *PLRE* 2: 892–893, "Fl. Plinta."

[51] *PLRE* 2: 396, "Epigenes."

[52] *PLRE* 2: 164–169, "Fl. Ardabur Aspar."

[53] Zuckerman, "L'empire," 171.

and Thrace in 447, the aristocrat senator, consul in 436, was despatched as an envoy to Attila (Priscus, fr. 9.2 [Blockley 236–237]). Over coming months, extending into years (447–450), the successive embassies exchanged between Romans and Huns involved in 447 the long-serving general and consul for 440, Anatolius, along with the Thracian general Theodulus,[54] then that of Maximinus and Priscus in 449. Next, as Attila had requested, came Anatolius again and the distinguished general and consul for 445, Nomus.[55] Finally, in 451, the emperor sent the senior court general Apollonius to negotiate with Attila.[56] By now it was clear that the emperor Marcian was terminating the tribute payments to the Huns and spurning them at every opportunity. Attila therefore refused to meet the imperial envoy.[57]

. . . in the West

The western court of Valentinian also deployed aristocratic officials whom Attila had come to know and trust. On one occasion (ca. 445), the imperial envoy was a court official named Cassiodorus, whose eloquence subdued the ferocity of the Hun king. He was an associate of the senior general Aetius, whose son Carpilio accompanied Cassiodorus to Attila, and grandfather of the famous sixth-century orator and administrator for the Gothic king Theodoric.[58] The Cassiodorii provide a timely example of a provincial family which emerged in the fifth century to become part of the governing aristocracy of Italy, while the increasing importance of the provincial aristocracy to the central government is also illustrated by the next known legation, in 449, which consisted of members of the local civil and military elite of Attila's neighbouring territory inside the Roman Empire, the provinces of Pannonia and Noricum. They were Promotus, the governor of Noricum, and the general Romanus,[59] Attila's secretary Orestes, who was accompanied by both his father Tatulus and his father-in-law Count Romulus,[60]

---

[54] *PLRE* 2: 84–86, "Anatolius 10"; 1105–1106, "Theodulus 2."

[55] *PLRE* 2: 785–786, "Nomus 1"; see also Brian Croke, "Anatolius and Nomus: Envoys to Attila," *ByzSlav* 42 (1981) 159–170.

[56] *PLRE* 2: 121, "Apollonius 3."

[57] Robert L. Hohlfelder, "Marcian's Gamble: A Reassessment of Eastern Imperial Policy toward Attila, AD 450–453," *American Journal of Ancient History* 9 (1984) 54–69.

[58] *PLRE* 2: 264, "Cassiodorus 2."

[59] *PLRE* 2: 926, "Promotus 1"; 946–947, "Romanus 2."

[60] *PLRE* 2: 1055, "Tatulus"; 949, "Romulus 2." Tatulus and Romulus were the grandfathers of the emperor Romulus Augustus installed by his father Orestes in 476:

and another of the secretaries provided for the Huns by Aetius, namely Constantius.[61] The most important western legation was that sent by Valentinian in 452, when Attila's attention had turned to Italy, following his defeat the previous year by the combined forces of Aetius and the Goths. Near Mantua, the embassy succeeded in turning Attila away from Italy. Pope Leo's participation in the embassy has resulted in his acquiring exclusive credit for taming the rampaging Hun king, and their direct confrontation became renowned in word and image. It is too often forgotten, however, that Leo was accompanied by two senior local aristocrats, namely the experienced ambassador and now praetorian prefect Trygetius[62] and the consul of 450, Gennadius Avienus, whom Sidonius Apollinaris later considered the most distinguished man in Rome after the emperor.[63]

If the channel of engagement between the Roman courts and Attila was limited and narrow, all the more so was the reverse channel, that between Attila and the Romans. During Attila's reign there were three Roman emperors, Valentinian III in the West and in the East Theodosius II, followed by Marcian, but the Hun king never came face to face with any of them. Dealings with emperors and their courts he left to his associates who were expert in Roman ways and Roman bureaucracy, men such as Constantius and Orestes. In doing so Attila was merely following the model of Hun kings before him: Charaton, for instance, whom the historian Olympiodorus met in 412[64] and Rua, who dealt with Roman envoys in 422 and 435.[65] The only Huns who ever travelled to Constantinople or Rome or Ravenna were few and had limited impact: Scottas, one of the leading Hun warriors, in 447;[66] Edeco, a highly regarded soldier and one of Attila's personal bodyguard, in 449;[67] Eslas, twice in 449, who had represented King Rua in negotiations with the imperial court in 435,[68] and finally a

---

Marjeta S. Kos, "The Family of Romulus Augustulus," in *Antike Lebenswelten: Konstanz – Wandel – Wirkungsmacht: Festschrift für Ingomar Weiler zum 70. Geburtstag*, ed. Peter Mauritsch et al. (Wiesbaden, 2008) 439–449.

[61] *PLRE* 2: 319, "Constantius 7."

[62] *PLRE* 2: 1129, "Trygetius."

[63] *PLRE* 2: 193–194, "Gennadius Avienus 4"; see also Susan Wessel, *Leo the Great and the Spiritual Rebuilding of a Universal Rome* (Leiden, 2008) 45–47.

[64] *PLRE* 2: 283, "Charaton."

[65] *PLRE* 2: 951, "Rua."

[66] Prisc. fr. 9.3 (Blockley 239); see also *PLRE* 2: 983, "Scottas."

[67] *PLRE* 2: 385–386, "Edeco."

[68] *PLRE* 2: 402, "Eslas."

senior Hun ruler named Berich.[69] Notwithstanding the limitations of surviving documentation, there is not a single record of any of these Hun envoys ever actually negotiating with Emperor Theodosius II, nor of any comparable engagement with Valentinian III, although the protocols of embassies would normally have at least required some ceremonial reception, such as Edeco having the Huns' letter read out in a formal palace audience in the presence of Theodosius.[70] Attila never permitted or encouraged the most illustrious of his own colleagues to become part of the Roman aristocracy. He never even forged close personal or family links with Roman aristocrats and the most senior imperial officials, East or West.

CONCLUSION

On the very first day of the year 400 two men celebrated the ceremonial commencement of their consulship, Stilicho at Rome and Aurelian at Constantinople. Both had been strong supporters of Theodosius I and owed their preferment to him. Stilicho was a military man and Aurelian the consummate civil administrator who had been prefect of the city (393–394) and was to be twice praetorian prefect of the East (399, 414–416).[71] Stilicho had secured his influence by marrying into the imperial family, while Aurelian's civic administrative ability led to his high honours, wielding authority for Theodosius I's young son Arcadius and his even younger grandson Theodosius II. Aurelian's son Taurus imitated his father's double prefectures (433–434, 445) and was consul in 428.[72] A century later on 1 January 500, two very different men entered on the same office, but both were at Constantinople: the Dalmatian Hypatius owed this honour to his kinship with the reigning emperor Anastasius and then went on to hold senior generalships for another thirty years;[73] the career of the Phrygian Patricius had reached a peak but he remained an influential general until the 520s.[74] The West was now ruled by the Gothic king Theodoric at Ravenna, and no consular candidate from the western aristocracy or royal family was

---

[69] *PLRE* 2: 225, "Berich."
[70] Prisc. fr. 11.1 (Blockley 242–230), enriched by the reconstruction of Kelly, *Attila*, 120–126.
[71] *PLRE* 1: 128–129, "Aurelianus 3."
[72] *PLRE* 2: 1056–1057, "Fl. Taurus 4."
[73] *PLRE* 2: 577–581, "Fl. Hypatius 6."
[74] *PLRE* 2: 840–842, "Fl. Patricius 14."

advanced for recognition at Constantinople. In the profoundly different worlds of 400 and 500, separated by enormous political, social, and cultural change in a diminished Roman Empire, their respective consuls illustrate the enduring power of dynasty and aristocracy throughout the fifth century.

7: Military Developments in
the Fifth Century

Hugh Elton

Military activity was fundamental to the fifth century, a period when the Roman Empire fell apart in the West but survived in the East. This chapter attempts to set out the basic elements of military affairs so that we can interpret events. It will show that the eastern Roman Empire survived not because its military practices differed from those in the West, but because the strategic situations differed. As the western Roman Empire lost territory over the course of the century, it could no longer recruit or pay for soldiers or the infrastructure to support them.

SOURCES

The basis of our knowledge of the Roman army during the fifth century is the *Notitia dignitatum* (Register of Dignitaries), an imperial administrative document dating from around 395 in the East, later in the West, which includes regimental names, the location of regimental headquarters for border troops, and allocations of field army regiments to field armies.[1] Although there are no surviving Roman historians of the fifth century with a particular interest in military affairs (like Ammianus Marcellinus in the fourth century or Procopius in the sixth), imperial laws preserved in the Theodosian and Justinianic *Codes* are useful, as are inscriptions, especially epitaphs, which give much information about

---

[1] Peter Brennan, "The Notitia Dignitatum," in *Les littératures techniques dans l'antiquité romaine*, ed. Fondation Hardt pour l'étude de l'Antiquité classique (Geneva, 1995) 147–178; Michael Kulikowski, "The *Notitia Dignitatum* as a Historical Source," *Historia* 49 (2000) 358–377.

regimental titles and ranks. There are also two military manuals, both couched as advice to emperors to address supposed defects in the army, but they are certainly not well-informed descriptions of contemporary practice. The first of these, Vegetius's *De re militari* (On Military Affairs), written at an unknown date between 383 and 450, contains a challenging fusion of practical material and an idealised legion in an attempt to improve the performance of contemporary infantry.[2] The second was a short work of tactical and organisational recommendations, also heavily influenced by the past, the *Epitedeuma* (Practices), written by Urbicius in the reign of Anastasius (491–518).[3]

ENEMIES

The Roman Empire was surrounded by enemies. In Europe the Romans called them all barbarians, using this generic term in part from a feeling of cultural superiority, but also because they saw few significant cultural differences among the groups.[4] At the beginning of the fifth century the barbarian tribes were still outside the Empire: along the Rhine various groups of Franks and Alamanni, on the Danube various Huns and Goths. By the end of the century, several barbarian kingdoms had been founded in the West, in Gaul (the Franks, Visigoths, Burgundians), but also in Italy (Ostrogoths) and most critically in Africa (Vandals). Although there was political development and a change in areas of settlement, barbarian organization, tactics, and equipment changed little in the fifth century. Armies remained composed mostly of unarmoured spearmen and had few archers or cavalry. No standing armies were created, and there is little evidence of units and ranks. Nor was there much skill in sieges or the development of a naval infrastructure. Logistics do seem to have improved, but this was more through the inheritance of the administrative structure of the Roman state than of any indigenous development.

No major change, furthermore, is visible in equipment or practice among the tribes on the lower Danube, where no kingdoms

---

[2] Michael Charles, *Vegetius in Context* (Stuttgart, 2007).

[3] Richard Burgess et al., "Urbicius' *Epitedeuma*: An Edition, Translation and Commentary," *Byzantinische Zeitschrift* 98 (2005) 35–74.

[4] Michael Maas, "Barbarians: Problems and Approaches," in *The Oxford Handbook on Late Antiquity*, ed. Scott F. Johnson (Oxford, 2012) 60–91; Greg Woolf, *Tales of the Barbarians* (Chichester, 2011).

were founded on Roman territory. The Huns even disappeared within twenty years of Attila's death in 453, and the head of one of his sons, Dengizech, graced the walls of Constantinople in 469. Their direct threat was mostly to do with Attila's leadership and proved to be ephemeral; the Huns were no more capable of bringing down the empire militarily than any other barbarian people. Though the Huns are sometimes described as being revolutionary because of their use of mounted archers or their composite reflex bows, neither was new to the Romans.[5] The Huns had some skill at siege warfare, as shown by the capture of Naissus in 441 or 442, but this was at the simple end of siege technology, however (towers and screens, rams and ladders), and was heavily dependent on Roman prisoners and deserters.[6] Logistics could be a weak point as well: when Attila fought in Italy in 452, he was forced to withdraw not by direct Roman military action but by a delay that led to problems finding food in a famine-struck landscape and by the outbreak of disease.[7]

On its eastern frontier the Romans faced a very different enemy, in the form of Sasanid Persia. The Sasanid Empire was an organised state that could challenge the Romans as equals. As in the eastern Roman army, Sasanid military practices appear little changed in the fifth century. Their armies were tactically dominated by armoured cavalry supported by light cavalry and some infantry. As a result of careful negotiation, peace between Roman and Persia lasted throughout most of the fifth century, except for brief wars in 421–422 and 441. Hostilities broke out again in 502–506. The city of Amida fell to a Persian assault in January 503, a tribute to Persian skills at siege warfare. After a Roman siege of Amida, including an unsuccessful attempt to tunnel under the walls, the city surrendered in early 505 and a negotiated peace followed in 506.[8]

---

[5] Rudi Lindner, "Nomadism, Horses and Huns," *Past and Present* 92 (1981) 1–19; Christopher Kelly, *The End of Empire: Attila the Hun and the Fall of Rome* (New York, 2009) 59–71; M. C. Bishop and J. C. Coulston, *Roman Military Equipment* (Oxford, 2006) 249; cf. Edward Luttwak, *The Grand Strategy of the Byzantine Empire* (Cambridge, Mass., 2009) 22–28.

[6] Roger C. Blockley, "Dexippus and Priscus and the Thucydidean Account of the Siege of Plataea," *Phoenix* 26 (1972) 18–27.

[7] Hydatius 154.

[8] Geoffrey Greatrex, "The Two Fifth-Century Wars between Rome and Persia," *Florilegium* 12 (1993) 1–14; Geoffrey Greatrex, *Rome and Persia at War, 502–532* (Leeds, 1998).

STRATEGY

From the surviving sources, as well as from fourth- and sixth-century writers, we are able to make some judgements about how fifth-century Roman emperors and generals wanted to fight. Roman strategy for much of the fifth century was built around defensive operations. In the East, emperors continued to fight in the same regions as their fourth-century predecessors. In the West, however, there were successive changes of strategic focus as territory fell from Roman control. The repeated attempts to reconquer Africa from the Vandals were an exception to this defensive strategy, though any attempt that was made did depend on available resources. There were rarely enough troops available in either part of the empire to fight wars on multiple fronts. The risks were so serious that Theodosius II abandoned a campaign against the Vandals in 441 because of a Hun attack on the Balkans. The danger of being overcommitted is shown by a series of calamities in the early fifth-century West, starting in 405 when Honorius was faced with an invasion of Italy by some Goths, then continuing with the crossing of the Rhine at the end of 406 by large numbers of Vandals, Alans, and Suevi. After this, Constantine III declared himself emperor in Britain, probably because of Honorius's inability to intervene on the Rhine because of commitments in Italy, and then crossed to Gaul. With an army that had been defeated twice by Theodosius I in civil wars in the past decade, and ongoing Gothic problems in Italy, Honorius was simply overwhelmed.[9] As the number of barbarian settlements in the empire multiplied, by the middle of the fifth century there were too many threats for western emperors to deal with.

Ideally, Roman generals preferred to avoid the risks of battle because the results were unpredictable and sometimes disastrous. At the battle of Adrianople in 378, for example, the emperor Valens was badly defeated by a force of Goths and was killed on the battlefield; it took his successor Theodosius I four years to restore order. Another example was the expedition launched against the Vandals in Africa in 468, which cost 64,000 pounds of gold and 700,000 pounds of silver.[10] This amount was roughly equal to two years of tax product from the eastern empire, yet the operation was unsuccessful. At a strategic level,

[9] Mark Humphries, "International Relations," in *The Cambridge History of Greek and Roman Warfare*, ed. Philip Sabin, Michael Whitby, and Hans van Wees (Cambridge, 2007) 235–269.
[10] Candidus, fr. 2.

avoiding battle could be done cheaply by paying subsidies to barbarians. This, however, could be politically awkward if seen as "paying tribute" to the enemy. Theodosius II was criticised for sending first hundreds, then thousands of pounds of gold annually to Attila the Hun. When Marcian succeeded Theodosius in 450, he refused to cooperate with Attila and pay the subsidies. This risked another Hunnic attack like the one that had reached Constantinople in 447.[11] When committed to fighting, it was thought better to avoid battle, wearing the enemy down slowly and outmanoeuvring them. The Romans liked to have a main force supported by other contingents in the same theatre. As well as easing supply and giving greater operational flexibility, there was the possibility of distracting the enemy, who might be confused as to the real objectives of the operation. Thus, when attacking an imperial rival Magnus Maximus in Italy in 388, in addition to his main force operations in Pannonia, Theodosius I also sent out two secondary attacks, a marine assault on Sicily and Italy and an expedition from Egypt to Africa.[12]

STRUCTURES

Both the eastern and the western emperor had an imperial army commanded by two equally ranked *magistri militum* (masters of soldiers). These forces were supplemented by regional armies, also commanded by *magistri militum*. Thus in 388 Theodosius I also had regional field armies in Illyricum, in Thrace, and the East, while his western enemy Magnus Maximus had an additional army in Gaul. In addition to these campaigning armies, other troops under the command of *duces* were deployed in forts around the borders of the empire.[13] The subject of numbers is difficult, but there were probably around half a million men under arms at the start of the fifth century, though campaign armies

---

[11] A. D. Lee, *War in Late Antiquity* (London, 2007) 119–122; Kelly, *End of Empire*, 140–147.

[12] *PLips.* 1. 63, *Griechische Urkunden der Papyrussammlung zu Leipzig* [*P. Lips.*], ed. Ludwig Mitteis (Leipzig, 1906).

[13] A. D. Lee, "The Army," *The Cambridge Ancient History* 13 (Cambridge, 1998) 211–237; Michael Whitby, "The Army c. 420–602," *CAH* 14 (Cambridge, 2000) 286–314; Hugh Elton, *Warfare in Roman Europe, AD 350–425* (Oxford, 1996); Martijn Nicasie, *Twilight of Empire* (Amsterdam, 1998); Philippe Richardot, *La fin de l'armée romaine (284–476) (Paris, 1998)*; Sabin, Whitby, and van Wees, ed., *The Cambridge History of Greek and Roman Warfare*, 233–458.

were usually between twenty and fifty thousand.[14] Almost all cities had walls, and frontier provinces contained numerous fortifications.

By the sixth century the Romans were placing a greater tactical emphasis on mounted troops, as reported in Procopius's account of Justinian's wars, while Mauricius's late-sixth century *Strategikon* (Generalship) focusses on cavalry warfare.[15] However, there is little sign in the fifth century of a rise in the numerical importance of cavalry, and the numbers of infantry in Roman armies remained high. In 478, for example, Zeno planned to deploy two thousand cavalry and ten thousand infantry from the army of Thrace, and six thousand cavalry and twenty thousand infantry from the imperial army based at Constantinople.[16]

Roman armies also included allied contingents, usually of barbarians hastily recruited on the frontiers. During the 388 campaign, Magnus Maximus used men from the Rhineland, while Theodosius's army included Goths, Alans, Iberians, and Armenians. Their use was partly to increase the available manpower to both emperors. However, Maximus was able to persuade some of Theodosius's recently settled Gothic soldiers to desert, so Theodosius probably thought it safer to have the rest of the Goths under his control rather than unsupervised. Last, the Roman Mediterranean fleet of oared galleys was strong, with a network of dockyards (especially at Ravenna and Constantinople) and naval suppliers.[17]

EQUIPMENT AND INFRASTRUCTURE

Whether Roman or barbarian, all of these troops would have looked similar in battle, equipped with large oval shields, mail shirts, helmets, and spears, with swords as secondary weapons, though Roman-supplied

---

[14] E.g., Michael Whitby, "Army and Society in the Late Roman World: A Context for Decline?," in *A Companion to the Roman Army*, ed. Paul Erdkamp (Oxford, 2007) 515–531, here 517; Warren Treadgold, *Byzantium and Its Army, 284–1081* (Stanford, 1995) 43–64.

[15] George Dennis and Ernst Gamillscheg, *Das Strategikon des Maurikios* (Vienna, 1981); trans. George Dennis, *Maurice's Strategikon* (Philadelphia, 1984).

[16] Malchus, fr. 18.2; John Haldon, *Warfare, State and Society in the Byzantine World, 565–1204* (London, 1999) 191–197; Hugh Elton, "Cavalry in Late Roman Warfare," in *The Late Roman Army in the Near East from Diocletian to the Arab Conquest*, ed. Ariel Lewin and Pietrina Pellegrini (Oxford, 2007) 377–381.

[17] John Pryor and Elizabeth Jeffreys, *The Age of the Dromon: The Byzantine Navy ca. 500–1204* (Leiden, 2006).

armies probably had more armoured men. Roman troops also would have had a more uniform appearance than barbarians, with regimental shield patterns and similar tunics and cloaks. Differences in organisation and practice were, however, much more significant. Roman field army troops were expected to serve for twenty years, were organised in regiments with a formal rank structure, carried out exercises, and were supported by an efficient logistical train.[18] For the Persian campaign in 503, the state provided wheat to the city of Edessa in Syria to bake rations for the campaigning army, a total of 630,000 *modii* (about 428 metric tons); in Illyricum, the regional *magister militum* led an army of 15,000 men and 520 wagons against the Bulgars in 499.[19] Roman training at both unit and army level is of particular significance. Although many individual barbarians had substantial individual military experience and talent, this was very different from the skills needed to manoeuvre armies, manage the construction of siege equipment or fleets, and to plan effective operations. Thus, even when barbarians were attached to Roman armies as allies and able to see the advantages provided by imperial infrastructure, this did not mean that they learnt how to organise a logistical system or exercise as an army. Such advantages did not guarantee victory, but it made Roman forces flexible and resilient.[20]

LEADERSHIP

The leaders of Roman regiments and armies came from inside and outside the empire. Contemporaries viewed the use of outsiders in various ways. Many soldiers probably saw it as a practical solution to problems in recruiting and as a means of recruiting the best men, while others (or even the same men at different times) might see it as a political issue, as a retreat from traditional practice. When the North African aristocrat Synesius visited Constantinople in 397, he wrote a speech "De regno" (On the Kingdom), which encouraged purging Goths from the army. He did not deliver this speech at the imperial court,

---

[18] Elton, *Warfare*, 89–117; Philip Rance, "*Simulacra pugnae*: The Literary and Historical Tradition of Mock Battles in the Roman Army," *Greek, Roman, and Byzantine Studies* 41 (2000) 223–275.

[19] Joshua the Stylite, *Chronicle*, 54; Marcellinus Comes, year 499.

[20] Philip Rance, "The *fulcum*, the Late Roman and Byzantine *testudo*: The Germanization of Late Roman Tactics?," *GRBS* 44 (2004) 265–326.

nor did problems in recruiting make such an ideology practical. Away from the court a decade later, Synesius mentioned a debate in the civic council of Cyrene in 407 in which he was opposed to "foreign" troops, but in 411 he praised the performance of a unit of Unnigardae, usually assumed to be Huns. Such complexities within the source material are often interpreted differently by historians.[21]

Many Roman officers were born outside the empire, though their careers could follow very different patterns. The Goths provide a good example of the choices available to the politically ambitious in the Balkans in the fifth century. When Theodosius I fought against Eugenius in Italy at the battle of the Frigidus in 394, his Goth allies were led by a Roman officer, Gainas, of Gothic origins. Gainas's success led to his promotion to *magister militum*. Then in 399, exploiting a Gothic revolt in Anatolia, Gainas forced the exile of several Roman civilian officials. However, in 400 popular unrest in Constantinople against Gainas's troops forced Arcadius to summon another Gothic *magister militum*, Fravitta, who defeated Gainas and replaced him. Gainas and Fravitta thus felt that Roman service gave them great opportunities, but not all Goths agreed. Before Theodosius left to fight against Eugenius in 394, he held a banquet attended by many Gothic leaders. Here Fravitta fell out so badly with another Goth, Eriulf, over this issue that he killed him.[22]

Alaric's career was very different from those of Fravitta and Gainas. He is first heard of fighting against Theodosius at the Hebrus in 388; in 394 he led some allied Goths in the campaign against Eugenius.[23] In 395, dismissed from Roman service at the end of the campaign and frustrated because he had not been given a Roman command, Alaric revolted and moved to Greece. The western general Stilicho landed in the Peloponnese in 397 to confront Alaric. However, he was undercut when Arcadius declared Stilicho a public enemy and then appointed Alaric as *magister militum*. East and West usually cooperated well, but

---

[21] Synesius, *Epistula*, 95, 78; Tim Barnes, "Synesius in Constantinople," *GRBS* 27 (1986) 93–112; Peter J. Heather, "The Anti-Scythian Tirade in Synesius' *De Regno*," *Phoenix* 42 (1988) 152–172; Alan Cameron and Jackie Long, *Barbarians and Politics at the Court of Arcadius* (Berkeley, 1993) 91–102, 127–142.

[22] Eunapius, fr. 59.

[23] J. H. W. G. Liebeschuetz, "Alaric's Goths: Nation or Army?," in *Fifth-Century Gaul: A Crisis of Identity?*, ed. John F. Drinkwater and Hugh Elton (Cambridge, 1992) 75–83, here 76–77; Claudian, *De VI consulatu Honorii*, 108–109; Peter Heather, *Goths and Romans* (Oxford, 1991) 195–198.

this was an exception; Alaric had now achieved success similar to that of Gainas and Fravitta.[24]

The choices open to Alaric, Fravitta, and Gainas were ultimately political, to fight for or against the Roman emperor, not cultural. There were few differences between them and other Balkan soldiers. Thus at the end of the fifth century, another Gothic leader, Theodoric the Amal, said, "a poor Roman plays the Goth, a rich [utilis] Goth the Roman."[25] Theodoric had founded his own kingdom on Roman soil, but still saw ethnicity as something that might be manipulated.

RANK-AND-FILE RECRUITMENT

The empire had perpetual problems in keeping its armies up to strength. Finding officers was easier than finding soldiers. An army half a million strong with men serving twenty-year terms required a minimum of twenty-five thousand recruits annually, before considering replacing men lost to disease, desertion, accident, and battle. It also needed to disperse any defeated enemies who were not massacred or enslaved. Although the empire levied recruits annually, this commitment was often commuted, a choice favoured by landowners who could keep their agricultural workforces intact.[26] Financial pressures made recruiting problems more serious in the West and though the process by which laws were recorded in the Theodosian Code is complicated, it is probably significant that all eleven laws on the subject of recruiting from 397 onwards were issued in the West, like the nine laws after 396 on deserters.[27] Although there were pressures to get enough men, the recruits had to be the right sort. The army had height standards (a minimum of 5 ft 7 in, about 5 ft 5 in or 1.65 m in modern measures).[28]

---

[24] Michael Kulikowski, Rome's Gothic Wars (Cambridge, 2007) 167–168.

[25] Anonymus Valesianus, 61; Patrick Amory, People and Identity in Ostrogothic Italy, 489–554 (Cambridge, 1997).

[26] A. H. M. Jones, The Later Roman Empiree, 284–602: A Social, Economic and Administrative Survey (Oxford, 1964) 614–623; Peter Sarris, Empires of Faith (Oxford, 2012) 80–82; Michael Whitby, "Recruitment in Roman Armies from Justinian to Heraclius (ca. 565–615)," in The Byzantine and Early Islamic Near East, vol. 3: States, Resources and Armies, ed. Averil Cameron (Princeton, 1995) 61–124; Elton, Warfare, 128–136; Peter Brennan, "The Last of the Romans: Roman Identity and the Roman Army in the Late Roman Near East," Mediterranean Archaeology 11 (1998) 191–203.

[27] Codex Theodosianus 7.13.12–22, 18.9–17.

[28] CTh 7.13. 3.

Nor were all Romans happy to serve or to lose their tenants (who were also taxpayers), so *coloni* (a group of long-term tenants) were also restricted from military service. So were *curiales* (town councillors), the backbone of local councils. Working for the emperor also brought privileges, and a law of 412 exempted most court officials from providing recruits from their estates, "for recruits must not be demanded from the resources of those men whose valour subjugates enemy captives for our triumphs,"[29] though an edict of 444 demanded recruits from most of these too, unless they came from Africa.[30] Western senatorial reluctance to provide recruits for these wars has often been criticised. The consequences were probably greater politically than militarily, but refusing to make sacrifices to assist the emperor meant that in a crisis such as Radagaisus's invasion of Italy, even slaves were offered freedom in return for service.[31]

There certainly were problems in recruiting, though whether these were significantly different from the early empire is unclear. There is no evidence of a shortage of manpower, but there were problems in recruiting and paying for soldiers. In some cases Romans adopted cheaper, short-term solutions. When a group of Goths, led by Radagaisus, was destroyed near Florence by Stilicho in 406, twelve thousand of his men entered Roman service. In other cases, problems in recruiting led to a focus on smaller numbers of high-quality troops, that is, generals were forced to do more with less.[32] Some of these men were elite barbarian cavalry regiments (known technically as *foederati*), like Synesius's beloved regiment of the Unnigardae.[33] Another response to recruiting problems was appointing private bodyguards (*bucellarii*) to generals, often numbering in the hundreds.[34]

These varying responses meant that the diversity of the manpower making up the army was more clearly visible than in the fourth century. Thus there was a separate church in Constantinople for use by "Arian"

---

[29] *CTh* 11.18.1.

[30] *Novellae Theodosiani*, 6.3.

[31] *CTh* 7.13.16, 17; John Matthews, *Western Aristocracies and Imperial Court* (Oxford, 1975) 276–278.

[32] Olympiodorus, fr. 9; Ilkka Syvänne, *The Age of Hippotoxotai: Art of War in Roman Military Revival and Disaster (491–636)* (Tampere, Finland, 2004) 192–193; cf. Haldon, *Warfare*, 216; Philip Rance, "*DRUNGUS*, ΔΡΟΥΓΓΟΣ and ΔΡΟΥΓΓΙΣΤΙ: A Gallicism and Continuity in Late Roman Cavalry Tactics," *Phoenix* 58 (2004) 96–130, here 125.

[33] Elton, *Warfare*, 91–94.

[34] Liebeschuetz, *Barbarians and Bishops*, 43–47.

Gothic soldiers.[35] Although Latin was the language of military administration, in practical terms it was used alongside Greek and Syriac in
much of the Near East. In Edessa in 396, a Gothic soldier who had
learned Syriac was billeted on a local family and married their daughter
Euphemia.[36] When Adid the Arab surrendered "to the Greeks" in 504,
he joined a polyglot group of Roman soldiers including other Arabs,
Goths, Huns, Armenians, Moors, and Laz.[37] Some Roman officers
were royalty among their own people: Bacurius, for example, who fell
at the Frigidus in 394, both *comes domesticorum* (count of the domes-
tics, i.e., head of the imperial staff officers corps) and a member of the
Iberian royal family, or the Burgundian prince Gundobaudes who was
patricius and *magister militum* in Gaul and Italy in the early 470s.

Other prejudices affected recruiting men and officers. In 408 Honorius wished to appoint the pagan Generidus as a *magister militum*.
Generidus refused, since a law had been passed banning pagans from
military service, The emperor offered to exempt him but Generidus
again refused; Honorius subsequently repealed the law and Generidus
was finally appointed.[38] Generidus was also a barbarian, but this seems
not to have troubled Honorius. Some even felt that more barbarians
were needed, not fewer. In late 409, Alaric sent an expedition to Africa,
but according to Zosimus it was not "a battleworthy force" since it contained no "barbarians"; clearly, Zosimus (or his contemporary source)
saw barbarians as better troops than Romans.[39]

POLITICS

Although Theodosius I led his own armies, few of his successors led
troops in battle. Majorian was an exception, though many, like Marcian,
Leo, and Zeno in the East and Avitus and Anthemius in the West,
had some military experience.[40] In the West, Honorius's failure to
lead allowed the *magister militum* Stilicho to dominate both court and
military politics. He was succeeded by other great generals, Constantius

---

[35] Rochelle Snee, "Gregory Nazianzen's Anastasia Church: Arianism, the Goths, and
Hagiography," *Dumbarton Oaks Papers* 52 (1998) 157–186.
[36] Francis Burkitt, *Euphemia and the Goth* (London, 1913).
[37] Joshua the Stylite, 75.
[38] Zosimus, 5.46.2–5.
[39] Zos. 6.7, 6.12.
[40] J. H. W. G. Liebeschuetz, "Warlords and Landlords," in Erdkamp, *Companion*, 479–
494, here 482; Whitby, "Army and Society," in Erdkamp, *Companion*, 526.

in the 420s, Aetius in the 430s to early 450s, and Ricimer from the 450s onwards. In the East, although Arcadius and Theodosius II were too young to campaign, generals were not able to dominate politics. However, some eastern generals, such as Aspar, had long periods of great political influence.[41] There were other changes. In the fourth century, ambitious generals seized imperial power in their own names, while in the fifth century they were generally content to be the power behind the throne, examples being Aetius, Ricimer, or Aspar. And in the later fifth-century West, some generals had little allegiance to anyone except themselves. When Majorian's *magister militum* in Gaul Aegidius was murdered in 463, his son Syagrius succeeded to his position as commander of the army, but now ruled part of northern Gaul in his own name.

The failure of the emperor to lead troops on campaign thus involved these generals in the politics of raising men and money. In 405, Stilicho had promised to make payments to Alaric that would have kept him out of Italy. When Stilicho failed to make the payments (because of the invasion of Radagaisus and the problems in Gaul), Alaric threatened to attack Italy. Since Honorius could not pay (probably because of the costs of fighting in Italy in Gaul), Stilicho extorted the money from a reluctant Senate in early 408. The political cost, however, was so great that a coup soon followed, leading to Stilicho's execution in August, and a damning story told by the victors; Jerome in a letter of 409 smeared Stilicho as a "half-barbarian traitor."[42] Whether Stilicho would have been successful against Alaric with a few thousand more men levied from Italian senatorial estates is uncertain, but raising men involved him directly with the Senate in a way that was not true of the generals of Theodosius I only a generation earlier.

Settlements

In 418 Honorius settled the Goths in Aquitania Secunda in Gaul (map 5a).[43] We have no details of the mechanics of this settlement, though settling them on imperial estates and *agri deserti* (land that was not taxed

---

[41] J. H. W. G. Liebeschuetz, *Barbarians and Bishops* (Oxford, 1990) 89, 94–95, 132; Liebeschuetz, "Warlords," 481–485.
[42] Jerome, *Epistula* 123.
[43] Thomas Burns, "The Settlement of 418," in Drinkwater and Elton, *Fifth-Century Gaul*, 53–63.

because uncultivated) could have been relatively simple administratively and would have had little impact on most landowners or the primary sources. It seems unlikely that the organisation of this settlement would have been administratively identical to other, later settlements elsewhere in Gaul, in Africa, or in Italy, themselves also poorly described.[44] As in 382, the 418 settlement reflected the Roman state's inability to destroy its enemies, but it was also a practical response to a current problem. If everything had worked as hoped, this settlement, and those of various Alans and Burgundians elsewhere in Gaul later, would have provided soldiers and also preserved Roman taxpayers. There was some initial success, and an expedition against the Vandals in Baetica in 422, led by the *magister militum* Castinus, included a number of allied Gothic troops. The campaign had to be abandoned, however, when the Goths deserted.

In earlier centuries such settlements had been absorbed, as often continued in the East. But the western empire had already lost much military capacity in the early years of the fifth century and the loss of tax income and of recruits from these settlements exacerbated the problem. This led to repeated losses of territory in the West, and by 440, the Romans had lost control of Britain and large parts of Gaul, Spain, Africa, and Illyricum. The Roman Empire had collapsed in the West before it had time to assimilate the settlers.[45]

FINANCES

Although much of the loss of territory came from settlements, other lands were lost to conquest, in particular in Illyricum, Spain, Britain, and most crucially Africa (see map 4a). The Vandal capture of Carthage in 439 caused more damage to the Roman Empire than either the battle of Adrianople in 378 or the sacks of Rome in 410 and 455. The loss of the tax revenues from Africa crippled the western empire. At the same time, the empire was now exposed to a new threat, naval raids in the Mediterranean especially against Italy and Greece. Roman emperors in

---

[44] Guy Halsall, *Barbarian Migrations and the Roman West, 376–568* (Cambridge, 2007) 422–454; Walter Goffart, "The Technique of Barbarian Settlement in the Fifth Century: A Personal, Streamlined Account with Ten Additional Comments," *Journal of Late Antiquity* 3 (2010) 65–98; Guy Halsall, "The Technique of Barbarian Settlement in the Fifth Century: A Reply to Walter Goffart," *JLA* 3 (2010) 99–112; Peter Sarris, *Empires of Faith* (Oxford, 2012) 58–68.

[45] Timo Stickler, "The *Foederati*," in Erdkamp, *Companion*, 495–514.

east and west did not take this loss lightly, and expeditions were launched or planned in 431, 441, and 461, when Majorian was unsuccessful with a fleet of three hundred ships. After this, in 468 the eastern emperor Leo sent a large force, exploiting the peace with the Persians and in the Balkans, a clear difference from 441, when Hun pressure on the Danube forced the abandonment of an expedition. Leo's expedition also failed, though the causes were the vacillation of the Roman commander and the Vandal king Geiseric's seizing of this opportunity, not Roman military incapacity. The immediate consequences were felt mostly in Constantinople. However, in the longer term the failure to recapture the lands that could provide a surplus of men and money sealed the fate of the western empire.

CONCLUSION

In the West, Odoacer deposed the last emperor Romulus in 476, returned the imperial insignia to Zeno in Constantinople, and ruled Italy as king. Although his territory was little different to that of recent western emperors, the infrastructure of the western armies had for the most part already collapsed. Eugippius's *Life of Severinus*, set in Noricum Ripensis, shows that forts and Roman garrisons continued to exist on the Danube even after the 450s, but even for this province, the end of the Roman Empire, and thus of central payment of these garrisons, was a noticeable event.[46]

Odoacer's seizure of power illustrates well what had happened in the western empire. Armies may have looked similar to the early years of the century, but the world in which they were fighting had changed dramatically. The centrality of the Roman state that characterised Theodosius's campaigns in Italy had disappeared. The campaigns against Magnus Maximus and Eugenius were over who was to be Roman emperor and involved setting half of the Roman world against the other half. A century later, the Roman Empire was just one of many powers in north Italy.

However, the western Roman Empire did not fall because it was defeated militarily. When well led and well supported, as was usually the case in the East, the effectiveness of the fifth-century Roman army remained high. The inability of the eastern Romans to force the various Gothic groups in the Balkans into submission in the 470s suggests a lack

---

[46] Eugippius, *Vita Sancti Severini*, 4, 11, 15, 20.

of resources, but this did not necessarily affect operational efficiency. In 479 it was reported to a *magister militum*, Sabinianus, in Illyricum that some Goths

> were making a leisurely descent from Candavia and that the Romans could hope to overwhelm most of them. Sabinianus himself took command of the cavalry and sent a considerable body of infantry on a roundabout route through the mountains, telling them where and when to put in their appearance. Then he dined, assembled his army and set out at nightfall. He attacked the Goths at daybreak when they were already on the move. . . . When the infantry appeared . . . according to plan, [the Goths] were routed. Some died attacking the cavalry, some the infantry. Sabinianus captured their wagons, 2000 in number, more than 5000 prisoners, and considerable booty.[47]

This event shows what the eastern Roman army was capable of in the late fifth century, with good scouting, exploitation of the landscape, and the coordination of two forces on a night march in difficult terrain. But it was a risky operation even for a trained army.

The Roman armies of the West and those of the East were little different at the start of the fifth century, but as the fifth century continued, the West lost too much territory to pay for or recruit a large army. There was an increasing use of allies and non-Roman recruits to compensate. This diversity of manpower, often described as barbarisation, occurred in both parts of the empire, but should not be confused with a decline in military effectiveness. As the state grew weaker, new choices, of whether to serve Rome or a barbarian king, began to emerge for aristocrats that from the 450s onwards made the collapse of the western empire inevitable. Geography and politics, not a failure of military structures, lay at the heart of western Roman collapse in the fifth century.

---

[47] Malch. fr. 20.226–248, ed. Roger C. Blockley, *Fragmentary Classicising Historians of the Later Roman Empire: Eunapius, Olympiodorus, Priscus and Malchus*, vol. 2 of 2 vols. (Liverpool, 1983).

8: LAW AND LEGAL CULTURE IN THE AGE OF ATTILA

Caroline Humfress

The long fifth century was an age of legal codification, from the *Code* and *Novellae* ("new laws") of the eastern emperor Theodosius II to the *Breviary* of the Visigothic king Alaric [II] (promulgated 506 or 507) and beyond. How we understand law and legal culture in the fifth- and early sixth century East and West tends to be tied to their respective political and governmental fates: strong centralism and a renewed Roman legal classicism in the East, versus disruption, fragmentation, and the emergence of new legal "ethnic" identities in the West. In the last decade or so, however, legal scholars have developed new empirical frameworks and theoretical perspectives that seek to challenge legal centralist traditions. This chapter explores the issues and insights raised by some of these new approaches from three, explicitly comparative, perspectives: lawmaking, legal culture, and microlaw.

LAWMAKING IN THE FIFTH CENTURY

Lawmaking is powermaking.

–Walter Benjamin

According to Mark the Deacon's fifth- or possibly sixth-century *Life of Porphyry* [Bishop] *of Gaza* (48), Theodosius II's first act of imperial command took place in Constantinople, before "multitudes of inhabitants like the waves of the sea," when he was nine months old. The ceremonial occasion was Theodosius's baptism in 402: shortly after emerging from the church into a city "hung with garlands and adorned with silks and gold vessels," the imperial retinue – which included patricians, *illustres*, and "every dignity," together with troops of soldiers – was halted by a formal petition from Bishop Porphyry. The palatine official responsible for carrying the infant Theodosius accepted Porphyry's written petition (as agreed in advance, so the *Life* tells us, with Theodosius's mother: the empress Eudoxia) and began to read out his requests for antipagan legislation, alongside pleas for privileges and financial support for the holy church at Gaza. According to the *Life*, the same Palatine official "then rolled [the petition] up, placed his hand under the head of the baby, made it nod in front of all, and shouted: 'The power of his majesty has granted the petition.'"[1] All who saw this were amazed (not least, the *Life* implies, Theodosius's father: the emperor Arcadius). Thirty-five years later, Theodosius II was centre-stage at another glittering imperial event in Constantinople: the wedding of his daughter, Aelia Eudoxia, to the western Roman emperor Valentinian III. It was shortly after these festivities that copies of the first-ever collection of Roman imperial law to bear the name of an emperor – the *Theodosian Code* (*Codex Theodosianus*) – were conveyed from Theodosius's "divine hand" to the praetorian prefects, with careful instructions for copying and distribution throughout both the East and West.[2] The wedding celebrations of October 437 were commemorated in a series of mosaics in the imperial palace at Ravenna; the Western praetorian prefect Faustus also referred to the ceremonies when he presented his copy of the *Code* (brought back with him from Constantinople) to a meeting of the Roman Senate, probably held on 25 May 438.[3] We have no record, however, in either words or images, of any *public* festivities or dedication ceremonies to celebrate the confirmation of Theodosius's

---

[1] Mark the Deacon, *Life of Porphyry of Gaza*, 48, trans. Claudia Rapp, "Mark the Deacon," in *Medieval Hagiography: An Anthology*, ed. Thomas Head (New York 2000) 53–75, here 67. The epigraph to this chapter is from Walter Benjamin, "Critique of Violence," in *Walter Benjamin: Selected Writings*, vol. 11: *1913–1926*, ed. and trans. Marcus Bullock and Michael W. Jennings (Cambridge, Mass., 2004) 236–252, here 248.

[2] *Gesta Senatus Romani de Theodosiano publicando*, 2–3, an excerpted copy of the records of the Roman Senate, trans. Clyde Pharr et al., *The Theodosian Code and Novels and the Sirmondian Constitutions* (Princeton, 1952) 3–4.

[3] For the date see Lorena Atzeri, *Gesta Senatus de Theodosiano publicando: Il Codice Teodosiano e la sua diffusione ufficiale in Occidente* (Berlin, 2008) 128–132; and A. J. Boudewijn Sirks, *The Theodosian Code* (Norderstedt, Germany, 2007) 198–214. John Matthews, *Laying Down the Law: A Study of the Theodosian Code* (New Haven, 2000) 4, discusses the mosaics at Ravenna.

Code.[4] Nor do we have any descriptions of the physical text itself being received and duly venerated by imperial magistrates throughout the eastern and western empire, in preparation for its provisions coming into legal effect. From that date, so Theodosius's *Novel* 1.1 states, no man was to be permitted "to cite an imperial law [from the age of Constantine up to the time of the *Code's* completion] in court and in daily legal practice, or to compose the instruments of litigation," except from officially certified copies of the *Codex* itself.[5]

The *Theodosian Code* is one of the most important sources to survive (albeit incompletely) from the Age of Attila. "In its present state it contains more than 2,500 [excerpted] texts on all aspects of the legal, administrative, social, and religious life of the late Roman Empire and is a constant resource for historians"; although, as John Matthews explains, the modern use of the *Code* has not always been supported by a consistent understanding of its nature, nor of how it was produced.[6] In terms of late Roman legal and administrative history, the *Theodosian Code* now tends to be viewed as both the outcome and statement of a new kind of Roman "governmentality" centred on the Eastern imperial court: rule-of-law values emanate outwards from the fifth-century Constantinopolitan palace complex, as they simultaneously point forwards in time to the Age of Justinian and his *Corpus iuris civilis*. The emerging dominant narrative in late Roman legal history is thus no longer one of decline, or the rise of "vulgar law," but instead tells a story of the fifth-century working-out of a monarchical style of legislative government first articulated during the Age of Constantine.[7]

---

[4] Theodosius II, *Novel* 1.1, addressed to praetorian prefect Florentius of the Orient and promulgated on 15 February 438. The latest constitution excerpted in the *Theodosian Code* appears at 6.23.4 and is dated 16 March 437.

[5] *Novellae Theodosii*, 1.1, sec. 3 (trans. Pharr, *Theodosian Code*, 487). Theodosius II sent an official collection of his Novels to Valentinian III in October 447 (see *Nov. Theod.* 2.1 and *Novellae Valentiniani*, 26.1).

[6] Matthews, *Laying Down the Law*, vii. Matthews's discussion of the incomplete textual transmission (and modern editing) of books 2–5 of the *Theodosian Code*, the books on "private law," is crucial. See also Timothy D. Barnes, "Foregrounding the Theodosian Code," *Journal of Roman Archaeology* 14 (2001) 671–685.

[7] On "vulgar law" see Detlef Liebs, "Roman Vulgar Law in Late Antiquity," in *Aspects of Law in Late Antiquity: Dedicated to A. M. Honoré on the Occasion of His Sixtieth Year of Teaching in Oxford*, ed. A. J. Boudewijn Sirks (Oxford, 2008) 35–53; on the rise of legally trained bureaucrats, see Tony Honoré, *Law in the Crisis of Empire, 379–455 AD: The Theodosian Dynasty and Its Quaestors with a Palingenesia of Laws of the Dynasty* (Oxford, 1998); and Jill Harries, "The Roman Imperial Quaestor from Constantine to Theodosius II," *Journal of Roman Studies* 78 (1988) 148–172.

The traditional Roman image of emperors and imperial magistrates responding to pleas, petitions, and concrete cases (as we saw in Mark the Deacon's vignette of baby Theodosius) remains dominant in the fifth-century literary, documentary, and epigraphic evidence.[8] The only surviving autograph of any Roman emperor is to be found signed at the end of a petition, written on papyrus and sent to Theodosius II by Appion of Syene, a Christian bishop from remote southern Egypt, sometime in the first quarter of the fifth century.[9] After the promulgation of the *Code*, Theodosius II and later emperors still issued responses directly to petitioners; they also carried on issuing constitutions, mostly in response to legal or administrative proposals (*suggestiones*) from imperial magistrates and other officials – who had themselves been petitioned by suppliants and litigants. As Synesius, bishop of Cyrene (Libya), explained in an early fifth-century letter addressed to the Dux Libyarum: "They [a unit of barbarian soldiers] make a request of you [the Dux] through me [the bishop], and of the Emperor through you."[10] Over eighty of Theodosius II's own post-437 constitutions survive in one form or another: most appear as excerpted texts in Justinian's *Code*, but thirty-six have been transmitted in their entirety, complete with preambles and executive formulae: two via the acts of fifth-century church councils and the remainder, with Visigothic interpretations, via the *Breviary* of Alaric. In these complete constitutions we see Theodosius II's chancellery responding – through the medium of letters to the relevant bureaucratic official – to concrete cases and petitions, for example concerning the security of land tenure in Armenia (*Nov. Th.* 5.3); on ownerless property (*Nov. Th.* 17.1–2) and the ownership of alluvial lands (*Nov. Th.* 20.1); as well as the restoration of property to municipalities (*Nov. Th.* 23.1). In terms of Roman private law (inheritance, family, property, contracts, commerce, etc.) and public administration, individual and group petitioners throughout the eastern

---

[8] Papyrological evidence: Jean-Luc Fournet and Jean Gascou, "Liste des pétitions sur papyrus des Ve–VIIe siècles," in *La pétition à Byzance*, ed. Denis Feissel and Jean Gascou (Paris, 2004) 141–196. Legal epigraphy: Denis Feissel, "Les actes de l'État impérial dans l'épigraphie tardive (324–610): Prolégomènes à un inventaire," in *Selbstdarstellung und Kommunikation: Die Veröffentlichung staatlicher Urkunden auf Stein und Bronze in der römischen Welt*, ed. Rudolf Haensch (Munich, 2009) 97–128.

[9] Denis Feissel and Klaas A. Worp, "La requête d'Appion, évêque de Syene, à Théodose II: P. Leid. Z révisé," *Oudheidkundige Mededelingen* 68 (1988) 97–111. For discussion see Fergus Millar, *A Greek Roman Empire: Power and Belief under Theodosius II, 408–450* (Berkeley, 2006) 22 and 63–64.

[10] Synesius of Cyrene, *Epistola* 78 (trans. Millar, *A Greek Roman Empire*, 60).

provinces looked to imperial officials for decisions on case-specific issues. As the preamble to *Novellae Valentiniani* 23.1, dated 22 May 443, states, "Often a remedy requested by one municipality, or one man, customarily occasions a general rule for correction of wrong." The Greek-speaking subjects of Theodosius II thus "found themselves in an organic relationship with a bilingual imperial administration in Constantinople, a relationship not just of 'government,' but of persuasion, protest, and the assertion of rights on the one hand, and of admonition, self-justification, and the threat of force or legal penalties on the other."[11] In fact during the Age of Attila, as we shall see below, law-making – and legal code-making – was part of a much broader rhythm of socio-political exchange between rulers and subjects, in both the Roman East and to an extent, the post-Roman West.

In his *History against the Pagans* (7.43), the early fifth-century Christian priest Orosius relates how, whilst in Palestine, he overheard a story told about the Visigothic king Athaulf, the son-in-law of Emperor Theodosius I and a "keen partisan of peace." According to a "devout, serious and sober man from Narbonne," Athaulf (when drunk) was fond of explaining his decision not to make the land of the Romans into the empire of the Goths because "after long experience, he had proved to himself that, because of their wild barbarism, the Goths were completely unable to obey the law and because he believed it wrong to deprive a state of laws (without which a state is not a state at all)."[12] In retelling this story Orosius was, of course, doing more than simply repeating a classic ethnographic contrast between the peaceful law and order guaranteed by civilised (Roman) rule and the chaotic lawlessness threatened by war-loving, stateless barbarians.[13] In Orosius's account it is (the "barbarian") Athaulf who decides to uphold the ("Roman") legal fabric, using the might of his Goths. Later fifth- and sixth-century Roman writers, on the other hand, depict "barbarian warlords" themselves granting privileges, confirming existing rights, and administering justice according to traditional petition-and-response patterns.

---

[11] Millar, *Greek Roman Empire*, 51.

[12] Orosius, *History against the Pagans*, 7.43.6–8, trans. Andrew T. Fear, *Seven Books of History against the Pagans* (Liverpool, 2010) 412.

[13] For discussion see Michael Maas, "Barbarians: Problems and Approaches," in *The Oxford Handbook of Late Antiquity*, ed. Scott F. Johnson (Oxford, 2012) 60–91.

Priscus of Panium, for example, provides an eyewitness account of Attila the Hun responding to throngs of petitioners at his village encampment on the Hungarian plain (Priscus, fr. 11.2 [Blockley 227]). After Attila's death, the rapid fragmentation of the Hun federation into "a complicated array of competing tribal groups" can be attributed, at least in part, to Attila's skilled control of patronage whilst alive.[14] In the (still officially Roman) West, the Gallo-Roman aristocrat and landowner Sidonius Apollinaris – writing from Toulouse around 455 to Agricola, son of Emperor Avitus – describes the Visigothic ruler Theodoric II hearing deputations and disputes on a daily basis, in the company of armour-clad nobles and guards dressed in skins (*Ep.* I.2.4–9). Over twenty years later we find Sidonius himself seeking influence at the Visigothic court of Euric, having otherwise failed in his attempts to secure a share of his mother-in-law's property (*Ep.* 8.9.).[15] The early sixth-century Burgundian *Book of Constitutions* (*Liber Constitutionum*, also referred to as the *Leges Burgundionum*) – a structured collection of royal edicts, some dating back to the reign of Gundobad (473–516), probably ratified by assembly at Easter 517 – shows Burgundian rulers making gifts of land, slaves, and legal privileges, but also adjudicating between the existing rights of (at least second- or third-generation) "Burgundian" freemen and "Roman" landowners.[16] The rulers of Vandal North Africa and Ostrogothic Italy developed broadly comparable strategies.[17] In terms of fifth- and early sixth-century power strategies, controlling access to law and justice (including deciding on legal privileges, petitions, and concrete disputes) is perhaps not as immediately obvious as bestowing gifts of land, slaves, and war booty – yet we see

---

[14] Michael Whitby, "The Balkans and Greece, 420–602," in *The Cambridge Ancient History*, vol. 14: *Late Antiquity: Empire and Successors, A.D. 425–600*, ed. Averil Cameron, Bryan Ward-Perkins, and Michael Whitby (Cambridge, 2001) 701–730, here 704.

[15] On Euric and land disputes see Jill Harries, "Not the Theodosian Code: Euric's Law and Late Fifth-Century Gaul," in *Society and Culture in Late Antique Gaul: Revisiting the Sources*, ed. Ralph Mathisen and Danuta Shanzer (Aldershot, 2001) 39–51.

[16] Peter J. Heather, "Law and Society in the Burgundian Kingdom," in *Law, Custom and Justice in Late Antiquity and the Early Middle Ages*, ed. Alice Rio (London, 2011) 115–154, with discussion of manuscripts and editions for the Burgundian legal material. Also Matthew Innes, "On the Social Dynamics of Barbarian Settlement: Law, Property and Identity in the Burgundian Kingdom" (unpublished paper, with thanks to the author).

[17] Vandal Africa: Jonathan Conant, *Staying Roman: Conquest and Identity in Africa and the Mediterranean, 439–700* (Cambridge, 2012); Ostrogothic Italy: Sean D. W. Lafferty, *Law and Society in the Age of Theoderic the Great: A Study of the Edictum Theoderici* (Cambridge, 2013).

the former being used, in different ways, across Roman, sub-Roman and non-Roman contexts alike.

One of the stimuli towards the official fifth-century codification of late Roman imperial constitutions was elite anxiety concerning the use of law and justice as tools of patronage. According to the traditional Roman concept of the "beneficial ideology" – which advertised power relations of mutual benefit to both ruler and ruled – Roman emperors and their official representatives were the ultimate bestowers of gifts and largess, as well as dispensers of justice (including acts of amnesty, *indulgentia*, in criminal matters).[18] As an eastern imperial constitution, given on 8 June 439, puts it: "We almost believe that We have received a favour whenever the occasion is presented to Us to grant a favour, and without any doubt We suspect that We have lost a day if it is not illuminated by the munificence of Our divinity"; imperial generosity, continues the text, "brings the merit of a man before God" and "holds first place among the imperial and highest virtues."[19] An earlier eastern constitution (*CTh* 1.1.14), issued in 393, clearly restated a fundamental principle of Roman jurisprudence: that general regulations should always be preferred to special grants of favour. Yet as we have already seen in Mark the Deacon's story about Theodosius II, a prearranged nod from an imperial infant – given in public before a crowd that included Palatine officials and Constantinopolitan senators – could secure special privileges and new imperial commands for a persistent and well-connected petitioner (in this case a Christian bishop).

To the Roman and Constantinopolitan senatorial aristocracy, the practice of enacting imperial constitutions in favour of individual interests–whether "legally" or "fraudulently" – was seen as a threat to their security of title to land.[20] When the Roman senators met in 438 to receive Faustus's copy of the *Theodosian Code* they sent a request to the emperors, via acclamation, "that no laws be promulgated in reply to petitions[(*preces*]"; according to the final (extant) acclamation recorded for that day: "All the rights of landowners are thrown into confusion by such surreptitious actions!"[21] It is also worth noting that the famous

---

[18] Vivian Nutton, "The Beneficial Ideology," in *Imperialism in the Ancient World*, ed. Peter D. A. Garnsey and C. R. Whittaker (Cambridge, 1978) 209–222. For the fifth and sixth centuries see Ralph Mathisen, "Adnotatio and Petitio: The Emperor's Favour and Special Exceptions in Early Byzantine Law," in Feissel and Gascou, *La petition à Byzance*, 25–34.

[19] *Nov. Theod.* 5.1pr (trans. Pharr, 491).

[20] Honoré, *Law in the Crisis of Empire*, 128 n. 65.

[21] *Gesta Senatus* 5 (trans. Pharr, 6).

426 definition of "general law" (*Cod. Just.* 1.14.2–3) and the so-called Law of Citations (*CTh* 1.4.3), promulgated by Valentinian III's chancellery at Ravenna, were part of a much more extensive constitution relating to inheritance, donations, and property law – addressed to the Senate at Rome.[22] Theodosius II's announcement to the Constantinopolitan senate three years later, that his legal commissioners would only collect and codify those imperial constitutions which rested upon the force of edicts or with "general force" (*sacra generalitas*) (*CTh* 1.1.5), may have been intended – in part – as a response to specific aristocratic disquiet. An excerpt from an imperial constitution issued ten years later, also addressed to the (Roman) Senate, suggests ongoing tension: henceforth the Senate was to be consulted about and to consent to all general laws that had previously been handled by the emperor and consistory (*Cod. Just.* 1.14.8).

The collective fates of eastern and western senatorial aristocrats diverged sharply during the course of the long fifth century. The classical idea that Roman civil law guaranteed (elite) general rights, above and beyond imperial authority, is still to be found in the rhetoric of fifth- and sixth-century imperial constitutions (according to *Cod. Just.* 1.14.4, of the year 429, submission to law is greater than the power to command). But it also found new expressions in the lawmaking of Visigothic, Burgundian, and Ostrogothic kings.

LEGAL CULTURE

> Legal culture is the term we apply to those values and attitudes in society which determine what structures are used and why; which rules work and which do not, and why.
> –Lawrence M. Friedman, "Legal Culture and Social Development"

In current sociolegal scholarship the term "legal culture" can refer to the role of law within culture, the impact of culture on law, or the idea of law *as* culture.[23] In the first section of this chapter I explored

---

[22] Twelve excerpts from this constitution survive: *Codex Justinianus*, 1.14.2; 1.14.3; 1.19.7; 1.22.5; *CTh* 1.4.3; 4.1.1; 5.1.8; *Cod. Just.* 6.30.18; *CTh* 8.18.9; 8.18.10; 8.19.1; 8.13.6 (see further Honoré, *Law in the Crisis of Empire*, 117, 124, and 250–251; Matthews, *Laying Down the Law*, 24–26).

[23] For further discussion of the concept see David Nelken, "Using Legal Culture: Purposes and Problems," in *Using Legal Culture*, ed. David Nelken (London, 2012)

fifth- and early sixth-century lawmaking in the context of (elite) cultures of power. In this section and the one that follows, I turn to the concept of legal culture itself, using the term in the broad sense suggested by Friedman in the quotation above.

The idea that law is somehow both determined by and determinative of culture has (implicitly) framed much of the modern scholarship on law and identity in the long fifth century. For the East, there are analyses of the complex relationship between rabbinical legal writing and Jewish identity, particularly with respect to late antique Mesopotamia and Palestine.[24] Recent studies on the Sasanian *Book of a Thousand Legal Decisions* (or the "Sasanian lawbook") – compiled in Middle Persian (Pahlavi) probably in the late sixth or early seventh centuries, but with commentaries on Avestan jurisprudence and material relating to concrete law cases going back to at least the fifth century CE – also have an explicit focus on law and culture and law as culture.[25] As does scholarship on the *Laws of the Christian and Just Kings* (the *Sententiae Syricae*): an unsystematic collection of 102 propositions from the constitutions of Diocletian, Constantine, and Leo, plus extracts from the (juristic) *Sentences of Paul*, extant only in Syriac translation from a Greek original, and studies on the *Syro-Roman Lawbook:* a comprehensive and probably late fifth-century collection of late Roman constitutions up to 472 with short extracts from juristic writing, surviving in Syriac, Arabic, Armenian, and Coptic manuscripts.[26] In all these cases, legal culture is seen to be determined by and determinative of "religious" values and attitudes, to different extents and effects.

In terms of the politically fragmented West, on the other hand, relevant scholarship has mainly focused on law in relation to ethnogenesis and ("barbarian") state formation.[27] How long did the customs or

---

1–51. The epigraph to this section is from Lawrence M. Friedman, "Legal Culture and Social Development," *Law and Society Review* 4 (1969) 29–44, here 35.

[24] Beth A. Berkowitz, "The Limits of 'Their Laws': Ancient Rabbinic Controversies about Jewishness (and Non-Jewishness)," *Jewish Quarterly Review* 99.1 (2009) 121–157.

[25] Simon Corcoran, "Observations on the Sasanian Law-Book in the Light of Roman Legal Writing," in Rio, *Law, Custom, and Justice*, 77–114 (with discussion of the manuscript tradition and modern editions).

[26] *Laws of the Christian and Just Kings:* Walter Selb, *Sententiae Syricae* (Vienna, 1990); *Syro-Roman Lawbook:* Yifat Monnickendam, "The Kiss and the Earnest: Early Roman Influences on Syriac Matrimonial Law," *Le Muséon* 125 (2012) 307–334 (with discussion of the manuscript tradition and modern editions).

[27] Andrew Gillett, "Ethnogenesis: A Contested Model of Early Medieval Europe," *History Compass* 4.2 (2006) 241–260, with further bibliography.

"customary law" of militarised ethnic groups survive within the new kingdoms of "the Franks," "the Anglo-Saxons," "the Visigoths," "the Burgundians," "the Ostrogoths," "the Vandals," and so on? Was law in the fifth- and early sixth-century West applied territorially (within the bounds of a given region or state), or did its operation depend on the principle of personality ("Burgundian" law for "Burgundians"; "Frankish" or "Salic" law for the Franks; "Roman" law for the "Romans" etc.)?[28] What role, if any, did Roman law and bureaucratic practices play in the transformation of western "ethnic" identities into (nation) state-like identities? To what extent did Christian clerics and institutional church structures act as "carriers" of Roman legal traditions? These kinds of questions tend to rely on a number of assumptions about law and legal culture that demand unpacking just as much as the concept of "barbarian identity" itself.

According to Ernst Levy, writing in 1950, the development of law in the western successor kingdoms should be understood according to an evolutionary scale of development: "When, in a period of growing prosperity, self-reliance, and ambition, a people goes through an awakening, when it refuses to lag behind others and yet realizes that its own legal habits or concepts are not adequate to meet the needs of the time, it naturally turns to a superior system and checks upon the experiences had under it."[29] This, in a nutshell, was Levy's explanation for Visigoths, Burgundians, and Ostrogoths' turning to the "superior system" of Roman law and beginning to compile their own written legal collections, including the *Breviary of Alaric*, also referred to as the *Lex romana visigothorum*, an official codification, with Visigothic interpretations, that brought the *Theodosian Code*, collections of later Novellae, and an epitome of the semiofficial late third-century Hermogenian and Gregorian codes together with juristic material (compare *CTh* 1.1.5 outlining the first, 429, project for the *Theodosian Code*); the *Lex romana burgundionum*, probably dating to the first quarter of the sixth-century and condensed from the same material as the *Breviary of Alaric*, possibly

---

[28] Discussion, with further bibliography, in John Matthews, "Roman Law and Barbarian Identity in the Late Roman West," in *Ethnicity and Culture in Late Antiquity*, ed. Stephen Mitchell and Geoffrey Greatrex (London, 2000) 31–45; and Patrick Wormald, "The *Leges Barbarorum*: Law and Ethnicity in the Post-Roman West," in *Regna and Gentes: The Relationship between Late Antique and Early Medieval Peoples and Kingdoms in the Transformation of the Roman World*, ed. Hans-Werner Goetz, Jörg Jarnut, and Walter Pohl (London, 2003) 21–53.

[29] Ernst Levy, "The Reception of Highly Developed Legal Systems by Peoples of Different Cultures," *Washington Law Review* 25 (1950) 233–245, here 244.

compiled privately as a teaching aid or with reference to a concrete situation; and the *Edict of Theodoric*, issued by the Ostrogothic ruler Theodoric "the Amal" (493–536).

For Levy, moreover, it was the "decadence" of late Roman legal techniques that made the reception of Roman law amongst the "youthful" primitive minds of the Goths possible: "It is more than doubtful whether Roman law would have given the Goths a chance if they had entered the scene 200 or 250 years previously. The then flourishing classical jurisprudence was too complicated and required too high a level of legal training to impress men who lacked adequate legal minds.[30] Levy's framework should be read as part of a much broader twentieth-century, colonial, discourse on "law and primitive societies." More recent scholarly interpretations range from the ideological (barbarian kings sought to mimic Roman forms of lawgiving as a means to legitimate and advertise their own power) to the pragmatic (the continued use of Roman law in the Visigothic, Burgundian, and Ostrogothic kingdoms was a practical working-out from the Roman provincial past, with Roman writings being "pruned, simplified and adapted" to fit contemporary needs).[31] If, however, we develop a more explicitly comparative approach to legal cultures in the fifth century, prompted in part by recent postcolonial legal scholarship, then new avenues of interpretation open up. There were no institutionalized lawschools in the empire of Attila, but that does not necessarily equate to a lack of legal culture *per se*.

"One experience shared by almost every 'barbarian' gens that survived as a post-Roman polity into the seventh century was the eventual adoption of a written *lex*," writes Patrick Wormald.[32] Drawing a contrast, however, between unwritten ("barbarian") customs and written ("Roman") law tends to imply that we are dealing with two discrete and fixed entities. As Martin Chanock argues with reference to the nineteenth-century colonial Central Africa, customary law is not a residue from the past, but a product of contemporary relationships.[33]

[30] Ibid, 237.
[31] "Ideological": Wormald, "The *Leges Barbarorum*"; "Pragmatic": Roger Collins, "Law and Ethnic Identity in the Western Kingdoms in the Fifth and Sixth Centuries," in *Medieval Europeans: Studies in Ethnic Identities and National Perspectives in Medieval Europe*, ed. Alfred P. Smyth (London, 1998) 1–23.
[32] Wormald, "The Leges Barbarorum," 21 (noting the Avars and "the Anglian and most Saxon peoples in Britain" as exceptions).
[33] Martin Chanock, *Law, Custom and Social Order: The Colonial Experience in Malawi and Zambia* (Cambridge, 1984).

Hence the ("ethnic"/"barbarian") customary law that has been identified in the early sixth-century *interpretationes* written by the compilers of
Alaric's *Breviary*, or in the royal edicts collected within the Burgundian
Book of Constitutions, should be approached as a product of contemporary power relations and specific situations – not as a reflection of some
kind of static, preliterate identity. Sidonius Apollinaris (*Ep.* 5.5, written before 467), for example, may have intended to polarize "Roman"
and "Burgundian" cultural identities in his description of Syagrius, the
"great-grandson of a [Roman] consul," as a "new *solon* of the Burgundians" – expounding laws in Gothic, exposing the barbarians' linguistic
barbarisms in their own tongue, and acting as a trusted advisor and
arbitrator in their legal dealings – but his letter actually speaks to fluid
and functional legal practices and relationships on the ground. We thus
need to think within a more carefully nuanced comparative framework
than oral or preliterate (barbarian) versus literate (Roman) law.[34]

Late Roman law texts do not simply survive as manuscripts; they
were produced, circulated, and used within a manuscript culture. If
petitioners or litigants, for example, wished to cite imperial constitutions or juristic interpretations in hearings before Roman bureaucratic
officials, they were expected to produce the relevant texts themselves.
The private copying of legal texts was thus essential to late Roman
forensic practice, as well as to juristic activity and legal teaching. Families, municipal officials, and imperial bureaucrats all kept (different
kinds) of legal and documentary archives, but how was their content to
be stabilized?[35] The Theodosian Code and the *Breviary of Alaric* were
official attempts at an answer. When Theodosius II referred to the compilers of his Code having "purged" the decrees of previous emperors of
"interpretations" we can plausibly imagine the Code's commissioners
literally expunging accreted marginalia (juristic comments, case-specific
notes, bureaucratic annotations, etc.) from the texts that they had collected, searching out any words that were written in the distinctive,
cursive hand of the late Roman chancellery (*Nov. Th.*1.1). The compilers of the *Breviary of Alaric*, on the other hand, added their own official
interpretations to all of the material that they collected, with the single
exception of Gaius's *Institutes*. Neither the Theodosian Code nor the

---

[34] For example, Robin Chapman Stacey, *Dark Speech: The Performance of Law in Early Ireland* (Philadelphia, 2007).

[35] Including the question of which emperors' decrees counted as legitimate: see the entry for 438 in the *Gallic Chronicle* (452).

Breviary of Alaric, of course, put an end to either the private copying of Roman legal texts or juristic activity.[36]

As Bruno Latour's legal ethnography suggests, things compel us to do things.[37] The "things," the material objects, of late Roman legal culture: the palimpsest manuscripts, the *codices,* the scribal inkstands, and so on, were tools and symbols that helped to maintain an ideology of Roman law as a distinct, institutionalized and specialized form of knowledge – including in areas in where the official Roman legal system (the lawcourts, the bureaucratic networks of imperial officials, the schools of law, among others) had ceased to operate. Without minimizing the disruption and fragmentation experienced in some areas, Detlef Liebs's studies of Roman jurisprudence in Gaul and Italy during the fifth century demonstrate a perhaps surprising level of continuity in juristic practice.[38] In the East and West, some legal experts – including those *prudentes* who were commissioned to make Theodosius II's Code and the *Breviary of Alaric* – were still trained to arrive at general legal principles through arguments from concrete cases. It is to the "microlaw" of legal cultures in action that we shall now turn.

MICROLAW

> Vahrič has said: I have learned that Adur-parzkar has said the following: "When I was going to the ordeal court, three women were sitting by the road and one of them said: "Master, decide this legal case."
>
> —*Book of a Thousand Legal Decisions*

Chapter 57 of the Sasanian *Book of a Thousand Legal Decisions* cites the jurist Vahrič repeating a story told by another jurist, Adur-parzkar: Three women who were sitting by the road stopped the jurist as he passed by and asked him for an on-the-spot opinion concerning money received as a loan by two people acting as joint guarantors. They then asked him further questions, which complicated the original query.

---

[36] Detlef Liebs, *Römische Jurisprudenz in Gallien (2 bis 8 Jahrhundert)* (Berlin, 2002); and Detlef Liebs, *Die Jurisprudenz im spätantiken Italien (260–640 n.Chr.)* (Berlin, 1987).

[37] Bruno Latour, *The Making of Law: An Ethnography of the Conseil d'Etat,* trans. Marina Brilman (Cambridge, 2009).

[38] As noted in Liebs, *Römische Jurisprudenz* and *Die Jurisprudenz.*

Adur-parzkar states: "And I stood and did not know what answer to give. And then one of them said: Master, do not hesitate but say truthfully 'I do not know.'"[39] Through their skillful questioning, the three women in the story demonstrate their own working knowledge of (Sasanian) legal principles, but the lesson that they offer to Adur-parzkar is one in how to behave correctly: according to expected social norms. As the modern legal sociologist Susan Sibley argues, socially constructed definitions of normal behavior, respectability, responsibility, and "the good person" are fundamental aspects of legal culture: "Rules about how to fight, or whether to fight, how to respond to insults and grievances, how to live with one's neighbors, are parts of elaborate and complex belief systems which varies among social groups."[40] "Normative" social rules effectively make legal culture on a microlevel.

Approaching law from the perspective of "law-in-practice" means thinking about social action that involves law. It is in this sense that the legal sociologist Marc Galanter defines "local legal culture" as the "complex of enduring understandings, concerns, and priorities shared by the community of legal actors (and significant audiences) in a given locality."[41] Hence for example, the fact that the "Albertini Tablets" – an archive of forty-five wooden tablets from Vandal Africa (493–496) relating to the sale of land and cultivation rights on a remote estate on the Algero-Tunisian border – refer to a technical Roman lease regulation from the early empire, probably has less to do with the late fifth-century Roman government's "insistence on its legal authority" and more to do with local rhythms of established legal practice between tenants and landlords.[42] Over time, the official (Roman) law became part of a shared "local" legal culture.

Documentary material, including legal epigraphy and juristic papyrology, provides a crucial resource for studying local legal cultures across the fifth century. For example, for the West there are the Ravenna papyri and the *Pizarras* from Visigothic Spain, in addition

---

[39] Quotation from Corcoran, "Observations on the Sasanian Law-Book," 91. The epigraph to this section is from *Book of a Thousand Legal Decisions*, 57.2–12, quoted from ibid.

[40] Susan S. Silbey, "After Legal Consciousness," *Annual Review of Law and Social Sciences* 1 (2005) 323–368, here 339.

[41] Marc Galanter, "Justice in Many Rooms: Courts, Private Ordering, and Indigenous Law," *Journal of Legal Pluralism and Unofficial Law* 19 (1981) 1–48, here 33.

[42] Hendrik Wessel, *Das Recht der Tablettes Albertini* (Berlin, 2003).

to material relating to concrete cases in the Theodosian and post-Theodosian *Novellae* and the Burgundian *Book of Constitutions*.[43] For the East, the relatively newly discovered papyri from Petra include some fifth- and early sixth-century material.[44] Papyri from Egypt, on the other hand, provide a number of records of fifth-century bilingual court proceedings before military as well as civil officials, in addition to other legal and "paralegal" material, such as copies of arbitration agreements and settlements (which first appear in larger numbers in the fifth century).[45] As juristic papyrologists have long acknowledged, these kinds of documentary sources reveal a complex (para-) legal culture, with individuals and groups conducting legal business and relationships between themselves in multilingual settings (Armenian, Syriac, Jewish Aramaic, Arabic, Coptic, and so on). Transacting business and trade across frontier zones or in specially designated places – Priscus (fr. 2 [Blockley 227]) refers to clauses in diplomatic treaties designating market towns where Huns and Romans could do business – must have created opportunities for multilingual and multilegal exchanges. Such practices, of course, were not unique to the fifth century: according to the Roman jurist Ulpian, writing in the third century CE, contracts and *fideicommissa* (trusts) could be made in any language provided that both parties understood what was being said, via an interpreter if necessary (Justinian, *Digesta Iustiniani*, 32.11 pr. and 45.1.1).

Specific legal forms could be used to transform an everyday occurrence – the making of a promise, the offering of a loan, a gift of property – into something that could then be viewed (plausibly) as a formal and official "legal" act, whether by other parties to the transaction, or by an official, or in a court hearing, and so on. As Marc Galanter states: "Law may be used as a cookbook from which we learn how to bring about desired results – disposing of property, forming a partnership, securing a subsidy."[46] Alongside his deployment of brutal violence and force, Attila the Hun made a number of effective uses of Roman

---

[43] Ravenna papyri: Jan-Olof Tjäder, *Die nichtliterarischen lateinischen Papyri Italien aus der Zeit 445–700* (Lund, Sweden, 1955–1982); Visigothic Pizzarras: Isabel Velázquez Soriano, ed., *Documentos de época visigoda escritos en pizarra (sigl. vi–viii)* (Turnhout, 2000).

[44] Casper J. Kraemer, *Excavations at Nessana III: The Non-Literary Papyri* (Cambridge, Mass., 1958) = *P. Nessana 3*; Antti Arjava, Matias Buchholz, and Traianos Gagos, eds., *The Petra Papyri III* (Amman, 2007) = *P. Petra 3*.

[45] Bernhard Palme, "Law and Courts in Late Antique Egypt," in Sirks, *Aspects of Law in Late Antiquity*, 55–76.

[46] Galanter, "Justice in Many Rooms," 12.

law in diplomatic negotiations; he also displayed a working knowledge of the Roman law of marriage (Prisc. fr. 20.3 [Blockley 307–309]) and the Roman law of property and theft (Prisc. fr. 11 [Blockley 263–265]). As Lauren Bento, a historian of nineteenth-century colonial law, states: "Legal ideas and practices, legal protections of material interests, and the roles of legal personnel (specialized or not) fail to obey the lines separating one legal system or sphere from another."[47]

If we are interested, as historians, in the relationship between law and life across the long fifth century, we need to think beyond legal centralism and "governmentality." We also have to allow for radical discontinuities, violence and fragmentation within our comparative microlaw frameworks. In other words, we need to ask how, when, where, and why (formal) law was "taken up," as well as how it was "laid down," across the Roman East *and* the post-Roman West.

---

[47] Lauren Benton, *Law and Colonial Cultures* (Cambridge, 2002) 8.

9: ROMANNESS IN THE AGE
OF ATTILA

Jonathan P. Conant

In 449 Attila sent a man by the name of Orestes to the imperial court at Constantinople as his ambassador. Orestes was Roman in origin, but unlike many of his compatriots in Hunnic territory he was not a captive of war. Rather, he came from a part of Pannonia that had been ceded to Attila in a treaty with the western Roman Empire in 433.[1] Orestes' service to the Hunnic khagan illuminates some of the ambiguities of Romanness in the Age of Attila. Like most free inhabitants of the fifth-century empire, Orestes had been born a Roman citizen. The potent combination of the loss of his natal province to Hunnic control and his own personal association with Attila might have called Orestes' continued Romanness into question; indeed, in his account of the mission, the contemporary diplomat and historian Priscus was only willing to concede that Attila's agent was a Roman by birth. But we have no real reason to believe that Orestes himself ever doubted his own Romanness. Orestes seems to have absorbed the prejudices of his society with respect to non-Roman populations, and he was offended when he was treated with less deference at the imperial court than was a leading Hun warrior. Like his birth, Orestes' language and culture tied him firmly to the Mediterranean empire. So did his family: both his father and his father-in-law remained on the Roman side of the frontier, and indeed in 449 both continued to serve the empire on diplomatic missions. Even in his political loyalties – his service to Attila

[1] Priscus, fr. 11.1, ed. Robert C. Blockley, in *The Fragmentary Classicising Historians of the Later Roman Empire: Eunapius, Olympiodorus, Priscus and Malchus*, 2 vols. (Liverpool, 1983). On issues of identity in Priscus's account, see esp. Michael Maas, "Fugitives and Ethnography in Priscus of Panium," *Byzantine and Modern Greek Studies* 19 (1995) 146–160.

notwithstanding – Orestes may have remained fundamentally Roman in his outlook, for with time he was to return to the empire, assume a generalship, and eventually install his son, Romulus Augustulus, on the western imperial throne – the last Roman emperor in the West.[2]

In the fifth century, individuals like Orestes found themselves compelled by circumstance to confront challenging questions about what – if anything – bound them to other individuals elsewhere in the larger Mediterranean world. In the East, the institutions of imperial government survived well into the Middle Ages, and as a result, the aspects of late ancient life that contemporaries most closely associated with being Roman – citizenship, loyalty and service to the emperor, the application of the law, allegiance to the imperially sanctioned faith, the pursuit of high culture, and so forth – remained less problematic insofar as they continued to be linked directly to the structures of empire. They will therefore concern us less here. In the West, by contrast, individuals who found themselves on the wrong side of the contracting imperial frontiers but who nevertheless continued to identify with the empire, its history, and traditions had to confront the uncomfortable question of what it was that made them Roman. When politics failed them, the answers they found were overwhelmingly cultural and religious. All three were uncertain categories: the empire was shrinking, but still continued to admit new populations into Roman citizenship; Roman culture provided only a weak basis for Roman identity; and Christian orthodoxy – claimed as the faith of Rome by emperors and ecclesiastics alike – was itself undergoing a process of definition that proved as divisive as it was unifying. As in the classical period, then, the changing circumstances in which Romans found themselves ensured that there was never a fixed definition of Roman identity in the fifth century; rather, Romanness provided a supple and adaptable concept that for a time provided a measure of continued unity to the Mediterranean world.

In the Age of Attila, Romanness was still imagined primarily in imperial terms. First and foremost, to contemporary observers, the emperors and their courts were *the* Romans *par excellence*. Following the death of Theodosius I in 395, the empire was divided into eastern and western halves, as it had been on occasion since the late Republic. Officials and authors on both sides of the Mediterranean recognized the legitimacy

---

[2] See A. H. M. Jones, John Martindale, and John Morris, eds., *The Prosopography of the Later Roman Empire, 260–395*, 3 vols. (Cambridge, 1971) 2: 811–812 s.n. Orestes 2.

of each other's rulers as emperors, just as they accepted eastern and
western consuls.³ The ideological significance of the city of Rome
ensured its continued importance to the making of western emperors
through the middle of the fifth century, notwithstanding its earlier
eclipse as the center of imperial power in the Mediterranean world.⁴
The Eternal City, of course, also maintained a privileged, though by
no means exclusive, relationship to the adjective "Roman." Though
the Roman Senate no longer had much practical power, pretenders to
the imperial throne such as Attalus (409–410) and, later, the strongman
Odoacer (476–493) continued to seek the legitimacy that it conveyed.⁵
The army, its soldiers, and its generals (in both halves of the empire)
also came readily to mind when fifth-century authors thought of things
Roman.⁶ In short, then, the empire and its institutions largely defined
Romanness in the minds of fifth-century witnesses.

Roman citizenship also provided a legal foundation for Roman
identity. Regardless of the language they spoke or of their ethnic, social,
or geographic origins, at the beginning of the fifth century most free
inhabitants of the Roman Empire enjoyed citizen status, the legacy of
an edict known as the Antonine Constitution issued by the emperor
Caracalla in 212.⁷ Roman citizenship continued to be prized throughout Late Antiquity, most significantly because it distinguished free (and

³ On emperors, see, e.g., Hydatius Lemicensis, *Chronicon*, 138 (Theodosius II) and
241 (Leo), ed. Richard W. Burgess, in *The Chronicle of Hydatius and the Consularia
Constantinopolitana* (Oxford, 1993); Prisc. fr. 31.1 (Avitus) and 36.1 (Majorian). On
Romanness and loyalty to the emperor, see Geoffrey Greatrex, "Roman Identity in
the Sixth Century," in *Ethnicity and Culture in Late Antiquity*, ed. Stephen Mitchell
and Geoffrey Greatrex (London, 2000) 267–292. On consuls, see Roger S. Bagnall,
Alan Cameron, Seth R. Schwartz, and Klaas A. Worp, *Consuls of the Later Roman
Empire* (Atlanta, 1987) 24–26.
⁴ On Valentinian III, see Hyd. 76 and Olympiodorus, fr. 43.1, ed. Blockley, *FCH*.
On Petronius Maximus, see Hyd. 155; see also Prosper of Aquitaine, *Chronicon*,
1375, ed. Theodor Mommsen, MGH AA 9 (Berlin, 1892). On Avitus, see Hyd.
156. Anthemius: Hyd. 231. Also the pretender Attalus: see Zosimus, *Historia nova*,
6.7.1, ed. François Paschoud, 3 vols. (Paris, 1971–1989); Olymp. fr. 6; Socrates
Scholasticus, *Historia ecclesiastica*, 7.10.5, ed. Robert Hussey, 3 vols. (Oxford, 1853);
Sozomen Scholasticus, *Historia ecclesiastica*, 9.8.1, ed. Joseph Bidez and Günther Christian Hansen (Berlin, 1960); and Prosp. 1238.
⁵ Attalus: Soz. 9.8.2. Odoacer: Malchus of Philadelphia, fr. 14, ed. Blockley, *FCH*; and
in general André Chastagnol, *Le Sénat romain sous le règne d'Odoacre* (Bonn, 1966).
⁶ See, e.g., Malch. fr. 20; Prisc. fr. 11.1, 11.2, 33.1, and 49; Olymp. fr. 7.4; Soz. 7.24,
8.4, 8.25, 9.4, 9.8.5; Soc. 7.18 and 7.20–21.
⁷ Cassius Dio, *Historiae romanae*, 78.9.5, ed. Ursul Philip Boissevain, 2nd ed., 5 vols.
(Berlin, 1955–1969); *Fontes iuris romani antejustiniani*, ed. Salvatore Riccobono,

freed) Romans from slaves. Citizenship also marked off Roman subjects from those who lived beyond the imperial frontiers, peoples who are dismissed collectively in our sources as "barbarians." (It bears emphasizing here that the contentious conceptual category of the barbarian was a construction of Greco-Roman ethnography and, no less than the concept of "Roman," lent itself to multiple interpretations.) Romans may have been distinguished too from recently arrived foreigners resident within the empire, though such individuals could certainly serve in the army, attain high military command, hold civil office, and generally make use of the late Roman legal system, indicating that those of non-Roman birth could gain the full rights of citizens. Roman status could also be lost. Elite men who tried to legitimate their children born to slaves or other very low-status mothers could be deprived of their own access to Roman law, for example, and at least a handful of practices regarded as corrupt could similarly result in loss of citizenship. Romans carried off into captivity in enemy raids also lost their citizen status, though in theory this could be recovered along with their freedom upon return to imperial territory.[8] Thus questions of citizenship and its acquisition, preservation, and loss remained very much alive, and had resulted in a citizen body that included not only freeborn Romans, but also freed slaves and "barbarians" who had achieved Roman standing.

In both the East and the West, the elite shared a clear sense of self-identification with the empire, its values, and its history. No one who has read Priscus's fragmentary history, for example, or the poems and letters of the Gallic aristocrat Sidonius Apollinaris can doubt that these men considered themselves to be Romans. Of course, both Sidonius and Priscus had also served in the imperial administration, an experience that doubtless reinforced their sense of identification with the empire. Indeed, office holding seems to have been central to the Roman aristocratic conception of the responsibilities and privileges

---

vol. 1: *Leges* (Florence, 1941) no. 88, 445–449; and Fritz M. Heichelheim, "The Text of the *Constitutio Antoniniana*," *Journal of Egyptian Archaeology* 26 (1941) 10–22.

[8] Peter Garnsey, "Roman Citizenship and Roman Law in the Late Empire," in *Approaching Late Antiquity*, ed. Simon Swain and Mark Edwards (Oxford, 2004) 133–155, and Ralph W. Mathisen, "*Peregrini, Barbari*, and *Cives Romani*: Concepts of Citizenship and the Legal Identity of Barbarians in the Later Roman Empire," *American Historical Review* 111 (2006) 1011–1040. See also, e.g., *Codex Theodosianus*, 1.32.1, 2.22, 3.30.4, and 4.6.3, ed. Theodor Mommsen (Berlin, 1905); and Kristina Sessa, "Ursa's Return: Captivity, Remarriage, and the Domestic Authority of Roman Bishops in Fifth-Century Italy," *Journal of Early Christian Studies* 19 (2011) 401–432.

of their social position.[9] On the other hand, an official affiliation of this sort was not essential to fostering a sense of Romanness among the elite. Thus the decurion and future bishop Synesius, a native of Cyrene, clearly self-identified with the empire despite never having held high office.[10] The Spaniard Orosius also considered himself a Roman, despite the fact that he cast a critical eye over the history of the empire.[11] So too the Syrian bishop Theodoret of Cyrrhus, who furthermore felt that a sense of elite Romanness was widespread enough that he could write to the urban magistrates in the eastern border region of Zeugma, rebuking them for allowing intermarriage between first cousins or among uncles and nieces, even though they had an imperial dispensation. This was the dissolute behavior of Persians, Theodoret chided, "not of Romans who are the nurslings of [Christian] piety."[12] At least among members of the ruling class, then, Romanness mattered.

The nonelite majority of the population could also share a sense of being Roman. To be sure, many of the imperial institutions exploited by the powerful were probably less accessible to poor and rural populations.[13] Yet, as the work of Lesley Dossey has also demonstrated, in late Roman North Africa, at least, the preaching of country bishops and their clergy exposed rural congregations to universalizing imperial and Christian ideals, which peasants could seek to make a reality by putting an end to their own illegal exploitation at the hands of unscrupulous members of social elites.[14] Moreover, as both the instrument and the symbol of imperial power, the army too remained central to Roman identity in Late Antiquity, and to judge from the military theorist Vegetius, the army of the late empire maintained its preference

---

[9] On Sidonius's writings and career, see Jill Harries, *Sidonius Apollinaris and the Fall of Rome, AD 407–485* (Oxford, 1994). On Priscus, see Blockley, *FCH*, 1: 48–70. On the aristocracy, see John Matthews, *Western Aristocracies and Imperial Court, A.D. 364–425* (Oxford, 1975; repr. 1998) 12–31.

[10] See, e.g., Synesius, *Oratio de regno*, Patrologia Greca 66, esp. ibid., 14; and Syn. *Epistulae* 73, 113, 127, and 129*, PG 66.

[11] Orosius, *Historiae adversum paganos*, 5.2.6, ed. Karl Zangemeister (Leipzig, 1889).

[12] Theodoret of Cyrrhus, *Epistola* viii, ed. Yvan Azéma, 4 vols. (Paris, 1955–1998) 1: 80.

[13] See, e.g., Christopher Kelly, *Ruling the Later Roman Empire* (Cambridge, Mass., 2004) 138–145; Joëlle Beaucamp, "Byzantine Egypt and Imperial Law," in *Egypt in the Byzantine World, 300–700*, ed. Roger S. Bagnall (Cambridge, 2007) 271–287; and Cam Grey, *Constructing Communities in the Late Roman Countryside* (Cambridge, 2011) 185–189.

[14] Leslie Dossey, *Peasant and Empire in Christian North Africa* (Berkeley, 2010) esp. 147–194.

for recruits from a rural background. Regions at the peripheries of Roman control – Illyricum, Thrace, Isauria, Armenia – may also have been specially targeted as recruiting grounds. Through discipline and training, peasants of diverse ethnic and linguistic origins were socialized alongside men from military families to their roles as soldiers and identities as Romans. The same could be true of barbarians, including both those settled on imperial territory and those recruited from across the imperial frontier.[15] Foreign origins were no impediment: it was loyalty and service to the empire that made the Roman.

In general, though, the practical ramifications of whatever empire-wide solidarity was forged by a sense of shared Romanness remained ambiguous at best. According to Priscus, for example, a treaty worked out between Attila and the empire in 443 required that captive Romans who managed to escape and flee back to imperial territory had to be returned to the Huns, unless those who received them paid twelve solidi in ransom. Attila was particularly insistent about the enforcement of this clause in Asemus, a fortress near the borders of Illyricum and Thrace, where the Huns had suffered a major defeat and lost much of the booty that they had accumulated on raids on imperial territory, including a number of Roman captives. The imperial ambassador to Attila and the commander of Roman forces in Thrace both wrote to the people of Asemus, commanding them either to pay the ransom for the freed captives or to return them to the Huns. The Asemuntians insisted that this was impossible, swearing that the liberated prisoners had returned to freedom – and did so, Priscus maintains, even though "there were Romans among them; for they did not think an oath sworn for the deliverance of men of their own stock [*genos*] was falsely sworn."[16] Priscus felt that the government of Theodosius II (408–450) was weak and ineffectual, and the moral that the historian seems to have wanted his readers to draw was that its unjust demands could, at least on occasion, be trumped by a virtuous sense of fellow feeling as Romans.

The captives freed at Asemus were lucky, though, for such a feeling was far from universal. Indeed, throughout Late Antiquity imperial

15 Peter M. Brennan, "The Last of the Romans: Roman Identity and the Roman Army in the Late Roman Near East," *MedArch* 11 (1998) 191–203. See also Bernhard Palme, "The Imperial Presence: Government and Army," in Bagnall, *Egypt in the Byzantine World*, 244–270. Vegetius: *Epitoma rei militaris*, 1.3, ed. Michael D. Reeve (Oxford, 2004).

16 Prisc. fr. 9.3.

legislation struggled to prevent Roman soldiers from keeping in slavery Roman captives who had been retaken from barbarians.[17] At some point in the 440s, Theodoret of Cyrrhus learned that a young aristocratic woman named Maria and her anonymous slave girl had been captured in the Vandal conquest of Roman Africa and sold into slavery in the bishop's own diocese. The slave girl's continued ministrations to her former mistress in their common servitude brought their story to light, and the local garrison raised the funds necessary to redeem Maria. Theodoret had not done so himself, he hurriedly explained to a fellow bishop, because he had been out of town at the time.[18] In the late 420s, Augustine similarly learned that slavers from elsewhere in the empire were active in Numidia, capturing freeborn citizens both in cities and in rural hamlets through violence and deceit, bribing corrupt imperial officials to look the other way, and illicitly shipping their victims across the Mediterranean for sale on distant slave markets. While Augustine, too, was conveniently out of town, his parishioners staged a raid on some slavers' ships and freed their captives, who were then returned to their families.[19] Perhaps, then, we should not have too dark a vision of the fate of Romanness in the fifth-century Mediterranean: at Asemus, Cyrrhus, and Hippo fellow citizens, soldiers, and bishops stood up for the freedom of these captives as Romans. But it would nonetheless seem that a sense of shared identity could hardly be relied upon to protect vulnerable members of Roman society from ill-treatment, even within the confines of the empire.

This stark reality was at the heart of some of the harshest criticism leveled by Romans at their own society in the fifth century. In a much-discussed passage from his history, for example, Priscus claimed to have had a chance encounter with a fellow Greek at the court of Attila. The Greek had been captured and enslaved in the Huns' attacks on the Danubian provinces, but had nonetheless managed to rise to a position of wealth and status within Hunnic society. Into this man's mouth, Priscus placed a pointed appraisal of Roman society: Romans were weakened by their reliance on a professional army led by cowardly generals rather than on the universal service under arms of all free men; in peacetime Romans suffered from severe taxation and the depredations of the wicked; and the law offered no redress, for the courts were corrupt and punished the poor while letting the rich go free. Priscus

---

[17] *Codex Iustinianus*, 8.50.12, ed. Paul Krüger, 8th ed. (Berlin, 1906); *CTh* 5.6.2.
[18] Theod. *Ep.* 70, 2: 152–154.
[19] Aug. *Ep.* 10*, ed. Johannes Divjak, CSEL 88 (Vienna, 1981).

claims to have jumped to the empire's defense, with the result that the Greek, weeping, admitted that the Romans' laws were just and their state was good, but that their rulers were corrupting the polity by not being as prudent as their predecessors – hardly a repudiation of his original censure.[20] More aggressively Christian critics such as Orosius and Augustine were less willing to cede to earlier generations the virtues that were supposed to have been the bedrock of Roman identity.[21] Priscus's western contemporary, Salvian of Marseille (ca. 400–ca. 480), went further still, writing that "vice and impurity are like a tie that unites the Roman people in common descent."[22] Salvian saw proof of this everywhere he looked: in the impiety of Romans, in their love of circuses and theaters, but above all in the corruption of their officials and in the despoliation of widows, orphans, and the poor. As a result of these injustices, Salvian fulminated, Romans were fleeing to the barbarians, and Roman citizenship, which once had been dearly valued, was now being repudiated. Roman iniquity had caused many throughout the empire – and above all in Spain and Gaul – no longer to be Romans.[23]

The collapse of imperial power across the West over the course of the fifth century ensured that the political definition of Romanness would enjoy its longest life in the eastern Mediterranean. There it survived, along with the empire that supported it, into the middle Byzantine period and beyond.[24] In the western Mediterranean, the disintegration of the empire left a class of people who felt themselves to be Roman, but for whom imperial power was at best a flickering and retreating shadow. As late as the 470s, the emperor Zeno is said to have praised Odoacer, the barbarian strongman and ruler of Italy, for maintaining "the order befitting the Romans."[25] Yet some years earlier the Galician bishop Hydatius had regarded the provincial landscape of Spain and Gaul with increasing pessimism. Thus, for example, in

---

[20] Prisc. fr. 11.2.

[21] Oros. passim, and Augustine, *De civitate Dei*, ed. Bernhard Dombart and Alfons Kalb, CCSL 47–48 (Turnhout, 1955). See also below, note 22.

[22] Salvian, *De gubernatione Dei*, 6.8.40, ed. Georges Lagarrigue (Paris, 1975): "uitiositas et impuritas quasi germanitas quaedam est hominum Romanorum." On Salvian, see Michael Maas, "Ethnicity, Orthodoxy and Community in Salvian of Marseilles," in *Fifth-Century Gaul: A Crisis of Identity?*, ed. John F. Drinkwater and Hugh Elton (Cambridge, 1992) 275–284.

[23] Salvian, *De gub. Dei* passim, esp. 5.5.21–23.

[24] See in general Anthony Kaldellis, *Hellenism in Byzantium* (Cambridge, 2007; repr. 2009) esp. 42–111.

[25] Malch. fr. 14.

the mid-460s, after the death of the Gallo-Roman general Aegidius, Hydatius wrote that "Goths soon invaded the areas that he used to protect for the Roman name."[26] Some years later, Hydatius claimed that a Gothic army had invaded the region of Lusitania in western Spain, attacking and pillaging both the region's new Suevic overlords and the Hispano-Roman provincials subject to them.[27] Despite the collapse of effective Roman power in these regions, Hydatius continued to think of their inhabitants as Romans. The abbot Eugippius later used the same term to refer to the population of the Upper Danube, though he also clearly felt that Roman control was no longer a reality there as Rugi, Alamanni, Thuringi, Goths, and Heruls struggled for ascendancy in the region.[28] North Africans living under Vandal dominion evidently continued to think of themselves as Romans, though the term's continued implications of self-identification with and loyalty to the empire now made it a politically loaded word, which Africans living under Vandal rule rarely applied to themselves in the later fifth or early sixth centuries.[29]

They were perhaps wise to do so, as the potential consequences of holding Roman loyalties could be deadly serious. The career of Boethius, an Italo-Roman statesman and philosopher, provides the most celebrated illustration of what could go wrong: he was executed for treason in 524 on the orders of the Ostrogothic king Theodoric.[30] A generation earlier, the North African lawyer and poet Dracontius was similarly imprisoned by the Vandal king Gunthamund for writing a poem of praise to a ruler whom he did not know, presumably an act prefatory to emigration from the Vandal kingdom.[31] In the 470s, Sidonius Apollinaris found that one of his relatives had been accused

---

[26] Hyd. 224: "Quo desistente mox Gothi regiones quas Romano nomini tuebatur <inuadunt>."

[27] Hyd. 240.

[28] Eugippius, *Vita sancti Severini*, 2.1, 8.1–2, 8.4, 27.1, 31.6, ed. Pius Knoell, CSEL 9 (Vienna, 1885), and, on the collapse of Roman power, ibid. 20.1.

[29] Jonathan Conant, *Staying Roman* (Cambridge, 2012) 186–193.

[30] On Boethius, see esp. Henry Chadwick, *Boethius: The Consolations of Music, Logic, Theology, and Philosophy* (Oxford, 1990) 1–68, and John Matthews, "Anicius Manlius Severinus Boethius," in *Boethius: His Life, Thought, and Influence*, ed. Margaret Gibson (Oxford, 1981) 73–89.

[31] Dracontius of Carthage, *Satisfactio ad Gunthamundum regem Wandalorum*, ed. Claude Moussy, in *Dracontius: Oeuvres*, vol. 2 (Paris, 1988) 176–191; however, see also Andy Merrills, "The Perils of Panegyric: The Lost Poem of Dracontius and Its Consequences," in *Vandals, Romans, and Berbers*, ed. Andy Merrills (Aldershot, 2004) 145–162.

of scheming to turn the people of Vaison against the Burgundian king Chilperic II in favor of the new western emperor Julius Nepos – a charge that caused Sidonius's family no small amount of apprehension.[32] As the interests of the emperors diverged from those of an array of new kings who claimed (with greater or lesser degrees of plausibility) to be their allies, the game of balancing competing political loyalties became an increasingly dangerous one to play.

To western observers, then, over the course of the fifth century, politics failed to provide a satisfactory answer to the question of what defined Romanness. That left them with the stuff of culture. Heirs to the classical ethnographic tradition, men like Sidonius and Dracontius felt that they knew a barbarian when they saw one, marked out (as they were thought to be) by their distinctive clothing, hairstyles, ornamentation, armor, and weapons.[33] Other aspects of material life figure less prominently in fifth-century reflections on signaling cultural difference.[34] Language, by contrast, was thought to be a distinguishing feature, though it was a nuanced one. Caracalla's third-century expansion of citizenship had welcomed into the Roman fold the veritable Tower of Babel that the empire's subject populations comprised, and to these tongues the opinions of the emperor's jurist, Ulpian, extended at least limited legal standing.[35] To be sure, Latin remained the language of law and government into the sixth century, and indeed, the language was probably more widely spoken and understood in the late Roman East than scholars have sometimes allowed.[36] Moreover, the imperial house of Theodosius had its origins in Spain and was succeeded in the East in the later fifth and sixth centuries by a string of emperors of predominantly Illyrian origins, a fact that probably ensured that Latin remained the language of power in Constantinople, just as it was in

---

[32] Sidonius Apollinaris, *Epistula*, 5.6, ed. William B. Anderson, 2 vols. (Cambridge, Mass., 1936), and see also ibid., 5.7; Harries, *Sidonius Apollinaris*, 231–232.

[33] See in general Walter Pohl, "Telling the Difference: Signs of Ethnic Identity," in *Strategies of Distinction: The Construction of Ethnic Communities, 300–800*, ed. Walter Pohl and Helmut Reimitz (Leiden, 1998) 17–69. However, see also Philipp von Rummel, *Habitus barbarus: Kleidung und Repräsentation spätantiker Eliten im 4. und 5. Jahrhundert* (Berlin, 2007).

[34] Kaldellis, *Hellenism*, 55. One exception is diet: see, e.g., Conant, *Staying Roman*, 62, 256, and 263–264.

[35] Justinian, *Digesta*, 32.1.11 and 45.1.1.6, in *Corpus iuris civilis*, ed. Paul Krueger, Theodor Mommsen et al. (Berlin, 1872), vol. 1.

[36] Claudia Rapp, "Hagiography and Monastic Literature between Greek East and Latin West in Late Antiquity," in *Cristianità d'occidente e cristianità d'oriente (secoli VI–IX)*, 2 vols. (Spoleto, 2004) 2: 1221–1280, here 1228–1238; Kaldellis, *Hellenism*, 69–74.

the West. Priscus indicates that Latin was the language of diplomatic and personal exchange between Romans and Huns in the fifth century; Greek, by contrast, was not widely spoken at Attila's court.[37] Even so, in the eastern Mediterranean, command of the Latin language and literary tradition do not seem to have been indispensible to the construction of Roman identity, which by and large appears to have been perfectly comfortable there in its Greek skin.[38] Much work remains to be done on ideas of Romanness among speakers of eastern vernaculars, but for them too language and Roman identity may not have been intimately linked.[39] Yet it was precisely through the cultivation of Latin letters that at least some aristocrats in fifth-century Gaul and Africa sought to maintain their Romanness under barbarian rule.[40]

The fate of *belles lettres*, however, also highlights something of the weakness of the aristocratic lifestyle as a way of distinguishing Romans and non-Romans in the changed world of the fifth-century West. As far as Sidonius Apollinaris was concerned, discussing literature with barbarians was an inversion of the world's proper order; but by the end of the fifth century it would seem that barbarians were in fact applying themselves to the Latin literary tradition, at least in Africa and apparently in Italy.[41] At the same point, Gallo-Roman aristocrats anxiously fretted that the study of letters was a dying pastime among their own social order.[42] Just as the new ruling class adopted and adapted those elements of the elite Roman way of life that they found most congenial,

---

[37] Prisc. fr. 11.2 and 13.3.

[38] See in general Kaldellis, *Hellenism*, 42–119.

[39] Fergus Millar, "Ethnic Identity in the Roman Near East, AD 325–450: Language, Religion and Culture," in Clarke, *Identities in the Eastern Mediterranean*, 159–176, here 159–160. On questions of language and identity in the Syriac world, see, e.g., Kevin Butcher, *Roman Syria and the Near East* (Los Angeles, 2003) esp. 270–334; Sebastian P. Brock, "Greek and Syriac in Late Antique Syria," in *Literacy and Power in the Ancient World*, ed. Alan K. Bowman and Greg Woolf (Cambridge, 1994) 149–161; and David G. K. Taylor, "Bilingualism and Diglossia in Late Antique Syria and Mesopotamia," in *Bilingualism in Ancient Society*, ed. J. N. Adams, Mark Janse, and Simon Swain (Oxford, 2002) 298–331. Thanks to Susan Ashbrook Harvey for these references.

[40] See, e.g., Ralph W. Mathisen, *Roman Aristocrats in Barbarian Gaul* (Austin, Tex., 1993) 105–118; Gregory Hays, "'*Romuleis Libicisque Litteris*': Fulgentius and the 'Vandal Renaissance,'" in Merrills, *Vandals, Romans, and Berbers*, 101–132.

[41] On chauvinism, see Sid. Ap. *Ep.* 2.1.2. Italy: ibid., 1.8.2. On Africa, see Dracontius, *Romulea*, 1.14, ed. Jean Bouquet and Étienne Wolff, in *Dracontius: Oeuvres*, vols. 3–4 (Paris, 1995).

[42] Mathisen, *Roman Aristocrats*, 105–110.

Roman provincials also began to pursue new avenues toward prominence and advancement, above all by emulating what they, in turn, found fashionable and alluring about the newcomers. In an earlier era, the cultural change that this entailed would unquestionably have taken place under the rubric of "Roman." But the dynamics of power had shifted profoundly in the fifth-century West, and one result was that the new cultural identities that began to emerge there were now imagined as Gothic, Burgundian, Frankish, and so forth. As Matthew Innes has cautioned, this was not just the result of a cozy politics of cultural accommodation: the establishment of barbarian kingdoms across the western Mediterranean undermined the social and economic foundations on which Roman aristocratic status had been built, encouraged the development of regional rather than panimperial elites, and erected legal systems in which Romans no longer enjoyed all the advantages.[43] In the fifth century, the effects of these transformations were only beginning to be felt; but in the long run, they were to provide individuals of wealth and prominence with no mean impetus to "go barbarian."

Religion was another matter. In 384 Symmachus, the urban prefect of Rome, had petitioned the young western emperor Valentinian II on behalf of the "Roman rites" (*romanae religiones*), by which he meant aspects of traditional Roman paganism.[44] Yet before the century was out, Symmachus's contemporary Jerome was referring to Nicene Christianity as "the Roman faith" (*fides romana*). To be sure, the priest most often applied the phrase specifically to the church of the city of Rome; but in the throes of doctrinal conflict Jerome could also seek to assure the patriarch of Alexandria of his own commitment to "the Roman faith, approved by the apostolic mouth, of which the Alexandrine Church prides itself to be a part."[45] As far as the theologian was concerned, the *fides romana* was Christian, Nicene, and shared across the Mediterranean.

Jerome was not alone. In the East, for example, the Syriac deacon Ephrem (ca. 306–373) similarly expressed strong loyalty to the church

---

[43] Matthew Innes, "Land, Freedom and the Making of the Medieval West," *Transactions of the Royal Historical Society* 16 (2006) 39–74.

[44] Symmachus, *Relatio*, 3.13, ed. Otto Seeck, MGH AA 6.1 (Berlin, 1883).

[45] Jerome, *Epistula*, 63.2, ed. Isidor Hilberg, CSEL 54–56 (Vienna, 1910–1918): "sed tamen scito nobis esse nihil antiquius quam Christiani iura seruare nec patrum transferre terminos semperque meminisse Romanam fidem apostolico ore laudatam, cuius se esse participem Alexandrina ecclesia gloriatur." See also Jer. *Ep.* 15.4.4 and 127.9.1; and Jerome, *Dialogus adversus Pelagianos*, prol. 2, ed. Claudio Moreschini, CCSL 80 (Turnhout, 1990).

of the empire.[46] The men's sentiments echoed the official imperial policy of their day. A string of emperors from Constantine onward had sought to promote officially sanctioned Christianity, and Theodosius I (379–395) in particular brought the force of imperial law to bear in a futile effort to unify Roman society behind the Nicene version of the faith. He had desired that all peoples subject to his authority give themselves over to the universal religion that Peter had taught and whose doctrine was preserved by the churches of Rome and Alexandria. Dissenters – labeled as heretics – were deemed deluded and insane.[47] Their meetings were banned, their places of worship were to be confiscated, and their clergy were not to be recognized.[48] Manicheans and Christian converts to paganism were further deprived of the right to make wills or receive inheritances. Apostates also lost their rank, dignity, and status, and were prohibited from providing legal testimony.[49] Toward the end of his reign, Theodosius went still further and banned pagan cult, both public and private.[50] Under later emperors, Jews and Samaritans also saw their rights as citizens eroded, most notably through their exclusion from public service.[51] In this sense, then, Jerome was right: insofar as the exercise of power could define a faith as Roman, by the end of the fourth century imperial patronage had secured that status for Nicene Christianity.

Nonetheless, neither imperial nor ecclesiastical rhetoric should blind us to the fact that religious pluralism survived in the late empire. Jews, Samaritans, and pagans continued to be dutiful imperial

---

[46] Sydney H. Griffith, "Ephraem, the Deacon of Edessa, and the Church of the Empire," in *Diakonia*, ed. Thomas Halton and Joseph P. Williman (Washington, D.C., 1986) 22–52 (thanks to Susan Ashbrook Harvey for this reference).

[47] *CTh* 16.1.2. On imperial religious policy, see A. H. M. Jones, *The Later Roman Empire, 284–602*, 3 vols. (Oxford, 1964; repr. Baltimore, 1986) 1: 165–169. On Theodosius, more generally, see David Hunt, "Christianising the Roman Empire: The Evidence of the Code," in *The Theodosian Code*, ed. Jill Harries and Ian Wood (Ithaca, N.Y., 1993) 143–158.

[48] *CTh* 16.1.3, 16.5.6, 16.5.8, 16.5.10–15, 16.5.19–22.

[49] *CTh* 16.5.7, 16.5.9, and 16.5.18 (Manicheans) and 16.7.1–5 (apostates).

[50] *CTh* 16.10.11–12. For practical implications, see Stephen Emmel, "Shenoute of Atripe and the Christian Destruction of Temples in Egypt," in *From Temple to Church*, ed. Johannes Hahn, Stephen Emmel, and Ulrich Gotter (Leiden, 2008) 161–201 (thanks to David Brakke for this reference).

[51] *CTh* 16.8.16 and 16.8.24; Theodosius II, *Novellae*, 3.2, ed. Theodor Mommsen and Paul M. Meyer, in *Codex Theodosianus*, vol. 2 (Berlin, 1905); and, in general, Amnon Linder, *The Jews in Roman Imperial Legislation* (Detroit, 1987) 67–86, and Jones, *LRE*, 1: 945–949.

subjects. Homoian or "Arian" Christians – who rejected the equality of God the Father and the Son, and who constituted the main rivals of the Nicene Church in Theodosius's day – maintained a strong presence in Constantinople throughout the fourth century and survived in the East until at least 538. By that point the Arian population of the imperial capital will have long consisted primarily of barbarian *foederati* and their families, though we also hear of an Arian by the name of Olympius who was murdered in 498 in the baths of the Helenianae in Constantinople for blaspheming the Trinity.[52] Arianism appears also to have been well established among Balkan provincials in the fifth century. It likely survived in Italy, too, and in Africa an Arian community existed in Hippo Regius at the time of Augustine's episcopate.[53] Salvian of Marseille was similarly aware of an "innumerable multitude" of Roman heretics, whom he considered to be worse than either Romans or barbarians.[54] The Christological debates of the fifth century further polarized the empire's Christian community, introducing new divisions between those who accepted and those who rejected, either in whole or in part, the decisions of the ecumenical councils of Ephesus (431) and Chalcedon (451); but as Richard Lim has observed, as long as these communities harbored hopes of imperial acceptance, they remained loyal to the empire.[55] Despite the imperial role in defining and enforcing orthodoxy, then, religion was not necessarily constitutive of Roman identity in a broad sense in the fifth-century empire.

However, the new kingdoms that replaced the Roman Empire in the western Mediterranean found orthodoxy in Arian Christianity, and consequently the concept of the Nicene confession as the *fides romana* took on a newly charged meaning there. In part this was because

---

[52] Soc. 6.8; Soz. 7.5–7 and 8.8; Neil McLynn, "From Palladius to Maximinus: Passing the Arian Torch," *Journal of Early Christian Studies* 4 (1996) 477–493, here 484; and Geoffrey Greatrex, "Justin I and the Arians," *Studia Patristica* 34 (2001) 72–81. On Olympius, see Victor Tonnennensis, *Chronicon* 80, ed. Carmen Cardelle de Hartmann, CCSL 173A (Turnhout, 2001).

[53] Augustine, *In Iohannis evangelium tractatus CXXIV*, 40.7, ed. Radbodus Willems, CCSL 36 (Turnhout, 1954); Augustine, *Sermo Morin Guelferbytanus* 17.4, Patrologiae cursus completus, Series Latina Supplementum 2: 582–585; Michel Meslin, *Les Ariens d'occident, 335–430* (Paris, 1967); McLynn, "From Palladius to Maximinus," 480–484 and 487; Patrick Amory, *People and Identity in Ostrogothic Italy, 489–554* (Cambridge, 1997) 245–247.

[54] Salvian, *De gub. Dei* 5.3.14.

[55] Richard Lim, "Christian Triumph and Controversy," in *Late Antiquity: A Guide to the Postclassical World*, ed. G. W. Bowersock, Peter Brown, and Oleg Grabar (Cambridge, Mass., 1999) 196–218, here 210.

many western provincial aristocrats, facing diminished prospects of secular advancement, sought what Avitus of Vienne referred to as "true and perfect nobility" in ecclesiastical office.[56] In part, though, it had to do with a rhetorical strategy – perhaps most aggressively pursued in Vandal Africa – whereby Nicene authors sought to associate Arianism with barbarism and Nicene Christianity with Romanness. In a world in which political Romanness was at best dangerous and at worst impossible, and in which culture provided an uncertain guide to distinguishing Romans from barbarians, Nicene polemicists suggested to believers wavering between constancy and conversion that they could stay Roman only through steadfastness in their faith.[57]

Circumscribing the parameters of what could legitimately define Romanness, then, was a highly charged endeavor in Late Antiquity. We would thus do well not to accept too uncritically the rhetoric of "Roman" and "barbarian" deployed in our fifth-century sources. This is even more the case with later sources reflecting on fifth-century events from a more distant vantage point, and therefore with a perspective inevitably distorted by changes in the precise meanings, resonances, and politics of Romanness. For Romanness was always political. In the fifth century, it continued to be defined primarily in terms of participation in the political culture of the empire. But the fracturing and eventual collapse of imperial power in the West also brought to the fore other conceptions of what it meant to be Roman, defined above all in terms of culture and faith. These distinct understandings of Romanness frequently – though by no means universally – overlapped, and in regions that had been lost to the empire, the latter two in particular provided enduring links with the imperial past.

Such links were not just a question of nostalgia: they could have practical uses as a means of creating a sense of similarity (or difference) between communities over time and space. An enraged Sidonius Apollinaris played on just such ties of heritage and culture and calling

---

[56] Avitus of Vienne, *In ordinatione episcopi*, vol. 1, ed. Rudolf Peiper, MGH AA 6.2 (Berlin, 1883). See, *inter alia*, Mathisen, *Roman Aristocrats*, 89–104; William E. Klingshirn, *Caesarius of Arles* (Cambridge, 1994); and Karl Friedrich Stroheker, *Der senatorische Adel im spätantiken Gallien* (Tubingen, 1948) 71–105.

[57] Conant, *Staying Roman*, 190–193, and Tankred Howe, *Vandalen, Barbaren, und Arianer bei Victor von Vita* (Frankfurt am Main, 2007) esp. 302–318.

his fellow Auvergnats "brothers to Latium" in a letter to Bishop Grae-
cus of Marseille excoriating him for his role in negotiating the official
transfer of the Auvergne from imperial to Visigothic control in 475.[58]
In the throes of a schism that divided their respective seats of power,
Gelasius, an African and the bishop of Rome – then under Ostrogothic control – wrote to the emperor Anastasius in Constantinople
as one Roman to another: "For, glorious son, I love, cherish, and
receive the Roman prince, just as [I was] born a Roman."[59] Writing in Africa itself, the ecclesiastical historian Victor of Vita probably
sought to precipitate an East Roman invasion of the Vandal kingdom
by highlighting the atrocities of barbarian rule in ways that played heavily on the association of Nicene Christians and Romans.[60] Earlier in
the century the Visigothic king Athaulf had worn a Roman military
cloak and other Roman clothes at his wedding to the emperor's half-
sister Galla Placidia, who had been captured when the Visigoths took
Rome in 410. The marriage took place in thoroughly Roman fashion
in Narbonne, at the house of a leading Gallo-Roman aristocrat, and was
attended by both Romans and Goths. Athaulf presented Placidia with
gold and jewels carried off from Rome; and when the couple later had
a son, they named him Theodosius, after his grandfather and his cousin,
both Roman emperors.[61] To judge from the account of the historian
Olympiodorus, such heavy-handed cultural symbolism was intended
primarily to signal Athaulf's friendship to the empire; but given the
king's choice of wedding gifts and the fact that the marriage itself had
taken place in the face of opposition from the western imperial administration, any such signal will have been underscored by a tacit assertion
of Roman powerlessness in the face of Gothic military might.[62] Moreover, contemporary observers could be quite sensitive to the perceived
cynicism of efforts to manipulate Roman forms for political ends, as
when Priscus learned that the western imperial court had granted Attila

---

[58] Sid. Ap. *Ep.* 7.7.

[59] Gelasius I, *Epistola*, 12.1, ed. Andreas Thiel, in *Epistolae Romanorum pontificum genuinae et quae ad eos scriptae sunt a S. Hilario usque ad Pelagium II* (Braunsberg, 1868):
"quia, gloriose fili, et sicut Romanus natus Romanum principem amo, colo, susci-
pio."

[60] Conant, *Staying Roman*, 191–193, in the light of Christian Courtois, *Victor de Vita
et son œuvre* (Algiers, 1954) 17–22.

[61] Olymp. fr. 24 and 26.1.

[62] Olymp. fr. 26.1 (friendship) and 22.1–3 (opposition); Peter J. Heather, *Goths and
Romans, 332–489* (Oxford, 1991) 219–220.

himself a sham Roman generalship as a ploy to disguise the tribute paid out to him as if it were military supplies.[63]

Appeals to the incorporative power of Rome did not always succeed. Attila did not become a loyal subject of the empire or fight in its defense, and Athaulf similarly did not establish Roman–Gothic friendship. Gelasius and Anastasius did not heal the schism between Rome and the eastern patriarchs. Sidonius and Victor each failed to secure the return of his province to the imperial fold. The fact that Romanness could be defined in many different ways, each probably equally valid depending on one's point of view, made it a remarkably flexible rhetorical device through which to appeal to a sense of commonality; but it also made such appeals easier to reject if the terms of one's definitions differed. Indeed, this was to be the shape of the future, as the lands that had once been unified under Roman imperial control drifted slowly but inexorably apart. Ultimately, then, its incorporative force failed; but through the fifth century the concept of Romanness continued to prolong a feeling of Mediterranean unity.

---

[63] Prisc. fr. 11.2, here 2: 278.

PART II

ATTILA AND THE WORLD
AROUND ROME

10: The Steppe World and the Rise of the Huns

Étienne de la Vaissière

The origin of the Huns in the steppe is a topic that has occupied historians for hundreds of years. In 1776, Joseph de Guignes wrote, at the beginning of the preface to his *Histoire générale des Huns, des Turcs, des Mogols, et des autres Tartares occidentaux:* "I propose to present in this work the history of an almost unknown people, which at different times established powerful kingdoms in Asia, Europe, and Africa. The Huns . . . who originated in a country in the north of China, between the rivers Irtish and Amur, gradually took control of all of Great Tartary." The argument of this founding father of Orientalism was based on nothing more than the similarity of the lifestyle of the European Huns, who invaded Roman Europe in the first half of the fifth century, and the nomadic Xiongnu, the chief enemy of the Qin and Han Chinese dynasties. The great nomadic empire formed by the Xiongnu in the Ordos region and Mongolia lasted from the third century BCE until the first century CE, before its ultimate defeat in Mongolia in 155 at the hands of other nomads, the Xianbei (map 2). The far eastern provenance of the Huns was also of great interest to intellectuals in the nineteenth century, who thought in terms of nation, people, bloodlines, and language. Through detailed analyses of Chinese sources these scholars tried to find more precise parallels between the name Hun and Xiongnu. They sought to pinpoint some of their tribal names, to identify their language, and to reconstruct the trajectory of their movement from Asia to Europe. In the face of this quest for origins, the study of the Huns who established themselves on the Hungarian plain in Europe, and especially what archaeology could reveal about them, seemed less important.

In reaction to this situation, O. Maenchen–Helfen, a Sinologist with a deep knowledge of Soviet archaeology and ethnology, tried after the Second World War to change the approach of research on the Huns of Europe. He strongly criticized the philological character of previous scholarship and its emphasis on names as well as its lack of interest in archaeological realities. He sought to create a new field of Hunnic studies that was disengaged from the question of origins.[1]

In the following pages, while I acknowledge the force of Maenchen-Helfen's arguments, I offer a primarily political hypothesis that addresses the still open question of origins and of whether or not the Xiongnu in any way were connected to Attila's empire.[2] I argue that a group of Hunnic tribes, once part of the former Xiongnu Empire, actually migrated westward in the middle of the fourth century, two centuries after the Xiongnu state collapsed in Mongolia. This does not mean that the Huns who arrived in Europe had not changed considerably in the course of their long migration. The complexity and fluid character of ethnogenesis is an accepted fact, seen especially in the formation of confederations on the steppe. The language of the Huns might have changed, too; Maenchen-Helfen was right that we cannot prove that their spoken tongue remained the same. What I will try to show in this chapter, however, is that in the course of their migration the Huns kept their name as a political reference point, and that this perceived connection is of great historical importance for understanding the Hunnic domination of the tribes of the Pontic steppe. Precise evidence from the early medieval steppe shows that migrating tribes made use of their prestigious name with its powerful reference to the imperial past to rule over smaller tribes less blessed by fortune and history.[3]

The origins of the Huns and their links to the world of the steppe are pertinent political questions that scholars have approached differently. I will attempt to clarify their conflicting opinions, first regarding

---

[1] Otto Maenchen-Helfen, "The Legend of the Origin of the Huns," *Byzantion* 17 (1945) 244–251; Maenchen-Helfen, "Pseudo-Huns," *Central Asiatic Journal* 1 (1955) 101–106; Maenchen-Helfen, "The Ethnic Name Hun," in *Studia Serica Bernhard Karlgren Dedicata*, ed. Soren Egerod (Copenhagen, 1959) 223–238. In distinguishing the question of origins from that of the organization of Attila's empire, this *Companion to the Age of Attila* validates Maenchen-Helfen's approach.

[2] On this point see Hyun Kim, *The Huns, Rome, and the Birth of Europe* (Cambridge, 2013).

[3] See the famous story narrated by Theophylact Simocatta on the fleeing Avars in the middle of the sixth century: Michael Whitby and Mary Whitby, ed. and trans., *The History of Theophylact Simocatta: An English Translation with Introduction and Notes* (Oxford, 1986) 189–190.

events in the fourth century and the arrival of the Huns in Europe, and then moving on to the links of the Europe-based Huns to the Central Asian steppe in the fifth century.

DID THEY COME FROM BEYOND THE VOLGA?

The first challenge is to prove that the Huns did indeed arrive from beyond the Volga and that they did so in Late Antiquity, not earlier. The classical sources place the origins of the Huns beyond the Sea of Azov but say very little more, and one might easily envisage a local ethnogenesis or at least a very ancient arrival in the region. Some Soviet scholars took this position.[4] The fourth-century historian Ammianus Marcellinus places the Huns far to the northeast (31.2.1): "The people of the Huns, but little known from ancient records, dwelling beyond the Maeotic [Azov] Sea near the ice-bound ocean." He adds, furthermore, that the Huns went as far as the lands of the Alans north of the River Don (31.2.12–13), "which divides Europe from the measureless wastes of Scythia [the steppe]." Jordanes, writing two centuries later in Constantinople, also placed the Huns' origin to the east of the Sea of Azov, between the Volga and the Don Rivers (Get. 5). But Ammianus, notably, adds: "This race of untamed men, without encumbrances, aflame with an inhuman desire for plundering others' property, made their violent way amid the rapine and slaughter of the neighbouring peoples as far as the Halani [Alans]" and defines some limits to the north of the Alans: "The river Tanaïs [Don], which separates Asia from Europe. On the other side of this river the Alans ... inhabit the measureless wastes of Scythia" (Amm. 31.2.12–13). The Huns clearly *arrived* in the Don-Volga region and were not native to it. No classical source contradicts Ammianus's assertion that the Huns were completely unknown to the Mediterranean world before the 370s, and that they appeared quite suddenly. The date conventionally assigned to their crossing of the Volga is around 370, but it could have been somewhat earlier. It is not known how much time the Huns spent in the region between the rivers Volga and Don, but it was undoubtedly less than a generation. No source, however, explains the reasons for their advance into the West. We may conclude that the Huns arrived in the Volga-Don region, having come from somewhere far to the east unknown to the Greek, Latin, and Syrian observers of the fourth century.

---

[4] Otto Maenchen-Helfen, *The World of the Huns* (Berkeley, 1973) 447 n. 21.

We may know the region where the Huns arrived, but not their point of origin or the path they took to reach the West. I believe that the Huns had an origin in Inner Asia, and more precisely from the regions surrounding the Altai Mountains; all the archaeological and textual evidence points in this direction as we will see. They could have taken any number of routes to reach the Don-Volga area from their far-eastern point of origin. Perhaps they crossed the Turgai Plateau if they came via Central Asia. (map 2.) An alternate route could have brought them down the Volga from the North, a detour from their point of origin in Asia. In this scenario, the Huns left the Altai, traversed the northern steppe, crossed the Ural Mountains where the city of Yekaterinburg now lies, and then pushed south along the Volga.[5] Their steppe way of life, however, precludes a northern origin in the forest zone. We turn now to eastern evidence for their eastern origins and their relation to the empire of the Xiongnu.

THE HUNS AND THE XIONGNU: THE CENTRAL ASIAN EVIDENCE

To address the question of the connection between the Huns known to Europeans in the West and the Xiongnu, we must examine two fundamental texts, written in the region of Dunhuang and Gansu on the borders between Central Asia and regions populated by Chinese (Han) people at the end of the third century and beginning of the fourth, by two direct witnesses, Zhu Fahu and Nanaivande.

The first text is a translation, composed by Zhu Fahu (his Chinese name), also known as Dharmarakṣa (his Indian name), a Buddhist monk and one of the main translators of Buddhist texts in China in the third century.[6] Zhu Fahu's family, which had came from Bactria (northern Afghanistan) and had lived in Dunhuang for generations, was typical of the wealthy merchants who had established Buddhism in China. Zhu Fahu moved to central China and participated fully in Chinese culture but maintained very close ties to Central Asia. He knew many of the languages of the region and regularly returned to Dunhuang.

---

[5] Miklòs Erdy, "An Overview of the Xiongnu Type Cauldron Finds of Eurasia in Three Media, with Historical Observations," in *The Archaeology of the Steppes*, ed. Bruno Genito (Naples, 1994) 379–438.

[6] Emil Zürcher, *The Buddhist Conquest of China* (Leiden, 1972) 65–70.

In two of his translations into Chinese of canonical Indian texts, Zhu Fahu renders the name of the Huṇa people as "Xiongnu" (*Taisho Tripitaka*, 11.310, 3.186).[7] "Huṇa" was not a common word in any Indian language, and his two mentions of it are the oldest known. The name reappears later in inscriptions that designate invaders from the Northwest who attack India in the fifth century, and in literary texts such as the *Mahābharata*. In one of Zhu Fahu's texts, the *Tathāgataguhya-sutrā*, the Huṇa are cited in a list that identifies the major peoples of Asia and those neighboring India: the Saka (from Seistan), Parthians, Tokharians (from Bactria), Greeks, Kamboja (mountain people of the Hindu Kush), Khasa (mountain people of the Himalayas), Huṇa, Chinese, Dards (from the Upper Indus), and others. The rest of the list enumerates ever more imaginary peoples. The structure of this list is absolutely clear. It begins by cataloguing all the foreign peoples that the Indian authors whom Zhu Fahu was translating could name. At the end of the list, these groups are juxtaposed with others who were either imagined or who came from a far distant and semilegendary past. The Huṇa would not have been placed in the first part of the list if they were not a people with an ethnic and geographic reality on the order of the Parthians, Bactrians, Greeks, and Chinese. The text indicates that the Huṇa were among the great peoples at the time of the list's original composition, which can be dated to the first century BCE or slightly thereafter. The list places the Huṇa among the political powers that bordered the Chinese in this period. Could they be the Xiongnu?

As noted above, Zhu Fahu used the word "Xiongnu" to translate the term "Huṇa" into Chinese. This is not a vague, generic Chinese formulation. All the terms in the Indian text are rendered word for word, either by translation or transcription.[8] Zhu Fahu did not consider Huṇa a generic name; he could easily have placed them further down the list, among the semihistoric peoples. He also could have simply transcribed the name, as he did the name of the Dards, or eliminated it and replaced it by another, as he did with many names. On

---

[7] See Sylvain Lévy, "Notes chinoises sur l'Inde, V: Quelques documents sur le bouddhisme indien dans l'Asie centrale," *Bulletin de l'École Française d'Extrême-Orient* 5 (1905) 253–305, esp. 289. See also Étienne de la Vaissière, "Huns et Xiongnu," *Central Asiatic Journal* 49.1 (2005) 3–26, esp. 11–13.

[8] Only the names exclusively connected to the Indian way of looking at things are replaced by others: just as the Pahlava are replaced by the Arsacid Parthians (Anxi), the Tukhara by the Yuezhi (the invaders of Bactria), the Yavana by the Greeks (Daqin, roughly eastern Roman Empire, in other words, the Hellenistic world), and the Chinese by the Qin.

the contrary, the use of the name Huṇa in these texts has a precise political reference to the Xiongnu and the period when they were the great nomadic adversaries of China and the principalities of Central Asia. It was perfectly logical for the Indian writers to include them in their lists, and perfectly normal for Zhu Fahu to render the name as "Xiongnu."

The second text is a letter written by a Sogdian merchant named Nanaivande, who, like Zhu Fahu, came from the circle of Central Asian merchants who traded between China, the steppe, and India. The Sogdian traders came from Sogdiana, an Iranian-speaking land of settled peoples located between the Amu Darya and Syr Darya rivers, and were the main merchants on the Silk Road from the fourth to the ninth century.[9] The letter allows us to equate one name with another, as in Zhu Fahu's text, though this time in reverse. In 1948, the Iranologist W. Henning published a copy of a letter dated to 313, which was sent by Nanaivande on the route from Gansu to Samarkand. This letter describes in apocalyptic terms the raids by Xwn (the accurate Sogdian transcription of what the western sources called Hun) on the main towns of northern China, ruining its economy and trade. Henning demonstrates beyond all possible doubt that the Xwn raiders from north China described in the letter were those that contemporary Chinese texts called Xiongnu, the very people who were at that time destroying the Qin dynasty.[10] We see, then, that around the year 300, "Xiongnu" was only the Chinese transcription of the name Hun used by the extremely well-informed members of the Central Asian mercantile communities who traveled the length and breadth of Asia.[11] "Hun/Xwn/Huṇa" were the exact transcriptions of the name that the Chinese, always eager to play on words and to condemn their great enemies from the north, had rendered as "Xiongnu," "howling slaves."

All the contemporary sources agree that the Huns of Europe of the fourth and fifth centuries were called Huns by everyone who encountered them and that they used this name to refer to themselves.

---

[9] Étienne de la Vaissière, *Sogdian Traders: A History* (Leiden, 2005).

[10] Walter B. Henning, "The Date of the Sogdian Ancient Letters," *Bulletin of the School of Oriental and African Studies* 12.3–4 (1948) 601–615. Nicholas Sims-Williams and Frantz Grenet, "The Historical Context of the Sogdian Ancient Letters," in *Transition Periods in Iranian History*, ed. Philippe Gignoux (Paris 1987) 101–122; La Vaissière, *Sogdian Traders*, chap. 2.

[11] On these mercantile and monastic communities, see la Vaissière, *Sogdian Traders*, chap. 3.

Furthermore, the name Hun never changes among all the populations affected by the extremely rapid advance of the Huns, whether in Europe or south of the Caucasus, proving that it was the Huns themselves who diffused the name. If the contemporary sources are correct, the Huns of Europe arrived there bearing the name that the Chinese transcribed as "Xiongnu," that is, "Hun."

HUNS AND XIONGNU: SOME ATTEMPTED COUNTERARGUMENTS

Only a reinterpretation of the use of the word "Xwn" by the Bactrian monk Zhu Fahu and the Sogdian merchant Nanaivande could sever the link between the Xiongnu and the Huns. Some commentators have tried to do so by invoking the accident of phonology[12] or the bad conservation of manuscripts.[13] Others have claimed that the word "Hun" was simply a generic term that had lost all precise meaning because it was applied to so many tribes.[14] The examples of generic use that these scholars cite, however, all come from sources written after the great invasion and so obviously cannot be used to refute earlier texts. While it is true that the term "Hun" became generic after the fifth century, that does not mean that it was so before then. Only the Iranologist H. Bailey has proposed a coherent line of refutation of the thesis that there was a link between the Huns and the Xiongnu.[15] He advances the hypothesis that the Sogdian "Xwn" was a name for the Hyaona, who were an enemy people mentioned in the *Avesta*, the sacred texts of Zoroastrianism. Bailey's idea is attractive, but lacks a philological basis. His thesis nonetheless was elaborated recently by S. Parlato.[16] According to her, the word had a literary, epic character, and was spread through the steppe by the bards from the Parthian empire. In the steppe world, she claims, the term was received with enthusiasm and served as a generic term for any nomadic and demonic enemy. In

---

[12] Paolo Daffinà, "Chih-chih Shan-Yü," *Rivista degli Studi Orientali* 44.3 (1969) 199–232.

[13] Maenchen-Helfen, "Pseudo-Huns."

[14] Denis Sinor, "The Hun Period," in *The Cambridge History of Early Inner Asia*, ed. Denis Sinor (Cambridge, 1990) 177–205, here 179.

[15] Harold Bailey, "Harahuna," in *Asiatica: Festschrift Friedrich Weller* (Leipzig, 1954) 12–21.

[16] Sandra Parlato, "Successo euroasiatico dell'etnico 'Unni,'" in *La Persia e l'Asia Centrale da Alessandro al X secolo* (Rome, 1996) 555–566.

other words, it was not the Huns who migrated, but a generic name that spread across the steppe in the context of a culture that spoke Iranian languages.

This hypothesis is not convincing, however. The steppe was not Zoroastrian, and it is hard to see how a secondary figure in the Avestic literature could have acquired such a presence. The theory overestimates the influence of these hypothetical Parthian minstrels wandering across the steppe in causing a name derived from Hyaona to be adopted from Asia to Europe. Moreover, if "Hun" was a generic term of Iranian origin, why would the Huns of Europe use it to refer to themselves? If one thing is clear, as Maenchen-Helfen showed years ago,[17] it is that the Huns did not speak Iranian languages. "Hun," then, cannot be a generic Iranian term.

I have demonstrated thus far that the Huns who arrived in Europe from 370 onward called themselves by the name transcribed in Chinese as "Xiongnu." Maenchen-Helfen cautioned against such reasoning on several occasions because it relied entirely on the evidence of names to establish identity. He argued instead that only ethnographic and archaeological evidence should be taken into account. His thesis is unacceptable, however. The political implications of a name must never be ignored; otherwise one would have to dismiss as negligible a good part of the history of political ideas. If the Rhomaioi of Byzantium could claim to be the political heirs of the Romans, then the Huns could equally claim to be the heirs of the Xiongnu. The steppe has the right to have political ideas and history, and we must not deny the Huns those important aspects of their identity.

IN CENTRAL ASIA

The Hunnic period of Central Asia's history lasted until Turks achieved preeminence in the 560s, and the details of this period's political history remain very confused. In this section I argue against the long-held belief that there were three successive waves of Huns in Central Asia, that of the Chionites in the 350s, the Kidarites in either the 370s or much more probably the 420s,[18] and the Hephthalites, whom Procopius calls

---

[17] Maenchen-Helfen, "The World of the Huns," 376ff. and 443.
[18] *Pace* Joe Cribb, "The Kidarites, the Numismatic Evidence," in *Coins, Art and Chronology*, vol. 2: *The First Millennium C.E. in the Indo-Iranian Borderlands*, ed. Michael Alram (Vienna, 2010) 91–146.

the White Huns, around 450 (Proc. 1.3.2–8). Instead, Chinese textual evidence shows that these groups had in fact been in Central Asia from the beginning of the great Hunnic invasions of the fourth century, and that some of them had stayed there for a generation before they crossed the Volga, while others stayed for a while to the north of the Caspian Sea. I will consider each group in turn.

The Chionites. In the 350s, the great Persian king Shapur II (r. 309–379) probably fought invading nomads at the Amu Darya river, which marked the northeast frontier of the Sasanian empire. That, at least, is what is implied by Ammianus Marcellinus, who was always attentive to the whereabouts of the Persian king of kings. At the same time, the dynasty of Kushanshah, a vassal of the Sasanids based in the territory of modern-day Afghanistan, came to an abrupt end. In 356 Ammianus gave the name Chionites to these eastern enemies of the Persians. In 359, however, after the Chionites had changed sides and made a new arrangement with the Persians, Shapur brought a force of them under the command of their king Grumbates to the siege of Amida, modern-day Diyarbakir (Amm. 16.9, 17.5, 18.6, 19.1).

The name "Chionites" is an Iranian plural form (with final -t) of "Hyon," a deformation of "Xwn" influenced by the name "Hyaona" mentioned earlier. In a similar manner, western writers in medieval times gave the name "Tartars" to the Tatars, the dominant element in the armies of the Mongol Empire, confusing them with the name of the ancient river of Hell from which they seemed to have emerged.

Chinese sources confirm the identification of Chionite and Hun. The dynastic histories, and especially the history of the northern Wei, called the *Weishu*, are the key to understanding what went on in Inner Asia in the middle of the fourth century. The northern Wei, who were themselves of nomadic origin, took special interest in Mongolia and Central Asia. Although the original chapter of the *Weishu* devoted to the Western neighbors of China was lost and later reconstituted from various quotations in Chinese historical literature by imperial scholars, some additional data from the original *Weishu* have been preserved in other works, especially an encyclopedia published in 801, the *Tongdian*. The *Weishu* mentions the conquest of Samarkand by the Xiongnu three generations before 457, which – if we use the traditional Chinese calculation of thirty years to a generation – places this conquest around 367, the same time that the Persians were fighting the Chionites (*Weishu*, 102.2270).

The Armenian historian Faustus of Byzantium tells us that Shapur II renewed the fighting against Chionite Huns on the eastern front in

368, using Armenian troops, and that he was strenuously attacked on several occasions by a "king of the Kushans" who reigned over the Bactrians (Faustus 5.7, 5.37).[19] Another Armenian text mentions the combat of the Armenian prince Babik of Syunik, sent by Shapur very probably also into Central Asia against a Hun called Honagur.[20]

The Kidarites: While some numismatists would like to place them in the 370s,[21] it is very clear from the combination of the Chinese and classical sources that the Kidarites were the dominant nomadic dynasty in Central Asia from the 420s to the 470s.[22] Even while maintaining their Hunnic identity, the Kidarites engaged and promoted the local past of the sedentary people they ruled, and they built cities on the Hippodamian grid plan in their empire. They also revived the title of king of the Kushans, assuming it for themselves.[23] We find this title on a seal bearing the inscription "King of the Oghlar Huns, king of the Kushans, prince of Samarkand"[24] that was made some decades after their installation in Central Asia.

The Hephthalites: The *Tongdian* also tells us that another group of Huns, the Hephthalites, arrived from the Altai Range sometime after the year 360.[25] They were destined to play an important role in the political history of Central Asia between 450 and 560. The Hephthalites and their subordinate confederation of tribes seem to have been more oriented to the nomadic world than the Kidarites. At least until the 520s, the Hephthalites continued to live as nomads in the high plateaus of what is now northwest Afghanistan. The Alkhon tribes,

---

[19] Translated in Nina Garsoïan, *The Epic Histories Attributed to P'awstos Buzand (Buzandaran Patmut'iwnk)* (Cambridge, Mass., 1989) 187–198 and 217–218.

[20] Movsês Daskhurants'i (or Kałankatvats'i), in *The History of the Caucasian Albanians by Movses Dasxuranci*, trans. Charles J. F. Dowsett (Oxford, 1961) 63–64; also Stephannos Orbelian, trans. in Marie-Félicité Brosset, *Histoire de la Siounie par Stephannos Orbelian* (St. Petersburg, 1864–1866) 24–25.

[21] Most recently Cribb, "The Kidarites."

[22] Kazuo Enoki, "On the Date of the Kidarites (I)," *Memoirs of the Research Department of the Toyo Bunko* 27 (1969) 1–26.

[23] Frantz Grenet, "Regional Interaction in Central Asia and North-West India in the Kidarite and Hephtalite Period," in *Indo-Iranian Languages and Peoples*, ed. Nicholas Sims-Williams (London, 2002) 203–224.

[24] Ahmad ur Rahman, Frantz Grenet, and Nicholas Sims-Williams, "A Hunnish Kushan-Shah," *Journal of Inner Asian Art and Archaeology* 1 (2006) 125–131, here 128.

[25] Étienne de la Vaissière, "Is There Any 'Nationality of the Ephthalites'?," in *Hephthalites*, ed. Madhuvanti Ghose and Étienne de la Vaissière, *Bulletin of the Asia Institute* 17 (2007) 119–137.

who dominated the southern wing of the Hephthalite confederation, lived mostly in southern Afghanistan and in northwest India. They issued coins showing their leaders with cranial deformation, their skulls elongated into a dome shape, presumably to distinguish themselves from other local peoples.[26] It is possible that the name Alkhon, if one accepts "Al-" as the Turkic for scarlet, means "the red Huns," those of the south, as opposed to the white Huns of the east (the Hephthalites), in a geographic scheme of colors native to the world of the steppe.

Thus we see on the basis of the *Tongdian* and other materials that the Hephthalites, far from being a new wave of nomads had been one of several groups of Huns that had been in Central Asia from the middle of the fourth century at the beginning of the great invasions. There are therefore no grounds for arguing in terms of successive waves; what we have are dynasties or tribal groupings coming to power in succession among the nomads who arrived in Central Asia during the second half of the fourth century. There was just one massive single episode of migration in the years 350–370, perhaps followed by some more limited movement during the fluid circumstances of the following decades.[27]

BETWEEN CENTRAL ASIA AND EUROPE

Our sources locate these different groups (Chionites, Kidarites, Hephthalites, and others) in Central Asia, but say almost nothing about the connections that the Huns may have retained with the steppe, north of sedentary Central Asia, in modern Kazakhstan, or with the Huns of Europe. The Kidarites are mentioned unreliably by Priscus as being on the eastern shore of the Caspian around 468 (Prisc. 51). Moreover, nothing is known of the northern reach of the Hephthalite empire. That it included Sogdiana, between the Amu Darya and Syr Darya rivers, is certain, but we do not know if the empire controlled the nomadic groups of present-day Kazakhstan. One trace of a northern connection dates reliably to the years 440–460 and shows that the Hephthalites were originally subjects of a power from the North, probably the Avars. We

---

[26] On the Alkhon, see Klaus Vondrovec, *The Coinage of the Iranians Huns and Their Successors from Bactria to Gandhara (4th to 8th Century CE)*, Studies in the Aman ur Rahman Collection, vol. 4, Vienna, forthcoming.

[27] La Vaissière, "Is There Any Nationality?"

learn this from Chinese texts that mention an incursion into Central Asia made by the Rourans, the dominant power of Mongolia in the fifth century and the early sixth, where they fought against Kidarites and subjected the Hephthalites (*Weishu*, 102.2275, 2277; *Beishi*, 97.3210; *Liangshu*, 54.812). An Armenian geographer refers to this same episode when he mentions the Hephthalites, the Warkhons, and the Alkhons not far from the Zeravshan River, on which the Sogdian capital Samarkand was situated. If the Alkhons lived further to the south in Afghanistan, the Warkhons are very probably the Rourans – the "Avars" of later sources. Byzantine writers of the second half of the sixth century call them Ouarchonitai or Varchonites (Menander 19.1).

Another piece of evidence from the same period makes a connection between Central Asia and the Pontic steppe. In 463, after the disintegration of Attila's empire, new tribal groups began to appear in the steppes. One of these groups passed through Central Asia. The fifth-century historian Priscus (Prisc. 40) writes: "At this time the Saragurs, Urogs and the Onogurs sent envoys to the eastern Romans. These tribes had left their native lands when the Sabiri attacked them. The latter had been driven out by the Avars who had in turn been displaced by the tribes who lived by the shore of the Ocean." Theophylact Simocatta, the early seventh-century Byzantine historian, mentions an Onogur city named Bakath, which was destroyed by an earthquake. Since Bakath is a Sogdian name, we may infer that the Onogurs had spent some time in Central Asia.

The different groups of Huns were firmly based in Central Asia at the middle of the fourth century. Thus they bring a unity of time and place to the question of the origins of the Huns of Europe. To summarize my argument so far, I have demonstrated that around 350, a group bearing the name Huns was active in the Kazakh steppe, some of whom moved south and others west, and that a Chinese text precisely ascribes to the Altai the origin of the migration of some of these tribes.

IN THE ALTAI MOUNTAINS AND THE MINUSINSK BASIN: THE QUESTION OF CAULDRONS

We have seen that one Chinese source on Central Asia, the *Tongdian*, wrote that among those making the great migration of the 350s, the

Hephthalites at least originated in the Altai region. It is thus logical to search in that region to see if these Chinese texts can be confirmed by archaeology or other texts.

The archaeological evidence from Central Asia is woefully meager. Hunnic cemeteries are poorly known,[28] and very little other material survives. Given the current state of knowledge the *Weishu* text can neither be confirmed or invalidated. The archaeological aspect of Hunnic/Xiongnu settlement in Central Asia is simply missing.[29]

The archaeological evidence for the Huns of Europe is quite different, however, and permits us to draw important inferences about their origin in East Asia. The chief evidence comes from the cauldrons that the Huns may have used for cooking, ritual purposes, or both. People of the steppe had used cauldrons since much earlier times, but the Hunnic vessels are quite distinctive, constituting a true archaeological marker.[30] They are bell-shaped and crudely made, with squared handles surmounted by ornaments in the shape of mushrooms. This evidence shows clear links to Inner Asia (that is the Altai Mountains, Mongolia, southern Siberia, and the northern part of China). A concentration of similar cauldrons occurs on the northern flank of the Altai Mountains and the Minusinsk Basin (map 2). In the Minusinsk region, furthermore, there are petroglyphs depicting the cauldrons, with the same protuberances on the handles, though these are rounded not squared. In Hungary as well as Asia these cauldrons were buried near springs or rivers, indicating a continuity of ritual and culture from the Minusinsk region to Hungary.[31]

In the absence of a complete typology of the evolution of the cauldrons' forms and their archaeological contexts, however, these observations must remain inconclusive albeit extremely suggestive. When the archaeological evidence is augmented by textual material to which we now turn, the case becomes virtually certain. This archaeological evidence, supported by the text that has the Hephthalites coming from

---

[28] See, however, Daniel Schlumberger, "La nécropole de Shakh tépé près de Qunduz," *Comptes-rendus des séances de l'année: Académie des inscriptions et belles-lettres* 108.2 (1964) 207–211.

[29] On Xiongnu archaeology, see most recently Ursula Brosseder and Bryan K. Miller, eds., *Xiongnu Archaeology: Multidisciplinary Perspectives of the First Steppe Empire in Inner Asia* (Bonn, 2011).

[30] Toshio Hayashi, "Hunnic Cauldrons," in *Studies on Ancient Cauldrons: Cultic or Daily Vessels in the Eurasian Steppes* (Tokyo, 2011) 341–382.

[31] Erdy, "An Overview."

the Altai, indicates a north Altaic provenance of the Hunnic groups who invaded Central Asia and Europe from 350 onward.

THE TEXT OF THE *WEISHU*

One other passage in the *Weishu* mentions that at the beginning of the fifth century, "remains of the descendants of the Xiongnu" (*Weishu*, 103.2290) were to be found far northwest of the Rouran, that is, in the area of the Altai. The quality of this information is beyond question. The *Weishu* is very parsimonious in its use of the term "Xiongnu," and these Xiongnu are the only ones in a list of neighbors of the Rouran. There are about forty occurrences of the term "Xiongnu" in the text, the greatest number of which are related to the Xiongnu of the south who settled in China, or to rhetorical comparisons with the Han Chinese. Mentions of contemporary Xiongnu still in the Altai as opposed to those in China are extremely rare. In chapters 102 and 103, which are dedicated to the countries of the West and North, that is the whole of the Xiongnu Empire, there are only three mentions in all. One is the text cited above; the second is found in the famous passage on the conquest of Samarkand by the Xiongnu (*Weishu*, 102.2270); and the third describes the struggles between a Kidarite king in Bactria and the Xiongnu (*Weishu*, 102.2277).[32] The fact that the *Weishu* mentions "remains of the descendants of the Xiongnu" is an extremely important piece of information. It had been argued that the Xiongnu identity totally disappeared in Inner Asia after their defeat of the second century, so that the European Huns could not have come from these regions, but this passage of the *Weishu* proves that this argument is false. The Xiongnu did indeed survive to the far north, albeit beyond the range of vision of the Chinese sources. That they did not form an empire, and were no more than weakened descendants of the ancient Xiongnu matters little; they had conserved their tribal identity.

We see then that three facts (the genetic connection between the cauldrons, the texts on the Hephthalites, and the text on descendants of the Xiongnu) all point to the Altai region as the starting point of the Huns' migration to Central Asia and to the West starting in the middle of the fourth century. This conclusion is supported by some entirely

---

[32] In this case, the Xiongnu here are probably the Warkhon mentioned in the Armenian geographical treatise, that is the Rouran/Avars, who incorporated the Xiongnu into their confederation.

independent scientific data that shows that during this period the Altai was the place of dramatic climatic change.

THE CLIMATE HYPOTHESIS

Recently published findings regarding accumulations of pollen in the lakes of the Altai Range tell of a sharp drop in temperatures combined with a rise in humidity that lasted from the middle of the fourth century through the sixth, causing significant change in the vegetation. Likewise, from 340, glaciers advanced in the valleys.[33] The accumulated snow destroyed herds of the high plateaux; although the Mongolian horse is able to dig through the snow to feed, this capacity is strictly limited by the depth of the snow cover, and contemporary ethnography has shown the enormous impact that prolonged winters and their blizzards can have on herds of horses – eight million horses, 20 percent of the stock, died for this reason in Mongolia in the winter of 2010. Chinese sources report Hun invasions from the Altai happening exactly in the middle of the fourth century, without giving any reason for their incursions. For a long time scholars specializing in nomad studies have postulated a major climatic event as the explanation of the size of the Hun migrations. We now see that such an event is well supported by rigorous paleoclimatological studies conducted quite independently of the work of historians. Quite plausibly additional factors contributed to the destabilization of Hun societies in the Altai region, but little is known of them. The north slope of the Altai was beyond the reach of knowledge for the Chinese observers, the only exception being the *Weishu* text mentioned above.

We know, meanwhile, that the Rouran/Avar kaghanate became active in the fourth century, even if its power only truly began to develop at the end of that century. We may interpret the passage from Priscus quoted above as a brief summary of the history of Inner Asia in the fourth century: the Sabiri could be the Xianbei (from Chinese characters pronounced *Sarbi at the time), chased out of Mongolia by the developing power of the Rouran/Avars, and chasing in their

---

[33] Frank Schlütz and Frank Lehmkuhl, "Climatic Change in the Russian Altai, Southern Siberia, Based on Palynological and Geomorphological Results, with Implications for Climatic Teleconnections and Human History since the Middle Holocene," *Vegetation History and Archaeobotany* 16 (2007) 101–118.

turn the tribes further west.[34] In this case, the Hunnic groups cited by Priscus (Saraguri, Urogi, and Onoguri) paused in the Kazakh steppe before moving further westward in the middle of the fifth century.

It is thus likely that we can recapitulate the historical trajectory of the Huns in the same way. The Huns were a confederation of peoples fleeing from their ancestral homeland, whose incursions into the West would disrupt the old patterns of the distribution of the nomadic tribes throughout the entire Kazakh steppe, creating a new nomadic landscape under the leadership of the Hunnic tribes. They left the north Altai in a context of major climatic change that caused distress among local societies and which undoubtedly would have had political consequences of which we have not even the most basic knowledge. Absorbing other tribal groups that they encountered along the way, the Huns bore down on the Kazakh steppe in the mid-fourth century. While one part of them, Chionites, Kidarites, Oghlar, Hephthalites, and Alkhon, established themselves in Sogdiana and Bactriana, other groups followed a route to the West and reached the Volga. Still others perhaps, remained in the steppe and did not reach the West until the middle of the fifth century. The admittedly tenuous evidence permits us to conclude that throughout this migration from the Altai to Europe they carried the old name of the most prestigious empires of the eastern steppe, the empire that the Chinese called Xiongnu.

THE HUNS AND THE SHATTERED EMPIRE

The problem then has shifted from the relationship of the Huns and the Xiongnu in the fourth century to the relationship of the fourth-century Xiongnu to the second-century Xiongnu. We possess a coherent set of independent textual and archaeological set of proofs for the fact that the Huns came from Inner Asia and bore the name transcribed by the Chinese as "Xiongnu." Whether they were the direct descendants of the Xiongnu of antiquity, as they claimed, is another question that historians have barely touched upon. What was the relationship between these fourth-century Xiongnu/Huns north of the Altai to the Xiongnu/Hun empire of antiquity? They called themselves Xiongnu/Huns, and that is how they were known by their neighbors

---

[34] An idea already put forward by Omelian Pritsak, "From the Säbirs to the Hungarians," in *Hungaro-Turcica: Studies in Honour of Julius Németh*, ed. Gyula Káldy-Nagy (Budapest, 1976) 22 and 28–30. Many thanks to Peter Golden for this reference.

in the Altai; it must be stressed that the extreme paucity of documentation does not allow us to go much beyond this. Very little information is available on the tribal reorganizations of Inner Asia after the final defeat of the Xiongnu/Huns in 155 by the Xianbei. The Xianbei, who were for over a century the dominant group on the steppe, are known to have incorporated Xiongnu/Huns into their ranks.[35] Likewise, the dominant power from the fourth century onward,the Rouran, justifiably bore a double name in the Byzantine sources as we have seen; they were the Varkhon, that is, the Avar Huns. Apparently, the breakup of the Xiongnu empire led to the inclusion of its tribal groups in the multiple political entities that succeeded them in the region. The Rouran khaganate was such an entity, associating Xiongnu/Hun tribes with War/Avar tribes. The name Xiongnu had not become generic in Inner Asia in the third or fourth century but in this case belongs to this specific historical moment. It is not surprising that some groups refused to be included in the larger groupings, but kept the name Xiongnu for themselves. We do not yet know how these Xiongnu established themselves and maintained their identity in a zone of settlement on the north slopes of Altai and in the Minusinsk Basin, that is to say, quite far to the northwest of what had been the heart of their ancient empire. These are understudied historical questions. Only careful research into the archaeology of the two centuries of history on the Mongolian steppe that separated the end of the Xiongnu Empire and the Hun migration will be able to show how this happened.

A THREE-STAGE HISTORY

Some clans or tribes of actual Xiongnu origin politically dominated the Huns of Europe – Attila's Huns – but they had long been chased from the Xiongnu homeland in Mongolia and the Ordos region to the northwest, to the Altai region. It is only this point of separation in time – these "missing" two centuries – that prevents us from identifying them directly with the imperial Xiongnu of an earlier era. We must conceptualize a history in three stages: first there were the imperial Xiongnu, whose empire ended in the second century; next we must distinguish these imperial Xiongnu from their northern descendants, who were based in the secondary core of the Altai Mountains and

---

[35] Peter Golden, *An Introduction to the History of the Turkic Peoples* (Wiesbaden, 1992) 69ff.

the Minusinsk Basin in the fourth century; third, we must in turn distinguish these northern Xiongnu from the groupings that resulted from the migration from there and established themselves in Central Asia and in the West. Despite all of the internal cultural developments and recombination of tribes and peoples implicit in this movement, we can be certain of political and to some extent cultural continuity among the Xiongnu–Huns.

11: NEITHER CONQUEST NOR SETTLEMENT: ATTILA'S EMPIRE AND ITS IMPACT

Christopher Kelly

I n late June 451, in the middle of France, the Huns came close to defeat. They faced a well organised coalition force: Roman troops, commanded by the experienced general Aetius, allied with Goths under their king, Theodoric. The Goths had been a permanent presence in the Roman Empire for eighty years; finally settled in 418 by the imperial government in the Aquitaine, they had gradually established (against considerable Roman opposition) an autonomous kingdom centred on Toulouse.[1] It was the threat of a Hun invasion that compelled cooperation. Writing his *On the Origin and Deeds of the Goths* a century later (and fourteen hundred miles away in Constantinople), the former bureaucrat, Jordanes, attributed the initiative to the western Roman emperor Valentinian III, whose flattering communiqué had drawn Theodoric into an alliance: "Bravest of nations, we are well advised to unite against this universal despot who wishes to enslave the whole earth. Attila requires no reason for battle, but thinks whatever he does is justified. . . . He deserves everyone's hatred since he is undoubtedly the common enemy of all. . . . Can you permit such arrogance to go unpunished? Since you are a military power, face your own troubles by joining together with us."

---

[1] Useful surveys of the Goths within the Roman Empire: Herwig Wolfram, *History of the Goths* (Berkeley, 1988) 117–171; Guy Halsall, *Barbarian Migrations and the Roman West, 376–568* (Cambridge, 2007) 180–217; Peter J. Heather, *Goths and Romans, 332–489* (Oxford, 1991) 147–224; Peter J. Heather, *The Goths* (Oxford, 1996) 97–178; Peter J. Heather, *The Fall of the Roman Empire: A New History* (London, 2005) 182–250; Michael Kulikowski, *Rome's Gothic Wars* (Cambridge, 2007) 100–184.

By June 451, the situation was serious. The Huns had crossed the Rhine (somewhere near modern Koblenz) and continued west three hundred miles as far as Orléans. The allied forces saved the city by constructing an extensive network of ditches and earth barriers in front of its walls. The Huns withdrew, shadowed by the Goths and Romans. The armies met a few days later at the end of June on the Catalaunian Plains, an unidentified location in Champagne, probably "near Troyes." The battle began in the early afternoon. The fiercest fighting was for possession of a ridge at the top of a steep rise. The Huns were pushed down the slope by the advancing Romans. Then, quickly rallying, Attila's troops surged dangerously across the flat ground in front of the ridge. "Hand to hand they fought, and the battle was fierce, convulsed, dreadful, unrelenting – like none ever recorded in times past." In the midst of this bloody chaos, the Gothic king, Theodoric, was killed. His son, Thorismud, strayed into the Hun lines and was only just rescued in time.

Fighting ceased at nightfall. The Huns withdrew to their camp behind a protective screen of wagons. In the middle of the Hun laager, Attila ordered saddles to be piled high. Here (if need be) he would fight to the death and throw himself onto a blazing funeral pyre "so that the overlord of so many people should not be taken by his enemies." But, in the end, such stirring bravado proved unnecessary. On the day after the battle, there was no fighting; the Romans and Goths blockaded the Hun camp and buried Theodoric. By the morning of the next day (the second after the battle), both the Goths and Romans had broken camp. Attila too left the Catalaunian Plains, retracing his route and marching as quickly as possible back to the Rhine.

Such an anticlimactic ending spoils a good battle narrative. It is fertile territory for conspiracy theories. The seventh-century Burgundian chronicler Fredegar suspected the Roman general, Aetius. The night after the battle (Fredegar alleged) Aetius went secretly to Attila and claimed that Gothic reinforcements would soon arrive. In return for ten thousand *solidi* (140 pounds of gold), he agreed to persuade Thorismud to withdraw. Aetius then went to Thorismud to warn him that Hun reinforcements would soon arrive. And (now all too predictably) in return for ten thousand *solidi* Aetius agreed to persuade Attila to withdraw; he advised Thorismud to return to Toulouse to secure his position as his father's successor. Jordanes also noted Aetius's advice and similarly sensed duplicity. Jordanes suspected that Aetius feared the consequences of a Gothic victory; with the Huns defeated "the Roman

Empire would be overwhelmed" by a triumphant and newly confident Gothic kingdom.[2]

In whatever way the withdrawal of all three armies is to be understood, the stalemate on the Catalaunian Plains neatly underlines the limits of Hun success. It is a reminder that the Huns never decisively defeated the Romans in pitched battle. They never conquered any Roman territory. They never settled within the empire. Hun objectives were completely different. Certainly by the 420s, the Huns were firmly established on the Great Hungarian Plain in the heart of Europe, the only area of grassland west of the Black Sea capable of supporting horses on any scale and an ideal base for military operations on both sides of the Rhine and Danube. As the Hun Empire expanded across northern Europe, it was successful in systematising the extraction of resources. It was not an interventionist Roman-style empire relying on the close administrative control of subjugated provinces and peoples. Rather, it was a parasitic state: the Hun Empire's success lay in its ability to adopt the culture of those it ruled (the opposite of the usual pattern of imperial domination), to cream off their wealth and manpower, and to consume the food they produced. The Hun state was a protection racket on a grand scale. The Huns' approach to the Roman Empire followed the same strategic logic. As the pattern of attacks (to be sketched in the following section) swiftly shows, their aim was to exploit the possibilities the empire offered for the rapid acquisition of significant amounts of booty. In sharp contrast to other groups (such as the Goths or Vandals) who pressed hard on Roman territory in the fourth and fifth centuries, the object of the often cruelly destructive Hun raids was neither conquest nor settlement. From that point of view, it was not in the Huns' interests to cause the breakup of the Roman Empire: that would have significantly reduced their opportunities for continued wealth extraction.[3]

---

[2] Jordanes, *Getica*, 184–218 (for the most detailed account); see too 186–188 (alliance), 194–195 (Orléans), 207–208 (fighting), 212–213 (Attila's camp), 215–216 (Aetius's advice to Thorismud); Fredegar, *Chronicle*, 2.53. Modern discussion: Ulf Täckholm, "Aetius and the Battle on the Catalaunian Fields," *Opuscula Romana* 7 (1969) 259–276; Christopher Kelly, *The End of Empire: Attila the Hun and the Fall of Rome* (New York, 2009) 244–252; Edward Thompson, *The Huns* (Oxford, 1948; repr. 1996) 148–156; Giuseppe Zecchini, *Aezio: L'ultima difesa dell'Occidente romano* (Rome, 1983) 266–272; Heather, *Fall of the Roman Empire*, 337–339.

[3] The political transformation of Hun society is discussed in Thompson, *The Huns*, 177–195; Heather, *Fall of the Roman Empire*, 324–333; Kelly, *End of Empire*, 59–71.

The Huns are first recorded by Roman historians as a migrating people pushing round the north and west of the Black Sea. According to Ammianus Marcellinus (the most important political historian of the fourth century), the disruption caused by the Huns' advance in the mid-370s was a significant factor pushing one group of Goths (the Tervingi) to cross the Danube and shelter in Roman territory. Ammianus's suggestion of a sudden, mass movement of Huns is most likely exaggerated. It is probably better to think of independent raiding parties under a variety of leaders moving slowly into the fringes of Europe across ten or twenty years.[4] In 376, imperial permission was granted for the Tervingi to cross the Danube, but their subsequent internment in refugee camps was so poorly managed by the Roman military authorities that it provoked an uprising. Forces under the eastern emperor Valens moved into the Balkans in summer 378. Attempts to suppress an escalating revolt failed. The armies clashed on 9 August at Adrianople (modern Edirne, 130 miles northwest of Istanbul). The overwhelming Gothic victory was the worst loss suffered by the Romans since Hannibal routed their legions at Cannae seven centuries earlier. Out of thirty thousand Roman troops, twenty thousand were killed. Most important, success at Adrianople secured the Goths a foothold within the empire. All subsequent efforts to expel or eliminate them failed.[5]

The Huns did not fight at Adrianople. Indeed, for the next fifty years (until the mid-430s) their impact on the Roman Empire was limited. It is usually assumed that during this period the Huns settled on the Great Hungarian Plain and established their own empire as far west as the Rhine and perhaps as far north as the Baltic.[6] Some Hun

The constraints and advantages of the Great Hungarian Plain are explored in Rudi Lindner, "Nomadism, Horses and Huns," *Past and Present* 92 (1981) 3–19; Denis Sinor, "Horse and Pasture in Inner Asian History," *Oriens extremus* 19 (1972) 171–183. On the archaeological difficulties of finding a distinctive material culture for the Huns in Europe, see István Bóna, *Das Hunnenreich* (Budapest, 1991) 134–139; Michel Kazanski, "Les Goths et les Huns: À propos des relations entre les barbares sédentaires et les nomades," *Archéologie Médiévale* 22 (1992) 191–221.

[4] Ammianus Marcellinus, 31.3; Peter J. Heather, "The Huns and the End of the Roman Empire in Western Europe," *English Historical Review* 110 (1995) 4–41, here 6–7; Heather, *The Goths*, 98–102; see below n. 13.

[5] Amm. *Res gest.* 31.4–13; Heather, *Goths and Romans*, 122–147; Kulikowski, *Rome's Gothic Wars*, 128–143; Halsall, *Barbarian Migrations*, 165–180; Noel Lenski, *Failure of Empire: Valens and the Roman State in the Fourth Century AD* (Berkeley, 2002) 320–367.

[6] Thompson, *The Huns*, 84–85; Otto Maenchen-Helfen, *The World of the Huns: Studies in Their History and Culture* Ed. Max Knight (Berkeley, 1973) 125–129; Jan Bemmann, "Hinweise auf Kontakte zwischen dem hunnischen Herrschaftsbereich in

warbands made themselves available for hire. In late 406, mercenaries under Uldin – the first Hun leader whose name is recorded – joined Roman forces in northern Italy to defeat another group of Goths, led by Radagaisus, who had crossed the Rhine near Mainz the previous winter. Two years later, in 408, Uldin – this time uninvited – pushed across the Danube into the Balkans. His raid was timed to take advantage of an uncertain political situation in Constantinople: Emperor Arcadius had died six months earlier, and his successor was his seven-year-old son, Theodosius II. According to the Christian historian Sozomen, Uldin's senior officers were prepared to negotiate a withdrawal recognising the superiority of "the Roman form of government, the philanthropy of the emperor, and his swiftness and open-handedness in rewarding the best men." No doubt it was the generosity of the boy-emperor's advisers that was the deciding factor.[7]

Uldin's raid set a pattern. In early 422, an unnamed Hun leader took advantage of continued Roman troop commitments in Persia – Theodosius had initiated a campaign the previous year – and marched south into Thrace (roughly modern Bulgaria). The incursion is reported only in one very brief entry in a sixth-century chronicle: "The Huns laid waste Thrace." This was clearly more than a cross-border raid; it forced the immediate recall of units from Mesopotamia. The threat of redeployment was sufficient to force an agreement with the Huns who withdrew on the promise of an annual payment of 350 pounds of gold. In 434, the Hun leader Rua (who may have been responsible for the incursion in 422) again pushed through Thrace and towards Constantinople. His timing took advantage of the continuing presence of a task force in North Africa. There the Roman army (a joint operation by both eastern and western imperial governments) had been slow to halt the advance of the Vandals who had crossed the Strait of Gibraltar in spring 429. But the Hun raid in the Balkans did not realise its objective. It was suddenly abandoned following Rua's unexpected death. Not all modern scholars have been convinced. As with most of the scattered and fragmentary material on the Huns in this fifty-year period, the

---

Südosteuropa und dem Nordem," in *Attila und die Hunnen*, ed. Historiches Museum der Pfalz Speyer (Stuttgart, 2007) 176–183. The problem in fixing the extent of the Hun Empire is the difficulty of determining whether the scatter of objects from northern Europe associated with the Huns and other steppe peoples is the result of conquest, mercenary hire, alliance, or trade.

[7] Italy: Marc. Com. 406.2–3; *Gallic Chronicle of 452*, 50–52; Balkans: Sozomen, 9.5 (with discussion in Maenchen-Helfen, *World of the Huns*, 59–72); see too Thompson, *The Huns*, 33–35, 37–38; Kelly, *End of Empire*, 68–69.

references to Rua's invasion can be jigsawed together in a number of different ways. The celebrations in Constantinople following the Huns' withdrawal are even less to the liking of rational-minded historians. There it was rumoured that Rua had been incinerated by a providential lightning bolt, his army stricken by plague, and the survivors scorched by giant fire balls.[8]

On Rua's death in 434, control of the Hun Empire fell to two of his nephews, Bleda and Attila. (The concentration of effective authority in one "royal family" may itself reflect a transformation of Hun society adapting to the demands of imperial rule.) The following year, the brothers formed an alliance with Aetius, commander of Roman forces in Italy and France. No doubt it was this close liaison that nearly twenty years later fuelled rumours of Aetius's double-dealing at the Catalaunian Plains. In 436, Roman forces assisted the Huns in the suppression of the Burgundians (occupying territory just to the west of the Rhine) who, four years earlier, had repelled a Hun invasion and killed its commander, Octar (Rua's brother, and the father of Bleda and Attila). Hun forces then assisted the Romans in their on-going campaign to contain the Goths in the Aquitaine. The Goths had taken advantage of the attack on the Burgundians to blockade the prosperous seaport of Narbo (modern Narbonne) eighty miles southeast of Toulouse. The siege was lifted by Huns and Romans, under the command of Aetius's deputy, Litorius. The hungry citizens of Narbo cheered the Hun horseman who each carried a sack of grain. The allied army continued the offensive and in 439 attacked Toulouse. Before the city walls, Litorius agreed to consult soothsayers, the last time in the history of the empire that a Roman general would countenance non-Christian rites before a battle. The

---

[8] Invasion of 422: Marc. Com. 422.3; Priscus, fr. 2. Invasion of 434: Theodoret, *Church History*, 5.36.4; Socrates Scholasticus, 7.43. The sequence and dating of the Hun attacks in the 420s and 430s are uncertain. I follow the elegant solution to a number of difficult problems proposed by Constantin Zuckerman, "L'empire d'Orient et les Huns: Notes sur Priscus," *Travaux et Mémoires du Centre de recherches d'hist. et civil. byzantines* 12 (1994) 159–182, here 159–163. For a radically different reconstruction, see Brian Croke, "Evidence for the Hun Invasion of Thrace in AD 422," *Greek, Roman, and Byzantine Studies* 18 (1977) 347–367. This revised order of events leads to a somewhat different understanding of the relationship between Huns and Romans (and the strategic connections with France and North Africa) to that advanced, for example, in Thompson, *The Huns*, 69–86; Maenchen-Helfen, *World of the Huns*, 76–94. For the Vandals in North Africa, see, succinctly, Averil Cameron, "Vandal and Byzantine Africa," in *The Cambridge Ancient History*, vol. 14: *Late Antiquity: Empire and Successors, A.D. 425–600*, ed. Averil Cameron, Bryan Ward-Perkins, and Michael Whitby (Cambridge, 2000) 552–569, here 553–559.

Huns predicted the outcome of significant events by scapulimancy, a ritual in which the carefully cleaned shoulder blades of a sacrificed animal are exposed to fire. (The pattern of cracks and fissures in the bone, caused by the heat, is then interpreted by a soothsayer.) But – to the undisguised joy of Christian historians, who found themselves in the unusual position of backing Goths against Romans – Litorius's decision to join battle was a poor one. A hard-fought encounter turned when he was captured; the Huns and Romans were routed; a few days later, Litorius was executed.[9]

The defeat of the Huns before Toulouse may have been an important factor in pushing Attila and Bleda to agree a non-aggression pact with the eastern imperial government. The settlement reached between Roman and Hun negotiators in winter 439 at Margum, a commercial town at the confluence of the Danube and Morava Rivers, stipulated the deportation of any Hun refugees who crossed the frontier, confirmed trading rights between the two states, and required the Romans to make an annual payment of seven hundred pounds of gold directly to Attila and Bleda. Theodosius and his advisers risked that the treaty would hold. North Africa was still their principal concern. In the same year (in October 439), the Vandals captured Carthage and gained access to one of the finest harbours in the western Mediterranean. The following year, a Vandal armada set sail for Sicily. Theodosius countered with an expeditionary force which sailed from Constantinople in spring 441 manned by units released from the defence of the Danube frontier. This was a careful decision that balanced the danger of a Hun incursion (now hopefully mitigated by an agreement with their new leaders) against Vandal aggression, which threatened to disrupt Mediterranean trade, the security of Rome, and (along the North African coast) the grain shipments from Egypt to Constantinople. It was also a miscalculation. Again, there is no coherent narrative account: a scatter of laconic and contradictory notices – often preserved only in much later Byzantine chronicles – and the surviving fragments of a *History* (focused on the 430s and 440s) by Priscus of Panium, a teacher of

---

[9] There is no straightforward account of the campaigns of the 430s; only a series of scattered and often frustratingly brief notices in the chronicles. On the Burgundians: *Gallic Chronicle of 452*, 118; Hydatius, 102; Prosper, 1322. On Litorius before Narbonne and Toulouse: Hyd. 101 and 108; and Prosp. 1324 and 1335. See too Thompson, *The Huns*, 72–79; Maenchen-Helfen, *World of the Huns*, 95–107; Kelly, *End of Empire*, 111–116; Zecchini, *Aezio*, 211–222. On scapulimancy, see Jord. *Get.* 196, with Maenchen-Helfen, *World of the Huns*, 269–270.

Greek rhetoric in Constantinople writing in the second half of the fifth century.

The Hun offensive began with the capture of the fortified trading post of Constantia (across the Danube from Margum) and – with the brusque dismissal of Roman attempts to negotiate alleged breaches of the treaty – continued down the Morava River valley, sacking Naissus (the birthplace of the emperor Constantine) and Serdica. The Hun advance was only halted by the recall of the Roman expeditionary force from Sicily. On the army's return in spring 442, the Huns retreated in good order back beyond the Danube. The cycle of Hun threat and Roman countermove was repeated at the end of 446. Attila, now sole leader of the Huns (Bleda is alleged to have been assassinated the previous year), sent envoys to Constantinople to demand the return of refugees and back-payment of the seven hundred pounds of gold a year agreed at Margum in 439. Theodosius refused. It was a reasonable response: there were no pressing military commitments elsewhere in the empire to deplete troop strength in the Balkans; the Danube defences had recently been reviewed and strengthened. Nor did Attila negotiate. The Huns quickly crossed the frontier and again advanced along the line of the Morava River.

Whatever the strategic balance of advantage, it was critically altered in the early morning of 26 January 447, when a severe earthquake shook Constantinople damaging or demolishing part of its walls. (The "Theodosian Walls" – named after the boy-emperor who had funded their completion in the early fifth century – made Constantinople one of the best protected cities in the Roman Empire.) The weakening of the city's defences forced a change in Roman tactics. Rather than risk one decisive encounter, the army was divided into three mobile units covering all possible land routes to the capital. As in 441–442, Roman historians, as if too shocked to offer more than a mere outline of the Huns' success in "plundering no fewer than seventy cities," again record only a handful of places attacked. Roman troop deployment failed to halt the Hun advance, but it did slow it down long enough for the imperial capital's defences to be repaired by gangs that worked day and night. The inscription on a greyish marble slab which celebrated "the triumphant building of these walls in less than two months" is still visible by the Mevlevihane Gate in Istanbul – where substantial stretches of the Theodosian Walls still stand.

Attila and the Huns never saw Constantinople. It was not worth risking a long siege or facing the problems of provisioning a stationary army in a region ruined by invasion and earthquake, and threatened by the outbreak of disease. Nor could the imperial capital be blockaded effectively without a fleet. The Huns swung north, sacking Marcianople (near the Black Sea) and turning west along the Danube. At the Utus River (about 150 miles west of Marcianople) Roman forces blocked the Huns' homeward march. No detailed account of the battle survives. The Romans were eventually defeated, but only after a long engagement with heavy casualties on both sides. Certainly, it was no easy Hun victory. Peace terms were agreed. Central to Attila's demands, as on every occasion in the previous decade, was the return of refugees and continued annual payments of gold: this time (according to Priscus) set at twenty-one hundred pounds a year with an additional six thousand to cover arrears. Attila also demanded the evacuation of a strip of Roman territory along the Danube, three hundred miles long and at its maximum extent five days' journey wide. In some places, the frontier was pushed back 120 miles. This depopulated buffer zone protected the Huns from a surprise attack and deprived the Romans of the natural defensive advantages of the Danube.[10]

The Huns did not attack the Balkans again. Perhaps Attila was unwilling to risk engaging the Roman army at full strength; perhaps he was satisfied with the scale of Roman payments; perhaps he recognised the low returns from raiding recently pillaged territory; perhaps he was unwilling to test the new régime in Constantinople under the emperor Marcian (proclaimed in mid-450 following Theodosius's unexpected death). In 451, the Huns invaded France, an expedition that ended with the stalemate at the Catalaunian Plains. In 452 – less than twelve months later – they invaded Italy, sacking Aquileia (sixty miles east of modern Venice) then moving down the Po valley to take Pavia and Milan. In late summer, near the River Mincio outside Mantua, Attila

[10] The framework of this reconstruction is Prisc. fr. 2 (treaty of Margum, 439), 6 (Constantia and Naissus), 9.3 (treaty of 447), 11.1 (evacuation of territory); Marc. Com. 441.3, 447.5 (Utus River); Theophanes 5942 (further discussed in Zuckerman, "L'empire d'Orient," 164–168); Maenchen-Helfen, *World of the Huns*, 112–116; and Kelly, *End of Empire*, 116–141 and 309–311. For alternative reconstructions, see Brian Croke, "Anatolius and Nomus: Envoys to Attila," *Byzantinoslavica* 42 (1981) 159–170; and Croke, "The Context and Date of Priscus Fragment 6," *Classical Philology* 78 (1983) 297–308; Thompson, *The Huns*, 86–103; Heather, *Fall of the Roman Empire*, 300–312. On the earthquake, see Marcellin. 447.1, Malalas, 14.22, *Chronicon Paschale* 450, along with Brian Croke, "Two Byzantine Earthquakes and Their Liturgical Commemoration," *Byzantion* 51 (1981) 122–147. See Bruno Meyer-Plath and Alfons Schneider, *Die Landmauer von Konstantinopel* (Berlin, 1943) 133, no. 35, for the inscription by the Mevlevihane Gate.

received a delegation headed by Pope Leo I. Regrettably, no eyewitness report survives. Later tradition (brilliantly captured in one of the frescoes painted by Raphael between 1512 and 1514 for the papal apartments in the Vatican) imagined a fearful Attila cowed by Leo's magnificence and the miraculous appearance of Saints Peter and Paul, who hovered above the pope's head brandishing swords. In deciding to retreat, Attila must also have taken into account the more immediately practical problems of provisioning the Hun army: harvests in many parts of Italy failed in 451 and again in 452, and in some rural districts a malarial epidemic had broken out. He may also have been aware of a hardening in policy in Constantinople. The emperor Marcian had stopped the payment of gold after the Hun retreat from France and in 452 (with the Hun army in Italy) led a successful small-scale expedition across the Danube: the first and only occasion that Roman forces fought Huns outside the empire.[11]

Marcian's provocative tactics were never tested. At the beginning of 453, Attila decided to take another wife. After the wedding, he feasted late into the night. The next morning he did not appear; his bodyguard found his new wife weeping over her husband's lifeless body. There was no wound. According to Jordanes (who noted that he had read the account in Priscus), it seemed that Attila had collapsed drunk in bed and haemorrhaged through the nose. The blood had drained into his throat, and he had choked to death in his sleep. Not all believed that Attila the Hun had died of a nosebleed. Some suspected his new wife of murder. Others (continuing an insistent theme) attributed the assassination to plotting by the Roman general Aetius. Certainly, Attila was the key to the stability of the Hun Empire. It did not long survive his death. The bitter rivalry amongst his three sons significantly weakened Hun dominance in northern Europe. In 454, on the banks of the Nedao (an unidentified river probably in modern Slovenia), the Huns were overwhelmed by a new confederation of peoples once part of their empire. Within twenty years (and less than a century after their appearance west of the Black Sea) the Huns ceased to be a major power on either side of the Rhine-Danube.[12]

[11] Aquileia: Jord. *Get.* 219–221; Procopius, *Vandal Wars*, 3.4.30–35; Leo and Attila: Prosp. 1367; epidemic: Hyd. 146; see too Maenchen-Helfen, *World of the Huns*, 129–142; Thompson, *The Huns*, 157–163; Kelly, *End of Empire*, 256–264. On Marcian's military activity, see Richard Burgess, "A New Reading for Hydatius' *Chronicle* 177 and the Defeat of the Huns in Italy," *Phoenix* 42 (1988) 357–363.

[12] Attila's death: Jord. *Get.* 254; Theophanes, 5946 (an accident); Marc. Com. 454.1 (Ildico or an accident); Malalas 14.10 (Ildico or an accident or Aetius's bribery). On

For some, the history of the Huns as briefly sketched out above might be rather disappointing. It is not an undiluted tale of carnage and crushing victory. The best case for the impact of the Huns on the Roman Empire is that Hun pressure on the fringes of Europe – well before Attila – was directly responsible for pushing the Goths across the Danube (both before and after the battle of Adrianople in 376) and for the displacement of Vandals, Goths (including those led by Radagaisus), and others across the Rhine between 405 and 408. The causal chain is not easily established. Indeed, it is difficult to reconcile, on the one hand, a rightly judged rejection of a mass invasion (a *Hunnensturm*), and on the other hand, an insistence that even so the impact of the Huns was the root cause of the movements of Goths and Vandals into the Roman Empire. One important concern is that as late as the 390s the bulk of the Huns was still well to the east of the Danube, probably around the Volga and Don. It is also difficult to demonstrate a substantial Hun presence west of the Carpathians – that is, on the Great Hungarian Plain – until after the Rhine crossings, and not securely until the 420s. Certainly, there was not yet the degree of control over strategy, the unity of purpose, and the consolidation of resources more clearly evident under Bleda and Attila in the 430s and 440s. For Peter Heather, "The Huns did not have to come west themselves to cause convulsions in more distant lands by indirect displacement." No doubt the (even distant) presence of the Huns was a factor in the movement of Goths and Vandals across the Danube and Rhine frontiers. But cause and effect seem significantly more geographically and chronologically attenuated than a claim for the central importance of the Huns' demands.[13]

In their dealings with the Roman Empire, the Huns did not embark on an unstoppable craze of slaughter and destruction. Far from it: as recorded by Roman historians, the major Hun incursions into

---

the collapse of the Hun Empire, see Thompson, *Huns*, 167–175; Maenchen-Helfen, *World of the Huns*, 144–168, Heather, *Fall of the Roman Empire*, 351–384; Heather, *The Goths*, 124–129; Peter Heather, *Empires and Barbarians: Migration, Development and the Birth of Europe* (London, 2009) 207–265.

[13] The case is most fully argued in Heather, "The Huns and the End of the Roman Empire," esp. 4–21 (quoting 9), and reiterated in Heather, *The Goths*, 98–109; Heather, *Fall of the Roman Empire*, 146–154 and 202–205. The alternative position (itself something of an overclaim in seeking to deny any connection with the Huns in the case of the Rhine crossings) is set out in Walter Goffart, *Barbarian Tides: The Migration Age and the Later Roman Empire* (Philadelphia, 2006) 73–118. For discussion of a range of possible causes behind the Danube crossings in the 370s, see Kulikowski, *Gothic Wars*, 123–128; and Halsall, *Barbarian Migrations*, 170–175.

the Balkans – and no doubt these should be seen against a background of frequent small-scale sorties – were remarkably risk-sensitive. In 408, Uldin's senior commanders were induced to withdraw; in 422, the recall (or threatened recall) of Roman troops from Persia provoked retreat; in 434, Rua's sudden death caused the Hun advance to be abandoned; in 441–442, the return of Theodosius's Sicilian expedition led to Attila's march back up the Morava River valley. The most serious attack in 447 was greatly advantaged by a severe earthquake that weakened Constantinople's defences and resulted in a (prudent) tripartite division of Roman forces. In the end, the imperial capital was secured and the Huns on their homeward march were forced into a difficult and costly engagement at the Utus River. In France, in 439, Huns (and their Roman allies) were defeated at Toulouse by Goths; in 451, the Huns withdrew, as did the Romans (and their Gothic allies), after one day of bruising combat on the Catalaunian Plains. In Italy, in 452, a shortage of supplies, the outbreak of disease, and pressure from Roman attacks across the Danube led to withdrawal.

This is by no means a catalogue of military compromise. Rather, given the Huns' limited war aims – plunder rather than conquest or settlement – this rhythm of raid and retreat was strikingly successful. The key was high mobility, as the moves from the Balkans to France to Italy over six campaign seasons (447–452) demonstrate, and a shrewd sense of when to attack and when to withdraw. The Hun leadership was quick to exploit Roman commitments elsewhere in the empire: in 422, against Persia; in 434 and 441–442, against Vandal expansion in North Africa. It also took good advantage of fragile political situations: in 408, the accession of Theodosius II; in 451, the delay in concluding an alliance between Romans and Goths after an uneasy (at best) relationship in the previous twenty years; in 452, the difficulty (never in the end tested) faced by the Roman imperial government in Italy in getting the Goths under Thorismud to cross the Alps. Equally, Hun commanders were not prepared to place their forces in difficult situations: they withdrew when faced with the possibility of disease, long supply lines, or a lengthy siege.

The Huns' great strength was as swift-moving raiders. They relied on a combination of rapid mobility (in attack and retreat) and deadly firepower. Hun warriors were able to shoot arrows repeatedly and accurately from horseback. They used a composite short bow about five feet long, its wooden core backed by sinews and bellied with horn; bone strips stiffened both the grip and the extremities (the "ears").

That combination of materials, the back resistant to stretch, the belly to compression, produced a powerful weapon.[14] But these advantages were significantly reduced when the Huns' operated as a more conventional fighting force – that is, more like Romans or Goths. In fixed positions, the Huns deployed conventional forms of siege warfare (perhaps learned from Roman prisoners of war).[15] Most striking, is the lack of Hun success in pitched battle: they were defeated before Toulouse in 439; they had a close and hard-fought victory at the Utus River; they managed only a stalemate at the Catalaunian Plains; after Attila's death, they were routed at the Nedao River.

These repeated failures underline the strategic sense of one of Attila's key tactics: the avoidance, as far as possible, of any large-scale engagement with the Roman army. In Jordanes' judgement, "Beneath his great savagery, Attila was a subtle man, and fought with diplomacy before he went to war."[16] Attila was also prepared to negotiate not to go to war. That again emphasises that Hun military aims were not the permanent acquisition of Roman territory or settlement within the empire. Rather (as repeatedly registered above) it was a matter of deciding on a portfolio of risks and opportunities – on both sides. In 447, after the most serious of the Hun incursions into the Balkans, the Roman government agreed to pay Attila twenty-one hundred pounds of gold a year. Some contemporaries (such as Priscus of Panium) regarded this willingness to pay rather than fight as a sign of an underlying moral weakness in Theodosius's approach to government.[17] To be sure, twenty-one hundred pounds of gold is a large amount; but to give a sense of scale, it is worth noting that (at least according to one early fifth-century historian) aristocratic families in Rome, who had accumulated property over generations, might reckon on an annual income of one thousand to fifteen hundred pounds of gold; and the very wealthiest, up to four thousand. It is also important to factor in the expense of war: in 468, Emperor Leo (Marcian's successor) sent a task force to North Africa in another attempt to dislodge the Vandals. The cost of the campaign was

---

[14] Maenchen-Helfen, *World of the Huns*, 201–258; Thompson, *The Huns*, 58–60; Bodo Anke, *Studien zur reiternomadischen Kultur des 4. bis 5. Jahrhunderts*, 2 vols. (Weissbach, 1988) 1: 55–65; Edward N. Luttwak, *The Grand Strategy of the Byzantine Empire* (Cambridge, Mass., 2009) 22–36.

[15] Michael Whitby, "The Army *c.* 420–602," in *CAH* 14: 708–709.

[16] Jord. *Get.* 186; Whitby, "The Army," 706–708.

[17] Prisc. fr. 9.3.

estimated at one hundred thousand pounds of gold – and it was a complete failure.[18] In this context, given the competing strategic demands of the 430s and 440s, Theodosius's foreign policy made good sense. He attempted to ensure the integrity of the northern frontier and the safety of the imperial capital while seeking to hold off a stable, if hostile, state beyond the Danube. Resource rich, the eastern Roman Empire purchased the opportunities it needed to allow its armies to counter security threats elsewhere; threats which could only be dealt with by armed force. In many ways it was easier for the Roman government to deal with enemies that wanted plunder rather than land. Indeed, one, perhaps ironic, advantage of the Huns was that (unlike the Goths in France, or the Vandals in Africa) they were willing to be bought off – at least until a shift in the balance of risk and opportunity.

This sense of a more complex relationship between Romans and Huns is strengthened by Priscus of Panium. The surviving fragments of Priscus's history offer a reasonably coherent account of a Roman embassy that met with Attila in summer 449 at his main residence on the Great Hungarian Plain. Most remarkably, this is a fascinating eye-witness account both of a diplomatic mission beyond the Danube and of a failed scheme – allegedly initiated by one of Theodosius's closest advisers – to have Attila murdered by his own bodyguard. Perhaps what is most striking about Priscus's narrative is its (self-conscious) concern to blur the boundaries between the "Roman" and the "barbarian" worlds. Attila is not shockingly ugly (short stature, small eyes, sparse beard flecked with grey, flattened nose, dark complexion); his palace compound comprised an orderly set of buildings, including a stone bathhouse; Attila's wife was prettily dressed, with a liking for expensive jewellery; royal feasts had their own recognisable protocols, and the well-cooked food was served on silver platters; Attila's conversation (particularly once he became aware of the assassination plot) was shrewd and

---

[18] Senatorial wealth is helpfully estimated in A. H. M. Jones, *The Later Roman Empire, 284–602: A Social, Economic, and Administrative Survey*, 3 vols. (Oxford, 1964) 2: 554–557 and 782–784; the figures quoted are from Olympiodorus, 41.2, with discussion of these calculations in Chris Wickham, *Framing the Early Middle Ages: Europe and the Mediterranean, 400–800* (Oxford, 2005) 162–163; and (on Leo's expedition) John the Lydian, *On the Magistracies*, 3.43, with further discussion on the costs of war in Doug Lee, *War in Late Antiquity: A Social History* (London, 2007) 105–106. On the relative cost of subsidies, see Roger Blockley, "Subsidies and Diplomacy: Rome and Persia in Late Antiquity," *Phoenix* 39 (1985) 62–74; Michael Hendy, *Studies in the Byzantine Monetary Economy c. 300–1450* (Cambridge, 1985) 254–264; and especially Lee, *War*, 119–122.

not without subtlety. Certainly – and Priscus was firm on this point – nothing he saw north of the Danube came close to the sophistication of Roman culture and the magnificence of its cities. But equally there was little to support a set of overdrawn contrasts between good and evil, civilisation and barbarism, virtue and tyranny.[19]

To be sure, Priscus was no apologist for Attila. In offering a more nuanced account of the Huns, he did not seek to excuse the brutality of their incursions into the empire. Near the beginning of their journey, the Roman party had made camp for one night at the now abandoned city of Naissus (on the edge of the buffer zone stipulated by Attila as part of the peace settlement in 447). Near the walls – shattered by battering rams in the Hun campaign of 441–442 – Priscus observed the riverbank still littered with the bleached bones of the slain.[20] That desolate and melancholy picture could be repeated. Neither Naissus or Marcianople, near the Black Sea, were rebuilt for a century; tradition holds that refugees from Aquileia moved along the coast to a sheltered lagoon and founded Venice.[21] In both East and West, the Huns burned undefended farms and villages to the ground and sacked a long list of cities, some strongly fortified. But it does not need the Huns to underline the cruelty of warfare. If their ruthlessness is not to be diminished, it must be put in context. And it requires a fine and difficult judgement to determine that a campaign with the aim of plunder is a worse, or a more morally indefensible, form of warfare than a campaign with the aim of conquest and permanent subjugation. For all the repeated attacks on the Balkans, and those in France and Italy (where, in many cases, it is more difficult to distinguish raiding from destruction) the Huns never conquered Roman territory. The political and economic damage inflicted by the Huns' attacks on the Roman Empire was significantly less than the damage that followed the permanent settlement of the Goths in the Aquitaine, or the Vandal invasion of North Africa. Nor did the Huns ever inflict a major defeat on a Roman field army. From that point of view, the Huns were significantly less successful than the

---

[19] Prisc. frs. 11–15; on the historian and his text, see Roger Blockley, *The Fragmentary Classicising Historians of the Later Roman Empire: Eunapius, Olympiodorus, Priscus and Malchus*, 2 vols. (Liverpool, 1981) 1: 48–70; Barry Baldwin, "Priscus of Panium," *Byzantion* 50 (1980) 18–61; Michael Maas, "Fugitives and Ethnography in Priscus of Panium," *Byzantine and Modern Greek Studies* 19 (1995) 146–160; for modern treatments of Priscus's embassy to Attila, see Thompson, *The Huns*, 108–136; Kelly, *End of Empire*, 151–214.

[20] Prisc. fr. 11.2.

[21] Constantine Porphyrogenitus, *On Imperial Government*, 28.

Vandals or the Goths, who at Adrianople in 376 were responsible for one of the greatest military disasters in the history of the Roman Empire.

Certainly, the persistence of the Huns' fiercesome reputation far outstrips their impact. They have always proved easy targets for Christian moralists (ancient and modern) and moralising historians (ancient and modern). Unlike the Vandals or the Goths, they were not Christian. Writing in the seventh century, the philosopher and theologian Isidore of Seville argued that Attila's attacks were part of God's plan for the correction of Christendom. The Huns were the "rod of divine anger" sent to scourge the unrepentant and "force them to turn away from the desires and errors of the age."[22] The Huns must always be seen through the eyes of others. Only a few words of the Hun language survive, no Hun literature, very little unambiguous material evidence, no explanation or justification of their actions or policies except by their enemies. The Huns' origin as nomads marks them out as a disturbing and alien presence in a settled Mediterranean world. As complete outsiders, and without a voice of their own, the Huns can always be persuasively imagined as the ultimate threat to the (self-proclaimed) virtues of civilisation.

---

[22] Isidore of Seville, *History of the Goths, Vandals, and Sueves*, 29. The biblical reference is to the *flagellum iundans* (the "overwhelming whip") of Isa. 28:15 and 18.

12: THE HUNS AND BARBARIAN EUROPE

Peter J. Heather

The Huns' European tour was brief but explosive. They first appeared northeast of the Black Sea in the 370s, and are last explicitly recorded as independent actors in the late 460s. The years in between saw the rise and fall of the most powerful political unit that non-Mediterranean Europe had ever seen, capable at its apogee of mounting campaigns from Constantinople to Paris. To understand the effects of this Hunnic century upon barbarian Europe, it is necessary to start from the broader patterns of development unfolding within it on the eve of the Huns' appearance.

Around 350, Barbarian Europe stretched from the east bank of the Rhine to the western slopes of the Urals, and from north of the Danube to the Arctic Circle. Its boundaries had been set by the limits of Roman expansion in the centuries either side of the birth of Christ, although there had been some fluctuations since (especially Rome's acquisition and loss of Transylvanian Dacia). Since the early nineteenth century, it has been traditional to attempt to categorise the population of this vast expanse of territory primarily according to its linguistic affiliations (Germanic, Iranian, Balto-Slav, Finno-Ugrian, etc.). But the lack of contemporary information means that the process always involved much retrojective guesswork. It also imposes clear boundaries onto worlds where multilingualism or creolisation may have been normal, and where even any discernible linguistic affiliation may reflect only that of a politically dominant elite.[1]

---

[1] These revisionist points are now broadly accepted; the attempt to impose clear distinctions on the past reflected the interests of eighteenth- and nineteenth-century German and Slavic nationalists. A good introduction (among many possibilities) is

A more visible and potentially more useful set of distinctions – given the fact that functioning political units sometimes formed across linguistic divides – has been provided by the efforts of many generations of archaeologists, especially, but not only, since the end of World War II. This work was often motivated by a desire to give extra substance to the old arguments about linguistic affiliation, but its cumulative effect has been to demonstrate something much more tangible about barbarian Europe in the first millennium. At the moment of Roman conquest, it actually fell into three broad east-west zones.[2] The first – broadly La Tène Europe – extended from the Atlantic to an area just east of Rhine and, in parts at least, north of the Danube; the second covered central Europe and southern Scandinavia as far east as the Vistula; and the third encompassed everything further to the north and east (map 1). If you analyse these zones in terms of such key indicators of what we would now label "development" as population density, settlement size and durability, extent of agricultural technology, complexity of material culture (pottery, jewellery, weaponry, etc.), evidence for economic exchange, and the scale and durability of political structures, the pattern is consistent. Under all these headings, La Tène Europe comes out as much more developed than the central zone, while northern and eastern Europe was operating at a much lower level still.[3]

By around 350 CE, there had already been important changes. Most of La Tène Europe had been long since swallowed up by Roman imperial expansion. The central zone, likewise, was now home to political units (often confederative in nature) of greater size and military power: the products of important developments in both agricultural technique and economic exchange, larger populations and settlements, and even some significant cultural transformations, such as the first appearance within these lands of Christianity and literacy. It had also significantly increased its geographical range as a result of an important expansion of its elites' domination into lands north of the Black Sea in the third century. Patterns of life in the third zone, however, as of yet showed almost no signs of change at all. Population groups from these regions do not figure in the narratives of military and diplomatic relations between Rome and its European peripheries, and, archaeologically, the

---

Patrick J. Geary, *The Myth of Nations: The Medieval Origins of Europe* (Princeton, 2002).

[2] Leaving aside the arctic North, where conventional agriculture was impossible.

[3] For more detailed analysis, with full bibliography, see Peter J. Heather, *Empires and Barbarians: The Fall of Rome and the Birth of Europe* (London, 2009) chap. 1.

fourth-century picture looks little different from the period at the birth of Christ. Whereas the second, central European zone of barbarian Europe had been ushered along a relatively intense process of development, probably as a result of its relations with the Roman state, outer Europe remained largely untouched.[4]

The broad outlines of what unfolded within barbarian Europe over the next hundred and fifty years after about 350 has also become clear. By 500 CE, the patterns of material culture characteristic of the central zone in the late Roman period had disappeared, or were fast disappearing, from all of Europe not only east and south of the Carpathians, but also in areas south of the Baltic and east of the Elbe. This astounding curtailment ruptured a process of continuous evolution stretching back over many centuries. Its overall historical significance shows up in the fact that the kinds of reasonably durable client state structures characteristic of the second zone in the late Roman period ceased to be a feature of the sixth-century, post-Roman landscape across very large parts of central and southeastern Europe. Correspondingly, the material cultural patterns characteristic of the third and least developed zone of old barbarian Europe now began to spread over a much wider area: broadly over all those areas of the old central zone where late Roman patterns were fast disappearing. And here, too, there is a clear intersection between history and archaeology. Coincident in date and geographical extent with the zone-three expansion discernible in the archaeological evidence, population groups at least dominated by Slavic-speakers (whose origins certainly lay somewhere within the old third zone) start to appear – for the first time – in regions bordering the Roman world (map 1).[5]

The key question all this poses is whether the clear chronological coincidence between the rise and fall of the Huns and this massive reconfiguration of barbarian Europe extends into a direct causal relationship. Different answers can be given to this question, but all depend upon three interrelated variables. First, the sometimes problematic and

---

[4] For more detailed discussion and full bibliography, see Heather, *Empires and Barbarians*, chap. 2.

[5] The pioneer here was the great Polish archaeologist Kasimierz Godłowski. See, e.g., "Das Aufhören der Germanischen Kulturen an der Mittleren Donau und das Problem des Vordringens der Slawen," in *Die Völker an der mittleren und unteren Donau im fünften und sechsten Jahrhundert*, ed. Herwig Wolfram and Falko Daim, Denkschriften der Österreichischen Akademie der Wissenschaften, phil.-hist. Kl. 145 (Vienna, 1980) 225–232. Heather, *Empires and Barbarians*, chaps. 7–8, provides more detail and full bibliography.

generally scant nature of the available source material poses interesting methodological dilemmas at certain key moments of historical reconstruction. Second and third, Hunnic history also involves taking a view on two of the most contentious issues in late antique historiography: migration and barbarian group identity. This chapter will argue the case for one particular vision of the Huns' impact, but will attempt to serve a broader purpose by explicitly identifying the four particular contexts where key intellectual choices have to be made.

376 AND AFTERWARDS

The Huns' first impact upon barbarian Europe is one dimension of the subject whose outlines, at least, are not seriously disputable, since it is documented in too wide a range of contemporary sources. In very broad terms, the intrusion of Hunnic military power overturned a Goth-dominated political order which had been established north of the Black Sea for several political generations. In the mid-370s, three major Gothic groupings – two of Tervingi and one of Greuthungi – were displaced by the direct and indirect effects of Hunnic attack. After periods of attempted resistance, all three appeared on the Lower Danube Roman frontier probably early in 376, with asylum in mind. Certainly the Tervingi and probably also the Greuthungi had also split into a number of constituent sub-groups as they decided how to respond to the emergent Hunnic power. Ammianus Marcellinus explicitly records that the split among the Tervingi was a direct result of Hunnic assault, with Alavivus and Fritigern using the issue to overthrow Athanaric. It is extremely unlikely that it can be methodologically correct, as has sometimes been argued, to date the split prior to the Huns' arrival on the basis of the non-contemporary and relatively ill-informed account of the mid-fifth century church historian, Socrates.[6]

[6] This is the first of the four key intellectual choices to be made. The main source is Ammianus Marcellinus (31.1–4), with independent confirmation of the main points in Eunapius of Sardis, frs. 41–49 (and largely following him, Zosimus, 4.20.3ff.); Ambrose, *Commentary on the Gospel according to St. Luke* 10.10; Socrates Scholasticus, *Ecclesiastical History*, 4.34; Sozomen Scholasticus, *Ecclesiastical History*, 6.37. Further discussion and full bibliography: Heather, *Empires and Barbarians*, 151–173. Noel E. Lenski, "The Gothic Civil War and the Date of the Gothic Conversion," *Greek Roman and Byzantine Studies* 36 (1995) 51–87, revived the case for dating the Tervingi split according to the evidence of Socrates rather than Ammianus, and larger hypotheses downplaying the importance of Hunnic attacks on the Tervingi have been built on the back of it: e.g., Guy Halsall, *Barbarian Migrations and the Roman*

Our evidence is less explicit on the size and nature of the groups involved in the action. This is a besetting problem in understanding the rise and fall of Hunnic domination, but, for the 370s, the evidence is again clear enough – just about – to have precluded major scholarly dispute in one important area. The sources are unanimous and explicit that the Gothic groups that came to the Danube in 376 were composed of individuals of all ages and both genders. They also insist that the Goths were extremely numerous, but what order of magnitude do we need to envisage? The contemporary historian Eunapius provides an overall figure of 200,000 individuals. This is not impossible, but Eunapius was less well-informed than Ammianus (he does not distinguish between Tervingi and Greuthungi), the figure is beautifully round, and how might it have been derived? The Tervingi of Alavivus and Fritigern were ferried across the river with Roman assistance, so that they might have been counted, but the Greuthungi crossed independently.[7] A more reliable minimum indication of scale is provided by the fact that these two Gothic groups together, plus some Hunnic and Alanic reinforcements, were able to destroy two-thirds of the eastern empire's elite field army at Adrianople in August 378. Competing estimates for the size of Valens's force range between fifteen and thirty thousand men, and the decisive outcome of the battle was certainly a fluke. Nonetheless, this strongly suggests that, at Adrianople, the Goths must have disposed of at least fifteen to twenty thousand warriors. And a mixed group that could field about twenty thousand warriors would have numbered, in total, somewhere between fifty and a hundred thousand individuals.[8]

West, 376–568 (Cambridge, 2007) chap. 6. There is a remote possibility that Socrates could be correct, but it is *much* more likely – given Ammianus's infinitely greater overall knowledge of Gotho-Roman affairs (Socrates had never heard of Alavivus, for instance) – that the church historian is merely confused. On the broader intellectual reasons behind this otherwise inexplicable recent preference for Socrates' account, see note 19.

[7] Eunapius, fr. 42: accepted by Noel E. Lenski, *Failure of Empire: Valens and the Roman State in the Fourth Century AD* (Berkeley, 2002) 354–355.

[8] For fuller discussion and bibliographical references, see Heather, *Empires and Barbarians,*151–155. No one is quite sure what multiplier to use for barbarian non-combatants (guesses usually range between four and five) and the size of Valens's army is much contested, but there is nonetheless no serious discord in the secondary literature. Even those who would generally downplay the significance of barbarian migration in the late Roman period accept that a minimum of several tens of thousands of people were on the move in a relatively compact mass: see, e.g., Halsall, *Barbarian Migrations,* chap. 6, or Michael Kulikowski, *Rome's Gothic Wars* (Cambridge, 2007) 123ff.

Traditional accounts of these events tended to suppose that the Huns involved in the action at this stage were similar to those of the Goths: large, mixed groups – a united "people" in the old sense of the word – sweeping across the northern Pontus to occupy everything east of the Carpathians. In fact, the contemporary evidence paints a consistent picture that the disruption of the 370s was caused by a series of independent Hunnic warbands, rather than by a "people" conducting a co-ordinated campaign of conquest. Our sources report various Hunnic groups fighting different enemies in different contexts (and as we have seen one group even fought with the Goths – for profit – at Adrianople), and other Goths – apart from the refugees of 376 – remained in control of territories north of the Black Sea into at least the early 390s. There was clearly no outright Hunnic conquest of the northern Pontus in the 370s, and little sign, correspondingly, of major disruption west of the Carpathians. Something, arguably the advanced design of the Huns' bow, had given them sufficient military edge to cause chaos among the established inhabitants of the northern Pontus while operating in quite small groups.[9]

At this point, from our sources' Roman point of view, matters went relatively quiet for a generation. One more Gothic group, led by Odotheus, attempted to cross the lower Danube in the summer of 386, but was heavily defeated, and, although some of its survivors were resettled on Roman soil, this was done on explicitly Roman terms, the force being broken up and dispersed across Asia Minor (not the Balkans) in relatively small units.[10] From a Roman perspective, the main Hun-related barbarian issue became what to do about the great Tervingi-Greuthungi coalition, which had defeated Valens at Adrianople. It has become fashionable recently to attempt to downgrade this problem by arguing, first, that the coherence of the group was not maintained in the peace treaty they negotiated with the emperor Theodosius in 382, and, second, that there was no substantial continuity between Valens's

---

[9] Jordanes, *Getica*, 48.248–249, composed two hundred years after the events, reports that the Goths were conquered by a Hunnic king called Balamber. But this is probably a confused memory of Theoderic the Amal's uncle Valamer: Peter J. Heather, "Cassiodorus and the Rise of the Amals: Genealogy and the Goths under Hun Domination," *Journal of Roman Studies* 79 (1989) 103–128. More contemporary sources indicate that, in the 370s and for some time afterwards, the action was carried forward by independent Hunnic groups, each with its own leadership: Heather, *Barbarians and Romans*, chap. 4 with full refs.

[10] See further Peter J. Heather, "The Anti-Scythian Tirade of Synesius' De Regno," *Phoenix* 42 (1988) 152–172.

killers and the Gothic force that Alaric led in revolt from 395 onwards. But while the sources may be unclear on the *details*, an extensive range of contemporary writers unanimously maintain both that there was a formal agreement in 382, and that its fundamental point (against the norms of established Roman policy) was to maintain a substantial measure of Gothic autonomy. Two independent contemporary witnesses also insist that, in 395, Alaric came to the fore at the head of the Goths of 382 in open revolt, and a continuous history for the settled Goths can be reconstructed without too much difficulty – again from contemporary sources – for the intervening thirteen years. The *onus probandi* thus remains firmly with those who wish to argue that Alaric's initial revolt represents something other than the continuation of a Gothic problem left unresolved by the compromises of 382.[11]

FRONTIER CRISIS ROUND 2

The relative peace on the frontier came to a dramatic end in the first decade of the fifth century with three further major barbarian intrusions onto Roman soil. A force led by Radagaisus invaded Italy in 405–406, to be followed across the Rhine into Gaul by a coalition composed primarily of Vandals, Alans, and Sueves in December 406. Finally, in 408–409 the Hunnic leader Uldin – previously a Roman ally – seized the east Roman fortress of Castra Martis. The sources concentrate almost exclusively upon the effects of these intrusions upon the Roman world, and there is no extant equivalent to Ammianus's clear if concise backstory of the purely barbarian events which preceded and caused the earlier intrusions of the mid-370s.[12] Recent debate has generated

---

[11] This is the second key moment of intellectual choice. See further Heather, *Empires and Barbarians*, 191–196, arguing against the case put forward by Michael Kulikowski, "Nation versus Army: A Necessary Contrast?," in *On Barbarian Identity: Critical Approaches to Ethnicity in the Early Middle Ages*, ed. Andrew Gillett (Turnhout, 2002) 69–84, and Halsall, *Barbarian Migrations*, 189–184. The revisionist case relies heavily on the highly problematic account of Alaric's early career in Zosimus (esp. 5.5.4) where the effects of this sixth-century author's confused attempt to join together his main sources – Eunapius and Olympiodorus of Thebes – are readily apparent; they include confusing Stilicho's separate campaigns against Alaric in 395 and 397, and wiping out a decade of Gothic history between 397 and 407. The potential impact of these problems on Zosimus's credibility is not discussed by Kulikowski or Halsall.

[12] The only remotely detailed accounts of events beyond the frontier are Zos. 5.26.3, which has confused the separate expeditions of Radagaisus and the Rhine crossing, and Gregory of Tours, *Histories*, 2.29, which was written over 150 years afterwards.

agreement, nevertheless, on some key points and brought more clearly into focus the interpretative choices that underlie the remaining points of difference.

Three major points now seem established. First, all three sets of intruders crossed into Roman territory from the Middle Danube region, west of the Carpathian Mountains. Radagaisus's invasion route ran through Noricum, making its point of origin clear, while the Vandals and Sueves had long occupied territories in that region. Second, many of the groups involved in these intrusions were again both very large and substantially mixed in composition. There has been some attempt to argue this time that the action was carried forward mainly by warbands – smaller groups composed almost exclusively of warrior males – but this position has not won more general acceptance, even amongst scholars who would otherwise seek to play down the importance of barbarian invasion in the late Roman period. For while none of the surviving numbers reported for any of these groups gives much cause for confidence, the amount they were able to achieve, against even large-scale Roman counter-attack, strongly indicates that Radagaisus and the Rhine invaders at least could dispose of military forces well into the ten-thousand-plus range. Likewise, while certainly general, such descriptions as our sources give of the participating groups do again firmly indicate that they were mixed in profile.[13] And in fact, to generate military forces of ten thousand plus, they would have needed to be. Zone 2 kings of the later Roman period maintained specialist warrior retinues of only a few hundreds of men; the region's still limited productive capacity could not generate sufficient surplus to support very large numbers of professional soldiery. In this world, larger forces could

[13] John F. Drinkwater, *The Alamanni and Rome, 213–496* (Oxford, 2007) esp. 323–324, and Andy Merrills and Richard Miles, *The Vandals* (Oxford, 2010) chap. 2, both think in terms of warbands, but neither argues a case against the extant evidence (which entirely opposes such a view). Halsall, *Barbarian Migrations*, 206, 211, and Walter A. Goffart, *Barbarian Tides: The Migration Age and the Later Roman Empire* (Philadelphia, 2006) chap. 5, who both otherwise look to downplay the importance of barbarian migration, nonetheless accept in broad terms the reported scale and nature of the action here. The best further confirmation of its massive scale is the size (a) of the forces the Romans had to mobilise against the invaders – according to Zosimus 5.26.4 (by now safely following Olympiodorus alone – Stilicho mobilised thirty regiments – *numeri* – against Radagaisus) and (b) of the manpower losses that subsequent engagements down to ca. 420 CE generated in the west Roman army; these are apparent in the *Notitia Dignitatum*: A. H. M. Jones, *The Later Roman Empire: A Social Economic and Administrative Survey*, 3 vols. (Oxford, 1964) app. 3.

be generated only by mobilising a wider swathe of a ruler's dependent population, many of whom would have their own families, whom they would not be ready to leave behind.[14]

Third, following these large-scale departures from the Middle Danube region, Huns in really large numbers are first documented west of the Carpathians. They were certainly there by 411, when Olympiodorus's embassy encountered not just warband leaders, but the Hunnic main body, controlled by a series of ranked kings. They may even have been there as early as 409, when the west Roman imperial authorities negotiated some large-scale Hunnic military assistance, but that is not certain.[15] But was the second stage of Hunnic intrusion into barbarian Europe – represented by their arrival west of the Carpathians in about 410 CE – cause or effect of the cluster of barbarian intrusions which disturbed Roman frontier peace just a little before, in 405–408?[16]

In the absence of specific information, there is plenty of room for reasonable doubt, but more general considerations suggest that the second stage of Hunnic intrusion was probably cause rather than effect of the second cluster of major barbarian frontier incursions. First, many of the participants in this second cluster – particularly the Goths who followed Radagaisus, and the Alani, who were the largest component in the Rhine crossing – had been living east of the Carpathians before about 370. Their presence in the Middle Danube in the first decade of the fifth century demonstrates that further population displacements must have in fact continued in barbarian Europe during that generation of apparent quiet on the Roman frontier. Then there is the analogy with the 370s. Given the degree of chaos that the arrival just of Hunnic raiding parties on the eastern fringes of barbarian Europe caused at that point, the arrival on the Great Hungarian Plain of the main body of Huns under royal leadership could only have been a powerful stimulus for its inhabitants to consider leaving.[17]

I first offered these thoughts in the mid-1990s, since when other scholars have suggested alternative lines of reasoning to argue that the

---

[14] For fuller discussion Heather, *Empires and Barbarians*, chaps. 3–4.

[15] The three points were first made by Peter J. Heather, "The Huns and the End of the Roman Empire in Western Europe," *English Historical Review* 110 (1995) 4–41. For their acceptance, see, e.g., Goffart, *Barbarian Tides*, chap. 5, and Halsall, *Barbarian Migrations*, 206ff.

[16] The third key choice that needs to be made.

[17] On the aggressive and exploitative nature of the Huns' relations with other groups in their orbit, giving those with an option every reason to move, see below.

arrival of the Huns west of the Carpathians was effect and not cause. In *Barbarian Tides*, Walter Goffart wondered whether Constantinople encouraged the invasions to head off Stilicho's ambitions towards East Illyricum, and suggested that the concessions granted the Goths in 382 would have encouraged other groups to aim for similar advantages. Guy Halsall, alternatively, argued that, from the early 390s – in face of financial constraint and political dislocation – the western empire cut off subsidies to its frontier clients. This Roman policy change generated a political crisis beyond the frontier which manifested itself in the intrusions of 405–408, and in turn created a power vacuum west of the Carpathians, into which the Huns eventually moved.

These are possible arguments, certainly, but not in the end convincing ones. There is no evidence either for Constantinople's having encouraged the invasions (one of which – that of Uldin – fell uninvited on eastern territory in any case) or for the cessation of subsidies. Indeed, if subsidies were the issue, then it was also the "wrong" barbarians who did the invading. Apart from the Sueves, Rome's main frontier clients did not move in 405–408, but stayed put and even, in the case of Franks versus Vandals, fought back hard against the intruders. There is some evidence that the treaty of 382 started to alter barbarian perceptions of Roman imperial power, but, again, this is unlikely to be the full story, since the Rhine invasion occurred even after Stilicho had crushed Radagaisus's expedition with ruthless efficiency. And more generally, neither argument explains why Goths and Alani were present on the Great Hungarian Plain in significant numbers in the first place. Particularly if you apply Ockham's razor and keep the events of the 370s in mind, seeing the Huns' arrival west of the Carpathians as cause rather than effect really is the only proffered explanation currently on offer that satisfactorily accounts for all of the available evidence.[18]

There is one more general historiographical point that is also worth making here. Up to the 1960s (much later in some academies), an extremely simple migration model was massively overused in archaeological explanation. As a mass of excavation data built up in the later nineteenth and early twentieth centuries, it became apparent that particular items of material culture often had distinct regional and chronological distributions. In the nationalist intellectual climate of those times, the conclusion was almost inescapable, based on this observation, that

---

[18] Goffart, *Barbarian Tides*, chap. 5, esp. 75–80 and 94–95; Halsall, *Barbarian Migrations*, 195–212. For more detailed discussion, see Heather, *Empires and Barbarians*, 177–184.

ancient "peoples" each had their own individual material cultures (so-called culture history). And if "peoples" had their own "cultures," this also suggested, whenever you observed a major transformation in an existing regional distribution pattern, that a new "people" must have moved in. Thus "culture history" contained an inherent tendency to explain material cultural change in terms of migration, and migration of a very particular type: the displacement of one "people" by another via a process of mass migration of groups mixed in age and gender, usually accompanied by what we would now call ethnic cleansing (the "invasion hypothesis"). Hugely influential, the model formed a bedrock of archaeological thinking in the first half of the twentieth century, when most of European pre-history was understood as one major invasion following another.

Since the 1960s, however, a huge amount of work has exposed its underlying fallacies. Pre-historic "peoples" (if they existed: a point to which I will return) did not each have their own material cultural repertoires, and material culture can be transformed – even profoundly – for many reasons other than population replacement. "New" or "processual" archaeology – which emerged in the Anglophone world in the 1960s – was particularly interested in how environmental adaption and evolving social structures might generate material cultural transformations; "post-processual" archaeology subsequently turned the spotlight more onto ideology: the impact of evolving human thought. All this is relevant to the Huns because, in a fierce response to the previous stranglehold of the culture history/invasion hypothesis paradigm, many – again particularly Anglophone – archaeologists have, since the 1960s, come to reject any tendency to explain anything in terms of migration. As Halsall's introductory textbook to early medieval cemeteries put it, to avoid migration in explanations of archaeological change "is simply to dispose of an always simplistic and usually groundless supposition in order to enable its replacement with a more subtle interpretation of the period." Note the contrast of "simplistic" and "groundless" (the world dominated by migration) with "more subtle" (anything else). Goffart, too, was highly influenced by this anti-migration zeitgeist in his overall rejection of the importance traditionally ascribed to the Germanic *Völkerwanderungen* as a major agent of change.[19]

---

[19] Amongst many other possibilities, Colin Renfrew and Peter Bahn, *Archaeology: Theories, Methods and Practice*, 5th ed. (London, 2008), offers an excellent introduction to the evolution of archaeological thought. The quotation is from Guy Halsall, *Early Medieval Cemeteries: An Introduction to Burial Archaeology in the Post-Roman*

This strong intellectual association between migration and a more primitive stage in archaeological interpretation is important on two levels. First, it helps explain why there is now such a strong tendency in some late antique scholarship (whatever the evidence might say) to play down the potential importance of migration. Second, and arguably more important in the long run, it has also minimised scholarly engagement with the burgeoning discipline of comparative migration studies, which (also since the 1960s) has entirely transformed understandings of the forms, motivations, and mechanisms of human population displacement. Total population replacement in one fell swoop (the invasion hypothesis) has never been observed in historical time, but other forms of more complex predatory intrusion certainly have (and continue in the world around us). The migration specialists' preferred definition of "mass" migration, for instance, is not total population replacement, but any level of migration which generates observable social stress at either or both ends of a migration flow. The motivations of observable migrants, likewise, turn out usually to comprise an interesting mix of the positive and negative, and you are explaining nothing unless you understand the fields of information and expectation which make movement in a very particular direction (as opposed to staying put, or going elsewhere) a *possible* answer to life's problems in any potential migrant's brain. The rejection of the invasion hypothesis was extremely necessary in its original intellectual context, but taking migration seriously doesn't have to be inherently "simplistic," if the phenomenon is engaged with fully (as, indeed, even some Anglophone archaeologists have begun to do).[20]

There is no good reason, therefore, to shy away from a conclusion that migration played an important role in a given sequence of events just because over-simple migration models were massively misused in the

---

West (Skelmorlie, U.K., 1995) 61. The influence of the archaeologists' rejection of migration upon Goffart's thinking is equally apparent in his *Barbarians and Romans, AD 418–584: The Techniques of Accommodation* (Princeton, 1980) chap. 1.

[20] An excellent introduction to migration studies is provided by the works of Robin Cohen: e.g., *Global Diasporas: An Introduction*, 2nd ed. (Cambridge, 2008); *The Cambridge Survey of World Migration* (Cambridge, 2010). For fuller discussion of the potential contribution of migration studies, see Heather, *Empires and Barbarians*, esp. chaps. 1 and 11, with refs. More measured, recent archaeological approaches to migration include Scott G. Ortman, *Genes, Language, and Culture in Tewa Ethnogenesis, AD 1150–1400* (Tempe, Ariz., 2009); Takeyuki Tsuda and Brenda Baker, eds., *Migration and Disruptions: Unifying Themes in Studies of Ancient and Contemporary Migrations* (forthcoming).

past. The emergence of Hunnic power did not generate total population replacements over large stretches of the European landscape, but there is no pressing reason not to believe what our sources are telling us explicitly in relation to the 370s and implicitly in relation to 405–408. In a process that was highly stressful and extremely dangerous for all concerned, the growth of Hunnic power in two distinct stages led many tens of thousands of individuals from the fringes of the Roman world to take to the road, many of whom eventually took the decision to try to re-establish themselves somewhere within the empire's borders. All told, this represents a huge initial Hunnic impact upon the old central zone of barbarian Europe as it had stood in the mid-fourth century, but there was much more to come.

EMPIRE AND COLLAPSE

From their first appearance, Hunnic groups showed a marked tendency to operate alongside others. Huns and Alans fought with the Goths at Adrianople, and, before their arrival en masse in the Middle Danube, Huns also appear combined with both "Carpo-Dacai" and Sciri.[21] As the Hunnic Empire grew, these confederative tendencies continued apace, until, in the time of Attila, they incorporated a significant cross-section of the population of barbarian Europe. An exhaustive list cannot be compiled, but Attila's Hunnic Empire certainly encompassed two and probably three separate groups of Goths, along with contingents of Gepids, Sarmatians, Heruli, Alans, Rugi, Suevi, and Sciri. In addition, other groups – such as Alamanni, Burgundians, and, perhaps, Thuringians and Lombards – fell under Hunnic influence at least occasionally, and Attila even attempted to interfere in one succession dispute among the Franks. Attaching all these other groups to their train underlay the astonishing military success of Attila and Bleda in the 440s.[22]

---

[21] At Adrianople: Amm. 31.8.4. "Carpo-Dacai": Zos. 4.34.6 (chap. 382); Sciri: Soz. 8.9.8, with *Theodosian Code* 5.6.3.

[22] Gothic groups: one was transferred by the Romans from Pannonia to Thrace in the 420s, while the Amal-led Goths were settled in Pannonia from the 450s: Peter J. Heather, *Goths and Romans, 332–489* (Oxford, 1991) 241–263; more Goths remained under Hunnic dominion in the late 460s: Prisc. fr. 49. The other larger groupings appear in Jordanes's narrative of Hunnic imperial collapse (focussed on the Amal-led Goths: *Get.* 50.259–255.282) or in surviving extracts from the history of Priscus of Panium, but note too the series of smaller migratory population fragments resettled

Generating this confederation again involved population displacement. Of the groups occupying territory west of the Carpathians by the later 450s, only the Gepids, Sarmatians, and Suevi had been there prior to the 370s. Somewhere in the course of empire building, the Huns' other subjects – three separate groups of Goths, along with Alans, Sciri, Heruli, and Rugi had all made their way to the Middle Danube. Because we have no detailed narrative sources, it is unclear how many of these groups initially moved to the Middle Danube independently (as the Goths and Alans involved in the invasions of 405–408 clearly did), and how many were resettled there by the Huns.[23] After Attila's death, likewise, two further generations of conflict – first between the Huns and their subjects, where the Gepids led the way, and then between various groupings of the Huns' now independent former subjects – spawned still more migration. In the mid-460s, the Amal-led Pannonian Goths destroyed the coherence of the Sciri, elements of whose surviving political leadership – notably Odovcar – and perhaps others in larger numbers, fled to Italy. This was at more or less the same moment that the sons of Attila, still with some subject groups attached (including other Goths), attempted to move onto east Roman territory. They were followed down this trajectory by the Amal-led Goths themselves in 473, which left the Gepids, Rugi, Suevi, and Heruli as the main competing powers still established in the Middle Danube. Odovacar subsequently destroyed the kingdom of the Rugi in 487 – many of the survivors moving south to join Theoderic the Amal's gathering Italian expedition – at which point the Heruli in the West and the Gepids in the East were left as the main protagonists. A final twist to the saga came roughly a generation later in 511 when Lombard forces moved south – probably from Bohemia and the Upper Elbe region – to destroy the kingdom of the Heruli. Some Heruli fled north, others south-eastwards into east Roman territory, leaving the Middle Danube divided between Lombard hegemony in the West, and Gepids still in the East.[24]

But what exactly was the scale of actual human displacement into and out of the Middle Danubian region behind this shifting pattern

---

by the Romans close to the Lower Danube frontier: Jord. *Get.* 50.265–256. For a more detailed account, see Heather, *Empires and Barbarians*, chap. 5.

[23] Jordanes, in *Get.* 50.264, claims that the Amal-led Goths at least did so, and the same may have been true of others.

[24] For a more detailed account of these manoeuvres, see Walter Pohl, "Die Gepiden und die Gentes an der mittleren Donau nach dem Zerfall des Attilareiches," in Wolfram and Daim, *Die Völker*, 239–305.

of political domination? Constructing an answer to this question was always difficult, given the sparse nature of the evidence, but it has recently acquired the added excitement of requiring the researcher to take a view on the other great bone of contention in late antique barbarian studies: the nature of non-Roman group identities.[25]

Traditional historiography envisaged that behind each of these labels there lay a "people": a culturally homogeneous, endogamous community maintaining strict boundaries between itself and any neighbours. When such a label moved, therefore, a significant act of migration would always have occurred by definition (it was such "peoples" that populated the old invasion hypothesis). No one now doubts that this was much too simple, and, again since the 1960s, this time under the direct stimulus from the social sciences, old views of ancient (and indeed modern) group identities have been rewritten. Individuals can have more than one potential group identity, and sometimes oscillate between them, often according to which identity currently offers the best life opportunities.[26] One strand of evidence from Attila's Hunnic Empire nicely illustrates such tendencies at work in the fifth century. While on his famous embassy, Priscus encountered an individual who had started life as a Roman merchant, before being enslaved by the Huns. He had subsequently prospered, paying his master for his freedom, to become nothing less than a fully fledged and happily married Hun occupying a position of considerable social status and prosperity. In similar vein, Priscus also encountered an inner elite of functionaries at Attila's court, many with Germanic names and probably also Germanic origins. And since the Huns themselves seem to have adopted the prevailing material cultural patterns of Rome's inner ring of largely Germanic-speaking clients, abandoning their own previous repertoire, then it has seemed to some scholars that there were no stable group identities within the Hunnic Empire at all. If that were the case, then the discernible movement of labels such as "Goth" or "Herul" need have involved little actual migration, an influential alternative vision being that of the ethnogenesis model, which envisages that actual movement

---

[25] The fourth and final key moment of choice.

[26] A key catalyst in the reception of such ideas in history and archaeology is Fredrik Barth, ed., *Ethnic Groups and Boundaries: The Social Organisation of Ethnic Difference* (Boston, 1969), but there are many good accounts of the identity debate drawing on much broader social scientific literature: see, e.g., Halsall, *Barbarian Migrations*, chap. 14. It is no coincidence that this intellectual revolution unfolded at the same time as the culture history paradigm was unravelling (above note 19).

involved a small identity-carrying elite, around whom an assorted mass of human flotsam and jetsam then assembled at the new destination.[27]

But here too, as with migration, something more needs to be said before an old simplicity (that group identities were essentially rigid) is replaced by a new but equally simple alternative (that group identities were essentially fluid). Read in full, the social scientific literature does not suggest that individuals can in all contexts and with equal freedom change their identities according to perceived life advantage. Sometimes institutionalised constraints do not allow them to, while in other contexts their own emotional dependence on an original group identity can get in the way. We are still a long way from the old world of singular, rigid group identities, but it does mean we need to look at the evidence more closely before just assuming that identities within the Hunnic Empire will always have been fluid. The former Roman merchant, for instance, is worth further comment. It was his Hunnic master's choice whether or not to free him in return for payment – not the merchant's – and he only had the wherewithal to conduct this transaction game because of booty he had won in warfare. How frequently this may have happened depends on how likely you think it is that Hunnic slaves could win enough booty and have a generous enough master actually to find freedom. Less often quoted is the story of two other Roman slaves Priscus encountered who were about to be gibbeted for using the chaos of battle to settle debts another way: they had killed their Hunnic master.[28]

More generally, the contemporary historical evidence is utterly consistent (a) that the Hunnic confederation came into being by conquest and intimidation, and (b) that it was Hunnic practice to exploit those they conquered. Hence (c), whenever opportunity arose (before Attila, as well as after his death) Hunnic subjects showed a marked desire to escape from Hunnic domination, which was sufficiently strong for

---

[27] Merchant: Prisc. fr. 11.2.422–435; cf. Istvan Bona, *Das Hunnenreich* (Stuttgart, 1991), on the archaeological picture more generally. Herwig Wolfram is particularly associated with the influential "ethnogenesis" model: see, e.g., *History of the Goths* (trans. Thomas J. Dunlap) (Berkeley, 1988). Gillet, *Barbarian Identity*, contains a series of essays responding critically to this model and its widespread adoption.

[28] Gibbeted slaves: Prisc. fr. 14. For my own views on the theoretical balance between fluidity and rigidity in identity, and some relevant early medieval evidence is set out with reference to the social scientific literature, see Peter J. Heather, "Ethnicity, Group Identity, and Social Status in the Migration Period," in *Franks, Northmen, and Slavs: Identities and State Formation in Early Medieval Europe*, ed. Ildar H. Garipzanov et al. (Turnhout, 2008) 17–50.

the Romans successfully to operate a consistent strategy of undermining overall Hunnic military power by attracting away disaffected subjects.[29] In this broader context, group boundaries as a whole were extremely unlikely to be very fluid. The Huns themselves had every interest in maintaining the size of their subject populations, since, as the case of Priscus's merchant shows, to recognise someone as a Hun was to grant that person a substantial increase in rights and status. Even within the subject peoples, moreover, identities were not just the product of individual choice. Many of the subject groups had complex social structures, comprising individuals in three broad (and heritable) status bands: free, semi-free (or freed), and slaves in descending order. Unless the fifth century was full of people who wanted to be slaves and semi-free, this strongly suggests that an individual's place within their overall group identity was often constrained.[30]

The position is much more interesting, therefore, than the grand simplicities either of complete rigidity or complete fluidity, making it important not to adopt a position a priori on the likely scale of migratory phenomena associated with the rise and fall of Hunnic power, but to look closely at the available evidence. The sources provide us with specific information, in fact, in only two cases. When they entered east Roman territory in the 472–473, having thrown off Hunnic domination, the Amal-led Pannonian Goths led by Thiudimer and his son Theoderic could field ten thousand plus warriors from a group which was substantially mixed in its age and gender profiles. This force was the result of a considerable and recent political reconfiguration. In the *Getica*, Jordanes preserves an interesting passage which shows the Amal king Valamer – Thiudimer's brother – defeating a series of rivals and uniting their followings probably in the mid- to late 450s to create the basis of the group as we know it better in the time of his nephew, Theoderic the Great. There may have been other, smaller moments of recruitment prior to 472–473, and there was to be another major one before the group left Roman territory for Italy in 489. But none of this takes away from the main point: by 473, we are looking at a mixed migration unit, which, allowing for non-combatants, must have numbered several tens of thousands of people.[31]

---

[29] Cf. Heather, *Empires and Barbarians*, chap. 5, esp. 230ff.

[30] See in more detail and with full references, Heather, "Ethnicity, Group Identity, and Social Status."

[31] Heather, *Goths and Romans*, 240–251, commenting esp. on Jord. *Get.* 48.246–252 (Valamer) and Malchus of Philadelphia fr. 20 (numbers). By the time Theoderic

Even after a series of reversals which can only have cost them manpower, likewise, the Heruli could still field around five thousand warriors in the mid-sixth century. A first defeat at the hands of the Lombards in 511 generated an initial split between some Heruli who went north and a second group who fled into Roman territory. The latter then split again in the 530s, with some leaving the empire for the kingdom of the Gepids, but could still generate two contingents respectively of three thousand and fifteen hundred men who found themselves on opposite sides of Lombard–Gepid conflict in 549. This suggests that original Herule military capacity, prior to 511, must have been in the five- to ten-thousand bracket, with a total group size, including non-combatants, amounting to several tens of thousands of individuals (certainly twenty thousand plus). Neither the Heruli nor the Pannonian Goths were simple "peoples" in the old sense of the word, and, indeed, the Huns probably interfered in the political organisation of many of their more closely governed subjects, so that political reconfiguration, as in the case of the Amals, may often have been part of re-establishing independence. But the figures we have for at least two of the groups who emerged from the Hunnic Empire are specific and plausible. In both cases, the migration processes involved groups of several tens of thousands.[32]

Two further points are worth emphasising. First, since the economy of the old central zone of barbarian Europe could not support full-time professional warriors in their thousands, it is not surprising that mobilising forces on such a scale should have involved many men with dependent families (as our sources report). Second, while the broader evidence suggests that the Pannonian Goths were probably the

moved on to Italy, he had added the Thracian Goths (again ten thousand plus warriors and a large number of dependents) and an unknown number of refugee Rugi to his following: Heather, *Goths and Romans*, chap. 9. Patrick Amory, *People and Identity in Ostrogothic Italy, 489–554* (Cambridge, 1997) 95–102, asserted that it was only Procopius of Caesarea, *Wars*, 5.1.6ff., who described Theoderic leading a large mixed force to Italy, as part of an argument that this exemplified a distorting migration topos at work. But the same picture of Theoderic's following appears in sources composed at his court, so that the argument is unconvincing: Ennodius, *Panegyric on Theoderic*, 26–27; *Life of Epiphanius*, 118–219 (cf. 111–212). For a more general response to the migration-topos hypothesis, see Heather, *Empires and Barbarians*, 578–609.

[32] Herul numbers in 549: Procopius, *Wars*, 7.34.42–43. Walter A. Goffart, *The Narrators of Barbarian History (AD 550–800): Jordanes, Gregory of Tours, Bede, and Paul the Deacon* (Princeton, 1988) 84ff., attempts to undermine Procopius's account of the Heruli, but the argument is unconvincing.

most powerful of the groups of Hunnic subjects to emerge on the Great Hungarian Plain in the 450s, the protracted and complicated struggle with their neighbours (Sciri, Heruli, Rugi, Gepids, etc.) does not suggest that they enjoyed an overwhelming numerical advantage in the struggles of the 460s. This in turn implies – if only indirectly – that each of those subject groups participating in the action must have been able to field military manpower at least on the scale of the Heruli. Even where there are no figures, therefore (as in the case of the departing Sciri or Rugi, or the arriviste Lombards), the general political narrative makes it reasonable to suppose that these population movements, too, will have been on broadly the same scale as those of the better-documented Pannonian Goths and Heruli.[33]

For all the deficiencies of our sources, therefore, there is good reason to suppose that the population movements associated with the rise and fall of Attila's empire in central Europe again involved many tens of thousands of people, moving in groups that were mixed in age and gender. These were not ancient "peoples" but units constructed in the complex political processes which precipitated the collapse of Hunnic hegemony in central Europe. Some, it seems, were interfered with more by the Huns (the sons of Attila still had some leaderless Goths in tow in the late 460s for instance), others rather less. The capacity of the Gepids to kick-start the process of subject revolt soon after Attila's death might well indicate that their leadership structures required less rearrangement than those of the Pannonian Goths, say, to produce a military capacity that was powerful enough to fend off Hunnic hegemony. Either way, and even if the Pannonian Gothic confederation was somewhat larger than its peers, the evidence of the Heruli combines with the general political narrative to indicate that none of the named successor entities can have been very small, so that every major act of politically generated population displacement – even where we do not have specific information (Sciri, Rugi, Lombards, etc.) – must have involved movement on the part of at least a few tens of thousands of individuals. If this is looking a little too like the old invasion hypothesis, it is worth stressing that even most of those modern commentators who generally wish to downplay the importance of migration in the late Roman period would allow that the events of 376 and 405–406 to 408 involved reasonably co-ordinated geographical relocation on the part of several tens of thousands of individuals deriving from the kinds

---

[33] For more detailed analysis and full references, see Heather, *Empires and Barbarians*, 238–256.

of societies then characteristic of the central zone of Barbarian Europe. That being so, there is no good reason why the same kind of societies should not have generated some similar moments of intense migratory activity in the decades either side of the death of Attila.

CONCLUSION: THE STRANGE DEATH OF GERMANIC EUROPE

In short, the direct Hunnic impact on the central zone of barbarian Europe as it stood around 350 was massive. The intrusion of Hunnic power into south-eastern and then central Europe prompted two major bouts of emigration, each involved many tens of thousands of people, and the rise and fall of the Hunnic Empire did the same again. Methodologically, this is a conclusion that it is not entirely straightforward to reach; as we have seen, there are four key moments where important intellectual choices have to be made. But the better – that is, more detailed and more contemporary – historical evidence, and the overall impact of the displaced groups upon the Roman Empire both strongly suggest that three distinct pulses of large-scale emigration from central Europe (amounting to a hundred thousand warriors plus, accompanied by numerous non-combatants) was the overwhelming effect of the Huns' century-long European tour, and neither the updated social scientific literature on group identity nor that on human migration offers any real reason why we should not accept what the sources report. This very broad conclusion then becomes central to understanding the final and, in some ways, most significant impact of the Huns on the broader patterns of life in barbarian Europe.

Within a political generation of the eclipse of independent Hunnic power, the old central zone of barbarian Europe was in the midst of drastic geographic collapse, which would see it confined more or less to areas west of the Elbe (map 1), while material cultural patterns previously characteristic of the old third zone replaced it over the vast tracts of central and south-eastern Europe. It is stretching credibility beyond breaking point to argue that the Hunnic-era population displacements from zone 2 did not play a major role in facillitating this astonishing transformation. Much of the expansion from zone 3 was driven forward by Slavic speakers, and, although this would change subsequently, a central characteristic of the early medieval Slavic world was that its population operated in a large number of much smaller units than the type of political entities that had become characteristic of the central zone by the late Roman period. It is a straightforward point, but one of great significance, that the smaller polities characteristic of the early Slavic world could never have spread so far over zone 2 without the disappearance from the region, under Hunnic prompting, of so much of the military and political muscle which had previously dominated it. These emigrations were not remotely large enough actually to have emptied the landscape, but they did remove from it many of the power structures which would have previously made Slavic expansion impossible. The overall effect of the Huns was thus to break down the barriers between old zones 2 and 3 of barbarian Europe: a key moment in the on-going equalisation of levels of development right across the European landscape which is much the biggest story of the entire first millennium.[34]

---

[34] On swift evolution of early Slavic society in contact with more developed neighbours, see Florin Curta, *The Making of the Slavs: History and Archaeology of the Lower Danube Region, c. 500–700* (Cambridge, 2001) esp. chaps. 6–7. For a more detailed review of the evidence for Slavic expansion with full references, see Heather, *Empires and Barbarians*, esp. 371–377 and chap. 8.

13: Captivity among the Barbarians and Its Impact on the Fate of the Roman Empire

Noel Lenski

Sacred Cups, Sirmian Prisoners, and the Complications of Captivity

During his imperial embassy to Attila in 449, Priscus of Panium and his fellow eastern diplomats discovered that they were being shadowed by a second embassy, sent by the western emperor Valentinian III. These envoys were attempting to pacify Attila over the disappearance of a collection of silver vessels that had originally been turned over to a Hunnic agent for the redemption of captives from the city of Sirmium. When the Huns had besieged that city in 441, its bishop had entrusted the vessels to a secretary of Attila named Constantius, on the understanding that Constantius would use them to pay for the ransom of the bishop himself or, if he perished, his fellow Sirmians. In the event, Attila's agent absconded with the cups to Rome, where he used them as security on a loan for gold. Never one to be deceived, Attila detected his secretary's deception and had him crucified. When he then learned that the vessels had been sold to the Roman church by the banker who had taken them as collateral from Constantius, he demanded that either the cups or the banker be turned over to him. The western embassy had come to explain why this was impossible: the banker had been entirely within his rights to sell off the security on this failed loan, and the cups were absolutely off limits for ransoming, "because it is not just for men to employ for their service chalices dedicated to God!" The ambassadors contended that Attila should simply accept their value in gold, but the Hun was not to be persuaded. This was bad news for the ambassadors, but it would have been far worse for the Sirmian captives, for there was now no hope of their regaining freedom.[1]

The failure of this diplomatic mission encapsulates well the fluid and confusing situation in which the Roman Empire found itself in the Age of Attila. By this period, Rome's empire was divided in two, and each half was growing weaker as it was forced to negotiate with barbarian leaders like the Hunnic king on their own terms. In this period, the Huns controlled the entire territory north of the central and eastern Balkans, and they were now using it as a base from which to drain Illyricum of its inhabitants city by city. As we shall see, this had a major impact on the region, denuding Rome's Danubian provinces of their producers by killing large numbers of provincials and moving most of those who survived north of the river. Most of these probably had no hope of return, for although ransom was a possibility, it was too expensive to be within reach of most individuals, and it always depended on temperamental negotiations that could break down for all sorts of reasons, including exasperating cultural misunderstandings, as happened in the case of the Sirmian captives. The net result was that the Age of Attila saw a tremendous increase in captivity and enslavement, which had a devastating impact on the lives of individuals and on the fate of the Roman Empire.[2]

This study attempts to elucidate the important impact captivity and enslavement had on the provincial territories bordering the Huns and then to allude briefly to the way this same problem affected other parts of the Roman Empire. It will begin by surveying the shifts that occurred as the Huns evacuated the Balkans of much of their population. It will then examine the economic impact of this demographic change using both textual and archaeological sources. Next it will explore the fate of these captives inside Hunnic territory. It will then widen its scope to examine briefly how the empire and the church dealt with this widespread problem, both in the Balkans and in other

---

[1] Priscus, *Excerpta*, 8.77–81, 137–143 (ed. Pia Carolla, *Excerpta et Fragmenta, Priscus Panita* [Berlin, 2008] = ed. Robert C. Blockley, *The Fragmentary Classicising Historians of the Later Roman Empire: Eunapius, Olympiodorus, Priscus and Malchus*, 2 vols. [Liverpool, 1983] 11.2).

[2] More on captivity in Late Antiquity at Noel Lenski, "Captivity and Romano-Barbarian Interchange," in *Romans, Barbarians and the Transformation of the Roman World*, ed. Ralph W. Mathisen and Danuta Shanzer (Farnham, U.K., 2011) 185–198. More on late Roman slavery at Kyle Harper, *Slavery in the Late Roman World, AD 275–425: An Economic, Social, and Institutional Study* (Cambridge, 2011).

territories directly impacted by barbarian invaders. Ultimately, it will provide a case study in the way that Rome's diminishing ability to protect its frontiers opened the door for non-Roman groups to exploit a population of largely sedentary and docile taxpayers by seizing them as either objects of ransom or exploitable slaves.

THE DEMOGRAPHIC IMPACT OF THE HUNNIC WARS ON THE BALKANS

The Hunnic invasions represented a major demographic event in the central Balkans. Although this region had been slower to urbanize than other parts of the empire and never became particularly populous relative to other regions, it had seen the rise of numerous cities in the first and second centuries. The Gothic invasions of 250–251 dealt a serious blow to Illyricum, killing as many as 100,000 of its inhabitants, carrying off thousands more into captivity, and destroying many fortresses and cities.[3] Nevertheless, in the fourth century, the region bounced back as the empire renewed its investment in the defense of border cities and the embellishment of provincial capitals.[4] This newfound prosperity was to change dramatically beginning with the Gothic uprising of 377, which resulted in the temporary occupation of northern Thrace by an independent barbarian protectorate. Even so, it showed considerable resilience down to the mid-fifth century when, beginning in the 430s, the increasingly self-confident Hunnic empire began treating Illyricum as a pawn in its relations with the empire.

The Huns were much more dangerous than the Goths because, notoriously, they were much more adept at siege operations.[5] This allowed them to conquer entire cities, whose surviving populations

---

[3] Dexippus fr. 22(16) (*Die Fragmente der griechischen Historiker*, ed. Felix Jacoby [Leiden, 1926] 2.A.405 no. 100); cf. Ammianus Marcellinus, *Res gestae*, 31.5.17. Zosimus, *Historia nova*, 1.24.2 confirms that Trebonianus Gallus's treaty with the Goths permitted them to carry their captives back to their territory.

[4] Andrew Poulter, "The Use and Abuse of Urbanism in the Danubian Provinces During the Later Roman Empire," in *The City in Late Antiquity*, ed. John Rich (London, 1992) 99–135.

[5] On the Hunnic invasions of the fifth century, see Otto Maenchen-Helfen, *The World of the Huns: Studies in Their History and Culture*, ed. Max Knight (Berkeley, 1973) 74–152; Edward A. Thompson, *The Huns*, ed. Peter J. Heather (Oxford, 1996) 69–176; Peter J. Heather, *The Fall of the Roman Empire: A New History of Rome and the Barbarians* (Oxford, 2006) 300–384.

they then took into captivity to serve either as slaves or, when these were redeemed for gold, sources of cash. With the large-scale invasion of Illyricum launched by Attila and his brother Bleda in 441, we learn of the capture of at least seven major cities: Sirmium (Sremska Mitrovica), Naissus (Niš), Singidunum (Belgrade), Viminacium (Kostolac), Margum (Orašje), Constantia (a fortress opposite Margum), and Ratiaria (Archar).[6] This catalog represents all the major fortress cities on the middle Danube, whose inhabitants were either exterminated or deported as captives. In the year following, Marcellinus Comes reports, "Bleda and Attila . . . ravaged the populations of Illyricum and Thrace,"[7] an indication that the Huns took advantage of their elimination of Rome's defensive emplacements in the region to pillage rural areas and enslave their inhabitants as well.

A treaty was negotiated in 443, but peace did not last more than four years. By 447 Attila, who now ruled alone after the death of Bleda, launched a second invasion, even larger than the first, which plundered as far east as the shores of the Pontus and Propontis and as far south as the pass of Thermopylae, leading to the capture of every city in the region except Heraclea/Perinthus and Adrianople.[8] The *Gallic Chronicler of 452* reports that some seventy cities were taken,[9] including Marcianopolis (Devnya), Philippopolis (Plovdiv), and Arcadioupolis.[10] This same invasion is described in gripping terms by the monk Callinicus, an eyewitness, who reports the murder and enslavement of so many provincials that "Thrace could never possibly have been repopulated as it was before."[11] The treaty that ended this conflict in 448 then called for the evacuation of any remaining Roman inhabitants from the right bank of the Danube in a swath stretching from Singidunum in the West, east to Novae (Svištov), and extending a distance of five days march south from the river.[12] This was an expanse some 500 kilometers wide by about 160 kilometers deep. Attila had thus created a zone of

---

[6] This list can be reconstructed from Marcellinus Comes, *Chronicon*, sub annum 441; Prisc. *Exc.* 2 (Carolla = 6.1 Blockley), 3.3 (Carolla = 9.1 Blockley), 8.77, 97–8, 176–7 (Carolla = 11.2 Blockley); cf. Theophanes, *Chronographia*, anno mundi 5942.

[7] Marc. Com. s.a. 442.

[8] Marc. Com. s.a. 447; Theophan. a.m. 5942. Jordanes, *Romana*, 331, reports generically of the destruction of all of Illyricum and Thrace and both Dacias, Moesia, and Scythia.

[9] *Chronicon Gallicum ad annum 452*, s.a. 447.

[10] *Chronicon Paschale*, p. 589; Theophan. a.m. 5942.

[11] Callinicus, *Vita Hypatii*, 52.3–9.

[12] Prisc. *Exc.* 7.2–4 (Carolla = 11.1 Blockley).

depopulation in the provinces bordering the central Danube that would have driven this area into an economic and demographic tailspin.

The textual sources provide only the vaguest information with which to reconstruct the quantitative scale of this problem. We can gain some idea of the possibilities from the *Syriac Chronicle to 724*, which reports that, when a group of Huns – from the Trans-Caucasus, and thus independent of the European Huns – invaded Anatolia in 395, they swept up 18,000 prisoners.[13] The numbers were likely considerably higher in the Balkans, both because Attila's raids were carried out over a series of years and because his Huns had much easier access to their long-settled homeland on the Hungarian plain, where they could transport their prisoners after having captured them. Procopius claims that the Balkans had been transformed into a "Scythian wasteland" because of successive invasions by the Huns, Sklaveni, and Antae beginning in the late 530s, each of which he claims had denuded the territory of 200,000 citizens.[14] On a similar scale, he reports that the Hunnic invasions that hit the Balkans in 539 resulted in the capture of 120,000 prisoners.[15] Although Procopius is not known for quantitative accuracy, numbers in the range of 100,000 to 200,000 captives – both in the time of Attila and again in the sixth century – are well within the realm of the possible. They certainly fit with calculations possible from the information given above for the number of cities taken. If we assume that each of the ten major cities cataloged above averaged 7,000 inhabitants, that each of the remaining sixty cities reported to have been captured in 447 by the *Gallic Chronicle of 452* averaged 1,000, and that the Huns captured an additional one-fourth as many people in the countryside, we arrive at approximately 166,000 Roman captives taken in the period of the 440s.

This number, large though it is, remains fully in keeping with other figures for mass enslavements preserved in sources from Antiquity and the early Middle Ages. To take just four examples: after the defeat of the Macedonians at the battle of Pydna in 167 BCE, the Romans took seventy cities and some 150,000 prisoners in Greece;[16] C. Marius's victories against the Cimbri and Teutones in 101 are said

---

[13] *Chronicon Miscellaneum ad annum 724* (Corpus Scriptorum Christianorum Orientalium Scriptores Syri 3.136–137 = 4.106–107). See also Jerome, *Epistle*, 60.16; Claudianus, *In Eutropium*, 1.242–51.

[14] Procopius, *Anecdota*, 18.17.21.

[15] Procopius, *Bella*, 2.4.4–11; cf. 7.11.13–16. See also Procop. *Bell.* 8.19.2 for the ongoing retention of tens of thousands of Roman captives by the Kotrigurs.

[16] Livy, *Ab urbe condita*, 45.34; Polybius, *Historiae*, 30.16; Strabo, *Geographica*, 7.322.

to have yielded 150,000 captives;[17] the capture of Jerusalem in 70 CE produced 97,000 captives[18] and inscriptions from Cyprus reveal that 170,000 prisoners were captured by the Ummayyads during their invasions of the island in 649 and 650.[19] In light of these comparanda, a figure between 150,000 and 200,000 Roman prisoners for Attila's Balkan campaigns seems well within the bounds of the believable.

THE ECONOMIC IMPACT OF THE HUNNIC DEMANDS FOR TRIBUTE AND RANSOM

The tragic depopulation of the territories neighboring the Danube also had a significant economic impact on the empire. It obliterated a generation of producers and taxpayers and brought about the loss of accumulated investments in urban and rural infrastructure. Precise data is lacking, but it seems clear that the Huns created an economic dead zone in the central Balkans in the mid-fifth century.

This devastation can be confirmed archaeologically. Although stratigraphic excavation in the Balkans has come into its own only in the last three decades, the few sites now explored using independently verifiable dating criteria tell a consistent story. German excavations conducted at the fortress of Iatrus on the lower Danube have shown that it was burnt to the ground and evacuated in the mid-fifth century.[20] British excavations at the civilian settlement of Nicopolis ad Istrum further south have shown that it too was burnt and abandoned at the same time.[21] Finally, the Polish team working at Novae has found that this town's headquarters building (*principia*) was also violently destroyed and abandoned in the mid-fifth century.[22] Following this destruction, significant reoccupation of the region began again only at the very end

---

[17] Livy, *Epitome*, 18.
[18] Josephus, *Bellum Judaicum*, 6.416.
[19] *Supplementum Epigraphicum Graecum*, 35.1471.
[20] Gerda von Bülow, "The Fort of Iatrus in Moesia Secunda: Observations on the Late Roman Defensive System on the Lower Danube (Fourth–Sixth Centuries AD)," in *The Transition to Late Antiquity: On the Danube and Beyond*, ed. Andrew G. Poulter (Oxford, 2007) 459–478, here 468–470.
[21] Andrew G. Poulter, *Nicopolis ad Istrum: A Roman, Late Roman, and Early Byzantine City. Excavations 1985–1992* (London, 1995) 33–37.
[22] Tadeusz Sarnowski, "Die Principia von Novae im späten 4. und frühen 5. Jh.," in *Der Limes an der unteren Donau von Diokletian bis Heraklios*, ed. Gerda von Bülow and Aleksandra Milčeva (Sofia, 1999) 56–63.

of the fifth century.[23] Evidence from forts in the province of Scythia Minor also points to widespread destruction in the mid-fifth century followed by rebuilding beginning in the reign of Anastasius.[24] Further construction is then reported by Procopius for the 530s and 540s, just on the eve of invasions by the Sklaveni, Antae, and Avars, that would again drive the region into economic collapse.[25] In sum, the archaeology of the Balkans indicates that Attila and the Huns wrought widespread destruction, which led to a lull in settlement and building activity from the mid- to the late fifth century.

The Hunnic invasions also cost individuals and families dearly by forcing them to redeem relatives from captivity. Our sources confirm that the Huns deliberately strove to capture those they believed to be from wealthy or powerful backgrounds since these could generate high ransoms.[26] We also know of a regular diplomatic traffic on the part of Romans carrying money to redeem prisoners.[27] Priscus reports that, on the embassy in 449, a Roman agent named Vigilas attempted to escape detection for having brought 100 pounds of gold with which to pay Edeco for assassinating Attila by claiming the money had been sent to redeem captives – as if this were entirely plausible.[28] We learn the potential costs of such arrangements from another passage in Priscus reporting how he and his fellow ambassador Maximinus were able to persuade Attila's lieutenant Onegesius to accept a bargain price of just 500 *solidi* (7 lbs of gold) in exchange for the wife of a man named Syllus and even to free Syllus's children gratis.[29] When Attila took Vigilas himself prisoner after discovering his involvement in the assassination plot, he insisted on a ransom of 50 pounds of gold.[30]

There were also costs to the state, which was obliged to pay tribute to the Huns in ever increasing amounts throughout Attila's lifetime. Priscus and Theophanes can be used to construct the financial terms

---

[23] On Iatrus, see von Bülow, "The Fort of Iatrus," 470. On Nicopolis, see Poulter, *Nicopolis ad Istrum*, 35–37. See also the inscription of Ratiaria confirming rebuilding there under Anastasius, *Année Épigraphique*, 1985.723 = *AE* 1988.983.

[24] Constatin Scorpan, *Limes Scythiae: Topographical and Stratigraphical Research on the Late Roman Fortifications on the Lower Danube* (Oxford, 1980) 123–125.

[25] Procopius, *Aedificia*, 4.5.1–7.21.

[26] Sozomenus, *Historia ecclesiastica*, 7.26.6–8; Prisc. *Exc.* 8.98 (Carolla = 11.2 Blockley).

[27] Prisc. *Exc.* 5.9–16 (Carolla = 9.3 Blockley); *Exc.* 14 (Carolla = 15.4 Blockley).

[28] Prisc. *Exc.* 8.1.2–3 (Carolla = 15.1 Blockley). Anticipating this ploy, Attila had forbidden the ambassadors to purchase Roman prisoners, barbarian slaves, or horses from the beginning, Prisc. *Exc.* 8.54 (Carolla = 11.2 Blockley).

[29] Prisc. *Exc.* 8.176–7 (Carolla = 14 Blockley).

[30] Prisc. *Exc.* 8.1, 14.3 (Carolla = 15.1, 4 Blockley).

of four major treaties settled between the Romans and the Huns in the mid fifth century, including sums owed in annual tribute as well as those for the redemption of Roman prisoners who had escaped their Hunnic captors without a ransom having been paid.[31]

To these figures could be added the 6,000 pounds of gold demanded by Attila just to strike a treaty in both 443 and 448.[32] One could also add the cost of ransoms paid for captives who had not escaped the Huns, figures which – as we have seen – were generally considerably higher. Even if we assume a low average of just 20 *solidi* per ransom (the cost of the average slave in this period),[33] this would amount to another 556 pounds of gold to ransom an additional 2,000 prisoners annually. Thus, in any given year the Huns were able to extract between ca. 900 and 3,000 pounds of gold from the emperor and his citizens, and in banner years like 443 and 448 as much as 9,000 pounds of gold.[34]

These numbers can be set in relation to other known figures for fiscal revenue from the period. We can determine from one of the *Novels* of Valentinian III that, in the first part of the fifth century, the provinces of Numidia and Mauretania Sitifensis generated a combined annual tax revenue of around 1,700 pounds of gold.[35] Hendy has estimated that the entire diocese of Africa – a larger administrative grouping of most of the late Roman provinces in the region – may have produced something on the order of 6,700 pounds of gold per year in taxes. This would

---

[31] For the treaty of 435 and the terms that preceded it, see Prisc. *Exc.* 1.1.3 (Carolla = 5 Blockley). For that of 443, see Prisc. *Exc.* 5.1–2 (Carolla = 9.3 Blockley). For that of 449/450, see Theophan. a.m. 5942 with Prisc. *Exc.* 14.2–4 (Carolla = 15.4 Blockley).

[32] Maenchen-Helfen, *World of the Huns*, 117, cf. Heather, *The Fall of the Roman Empire*, 307–308, believes that these sums were meant to cover arrears from previous years when the Romans had refused to pay their tribute obligations. This is nowhere to be found in the sources, which make it clear that these one-time payments were demanded by Attila to cease hostilities, cf. Prisc. *Exc.* 5.1 (Carolla = 9.3 Blockley); Theophan. a.m. 5942. Constantin Zuckerman, "L'empire d'orient et les Huns: Notes sur Priscus," *Travaux et Mémoires du Centre de recherches d'hist. et civil. byzantines* 12 (1994) 159–182 offers an important, if not entirely convincing, revisionist reading of these treaties.

[33] See Kyle Harper, "Slave Prices in Late Antiquity (and in the Very Long Term)," *Historia* 59 (2010) 206–238.

[34] The unusually large amount of tribute in gold paid to the Huns is also reflected in hoards from Siebenbürgen, see Kurt Horedt, *Siebenburgen im Frühmittelalter* (Bonn, 1986) 53–57.

[35] *Novellae Valentiniani*, 13.5, with Michael Hendy, *Studies in the Byzantine Monetary Economy c. 300–1450* (Cambridge, 1985) 173.

mean that, in an average year, Attila was consuming the equivalent of the annual tax revenues of two to four African provinces and at times as much as the entire African diocese.[36] These were sizable figures, especially considering that, simultaneously, the Huns were diminishing fiscal revenues by nearly as much as they were consuming in tribute and ransoms, for they had cut off much of Illyricum from the reach of the Roman tax-collecting apparatus and had systematically purged it of taxpayers. Kelly has downplayed the overall financial impact of Hunnic demands for gold on the imperial fisc, but in an economic system with very limited annual growth and a tightly constrained imperial budget, the financial pressure created by the Huns' demands for gold was surely greater than he projects.[37] It is of import for this study that a significant percentage of these costs (25 to 50%) were paid out in ransoms.

TABLE 13.1. *Financial Terms of Four Hunnic Treaties*

	Tribute (lbs. Gold / Year)	Retroactive Ransom (Gold Solidi / Prisoner)	Cost to Ransom 2,000 Prisoners Annually (lbs. Gold / Year)	Estimated Total (lbs. Gold / Year)
Pre-435	350	unknown	unknown	350 +
435	700	8	222	922
443	2,100	12	333	2,433
449	1,000	12?	333	1,333

THE FATE OF ROMAN PRISONERS AMONG THE HUNS

I argued above that the Huns captured over 150,000 prisoners from Roman territory in the early fifth century, and it is likely they took many thousands more captives from other peoples outside the Roman Empire about whose conflicts with the Huns we know almost nothing.

[36] Hendy, *Studies*, 164–171, argues that the annual revenue of the eastern prefecture in the age of Justinian may have reached 55,000 lbs of gold annually, meaning that the Huns were consuming anywhere between 2 and 15 percent of the value of tax revenue available to the eastern emperor.

[37] See Christopher Kelly, *The End of Empire: Attila the Hun and the Fall of Rome* (New York, 2009) 141–148.

If the argument above is correct in assuming that only a small percentage of these captives were ever ransomed, what, we might ask, became of the remaining prisoners?

Any attempt to answer this question must begin with an examination of the Hunnic economy. The success of the Huns in conquering the peoples living north of the Danube in the late fourth century and of then turning the Roman Empire into a harvesting ground for captives and tribute in the fifth clearly had an economic and social impact on the Huns themselves.[38] There is every indication that the Hunnic aristocracy maintained its attachment to its pastoralist roots and above all to the horse throughout the Age of Attila. As their herds of horses – as well as sheep and goats – grew, they required considerable labor to manage, and it is here that many of their captives must have been put to work as herders and grooms. In a comparative study of 186 premodern societies, Patterson has shown that pastoral economies regularly deploy slave labor to manage their herds, so much so that pastoral societies are significantly more likely to employ slave labor than societies employing any other subsistence strategy, including agriculture.[39] Moreover, much of the territory controlled by the Huns was just as suited to intensive agriculture as pastoralism, and most of this land continued to be cultivated not by the Huns themselves, but by peoples under their suzerainty, including Goths, Gepids, Heruls, Sciri, and Rugi. These subject peoples probably also drew from the plentiful supply of Roman prisoners created by the Hunnic wars – wars in which they themselves also fought alongside the Huns.[40]

While the use of captives as slaves in primary production seems likely, we have no positive confirmation of this in our very limited sources for Hunnic life. Indeed, the only source that provides any indication of how the Huns used their captives and slaves is the famous passage of Priscus describing his embassy to Attila's court in 449. Here we see the Huns regularly employing slaves as household servants,

---

[38] For what follows, see Rudi P. Lindner, "Nomadism, Horses and Huns," *Past & Present* 92 (1981) 3–19.

[39] Orlando Patterson, "Slavery, Gender and Work in the Pre-modern World and Early Greece," in *Slave Systems, Ancient and Modern*, ed. Enrico Dal Lago and Constantina Katsari (Cambridge, 2008) 32–69, here 46.

[40] For Germanic traditions of slaveholding, see Noel Lenski, "Captivity, Slavery, and Cultural Exchange between Rome and the Germans from the First to the Seventh Century CE," in *Invisible Citizens: Captives and Their Consequences*, ed. Catherine Cameron (Salt Lake City, 2008) 80–109.

cupbearers, orderlies, and even bath attendants.[41] This was a society in which people could afford to maintain numerous slaves to look after their every need,[42] but Priscus also attests to much more pragmatic uses for Hunnic slaves. Those few with skills and education inculcated in the Roman Empire prior to their captivity served their masters as secretaries, accountants, and even architects in an increasingly elaborate and stratified economy.[43] We also have two attestations to the Huns' use of their slaves as combatants in their wars against the Roman empire and beyond it.[44] The Huns had thus adopted slave labor in varying forms and functions, not unlike their Roman neighbors. Attila is reported to have conceived of his relationship to his subjects and even to the Roman Empire as analogous to that of a master to his slaves.[45] Slavery was thus a normal part of life among the fifth-century Huns.

Captive-taking and slaveholding were, of course, not unique to the Huns. Indeed, these are phenomena that occur with great regularity across world cultures, and particularly among pastoralist peoples.[46] This was true, for example, of Rome's pastoralist neighbors on its frontier with the Syrian and Arabian desert, nomadic Arabs known generically as Saracens.[47] It was true as well of those steppe peoples – also referred to in the sources as Huns – who followed the fifth-century Huns as invaders of the Byzantine and Sasanian empires.[48] The mobility of

---

[41] Prisc. *Exc.* 8.86, 88, 93, 131, 151–163 (Carolla = 11.2 Blockley); cf. Jordanes, *Getica*, 49 (254). On the historiographical background of Prisc. *Exc.* 8, see Michael Maas, "Fugitives and Ethnography in Priscus of Panium," *Byzantine and Modern Greek Studies* 19 (1995) 146–160.

[42] See, for example, the African dwarf and court jester Zercon, acquired as a slave by Attila's brother Bleda, Prisc. *Exc.* 8.169–170, 11 (Carolla = 11.2, 13.2 Blockley).

[43] For captive secretaries, see Prisc. *Exc.* 8.174–75 (Carolla = 14 Blockley). For a captive slave architect, see Prisc. *Exc.* 8.86 (Carolla = 11.2 Blockley). More examples of Hunnic secretaries, some of whom were free, at Prisc. *Exc.* 8.36, 44 (Carolla = 11.2 Blockley); *Anonymus Valesianus II*, 38.

[44] Prisc. *Exc.* 8.99, 190 (Carolla = 11.2, 14 Blockley). More on slave combatants in various late antique cultures at Noel Lenski, "Schiavi armati e formazione di eserciti privati nel mondo tardoantico," in *Ordine e sovversione nel mondo greco e romano*, ed. Gianpaolo Urso (Pisa, 2009) 145–175.

[45] Prisc. *Exc.* 12, 19 (Carolla = 15.2, 23.1 Blockley); *Chron. Pasch.* p. 587; Jord. *Get.* 52(268–269).

[46] See for example James Brooks, *Captives and Cousins: Slavery, Kinship, and Community in the Southwest Borderlands* (Chapel Hill, 2002).

[47] Noel Lenski, "Captivity and Slavery among the Saracens in Late Antiquity (ca. 250–630 CE)," *Antiquité Tardive* 19 (2011) 237–266.

[48] Procop. *Bell.* 2.4.6–11; 7.11.13–16; Agathias, *Historiae*, 5.13.1–4; John Malalas, *Chronographia*, 18.129.

pastoralists and their experience transporting livestock – among which we might number human prisoners – overland to foreign territory gave pastoralists advantages as slavemakers.

Nevertheless, pastoral societies often differ from agriculturalists in that they tend to integrate their captives into their own social framework quite rapidly. This was certainly true of the Greek businessman from Viminacium met by Priscus in 449, who was wearing Hunnic clothing and speaking Hunnic. This man had gone from prisoner, to slave, to full member of Hunnic society in less than a decade.[49] It is also reflected in the only other source we have that intimates details about the life of Hunnic captives. In two epistles to the church of Aquileia, Pope Leo the Great proffers advice on how to reintegrate individuals who had been captured from that city by the Huns in 452 but had managed to return home some six years later. These had apparently been made to participate in Hunnic religious celebrations, and the children among them seem largely to have forgotten their Roman past.[50] The Huns evidently converted many of their captives rather quickly from outcasts to insiders.[51]

CAPTIVITY AND REDEMPTION AS A FIFTH-CENTURY PREOCCUPATION

Attila depopulated the Balkans with large-scale captive taking, but the Romans had experienced similar damage before. Marcus Aurelius, for example, had to negotiate the release of some 100,000 Roman citizens being held in captivity by the Iazyges, predecessors of the Huns on the Hungarian Plain.[52] Nevertheless, the collapse of the imperial frontiers beginning with the battle of Adrianople in 378 had initiated a cycle of depredation and captivity that was quite unprecedented in duration and

---

[49] Prisc. *Exc.* 8.94–100 (Carolla = 11.2 Blockley).

[50] Leo Magnus, *Epistulae*, 159, 166. On the Hunnic capture of Aquileia, see Marc. Com. s.a. 452; Jord. *Get.* 32(219–222). It should be remembered that the Huns sacked numerous cities on Attila's western campaign in 451–452, but they appear not to have been as interested in captive-taking – most likely because captives would have represented too great an impediment to their expeditionary force, cf. Jord. *Get.* 32(222); *Suidas*, M 405 s.v. Μεδιόλανου; Paulus Diaconus, *Historia Romana*, 14.9–12; Ps. Maximus Taurinensis, *Homiliae*, 94 (Patrologia Latina 57.469–472).

[51] We also learn of those who were cheated of their ambitions for liberation and cast into more abject slavery, as at Prisc. *Exc.* 8.86 (Carolla = 11.2 Blockley).

[52] Dio Cassius, *Historiae*, 71.16.2.

extent. The attacks of Attila and the Huns were thus the culmination of a series of incursions by barbarian invaders, the cumulative impact of which had gradually ground down the tax and population base of certain provinces and eventually split them from Roman political control altogether.[53]

In the face of this sustained threat, the Roman government was forced to amplify its responses to the problem of captivity. We have already seen that the eastern emperor negotiated reduced prices for the redemption of those Hunnic captives who had escaped to Roman territory before a ransom had been paid. We can also catalog a number of other instances where the state was directly involved in the liberation of captives through direct negotiation with barbarian nations.[54] In addition the state relieved some of the pressure created by the marked increase in the number of Romans held in captivity by modifying the laws on *postliminium* – the Roman legal right allowing citizens to regain their civic rights once freed from captivity. In a law of 409, issued in the aftermath of the second Visigothic siege of Rome, Honorius introduced a new provision that fundamentally altered the once black-and-white division between free and slave in the realm of *postliminium:* those who escaped captivity or were ransomed by relatives with no expectation of recompense gained full freedom immediately; but those ransomed for a price by a third party who wanted the money restored could be forced to repay that price or to work it off for a period of five years in indentured servitude.[55] This new measure will have encouraged the redemption of Roman prisoners, but also their exploitation, as investor-redeemers sought to profit from others' misfortune by exploiting their labor uncompensated for five full years.[56]

One of the most important shifts in the period was the involvement of the Christian church in the process of ransoming. Taking as their cue the scriptural passage in which Christ claims to have come

---

[53] See the chapter by Peter Sarris in this volume.

[54] Dio Cass. 71.11.1–2, 16.2, 72.2.2; *Anonymus Valesianus,* I, 21; Julianus, *Epistula ad Athenienses,* 8 (280C–D); Libanius, *Oratio,* 18.78–79; Amm. 18.2.19; Zos. 3.4.4–5.1; Eunapius, *Historiae,* fr. 19 (Blockley); Malchus, fr. 5 (Blockley).

[55] *Codex Theodosianus,* 5.7.2 = *Codex Justinianus,* 1.4.11 + 8.50.20 = *Constitutio Sirmondiana,* 16. Prior to this, those freed appear to have owed the price of their redemption to the redeemer but could not, apparently, be held in servitude legally. See *Cod. Just.* 8.50.2 (a. 241); 8.50.6–7 (a. 291); 8.50.17 (a. 294), on which, see Serena Connolly, "Roman Ransomers," *Ancient History Bulletin,* 20 (2006) 115–131.

[56] Nor were the redeemers always willing to set these servants free after five years; see Gregorius Magnus, *Epistulae,* 3.40, 4.17, 7.21, cf. 9.52.

"to proclaim freedom for prisoners" (Lk. 4:18; cf. Is. 61:1–2), Christian leaders responded to the increased threat of captivity beginning in the late fourth century by becoming brokers in the negotiation of money ransoms for those taken into captivity by barbarian enemies. Ambrose paved the way for this in the aftermath of Adrianople when he melted down sacred vessels from the church of Milan in order to generate revenue with which to buy back captives from the Goths.[57] From this point on, we can catalog scores of instances through the sixth century and beyond in which bishops used church revenues or accumulated ecclesiastical wealth to pay off barbarian captors for the release of prisoners.[58] In other instances, they took up collections from congregants toward the same ends.[59] Nevertheless, the system could be abused. This we have seen already in the vignette at the beginning of this chapter in which Attila's secretary Constantius had exploited the custom of ecclesiastical ransoming by pilfering Sirmium's church plate for his own profit. The incident was clearly not unique, for by the time of Justinian, several laws had been issued tightly regulating the use of church vessels for the redemption of captives.[60] Ecclesiastical redemption was thus a social imperative, but the very urgency created by the call to free prisoners opened the door to exploitation and thus necessitated regulation.

Private individuals also became involved. For many – probably most – this entailed above all redeeming one's own relatives. Such, for example, was the case with Syllus, and this also constituted the basis

---

[57] Ambrosius, *De officiis*, 2.70; 136–143; cf. Paulinus, *Vita Ambrosii*, 38 (*PL* 14.43); Ambrosius, *Epistulae*, 73(18).16 (Corpus Scriptorum Ecclesiasticorum Latinorum 82.43, ed. Otto Faller and Michaela Zelser [Vienna, 1968–1990]).

[58] For lists of sources, see William E. Klingshirn, "Charity and Power: Caesarius of Arles and the Ransoming of Captives in Sub-Roman Gaul," *Journal of Roman Studies* 75 (1985) 183–203; Lenski, "Captivity and Romano-Barbarian Interchange," 189–190.

[59] This practice as attested already in the third century under Cyprian of Carthage, *Epistulae*, 62.4 (Corpus Christianorum Series Latina 3C.384–388, ed. Gerard Diercks [Turnhout, 1994–1996]). It continued throughout Late Antiquity, e.g., Patricius, *Epistula ad milites Corotici* 14–15 (Sources Chrétiennes 249.146–147, ed. and trans. Richard P. C. Hanson [Paris, 1978]); Procop. *Bell.* 2.5.26–33, 13.1–6.

[60] Cod. Just. 1.2.21 (a. 529); *Novellae Iustiniani*, 7.8 (a. 535), 65.1 (a. 538), 120.9–10 (a. 544); cf. *Concilium Clippiacense*, a. 626–627, can. 25 (CCSL 148A.296). For efforts by clergy to observe these laws strictly, see Pelagius, *Epistulae*, 39 (ed. Samuel Loewenfeld, *Epistolae pontificum Romanorum ineditae* [Leipzig, 1854; repr. Graz, 1959] 20); Gregorius Turonensis [Gregory of Tours], *Historia Francorum*, 7.24; Greg. Mag., *Ep.* 7.13.

of Vigilas's excuse for having brought so much money into Hunnic territory – it was sent by the families of captives for their redemption.[61] In other instances, lay Christians otherwise unaffiliated with the church are attested offering money to redeem captives as a means of expressing piety.[62] Some wealthy laypeople even established endowments toward this end. Perhaps our best example of this comes not from the Balkan frontier – where our evidence is very scanty – but from an Egyptian papyrus of 567 recording the will of Flavius Theodorus who left to the White Monastery of Atripe considerable real estate holdings whose income was to be used for pious works, including the redemption of captives.[63] The White Monastery was well chosen, for it had a history of involvement in the redemption of captives going back to the days of its founding abbot, Shenoute. When in the mid-fifth century a group of "Ethiopian" barbarians invaded upper Egypt, destroyed settlements, and carried off prisoners, Shenoute responded to the crisis by establishing an emergency refugee camp. His treatise "On the Invasion of the Ethiopians" catalogs in minute detail how he fed, clothed, and sheltered some 7,500 fugitives at great expense to himself and his monastery. The single biggest cost on his ledger – more even than the grain needed to feed this small city of starving people – was the redemption of 100 captives, which cost him a total 1,000 *solidi* (almost 14 pounds of gold).[64] At 10 *solidi* apiece, the captives were redeemed at the average price paid to the Huns at around the same time for the redemption of escaped prisoners. Thus in Egypt, as in the Balkans and indeed elsewhere, Roman provincials were pulled into redemption rackets whereby increasingly powerful and belligerent peoples exploited both the relative vulnerability and the relative wealth of the empire to turn the victims of warfare into sources of money.

These empire-wide responses to the problem of captivity make it clear that this was an issue that affected not just the Balkans in the

---

[61] For other examples, see Malch. fr. 6.2; Greg. Mag. *Ep.* 7.35.

[62] Venantius Fortunatus, *Carmina*, 2.11.15–18, 3.11.10–11, 4.27.15–16, 6.4.21–22; Sidonius, *Epistolae*, 4.11.4; Greg. Mag. *Ep.* 5.46, 7.23, 25, 8.22.

[63] *Papyrus grecs d'époque byzantine*, ed. Jean Maspero (Paris, 1913) 3.67312. See also *Nov. Just.* 65.1 (a. 538); *Concilium Aurelianense*, 1 (a. 511), can. 5 (CCSL 148A.6–7).

[64] Shenoute, *De Aethiopum invasionibus*, 1–3 (ed. John Leipoldt and E. Walter Crum, Corpus Scriptorum Christianorum Orientalium Scriptori Coptici 2.4.67–77/37–41 [Leuven, 1908]); cf. *Besa: The Life of Shenoute*, 89–90 (ed. John Leipoldt and E. Walter Crum, CSCO SC 2.2.43–44 [Leuven, 1906]), with Ariel G. López, *Shenoute of Atripe and the Uses of Poverty: Rural Patronage, Religious Conflict, and Monasticism in Late Antique Egypt* (Berkeley, 2013) 57–63.

time of the Huns, but the later Roman Empire in general. In the fifth century alone, the same story could be told of captivity to the Vandals, the Goths, and the Burgundians in the West and the Saracens, Persians, and Austuriani in the East. Nor did the collapse of the Hunnic Empire put an end to the problem on the Danube frontier, for the power vacuum created by the disappearance of Hunnic central control fomented new hostilities among the many ethnicities they had formerly ruled and resulted in a continuation of the cycle of violence and enslavement in the region, if only under a new set of mutually hostile groups.[65] Captivity and enslavement to barbarian peoples had, in other words, become a problem of epidemic proportions. The gradual collapse of Roman territorial hegemony fragmented the greater Mediterranean basin into a patchwork of jurisdictions, hemming Roman citizens within ever-shrinking territories surrounded by hostile neighbors who readily exploited the growing weakness of the Roman military to raid these remaining territories for human subjects.

CONCLUSION

The Age of Attila was thus one of tremendous upheaval for many Roman provincials. To be sure, neither Attila nor any other barbarian group single-handedly dealt a death blow to Rome's empire. But for many individuals, and often for entire cities and even regions, Rome's loss of military control over its former provinces carried with it devastating consequences as peoples were slaughtered or swept up into captivity. In the mid-fifth century, the northern Balkans suffered as the Huns moved through and culled well over 150,000 inhabitants as prisoners. The resulting destruction and depopulation created a sort of wasteland that rendered this area largely unproductive for the next half-century. The individuals caught up in this storm, if they survived the initial attack, were then transported into barbarian custody where they either served as slaves or, if they were lucky, were redeemed by family members, private individuals (often looking for a profit), or the church. Nevertheless, negotiations over ransoms were always tenuous and were sadly liable to failure in the face of misunderstandings or sheer corruption. This did not stop both state and church from working to maximize the chances for redemption. Ultimately, however, the problem was so widespread across the Mediterranean in this period that the

[65] See Eugippius, *Vita Severini*, 8.1–6, 9.1–3, 10.1–2, 19, 24.1–3, 31.1–6.

net outcome was surely a sizeable increase in the number of individuals held in captivity or slavery. Rome itself was, of course, a slaveholding power of long distinction, but ironically, as its power declined and its ability to protect its subjects diminished, these became increasingly subject to slavery themselves.

14: MIGRATIONS, ETHNIC GROUPS, AND STATE BUILDING

Walter Pohl

I n the Age of Attila, new kingdoms began to form on the territory of the western Roman Empire.[1] This was a gradual process,
punctuated by wars and usurpations. In 416, the Visigoths, after
long marches through the Balkans, Italy, and Gaul, and repeated negotiations with government officials, were settled by Roman authorities in
Aquitaine. At the same time, Vandals, Alans, and Suebi imposed a precarious control over much of Hispania. In 429, Vandals and Alans moved
to Africa, and, when they conquered Carthage in 439, the Vandal kingdom extended over most of the African provinces. In the 440s, after a
crushing defeat by Huns in Roman service, the Burgundians obtained
land in the southeast of Gaul around Lyons and Geneva. At around
the same time, Angles and Saxons seem to have begun spreading across
the eastern half of the British Isles. When the Hun empire fell after
the death of Attila, several new kingdoms emerged from its remains:
most notably, that of the Ostrogoths who eventually conquered Italy
in 493, but also a chain of smaller, and mostly very short-lived realms
along the Danube, governed by Rugians, Heruls, Suebi, Sarmatians,
and Gepids. Towards the end of the fifth century, two of the most successful peoples began to extend their rule: the Franks in northeastern
Gaul, who conquered most of Gaul under their king Clovis around

[1] For an overview, see Herwig Wolfram, *The Roman Empire and Its Germanic Peoples*
(Berkeley, 1997); Walter Pohl, *Die Völkerwanderung*, 2nd ed. (Stuttgart, 2005); Peter J.
Heather, *The Fall of the Roman Empire: A New History* (London, 2005); Guy Halsall,
Barbarian Migrations and the Roman West, 376–568 (Cambridge, 2007). The research
leading to these results has been conducted in the context of the Austrian Science
Fund (FWF) Project F 42-G 18 – SFB "Visions of Community" (VISCOM).

500, and the Lombards in Pannonia, from where they would eventually move to Italy in 568.

The stories about the migrations of Huns, Goths, Vandals, or Burgundians have been enriched by successive generations, in Nordic sagas and medieval chivalric epic, by the emphatic identification of early modern German humanists with what they regarded as their fore-fathers, or, in the Romantic period, by vivid images of wandering tribes in search of new homelands. All of these layers have added to the wide appeal and the load of positive or negative emotions connected with the master narrative of the migration period. This again pro-vided the basis for its appropriations in nationalistic movements, most of all, in the identification of ancient Germanic warriors with modern Germans.[2] On the other hand, images of waves of barbarian immigrants and of their destructive sweep through the civilized Roman world were always available for negative stereotypes of migrants. Most educated people nowadays would rather identify with late Roman civilization than with the immigrants that threatened it – an "us" against "them" that seems increasingly familiar to Europeans and North Americans today. Once again, the kaleidoscope history of the end of the Roman Empire in the West is about to acquire a new, highly charged signif-icance. This emotional charge of identification or condemnation still overshadows scholarly debates today.[3] Ethnicity, migration, and barbar-ian state-building are highly controversial topics. This is not the place to do justice to all the individual contributions to these discussions; rather, this essay will briefly sketch some of the basic problems, and look at different ways to address them.

Several contested issues are intertwined in these debates, and it is hard to disentangle them.[4] First, there is the old debate about why and how the Roman Empire fell, which was made popular by Edward Gibbon in the later eighteenth century: was it for internal reasons, such as a decline in population, the loss of traditional political and military virtues, the impact of Christian otherworldliness, civil strife that got out of hand, natural disasters, or prolonged economic crisis? Or were the barbarian invasions directly responsible for the end of imperial rule

[2] Patrick J. Geary, *The Myth of Nations: The Medieval Origins of Europe* (Princeton, 2002).

[3] Ian N. Wood, *The Modern Origins of the Early Middle Ages* (Oxford, 2013).

[4] Walter Pohl, "Rome and the Barbarians in the Fifth Century," *Antiquité Tardive* 16 (2008): 93–101; and see the contribution by Michael Maas in this volume.

in the West?[5] Second, there was disagreement about the extent of the rupture between antiquity and the Middle Ages. Some scholars maintained that the end of empire in the West in 476 was little more than a regional regime change, while the Roman Empire in the East continued to rule extensive, if shrinking stretches of land for almost another millennium. In the late twentieth century, the focus of research shifted to the long-term process of social and cultural change that could also help to explain the political ruptures: a fundamental but gradual "transformation of the Roman World."[6] This transformation was not simply a process of decline, and much recent research has underlined the creative impulses and robust culture of the ages of Attila and of Justinian.[7] Recent critics of the "transformation" model have returned to the paradigm of a catastrophic "end of civilization."[8] Of course, many features of classical civilization faded out in the fifth century. But was that simply the result of barbarian invasions? Or could the barbarians only grab power in many provinces because something fundamental had already changed in the Roman west? The significance of migrations, ethnicity, and state-building should be discussed in the context of these complex changes. Scholars may legitimately highlight one or the other of its aspects, but monolithic explanations are unlikely to help our understanding.

MIGRATION

Traditionally, the period at the end of antiquity has been described as "the" migration period, or, in German, *die Völkerwanderungszeit:* it was "the" migration at the beginning of "our" European history, usually dated to the time between the appearance of the Huns in around

---

[5] For an overview of all previous explanations, see Alexander Demandt, *Der Fall Roms: Die Auflösung des römischen Reiches im Urteil der Nachwelt* (Munich, 1984).

[6] Ian N. Wood, "Report: The European Science Foundation's Programme on the Transformation of the Roman World and Emergence of Early Medieval Europe," *Early Medieval Europe* 6 (1997) 217–227; Walter Pohl, ed., *Kingdoms of the Empire: The Integration of Barbarians in Late Antiquity*, The Transformation of the Roman World 1 (Leiden, 1997).

[7] See, for instance, Peter R. L. Brown, *The Rise of Western Christendom: Triumph and Diversity A.D. 200–1000*, 2nd ed. (Cambridge, Mass., 2003); Michael Maas, ed., *The Cambridge Companion to the Age of Justinian* (Cambridge, 2005).

[8] Bryan Ward-Perkins, *The Fall of Rome and the End of Civilization* (Oxford, 2005).

375 and the movements of the Lombards and the Avars in 568. Many modern images of migrations, and the corresponding anxieties, were shaped in the period when Goths, Huns, and Vandals stood in the limelight. The period is therefore important for a history of perceptions. Migrations are not simply social facts, but abstractions that subsume certain events, movements, and experiences and give them an overall explanation. To describe the origin of the medieval and modern West, however, the grand narrative of "destructive/foundational migrations" is at best misleading. The brief existence of the kingdoms of the Goths, Huns, Vandals, or Burgundians stands in remarkable contrast to their prominence in successive historical writing. The ruling elites of the barbarian kingdoms on Roman soil were small minorities, who sometimes imposed their names on the territories (France, Burgundy, Lombardy), but eventually became romanized. As to the numbers of migrants, the "migration period" is not exceptional in European history. The Roman Empire had already moved large numbers of slaves, soldiers and settlers throughout its sphere of power. And the medieval period also witnessed a steady flow of populations, not only of military elites (Normans, Hungarians), but also of colonists (German, English), precarious minorities (Jews, Roma), or mobile social groups. The Age of Attila was not "*the* great migration" that fundamentally reshuffled European populations, and the temptation to link genetic particularities in some European regions to these changes has little to recommend it from a historian's perspective. It is likely that the study of ancient DNA, stable isotope analysis and other new scientific methods will bring further insights into routes and impact of fifth- and sixth-century migrations, but not about ethnic identities in the period, which are not determined by the genes.[9]

What was the impact of the migrations? In most Roman provinces, there was no major change of populations. Apart from the specific British case, the boundary between Germanic and Romance languages formed at relatively little distance inside the former Rhine and Danube frontier. What mattered politically was the gradual replacement of a Roman military by barbarian warriors, up to the highest officers. Migrating peasants (such as the so-called *Gothi minores* settled in the Balkans) did not challenge the Roman order. Immigrant warriors often were integrated in the flexible imperial military system, but eventually

---

[9] Patrick Geary, "Using Genetic Data to Revolutionize Understanding of Migration History," *IAS eNews, Spring 2013*, http://www.ias.edu/about/publications/ias-letter/articles/2013-spring/geary-history-genetics, accessed 17 July 2013.

they could change the balance of power. The barbarians also had an impact on what we could call the social imagination. Many Roman sources of the period reflect the presence of barbarians in Roman heartlands: not only historiography, but also imperial law, the sermons of Augustine, the letters of the church father Jerome or of the Gallic aristocrat Sidonius Apollinaris, a moral treatise by Salvian of Marseille, or the *Lives* of Severinus of Noricum or Germanus of Auxerre. On the other hand, it is also remarkable in which cases the events were met with comparative silence. In 406, Vandals, Alans, and Suebi crossed the Rhine and moved across Gaul into Spain; we would regard this as one of the major migrations of the period, but it received little notice in contemporary accounts. The only details come from a letter that Jerome wrote in distant Palestine.[10] In the same years, several Roman usurpers operated in Gaul, among them Constantine III, who removed the Roman troops from Britain in 407. Contemporary writers concentrate on their complicated maneuvres, in which the barbarians hardly featured. Perhaps the "Vandalism" (a word coined in the polemics of the French Revolution) of the Vandals did not exceed the expectable.[11] At the time, nobody could have foreseen that the next Vandal generation would conquer Rome's richest province, Africa, and establish their kingdom in one of the centers of the Mediterranean world, Carthage. In contemporary perspective, the real power games were between contenders for empire, not between Romans and barbarians.

How strong were the invading barbarian armies? When, in 376, Goths retreating before the Huns crossed the Danube into the empire, "the ill-omened officials who ferried the barbarian hordes often tried to reckon their number, but gave up their vain attempt."[12] Contemporary accounts often exaggerate the numbers of the barbarians; but rarely do they underline as frankly as here that attempts to calculate the numbers of "a countless swarm of peoples" had failed. Only sometimes do we get likely numbers. In May 429, the Vandals (and other barbarians) under

---

[10] Jerome, *Epistula* 123.16, ed. Isidor Hilberg, *Sancti Eusebii Hieronymi Epistvlae: Epistulae Pars III, CXXI–CLIV* (Vienna, 1996) 93.

[11] This is controversial, but there is little textual or archaeological evidence for extraordinary devastation in Gaul; see Walter Goffart, *Barbarian Tides: The Migration Age and the Later Roman Empire* (Philadelphia, 2006) 73–118; Andy Merrills and Richard Miles, *The Vandals* (Chichester, 2010) 35–41; John F. Drinkwater and Hugh Elton, *Fifth-Century Gaul: A Crisis of Identity?* (Cambridge, 1992); and Roland Steinacher, *Die Vandalen: Aufstieg und Fall römischer Barbaren* (Stuttgart, forthcoming).

[12] Ammianus Marcellinus, *Rerum gestarum libri*, 31.4.6, ed. and trans. John C. Rolfe, *Ammianus Marcellinus* (Cambridge, 1935) 3: 405.

their king Geiseric crossed the Straits of Gibraltar. Victor of Vita reports that Geiseric had his entire people counted, men, women, children, and slaves, and they were eighty thousand individuals, not warriors, as Victor underlines.[13] Procopius has the same number, but supports the interpretation that Victor rejects: Geiseric, he writes, had the "Vandals and Alans arranged in companies, appointing over them no less than eighty captains, whom he called *chiliarchs*, making it appear that his host of fighting men in active service amounted to eighty thousand. And yet the number of the Vandals and Alani was said in former times, at least, to amount to no more than fifty thousand men. However, after that time by their natural increase among themselves and by associating other barbarians with them they came to be an exceedingly numerous people."[14] Procopius was aware of the changes in size and composition of barbarian armies, but Victor's numbers are more likely. Belisarius's army that conquered the Vandal kingdom in 533–534 amounted to about twenty-five thousand men.[15] This corresponds to other estimates for the size of large late Roman and barbarian armies. If it really were eighty thousand who crossed the Straits of Gibraltar in 429 they may have consisted of about fifteen to twenty thousand Vandal and Alan warriors, perhaps ten thousand more men who could take up arms if necessary (adventurers, servants, low-status Romans trying to improve their lot, and fugitive slaves), and about fifty thousand women, children, old men, and slaves. Some scholars, however, have argued for lower figures.[16]

Like the Vandals, few barbarian groups came into the Roman Empire directly from distant regions; most of them had already made some experience with the Romans when they attacked. That is even true for the Huns, who only launched their major campaigns against Roman provinces under Attila, more than sixty years after they had settled in the vicinity. Attila had a Roman secretary and was familiar

[13] Victor Vitensis, *Histoire de la persécution vandale en Afrique suivie de La passion des sept martyrs, Registre des provinces et des cités d'Afrique* 1.2, ed. and trans. Serge Lancel (Paris, 2002) 96–98.
[14] Procopius, *De bello Vandalico* 3.5.18f., ed. and trans. Henry B. Dewing, *History of the Wars* (Cambridge, Mass., 1970) 3: 53.
[15] Proc. *BV* 3.11, Dewing 101–111.
[16] Walter Goffart, *Barbarians and Romans, AD 418–584: The Techniques of Accommodation.* (Princeton, 1980) 231–235; but see John H. G. W. Liebeschuetz, "*Gens* into *Regnum*: The Vandals," in *Regna et Gentes: The Relationship between Late Antique and Early Medieval Peoples and Kingdoms in the Transformation of the Roman World*, ed. Hans-Werner Goetz et al., The Transformation of the Roman World 13 (Leiden, 2003) 67ff.

with Roman politics, and he knew how to organize a military expedition against imperial territory, although he never attempted to stay. Only rarely did large barbarian armies invade the empire without much knowledge of what they would encounter – that is usually a sign that they were pushed, and not pulled by the opportunities that the empire could offer. The year 406–407 seems to have been such a case, when both the Goth and "real Scythian" Radagaisus (as Orosius calls him) and the Vandals, Alans, and Suebi invaded, probably displaced by the Hun advance into the Carpathian basin.[17] But twenty years later, when Geiseric had taken power, a new generation of Vandal warriors was in charge. They had grown up on Roman soil and were more familiar with Roman ways. Unlike Alaric the Visigoth about twenty years earlier, Geiseric managed to cross over to Africa with tens of thousands of people, a considerable logistic achievement.

All barbarian kings who managed to establish a relatively stable barbarian realm on Roman soil had already grown up there, and their peoples had spent at least twenty to thirty years in Roman provinces, usually as federates of the Roman army. The Visigoths reached a permanent settlement in the kingdom of Toulouse about forty years after they had crossed the Danube under pressure from the Huns; the Burgundians spent a similar period on the Roman side of the Middle Rhine before founding their kingdom around Lyons and Geneva; Theoderic, who had grown up as a hostage in Constantinople, led the Ostrogoths to Italy thirty-five years after they had been established as federates in Pannonia; and Clovis, who unified the Frankish kingdom around 500, was the son of Childeric, Roman commander at Tournai. One had to know how to rule over Romans, and perhaps more important, how to profit from the Roman system. Only the Angles and Saxons who came to Britain may have been less familiar with Roman ways, and it seems to have taken them a long time to establish their rule over parts of the island through an unstable succession of alliances and wars with the sub-Roman British kingdoms and with each other.

Barbarian migrations into the Roman world were a process full of war and plundering, conflict and bloodshed, and we should not forget that. More often than not, the conflict was not between Romans and invaders, but developed along different lines. Some of the bloodiest battles of the period were fought between contenders for the Roman

[17] Peter J. Heather, *The Fall of the Roman Empire: A New History* (London, 2005) 192–209; Orosius, *Historiae adversum paganos*, 7.37.9, ed. Karl Zangemeister (Leipzig, 1889) 539.

imperial throne, for instance, the battle at the Frigidus in which, in 394, Theodosius "the Great" destroyed the army of the pretender Eugenius. Thousands of Goths fell on the Theodosian side, thousands of Franks led by the educated Frank Arbogast died for Eugenius. Likewise, barbarian rivals fought endless wars with each other, often spurred by Roman money and diplomacy. In the 410s, the Christian historiographer Orosius welcomed as one of the most fortunate events in all of Roman history the fact that Visigoths and Vandals were decimating each other in Spain.[18] Such conflicts continued throughout the period: on the Catalaunian fields, both Aetius's and Attila's armies consisted mainly of barbarians, most prominently, of Goths; Odoacer destroyed the kingdom of the Rugi in 487; Theoderic the Ostrogoth destroyed Odoacer in 493; the Frank Clovis defeated the Visigoths in 508, and so on. One of the few all-out wars of the empire against barbarians was waged between Justinian's Byzantine armies and the Ostrogoths in Italy between 535 and 554; and that had been started by the Roman side to oust the highly romanized Goths from power, and was conducted largely by barbarian troops in Byzantine service.

Since the fourth century, barbarian soldiers had largely replaced Roman citizens in the army. These had to pay a tax in exchange for their military duties, and it had become much more profitable for the Roman state to draft ambitious barbarian warriors than often unwilling provincials.[19] Huns, for example, soon became attractive as army units and as bodyguards for Roman aristocrats. Later, Attila attempted to stop any movement from his realm to the empire, and repeatedly insisted on the return of fugitives from the Roman Empire, who were then executed with exemplary cruelty (some members of the royal clan were crucified immediately after they had been handed over).[20] There was a lucrative market for soldiers: a strong pull-factor in the migration of barbarian warriors to Roman territory. Since the late fourth century, barbarians increasingly came in large groups under their own leaders, and entered Roman service as fixed units. They were in a better position to negotiate with the imperial authorities, and to exert pressures to obtain additional benefits. Especially Gothic groups used the full range of opportunities between loyal service for Rome, negotiations for better

---

[18] Oros. *Hist.* 7.43, 565.

[19] Hugh Elton, *Warfare in Roman Europe, AD 350–425* (Oxford, 1996).

[20] Priscus, fr. 2, fr. 9.1, fr. 9.3, ed. Roger C. Blockley, *The Fragmentary Classicising Historians of the Later Roman Empire: Eunapius, Olympiodorus, Priscus and Malchus*, 2 vols. (Liverpool, 1983) 2: 227, 234, 238.

conditions, threats, reprisals, and full-scale raids. Regular supplies, better pay, and higher rank for the leader then meant the chance to attract a stronger following. Those barbarians who had been most successful as allies (*foederati*) and competitors within the Roman system were the ones who eventually built their kingdoms on west Roman territory.

ETHNIC GROUPS

The Romans distinguished the barbarian groups that they were confronted with by ethnic names.[21] This was a coherent system of perceptions, and it is only rarely that we find other, mostly vague definitions in the sources ("the barbarians in these parts," "those who followed X"). For a long time, modern scholarship has taken this ethnic language as a direct testimony of self-assured ethnic groups. But it is not that simple. The Romans, like the Greeks before them, distinguished their barbarian neighbors by ethnic categorization, whereas they mostly described the inhabitants of the classical world by their city or their polity. The ethnic denomination of the barbarian "others" was a complex process. Some of the names were ethnographic classifications, such as "Germans" or "Scythians," based on territory and lifestyle. They hardly corresponded to any late antique self-identification – it is unlikely that the Franks regarded themselves as Germans or the Huns as Scythians, or the Goths as either of them (in the sixth century only, Cassiodorus and Jordanes constructed a grandiose history of the Goths in which they identified them with the ancient Scythians, Getae, and Dacians). Other names in the sources were literary reminiscences, and late antique panegyrics are full of lists of long-gone peoples reputedly annihilated by an emperor. Nevertheless, most ethnic names reflect consistent contemporary usage. It is often hard to prove that they were also used for self-identification, simply because genuinely barbarian voices are rather rare in the fifth century, apart from a few inscriptions and highly rhetorical speeches in the histories.

Some scholars have used the relative lack of self-identifications in our sources to argue that ethnic identities were rather meaningless in the period, a mere literary convention.[22] However, the barbarian

---

[21] For the following, see Walter Pohl, "Introduction: Strategies of Identification: A methodological profile," in *Strategies of Identification: Ethnicity and Religion in Early Medieval Europe*, ed. Walter Pohl and Gerda Heydemann (Turnhout, 2013) 1–64.

[22] For instance, Goffart, *Barbarian Tides*.

gentes were very much part of the everyday political reality of fifth-century Rome. The Romans may have underestimated the dynamic that growing military forces of barbarian origin within their empire could develop, or treated some of them rather inadequately. They could not, however, afford to use a completely imaginary system of names to distinguish among them. Ethnicity is not a quality that particular groups have or have not; it is a system of distinctions that allows defining social groups in relation to each other. Such distinctions are necessarily fuzzy, and they become even fuzzier in times of uncertain or shifting identities, which was certainly the case in the fifth century. Yet they allow group members or newcomers to identify with a group, and outsiders to know with whom they are dealing. Communication between Romans and barbarians was intense, and Roman officers and diplomats had to have a differentiated knowledge of their adversaries. An author-diplomat such as Priscus was very well informed about the Huns. Mistakes could be fatal, as he noted repeatedly: for instance, Roman diplomats had distributed presents among the leaders of the Akatzirs (a Hunnic people north of the Black Sea) not quite according to their current status in the tribal hierarchy. As a result the pro-Attila faction among them came to power.[23] In another case, the Romans got it almost right: Attila's Roman secretary Orestes had complained on a mission to Constantinople that his colleague Edekon had been invited to dinner without him; but the interpreter Vigilas explained to Priscus that Edekon was a Hun, whereas Orestes, although powerful, was only Attila's Roman servant.[24] Being "of Hun origin" counted. It is ironic that Edekon is later attested as Edica, king of the Sciri, and it was his son Odoacer whose military coup removed Orestes and his son, the last western emperor Romulus Augustulus, from power in 476. Odoacer is variously identified in our sources as Scirian, Turcilingian, Thuringian, Herul, or Goth, but not as a Hun. Ethnic identities could change, and they could also remain somehow ambiguous; Odoacer may have deliberately left his identity open in order to appeal to his army, which comprised all these components. That does not mean that ethnicity did not matter – in Odoacer's case, it probably reflected the continuing significance of ethnic identities in his army.

This is what makes understanding late ancient ethnicity so difficult: ethnic identities were not clearly circumscribed and could change. They might matter to some and not to others, and they were distorted

---

[23] Prisc. fr. 11.2 (Blockley 247).
[24] Prisc. fr. 11.2 (Blockley 249).

by outdated conventional names, ethnographic perceptions, and literary fabrications. Last but not least, we have relatively little evidence what people called themselves. Still, it would be wrong to conclude that ethnicity was insignificant. Changes of identity do not invalidate the importance of having an identity. The anthropologist Fredrik Barth, in his 1960s studies of the Pathans, noticed that the boundaries between ethnic groups were frequently crossed; such changes in ethnic identity did not erode, however, but reinforced the ethnic boundaries.[25] Most major barbarian figures of the period get clear ethnic labels in the sources, and their use is relatively consistent in different texts. The Huns are a good example that identifications remain relatively coherent even between sources that are unlikely to be derived from each other, for they appear not only in Latin and Greek, but also in Armenian, Iranian, and Sogdian texts. Furthermore, it is quite likely that these "Huns" corresponded with the Xiongnu of the Chinese sources in some way (see la Vaissière's chapter in this volume). Fifth-century coins from a Hun kingdom in the periphery of the Sasanian empire bear the legend "HWN," offering a rare case of Hun self-identification.[26] An indirect example is found in Priscus, where the Roman officer Chelchal is quoted saying that he was proud of his Hunnic origin.[27] The exact relations between the European Huns, the Central Asian Huns of the fourth century and the earlier Xiongnu are debatable, but the Huns who arrived in 375 are surely part of a general movement of Hunnic groups in the period. Whether they were of predominantly Xiongnu origin is not a very meaningful question. They may very well have been a mixed group of refugees, fleeing from power struggles farther east, who had adopted the most prestigious name available on the steppe, like many other steppe peoples. What mattered is how they were identified, and identified themselves. When the Avars arrived from Central Asia in the sixth century, a Byzantine chronicler reported that in fact they were only Pseudo-Avars and had wrongly adopted that awe-inspiring name; but the name stuck.[28] That does not prove that ethnicity was

[25] Fredrik Barth, ed., *Ethnic Groups and Boundaries: The Social Organization of Culture Difference* (Oslo, 1969).

[26] Walter Pohl, "Huns, Avars, Hungarians: Comparative Perspectives Based on Written Evidence," in *The Complexity of Interaction along the Eurasian Steppe Zone in the First Millennium AD*, ed. Jürgen Bemmann and Michael Schmauder (forthcoming).

[27] Prisc. fr. 49 (Blockley 357).

[28] Theophylactus Simocatta 7.7, 7.8, ed. and trans. Michael Whitby and Mary Whitby, *The History of Theophylact Simocatta: An English Translation with Introduction and Notes* (Oxford, 1986) 187–189.

meaningless: on the contrary, it was important enough to make faking it worthwhile.

What ethnicity can help to explain is the relatively greater coherence of ethnic groups as compared to the very diverse group of recruits who filled the ranks of "normal" armies or retinues. When the Roman count (*comes*) Bonifatius died, he told his followers to join his arch-rival Aetius, and his wife, to marry him. Likewise, when Stilicho or Aetius were killed, their armies dissolved or went over to a rival. After the deaths of Alaric and Athaulf, however, their Goths elected new kings and stayed together even in situations when royal succession was highly contested. Being a *gens*, a people, seems to have made an important difference.[29] Recent exploits surely contributed to this shared identity; yet Aetius's troops had also been through many battles together. We do not know whether origin stories mattered, and which ones, but it is unlikely that all memories of pre-Roman times had been erased. Military exploits alone were not a sufficient basis for building a kingdom, and neither was personal loyalty to a warlord. Except for the short-lived rule of Odoacer and a few ephemeral regional Roman realms in Gaul and Spain, all post-Roman kingdoms became known by their ethnic labels. On the other hand, they were not simply the creation of self-confident Germanic peoples, as former generations of scholars believed. At least as much, as will be argued below, these kingdoms stabilized and shaped the ethnic identity of the barbarian-Roman elites that governed them.[30]

BUILDING KINGDOMS

In fifth-century Europe, Attila's kingdom was an exception. In many respects, it followed the model of empires as they existed in the vast Central Asian steppes: an enormous, but rather volatile concentration of mobile warriors who flocked around a center of power that could give its expansionist dynamic a sense of direction and successful

---

[29] Claudian, *De IV consulatu Honorii Augusti C. Claudiani*. 474, ed. and trans. Maurice Platnauer (London, 1922) 1: 320; Zosimos, *Historia nova*, 5.5.4, ed. François Paschoud, vol. 3 (Paris, 1986) 11. Walter Pohl, "Pistis e potere: Coesione etnica negli eserciti barbarici nel periodo delle migrazioni," in *Archeologia e storia delle migrazioni: Europa, Italia, Mediterraneo fra tarda età romana e alto medioevo*, ed. Carlo Ebanista and Marcello Rotili (Cimitile, 2011) 55–64.

[30] Hans-Werner Goetz, Jörg Jarnut, and Walter Pohl, eds., *Regna et Gentes: The Relationship between Late Antique and Early Medieval Peoples and Kingdoms in the Transformation of the Roman World*, The Transformation of the Roman World 13 (Leiden, 2003).

leadership. Such a steppe empire consisted of various groups, clans, and peoples with different status, governed by a ruling dynasty or clan (in Priscus's terminology, the "royal" or "imperial" Scythians – he uses the Greek word *basilikós*, which is also used for the emperor). Its formidable military power could hold all subjects and neighbors in check, secure victory and plunder in war, and put such pressure on a sedentary empire that it preferred to buy peace at exceptional cost by paying a tribute only thinly disguised as "presents" or rewards for military service. The ruler of such a steppe empire could use the influx of gold, silver, and prestige goods to demonstrate his invincibility, and to keep his warriors satisfied by gifts and benefits. Food and the necessities of daily life were procured by a traditional pastoral economy, and by the agricultural production of the subject populations, in part resettled near the core areas of the empire. These steppe empires usually exhausted their expansive dynamic within a few generations, and were soon replaced by another one.[31]

Attila's kingdom corresponded to the model, but with some interesting differences. In spite of their dramatic impact when they arrived in Europe, the Huns did not establish a unified empire at first. Several kings and leaders seem to have coexisted, each with limited powers. Only in the 430s did the Huns begin to pose a threat to the Roman Empire, and Attila's empire reached the apex of its glory a few years before his death and the dissolution of the kingdom. Unlike many of the steppe empires bordering on Sasanian Iran or China, Attila obviously did not aspire to conquering imperial territories and to appropriating its infrastructure, its cities, fortresses, mints, or tax systems. When his raids had depopulated a broad strip of Roman land south of the Danube, he even requested that it should not be resettled. The expeditions to Gaul and Italy in 451 and 452 indicate that the range of strategic options under these premises were limited. Paradoxically, many powerbrokers of the future met at Attila's court, men whose sons would follow a very different strategy, and who were to rule Italy for more than half a century: Orestes, father of the last western emperor; Odoacer's father Edekon; and the Ostrogothic king Thiudimir, father of Theoderic "the Great." Yet none of them followed Attila's model of an empire outside

---

[31] Otto Maenchen-Helfen, *The World of the Huns: Studies in Their History and Culture*, ed. Max Knight (Berkeley, 1973); Walter Pohl, *Die Awaren: Ein Steppenvolk in Mitteleuropa 567–822 n. Chr.* (Munich, 2002); Peter B. Golden, *Central Asia in World History* (Oxford, 2011); Nicola Di Cosmo and Michael Maas, eds., *Eurasian Empires: Rome, China, Iran, and the Steppe in Late Antiquity, ca. 250–650 C.E.* (forthcoming).

the Roman empire.[32] In the meantime, Attila's sons, and increasingly, other "Hunnic" steppe peoples lived in an unstable landscape of regional kingdoms and powers north of the Black Sea, until the Avars built a similar empire from the 560s onward.[33]

The future post-Roman kingdoms began more inconspicuously than Attila's empire. The Visigoths were the pioneers of a stable settlement by treaty of a barbarian army in a Roman province. They were granted the province of Aquitania, but it had taken almost a generation of conflicts and negotiations before this arrangement was reached, and it entailed the consent of at least part of the Roman elite in Gaul.[34] In theory, the Visigoths represented imperial rule, and in practice, they controlled, but were also dependent on, the Roman administration in their province. This arrangement did not bring lasting peace, for the Goths tried to extend the area of their control, while Roman commanders and other barbarian groups strove to contain them. The stable settlement of barbarians, however, resulted in limiting the range and intensity of military conflict. The Visigothic "kingdom of the empire" gradually slipped out of imperial control, but as most other barbarian kingdoms, it continued, and eventually down-sized the Roman administration and its tax system.[35]

The situation was much more precarious in Hispania, where Vandals, Alans, and Suebi had carved out rough areas of dominance in endemic conflict with each other, with Roman commanders, and with the Visigoths who repeatedly attacked them with or without an imperial mandate. It is an example of an integration that never quite worked, so that King Geiseric decided to move on. When his Vandals and Alans crossed over into Africa in 429, there were rumors that the Roman governor Boniface had called them in to assist him in internal struggles. But they came as conquerors, not by way of a negotiated settlement – a rare case. Still, Geiseric found ways to collaborate with the Roman administration, and to settle his army comfortably without disrupting the provincial economy too much. The Vandal kingdom threatened the grain supplies for Rome, which had come from Africa, cut off the tax proceeds from one of the richest provinces, and challenged imperial naval control over the western Mediterranean – severe blows for the

---

[32] For the "Hunnic alternative," see Herwig Wolfram, *The Roman Empire and Its Germanic Peoples* (Berkeley, 1997).

[33] Pohl, "Huns, Avars, Hungarians."

[34] Roger Collins, *Visigothic Spain, 409–711* (London, 2004).

[35] Walter Pohl, ed., *Kingdoms of the Empire: The Integration of Barbarians in Late Antiquity*, The Transformation of the Roman World 1 (Leiden, 1997).

empire. Still, Emperor Valentinian III tried to come to terms with Geiseric, whose son Huneric was then married to a Theodosian princess. When Attila died and his empire collapsed, the Vandal kingdom seemed to be built on much more solid ground; in 455, Geiseric directed his fleet to Rome to avenge the murder of Valentinian III, and had the city plundered for two weeks.

Whereas the Visigothic kingdom was built on negotiations, and that of the Vandals on conquest, the Burgundian kingdom in southeastern Gaul started with defeat.[36] In the 440s, the Roman general Aetius transferred them from the agitated Rhine frontier to a quieter province further inland. They were to provide military services when required, and indeed, members of the Burgundian royal family repeatedly took high military office. In the last years of the western empire, their later king Gundobad acted as military commander and impresario of power in Ravenna for some time, until he withdrew to Burgundy. In these years, the elites of the Burgundian kingdom had no sense that something fundamental had changed. The sixth-century *Lives of the Jura Fathers* underline how the Burgundian king Chilperic in circa 470 publicly criticized the ascetic abbot Lupicinus for having prophesied the collapse of the Roman order in the province, and shouted at him: "Are you not the impostor who . . . proclaimed to this region and to our fathers that ruin was imminent? Why, then, I ask you, have terrible predictions that you made publicly not been confirmed by any unfortunate event? Explain that to us, you false prophet!"[37] In these kingdoms, the empire was still a reality, although mediated through barbarian kings and officials who were often more accessible than the distant imperial court. It is remarkable that although the kingdoms of the Visigoths, Vandals, and Burgundians had been established under very different conditions, their basic policies and political conduct did not differ fundamentally. Their kings were proud of their rule over imperial territory, but still operated within the imperial framework.

The texts routinely use ethnic labels for these kingdoms, and ascribe agency to the *gens*, the people. The *gentes* wage war, conclude peace, extend their kingdoms, elect their kings, are friend or foe to the empire. These perceptions of practical politics do not quite correspond

---

[36] Reinhold Kaiser, *Die Burgunder* (Stuttgart, 2004).

[37] *Vitae Patrum Iurensium*, trans. Tim Vivian, Kim Vivian, and Jeffrey Burton Russell, *The Life of the Jura Fathers: The Life and Rule of the Holy Fathers Romanus, Lupicinus, and Eugendus, Abbots of the Monasteries in the Jura Mountains*, 2.92–95 (Spencer, Mass., 1999) 144ff.

to the formal self-representation of the new rulers. In the fifth century, they rarely advertised the ethnic background to their rule. They mostly used *rex* (king) as their title, without any ethnic qualification. This is understandable, because they claimed to rule not only over their own people, but also over other barbarians and over a vast majority of Roman provincials. To call oneself king of the Goths (*rex Gothorum*) or Vandals would have implied a limitation of their rule. Still, in certain occasions, the ethnic title is also attested. A North African inscription, for instance, gives Huneric's title as *rex Vandalorum et Alanorum;* it was a time when Geiseric's son, husband of a Theodosian princess, had to secure the loyalty of his more traditionally minded nobles.[38] Around 500, a seal ring of the Visigothic king Alaric II conserved in the Vienna Kunsthistorisches Museum gives his title as *rex Gothorum.*[39] In some manuscripts of Burgundian law, Gundobad is presented as *rex Burgundionum.*[40] The use of the title was obviously situational, and depended on the audience. It took centuries until the use of the ethnic title as self-representation became standard.

This is not surprising, the political situation was complex and in many ways experimental. The *gentes* had been regarded as barbarians, pagans (*gentes* or gentiles was the Christian term for them), minorities, and outsiders. Now they ruled over large swaths of imperial territory. We still do not understand properly why and how this change to hegemonic ethnicity happened. Why were the new kingdoms not simply defined by dynasty or province?[41] For a long time, scholars have taken it for granted that the conquerors should assert their ethnic identities in their new kingdoms. However, the contemporary sources attest to little ethnic self-assertiveness. Yet ethnic identity could now offer privilege, and the new rulers had to be careful to control access to what later on, in Ostrogothic Italy, was to be called *libertas Gothorum,* the

[38] Vict. Vit. 2.8 (2.9); 3.3, 125, 175; Herwig Wolfram, *Intitulatio I: Lateinische Königs- und Fürstentitel bis zum Ende des 8. Jahrhunderts* (Graz, 1967) 79.
[39] Kunsthistorisches Museum Wien, "Gemme: Siegelstein Alarichs II., König der Westgoten," Kunsthistorisches Museum Wien, Bilddatenbank, http://bilddatenbank.khm.at/viewArtefact?id=71108, accessed 16 July 2013.
[40] *Leges Burgundionum*, Praef., Extravagantes XIXf., ed. Ludwig Rudolf von Salis (MGH LL Nat. Germ. 2, 1, Hannover, 1892), 29; 118f.; Ian N. Wood, "Ethnicity and the Ethnogenesis of the Burgundians," in *Typen der Ethnogenese unter besonderer Berücksichtigung der Bayern* 1, ed. Herwig Wolfram and Walter Pohl (Vienna, 1990) 53–69.
[41] Walter Pohl, "Introduction: Ethnicity, Religion and Empire," in *Visions of Community in the Post-Roman World. The West, Byzantium and the Islamic World, 300–1100,* ed. Walter Pohl et al. (Farnham, U.K., 2012).

freedom of the Goths.[42] The *gens* had to be big enough to impose its rule and small enough to provide a fair share in the benefits. It was this innovative political role that made ethnic identities significant in a new way. Visigoths and Burgundians issued their own law codes, Goths and Vandals distinguished themselves by their Arian creed, and all of this was part of a complex effort to maintain difference in a process of integration into the Roman and Christian world. The Age of Attila saw the beginning of a specifically European process: the development of a political landscape structured by ethnic (and later, national) distinctions.[43] That was not the natural result of a "migration of peoples." It was the eventual outcome of arrangements between the Roman elites and ethnically defined armies that gave them control over Roman provinces.

---

[42] Herwig Wolfram, *History of the Goths* (Berkeley, 1985) 301.

[43] Walter Pohl, "Introduction: Christian and Barbarian Identities in the Early Medieval West," in *Post-Roman Transitions: Christian and Barbarian Identities in the Early Medieval West*, ed. Walter Pohl and Gerda Heydemann (Turnhout, 2013).

15: KINGDOMS OF NORTH AFRICA

Andy Merrills

Where is Africa, that for the whole world was like a garden of pleasures? Where are her many districts? Where are her great and most splendid cities?[1]

D
e tempore barbarico (On Barbarian Times) by Bishop Quodvult-deus of Carthage was a valedictory sermon on the charmed existence of Roman North Africa, in the face of the Vandal occupation of the 430s. For centuries, Roman North Africa had indeed been a rich region: its vast surplus of grain, olive oil, and wine had long been shipped to feed the hungry bureaucracy of the western Roman Empire, and its towns witnessed an efflorescence of Latin literary culture, both secular and Christian. The military presence in the region had also been comparatively light, and it had been spared the political convulsions which beset the northerly provinces of the empire in the third century and in the early decades of the fifth. If North Africa was scarcely a prelapsarian Paradise – bitter sectarian disputes had been common in the fourth century, and sporadic frontier warfare was endemic – it remained a uniquely privileged region in the later Roman world.

The fifth century was to change this dramatically, but not in the way which Quodvultdeus or his parishioners might have feared. The Vandal occupation of Carthage in 439, and the formal establishment of their kingdom three years later, marked the foundation of a remarkably effective successor state, which was to last for almost a century. Simultaneously, margraves along the old Roman frontier asserted their own military and political authority in the shadow of the empire.

[1] Quodvultdeus, De tempore barbarico, 2.5.4: "ubi est Africa, quae toto mundo fuit velut hortus deliciarum? . . . ubi tantae splendissimae civitates?"

These Vandal and Moorish kingdoms rapidly made their presence felt on the world stage – joint raids throughout the Mediterranean in the middle decades of the century reminded nervous contemporaries of the dark days of the Punic Wars – but it was in Africa itself that this transformation was most apparent. Changing political rule created tensions within the region – most obviously in a series of poorly documented conflicts between the new polities at around the turn of the sixth century, and in the sporadic religious persecution which marked the Vandal kingdom in particular. Yet "the great and most splendid cities" of North Africa continued to flourish into the fifth century and beyond, the economy remained buoyant under the Vandals and Moors, and the region remained an important cultural centre down to the sixth century (map 6).

THE VANDAL KINGDOM

The Vandal Kingdom is the best-known of the polities which developed in North Africa over the course of the fifth century, and was the most visible to contemporary observers elsewhere in the Mediterranean (map 4a).[2] In 428 or 429, a disparate warband under the leadership of King Geiseric abandoned their holdings in Baetica and Mauretania Tingitania and moved east into the heartland of Roman Africa. They captured Hippo in 430, and were formally settled in Numidia in 435, but it was only with the sack of Carthage in 439 and the imperial treaty of 442 that their presence in the region was emphatically established. The history of the kingdom that followed can be broadly divided into two phases, which map closely onto the reigns of the kings of the ruling Hasding dynasty. The Vandals experienced an initial period of spectacular success under Geiseric (d. 477), which was followed by a long period of consolidation (or contraction) under his successors Huneric (477–484), Gunthamund (484–496), Thrasamund (496–523), and Hilderic (523–530). The last king, Gelimer (530–534) rebelled against Hilderic, and

---

[2] Christian Courtois, *Les Vandales et l'Afrique* (Paris, 1955), and Ludwig Schmidt, *Geschichte der Wandalen* (Leipzig, 1901), remain fundamental on the Vandal kingdom. See also María Elvira Gil Egea, *África en tiempos de los vándalos: Continuidad y mutaciones de las estructuras sociopolíticas romanas* (Alcalá de Henares, 1998); Guido M. Berndt, *Konflikt und Anpassung: Studien zu Migration und Ethnogenese der Vandalen* (Husum, Germany, 2007); and Andy Merrills and Richard Miles, *The Vandals* (Chichester, 2010).

thereby prompted military intervention from Justinian's Constantinople. This was not the first imperial action against the Vandals – earlier campaigns in 441, 460 and 468–470 had ended in humiliating failure – but it proved to be devastating. Within months, the Vandal presence in North Africa and the western Mediterranean was eradicated, and the Byzantine bridgehead in the West had been established.

The Vandals are best remembered for the more violent episodes in their history, particularly the sack of Rome in 455 and the persecution of Nicene Christians, in the name of their own Arian faith. But Vandal North Africa was by no means a bleak dystopia. After some interruption in production patterns at the start of the occupation, the economy continued to flourish down to the early sixth century, and African exports continued to be found throughout the Mediterranean.[3] While this trade did eventually decline, this was the result of changing patterns of consumption, rather than failures of production or distribution.[4] The Vandals were generally competent economic caretakers: indeed Gunthamund has been credited with substantial fiscal and monetary innovation, which was emulated in Constantinople.[5] Literary culture also prospered under the Vandals, thanks to the continuation of the region's schools. Some of the most important late Latin poetry and prose was produced in the region, and Vandals proved themselves to be adept pupils as well as patrons of the arts. Viewed from a wide perspective, the general picture of Vandal North Africa is one of cultural and physical continuity, rather than disruption and decline.[6]

The success of the Vandal kingdom, and its survival for almost a century, depended almost entirely upon foundations laid by the treaty of 442, in which the imperial government of Valentinian III formally recognised the new state.[7] There can be little doubt that the first months of the Vandal invasion had been brutally violent. Our sources speak of atrocities committed on the local population in the 430s and of the terrified flight of those who had the means to escape.[8] While historians

---

[3] Chris Wickham, *Framing the Early Middle Ages* (Oxford, 2005) 720–728; Merrills and Miles, *Vandals*, 141–176.

[4] Wickham, *Framing*, 725–726.

[5] Merrills and Miles, *Vandals*, 168–175.

[6] Yitzhak Hen, *Roman Barbarians: The Royal Court and Culture in the Early Medieval West* (London, 2007) 67–74.

[7] Prosper of Aquitaine, *Chronicle*, 1347 a.442. Merrills and Miles, *Vandals*, 66–70.

[8] Possidius, *Vita Augustini*, 28–30; Victor Vitensis 1.3–7; Theodoret, *Epistolae*, ed. and trans. (into French) Yvan Azéma, Sources Chrétiennes C 40, 98, 111, and 429 (Paris, 1964–1998) 22, 29–36, 70; Valentinian III, *Novellae*, 2, 12, 13.6.

writing in later years certainly exaggerated the physical destruction caused in the occupation of Carthage, the capital did suffer at the hands of the invaders, and field survey data suggest that rural production also experienced something of a hiccup at around the same time.[9] Yet the settlement of 442 effectively transformed Geiseric's followers from a mobile field army to a settled aristocracy, and furthermore consolidated the king's own position – and that of his family – within his new kingdom.

Land redistribution was central to both of these ambitions.[10] Historically, much of the agricultural land within North Africa had been owned by the imperial house, or by Italian senatorial families. Following the occupation, these estates were effectively unclaimed, and so too were the holdings of those families who had fled North Africa during the 430s.[11] Geiseric divided these estates up among his followers, and declared them to be both heritable and exempt from taxation in perpetuity.[12] In due course, the possession of these "Vandal estates" was to become a defining feature of the group's social and ethnic identity, and their heritable status was a jealously guarded privilege. At more or less the same time (our sources are frustratingly imprecise on the issue), the king substantially reorganised his army, instituting or formalising the new rank of *chiliarch* (nominally commander of one thousand men).[13] This may have been prompted by practical necessity: a new kingdom with a large fleet and a freshly minted peace treaty has rather different strategic ambitions from a peripatetic warband. But it also helped to ossify the social and political position of the individuals under the king's command, and may have been closely integrated with the division of lands.[14] The Vandals were given a physical stake in the new kingdom.

The settlement treaty also solidified Geiseric's own position, and that of his sons. Our sources are clear that the "Vandal estates" were limited to Africa Proconsularis – that is the territory immediately

---

[9] On Carthage, see Vict. Vit. 1.7. On rural production, see Merrills and Miles, *Vandals*, 148–149 with references.

[10] Land settlement in this period is a contentious issue. See Yves Modéran, "L'établissement territorial des Vandales en Afrique," *Antiquité Tardive* 10 (2002) 87–122 with discussion.

[11] Vict. Vit. 1.14; Ferrandus, *Vita S. Fulgentii*, 1; Gil Egea, *África*, 259–262.

[12] Vict. Vit. 1.13; Procopius, *De bello Vandalico*, 3.5.11–15; cf. also Vict. Vit. 1.35; Proc. *BV* 4.14.8.

[13] Proc. *BV* 3.5.18. Cf. Gil Egea, *África*, 333–334, for discussion.

[14] Vict. Vit. 1.30–36 refers to the estate of a Vandal *millenarius*, but the link between estate and rank is not explicit.

surrounding Carthage. Landholdings further afield – in Byzacena or Numidia – Geiseric kept for himself, or distributed amongst members of his family.[15] This secured the financial position of the Hasdings, but also underscored the distinction between the ruling family and the most senior of their aristocratic supporters. Developing this still further, Geiseric established royal courts for himself and his sons and formulated a law of royal succession which explicitly excluded Vandals who were not from the Hasding line.[16] Most spectacularly of all he arranged the betrothal of his son Huneric to Valentinian's daughter Eudocia as a condition of the imperial peace treaty. This diplomatic coup caused some consternation elsewhere in the Mediterranean – Huneric had previously been engaged to a Visigothic princess whom Geiseric disfigured before expelling her from the kingdom – but it was a tremendous boon to the Vandal royal house.[17] At once financially secure, materially distinguished from their followers and ideologically bound to the imperial family, the Hasding house were in an exceptionally strong position after 442. Unsurprisingly, some prominent Vandals were hostile to Geiseric's arrogation of power and revolted, but the rising was crushed with little difficulty.[18] This was to be the last domestic rising within the kingdom for almost a century.

Geiseric's initial success was founded upon his skill as a military leader, and these talents resurfaced in the later years of his reign. The political upheaval which followed the assassination of Valentinian III in 455 threatened Geiseric's diplomatic plans, and introduced the opportunity for an aggressive foreign policy. In that year a combined force of Vandals and Moors sacked Rome and Eudocia was brought back to Carthage in the treasure ships, along with her mother and sister, (and a substantial amount of plunder).[19] In the same year, Geiseric launched an ongoing maritime campaign which was to bring Sardinia, Corsica, the Balearics, parts of Sicily, and large sections of the North African coast under his direct control, and which harassed the coastal communities of Italy and the Adriatic for more than two decades.[20] The strategy was

---

[15] Vict. Vit. 1.13.
[16] On the law of succession see Andy Merrills, "The Secret of My Succession: Dynasty and Crisis in Vandal North Africa," *Early Medieval Europe* 18.2 (2010) 135–159.
[17] Jordanes, *Getica*, 184.
[18] Prosp. 1348 a.442.
[19] Courtois, *Vandales*, 194–196. Proc. *BV* 1.5.4 provides the most vivid account of the sack.
[20] Merrills and Miles, *Vandals*, 116–124.

a dangerous one, and two major imperial expeditions were mounted in response, the first under Majorian in 460, the second a combined eastern operation in 468–470.[21] But Geiseric's African stronghold held, and the king's position was solidified still further among his followers and allies. This sporadic warfare was only brought to a halt in 476–477 when Geiseric, mere months before his death, signed a peace treaty with the eastern empire and came to terms with Odovacer over the rule of Sicily.[22] Thereafter, Vandal foreign policy was more muted. Thrasamund fostered close connections with Ostrogothic Italy, through his marriage to the princess Amalafrida, but largely surrendered his claim to Sicily as a result. Nevertheless, the Vandal thalassocracy remained strong. At the time of the Byzantine invasion in 533, Sardinia, Corsica, and the Balearics remained under Vandal control, along with the rump territories of North Africa.[23]

The Vandals integrated readily within Roman-African society; indeed the "Vandal" identity which emerged over the course of the fifth century was profoundly shaped by its North African setting.[24] The group that occupied Carthage in 439 were essentially a mercenary warband, whose unity was determined largely by their shared deference to Geiseric. The cohesive corporate identity of the group – the means by which this variegated army became recognised as "the Vandals" by outside observers, and began to see themselves as more than an alliance of convenience – took time to emerge, and remained in a constant state of development.[25] Certain aspects of this group identity were proudly distinct from local "Carthaginian" or "Roman" cultural traditions, but these were surprisingly few. A distinct Vandalic dialect of the Gothic language was known, although its use may have been restricted to proper names by the end of the Vandal period. The only surviving fragments of the language are an allusion to an Arian liturgy and a joke in a Latin epigram.[26] Latin probably remained the *lingua franca* of government, and although there are references to translators in the texts,

[21] Discussed (with references) in Merrills and Miles, *Vandals*, 119–123.
[22] Malchus, fr. 5; Proc. *BV* 4.7.26; Vict. Vit. 1.14.
[23] Merrills and Miles, *Vandals*, 129–140.
[24] Berndt, *Konflikt*, 175–256; Merrills and Miles, *Vandals*, 83–108; Jonathan Conant, *Staying Roman: Conquest and Identity in the Mediterranean 439–700* (Cambridge, 2012) 19–66.
[25] Berndt, *Konflikt*, 260–263; Cf. Proc. *BV* 3.5.21–22.
[26] Nicoletta Francovich Onesti, *I Vandali: Ligua e storia* (Rome, 2002).

prominent Vandal figures were generally expected to communicate in the language.

In other ways, the Vandals simply adopted the established conventions of the Romano-African aristocracy. The Vandals were concerned, not with defining their identity in opposition to the existing "Roman" populace of North Africa, as has frequently been assumed, but rather in establishing their position among the privileged elite of this society. The distinction between "Vandal" and "Roman" was a less significant fissure within North Africa than were long-established distinctions between rich and poor. This is not to suggest that "Vandal" identity was meaningless in fifth- and sixth-century Africa. Individuals were certainly proud of the wider identity that their military profession, privileged rights of land ownership, unusual names or family histories might signify. But well-established symbols of Roman or African identity were also adopted with alacrity. When we read of Vandals who patronised Latin literature, who commissioned paintings of themselves on hunts, or who engaged in theological debate, this does not reflect a "Romanisation" of the Vandals as has often been assumed, but rather the emergence of a distinct cultural identity within a post-Roman world.[27] Equally, when individual Vandals aspired to comparison with Achilles – as happened more than once – this was neither a betrayal of "Germanic" ideals of masculinity nor an arch irony on the part of classically educated writers, but a meaningful inheritance of shared aristocratic ideals.[28] Significantly, the reverse was also true, and Romano-Africans frequently sought access to this "Vandal" aristocratic power through the emulation or appropriation of its outward symbols. When the Catholic historian Victor of Vita denounced the typically "barbarian" clothing worn by courtiers, or reminded his readers that the Vandals should be ostracised for their barbarism, his shrill denunciations were necessary simply because their social integration had been so successful. As Victor makes clear, "barbarian" clothing was worn just as readily by Catholic Romans as by Arian Vandals.[29]

The smooth functioning of the Vandal kingdom depended upon the collaboration of existing social elites. The fact that North Africa

---

[27] Proc. *BV* 4.6.5–9 is the *locus classicus* here, which has often been misinterpreted. Cf. Merrills and Miles, *Vandals*, 99–102 and the references therein.

[28] Achilles – Parthemius, *Rescriptum ad Sigisteum;* Proc. *BV* 3.9.2.

[29] Vict. Vit. 2.8–9. See esp. Philipp von Rummel, *Habitus Barbarus: Kleidung und Repräsentation spätantiker Eliten im 4 und 5 Jahrhundert* (Berlin, 2007) 183–191, and Berndt, *Konflikt*, 238–244, on this episode.

continued to flourish throughout the fifth century testifies to this success. Inevitably, our sources for the day-to-day government of the kingdom are fragmentary, but certain broad patterns may be identified. As was the case elsewhere in the Mediterranean, the royal court was the centre of government. It was here that laws were promulgated, ambassadors received and state policy instituted.[30] The court was normally situated in the old provincial governor's palace on Byrsa Hill in the very centre of Carthage, but the rural estates of the Hasdings were also important secondary foci.[31] Geiseric's immediate entourage at court was marked by its variety. We read of individuals with Germanic names who enjoyed particular influence at court, including some with rather baffling titles.[32] Equally, Geiseric found room for aristocratic exiles from other Mediterranean kingdoms, Arian bishops, and a considerable number of aristocrats from local African families, including some of the richest individuals in the kingdom. Huneric, who may have spent time as a hostage at the court of Valentinian III, and hence may have been influenced by conventions of royal life elsewhere in the Mediterranean, continued his father's broad-minded approach, although he took care to expel several of Geiseric's trusted advisors upon his accession, whom he may have regarded as a political threat.[33]

Outside the court, Vandal kings were content to leave existing administrative systems in place, and probably proved to be better patrons of the local aristocracy than the old imperial system had been.[34] Where plum governmental positions in Africa had previously been distributed to favourites from elsewhere in the empire, regional autonomy after 442 ensured that local families who were supportive of the Vandals found unprecedented opportunities available to them. This was particularly true in Byzacena and Numidia (and later parts of Tripolitania and Mauretania), which were ruled from Carthage, but which did not experience extensive Vandal settlement. We know of two African proconsuls, Pacideius and Victorinianus, both of whom came from the old aristocracy, and both of whom held office in the third quarter of the fifth

---

[30] Hen, *Roman Barbarians*, 67–74.

[31] On Brysa Hill, see Anna Leone, *Changing Townscapes in North Africa from Late Antiquity to the Arab Conquest* (Bari, Italy, 2007) 157.

[32] Merrills and Miles, *Vandals*, 77–81. Peculiar titles include *praepositus regni* [Victor, *Historia Persecutionis* 2.29, 2.43]; *referendarius* [*Anthologia Latina*, S.375]; *primiscriniarius* [*Anth. Lat.* S.248].

[33] Huneric at Ravenna – Proc. *BV* 3.4.13; expulsions – Vict. Vit. 2.12–16. Cf. Merrills, "The Secret," 143–148.

[34] Conant, *Staying Roman*, 143–146.

century. Other provincial responsibilities were held by *Iudices* (judges), who probably oversaw administrative as well as legal duties, and in certain circumstances *comites* (counts). Municipal aristocracies also seem to have flourished, and proudly erected inscriptions celebrating their titles and achievements. While it is sometimes difficult to reconcile this self-promotion with the realities of civic administration on the ground, it seems clear that there was considerable political continuity under the Vandals.[35] At the very least, taxes continued to be collected, towns continued to function as foci for local pride and identity, and the hinterland of the Vandal kingdom continued to flourish economically.

Religion posed greater problems. Geiseric (and we may assume the majority of his followers) were adherents of Arian Christianity, and thus found themselves in opposition to the Nicene Church in Carthage. This established faith had earned its position only after the brutal internecine conflict of the fourth and early fifth centuries, and this ideological inheritance did much to set the old episcopal hierarchy at odds with the new Arian aristocracy. Certainly relations between church and crown were more strained in North Africa than in any other part of the old western empire. Under Geiseric religious conflict was largely restricted to the confiscation of church lands in Africa Proconsularis, and the dismissal or exile of some secular figures who advertised their Nicene faith.[36] The African church resisted through sermons and treatises, which frequently invoked the martyrological traditions which had been so firmly established in previous centuries. Under Huneric, this war of words tipped over into direct physical persecution, although it is sometimes difficult to distinguish between religious policy and the political purges which marked his unstable reign. This conflict reached a climax in 483–484, when many Catholic clerics were exiled from Africa Proconsularis to the frontier regions of the kingdom, and some believers were killed. The precise number of martyrdoms is disputed, but the episode certainly cast a pall upon the Vandal kingdom.[37]

---

[35] Merrills and Miles, *Vandals*, 79–81.

[36] Yves Modéran, "Une guerre de religion: Les deux Églises d'Afrique à l'époque vandale," *AnTard* 11 (2003) 21–44.

[37] Danuta Shanzer, "Intentions and Audiences: History, Hagiography, Martyrdom and Confession in Victor of Vita's *Historia Persecutionis*," in *Vandals, Romans and Berbers: New Perspectives on Late Antique North Africa*, ed. Andy Merrills (London, 2004) 271–290, here 284.

Religious policy was more varied under the later Vandal kings. We know little of Gunthamund's faith, and Procopius's brief statement that the king simply continued the policies of his predecessor probably betrays a similar ignorance on the part of that historian.[38] Thrasamund did engage actively with the problem of religion. In his reign, many prominent Catholic bishops were sent into exile on the Vandal-held island of Sardinia – a policy which had the happy side-effect of transforming that island for a few decades into an unlikely hotbed of Christian activism. Thrasamund was also interested in the theology of the dispute, and personally discussed the issue with the churchman Fulgentius of Ruspe.[39] In the event, these staged debates came to nothing, and the king was adamant that his nephew and successor Hilderic maintain his adherence to the ancestral faith. Hilderic converted almost immediately to Catholicism, however, a shift that may have been motivated in part by his cultural sympathies with the imperial court (as the grandson of Valentinian III by way of his mother, Hilderic had personal reasons for this), and by his cooling relations with the Ostrogothic court of the Arian Theoderic. With Hilderic's accession, the bishops finally returned from exile, and prepared their church for the onslaughts to come with the Byzantine occupation of the 530s.[40]

Convincing explanations for the peculiar religious history of Vandal Africa are hard to come by. Although Arianism proved popular among the new military aristocracies of the post-Roman West, North Africa was the one region in which this was manifested in active persecution of the Nicene majority. It is certainly possible that the Vandal kings regarded the episcopal hierarchy as the greatest threat to their royal power, and that exile proved a tempting strategy: certainly social and political integration seems to have been effected most successfully when the more outspoken Nicenes were safely out of the picture.[41] But such pragmatism discounts the depth of the faith within North Africa, among locals and Vandals alike. Instead, it seems more reasonable to look to the long tradition of sectarian conflict in the region to explain the problems of the later fifth century. Not only were the members of the African church unusually sensitive to their rich history of confession

---

[38] Proc. *BV* 3.8.7.
[39] Hen, *Roman Barbarians*, 87–92.
[40] Merrills and Miles, *Vandals*, 228–255.
[41] Richard Miles, "The Anthologia Latina and the Creation of Secular Space in Vandal North Africa," *AnTard* 13 (2005) 305–320.

and martyrdom, and hence perhaps more likely than others to come into conflict with a hostile secular establishment, they were also well attuned to seeing their history represented in vivid terms of sectarian persecution. Religious disagreements between the Vandals and their new subjects were certainly very real, and the sufferings of those who experienced persecution directly are not to be dismissed lightly, but the truth is that the Vandals occupied a region that was long-familiar with intense religious hatred, and came under the attention of writers who were acutely conscious of a strong sectarian tradition of authorship. Chief among these was, of course, Victor of Vita, who wrote his evis-cerating *History of the Vandal Persecutions* in around 486 – only a year or two after Huneric's bloodiest period of religious violence.[42] Crucially, this text was not simply a passive record of the recent past, it also had an active agency of its own, both as a reminder of long-standing traditions of religious intransigence, and as an incitement to further resistance to the Arian regime. In this, it drew upon the well-worn tropes of marty-rological literature, for an audience to whom such works were a familiar feature of their worship. Sectarian conflict may have taken an unusual and bloody new form under the Vandals – and there is good reason to suppose that the persecution of 483–484 was the bloodiest that Africa had experienced since the end of the Great Persecution in 306 – but it was not itself especially novel, and it was this which gave Victor's work its power. State and regional power had long been negotiated in terms of religious conflict in Africa, and local disputes had long been articu-lated through sectarian hatred. This continued under the Vandals – as did local forms of collaboration and social interaction.[43]

KINGS OF MOORS AND ROMANS

The Vandal kingdom occupied only a relatively small area of what had once been Roman North Africa. Outside the agricultural zone of Africa Proconsularis and Byzacena and a small handful of garrison towns, true power devolved to the localities. The extant evidence for the history of

[42] On Victor's text and its relation to the African martyrological tradition, see esp. Tankred Howe, *Vandalen, Barbaren und Arianer bei Victor von Vita* (Frankfurt am Main, 2007), and Shanzer, "Intentions."

[43] See esp. Brent Shaw, *Sacred Violence: African Christians and Sectarian Hatred in the Age of Augustine* (Cambridge, 2011).

these large regions is fragmentary and often confusing. Augustine's letters hint at the emergence of marcher lords in the frontier regions in the first decades of the fifth century, and a handful of legal sources help to clarify this, but these polities only come into focus for a few years in the middle of the sixth century. For around fifteen years after the Byzantine defeat of the Vandals in 533–534, and their occupation of Carthage, the imperial forces fought a prolonged campaign against a shifting alliance of Moorish states in Numidia, southern Byzacena, and Tripolitania. Our principal sources for this conflict are Procopius's *Vandal Wars* and the Latin epic *Iohannis* by the African poet Corippus. Neither of these works is unproblematic: both view the conflict from a resolutely imperialist perspective, and frequently cast the conflict in anachronistically classicising terms. Nevertheless through careful scrutiny of the texts we can identify a small number of powerful dynastic rulers along the old frontier, who articulated their power through a pattern of alliance and federation, and thereby positioned themselves with respect to Carthage (and to one another).[44]

It is hard to know how far this brief glimpse of a dynamic political system, imperfectly understood even for the mid-sixth century, can be used to inform our understanding of the mid-fifth. Allusions to the Moorish kingdoms in the texts of the Vandal period are generally brief and allusive. Many sources refer to the involvement of Moorish federates in Vandal raids under Geiseric, and it is likely that military alliances, however they were articulated, did much to keep the peace between these African neighbours.[45] Certainly once the raids into the Mediterranean stopped in the later 470s, tensions seem to have increased on the southern frontiers. Parts of Numidia seem to have ceded successfully under Huneric, and Thrasamund and Hilderic fought more or less constant border skirmishes in Tripolitania and Byzacena. Yet for the expression of power within the Moorish polities themselves, we are dependent upon a small number of inscriptions and some remarkable monumental architecture.

Two inscriptions have dominated discussion of the post-Roman Moorish states. The better known is the so-called Altava inscription. This can be dated firmly to 508, and comes from the area of the old frontier road close to the provincial boundary between Mauretania

---

[44] Yves Modéran, *Les Maures et l'Afrique Romaine (IVe–VIe siècle)* (Rome, 2003) studies Moorish society in detail, with Procopius and Corippus as his points of departure.

[45] Merrills and Miles, *Vandals*, 124–125.

Caesariensis and Mauretania Tingitana. This inscription is dated to the provincial year of 469, which is equivalent to 508 CE:

> For the salvation and security of Masuna, King of the Moors and Romans.
>
> A fort built by Masgiven, prefect of Safarus, (and Idrus, Procurator of Castra Severiana?) who was placed there by Masuna of Altava. And Maximus, the procurator of Altava finished it. Dated to the provincial year 469.[46]

Much about this inscription is profoundly imperial in tone – it is clearly a dedicatory text and was intended to be displayed on the structure that it commemorates; it was written in Latin with relatively familiar conventions of abbreviation; it was dated according to the well-established system of provincial years and it names three officials who bear imperial-sounding titles. And yet, as its opening line proclaims, the inscription and the *castrum* were both erected in honour of Masuna, "King of the Moors and Romans," and in a region far beyond imperial control. Frustratingly, little else is known of Masuna's kingdom, and it is not clear whether Altava was at the heart of the polity, or at one of its frontiers. It may be that Masuna was one of the predecessors of Mastinas (or Mastigas) whom Procopius identifies as the ruler of much of Mauretania some twenty or thirty years later, but this is speculative, (and Procopius's account of Mastinas itself is scarcely straightforward).[47] Viewed in isolation, Masuna appears as an autonomous ruler who sought to articulate his authority in a recognisably imperial form. It is possible – even likely – that "King" Masuna performed his authority in different ways before different audiences, and that he limited his "pseudo-Roman" display to the peculiarly classical register of the dedicatory inscription, but the fact that he did so is sufficient testimony to the imperial foundations upon which a substantial part of his authority was built.

---

[46] *Corpus Inscriptionum Latinarum* 8.9835: PRO SAL[UTE] ET INCOL[UMITATE] REG[IS] MASUNAE GENTI[IUM] | MAUR[ORUM] ET ROMANOR[UM]. CASTRUM [A]EDIFIC[ATUM] A MAS | GIUINI PR[A]EF[ECTO] DE SAFAR (?) IDER PROC[URATORE] CAST | RA SEUERIAN[A] QUEM MASUNA ALTAUA POSUIT | ET MAXIM[US] PROC[URATOR] ALT[AUAE] PER-FEC[IT] [ANNO] PP[ROUINCIARUM] CCCCLXVIIII.

[47] Proc. *BV* 4.13.19; 4.20.30–31. For discussion see Modéran, *Maures*, 377–383.

The second important inscription comes from the northern region of the Aurès Massif, in what is now south eastern Algeria, and what used to be on the south-western fringes of the Vandal Kingdom. This text commemorates Masties, who states that:

> I, Masties, *dux* for 67 years and *imperator* for 10 years, never perjured myself nor broke faith with either the Romans or the Moors, and was prepared in both war and peace, and my deeds were such that God supported me well.
>
> And I, Vartaia, have erected this monument with my brothers, for which I spent 100 *solidi*.[48]

Sadly, the original context of the inscription (and hence its purpose) is unknown. The letter forms suggest a fifth- or sixth-century origin, but precise dating can only be inferred from hints in the text.[49] Most commentators agree that Masties's original appointment as *dux* was probably an external one – that he was made a duke of this lawless region by Roman or Vandal authorities in Carthage. Then, after sixty-seven years (or fifty-seven if he held the titles concurrently), Masties became an *imperator* – by this period a pretension to imperial authority that must represent a declaration of autonomy from the African capital. The most persuasive context for this self-elevation is the reign of the Vandal king Huneric (477–484). Procopius states that there was a substantial revolt in the Aurès mountains in this period, and that Vandal authority in the highlands was lost thereafter.[50] Huneric's elevation coincided with a period of peace between the Vandals and the Mediterranean powers, and hence brought an end to the maritime campaigning which had once seen Vandals and Moors fight as allies: with no prospect of plunder to bind him to Carthage, Masties is more likely to have asserted his independence. If this dating is to be trusted, then the long-lived Masties was originally proclaimed *dux* in the 420s, held this position throughout the dramatic political changes of the mid fifth century, and declared his independence in the later 470s or 480s. In the last years of the fifth century, Vartaia and his brothers then erected the monument,

---

[48] D.M.S. EGO MASTIES DUX | ANN[IS] LXVII ET IMP[E]R[ATOR] ANN[IS] X QUI NUN | QUAM PERIURAVI NEQUE FIDE[M] | FREGI NEQUE DE ROMANOS NEQUE | DE MAUROS, ET IN BELLU PARUI ET IN | PACE, ET ADVERSUS FACTA MEA | SIC MECU[M] DEUS EGIT BENE.

[49] On Masties see esp. Modéran, *Maures*, 398–415 and the bibliography therein.

[50] Proc. *BV* 3.8.1–2.

(or modified it), and hence associated their own authority with that of the long-lived Moorish ruler.[51]

Masuna and Masties are known to us through the chance survivals of two inscriptions: there must have been many similar rulers who claimed authority in the extended frontier regions throughout the fifth and sixth century, and other fragmentary inscriptions support this assumption.[52] While both inscriptions are exceptional as historical sources, then, we should not necessarily assume that Masuna and Masties enjoyed unrivalled military power on the African frontier. It is clear that both rulers were powerful, and that they derived at least some of their authority from the privileged connections that they enjoyed to the old imperial framework of Rome, either by declaring their rule over "the Romans," or their alliances with them. Both also explicitly asserted their own political autonomy, albeit in language that would have been familiar to generations of imperial subjects. Beyond this, we can only speculate. In due course fieldwork in Algeria should develop our knowledge of the Moorish polities considerably: we will be able to consider the extent to which the practices of everyday life continued or changed in this period, and may gain some understanding of the social, economic, and religious life of these communities.

DJEDARS

The expression of late Roman political ideology in a profoundly local register is illustrated particularly clearly by the Djedars (literally: "structures"), of the fifth, sixth, and seventh centuries.[53] [Figure 15.1] These are thirteen spectacular monumental tombs located south of the modern Algerian city of Tiaret, and close to the old frontier road of Mauretania Caesariensis. They stand in two groups. The older is a cluster of three tombs on a spur of the Djebel Lakhdar, which may be dated broadly to the fifth century on the strength of a fortuitous carbon 14

[51] Modéran, Maures, 412–413.
[52] See, for example, CIL 8.8379 and 20216 from the Little Kabylia, which commemorates a rex gentis ucutaman[orum].
[53] Fatima Kadra, Les Djedars: Monuments funéraires Berbères de la région de Frenda (Algiers, 1983); Jean-Pierre Laporte, "Les djedars, monuments funéraires berbères de la region de Frenda et de Tiaret," in Identités et culture dans l'Algérie Antique, ed. Claude Briand-Ponsart (Rouen, 2005) 321–406.

FIGURE 15.1 Djedar A, on the Djebel Lakhdar near modern Tiaret, Algeria, fifth century. Courtesy of Corisande Fenwick.

sample, and the letter-forms of its dedicatory inscription.[54] The ten later structures were built on the Djebel Araoui to the south, and cannot have been erected before the middle of the sixth century at the earliest. The Djedars vary considerably in size and complexity, but are essentially colossal stone *tumuli*, almost certainly intended as funerary monuments. All of them have roughly rectilinear masonry platforms up to four metres in height, surmounted by a built pyramid; several have external "courtyards" created by smaller peripheral walls, and the larger structures also have internal corridors and chambers of varying complexity. The two largest Djedars were the first of each cluster to be erected. Djedar A on the Djebel Lakhdar has a rectangular masonry plinth around thirty-five metres in length and a little under four metres in height, it contains eight internal chambers, connected by a rectilinear corridor. Djedar F on the Djebel Araoui has a base of around forty-five metres square and contains twenty internal chambers, including dressed stone corridors and two well-decorated focal burial chambers. Traces of wall-painting are still evident on one of the burial chambers in Djedar

<hr />

[54] Kadra, *Djedars*, 332; Laporte, "Djedars," 360.

F, and detailed descriptions from the nineteenth century (when the paintings were in a better state of preservation) suggest strongly that they represented Christ the Good Shepherd.[55]

Two of the three Djedars on the Djebal Lakhdar were ornamented with dedicatory inscriptions in Latin; these were made *in situ* and occupy prominent positions on the eastern walls of each structure. Sadly, they are virtually illegible, but recent readings have tentatively identified the words *egregiu[s]* and *duc/dux* in lines 2 and 4 of the Djedar A inscription, and the words *filiv[s?]* and *+matri* appear on different fragments from Djedar B.[56] The Djebel Araoui group includes no such dedication, but the construction of Djedar F did include the re-use of seven Christian funerary epitaphs, which can be dated securely to the second half of the fifth century, and presumably came from a cemetery nearby.[57] Both groups of Djedars include varied decorative imagery (both internal and external) as well as masons' marks which take the form of proper names carved in Latin characters, as well as other symbols.

Viewed together, the Djedars promise a tantalising glimpse of new forms of aristocratic power on the old frontier. If only the Djebel Lakhdar group survived, it would still tell us a great deal. The erection of the tumuli represented a substantial logistical operation, which left an indelible mark on the landscape. The Djedars still look down on the Algerian highway, and may have similarly dominated the old frontier road. They may also have been the focus of funerary or other cults after their erection. Crucially, the monuments were erected by a society which was long familiar with the conventions of Roman imperial power. If tentative readings of the inscriptions can be trusted, it would seem that the occupant of Djedar A was a military appointment, and paraded this status proudly. Similarly, the fragments from Djedar B hint at both the dynastic connections between the different structures and the Christian faith of those who built them. At the very least, the Djebel Lakhdar group testifies to a vibrant aristocracy in the fifth century with political ideologies similar to those expressed in the Masuna and Masties inscriptions.

The erection of the second Djedar cluster on the Djebel Araoui complicates this image further. The re-use of Christian epitaphs within

---

[55] Discussed in Laporte, "Djedars," 376–379.

[56] Text at ibid., 352, 359. Recent photographs of the site by Corisande Fenwick demonstrate conclusively that the inscription on Djedar A was made in situ. I am grateful to her for allowing me to see those images.

[57] Laporte, "Djedars," 380.

the construction of Djedar F is evidence for the continued vibrancy of the faith in this part of the frontier in the fifth century, but also demonstrates beyond reasonable doubt that there was a substantial hiatus – perhaps of up to a century – between the construction of the last Djedar on the Djebel Lakhdar and the first on the Djebel Araoui. We cannot know what caused this break: it may have been civil unrest, wider political changes or dynastic upheaval.[58] But the revival of Djedar construction, and the establishment of the new cluster of monuments on a second spur of land, can only be read as the conscious reinvention of a local expression of power. The occupant of Djedar F may have occupied the largest and most spectacular of the Tiaret "structures," but he deferred to local tradition when he had this built. Whatever the direct relation was between the individuals commemorated on the Djebel Araoui and their predecessors, both groups combined familiar imperial forms of political display (including inscribed stone and Christian imagery of different kinds), with emphatically local traditions of power. Precisely how these monuments related to the well-populated and fertile lands around them, and how the other members of this Romano-African society lived their lives, will only be revealed with the resumption of archaeological survey in the area. But the monuments themselves testify to a vibrant tradition of political and religious display.

Had they been erected virtually anywhere else in the old western empire, the Djedars would be familiar features of modern scholarship on the post-Roman world. The fact that they are little known is emblematic of the neglect of North African history in the period between Augustine's death and the Arab Conquest. Yet for all their strangeness, the Djedars tell a familiar story. The fifth and sixth centuries witnessed a political fragmentation in North Africa – as the Vandal kingdom declared autonomy in Carthage so too did countless Moorish polities in Tripolitania, Byzacena, Numidia, and the Mauretanias. These African kingdoms developed their own ideologies and institutions, and some we understand rather better than others. Yet diverse as they may have been, all of them were profoundly influenced by the legacy of the old empire. It was only with the Byzantine conquest of Africa in 533–534, and the outbreak of a new wave of wars that the complexity of this imperial legacy became evident.

[58] Ibid., 395–396.

16: THE REINVENTION OF IRAN: THE SASANIAN EMPIRE AND THE HUNS

Richard Payne

The Iranian Empire encountered an unfamiliar kind of Hun on its northeastern frontiers in the latter half of the fourth century. Migrating from the steppes south of the Altai Mountains as heirs of the Xiongnu imperial tradition, these Huns came not to raid but to rule.[1] If some nomadic warriors sought positions as mercenaries in the service of the king of kings, others took control of Balkh and Kabul, once strongholds of the Iranian Empire, as well as Sogdian cities such as Samarkand, Bukhara, and Chach just beyond its former limits.[2] With few geographical barriers to prevent nomadic armies from entering the Iranian plateau, the heart of the empire was now exposed to the steppe.[3] Unlike the more famous armies of Attila that the Romans encountered, the Huns in Central Asia combined the best of steppe and sedentary state structures, adapting the administrative and ideological institutions

---

[1] See Étienne de la Vaissière, chapter 10 in this volume.

[2] The chronology of Joe Cribb, "The Kidarites, the Numismatic Evidence," in *Coins, Art and Chronology II: The First Millenium C.E. in the Indo-Iranian Borderlands*, ed. Michael Alram (Vienna, 2010) 91–146, who places the end of Iranian rule in Balkh and Kabul in the 380s, takes precedence over Frantz Grenet, "Regional Interaction in Central Asia and Northwest India in the Kidarite and Hephthalite Periods," in *Indo-Iranian Languages and Peoples*, ed. Nicholas Sims-Williams (Oxford, 2002) 203–224; Étienne de la Vaissière, "Is There a 'Nationality of the Hephthalites'?," *Bulletin of the Asia Institute* 17 (2003) 119–132.

[3] James Howard-Johnston, "The Sasanians' Strategic Dilemma," in *Commutatio et contentio: Studies in the Late Roman, Sasanian, and Early Islamic Near East*, ed. Henning Börm and Josef Wiesehöfer (Düsseldorf, 2010) 37–70.

they inherited to their own purposes. The Kidarite (ca. 360–457) and Hephthalite (ca. 457–560) dynasties, in particular, created states that continually humbled the Iranian Empire, destabilizing both its frontiers and its ideological foundations.

Yet the Iranian empire endured the ensuing crisis with institutions, elite networks, and an ideological apparatus to support the expansionist ambitions of the sixth-century kings of kings. What is remarkable about the fifth-century Iranian Empire is its survival in the face of unprecedented and unforeseen external threats that exacerbated internal conflicts. The aristocracies of the Caucasus famously rebelled against the ruling Sasanian dynasty in 451 and 482, enlisting the Huns as allies and mercenaries.[4] In explaining the endurance of the empire, we need to attend to the ideological innovations through which the kings of kings adapted to the unfavorable circumstances of the age and reconsolidated aristocratic networks. The present chapter will argue that the highly malleable idea and ideology of Iran enabled the court to mobilize the aristocratic houses of the empire in its defense. For the political turmoil that accompanied the collapse of the empire in the East inspired courtly literary specialists to expand upon the corpus of Zoroastrian cosmological and mythical-historical traditions to provide new modes of representation and models for political action. To comprehend the geography, peoples, and political actors beyond the empire's eastern frontier, Iran's political decision-makers depended upon the ideology of Iran rather than any systematically gathered geographic or ethnographic knowledge. Developed on the basis of the Avesta, the orally transmitted body of Zoroastrian religious knowledge from the first millennium BCE, the cosmological concept of Iran proved to be an adaptable ancillary to empire. But for Iran to endure, it had to be reinvented.

---

[4] Hun mercenaries from north of the Caucasus played a major role in the Armenian rebellion of 450 and the Armenian and Georgian rebellion of 482: Ełiše, *Vasn Vardanants' ew Hayoc' Paterazmin*, ed. Ervand Ter-Minasean (Yerevan, Armenia, 1957) 78, 127–128, 134, 141–142, and *History of Vardan and the Armenian War*, trans. Robert W. Thomson (London, 1982) 130, 180, 185, 192–193; and Łazar P'arpec'i, *Patmut'iwn Hayoc'*, ed. Galust Ter-Mkrtchean (Tbilisi, Georgia, 1904) 119–121, and *History of the Armenians*, trans. Robert W. Thomson, *The History of Łazar P'arpec'i* (Atlanta, 1991) 173–175. On the rebellions, see now Nina Garsoïan, "La politique arménnienne des sassanides," in *Trésors d'Orient: Mélanges offerts à Rika Gyselen*, ed. Philippe Gignoux et al. (Paris, 2009) 67–79, emphasizing the political as opposed to the religious dimensions of the conflicts.

The Idea of Iran and Turan

The early Sasanian kings of kings claimed to unite the civilized population of the world and to subordinate all outside powers, especially
Rome, to Ērānšahr, "the empire of the Iranians."[5] The "Iranians" in
question were the mythical-historical kings of the Avesta and their supposed successors, the Sasanians, not an ethnic group.[6] From the fifth
century, Iran came to be defined in opposition to Turan, the Central
Asian lands beyond its eastern frontiers that formed the homeland of
the Iranians' mythical enemies. As the kings of Airyana Vaejah in the
Avesta, the model for Ērānšahr, ruled the entire world, the idea of
Iran the Sasanians invented required them to unify humanity politically. This universalist ideology did not envision the incorporation of
non-Iran into Iran, but rather non-Iran's recognition – often through
tribute – of the Iranian rulers' role as the source of legitimate political
power. If the early Sasanians could display their subjugation of Rome
and – on the newly discovered rock relief at Rag-i Bibi in Bactria –
India on monuments and coins, there were to be few victories to
vaunt in the fourth and fifth centuries.[7] The Huns' conquest of hitherto Iranian lands made the illusion of universal sovereignty difficult to
maintain. Iranian elites, moreover, considered their nomadic counterparts the uncivilized agents of the evil deity Ahreman. Defeat at their
hands had the potential to vitiate Sasanian claims to be the rulers of
Ērānšahr.[8]

After the Kushano-Sasanian subkingdom that had ruled the Iranian East since at least the reign of Shapur I yielded to the Kidarite
Huns in the 370s, the kings of kings struggled merely to retain their
strategic hold on the Merv Oasis, not to regain these regions so rich in
taxable lands and trading routes.[9] In the 420s, Wahram V Gor undertook a campaign from Gurgan against the Kidarite Huns that the Iranian

---

[5] Artur Christensen, *L'Iran sous les Sassanides* (Copenhagen, 1936) 200–235.

[6] Gherardo Gnoli, *The Idea of Iran: An Essay on Its Origin* (Rome, 1989).

[7] Matthew P. Canepa, *The Two Eyes of the Earth: Art and Ritual of Kingship between
Rome and Sasanian Iran* (Berkeley, 2009) 53–78; Frantz Grenet, "Découverte d'un
relief sassanide dans le nord de l'Afghanistan," *CRAI* (2005) 115–135.

[8] Bruce Lincoln, "Human Unity and Diversity in Zoroastrian Mythology," *History of
Religions* 50 (2010) 7–20.

[9] James Howard-Johnston, "The Late Sasanian Army," in *Late Antiquity: Eastern Perspectives*, ed. Teresa Bernheimer and Adam Silverstein (Oxford, 2012) 87–127, here
98–99.

historiographical tradition vaunted as a decisive victory.[10] The heroic king, however, appears rather modestly to have secured Merv.[11] Iranian control of Khurasan was sufficiently precarious for Yazdgird II to have had to campaign continuously from about 440, without succeeding to stabilize the northeastern frontier to which he was forced to return until the end of his reign in 457. His successor, Peroz, temporarily reconquered Bactria from the Kidarites in 467 and issued a gold dinar at Balkh with a Bactrian legend, "Peroz king of kings."[12] This coin embodied a vision of an Iran returned to its third-century grandeur that was not to be. Humiliating defeats at the hands of the Hephthalites in 474–475 and 484 removed not merely Bactria, but Merv itself from the remit of Iran. Iranian silver drachms ceased to be minted at Merv in 484, only to recommence in the first decades of the sixth century.[13]

Archaeological, numismatic, and sigillographic sources show how the Huns sought to rule the territories as kings no less majestic than their Iranian counterparts. In recently published sealings a Hun declared his political ambitions: "Lord Ularg, the king of the Huns, the great Kushan-shah, the Samarkandian, of the Afrigan (?) family."[14] Representing the "king of the Huns" in the guise of an Iranian Kushan-shah, the sealing demonstrates the Huns' rapid appropriation of Iranian imperial symbolism and titulature. In their coinage, too, this first generation of Hun rulers continued Iranian modes of representation, with the exception of inscriptions that announced the name of a new Hun dynasty, the Kidara, and the replacement of Iranian beards with clean-shaven faces. The Hun king, moreover, based himself within the city of

[10] Al-Dīnawarī, *Kitāb al-akhbār al- ṭiwāl*, ed. 'Abd al-Mun'im 'Āmir (Cairo, 1960) 56–57.

[11] Boris Marshak, "K Voprosu o Vostochnikh Protivnikakh Irana," *Strany i Naroda Vostoka* 10 (1971) 58–66, here 60–61.

[12] Nicholas Sims-Williams, "The Sasanians in the East: A Bactrian Archive from Northern Afghanistan," in *The Sasanian Era: The Idea of Iran*, vol. 3, ed. Vesta Sarkhosh Curtis and Sarah Stewart (London, 2008) 88–102, here 94–95.

[13] Rika Gyselen, "New Evidence for Sasanian Numismatics: The Collection of Ahmad Saeedi," in *Contributions à l'histoire et la géographie historique de l'empire sassanide*, ed. Rika Gyselen (Bures-sur-Yvette, 2004) 49–140, here 61.

[14] Aman ur-Rahman, Frantz Grenet, and Nicholas Sims-Williams, "A Hunnish Kushan-shah," *Journal of Inner Asian Art and Archaeology* 1 (2006) 125–131; Judith A. Lerner and Nicholas Sims-Williams, *Seals, Sealings and Tokens from Bactria to Gandhara (4th to 8th Century CE)* (Vienna, 2011) 72–74.

Samarkand, a stronghold of the Sogdian mercantile network. The Sogdians worked as closely with the Huns as they would with the Turks in the sixth century, to the extent that Hun (*xwn*) became a common personal name in Sogdian inscriptions.[15] It was the administratively adept Sogdians that could draft documents in Middle Iranian languages, staff mints, and introduce new rulers to the symbolics of Iranian power. Hun rule marked the beginning of the flourishing of the Sogdian cities of Samarkand, Bukhara, Paykend, and Panjikent.[16] In previously Iranian territories, the fifth-century Bactrian documents show that Huns continued to collect the land tax, and the local aristocracies continued to wield Iranian administrative titles and offices.[17] Far from the destructive *xyōnān* of the Iranian accounts discussed below or the marauding barbarians of the Roman historians, the Hun kingdoms of post-Iranian Central Asia were city-based, tax-raising, ideologically innovative states the kings of kings found themselves hard pressed to unseat.[18]

These tendencies were characteristic of the various Hun successor states. The early fifth-century Hun king of the Kushans likely belonged to, or was at least associated with, the Kidarite dynasty.[19] Based in the formerly Iranian province of Bactria and in Gandhara the ruler proclaiming himself "Kidara king of the Kushans" – and presumably his dynastic successors – effectively repulsed the campaigns of Wahram V (420–438) and Yazdgird II (438–457). Alongside Kidara and his successors, a possibly related dynasty known as the Alkhan Huns established itself in Kabul in 388 and subsequently displaced the Kidarites in Gandhara. From the middle of the fifth century, a distinctive Alkhan coinage devoid of Iranian symbolism and displaying Hun rulers with elongated foreheads downgraded Iranian traditions in the Kabul region, which had formed an integral part of the empire less than a century before.[20] At roughly the same time, another group with similarly distinctive coinage

---

[15] Étienne de la Vaissière, *Sogdian Traders: A History* (Leiden, 2005) 107–110.

[16] Frantz Grenet, "Crise et sortie de crise en Bactriane-Sogdiane aux IVe–Ve siècles: De l'héritage antique à l'adoption de modèles sassanides," in *La Persia e l'Asia Centrale da Alessandro al X Secolo*, ed. W. Belardi et al. (Rome, 1996) 367–390; cf. Procopius, *De bello Vandalico*, ed. and trans. Henry B. Dewing, *History of the Wars*, 5 vols. (Cambridge 1914) 1: 14–15.

[17] Sims-Williams, "The Sasanians in the East," 92–93.

[18] For Hephthalite taxation, see Nicholas Sims-Williams, *Bactrian Documents from Northern Afghanistan*, vol. 1: *Legal and Economic Documents* (Oxford, 2000) 50–61, 162–163.

[19] Cribb, "The Kidarites, the Numismatic Evidence," 97.

[20] Michael Alram and Matthias Pfisterer, "Alkhan and Hephthalite Coinage," in *Coins, Art and Chronology*, vol. 2: *The First Millenium C.E. in the Indo-Iranian Borderlands*, ed. Michael Alram et al. (Vienna, 2010) 13–38.

came to dominate Bactria: the Hephthalites. In all likelihood a Hun dynastic grouping akin to the Kidara and Alkhan, the Hephthalites emerged from a base in Tokharistan to develop the most resilient of Hun states, which at its height in the sixth century would rule Sogdia, Bactria, and Gandhara and extend its reach as far afield as the Tarim basin and northwest India.[21]

Hun states demanded something the kings of kings could not provide without compromising his position as ruler of Iran: tribute. According to Priscus, the Kidarite Huns had demanded regular deliveries of tribute from the kings of kings, which were reportedly rendered with satisfactory regularity until Yazdgird II refused payment.[22] The submission of tribute to another ruler was a perversion of the natural order according to which the Iranians disbursed power on a global scale. The humiliation of Iran was put on grand display in the year 474, when the king of kings Peroz was taken captive by the Hephthalite Huns. To redeem himself from Hun captivity, Peroz submitted thirty mule loads of silver drachms to the Hephthalite king. The sums involved were modest in comparison with late antique diplomatic subsidies or state revenues. But rumors of a caravan delivering tribute from the Iranian court to the Huns spread across the Iran and the Mediterranean worlds, as far as Sidonius Apollinaris in Gaul.[23] On the basis of these coins, the Hephthalite kings adopted the winged, triple-crescent crown Peroz wore on coins minted after 474, suggesting they had assumed the rightful rulership of Iran.[24] From the late fourth century until the Turks, at Sasanian instigation, conquered the Hephthalites in 557, Iran was subordinate to Turan.

In this context we can appreciate the urgency of Peroz's brazen campaign of 484 as an attempt to restore the cosmologically appropriate relationship between Iran and Turan. Marching deep into unfamiliar territory with forces that included some of the greatest nobles of the empire, Peroz led his forces into a trench the Hephthalites had concealed. The Iranian army was annihilated and the body of Peroz was

---

[21] La Vaissière, "Is There a 'Nationality' of the Hephthalites?"

[22] Priscus, *Historia*, ed. and trans. Roger C. Blockley, *The Fragmentary Classicising Historians of the Later Roman Empire: Eunapius, Olympiodorus, Priscus and Malchus*, 2 vols. (Liverpool, 1983) 2: 348–349.

[23] Nikolaus Schindel, *Sylloge Nummorum Sasanidarum, Paris-Berlin-Wien*, vol 3.1: *Shapur II. – Kawad I. / 2. Regierung* (Vienna, 2004) 397, 416–417.

[24] Etsuko Kageyama, "The Winged Crown and the Triple-Crescent Crown in the Sogdian Funerary Monuments from China: Their Relation to the Hephthalite Occupation of Central Asia," *JIAA* 2 (2007) 11–23.

never recovered. The courtly mint, too, disappeared.[25] No other event in the history of the Sasanian dynasty so clearly vitiated the pretensions of Ērānšahr, and contemporaries were aghast at the foolhardiness of the king of kings.[26] Nevertheless, the Karinid Sukhra was able immediately to raise a new army to prevent the Hephthalites from capitalizing on their success.[27] Despite its catastrophic outcome, Peroz's fateful 484 campaign bore witness to the strength of the ideological and material structures erected in the course of the fifth century, which could continue to function despite the disappearance of the empire's mobile center, the king of kings and his court.

KAYANIANS, *XYŌNĀN*, AND HUNS: MYTH AND HISTORY

The Huns' challenge to the idea of Iran required a response. In the coinage of fifth century, we find the lineaments of major ideological innovation. From the reign of Ardashir I onward, Iranian silver drachms consistently presented the Sasanians as "Mazda-worshipping divine kings of kings of the Iranians and the non-Iranians whose lineage is from the gods." This consistency ceased abruptly with the accession of Yazdgird I in 399, who introduced the title *rāmšahr*, "[bringer of] imperial peace," before "king of kings."[28] Since the mythical king Wishtasp, the patron of Zoroaster, held the title *rāmšahr*, its appearance on Yazdgird I's coinage marks the first Sasanian attempt expressly to model the dynasty after the Kayanian royal dynasty of the Avesta.[29] Wahram V continued his father's practice, and Yazdgird II made the equation of Kayanian and Sasanian explicit with his simplified title,

---

[25] Nikolaus Schindel, *Sylloge Nummorum Sasanidarum Israel* (Vienna, 2009) 35.

[26] Łazar P'arpec'i, *Patmut'iwn Hayoc'*, ed. Ter-Mkrtchean, 155, and trans. Thomson, 214–215.

[27] Al-Ṭabarī, *Ta'rīkh al-rusul wa'l mulūk*, ed. Michael de Goeje (Leiden, 1879–1901) 879–880, trans. Clifford Bosworth, in *The History of al-Ṭabarī*, vol. 5: *The Sāsānids, the Byzantines, the Lakmids, and Yemen* (Albany, 1999) 120–121; al-Dīnawarī, *Kitāb al-akhbār al-ṭiwāl*, ed. al-Mun'im 'Āmir, 60.

[28] Schindel, *Sylloge Nummorum Sasanidarum*, 3.1: 320–321.

[29] Touraj Daryaee, "History, Epic, and Numismatics: On the Title of Yazdgerd I (*rāmšahr*)," *American Numismatic Journal* 15 (2002) 89–95; and Iris Colditz, "Altorientalische und Avesta-Traditionen in der Herrschertitulatur des vorislamischen Iran," in *Religious Themes and Texts of pre-Islamic Iran and Central Asia: Studies in Honour of Professor Gherardo Gnoli*, ed. Carlo Cereti et al. (Wiesbaden, 2003) 61–78.

"Mazda-worshiping Kayanian [*kay*] Yazdgird."[30] Subsequent Sasanians would continue to identify themselves as Kayanian, explicitly or implicitly, in the coins, seals, historical texts, and other media the court produced.

These shifts in royal titulature attest to a profound reorientation of Iranian kingship. Identification with the Kayanians signaled the embrace of Avestan models for political practice that aimed to address the ideological crisis the loss of the Iranian East precipitated. It was, indeed, during this period that Zoroastrian scholars with courtly patronage began to record in Middle Persian mythical historical traditions that had hitherto circulated orally. Between Yazdgird I's designation as *rāmšahr* and Yazdgird III's (633–651) final redaction of a *Book of Kings*, courtly literary specialists expanded upon the allusive references to the activities of Kayanian kings in the Avesta to create the mythical history of Iran best known from Firdawsi's *Shāhnāmeh*.[31]

Why did the fifth-century court elevate these sacred historical kings as the foremost exemplars for the Sasanians? Kayanian history was primarily a story of confronting and, in the course of a multigenerational struggle, overcoming Ahremanic enemies from the East, who despite their demonic dispositions managed to challenge the supremacy of the Iranian kings of kings. Wishtasp, in particular, was celebrated in the Younger Avestan *Zamyād Yašt* – and in the Middle Persian *History of Zarēr* – for defeating the "evil and oppressive" *xiiaona-* (Avestan) or *xyōnān* (Middle Persian) led by their king Arjasp.[32] Sasanian literary specialists identified the Huns as the enemies of Wishtasp, the *xyōnān*. The fourth-century Roman historian Ammianus Marcellinus recounted how Shapur II campaigned against "Chionites" (*chionitae*) from 351 to 358.[33] Ammianus' reference has given rise to a historiography on the identity of Chionites as a group, or branch of Huns, but the term is merely an Iranian description of the Huns as a collective. "Chionite" Latinized the Middle Persian ethnonym *xyōn*, which was in turn a rendition of the Avestan *xiiaona-*. The term's appearance

---

[30] Schindel, *Sylloge Nummorum Sasanidarum*, 3.1: 369–370.

[31] Ehsan Yarshater, "The Iranian National History," in *The Cambridge History of Iran*, vol. 3.1: *The Seleucid, Parthian and Sasanian Periods*, ed. Ehsan Yarshater (Cambridge, 1983) 359–477.

[32] *Zamyād Yašt*, ed. and trans. Almut Hintze, in *Zamyād Yašt: Introduction, Avestan Text, Translation* (Wiesbaden, 1994); and *Ayādgār ī Zarērān*, ed. and trans. Davoud Monchi-Zadeh, *Die Geschichte Zarēr's* (Uppsala, Sweden, 1981).

[33] Ammianus Marcellinus, *Rerum gestarum libri*, ed. and trans. John C. Rolfe, *Ammianus Marcellinus*, 3 vols. (Cambridge, 1935–1939) 1: 240–243.

in Ammianus shows how the Iranians perceived and represented the Hun invaders, as the enemies of Zoroaster and his kings in the Avesta. The coincidental correspondence between "Hun" and *xyōn* facilitated the former's rebranding as the agents of Ahreman.[34] Both the Huns and the *xyōnān* also possessed the "broad fronts," elongated foreheads, characteristic of nomadic warriors.

In applying the label *xyōn* to their fourth- and fifth-century enemies in the East, Iranian literary specialists elevated the Huns to the status of Iran's primordial adversary. In the history of the Kayanian dynasty, the Sasanians found Iranian kings of kings that faced enemies as overwhelming as the Huns who managed, ultimately, to vindicate themselves as the sovereigns of Iran. This was a story of an Iran embattled that nevertheless emerged victorious, a myth the Sasanians would, in time, successfully reenact.

THE ARISTOCRACIES AND THEIR KINGS OF KINGS

The primary audience for these new narratives were the aristocrats who provided Iran with the cavalry based armies needed for its campaigns whether against the Huns, Romans, or others. Although there was a generally operative consensus according to which only a man from the house of Sasan could rule, Iranian aristocracies frequently intervened to depose ineffective rulers.[35] There was a language of legitimate rebellion, to which humbled Sasanians were vulnerable for having failed to secure the unity of Iran.[36] Ardashir II (379–383), Shapur III (383–388), Wahram IV (388–399), and Yazdgird I (399–420) were either deposed

---

[34] Carlo Cereti, "Xiiaona- and Xyôn in Zoroastrian Texts," in *Coins, Art and Chronology*, vol. 2: *The First Millenium C.E. in the Indo-Iranian Borderlands*, ed. Michael Alram et al. (Vienna, 2010) 59–72.

[35] Philip Huyse, "Die königliche Erbfolge bei den Sasaniden," in *Trésors d'Orient: Mélanges offerts à Rika Gyselen*, ed. Philippe Gignoux et al. (Paris, 2009) 145–157; and Henning Börm, "Das Königtum der Sasaniden – Strukturen und Probleme. Bemerkungen aus althistorischer Sicht," *Klio* 90 (2008) 423–443.

[36] Zeev Rubin, "Nobility, Monarchy, and Legitimation under the Later Sasanians," in *The Byzantine and Early Islamic Near East*, vol. 6: *Elites Old and New in the Byzantine and Early Islamic Near East*, ed. John Haldon and Lawrence Conrad (Princeton, 2004) 235–273; Christensen, *L'Iran sous les Sassanides*, 248–252, 268; Parvaneh Pourshariati, *Decline and Fall of the Sasanian Empire: The Sasanian-Parthian Confederacy and the Arab Conquest of Iran* (London, 2009) 57–58.

or killed for inspiring noble opposition.[37] The three subsequent kings of kings were more effective at achieving consensus, but their successions were hard-won. Wahram V Gor had to rely on the support of the Arabs with whom he had been raised and perished under circumstances no less ambiguous than those of his father.[38] If Yazdgird II enjoyed the first uncontested succession in six decades, Peroz had to enlist the Hephthalites, who would later become his enemies, to defeat his fraternal rival in 457.[39] The tumultuous history of the dynasty superficially lends support to the view that the kings of kings were weak and unable to realize their ambitions in the face of a recalcitrant aristocracy. Noble houses such as Mihran, Karen, and Suren possessed ancestral territories as extensive, genealogies as glorious, and martial abilities as impressive as those of the house of Sasan, leading Parvaneh Pourshariati and Zeev Rubin to argue that we are dealing with a confederacy of autonomous aristocratic factions rather than an empire united in the service of the king of kings.[40] Real power, in this view, was always in aristocratic hands, and the aristocracy was always a centrifugal force.

But the opposition of aristocratic and royal power in the analysis of Iranian political history downplays the loyalty of the great noble houses to the ruling house from Ardashir's accession to Husraw II's deposition in 628. With the exception of the rebellion of Wahram VI Chobin in 589, the great nobles placed a Sasanian on the throne whenever they intervened to depose a ruler. Four centuries of faithfulness well demonstrate how much these families believed their destinies to be intertwined with that of the royal dynasty. As Karin Mosig-Walburg has recently insisted, we need to replace the binary opposition between aristocracy and royalty with the analysis of different competing groups of nobles.[41] Moreover, if real power did indeed reside with the landed aristocracies, imperial institutions will have expanded not at the expense

---

[37] Al-Ṭabarī, *Ta'rīkh al-rusul wa'l mulūk*, ed. de Goeje, 845–850, trans. Bosworth, 67–69, 73.

[38] Ibid., 858–863, trans. Bosworth, 86–93.

[39] Al-Dīnawarī, *Kitāb al-akhbār al-ṭiwāl*, ed. al-Mun'im 'Āmir, 58–59; al-Ṭabarī, *Ta'rīkh al-rusul wa'l mulūk*, ed. de Goeje, 873, trans. Bosworth, 110; Firdawsī, *Šāhnāmeh*, vol. 7, ed. Djalal Khaleghi-Motlagh (New York, 2007) 10–11, trans. Julius Mohl, *Le Livre des Rois*, vol. 6 (Paris, 1976) 89; Ełiše, *Vasn Vardananc' ew Hayoc' Paterazmin*, ed. Ter-Minasean, 197, trans. Thomson, 242.

[40] Zeev Rubin, "The Sassanid Monarchy," in *The Cambridge Ancient History*, vol. 14: *Late Antiquity: Empire and Successors, AD 425–600*, ed. Averil Cameron, Bryan Ward-Perkins, and Michael Whitby (Cambridge, 2000) 638–661.

[41] Karin Mosig-Walburg, "Königtum und Adel in der Regierungs Zeit Ardashirs II., Shapurs III., und Wahrams IV.," in *Commutatio et contentio: Studies in the Late*

of, but rather through the cooptation of, aristocracies great and small, transregional and provincial. If a king of kings wished to levy taxes on a province, to rally a host against the Huns, or to establish a frontier military commandery in the Caucasus, he needed men of great noble lineage commanding men and material to do so.

The great nobles readily lent their support in exchange for the power and prestige that came with imperial order. Mihr Narseh, a member of the Parthian Suren family, served Yazdgird I, Wahram V, and Yazdgird II as *wuzurg framādār*, "great commander," the highest office in the empire, marshaling military forces and presiding over the administration for kings of kings so frequently on campaign.[42] His agnates likewise occupied religious, fiscal, and military offices. An exceptionally well-documented case of a great noble house in imperial service, the example of the Surenids reveals how strenuously aristocrats could work to defend and extend the empire. There were other houses equally eager for imperial offices.[43] Our best evidence for this is the corpus of Sasanian seals and sealing that officials used to authorize documents. Although there is precious little sigillographic evidence for the administration datable to the fourth or fifth centuries, the sixth-century seals are those of a transregional elite that imagined its powers as resulting from service to the state. These men boasted of their offices, presented themselves wearing the headgear to which their offices entitled them, and only occasionally vaunted their aristocratic lineage alongside their imperial title.[44] Fifth-century nobles such as Mihr Narseh were the predecessors of this sixth-century state aristocracy.

There was precedent for their behavior in the mythical-historical traditions of the Kayanians, in which Parthian dynasts feature as the purveyors of the men, material, and leadership the kings of kings needed to defend Iran against the *xyōnān*. If Kayanians directed the struggle,

Roman, Sasanian, and Early Islamic Near East, ed. Henning Börm and Josef Wiesehöfer (Düsseldorf, 2010) 159–198.

[42] Al-Ṭabarī, *Ta'rīkh al-rusul wa'l mulūk*, ed. de Goeje, 849, 866–867, 868–872, trans. Bosworth, 72, 99, 103–106; Nina Garsoïan, "Une coïncidence supplémentaire entre les sources arméniennes et perses: Le cas du grand vizir Mihr Narseh," *Revue des Études Arméniennes* 27 (1998–2000) 311–320; Pourshariati, *Decline and Fall of the Sasanian Empire*, 60–65; Rika Gyselen, *Great-Commander (wuzurg-framadār) and Court Counsellor (dar-andarzbed) in the Sasanian Empire (224–651): The Sigillographic Evidence* (Rome, 2008).

[43] Eliše, *Vasn Vardananc' ew Hayoc' Paterazmin*, ed. Ter-Minasean, 197, trans. Thomson, 242.

[44] Rika Gyselen, "Primary Sources and Historiography of the Sasanian Empire," *Studia Iranica* 38 (2009) 163–190, 165–170, and 173–178.

legendarily heroic men such as Godarz, Tus, and Karen delivered them victory. In the mythical histories emanating from the fifth century court, nobles initiated and directed military campaign as often as the kings the kings themselves. The nobles also selected their rulers. These stories, Theodor Nöldeke suggested, projected fifth-century events into the mythical age.[45] We can discern this phenomenon most clearly in al-Ṭabarī's account of the noble Sukhra, who liberated the men held captive by the Hephthalite ruler after the defeat of Peroz in 484. A Karinid, Sukhra claimed descent from the heroes Karen and Tus that had rescued Iranian kingship after the archetypal Turanian Afrasyab had slain king Nawdhar, in circumstances too similar to those of Peroz's death for the resemblance to be coincidental.[46] Here we have a late fifth-century aristocrat – who came to play as active a role as Mihr Narseh in the imperial administration – identifying himself with mythical heroes famous for serving the kings of kings. The Kayanian history of Iran at war with Turan bound the great noble houses ever more tightly to the Sasanians at a time when their commitment to Ērānšahr was indispensable. Sasanian and aristocratic dynasties began to articulate their interdependence in the course of Iran's encounter with the Huns.

A SHIFTING FRONTIER: THE GREAT WALL OF GURGAN AND THE MOBILIZATION OF THE IRANIAN MILITARY

The results of this renewed relationship are evident in the infrastructural projects of the fifth century. Chief among these was the Great Wall of Gurgan, which reveals the scale and the strategy of the elusive Iranian military. In the latter half of the fifth century, the Iranians began to construct a wall that would, by the century's close, extend 195 kilometers from the Kopet Dagh Mountains to the Caspian Sea, with at least thirty-thee forts. The excavators estimate that between fifteen thousand and thirty thousand troops were stationed at the wall.[47] An

---

[45] Theodor Nöldeke, *Das iranische Nationalepos* (Berlin, 1920) 14.

[46] Al-Ṭabarī, *Ta'rīkh al-rusul wa'l mulūk*, ed. de Goeje, 877–878, trans. Bosworth, 117.

[47] Hamid Omrani Rekavandi, Eberhard W. Sauer, Tony Wilkinson, et al., "An Imperial Frontier of the Sasanian Empire: Further Fieldwork at the Great Wall of Gurgan," *Iran* 45 (2007) 95–136, 130; Hamid Omrani Rekavandi, Eberhard W. Sauer, Tony Wilkinson, et al., "Sasanian Walls, Hinterland Fortresses, and Abandoned Ancient Irrigated Landscapes: The 2007 Season on the Great Wall of Gurgan and the Wall of Tammishe," *Iran* 46 (2008) 151–178.

additional fifty to sixty thousand mobile forces including cavalry were prepared to campaign from larger forts in the wall's hinterland. Fifth-century aristocratic estates have also been excavated in the transitional zones of Khurasan between the Kopet Dagh and Merv, a *dastgird* (aristocratic estate) at Bandian and a residence with a fire temple at Mele Hairam.[48] At the same time, two mud-brick walls were constructed between the Caucasus Mountains and the Caspian Sea at Derbend (where imposing stone fortifications would replace mud-brick in the sixth century) and at Ghilghilchay in Azerbaijan, both to resist Hun incursions from the North and to control the aristocracies of Caucasian Albania.[49] The recent survey of the Mughan Steppe (ancient Balāsagān) in Azerbaijan conducted by Jason Ur and Karim Alizadeh has demonstrated the construction of a network of fortified settlements in the latter half of the fifth century.[50] Even if the evidence for the financing of the fortifications and the armies that manned them remains inadequate, these studies reveal that "the Sasanian army in the fifth and sixth centuries was substantially stronger, in terms of numbers and organization, than had previously been thought... an equal to its late Roman counterpart."[51]

The Great Wall of Gurgan was a material manifestation of courtly myth making. The walls represented an important, even necessary, ideological development: a newfound ability to define the limits of Ērānšahr. In various recensions of the *Book of Kings* traditions, the Kayanians Wishtasp and Manushchihr are reported to have set a boundary between Iran and Turan. The heroic archer Arash, mentioned in the Avesta, shot an arrow from the Alburz Mountains that reached beyond Merv to the edge of Khurasan, marking the limit of Iran at the Oxus.[52] In a similar account, Spandyad the son of Wishtasp struck his lance into the ground at Balkh and warned the *xyōn* king that to advance further

---

[48] Philippe Gignoux, "Les inscriptions en moyen-perse de Bandiān," *Studia Iranica* 27 (1998) 251–258; Barbara Kaim, "Où adorer les dieux?: Un spectaculaire temple de feu d'époque sassanide," *Les Dossiers d'archéologie* 317 (2006) 66–71.

[49] Askar A. Aliev, Murtazali S. Gadjiev, M. Gaye Gaither, et al., "The Ghilghilchay Defensive Long Wall: New Investigations," *Ancient West and East* 5 (2006) 143–177.

[50] Karim Alizadeh, "Ultan Qalasi: A Fortified Site in the Sasanian Borderlands (Mughan Steppe, Iranian Azerbaijan)," *Iran* 49 (2011) 55–77; *History of Karka d-Beit Slok*, ed. Paul Bedjan, *Acta martyrum et sanctorum*, vol. 2 (Paris, 1891) 507–335, here 518.

[51] Rekavandi et al., "An Imperial Frontier of the Sasanian Empire," 131; and James Howard-Johnston, "The Late Sasanian Army," 108–113.

[52] Theodor Nöldeke, "'Der beste der arischen Pfeilschützen' im Awestâ und im Tabarî," *Zeitschrift der Deutschen Morganländischen Gesellschaft* 35 (1881) 445–447.

would constitute an invasion of Iran.[53] Wahram V, in turn, was believed to have reestablished such a boundary in the vicinity of Merv subsequent Sasanians sought to maintain.[54] Regions that the Iranians had once notionally – but never administratively – included in their empire, such as Khwarezm and Sogdia, became territories of the *xyōnān*, firmly excluded from Iran.[55] A physical and imaginative barrier between Iran and Turan came to stand in territories that had been, in the preceding two centuries, zones of fluid and overlapping sovereignties. The ideology of Iran contained within its resources models for defining a frontier in a space that previously embodied its aspirations to an empire without end.

The fortifications of Gurgan and Azerbaijan attest to the effective mobilization of men and materials in the empire's service. It is only in Armenia that we can analyze the processes through which nobles were compelled to dedicate resources to Iran. The rich Armenian historiographical tradition of the sixth-century describes how sometimes recalcitrant aristocracies – often of the same Parthian lineage as their grander counterparts on the Iranian plateau – were persuaded to gather cavalry for campaigns in the east, specifically in Gurgan.[56] Early in his reign, Yazdgird II delivered a letter to the nobles, known as *nakharars*, that shows how an army was raised: the nobles receiving the letter were expected to gather a cavalry force and to meet the king of kings in Khurasan.[57] Armenian *nakharars* could summon forces ranging from

---

[53] *Šahrestānīhā ī Ērānšahr*, ed. and trans. Touraj Daryaee, *Šahrestānīhā ī Ērānšahr: A Middle Persian Text on Late Antique Geography, Epic, and History* (Costa Mesa, Calif., 2002) 13.

[54] Al-Ṭabarī, *Taʾrīkh al-rusul waʾl mulūk*, ed. de Goeje, 864, trans. Bosworth, 96. Ananias Širakacʿi (*Ašxarhacʿoycʿ*, trans. Robert Hewsen, *The Geography of Ananias of Širak* [Wiesbaden, 1992] 74), places the frontier at the Hari Rud.

[55] Early Sasanians claimed regions beyond the Oxus, but seem never to have received more than token recognition from them: A. I. Kolesnikov, "Dopolnitelnie Istochniki po Istorii Rannesrednovekovovo Irana i Evo Vostochnikh Sosedei," in *Tsentralnaya Aziya ot Akhemenidov do Timuridov: Arkheologiya, Istoriya, Etnologiya, Kultura*, ed. V. P. Nikonorov (St. Petersburg, 2005) 112–115.

[56] See Robert Thomson, "Armenian Ideology and the Persians," in *La Persia e Bisanzio*, ed. Antonio Carile (Rome, 2004) 373–389, on Armenian historiography; and Scott McDonough, "A Question of Faith?: Persecution and Political Centralization in the Sasanian Empire of Yazdgard II (438–457 CE)," in *Violence in Late Antiquity: Perceptions and Practices*, ed. Harold A. Drake (Aldershot, 2007) 69–81, on the Armenian rebellions.

[57] Ełiše, *Vasn Vardanancʿ ew Hayocʿ Paterazmin*, ed. Ter-Minasean, 9–11, trans. Thomson, 63–65.

a few dozen to a few thousand men, numbers probably typical for the military manpower at the disposal of aristocratic houses across the empire.[58] It was the task of great men personally loyal to the king of kings to mobilize, equip, and lead the contingents that convened to form Iranian armies. The nobles obliged Yazdgird II's request, marching their troops into the distant and unfamiliar terrain of the northeast.

To persuade Armenian nobles to provide cavalry for his eastern campaign, Yazdgird II boasted of his successful subjugation of Rome: "Without causing you any trouble we marched into the land of the Greeks, and without warfare by our loving benevolence we subjected the whole land to us in servitude."[59] The symbolic submission of Rome, not military victory, was presented to the *nakharars* as vindication of the king of kings' claim to universal sovereignty. By demonstrating their effective rulership through the subjugation of the Romans, the Sasanians gained the military service of the great Armenian houses and the lesser nobles of the Caucasus subordinate to their authority. It was through the communication of their ongoing realization of the idea of Iran that the Sasanians mobilized the vast armies evident in the excavations of Gurgan.

ROME AND IRAN: A FRATERNAL PARTNERSHIP

Although Yazdgird II represented the Romans as Iranian subjects, Iran's relations with the Roman Empire became unprecedentedly amiable in the fifth century. With the East in crisis, the court pursued peace with the empire against which the kings of kings had hitherto maintained a nearly unceasing antagonism: Rome. The empire could not afford to campaign on two frontiers simultaneously. In 388 Iranians and Romans settled their long-standing dispute for control of the Armenian provinces and agreed to respect one another's distinct zones of influence.[60] In the following decades, Yazdgird II received Marutha the bishop of Maipherqat as a Roman envoy and elevated what would

---

[58] K. N. Yuzbashian, *Armyanskaya Epopeya v Veka: Ot Avarairskoi Bitvi k Soglasheniyu v Nuarsake* (Moscow, 2001) 24, 46.

[59] Ełiše, *Vasn Vardananć ew Hayoc' Paterazmin*, ed. Ter-Minasean, 9, trans. Thomson, 64.

[60] Roger C. Blockley, "The Division of Armenia between the Romans and the Persians at the End of the Fourth Century A.D.," *Historia* 36 (1987) 222–234, 232.

become the East Syrian Church to a position of privilege in a Zoroastrian Empire.[61] The king of kings was even invited to serve as the guardian of the emperor Arcadius's son.[62]

The rapid reinvention of Rome as Iran's partner depended on the Avestan tradition.[63] In the era of the primordial kings, Fereydun had divided the world's seven climes among his three sons, Iraj, Salm, and Tur, each of whom assumed a realm that corresponded with the three imperial powers of Late Antiquity. If the descendants of Iraj ruled the central clime of of Iran, the Roman emperors descended from his brother Salm. This paradigm permitted the kings of kings to describe the Roman emperors as their brothers and, most famously, their partnered kingdoms as the two great powers of the civilized world.[64] The fraternal partnership was, nevertheless, unambiguously hierarchical.[65] Rome ruled its territories legitimately, but only on the authority of the Iranian kings of kings. Peace between Rome and Iran depended as much on mutual ignorance or self-delusion as on active collaboration on matters of shared interest. The idea of Iran nevertheless permitted the Sasanians to recast their previously sworn enemy as a brother and partner, leading to the intensified diplomatic contact and cultural exchange characteristic of the fifth and sixth centuries.

At the same time, the Sasanian court came to demand recognition of Iran's superior position, through the payment of tribute. In the late fourth century, the court began to request assistance from the Romans to defend against Hun incursions in the Caucasus that threatened Roman Anatolia as much as Iran.[66] Roman envoys accordingly submitted payments of approximately 500 lbs of gold at irregular

---

[61] Elizabeth Key Fowden, *The Barbarian Plain: Saint Sergius between Rome and Iran* (Berkeley, 1999) 53–54; Scott McDonough, "Bishops or Bureaucrats?: Christian Clergy and the State in the Middle Sasanian Period," in *Current Research in Sasanian Archaeology, Art, and History*, ed. Derek Kennett and Paul Luft (Oxford, 2008) 87–92.

[62] Proc., *BP*, ed. Dewing, I. 2.1–10.

[63] M. Rahim Shayegan, *Arsacids and Sasanians: Political Ideology in Post-Hellenistic and Late Antique Persia* (Cambridge, 2011) 21–29.

[64] Nina Garsoïan, "Byzantium and the Sasanians," in *The Cambridge History of Iran*, vol. 3.1: *The Seleucid, Parthian, and Sasanian Periods*, ed. Ehsan Yarshater (Cambridge, 1983) 568–592, here 575–576.

[65] Touraj Daryaee, "Sasanians and their Ancestors," in *Proceedings of the 5th Conference of the Societas Iranologica Europaea*, ed. Antonio Panaino and Andrea Piras (Milan, 2006) 387–393.

[66] John Lydus, *De magistratibus*, ed. and trans. Anastasius Bandy, *Ioannes Lydus on Powers* (Philadelphia, 1983) 212–213.

intervals.[67] Viewed as diplomatic subsidies by the Romans, for the Sassanians these payments were unambiguously tributary, evidence of Roman subordination.[68] Roman failures to submit gold rendered a king of kings' internal political position even more precarious, and Theodosius II's outright refusal compelled Yazdgird II to invade Roman territory in 441. The emperors Leo and Zeno were less and less willing to dispatch gold to Iran as the Romans became more aware of the payments' tributary significance and began to view their neighbor as the "pagan" enemy of a Christian empire.[69] With Peroz in peril on the eastern frontier in 484, Zeno again refused payments, signaling a hiatus in the flow of Roman gold eastward until Kawad's great campaign of 501 that inaugurated a century and a quarter of unremitting Roman-Iranian conflict. In the sixth century, the pursuit of Roman tribute as a form of recognition of Iranian universal sovereignty was the main goal of the Iranian campaigns against the Romans.

CONCLUSION

Despite their inability to repel he Huns from the East, the Iranian Empire managed to surmount its crises in the fifth century through the construction of an aristocratic consensus around the Sasanian dynasty as the rulers of Ērānšahr. It was the willingness of these men to march with Wahram V, Yazdgird II, and Peroz against the Hun states that prevented the overrunning of the Iranian plateau, and the end of Iran as a cosmological project. This consensus, in turn, depended on a reinvention of Iran. On the one hand, the invocation of the Avestan conflict between Iran and Turan, between ērān and xyōnān, enabled the court to account for its catastrophic losses and to erect fortified frontiers that would prevent the further erosion of imperial authority. On the other, the establishment of fraternal relations with Rome reinforced the dependence of the Roman emperor on the king of kings in Iranian ideology. We thus find the Sasanian court producing gold coins out of Roman tributary payments as special issues precisely when a

---

[67] Zeev Rubin, "The Mediterranean and the Dilemma of the Roman Empire in Late Antiquity," *MHR* 1 (1986) 13–62, 39–42.

[68] Henning Börm, "'Es war allerdings nicht so, dass sie im Sinne eines Tributes erhielten, wie viele meinten . . .': Anlässe und Funktion der persischen Geldforderungen an die Römer (3. bis 6. Jh.)," *Historia* 57 (2008) 327–346.

[69] Fergus Millar, *A Greek Roman Empire: Power and Belief under Theodosius II (408–450)* (Berkeley, 2006) 73–75.

king of kings sought to rally the aristocratic families on a campaign against the *xyōnān:* Peroz's gold coinage.[70] Peroz, who had submitted embarrassing sums to the Hephthalites after his 469 defeat, extended these gold coins to the aristocracies as evidence of continued ability to superintend power globally. Just as his Kayanian forebearers had experienced momentary failures in their centuries-long struggle with Turan, so too would the Sasanian kings of kings ultimately restore Iran to its rightful place as the unquestioned universal sovereign expediting the world's eschatological renewal. With Iranian elites so committed to this cosmological framework, the death of Peroz at the hands of the Huns in 484 was in the final analysis an event of little consequence. Sukhra, a man of the ancient house of Karen as mighty as any Sasanian, placed the king of kings' surviving son on the throne, rather than dispensing with a dynasty that had so humiliated Iran. Six decades later, Husraw I would decisively defeat the Hephthalite Huns and restore, however temporarily, Iranian political authority in Central Asia. The embattled empire of the fifth century engineered the foundations – infrastructural, ideological, and social – of the expansionist empire of the sixth.[71]

---

[70] Schindel, *Sylloge Nummorum Sasanidarum,* 3.1: 401.
[71] The author would like to thank Lesha Shah for her help in completing the chapter.

PART III

RELIGIOUS AND CULTURAL
TRANSFORMATION

17: ASCETICS AND MONASTICS IN THE EARLY FIFTH CENTURY

Susanna Elm

Though Constantine had made Christianity a legitimate religion, it became securely established only after the death of the last pagan emperor, Julian, in 363. Julian's successor in the East, after a brief interlude, was the unlucky Valens. Mindful of the turmoil under Julian, Valens made conversion to Christianity obligatory for the Gothic Tervingi and Greuthungi who wanted to settle in the empire.[1] His form of Christianity has been labeled "Arian," and these Goths too became Arian Christians. Theodosius I, who succeeded as emperor after Valens's defeat at Adrianople, instead declared what he called Catholic Christianity the religion of the empire. Such imperial shifts sharpened the already tense debates over right Christian belief and orthodoxy, and made them a dominant feature of the late fourth and early fifth century.

These debates also posed a significant challenge to Christian asceticism and monasticism. Ascetic and monastic leaders often engaged directly in theological debates, because when they wrote about the right form of Christian belief they were also writing about the right way to live it as ascetics and monastics.[2] As a consequence, the ascetic and monastic insiders of the second and third generation subjected earlier forms of the ascetic life to intense scrutiny. Their efforts to reform

---

[1] Socrates Scholasticus, *Historia ecclesiastica*, 7.33.4; Peter J. Heather, *Goths and Romans, 332–489* (Oxford, 1991) 127–128; Stefan Esders, "Grenzen und Grenzüberschreitungen: Religion, Ethnizität und politische Integration am Rande des oströmischen Imperiums (4.–7. Jh.)," in *Gestiftete Zukunft im mittelalterlichen Europa*, ed. Wolfgang Huschner and Frank Rexroth (Berlin, 2008) 3–28, esp. 5–13.

[2] For further references to these theological debates, see Christopher Beeley, *The Unity of Christ: Continuity and Conflict in Patristic Tradition* (New Haven, 2012).

their own ascetic and monastic practices, including ascetic marriage, are the subject of this chapter. I will focus on a few of these reformers, men from Egypt, Southern Gaul, Rome, and Constantinople, to illustrate the consolidation of earlier ascetic and monastic experiments into institutions that differed regionally, east to west, and which were shaped by the challenges and opportunities presented by the long reign of Theodosius II and the movements of Attila and his Huns.

By the mid-fifth century, ascetic and monastic life had become an intrinsic part of the social fabric of the Roman Empire across all geographic regions. The regional differences just mentioned were apparent, but dense networks, displacements, and voluntary movements by ascetic experts assured an exchange of information throughout the empire; east and west, ascetic and monastic leaders such as Shenoute, Cassian, Salvian, Leo, Dalmatius, and Nestorius wanted to reform, adjust, fine-tune, and control the relations between ascetics, monastics, bishops, and society at large. The distribution of wealth toward monks, among monks, and from ascetic and monastic intuitions to others, played a key role in these changes. At stake were issues of social status within ascetic and monastic communities and how they related to ascetic discipline, which also included sexual abstinence. Also controversial was the extent to which the rigor of the ascetic few ought to be emulated by all Christians. The breakdown of public order caused by the barbarian invasions in the wake of Valens's defeat at Adrianople prompted the reformers to advocate a heightening of ascetic discipline that they all considered a precondition for their own involvement in the world so evidently in crisis. But Salvian and Leo, both of whom had encountered barbarian invaders face to face, went further. For them, a more rigorous ascetic discipline, including stricter dispersal of wealth, was only a first step, because the extent of the disaster facing their world required that all Roman Christians change their lives to do penance through a more rigorous adherence to God's demands.

EGYPT: SHENOUTE OF ATRIPE AND HIS MONASTIC FEDERATION

Around 465 a man died in the deserts of Egypt whose life spanned the entire period under discussion. In 371, when he was about ten years old, he joined a monastery located outside the modern town of Sohag, ancient Atripe, on the west bank of the Nile. When he died, he had for decades been the leader of a federation of monastic communities of some four thousand men and women, and he entered history as the archimandrite, or monastic leader, Shenoute of Atripe.[3] Shenoute also produced a large body of writings, in which he refers to a number of events that occurred in his long lifetime. He recounts, for example, a series of hostile encounters that reached their apogee around 400 with a local potentate called Gesios, who engaged in pagan practices and ruthlessly exploited his peasants. We learn that later, in 431, Shenoute joined Cyril, bishop of Alexandria, to travel to Ephesus to oppose Nestorius, bishop of Constantinople. Shenoute also reports overseeing the construction of a church for his communities between 450 and 455, and dealing with the fall-out of significant "barbarian" invasions from the South soon after the completion of that church, when his federation sheltered numerous refugees from nearby villages.[4] The most consequential event of Shenoute's life occurred, however, in the early 380s. At some point, the young Shenoute, already a *monachos* of the White Monastery at Atripe for about a decade, left his community to retire into the nearby desert.[5]

Monastics (sing. *monachos*, pl. *monachoi*) were men and women whose life was dominated by a desire to discipline their body through rigorous training, or *askesis*, in chastity, fasting, and prayer so that their souls would be pure. In practice, such discipline could be followed alone or in a community with others, in which case it also included obedience and submission to the will of the community's leader, occasionally codified in a rule. As Shenoute's retreat into the desert shows, some communities allowed for a combination of both forms: members could live in isolated cells but still be connected to the community, so that they too were compelled to discipline through obedience. Shenoute's removal to such a cell, where he remained for the rest of

---

[3] Stephen Emmel, ed., *Shenoute's Literary Corpus*, 2 vols., Corpus Scriptorum Christianorum Orientalium 599–600, subsidia 111–112 (Louvain, 2004) 1: 4–13, Bentley Layton, "Social Structure and Food Consumption in an Early Monastery: The Evidence of Shenoute's *Canons* and the White Monastery Federation, AD 385–465," *Muséon* 115 (2002): 25–55.

[4] Events in Shenoute's life are notoriously difficult to date. Shenoute, *Canon 7*, in Emmel, *Literary Corpus*, 1: 178–204, 2: 582–593; Stephen Emmel, "From the Other Side of the Nile: Shenoute and Panopolis," in *Perspectives on Panopolis: An Egyptian Town from Alexander the Great to the Arab Conquest*, ed. Arno Egberts, Brian P. Muhs, and Joep van der Vliet (Leiden, 2002) 95–113, here 100–109; Rebecca Krawiec, *Shenoute and the Women of the White Monastery: Egyptian Monasticism in Late Antiquity* (Oxford, 2002) 3; Peter Grossmann, *Christliche Architektur in Ägypten*, Handbook of Oriental Studies 62 (Leiden, 2002) 528–529.

[5] Emmel, *Literary Corpus*, 1: 7.

his life while leading the monasteries of his federation, was prompted, he claims, because God had revealed to him that some fellow *monachoi* had transgressed three of the central features of this discipline. They had disobeyed their then leader, stolen and hoarded food (thereby breaking dietary restrictions), and may have engaged in homoerotic acts.[6] According to Shenoute, the leader had failed to address these lapses adequately. Shenoute's highly public "flight" underscored his protest and demonstrated his greater competence to lead because his revelations about the monks' transgressions were subsequently confirmed and his flight attested to his commitment to these rules. This is a crucial point: all of Shenoute's subsequent writings reflect his self-conception as a prophet sent by Heaven to reform his own monastic community and to spare no effort to ensure that those whom he guided after his successful protest recognized what true ascetic discipline meant.[7]

As Caroline Schroeder has shown, "Shenoute envisioned the monaster[ies of his federation] as one corporate body in which the individual monks (both male and female) are its members."[8] Because Shenoute considered all bodily defilements sin, the individual male and female monk's bodily purity (or lack thereof) became the measure of the purity of the whole: the health of the entire monastic body depended on the purity of each of its members and vice versa. As a consequence, Shenoute made no difference between his male and female monks as ascetics. The pollution of sin could spread with equal ease in carriers of either gender, as could the salvific power of proper ascetic discipline. In

---

[6] Shenoute, *Canon* 1, 90.13–14, in *Sinuthii Archimandritae Vita et Opera Omnia*, ed. Johannes Leipoldt with Walter E. Crum, 3 vols. (numbered 1, 3, and 4) (Paris, 1906–1913) 3: 195–196; Stephen Emmel, trans., "Shenoute the Monk: The Early Monastic Career of Shenoute the Archimandrite," in *Il monachesimo tra eredità e aperture: Atti del simposio "Testi e temi nella tradizione del monachesimo cristiano" per il 500 anniversario dell'Istituto Monastico di Sant'Anselmo, Roma, 28 maggio–10 giugno 2002*, ed. Maciej Bielawsi and Daniël Hombergen (Rome, 2004) 151–174, here 165–166; see Emmel, *Literary Corpus*, 1: 125–145, 2: 558–565, for the codicological reconstruction.

[7] For a discussion of Shenoute's self-presentation as prophet, see David Brakke, "Shenoute, Weber, and the Monastic Prophet: Ancient and Modern Articulations of Ascetic Authority," in *Foundations of Power and Conflicts of Authority in Late Antique Monasticism*, ed. Alberto Camplani and Giovanni Filoramo (Louvain, 2007) 47–73. See also Shenoute, *Canon* 1; and Caroline Schroeder, "Prophecy and *Porneia* in Shenoute's Letters: The Rhetoric of Sexuality in a Late Antique Egyptian Monastery," *Journal of Near Eastern Studies* 65 (2006) 81–97.

[8] Caroline Schroeder, *Monastic Bodies: Discipline and Salvation in Shenoute of Atripe* (Philadelphia, 2007) 3.

this, all Shenoute's ascetics were brothers and sisters.[9] Men and women in Shenoute's federation occupied different monastic compounds, and he interacted with both only through specially chosen, male intermediaries. In the case of the women's compounds, these male intermediaries were connected to the women, especially the female leader, through biological kinship (*kata sarx*). Shenoute's writings make it clear that his federation housed entire families. This was by no means unusual. But whereas Pachomius, an earlier Egyptian monastic leader whom scholars have often, and all too easily, considered Shenoute's intellectual precursor, permitted married and otherwise related monastics to visit each other, for example "if some paternal inheritance was due them," Shenoute was far stricter. For him, monastic community overrode all other ties absolutely.[10]

Shenoute's use of the language of family and his concept of the intensely reciprocal relation between the individual male or female monastic's body and the body politic of the federation are the ordering principle that accounted for both the individual's place within the federation and for the interaction between male and female monastics. Though everyone was equal in their asceticism and hence called to observe the prescribed ascetic discipline with equal rigor or else face appropriate disciplinary reprisals, the monasteries were organized according to a strict hierarchy, with each member assigned his and her proper, gendered role. Shenoute was the head, and his authority and power were indisputable.

As such, Shenoute was a player within the power structures of late Roman Egypt. He was an ordained presbyter, his federation was economically self-sufficient,[11] and he acted as local patron, for example when sheltering refugees (who lived alongside his monastics without any fear of defiling the latter; their reciprocal roles were such that the boundaries separating his monastics from the lay population

---

[9] Krawiec, *Shenoute and the Women*, 92–119.

[10] Pachomius, *Rule*, 143; Armand Veilleux, *Pachomian Koinonia*, 3 vols. (Kalamazoo, 1980–82) 2: 166–167; Krawiec, *Shenoute and the Women*, 161–174; Schroeder, *Monastic Bodies*, 115–116; Caroline Schroeder, "Child Sacrifice in Egyptian Monastic Culture: From Familial Renunciation to Jephthah's Lost Daughter," *Journal of Early Christian Studies* 20 (2012) 269–302.

[11] Ariel Lopez, *Shenoute of Atripe and the Uses of Poverty: Rural Patronage, Religious Conflict, and Monasticism in Late Antique Egypt* (Berkeley, 2013) 46–69; and especially Ewa Wipszycka, "Les formes institutionelles et les formes d'activité économique du monachisme égyptien," in Camplani and Filoramo, *Foundations of Power*, 109–154.

were porous).[12] Further, his understanding of the ascetic body as trans-
formable and essential for salvation embodied, and developed, the Trinitarian orthodoxy of the Alexandrian see. Despite his radical notions
of purity Shenoute maintained the social status quo. Thus, the ascetic
equality of women did not correspond to their institutional place within
the confederation, which mirrored that of women in general. Spir-
itually, the physical purity of the chosen male and female monastics
functioned as a healing remedy for all in Shenoute's care, all orthodox Christians who were themselves the body of Christ.[13] Rather than
an intellectual follower of Pachomius, Shenoute was the leader of a
powerful institution in his own right, which had a real impact on its
surroundings.[14]

Scholars have often considered Shenoute a true outlier, because
he wrote only in Coptic (though he had a Greek education), used a
highly evocative prophetic language, and was very harsh in his criticism
of pagans, heretics, and those he disciplined within his confederation.
Upon closer analysis, however, Shenoute is far more representative of
the early to mid-fifth century than has been recognized. His federation
and, even more so, the manner in which Shenoute represented himself
encapsulate several key tendencies of that period. In the early phases
of the ascetic movement, above all in Egypt, ascetic individuals, mostly
laypeople, who practiced various forms of asceticism by themselves or in
small communities, in cities, and in the countryside such as the desert,
were often represented by our sources as standing "outside" the world
and in tension and outright conflict with members of the clergy and
the civic powers.[15]

Shenoute also thought of himself as a charismatic "outsider," an
ascetic prophet, and he too lived as a hermit. But as hermit, he exercised
undisputed authority over his own monastics and over nonmonastic

---

[12] In Emmel's words, the monastics were "caring for the needs of the refugees' bodies
out of concern for the needs of their souls": Stephen Emmel, "The Historical
Circumstances of Shenoute's Sermon God is Blessed," in *Themelia: Spätantike und
koptologische Studien Peter Grossmann zum 65. Geburtstag*, ed. Martin Krause and Sofia
Schaten (Wiesbaden, 1998) 81–96, here 88.

[13] Schroeder, *Monastic Bodies*, 17–18, 117, 128–157.

[14] The relation between Pachomius and Shenoute that earlier scholars have posited
appears increasingly problematic; Layton, "Social Structure."

[15] Samuel Rubenson, "Argument and Authority in Early Monastic Correspondence,"
in Camplani and Filoramo, *Foundations of Power*, 75–87; David Brakke, "The Making
of Monastic Demonology: Three Ascetic Teachers on Withdrawal, and Resistance,"
Church History 70 (2001) 19–48; Susanna Elm, *Virgins of God: The Making of Asceticism
in Late Antiquity* (Oxford, 1994).

Christians, laypersons and members of the clergy – in sum, all whom he considered within his extensive sphere of influence. He exhibited no tension or conflict between ascetic withdrawal and active engagement in the world.[16] To the contrary, his ascetic discipline, the size of his monastic federation, and his prophetic gifts legitimated his authority, destined to be exercised inside and outside his federation. Strict ascetic discipline became the precondition for correct leadership of all Christians, monastics and others, and such discipline had to increase in rigor the greater the monastic's involvement in the affairs of the world. This seeming paradox – that an increase in ascetic stricture, in actual withdrawal from the world, increasingly became the prerequisite for active participation and interference in worldly affairs – lies at the heart of the fifth-century monastic movement, of which Shenoute is our first example.[17]

SOUTHERN GAUL: CASSIAN AND SALVIAN OF MARSEILLE

The second case study brings us to an entirely different part of the world, the Rhineland and southern Gaul in the 420s to the 440s. Here, ascetic and monastic reformers such as Salvian of Marseille sought to enforce greater physical and spiritual purity because their troubled world encountered the barbarians directly. This world in crisis was, they felt, in dire need of the monks' active participation, because only a monastic's pure body could sanctify the body politic such that it might withstand near certain doom. Salvian, who lived from about 400 to the 480s, came to southern Gaul, the modern Provence, in the 420s as a refugee after the gruesome collapse of the Rhine frontier. Salvian had seen rows of corpses piled up outside the walls of Trier, and one of his female relatives and her son had been left destitute in Cologne, dependent on the benevolence of the new Frankish leading ladies.[18] When Salvian fled south, he was married and had a daughter. He and his wife were *conversi*, converts to asceticism, against the intense opposition of his wife's pagan

---

[16] Wipszycka, "Formes institutionelles," 142–146.

[17] Conrad Leyser, *Authority and Asceticism from Augustine to Gregory the Great* (Oxford, 2000).

[18] Salvian, *De gubernatione Dei*, 6.15.94, and Salvian, *Epistula* 1.5–6, both in *Salvien de Marseille: Oeuvres*, 2 vols., Sources Chrétiennes 176 and 220, ed. Georges Lagarrigue (Paris, 1971, 1976); Hubert Fischer, *Die Schrift des Salvian von Marseille "An die Kirche"* (Frankfurt, 1976) 11.

parents.[19] Marseille had not been Salvian's first stop, however. Upon reaching the South, he joined the monastic community on the island of Lérins, the Ile Saint Honorat, accompanied by his family (Salv. *Ep.* 4.5).

Although surrounded by post-Roman, barbarian kingdoms of which Salvian had had firsthand experience, the region from Lyon to Marseille remained a relatively peaceful Roman imperial enclave until the 470s.[20] Marseille, partially as a result of the collapse of imperial rule in Gaul, increased in importance as a harbor and became a magnet for Christian intellectuals, not least because of its proximity to the famous monastery on Lérins.[21] In the 420s, those Christian intellectuals included John Cassian, a man with extensive experience of Egyptian and Greek monastic practices.[22] Between 426 and 428 Cassian addressed a series of sermons, *Collationes* or *Conferences*, to Honoratus, the founder of the monastery on Lérins, where Salvian had recently arrived.[23] Cassian intended these *Collationes* (which followed an earlier work, the *Institutes*, addressed to another Provençal abbot) polemically as a tool for reforming monastic life on Lérins. He declared that these sermons contained the direct teachings of leading Egyptian ascetics and monastics, among whom Cassian had lived for some fifteen years. For Cassian, these teachings were essential to instruct those he considered mere amateurs.[24]

It is important to keep in mind that Salvian on Lérins experienced the monastic life as practiced by Honoratus and his companions, many of whom, like Salvian, belonged to the Gallic elite. However, at Lérins, Salvian also encountered Cassian's calls to reform just that life, and, as we shall see, he reacted to both influences. Cassian and later Salvian did not advocate a lessening of the monasteries' interaction with the world;

---

[19] Sal. *Ep.* 4.6.

[20] Peter Brown, *Through the Eye of a Needle: Wealth, the Fall of Rome, and the Making of Christianity in the West, 350–550 AD* (Princeton, 2012) 411.

[21] Friedrich Prinz, *Frühes Mönchtum im Frankenreich* (Munich, 1965) 52–53; Lagarrigue, *Salvien de Marseille*, 1: 10–12.

[22] Richard Goodrich locates Cassian in Marseille around 429: *Contextualizing Cassian: Aristocrats, Ascetics, and Reformation in Fifth Century Gaul* (Oxford, 2007) 211–234.

[23] Eugène Pichéry, *Jean Cassien: Conférences*, 3 vols, Sources Chrétiennes 42, 54, 64 (Paris, 1955, 1958, 1959); Jean-Claude Guy, *Jean Cassien: Institutions cénobitiques*, SC 109 (Paris, 1965).

[24] Goodrich, *Contextualizing Cassian*, 2–4, 32–116; for the increasing connectivity between eastern and western bishops and monastics, despite increasing regionalization, see Maribel Dietz, *Wandering Monks, Virgins, and Pilgrims: Ascetic Travel in the Mediterranean World, AD 300–800* (University Park, Pa., 2005) 69–106.

on the contrary, they sought to highlight and enforce a greater physical and spiritual purity because it was the monastics' role to sanctify the whole of Christ's body through their own, pure body. This required an inner discipline that intensified in severity, in *actual* renunciation, the closer the monastics' ties were to the Christian body; such ties had to increase the more Christ's body was under pressure and in need of salvation, which in turn increased the need of ascetic discipline.[25]

For Cassian, asceticism in a monastic community signified complete equality of all. For him, however, such ascetic equality was not so much one between the sexes but rather among socially diverse persons.[26] Granted, all monks at Lérins were obliged to work with their hands, but many wealthy monks had brought their slaves with them (together with their other donations), whose labor soon turned the inhospitable island into a high-yielding agricultural complex.[27] Such upper-class "asceticism" was anathema to Cassian. For him, to enter into a monastic community meant to be stripped of everything, including all family ties, "so that, apart from the will of the leader, hardly any will should be alive in us."[28] To become a monk meant to become part of the "body of the brotherhood," and that body was poor.[29] Avarice and its results, such as theft, overeating, and the hoarding of food were sinful pollution that infected the monastic body through the bloodstream of each member.[30]

Cassian, like Shenoute, and later on Salvian (though with a twist), addressed his criticism to existing monastic communities as one ascetic and monastic expert to his peers in the same profession.[31] Like Shenoute's federation, the monastery on the island considered itself separate from the "world." But such separation was the vantage point from which monastic leaders like Honoratus, Cassian, and Shenoute (things were different for ordinary monastics) interacted fully with the powers of the day. The wealthier and more elite monastics at Lérins interacted

---

[25] Goodrich, *Contextualizing Cassian*, 155–157.
[26] Ibid., 184–207.
[27] *Regula quattuor patrum*, 2.35; Adalbert de Vogüé, *Régles des saints pères*, Sources Chrétiennes 298, 2 vols. (Paris, 1982) 1: 192.
[28] Cassian, *De institutis coenobiorum*, 12.32.1; Goodrich, *Contextualizing Cassian*, 177–181.
[29] Cass. *Inst.* 4.5.
[30] Ibid., 7.13.
[31] Goodrich, *Contextualizing Cassian*, 4–6; Leyser, *Authority and Asceticism from Augustine to Gregory the Great*, 33–59; Philip Rousseau, *Ascetics, Authority and the Church in the Age of Jerome and Cassian*, 2nd ed. (Notre Dame, 2010).

directly by becoming bishops in cities near and far; one was bishop of Geneva. Monastic elites, then, leaders within their community, were successful players in their region's economy and confronted the ravages of invasions by sheltering refugees. Indeed, the very success of these monastic leaders within their regional power structure propelled the calls for internal reform by some of the leaders themselves, often belonging to the second or third generation of monastics, persons such as Shenoute, Cassian, and Salvian.

Of these men, Salvian of Marseille linked the absolute purity of the monastic body and its spiritual (and actual) separation the most tightly to the salvation of the entire Christian body politic. He, too, addressed first and foremost his fellow ascetics and monastics in southern Gaul, but then he extended his criticism outward with great urgency.[32] By the time he wrote his first known work, *Ad ecclesiam*, or *To the Church*, between 435 and 439, Salvian had become a priest in Marseille, and he addressed his works to fellow monastics from Lérins, by then bishops in Lyon and Geneva, far closer to the frontier than Marseille.[33] At that point, the Vandals controlled North Africa, the bread basket of Rome and the Western Empire; and "Romans out there" who no longer wished to be subjects of Rome, lawless persons known as Bacaudae, were wreaking havoc of the kind Salvian had witnessed firsthand in Cologne and Trier.[34] Confronted with such devastation Salvian concluded that "the Christians of the empire had abandoned God . . . [and that t]he empire might fall because the church had already fallen."[35]

Whereas Shenoute and Cassian, each in his own way, had called on their peers to intensify their monastic purity and discipline so that the elect monks could heal the world around them through their own ascetic practice, Salvian went further by equating ascetic reform with that of the entire church: only if the Christians of the empire reformed their misguided ways (with the help of the true monks) could they arrest the utter collapse of what remained of Rome. Salvian directed his

---

[32] Brown, *Through the Eye*, 434.

[33] Ibid., 435–436.

[34] *Ilic Romani*, in Sal. *De gub.* 5.8.37; Salvian, *Ad ecclesiam*, in Larrigue, *Salvien de Marseille*, 1: 135–345; Andy Merrills and Richard Miles, *The Vandals* (Chichester, 2010) 141–176; John F. Drinkwater, "The Bacaudae of Fifth-Century Gaul," in *Fifth-Century Gaul: A Crisis of Identity?*, ed. John F. Drinkwater and Hugh Elton (Cambridge, 1992) 208–217, with further bibliography.

[35] Brown, *Through the Eye*, 434–435.

harshest criticism toward ascetics and monastics who failed to comprehend fully what their profession entailed, and mistook the monastic life
as a slight modification of their elite customs. Such monastics continued to cling to their property and kin. Monastic leaders, high-ranking
clergy, and wealthy laypersons, moreover, incorporated the ascetic life
into their family financial planning to safeguard their personal estates.
Young men and women were sent by their families into the ascetic life,
but only after they had forfeited their share of the parental estates, their
renunciation thus preserving the shrinking properties of the wealthy.[36]

For Salvian, such behavior threatened the economic survival of the
monastic communities and the sanctuary they provided the displaced;
in doing so, it threatened the survival of the church and the collapsing
empire. And the worst of those engaged in such avarice (*Avarice* was the
original title of *Ad Ecclesiam*) were the monastics themselves. Ascetics
who came already stripped of their properties in favor of their kin could
not, in fact, renounce and were thus bereft of their chance to live their
true monastic vocation, namely to renounce in such a way that the
poor, the widows, and the monastic communities were provided for.[37]

Salvian's next work, *De gubernatione Dei*, or *The Governance of God*,
was aptly known to his contemporaries as *Judgment in the Here and Now*
(*De praesenti iudicio*).[38] It resonates with the rigor of Shenoute, echoed
by Cassian, in its demand for absolute obedience to God's commands in
face of the present dangers, but those Salvian called to such obedience
were not only the monastic few, but all Christians. Now more than ever
all should obey the same divine laws, the same discipline, to live justly
and purely, with compassion and humanity.[39] Such a life included the
just use of all that God gave to people, especially their earthly goods
and family. The wealthy must not waste their funds on spectacles in the
arena while corpses were rotting among smoldering ruins, nor shame

---

[36] Sal. *Ad eccl.* 3.13. 57–58; *Novella Maiorani*, 6, in Theodosius, *Theodosiani libri XVI cum
Constitutionibus Sirmonianis et Leges novella ad Theodosianum pertinentes*, ed. Theodor
Mommsen and Paul M. Meyer (Berlin, 1905); the laws, issued in 458, stipulated that
young girls should not be forced to take the veil. Jan Badewien, *Geschichtstheologie
und Sozialkritik im Werke Salvians von Marseilles* (Göttingen, 1980) 113–116; Sam J.
B. Barnish, "Transformation and Survival in the Western Senatorial Aristocracy, c.
AD 400–700," *Papers of the British School at Rome* 66 (1988) 120–155; Kate Cooper,
The Fall of the Roman Household (Cambridge, 2007) 112–114.

[37] Sal. *Ad eccl.* 3.4.21.

[38] Written in 439 and unfinished; the original title is given in Gennadius, *De viris
illustribus* 68.

[39] Sal. *Ad eccl.* 1.2.9, 1.4.19–20; Badewien, *Geschichtstheologie*, 139–143.

their wives by sleeping with their concubines, slaves, and prostitutes. Such misdeeds violated divine law, and the troubled times left no doubt as to the extent of God's punishment for those who disobeyed him.[40]

Salvian's clarion call for rigorous discipline of monastics and all other Christians (though differing in degree of severity) emanated from his identification of Rome and Israel. Rome, the new Israel, suffered the devastation of the present as divine punishment because it, too, had disobeyed God's Law. This was the price Christian *Romans* had to pay. *Roman* ascetics and monastics were the worst and the best of the lot. Their failings amplified those of the body politic at large, but those who lived according to God's commands were the sole low bulwark safeguarding the remaining realm.[41] "The Romans were once the strongest of all, now they are powerless. . . . Now we are tributary to the barbarians. . . . Our entire safety is up for sale."[42] For Salvian, the barbarian Vandals, Visigoths, and Goths – all Arians – were merely the executors of God's judgment. Because they had never received full knowledge of the divine truth they also received less blame. As Michael Maas has shown, Salvian believed that the Romans were the prime object of divine punishment, not because of factors such as whether one was Roman or barbarian, orthodox or heretical, but because of their moral behavior.[43]

Salvian's call for the monastics and ascetics to reform so that they could save the church and the remains of the Roman Empire highlights a question that had troubled the ascetic movement since its inception: to what extent ought ascetic discipline be demanded of all Christians? All along, ascetic pioneers had proclaimed their way of life *the* model for all Christians, but the degree of rigor involved was debated, and radical demands soon moderated.[44] Elite ascetic practitioners enticed their peers by portraying the ascetic life as a nobler version of the aristocratic *otium*, or withdrawal to the country estate, in a way that was particularly attractive to many of the elites and the newly rich aspiring

[40] Sal. *De gub.* 6. 49, 71, 88; 7.15–20; Badewien, *Geschichtstheorie*, 83–96.

[41] Sal. *De gub.* 3. 3.14; 7.14. 58.

[42] Ibid., 6.18.93; Badewien, *Geschichtstheorie*, 149–150; David Lambert, "The Use of Decay: History in Salvian's De gubernatione Dei," *Augustinian Studies* 30 (1999) 115–30; Brown, *Through the Eye*, 442–443.

[43] Michael Maas, "Ethnicity, Orthodoxy, and Community in Salvian of Marseilles," in Drinkwater and Elton, *Fifth-Century Gaul*, 275–284.

[44] Daniel Caner, *Wandering, Begging Monks: Spiritual Authority and the Promotion of Monasticism in Late Antiquity* (Berkeley, 2002).

to the very top.[45] In the early fifth century, men like Shenoute and Cassian disrupted such a stance profoundly: for them, to become an ascetic and a monastic meant real renunciation of wealth and status, true equality in utter dependence on the community and its leader, who, just like God, commanded absolute obedience.[46]

However, Shenoute and Cassian's calls for such rigor had been directed to monastics; Salvian, by contrast, extended them once again to all Christian Romans. Reacting to his times, Salvian differed from earlier "reformers." Whereas Cassian, for example, called for a complete renunciation of all wealth before entering the monastic community, Salvian insisted that elite ascetics must donate their wealth to the community upon entering it, even though this would preserve their social privilege.[47] Rather than echoing the mainstream of elite asceticism, Salvian's insistence on donations by wealthy monastics to the church (which earlier scholars deemed a prime example of "the clerical art of extortion")[48] was instead a call to resist the ferocious burden of Roman taxation. Wealthy, elite Romans, Salvian's prime targets, had shifted the extraordinarily heavy tax burdens entailed by Aetius's costly push-back of the barbarians during the 430s and 440s down to the lesser, local elites – men such as Salvian – to devastating effect. For Salvian, therefore, Rome and its elites had been so unjust that it was far better to give to monastics than to an empire so depraved that free Romans would rather be enslaved to barbarians than to the tax collector.[49]

---

[45] Goodrich, *Contextualizing Cassian*, 19–31; Roberto Alciati and Mariachiara Giorda, "Possessions and Asceticism: Melania the Younger and Her Slow Way to Jerusalem," *Zeitschrift für Antikes Christentum* 14 (2010) 425–444; Julia Hillner, "*Domus*, Family, and Inheritance: the Senatorial Family House in Late Antique Rome," *Journal of Roman Studies* 93 (2003) 129–145; Julia Hillner, "Clerics, Property, and Patronage: The Case of the Roman Titular Churches," *Antiquité Tardive* 14 (2006) 59–68; Michele Salzman, "Competing Claims to *nobilitas* in the Western Empire of the Fourth and Fifth Centuries," *Journal of Early Christian Studies* 9 (2001) 359–385; for the East, see Susanna Elm, *Sons of Hellenism, Fathers of the Church: Emperor Julian, Gregory of Nazianzus, and the Vision of Rome* (Berkeley, 2012).

[46] Such calls for dependence and obedience were at the heart of the so-called Pelagian controversy. Although these and related theological concerns are present in the work of Cassian and Salvian, this is not the point of this chapter; Badewien, *Geschichtstheorie*, 176–199; Elizabeth Clark, *The Origenist Controversy: The Cultural Construction of an Early Christian Debate* (Princeton, 1992).

[47] Brown, *Through the Eye*, 438.

[48] Edgar Loening, *Geschichte des deutschen Kirchenrechts*, vol. 1: *Das Kirchenrecht in Gallien von Constantin bis Chlodovech* (Strassburg, 1878) 235.

[49] Sal. *De gub.* 5.6.24; 5.5.22–23; Guy Halsall, *Barbarian Migrations and the Roman West, 376–568* (Cambridge, 2007) 250; Hugh Elton, "Defense in Fifth-Century Gaul," in

THE CITY OF ROME: BISHOPS, ASCETICS, AND THE HOUSEHOLD – LEO AND PROSPER

From the 440s onward, Rome was central to the emerging story of asceticism and monasticism. Though the imperial court had resided since 402 in Ravenna, Rome between 440 and 476 (from the emperor Valentinian III to Odoacer) was once again "the head of our empire."[50] Indeed, Valentinian III spent more time in Rome than any emperor since Maxentius (r. 306–312), and he and other emperors were important founders and benefactors of splendid basilica churches. The emperor's presence also underscores the lasting impact of the Roman senatorial aristocracy. Mindful of these two powerful players, recent scholarship no longer focuses solely on the bishop or pope, but paints a picture in which the emperors, Rome's aristocracy, the bishop, and the subelites, that is, the military, the imperial administration, and the clergy, all jostle for space within a changing world.[51] What all members of these competing spheres had in common was the *domus*, the Roman household.[52] Indeed, the history of fifth-century asceticism, monasticism, and the bishop in Rome is one of competition for the control of households, in particular of that of the subelites, who provided most of Rome's bishops and clergy. Over time, the bishops accumulated more and more control. But it was not until the end of the fifth century, when bishops came for the first time from the senatorial aristocracy, that the household of the bishop, the *domus ecclesiae*, really assumed dominance. Only then did the imperial presence wane and we begin to see a papacy with a real impact on Rome's aristocracy.[53]

Drinkwater and Elton, *Fifth-Century Gaul*, 167–176; Cam Grey, "Salvian, the Ideal Christian Community and the Fate of the Poor," in *Poverty in the Roman World*, ed. Margaret Atkin and Robin Osborne (Cambridge, 2007) 168–182.

[50] *Novella Valentiniani III* 5; Andrew Gillett, "Rome, Ravenna, and the Last Emperors in the West," *Papers of the British School at Rome* 69 (2001) 131–167; Mark Humfries, "Valentinian III and the City of Rome (425–55): Patronage, Politics, Power," in *Two Romes: Rome and Constantinople in Late Antiquity*, ed. Lucy Grigs and Gavin Kelly (Oxford, 2012) 161–182.

[51] Susan Wessel, *Leo the Great and the Spiritual Rebuilding of a Universal Rome* (Leiden, 2008) 5–6.

[52] Federico Marazzi, "Rome in Transition: Economic and Political Change in the Fourth and Fifth Centuries," in *Early Medieval Rome and the Christian West*, ed. Julia Smith (Leiden, 2000) 21–41.

[53] These developments occurred during the episcopacies of Simplicius (468), Felix III (483), Gelasius (492), and Symmachus (498); Felix was the first senatorial bishop. Kristina Sessa, *The Formation of Papal Authority in Late Antique Italy* (Cambridge, 2012)

The story of asceticism's emergence in Rome has often been told. It is that of a highly aristocratic endeavor, in which some ambitious noblewomen (and a few of their husbands), who would have liked to become even more noble but had not quite succeeded in the marriage plot, decided to invite expert Christian ascetics into their houses and their patronage networks to lead a life of elite personal renunciation (of sex rather than wealth), so that their splendid status would become even nobler in a new Christian way.[54] These ascetic women, mostly widows and their virgin daughters, are well known – examples are Melania, Marcella, Paula, Eustochium, and Demetrias – as are those of their spiritual advisors – Jerome, Rufinus, Pelagius. Because of the writings of these advisors, these aristocratic circles have dominated scholarship on Rome's ascetic scene to the detriment of the silent ascetic majority: members of the clergy and their households, who often practiced a married ascetic life. Julia Hillner has recently made it clear that much of the wealth that accrued to the Roman churches (especially as *tituli*, that is, churches that the bishop's church had acquired as their property) in the early fifth century originated far less than had been assumed with the noble ascetic ladies than with the imperial household, and above all with these ascetically married clerics.[55] Such persons did not always look favorably on the ascetic rich and unmarried, especially not when the latter were deemed superior.[56]

The rise of ascetically married clerics during the latter part of the fifth century represent the face of Roman asceticism (and monasticism, which awaits further study), a form of Christian life based on solid landholdings that increasingly guaranteed the church's economic and political autonomy from the emperor and the resiliently pagan

---

103–109; Hillner, "*Domus*, Family, and Inheritance"; Hillner, "Clerics, Property, and Patronage"; Cooper, *Fall of the Roman Household;* Michele Renee Salzman, *The Making of a Christian Aristocracy: Social and Religious Change in the Western Empire* (Cambridge, 2002) 200–219.

54 Georg Jenal, *Italia ascetica atque monastica: Das Asketen-und Mönchtum in Italien von den Anfängen bis zur Zeit de Langobarden (ca. 150/250–604)*, 2 vols. (Stuttgart, 1995) 1: 28–93, 318–461, 474–493; Brown, *Through the Eye*, 259–307; Christiana Sogno, "Roman Matchmaking," in *From the Tetrarchs to the Theodosians: Later Roman History and Culture, 284–450 CE*, ed. Scott McGill, Christiana Sogno, and Edward Watts (Cambridge, 2010) 55–72.

55 Brown, *Through the Eye*, 253; A. J. Boudewijn Sirks, *Food for Rome: The Legal Structure of the Transportation and Processing of Supplies for the Imperial Distributions in Rome and Constantinople* (Amsterdam, 1991) 325–330, 367–368, 383.

56 David Hunter, *Marriage, Celibacy, and Heresy in Ancient Christianity: The Jovinianist Controversy* (Oxford, 2007).

aristocracy.[57] Toward the end of the fifth century, this rise culminated in the emergence of the managerial bishop, increasingly of aristocratic background. These men were indeed popes. Two factors coincided to achieve this rise. On the one hand, the wealth of the lay households, from which the Roman clergy was recruited and which bishops sought to control, derived from landholdings that became, after 450, increasingly concentrated closer to Rome in southern Italy, Gaul, and Dalmatia. These consolidated estates – including the estates owned by the church – were less wealthy overall than the estates of the Roman aristocracy in earlier times, who had owned estates empire-wide, but the fact that they were closer together permitted tighter control by their owners. This development was paralleled by the Roman bishops' increasing interests in household management. The focus of this managerial intent was the bishop's own expanding household (or better, estates), which included family members, young wards over whom the bishop held *tutela*, and slaves. A second sphere of episcopal management (or interference) were the households of Rome's married, ascetic clerics.[58]

Classic Roman household management focused on sexual relations and money, and managing the clerical households was no different. Hence, for the bishops, the establishment and control of ascetic principles within clerical households was of central importance. Higher clergy were increasingly pressured to forgo sexual activity after ordination (those already ordained were prohibited from marrying) and to have married only one wife, who herself had been married only once.[59] These and similar stipulations regulating ascetic, clerical marriages were a continuous feature of Roman episcopal regimes and had numerous practical implications, especially for the higher clergy, requiring constant regulations.[60] This was so because proper control of one's household

---

[57] Claire Sotinel, "Les évêques italiens dans la société de l'antiquité tardive: L'emergence d'une nouvelle élite?," in *Le trasformazioni delle "elites" in età tardoantica*, ed. Rita Lizzi Testa (Rome, 2006) 377–404; Sessa, *Formation*, 104–109.

[58] Those of laypersons received far less attention. L. Cracco Ruggini, "La Sicilia e la fine del mondo antico (IV–VI secolo)," in *La Sicilia antica*, vol. 2.2: *La Sicilia Romana* (Naples, 1980) 483–524, here 493; Hartmut G. Ziche, "Administrer la propriéte de l'église: L'évêque comme clerc et comme entrepreneur," *AntTard* 14 (2006): 69–78.

[59] For epigraphic evidence Sessa, *Formation of Papal Authority*, 175–176 and 177–182.

[60] *Codex Theodosianus*, 16.2.44 (Honorius, 420). Leo, *Epistula*, 4.2, insisted that priests could only marry once, and in *Ep.* 4. 3 and 14.3–4 extended these requirements to subdeacons. The intensity of the regulations also reveals the degree of resistance.

through the right choice of partner and evidence of sexual purity and marital chastity after ordination was a mainstay of clerical, and hence episcopal, authority that set members of the clergy apart from laypersons. Hence, the bishops' principal focus in fifth-century Rome was the married ascetic life of the clergy rather than the aristocratic ascetic circles with their experts, mentioned above, or the monastic ascetic life.[61]

Wealth was the second focus of episcopal household management. Clerical householders routinely "confused" and intermingled their own properties and those the church had accumulated, often from donations by lay and clerical persons for their salvation, and they used the vaguely defined church properties to further their personal, family interests.[62] To ensure fiscally proper household management, the Roman church required its clergy, beginning in the fifth century, to list private property-related documents (such as wills, transfers, manumissions, deeds) in its archives, a practice akin to the listing of all such transactions by Roman property owners in the municipal offices, but it took well into the seventh century to establish the practice.[63] Still, bishops and higher clergy frequently considered their office as something to bequeath to their kin, treating the *domus ecclesiae* just as they would their own family household: dynastically.[64]

Episcopal intervention in fifth-century Rome focused on the clerical households; intervention in lay households was far more subtle and confirms that on the whole the Roman aristocracy remained loyal to its glorious past. Whereas streams of elite donations bolstered the monasteries and churches of Constantinople, Roman senators, for example in

---

[61] Jenal, *Italia ascetica*, 91–93, has identified only two male monastic complexes (though he assumed that more exclusively male ascetic communities must have existed), founded under Sixtus (432–440) and Leo (440–461).

[62] Julia Hillner, "Families, Patronage and the Titular Churches of Rome," in *Religion, Dynasty, and Patronage in Early Christian Rome, 400–800*, ed. Kate Cooper and Julia Hillner (Cambridge, 2007) 190–224; Federico Marazzi, *I "Patrimonia Sanctae Romana Ecclesia" nel Lazio (secoli IV–X): Strutture amministrative e prassi gestionale* (Rome, 1998) 50–53; Roberta Mazza, "Tra oriente e occidente: La gestione del *patrimonium Petri* in Italia meridionale," in *Paessagi e insediamenti rurali in Italia meridionale fra tardoantica e altomedioevo*, ed. Giuliano Volpe and Maria Turchiano (Bari, 2006) 703–714, here 704–707.

[63] Pierre Toubert, "'*Scrinium*' et '*Palatium*'": La formation de la bureaucratie romano-pontificale aux VIII–IX siècles," in *Roma nell'alto medioevo*, ed. Centro italiano di studi sull'alto Medioevo (Spoleto, 2001) 57–119, here 61–65.

[64] Leo *Serm.* 3.1; Walter Ullmann, "Leo I and the theme of Papal Primacy," *Journal of Theological Studies* n.s. 11 (1960) 25–51, here 33–36.

438, refurbished the Colosseum.[65] Yet, during the fifth century more aristocrats and their wealth went over to the churches. Thus, in 433, a certain Anicia Demetrias, who in her youth had received letters from Jerome and Pelagius, received another letter, perhaps from Prosper of Aquitaine. By then Demetrias lived an aristocratic life of ascetic *otium* in her villa near the Via Latina, where she had endowed a martyr's shrine to Saint Stephen.[66] Prosper, who had come to Rome to become an adviser to the bishops, informed Demetrias that she did not own her wealth but administered it as God's estate manager, or *procurator*. Therefore, she ought to distribute the revenues of her prudent management "for the useful purposes of the church," including the poor.[67]

Such language, when put into practice, increased the flow of wealth toward the church, and became increasingly urgent while Leo was bishop (440–461), for reasons similar to those that prompted the admonitions of Salvian of Marseille. Faced with Vandal threats in 442, the Hunnic alliance in 452, and the Vandals again under Geiseric in 455, Leo extended to all Romans his messages of ascetic discipline and the proper distribution of wealth, first addressed to the clerical household and ladies such as Demetrias. God, he argued, required Rome's penance through acts such as communal abstinence and almsgiving throughout the liturgical year. Such alms benefited both the impoverished citizens of Rome who had previously enjoyed the privilege of the *annona*, or food supply, now distributed through the means of the church, and the truly poor. Thus, by emphasizing the continuous ascetic discipline and appropriate dispersal of wealth of the elect, including the married clergy, and by introducing temporary penances throughout the year, in which such discipline was observed collectively by all Romans, Leo created a new, Christian *populus Romanus*, independent of the old aristocracy.[68]

---

[65] Silvia Orlandi, *Epigrafia anfiteatrale dell'occidente romano*, vol. 6: *Roma* (Rome, 2004) 102–118, 545–563; Averil Cameron, *The Last Pagans of Rome* (Oxford, 2011) 231–272, 567–626, argues for less aristocratic loyalty to old religious mores.

[66] For Prosper's authorship, see Mary K. C. Krabbe, *Epistula ad Demetriadem de vera humilitate* (Washington, D.C., 1956); Bronwen Neil, "Leo I on Poverty," in *Preaching Poverty in Late Antiquity*, ed. Pauline Allen, Bronwen Neil, and Wendy Mayer (Leipzig, 2009) 171–203, esp. 195–196.

[67] Prosper, *De vera humilitate*, 5; Norman W. James, "Leo the Great and Prosper of Aquitaine: A Pope and His Adviser," *JTS* n.s. 44 (1993) 554–584.

[68] Michele Renee Salzman, "Leo in Rome: The Evolution of Episcopal Authority in Fifth-Century Rome," in *Istituzioni, carismi ed esercizio del potere (IV–VI secolo d.C.)*, ed. Giorgio Bonamente and Rita Lizzi Testa (Bari, 2010) 343–356; Salzman, "Leo the Great: Response to Crisis and the Shaping of a Christian *Cosmopolis*," in *The Transformation of City and Citizenship in the Classical World: From the Fifth Century BCE*

CONSTANTINOPLE: ARCHIMANDRITES AND THE CITY – ALEXANDER, DALMATIUS, NESTORIUS

What, then, about the other imperial capital, Constantinople? The East, though less deeply affected, had not escaped the consequences of Adrianople either. In 395, Gothic, Vandal, and Hunnic forces – whom Jerome described as "Caucasian wolves" or "White Huns" – invaded the eastern provinces, capturing monasteries and causing rivers to run red with blood.[69] These calamities were exacerbated by natural disasters that exceeded the incidence of famine typical for subsistence economies. We know of harsh famines in 383–385 around Antioch, 396 in Gaza, 440–446 in Constantinople, and, between 431 and 451 in Jerusalem.[70] Such disasters may well have caused the uprising of native Isaurians in Pamphylia and Cilicia in 405, who acted much like the roving bands of Bacaudae in the West: "They spared neither city nor village, but plundered and burned all they could seize."[71]

Famine, invasions, and disruptions of public order led to dislocations, and it is no surprise that our sources convey their authors' increasing preoccupation with vagrants, beggars, and the utterly dispossessed. As Daniel Caner has shown, concerns with wanderers and beggars and their relation to monks became central themes for urban asceticism and monasticism, above all in fifth-century Constantinople. What was the right kind of urban monastic life? Should monks lead the life of charismatic masters of poverty who, alone or in groups, exchanged spiritual blessings for physical sustenance in a new, "miraculous" economy?[72] Or should they rather follow the ascetic ideal that the fifth-century

---

to the Fifth Century CE, ed. Harold Drake and Claudia Rapp (Cambridge, 2014) 183–201; Bronwen Neil, "Blessed Are the Rich: Leo the Great and the Roman Poor," Studia Patristica 44 (2010) 533–548.

[69] Jerome, Epistula 60.16.2–4; John Matthews, The Roman Empire of Ammianus (Baltimore, 1989) 304–382.

[70] Philostorgius, Historia ecclesiastica, 11.7; Evelyne Patlagean, Pauvreté économique et pauvreté social à Byzance, 4–7ème siècles (Paris, 1977) 75–84; Peregrine Horden and Nicholas Purcell, The Corrupting Sea: A Study of Mediterranean History (Oxford, 2000) 152.

[71] Theodoret, Historia religiosa, 10.5; Matthews, Roman Empire, 362–367; Patlagean, Pauvreté, 297–298.

[72] Caner, Wandering, Begging Monks, 166–167, cites the first law against vagrant beggars in 382; Daniel Caner, "Toward a Miraculous Economy: Christian Gifts and Material 'Blessings' in Late Antiquity," JECS 14 (2006) 329–377; Noel Lenski, "Valens and the Monks: Cudgeling and Conscription as a Means of Social Control," Dumbarton Oaks Papers 58 (2004) 93–117.

Constantinopolitan church historian Sozomen ascribed to "the great [Egyptian] monk Antony": "It is agreed by all that he brought [the ascetic life] to the pitch of discipline and perfection.... He bestowed his patrimony on his villagers and distributed the rest of his property to the poor," showing that it was a hallmark of good ascetic practice "not just to strip oneself of wealth, but to disperse it properly."[73]

Constantinople as Christian capital (as described by Richard Krautheimer)[74] emerged in full form during the reign of Theodosius I and especially Theodosius II. This "new Rome" was a different place from the old.[75] Its elite never reached the dizzying heights of the old Roman senatorial aristocracy, but belonged to the kind of group that, in Rome, formed the subelite, persons whom Peter Heather has called "the new men": the curial classes, the imperial administration, and the military. These new elites, who often came from far-flung provinces, had amassed great wealth, profiting from the age of gold Constantine had initiated, and they were mostly Christian: the prime recruiting group for Christian leadership.[76]

The evolution of asceticism and monasticism in late fourth- and early fifth-century Constantinople reflects these differences. We know of one ascetic, monastic community that evolved out of the estate of a wealthy Constantinopolitan woman, Olympias, at the end of the fourth century, alongside other, lasting female communities that appear to have been founded by women who came from elsewhere.[77] Likewise, many male ascetic and monastic leaders, or archimandrites, in Constantinople

---

[73] Sozomen, *Historia ecclesiastica*, 1.13.1–10; cited in Caner, *Wandering, Begging Monks*, 6.

[74] Richard Krautheimer, *Three Christian Capitals: Topography and Politics* (Berkeley, 1983) 41–68.

[75] Brian Croke, "Reinventing Constantinople: Theodosius I's Imprint on the Imperial City," in McGill, Sogno, and Watts, *From the Tetrarchs to the Theodosians*, 241–264; Steffen Diefenbach, "Zwischen Liturgie und *civilitas*: Konstantinopel im 5. Jhd. und die Etablierung eines städtischen Kaisertums," in *Bildlichkeit und Bildort von Liturgie: Schauplätze in Spätantike, Byzanz und Mittelalter*, ed. Rainer Warland (Wiesbaden, 2002) 21–47; Gilbert Dagron, *Naissance d'une capitale: Constantinople et ses institutions de 330 à 451* (Paris, 1974).

[76] Peter J. Heather, "Senators and Senates," in *The Cambridge Ancient History*, vol. 13: *The Late Empire, AD 337–425*, ed. Averil Cameron and Peter Garnsey (Cambridge, 1998) 184–210; Filippo Carlà, *L'oro nella tarda antichità: aspetti economici e sociali* (Turin, 2009) 117–157; Jairus Banaji, *Agrarian Change in Late Antiquity: Gold, Labor, and Aristocratic Dominance* (Oxford, 2001, repr. 2007) 39–88.

[77] *Vita Olymp.* 5.413.14–16, 414.25; *Vita Hypatii*, 18. 132.3–6; *Vita Matronae*, 8.794 D; Dagron, *Naissance d'une capitale*, 490–491, 505–506.

arrived from outside the city to establish thriving communities in a few, short years.[78] Some had been in the military, others came from provinces so remote they spoke no Greek, while others were members of the elites in Antioch who came once the new Rome was securely on the ascendant.[79] Some of these ascetic leaders drew the attention of our sources (perhaps to the detriment of many other more moderate ones) because of their highly experimental practices. Thus, a highly learned Egyptian monk, Ammonius, displayed brandings on his body and even cut off his ear, a feat that gained him an audience with the empress; another monk, Alexander, and his followers stressed all-night prayer and a rigorous asceticism that including absolute poverty, begging, and lavish giving to the urban poor.[80]

Such ascetic feats opened two avenues for success in the city: daily support by many citizens and elite patronage, both in exchange for spiritual blessings. Elite patronage provided monastic leaders and their communities visibility, political support, a potential entree to the court, and economic sustainability.[81] Thus, one of the most influential monasteries in the fifth century, the Dalmation, was supported by two imperial administrators, who were significant sponsors of its founder, Isaac, a Syrian. Isaac was eventually succeeded by Dalmatius, who gave the monastery its name; he was a married member of the military before he and his son joined Isaac's monastery.

Many monastic compounds, like Dalmatius's, were located on the estates of their elite sponsors just outside the city walls. Even though many monastic and ascetic leaders and their communities enjoyed elite and even imperial patronage, and as a result had significant public influence, the ever-increasing role of Constantinople as the center of world power demanded that archimandrites be seen as distant, ideologically and physically, from those in power. This was crucial because

---

[78] Soz. *Hist. eccl.* 4.3.2; Gilbert Dagron, "Les moines et la ville: Le monachisme à Constantinople jusqu'au concile de Chalcédoine (451)," *T&MBZ* 4 (1970) 229–276, here 239–257; Peter Hatlie, *The Monks and Monasteries of Constantinople, ca. 350–850* (Cambridge, 2007) 33–41, 62–65. Unlike in Rome, there are almost no archaeological remains of early Constantinople, so much of the history of early monasticism has to be reconstructed from hagiographical sources; Hatlie, *Monks and Monasteries*, 17–21.

[79] Dagron, "Les moines," 254–255.

[80] Palladius, *Historia Lausiaca*, 11.32.18–34.16; *Vita Alexandri Akoimetou*, 26–27, 42–43; *V. Hypatii* 41.1–5; Nilus of Ancyra, *De voluntaria paupertate*, Patrologia Graeca 79.968C–1060D; Caner, *Wandering, Begging Monks*, 126–137; Hatlie, *Monks and Monasteries*, 66–68.

[81] Hatlie, *Monks and Monasteries*, 79–81.

Constantinople continued to attract ascetic risk takers and experimenters, who came alone or in groups, and who did not fail to challenge those who had sided too much with the powers of the day. Alexander, mentioned above, is an example. He and his followers arrived in Constantinople in 424, soon displayed rigorous ascetic discipline, including absolute poverty, and, far from seeking elite patronage, openly challenged the city's magistrates and the ascetic establishment.[82] Within two years, Alexander's followers had tripled. However, their success was also the cause of their rapid downfall. In 428, the bishop and the magistrates dispersed Alexander's community by force; only the involvement of another well-established ascetic leader and the emperor's sister prevented their complete dissolution, but they had to relocate far away from the city.[83]

Alexander's story, as Daniel Caner has shown,[84] is indicative of the tensions characteristic of fourth- and fifth-century monasticism and asceticism in Constantinople. The city and its elites, the bishop, and the imperial court, supported and encouraged individual charismatic ascetics and their followers, men and women who were often newcomers. Engaged in an economy where spiritual blessings were exchanged for physical sustenance provided by the wealthy or by many of the city's ordinary inhabitants, these ascetics were welcomed as long as they adhered to certain limits. Their numbers could not become too disruptive; they could not challenge those in power too openly; and they had to find an arrangement with the bishop of the city, who in turn could ill afford to alienate the archimandrites and their communities just outside the walls.

A number of spectacular conflicts, like that of Alexander or the one that pitted Dalmatius against Bishop Nestorius in 431, illustrate how quickly this delicate balance could break down. Nestorius had become bishop in 428. Soon after his ordination, he began to pressure "those who had been separated from their monasteries by reason of their lives and strange manners, and had for that reason been expelled [from their original monasteries]" to reform. Nestorius considered monks who wandered about, openly displaying their ascetic feats, improper and ordered that they remain inside their monastic compounds. Such moves alienated the (lay) monastic leaders, their followers, and their

---

[82] Caner, *Wandering, Begging Monks,* 142.
[83] Hatlie, *Monks and Monasteries,* 71; Caner, *Wandering, Begging Monks,* 137–156, 199–212.
[84] Caner, *Wandering, Begging Monks,* 126–149.

wealthy and influential patrons.[85] By 430, Nestorius had been removed from his see, with the help of Cyril of Alexandria, who had arrived in Constantinople with other archimandrites, including Shenoute of Atripe. But the coup de grace came in 431, when Dalmatius left his monastery for the first time in forty-eight years, and, accompanied by his monks, who numbered in the hundreds, marched to the imperial palace to demand that Theodosius II withdraw his support for Nestorius. The emperor gave in to Theodosius's demand, and Nestorius's loss of power was complete. Faced with an independent monastic leader in control of a sizeable monastic federation just outside the city, neither bishop nor emperor could stand firm.[86]

In 451, however, alliances shifted. In the intervening decades, continuing theological disputes had led to an escalation of open, monastic interference in the affairs of the city – inside the city rather than on the outskirts – and to increasing rivalries among monks. The matter came to a head just before the Council of Chalcedon, across the sea from Constantinople. This time, the bishop of the city and the emperor maintained a united front. The result is encapsulated by the council's fourth canon: "Those who truly and sincerely adopt the solitary life [will] be considered worthy of honor. But since some have used the monastic cover to throw church and civil affairs into confusion, moving indiscriminately around the cities, even making it their business to establish monasteries for themselves, let no one anywhere establish a monastery . . . against the will of the city's bishop. . . . But the bishop of the city must make the necessary provisions for the monastery."[87] The monks were to be kept inside their monasteries and be provided for by the bishop: they were to become a part of the episcopal power structure.

We see, therefore, that the monastic federations of early fifth-century Constantinople, Shenoute's urban counterparts, emerged in a climate of ascetic experimentation, in which a combination of charismatic flair and elite patronage allowed men and women from the far-flung regions of the empire to flourish (presumably side by side with many others who did not attract our sources' attention). Established communities, continually challenged by newcomers, grew in importance if their leaders managed to strike the right balance between ascetic

---

[85] Nestorius, *Liber Heraclidis* 2.1; Caner, *Wandering, Begging Monks*, 213.
[86] Dagron, "Les moines," 253; Hatlie, *Monks and Monasteries*, 81–91.
[87] Council of Chalcedon, can. 4; its effectiveness prior to Justinian is open to debate; Hatlie, *Monks and Monasteries*, 45–57, 72–89, 110–113.

purity, rigor, and withdrawal (for example, by settling on the edge of the city), and political involvement. They had to maintain their visible independence from the powers of the day (for example, by remaining strictly within their compounds) without relinquishing their active public role, a feat often achieved by their followers' visibility as wandering, begging monks within the city. Another important means by which they could demonstrate both ascetic rigor and public engagement was alms giving and intercession for the urban poor (as in other parts of the empire). During the first half of the fifth century, several successful male and female leaders allowed monastics and ascetics in the city to flourish, reaching numbers as high as ten thousand, until factionalism led to a first consolidation under episcopal control in 451. But the first half of the fifth century was just the beginning. Much had been set in motion by men like Shenoute, Salvian, Leo, Dalmatius, and Nestorius, but it took several additional generations to come to full fruition under others such as Gelasius, Gregory the Great, and Justinian.

18: Religious Doctrine and Ecclesiastical Change in the Time of Leo the Great

Susan Wessel

I n the late summer of 452, Leo the Great, bishop of Rome (pope,
440–461) met with Attila at the River Mincius in northern Italy.[1]
Ever since Attila's defeat at the battle of the Catalaunian Fields in
Gaul fourteen months before, the Hun and his coalition of forces had
sought vengeance against the Roman Empire. They stormed through
the cities of northern Italy, destroying houses and churches, burning
property, and killing untold numbers of lay people and clergy. Despite
this show of strength the Huns were badly weakened, and Pope Leo
came away triumphant from the negotiations. Attila agreed to withdraw
his troops across the Danube and promised to make peace.

The pope's secretary, Prosper of Aquitaine (d. ca. 463), attributed
Attila's sudden retreat to the power of the church in the person of Leo,
dressed in his priestly robes. We need not accept this explanation, yet it
speaks volumes about the shifting ecclesiastical-political structures of the
mid-fifth century. Prosper presents Leo, acting in his papal capacity, as
the sole authority in secular politics and diplomacy, going well beyond
any previous author in showing the moral authority of the bishop of
Rome and his role in the governing of the state. He illustrates the
convergence of ecclesiastical and secular power in the bishop of Rome
at mid-century while offering a stunning rebuke of the Roman imperial
political apparatus.

---

[1] I shall refer to Leo both as bishop and as pope, the latter being merely an honorary title
until the beginning of the seventh century, when it was used formally to designate
Pope Boniface III in 607. Leo was one of only two popes to receive the title "the
Great," the other being Gregory the Great (pope, 590–604).

Prosper viewed the Huns' invasion of Italy as a strategic failure on the part of Aetius, the Roman commander at the Catalaunian Fields, who had underestimated the Huns' appetite for revenge. He says that as soon as Aetius realized the extent of his error, he and the emperor Valentinian abandoned Italy, leaving the region vulnerable to its enemies. When Prosper reports that Attila was moved by his encounter with Leo to retreat peacefully across the Danube, he suggests that the divine power of the church had filled the power void left by Aetius and the emperor. The meeting, as Prosper tells it, illustrates papal ecclesiastical power extending into the secular sphere at a time when the imperial court and army had failed the Roman people.[2]

During the first half of the fifth century, as we have seen in other chapters, the Roman imperial administration collapsed in western Europe, with much loss of life and property. These harsh and bitter circumstances created a feeling of helplessness among the population, which could no longer count on imperial assistance. In the midst of this turmoil, when the empire was fragmenting and its various parts were spinning off in different ways and contexts, the bishops of Rome gradually came to understand the papacy as the center of Christendom. Leo's diplomatic meeting with Attila, in which the papacy replaced the political void left by the fleeing emperor with ecclesiastical sentiments and imagery, illustrates these developments in microcosm.

This chapter explores how the papacy enlarged its self-understanding on the world stage by examining (1) its doctrinal formulations in the context of sociopolitical change; and (2) the shifting doctrinal and ecclesiastical relationships between the papacy and the provincial churches. I argue that it is misleading to think of the papacy as extending its power indiscriminately in the face of resistance by provincial churches. The evidence calls for the more nuanced picture of an emerging Christendom tentatively united by its doctrinal commitments and its ecclesiological self-understanding. That this ideal of unity ultimately failed speaks to the overwhelming forces of fragmentation, seen for example in the Egyptian and Syrian churches that articulated doctrines and practices that rejected those of Rome.

---

[2] Leo's actions carry forward ideas about the role of the papacy that were later articulated by Pope Gelasius (pope, 474–491), who envisioned the world being governed by two powers, the power of kings who govern the world and the more significant sacred authority of priests who exercise power over the kings' salvation. The power Gelasius claimed in matters of religion eventually extended to secular policy: he himself is reported by the *Liber pontificalis* in about 494 to have saved the inhabitants of the city of Rome from famine.

RELIGIOUS DOCTRINE IN THE CONTEXT OF SOCIO-POLITICAL CHANGE

During the upheavals and barbarian settlements of the fifth century, certain prominent Christians noted the suffering of their parishioners and felt that a pastoral and theological response was needed.[3] Leo's sermons are filled with references to the anxieties of the day, which he attempts to alleviate by comforting his congregations, by organizing poor relief for those in need, and, above all, by developing a Christology that defined precisely what it meant for suffering humanity that Christ had lived and died as a human being: "Who then does not recognize the stages of his own life in him? Who does not see that his taking of food, his rest in sleep, his anxiety [*sollicitudo*] in sorrow, and his tears of compassion made his form that of a servant?"[4]

It was not enough for Leo merely to identify aspects of the life of Jesus that were similar to the experiences of Christians. Leo made the humanity of Christ both accessible and theologically relevant to mid-fifth-century Christians with the doctrine known as the *communicatio idiomatum*, or the exchange of idiomatic properties.[5] Each of the natures, the divine and the human, was complete in its respective attributes and interrelated by the unity of Christ's person, so that the impassive divinity and the suffering humanity were mutually present, without causing the other to undergo change. Although Augustine had conceived of this paradoxical intermingling of the divine and the human in the person of Christ, Leo brought it to fruition with the precision of his doctrine and the sensitivity by which he considered the human expression of Christ's suffering. Because the *communicatio idiomatum* enabled the fullness of divinity to be present in the human actions of Christ, late antique

---

[3] Eric R. Dodds has suggested that people in the third century were deeply disillusioned as a result of that century's sociopolitical decline. Peter Brown has observed, however, that people were likely no more disillusioned than they had been in the periods of so-called prosperity. Eric R. Dodds, *Pagan and Christian in an Age of Anxiety* (Cambridge, 1965) 137; Peter Brown, *The Making of Late Antiquity* (Cambridge, Mass., 1978) 5. In suggesting that people suffered – and were perceived as suffering by their pastors – during the upheavals of the fifth century, I do not mean to revive Dodds's thesis for the fifth century.

[4] Leo, *Sermon* 66.4, 10 April 453, ed. Antoine Chavasse, *Sancti Leonis Magni Romani pontificis tractatus septem et nonaginta*, Corpus Christianorum Series Latina 138–138a (Turnhout, 1973). See also Leo *Serm.* 65.2, 8 April 453.

[5] Leo, *Epistle* 28.4, 13 June 449, ed. Philipp Jaffé, *Regesta Pontificum Romanorum ab condita ecclesia ad annum post Christum natum* (Leipzig, 1885) 423. Cf. *Serm.* 54.2, 5 April 442.

Christians were able to identify with the suffering of Christ and to experience him as immanent in their lives.

The suffering of Jesus on the Cross had been interpreted theologically as early as Paul and the Gospels. Leo, however, imbued what he perceived to be the anxieties caused by the barbarian settlements with theological significance by identifying people's suffering with the extraordinary suffering of Christ. If Christians in the time of the Gospels were to take up the Cross and follow Jesus, in the time of Leo they were to recognize the suffering of Christ in their interior lives. Their fear, anxiety, sorrow, and tears were the natural expression of the Christian emotional life because Christ had experienced the suffering of the human condition on the Cross.[6] Christians now had a vivid example of a feeling Christ, through which their suffering acquired theological meaning.

Among the Christologies that Leo rejected were the docetic views of Eutyches and the two-person Christ of Nestorius. For different reasons, each of them failed to respond adequately to the pastoral and existential needs of a Christian flock enduring the sociopolitical changes caused by the collapse of Roman rule and the settlement of new peoples on Roman territory.

Eutyches was the leader of a large monastery in Constantinople, who had been condemned by Flavian, the patriarch of Constantinople, in a local council held in November 448 for teaching heretical views. When Leo received the report of the council, he concluded that Eutyches was a docetist who believed that the body of Christ was not of the same substance as human flesh and was not composed of human matter. Being such a docetist, Eutyches would not have acknowledged that Christ had suffered the emotional pain of a real person. And without that acknowledgment, there would have been no correspondence between the emotional life of Christ and the perceived anxieties of Christians and, therefore, no theological basis on which to pastor their needs.

Originally a preacher from Antioch, Nestorius was the patriarch of Constantinople (10 April 428–August 431), who was deposed and sent into exile to the Great Oasis in Egypt for subscribing to Christological views that the Council of Ephesus (431) determined were heretical (see table 18.1: Major Councils). Like many of Nestorius's critics before him,

---

[6] Christians were to imitate the suffering of Christ's passion and resurrection, "so that among the dangers of the present life we might not so much wish to avoid them by escaping as to overcome them by enduring." Leo *Serm.* 67.6, 28 March 454.

TABLE 18.1. *The Major Councils of the Early Church*

Councils	Year and Location	Summary
First Council of Nicaea	325, Nicaea (present-day Iznik, Turkey)	First ecumenical council, which composed the Nicene Creed and determined that Arianism was a heresy.
341 Synod at Rome	341, Rome, Italy	The synod defeated Arianism and exonerated Athanasius, formerly bishop of Alexandria, of prior claims against him from the 334 and 335 Synods of Caesarea and Tyre.
Council of Sardica in Illyricum	343 – 344, Sardica (present-day Sofia, Bulgaria)	The council ruled that all important doctrinal decisions should be reached by a major council. It also set standard practices for bishops regarding recruitment, residence, and transferral to another diocese.
Council of Saragossa	380, Saragossa (present-day Zaragoza, Spain)	The council condemned Priscillianism as a heresy.
First Council of Constantinople	381, Constantinople (present-day Istanbul, Turkey)	Second ecumenical council, which expanded upon the Nicene Creed, denounced Macedonianism and Apollinarianism, and confirmed the Holy Spirit was divine.
Council of Carthage	418, Carthage (suburb of present-day Tunis, Tunisia)	The council, which resulted in the Code of Canons of the African Church, denounced Pelagianism.
First Council of Ephesus	431, Ephesus, Turkey	Third ecumenical council, under the direction of Cyril of Alexandria, denounced the teaching of Nestorius of Constantinople and confirmed the Virgin Mary was the *Theotokos*.
448 Synod at Constantinople	448, Constantinople (present-day Istanbul, Turkey)	Patriarch Flavian of Constantinople excommunicated the Archimandrite Eutyches for denying that Christ has two natures, human and divine.
Council of Chalcedon	451, Chalcedon (present-day Kadıköy, Turkey near Istanbul)	Fourth ecumenical council, which reversed the Second Council of Ephesus (449), known as the Robber Council, and defined Christ as having two natures united in one person.

Leo thought that his Christology made Christ out to be only a man because he, Nestorius, had failed to describe adequately how the human and divine natures in Christ were related to one another. Nestorius had been eager to preserve the divinity of Christ, fearing that "the hypostasis of the God Logos [might be] confused with the changeableness of the fleshly [hypostasis]."[7] That led him to follow the teachings of his native school of Antioch in assigning the sayings of Christ in Scripture either to the human nature or to the divine. Although his critics thought this method of exegesis promoted a doctrine of two, disconnected Sons, Nestorius was actually quite committed to joining the two natures in a unified person. For Leo, however, Nestorius lacked the theological insight needed to articulate such a unity and to relate the suffering of the incarnate Christ to the experiences of Christians.

While for Augustine and those such as Athanasius in the eastern churches the purpose of the Incarnation was to make human beings divine, for Leo its purpose was to elevate human beings by embracing and ministering to their lowliness and fragility. Amid the disorder and uncertainty in the wake of the Vandals' conquest of North Africa in 429, Leo preached that Christ had cured human weakness, anxiety, and suffering by fully participating in and experiencing such emotions on the Cross: "He cured the emotion of our infirmity by participating in it; he drove away the anxiety in the experience of suffering by undergoing it."[8] This was Leo's pastoral response to the needs of his flocks as they faced the challenges posed by the barbarian settlements. It was also the vision of Christ he negotiated with the provincial churches.

SHIFTING DOCTRINAL AND ECCLESIASTICAL RELATIONSHIPS BETWEEN ROME AND THE PROVINCIAL CHURCHES

The regions of the Roman Empire that the mid-fifth century papacy came into contact with, including North Africa, Gaul, Spain, Constantinople, Egypt, and Syria (each of which will be considered here), responded differently to the political changes that were taking place and to the role of the papacy and its teachings in the light of those changes. Sometimes the provincial churches turned to Rome for guidance, while

---

[7] Severus of Antioch, *Liber contra impium Grammaticum*, 2.32, ed. Joseph Lebon, *Severi Antiocheni liber contra impium Grammaticum*, Corpus Scriptorum Christianorum Orientalium 111–112 (Louvain, 1929–1952), here 101–102.

[8] Leo, *Serm.* 54.4: "nostrae infirmitatis affectus participando curabat, et poenalis experientiae metum subeundo pellebat"; in the edition of Antoine Chavasse, *Sancti Leonis Magni Romani pontificis tractatus septem et nonaginta*, CCSL 138–138a (Turnhout, 1973) 320, lines 74–76. This inspired Leo's vision of a Christian renewal of Rome. See Robert A. Markus, *The End of Ancient Christianity* (Cambridge, 1990) 127.

at other times they were determined to express their self-understanding in doctrines and practices that were openly hostile to Rome. A longing for ecclesiastical and doctrinal unity, expressed by a certain willingness to write letters to Rome asking for advice (as in North Africa, Gaul, Spain, and Constantinople), held back the forces of fragmentation, which this volume explores, until the ideal of unity was no longer feasible (as in Egypt and Syria, and to a lesser extent, Spain).

North Africa

North African Christians were particularly fraught with ambivalence when it came to defining the contours of their relationship with Rome. Sometimes they expressed a spirit of autonomy that was nurtured by the region's relative prosperity,[9] while at other times they longed to connect their understanding of themselves and their religion with the world of Christendom.[10]

The Donatists, religious zealots who had refused to readmit to Catholicism those who had lapsed during the persecutions of the emperor Diocletian (r. 303–305), appealed to the African fascination with religious enthusiasm. When North Africa came under Vandal rule in 429, however, the Donatists failed to articulate a church organization that might have addressed the challenges the Christians faced under the Vandals, who had converted to Arianism. Catholic bishops were persecuted, church property was confiscated, and Catholic rites were prohibited throughout the period being considered here, first under King Geiseric, and then under his successor Huneric.[11] The Vandal kings may have found the Arian belief that Christ was subordinate to

---

[9] On the social and political context of heretical movements, see Brent Shaw, *Sacred Violence: African Christians and Sectarian Hatred in the Age of Augustine* (Cambridge, 2011) 829–831.

[10] The rise of Christianity in Africa should not be connected to a resurgence of the local culture. Peter Brown, "Christianity and Local Culture in Late Roman Africa," *Journal of Roman Studies* 58 (1968) 85–95; John Ferguson, "Aspects of Early Christianity in North Africa," in *Africa in Classical Antiquity: Nine Studies*, ed. Lloyd A. Thompson and John Ferguson (Ibadan, Nigeria, 1969) 189.

[11] Yves Modéran, "Une guerre de religion: Les deux églises d'Afrique à l'époque Vandale," *Antiquité Tardive* 11 (2003) 21–44, here 23, 25; F. Bashuth Mapwar, "La résistance de l'Église catholique à la foi arienne en Afrique du Nord: Un exemple d'une église locale inculturée?," in *Cristianesimo e specificità regionali nel Mediterraneo latino (sec. IV–VI)* (Rome, 1994) 189–213, here 199; Andy Merrills, "Kingdoms of North Africa," in this volume.

God an effective way to support the political hierarchy of kingship, in which all members of the government were subordinate to the king. The subordinationist theology of Arianism confirmed their political ideology. The Donatists' failure to accommodate the theological and organizational needs of Catholics struggling to articulate their identity under Arianism resulted in their being suppressed eventually by the Catholic opposition, which had collaborated with Roman imperial forces.

Pelagianism, named for its founder Pelagius (354–420 to 440) who taught that people were capable of choosing between good and evil without the assistance of divine grace, provided another occasion for an alliance between North Africa and Rome. The anti-Pelagian bishops of Africa conspired with the anti-Pelagian bishops in Rome to defeat their common adversary.[12] This relationship was confirmed when Boniface (pope, 418–422) and Caelestine (pope, 422–432) ratified the African canons issued by the Council of Carthage in 418, a move that signaled to the African church that Rome approved of its teachings and assured the papacy that the Africans deferred to its judgment.

The complexity of the Roman-African alliance was revealed one year later, when the Africans decided to limit papal jurisdiction in Africa because they resented the papacy's attempt to enforce its decisions there. Although such behavior on the part of the Africans might appear to be capricious, it was in fact consistent with their tendency to ally themselves with the papacy when it served their provincial concerns.[13] No matter how rebellious their decision seemed there was no intent to reject the Roman primacy of which the Africans had availed themselves successfully during the Donatist and Pelagian controversies.

In the course of Leo's papacy the North African churches continued to evolve with respect to their relationship to Rome from being a distant object of papal disapproval to participating voluntarily in the extension of papal hegemony. This gradual shift can be discerned in the only surviving letter that Leo wrote to the African bishops of Mauritania and Caesariensis.[14] Textual evidence reveals that the letter is actually two letters combined. The first part suggests that Leo had approached the province critically and on his own initiative, and the second that

[12] Christopher Ocker, "Augustine, Episcopal Interests, and the Papacy in Late Roman Africa," *Journal of Ecclesiastical History* 42 (1991) 179–201, here 179.

[13] Ibid., 181. See generally Christian Courtois, *Les Vandales et l'Afrique* (Paris, 1955) 175–176.

[14] Leo *Ep.* 12, 10 August 446, *Cum de ordinationibus*, ed. Jaffé 410.

the Mauritanian bishops had sought Rome's guidance voluntarily and were ready to abide by its judgment.

It is worth mentioning that every papal decretal contained in this letter is consistent with the canons of the Council of Sardica in Illyricum (343 or 344). This was the council whose canons had been accepted in Rome as just as binding as the canons of the Council of Nicaea (325) and that "granted the papacy the authority to function as a 'court of appeals' in the Western Church."[15] The problem was that most of the North African bishops had rejected the Council of Sardica. From Athanasius we learn that only 170 bishops and clergy met at the Council of Sardica, which many – including the African bishops – believed was insufficient to make its canons universally binding. The African bishops' dismissal of Sardica changed after the Vandal conquest of Carthage in 439 disrupted the ecclesiastical hierarchy of the region. Bereft of their local leadership and oppressed by the Arian Vandals, the African bishops were prepared, by the time of Leo, to overlook the irregularities they had perceived in the Sardican council and to follow the judgments of Rome.[16]

Gaul

The attitude toward Rome in Southern Gaul was similarly fraught with ambivalence. In 418, less than a decade after Alaric sacked the city of Rome in 410, the Roman imperial administration invited the Goths to settle as a federation along the western seaboard of Gaul, a region that extended from Toulouse to the area north of the Bordeaux valley.[17] The Goths had fought for Rome in northern Spain, where they helped subdue the Alans and Vandals. As settlers in Gaul they were asked to address the threat of civil unrest and assist Rome against the Vandals. The Romans thought that granting them territory was an efficient way to exploit their military resources and control their movements.

---

[15] Ocker, "Augustine, Episcopal Interests," 179 and n. 3.

[16] Trevor Jalland, *The Life and Times of St. Leo the Great* (New York, 1941) 112.

[17] Elizabeth Allison Thompson, "The Settlement of the Barbarians in Southern Gaul," *JRS* 46 (1956) 65–75, here 65; Hagith Sivan, "On Foederati, Hospitalitas, and the Settlement of the Goths in A.D. 418," *American Journal of Philology* 108 (1987) 759–72, here 770. Whether those lands included or were limited to tax revenues is uncertain. See Thomas S. Burns, "The Settlement of 418," in *Fifth-Century Gaul: A Crisis of Identity?*, ed. John F. Drinkwater and Hugh Elton (Cambridge, 1992) 53–63, here 57–58.

The plan failed. The Gothic king, Theodoric, attacked the city of Arles in 425 and Narbonne in 436. These assaults signaled to the Gallic people that the alliance between the empire and the Visigoths – as the Goths were called after they settled in the West – was precarious and that their political interests did not necessarily coincide. The Roman administration did not have the resources to deal with the threat that the Visigoths posed in Gaul. In the light of Rome's military weakness, the Gallic people both longed for and resented the imperial administration that was supposed to protect them.

Against this larger political backdrop Leo became involved in a controversy with one of Gaul's leading bishops, Hilary of Arles, over Hilary's exercise of episcopal power in northern and southern Gaul. Hilary wanted to exercise the same extensive jurisdictional privileges and rights of honor that his predecessor Patroclus had exercised and that Leo claimed had been canceled. The controversy raised larger questions about Rome's hegemony over the western provincial churches, as well as the shape that such hegemony might take: in what sense might Rome be regarded as the center of Christendom when the empire was fragmenting in the wake of the barbarian settlements? What influenced the shifting relationships between Rome and the provincial sees?

Both questions come into sharper focus when we consider Hilary of Arles, a man who apparently longed for order and stability at a time when the Gallic way of life was being challenged by the barbarian settlements. Gaul needed Rome in order to feel connected to the rest of Christendom. But Gaul also longed for Rome to acknowledge its competence to address the problems that troubled it. Raymond Van Dam has remarked that the appearance of usurping emperors in the outlying regions of early fifth-century Gaul did not mean that Gallic society was either hostile or indifferent to Roman political authority.[18] People craved order, and the uprisings the imperial government viewed as revolts were actually "attempts by local citizens to revive a Roman administration that was abandoning them."[19] The Gallic citizenry came

---

[18] Raymond Van Dam, *Leadership and Community in Late Antique Gaul* (Berkeley, 1985) 53. On Hilary and intra-Gallic politics, see Ralph Mathisen, "Hilarius, Germanus and Lupus: The Aristocratic Background of the Chelidonius Affair," *Phoenix* 33 (1979) 160–169, here 167. See also "The 'Affair' of Hilary of Arles (445) and Gallo-Roman Identity in the Fifth Century," in Drinkwater and Elton, *Fifth-Century Gaul*, 239–251.

[19] Van Dam, *Leadership and Community*, 53.

to understand themselves as capable of shaping their destiny in a way that sensitively acknowledged their dependence on the culture and institutions of Rome. A similar longing for order and structure influenced the region's relationship to the papacy.

It is worth noting that after Hilary died in 449, Leo restored the broad jurisdictional privileges to the bishopric of Arles that he had earlier withdrawn amid controversy. The recognition from Rome that Hilary had asked for was now being given to his successor. And when Leo died in 461, the new pope, also named Hilary (pope, 461–468), continued Leo's policies in the region, recognizing the next bishop of Arles, Leontius, as a papal representative. The new bishop functioned as a quasi-vicar of the apostolic see, who was to maintain ecclesiastical discipline and convene yearly councils. Far from rejecting papal hegemony, this meant that the see of Arles had willingly integrated its hierarchy into the Roman model of ecclesiastical leadership.

Spain

The alliance that developed between Rome and a few of the Catholic bishops of Spain was the result of opposing a common enemy, the Priscillianists. These were followers of an aristocratic layman named Priscillian, who, beginning in the 370s, taught a rigorous asceticism and promoted an expansive interpretation of the biblical canon. The Catholics perceived him and his followers as threatening to the episcopal hierarchy of Spain, several members of which gathered at Saragossa some ten years later (380) to curtail a variety of asceticism that had reached "out of the towns and into the country, where the bishops could not control it."[20] Over the course of the next six years (from the Council of Saragossa in 380 until Priscillian was executed by the civil authorities at Trier in 386) the Catholic hierarchy no longer viewed Priscillian merely as the rigorous ascetic whose practices undermined episcopal authority, but as the much more dangerous heretic who subscribed to a cosmological dualism, read apocryphal books, and held secret meetings.

Leo's encounter with the Priscillianism presented to him by the Catholic bishops of Spain was the occasion for his articulating a theology of the human person. The soul is not identical to God (contrary to the Priscillian view described to him by the Spanish bishops) because a vast ontological distance separated the ultimate, unchangeable being of

---

[20] Michael Kulikowski, *Late Roman Spain and Its Cities* (Baltimore, 2004) 248–249.

divinity from the contingent, mutable nature of everything that is part of creation. As the *locus* of the passions, the soul is the place in the human person to which ascetic practice is addressed. Following a trajectory that began with the Trinitarian debates of the fourth century, Leo separated the ontological status of the human soul from the immutable nature of divinity.[21]

While opening one chasm, Leo and his contemporaries closed another. They diminished the seemingly insurmountable distance between God and humanity by insisting upon a Christ whose humanity was in nearly every respect a faithful reproduction of the vicissitudes of human frailty. Priscillianists threatened this precarious juncture between the human and the divine that occurred when God became a human being and, therefore, failed to extricate humanity from the deplorable conditions of its existence.

Leo pulled out all the polemical stops to suppress the heresy: he made them sound like Docetists for allegedly rejecting the reality of Christ's incarnation, death, and resurrection; like Arians for subjecting Christ to human progress; like Paul of Samosata and Photinus for maintaining that Christ began in his mother's womb; and like Manichaeans for refusing to admit the resurrection of the body. Their alleged cosmological dualism, their rigorous asceticism, their reading of apocryphal books were interpreted as undermining the role of Christ in redeeming fallen humanity. If humanity consisted in a soul that was divine, a body that did not resurrect, a capacity for moral responsibility that could be realized only in the context of the moral failings and achievements of an earlier life, then humanity's transgressions were not redeemed, its suffering not assuaged, and the chasm between God and creation would not have been overcome. The cosmological rupture between divinity and humanity, which Leo's Priscillianists attempted to address by making the human soul an exact reproduction of the divine, could be resolved only by acknowledging the fullness of humanity in the Incarnation.

Leo attributed the rise of Priscillianism in Spain (the "secret treachery" mentioned below), some sixty years after Priscillian's execution, to the deteriorating political conditions that were the result of the invasions: "Many provinces have been preoccupied with the enemy invasions, and the stormy wars have prevented the laws from being executed. Travel has become difficult among God's bishops and meetings rare; because of the general disorder, secret treachery runs

---

[21] Virginia Burrus, *The Making of a Heretic: Gender, Authority, and the Priscillianist Controversy* (Berkeley, 1995) 70.

rampant."[22] The dismantling of the ecclesiastical and political organization was partly the result of the treaty (438) between the Gallaecians in the North and their political adversaries, the Suevi. It was a dubious peace that spared the Gallaecians and their neighbors from continuous wars, while unburdening the Suevi to pursue their conquests throughout the rest of Spain.

Although Leo's remarks about the overall state of political disarray were valid, they also served a deeper rhetorical purpose. By imputing the rise of Priscillianism in Spain to the dismantling of its political organization and to the forces of disintegration he described, Leo vindicated an ecclesiastical hierarchy that had failed to stop the heresy. The Priscillianists were sufficiently established among the Spanish ecclesiastical hierarchy that only some of its members were willing to condemn the heresy's failure both to recognize the fullness of Christ's humanity and to close the rupture between God and human beings.

Constantinople

As in North Africa, Gaul, and Spain, the relationship between Rome and Constantinople was shaped by their different historical and ecclesiastical situations, rather than by their competing claims to power. Constantine established the city of Constantinople upon the old city of Byzantium in 330 and fashioned it as the New Rome and as the heir to Roman virtues. In 381, the Council of Constantinople made the first attempt to solidify this ideology in a canon elevating Constantinople to the second place after Rome.

These ideals were still pertinent when Leo came into contact with the patriarchate of Constantinople in the middle of the fifth century. In the twenty-eighth canon of the Council of Chalcedon in 451, Constantinople assumed equal privileges to Rome and ratified the canon of 381 that assigned itself the second place after Rome among the patriarchal sees.[23]

While Leo interpreted the canon as an audacious move to undermine the Roman primacy, the authors of the canon probably

---

[22] Leo *Ep.* 15, intro., 21 July 447, ed. Jaffé 412. "Ex quo autem multas provincias hostilis occupavit irruptio, et executionem legum tempestates interclusere bellorum. Ex quo inter sacerdotes Dei difficiles commeatus et rari coeperunt esse conventus, invenit ob publicam perturbationem secreta perfidia libertatem."

[23] See André de Halleux, "Le décret Chalcédonien sur les prérogatives de la nouvelle Rome," *Ephemerides Theologicae Lovanienses* 64 (1988) 288–323, here 303.

wished only to legitimize certain long-standing jurisdictional practices. For some time, Constantinople had been responsible for ordaining metropolitans for the provinces of Asia Minor, Pontus, and Thrace. Prior to Chalcedon, however, the only canonical basis for the custom was the third canon of the Council of Constantinople. The bishops at Chalcedon wished to ratify and make explicit the self-understanding that the Council of Constantinople had alluded to seventy years earlier.

There were practical reasons for the church of Constantinople to seek legitimacy for its customs. Upon the death of certain bishops in the provinces of Asia Minor, Pontus, and Thrace, disorder had arisen when men contended for the privilege of becoming the next bishop. The Constantinopolitans felt that promulgating a canon that acknowledged their authority to make episcopal consecrations would help ensure a smooth succession of power among the bishoprics.

It is worth mentioning that the Church of Constantinople based its claim for being the second see after Rome upon the principle of apostolic succession. In contrast to the twenty-eighth canon of Chalcedon, which argued that the church should enjoy privileged status for its proximity to imperial power, the clergy and bishops of the Church of Constantinople thought that Leo himself had conferred the apostolic privilege upon them. Perhaps they meant that Leo acknowledged their privileged status when he defended their bishop, Flavian, against Dioscorus, the bishop of Alexandria, their rival see. Perhaps they thought that Rome honored them with the apostolic privilege when it placed its representative, known as an *apocrisiarius*, there. Or perhaps they simply wished to justify what they had already resolved to do. Whatever their reasons, they understood that the principle of apostolic succession should be the basis for the jurisdictional claims they were making. However far apart events had taken them, the sees of Rome and Constantinople saw the legitimacy of their actions in the light of a shared apostolic past.

The relationship between Rome and Constantinople was, nevertheless, fraught with contradictions. For example, when Nestorius served as the patriarch of Constantinople in 429, he tried to secure the support of Caelestine, the bishop of Rome, against his rival, Cyril of Alexandria, by writing a letter to Caelestine describing his theological views. Instead of winning his approval, Nestorius succeeded merely in assuring his own condemnation. Not only was his doctrine difficult for Caelestine to comprehend, but also Nestorius, apparently unaware of the Pelagian controversy in the West, had made the serious tactical error of mentioning the Pelagians he had welcomed into his church.

Caelestine concluded that Nestorius was a Pelagian sympathizer and told Leo, then a deacon, to commission John Cassian to write a treatise against him for his Pelagian-like views.[24]

The case of Anatolius, who became the bishop of Constantinople in 449 after Flavian died in exile, serves as another example of the intricacies of the relationship between Rome and Constantinople. Leo perceived Anatolius as a self-serving, ambitious upstart who had been consecrated by a heretic and had converted to orthodoxy merely to secure his position as bishop of the imperial city. His contempt for the bishop was rooted in his view that Anatolius's ambition had exceeded his rank and had resulted in his illegally coercing certain bishops to assent to canon 28.[25] As in the case of Nestorius, Rome contained the consequences of Anatolius's disobedience by limiting it to the personal tragedy of his own incompetence. The broader contours of the relationship between Rome and Constantinople remained intact, because each needed the other to maintain the ideal of Christian unity.

Egypt and Syria

The relationship between Egypt and Rome shifted dramatically from the close collaboration of the mid-fourth century to the utter indifference of the late fifth century, as Egypt seceded from the churches that subscribed to the Council of Chalcedon and to the Leonine Christology that was its doctrinal foundation. Athanasius had established close ties with Rome when he and Julius, the bishop of Rome (pope, 337–352), collaborated to defeat Arianism at a Roman synod held in 341. Those ties were renewed when Cyril of Alexandria and Caelestine conspired against Nestorius at the Council of Ephesus in 431. The legend that a disciple of Peter, Saint Mark of the Gospel, had founded the Alexandrian see also united the two churches.

Leo attempted to draw upon this history in order to secure the continuing presence of the Council of Chalcedon and its two-nature Christology in Egypt. He failed miserably. Previously, he had asked two bishops of Alexandria, Dioscorus and Proterius, to observe the

---

[24] John Cassian, *De incarnatione Domini contra Nestorium*, Patrologia Latina 514, ed. M. Petschenig and G. Kreuz, CSEL 17 (Vienna, 2004) 235–391; Marie-Anne Vannier, trans., *De incarnatione: Jean Cassien, Traité de l'Incarnation contre Nestorius*, Sagesses Chrétiennes (Paris, 1999).

[25] Leo *Ep.* 105.2, ed. Jaffé 482; "Epistula Leonis papae ad Pulcheriam augustam (d. 22 m. Mai a. 452)," ed. Eduard Schwartz, *Acta Conciliorum Oecumenicorum*, 4 vols. in 27 parts (Berlin, 1914–) 2: 4, 58.

practices of the Roman church.[26] Dioscorus was to keep fixed days for ordaining priests and deacons, and he was not to repeat the Eucharist during the great festivals. Proterius was to set the date for Easter in conformity with the practice of Rome. But a fissure in the relationship began to reveal itself after the Council of Chalcedon when Proterius, in spite of Leo's recommendations to the contrary, refused to conform to Roman practice. Because he was at best a nominal Chalcedonian, Proterius had little interest in what Rome had to say in matters of theology and practice. For Rome to challenge the customs of the Alexandrian church was, in his mind, to make demands that were well beyond its jurisdictional privileges. Whether Proterius's Chalcedonian successor, Timothy (II) Salophaciolus, was similarly inclined to disregard the directions that Leo issued is impossible to say because no letters from him survive. That most of Egypt had by this time (460) no interest in the views of Rome and of the imperial church is evident from the fact that only ten Egyptian bishops sympathetic to Chalcedon could be found to consecrate Timothy II.

Some of the Syrian Christians of the fifth century were just as unwilling as the Egyptians to define themselves in relation to Rome. Although it is true that Theodoret of Cyrrhus (d. ca. 457) championed the primacy of Rome, and by implication its two-nature Christology, when he said that its see had never been tainted by heresy, there were non-Chalcedonian followers of Eutyches in Syria, as there were in Egypt, who wanted nothing to do with Rome or its Christological views. After Chalcedon, the Syrian churches had split. There were those like Theodoret who accepted the two-nature Christology of Chalcedon and those like the Eutychians who rejected it as failing adequately to exclude the possibility of Nestorianism. Following the early teachings of Cyril of Alexandria, the Eutychians of Syria believed that a one-nature Christology – what we now call miaphysitism – captured the mystery of the divine and human aspects of Christ.

Perhaps the one-nature Christology of Egypt and Syria, which emphasized the divinity of Christ, supported their austere variety of asceticism, through which the human person was transformed into a God-man being that resembled Christ. While it is true that the West practiced asceticism, it was generally in the context of a common monastic life that valued moderation and criticized the extreme practices of the East. The two-nature Christology, which Leo defined and the Western and Eastern Chalcedonian churches accepted, supported

---

[26] See Leo *Ep.* 9 (21 June 445), ed. Jaffé 406.

the notion that the experience of human suffering connected people to the suffering of Jesus on the Cross. Among the Miaphysites of Egypt and Syria, in contrast, suffering in the form of austere ascetic practice was a means of transformation into, rather than connection with, the divinity of Christ. Insofar as they did not share the West's experience of the barbarian settlements, they did not need to subscribe to a two-nature Christology to overcome their suffering.

Despite the fact that Egypt and Syria were to secede from the Chalcedonian churches after 451, Leo's achievement was to mobilize the bishops and persuade the emperors that no new council should be given the opportunity to undermine what he had hoped would be the universal Council of Chalcedon. While Leo's notion of a unified Chalcedonian church was unable to encompass the theology and practice of the Egyptian and Syrian churches, it confirmed his view of Rome as the exclusive guardian of a two-nature Christology that gave meaning to the experience of human suffering as it unfolded amid the changes and uncertainty that people were experiencing in the West.

CONCLUSIONS

By the mid-fifth-century, Leo's Christological formulation of a fully articulated and interrelated divine and human Christ had been accepted at the Council of Chalcedon as the standard of orthodoxy. His understanding of the suffering, human nature in Christ not only built upon the Christology of his predecessors, but also gave theological meaning to what he perceived to be the anxieties of his day. In the context of the shifting power relationships I have outlined above, in which the provincial churches sometimes collaborated with Roman hegemony and at other times opposed it, Leo attempted to bring this Christology to bear upon each of the regions of the Empire. Egypt and Syria, as well as a majority of the Spanish hierarchy, resisted the vision of Christ that Leo advocated, while North Africa, Gaul, and Constantinople continued to seek Rome's guidance and to negotiate the ideal, if not the reality, of a unified church.[27]

---

[27] This essay develops themes I explored in my book *Leo the Great and the Spiritual Rebuilding of a Universal Rome* (Leiden, 2008). I am grateful to Paul Brazinski for his help in preparing the manuscript and to Michael Maas for his comments.

19: CHRISTIAN SERMONS AGAINST PAGANS: THE EVIDENCE FROM AUGUSTINE'S *SERMONS* ON THE NEW YEAR AND ON THE SACK OF ROME IN 410

Michele Renee Salzman

Constantine's conversion to Christianity in 312 marked the beginning of two centuries of religious change, as Christian emperors started the process of disengaging traditional religion (paganism) from the Roman state. Over the course of the fourth and early fifth centuries, Constantine's successors passed laws outlawing certain rites, focusing primarily on animal sacrifice and idol worship, and eventually closed the pagan temples. Christian opinion makers – bishops and monks – encouraged the Roman emperors to take these actions. However, because "paganism" was never a unified religion but rather incorporated a wide range of rites, beliefs, and practices, it was not possible to outlaw "paganism per se," however harsh the penalties became for practicing individual rites.[1] Hence, some Romans continued to practice some traditional religious rites through the fifth century, though those who did so were increasingly marginalized. This somewhat nebulous legal situation also helps to explain why, in the fifth century, Christian bishops continued to produce antipagan sermons. These sermons are of importance in understanding the Christianization of the empire and also developments in the late Roman traditional religion, paganism. There is no consensus, however, about the

---

[1] As Maijastina Kahlos remarked, "Late Antiquity saw, as a tool of Christianization, the creation of 'paganism.'" See Maijastina Kahlos, *Debate and Dialogue. Pagan and Christian Cultures, c. 360–430* (Aldershot, 2007) 18.

interpretation of these sermons or the evidence they provide for religion and society in the fifth-century empire.

Some historians read the antipagan sermons of Christian bishops and monks as direct evidence for the continuation of pagan religious activities into the fifth century.[2] Others, however, have challenged the "reality" of the antipagan rhetoric in these sermons and read them rather as exaggerated rhetorical exercises, aimed at preserving the integrity of the Christian community.[3] Moreover, since these sermons were attacking private rites and "not the continuing performance of official, public ceremonies or processions"; other scholars tend to dismiss the religious nature of the rites by viewing them as "simply popular traditions extending back before Christian times."[4] In this chapter, I present the antipagan sermons of fifth-century Christian bishops in a somewhat different light, by correlating such invective with broader religious and historical trends.[5] I focus in particular on two sets of sermons delivered by Augustine that deal with the New Year and with the sack of Rome in 410. Before turning to the particular information on rites and attitudes provided by these texts, I want to make three general points about my approach.

First, by reading these antipagan sermons closely and in the light of other evidence, I argue that we can get a sense of how non-Christians adapted to Christian times, and what practices and activities were now part of what it meant to be a "pagan." Admittedly, our understanding of paganism derives from mostly hostile Christian sources. We should, consequently, be aware that these texts include a certain degree of rhetorical exaggeration on the part of Christian preachers who were intent on demonizing pagan rites to their congregations and painting

---

[2] John Scheid, "Les réjouissances des calends de janvier d'après le *sermon* Dolbeau 26: nouvelles lumières sur une fête mal connue," in *Augustin prédicateur (395–411)*, ed. Goulven Madec (Paris, 1998) 353–365; and Fritz Graf, "Fights about Festivals: Libanius and John Chrysostom on the *Kalendae Ianuariae* in Antioch," *Archiv für Religionsgeschichte* 13 (2012) 175–186.

[3] Alan Cameron, *The Last Pagans of Rome* (Oxford, 2011) 788; and Richard Lim, "Augustine and Roman Public Spectacles," in *A Companion to Augustine*, ed. Mark Vessey (Chichester, 2012) 138–150.

[4] Cameron, *The Last Pagans*, 788. Similarly, Robert A. Markus, *The End of Ancient Christianity* (Cambridge, 1990), 14, makes a further distinction: "Among practices disapproved by clergy we need to allow for a distinction between those which their congregations regarded as harmless customs without religious significance – as for example, many claimed the observances of the New Year clebrations to be – and customs that they thought properly carried over from pagan into Christian cult."

[5] Markus, *The End of Ancient Christianity*, passim, for this approach.

pagans as "the moral other."[6] But from the point of view of the historian, it is important to remember that the bishops' rhetoric resonated with their respective audiences because the rites and attitudes of the people who practiced what was now denigrated with the label "pagan" were familiar enough in daily life to their audience. Without such familiarity, this rhetoric would not make sense.[7] Hence, I suggest, because pagans were still a recognizable presence, Christian bishops continued to deliver antipagan sermons even as they worked to widen the category of actions, beliefs, and rites they deemed pagan and hence problematic.

Second, the antipagan rhetoric adopted by a number of Christian bishops attacking such pagan events as New Year celebrations does not represent the only or perhaps the typical Christian perspective on pagans and their practices. Many Christians and Christian emperors were happy to allow or even participate in New Year rituals, viewing them rather as traditional elements of civic life and devoid of problematic associations. Yet bishops delivered sermons against such practices, insisting that these were pagan precisely because they wanted to change the habits and activities of their congregations as well as to influence prospective converts.

Third, while it is certainly true that many of the pagan practices and rites that came under attack were no longer state-supported, many of them were still important communal events. As such, they offered alternative, and at time competing, avenues for religiosity. Christian bishops were, with reason, concerned about the participation of their Christian congregants in such rites. Indeed, since many congregants had only recently converted to Christianity, the bishops' desire to prevent apostasy especially in times of crisis was quite understandable. Nor should we view the bishops' focus on private practices and attitudes of traditional religionists as irrelevant for understanding public religion, pagan or Christian. Rather, we should place their concern within fifth-century religious developments more broadly. Indeed, many bishops across the empire, as Kristina Sessa has argued for the bishops of Rome, adopted a model of leadership influenced by New Testament language of stewardship that continued previously established Roman values and practices associated with the elite household; just as the steward was the householder's appointed agent who oversaw his property and people,

---

[6] Rhys Williams, "Politicized Evangelicalism and Secular Elites: Creating a Moral Other," in *Evangelicals and Democracy in America*, vol. 2: *Religion and Politics*, ed. Steven Brint and Jean Reith Schroedel (New York, 2009) 145–146.

[7] Ibid., 151.

so the bishop as the steward of God oversaw people and property in domestic as well as ecclesiastical settings.[8] It was as an extension of their role as stewards of the people that the bishops preached against private rites practiced by Christians and pagans.

To see more clearly how these processes of religious change worked, I will discuss in the first part of this chapter a group of sermons delivered by bishops across the empire attacking pagan rites associated with the New Year's Day celebrations. Of particular interest is Augustine's recently discovered *Sermon against the Pagans*, delivered in Carthage or Hippo on 1 January 404, for in it he provides the fullest attack on pagan rites associated with the New Year in the West.[9] Other Christian leaders in the West, also preached against New Year rites as "pagan," including notably Maximus, bishop of Turin (390–408 or 423); Peter Chrysologus, bishop of Ravenna (433–450); and Caesarius, bishop of Arles (502 or 503–543); as well as eastern leaders, including Asterius, bishop of Amaseia (in modern Turkey, 380 or 390–410), and John Chrysostom, likely during his time as priest in Antioch (386–398) rather than during his bishopric in Constantinople (398–404).[10] The range of responses to the New Year celebrations suggests how widespread the perception was among Christian opinion leaders that the practices on this day were pagan and hence of concern for reasons that went beyond the local. In the second part of this chapter, I turn to Augustine's antipagan rhetoric in sermons that dealt with the 410 sack of Rome, a pivotal moment for Christians and pagans trying to understand this catastrophe.

---

[8] For the bishops of Rome, see Kristina Sessa, *The Formation of Papal Authority in Late Antique Italy* (Cambridge, 2012) 1–62 and 87–126.

[9] Augustine, *Sermon 198*, trans. Edmund Hill, in *The Works of St. Augustine: A Translation for the 21st Century, Sermons*, vol. 3.8 (273–305 A) (New York, 1997) 180–237. Throughout this chapter I refer to this as *Sermon 198*, to follow the English numeration; the sermon is usually cited as *Sermon 26 Dolbeau* since it was first published by François Dolbeau, "Nouveaux sermons de saint Augustin pour la conversion des païens et des donatistes IV," *Recherches Augustiniennes* 26 (1992) 69–141, repr. François Dolbeau, ed., *Augustin d'Hippone: Vingt-six sermons au peuple d'Afrique*, Collection des Études Augustiniennes, Antiquité 137 (Paris, 1996) 345–417. I cite all other sermons of Augustine from the volumes translated by Hill unless otherwise noted.

[10] For Augustine, see note 9 above; for Caesarius, see his *Sermons 192* and *193*, and note 23 below. For Maximus of Turin, see his *Sermon 98*; for Asterius, see his *Homily 4*, ed. Cornelis Datema, *Homilies 1–44 of Saint Asterius of Amaseia* (Leiden, 1970), 39–43; for John Chrysostom, see his *On the Kalends* (Patrologia Graeca 48, 951–62).

By reading the sermons of Augustine, in particular, against the grain, we can gain a better understanding of the kinds of practices, emotions, and arguments that not only Christians but also pagans were expressing across the fifth-century empire. These are important indicators that the rites of traditional religion persisted into the Christian times of the fifth century.

BISHOPS AGAINST PAGAN RITES FOR THE NEW YEAR

In his *Sermon against the Pagans* delivered in Carthage or Hippo on 1 January 404, Augustine mocks pagan practices and beliefs about this first day of the new year in order to draw sharp contrasts with how Christians ought to behave:

> Are you going to join today in the celebration of good luck presents with a pagan, going to play at dice with a pagan, going to get drunk with a pagan?... They give good luck presents: as for you, give alms (Luke 11:41). They entertain themselves with lascivious songs; as for you, entertain yourselves with the words of the scriptures. They run off to the theater, you people to church; they are getting drunk; you see to it that you fast. If you do all this, you have genuinely sung, "Save us Lord our God, and gather us from among the nations."[11]

Augustine presents these practices as fundamentally flawed; they are based on a false belief that demons exist, whereas the Christian lifestyle is based on true belief in God. Being a Christian, according to Augustine, requires the complete separation from such pagan behavior in order to be true to Christian beliefs: "So if you believe something different from them, hope for something different, love something different, you should prove it by your life, demonstrate it by your actions."[12] According to Augustine, the demons take pleasure in all these pagan activities: "The pagans rejoice in the mad frenzy of the chariot races, in the cruelty of the amphitheater, in the unrelenting rivalries of those who take up quarrels and disputes, to the point of open hostilities, on

[11] Augustine, *Sermon* 198.2.
[12] Ibid.

behalf of pestilential persons, on behalf of a comedian, an actor, a clown, a charioteer a hunter. When they do these things, it's as though they were offering incense to demons from their hearts. These spirits, you see, given to seduction, rejoice in the people that have seduced."[13] Some of the practices Augustine lists took place on other holidays as well, but that does not diminish the vehemence of Augustine's denunciation of the New Year's Day festivities.

Admittedly, the fact that Augustine and a number of his contemporary bishops saw games, chariot races, and theatrical shows as pagan did not deter many Christians from enjoying such activities, even later under the orthodox emperor Justinian.[14] And it is worth noting that the Kalends of the New Year (the first of January) had been one of the few holidays – along with the anniversaries of the founding of Rome and Constantinople, the seven days before and after Easter, Sundays, and imperial birthdays – on which legal business was suspended, as mandated in a rescript of 389 (Theodosian Code 2.8.19) by the Christian emperors Valentinian, Theodosius, and Arcadius. This official position, accepting the continuing status of these holidays, may have fueled the ire of Christian bishops, for we hear in several sermons how the New Year celebrations were pagan and hence harmful to Christian communities.[15] Indeed, part of the bishops' concern was that the festivities and games on the New Year were offering clear alternatives to Christian worship services. In response to the criticism of bishops such as Augustine, a law of 400 (Theodosian Code 2.8.23) stipulated that public spectacles could not be displayed on Sundays, so that there would be no conflict with the observance of important Christian holidays. And in 401, a synodal decree of the Council of Carthage (*Registri ecclesiae Carthaginensis* 60; *CCSL* 149.197) enacted this same ban.

But there are some specific practices associated with New Year celebrations that Augustine highlights as especially problematic. One of the distinctive Roman practices of the New Year was the giving of private gifts – *strenae* (*Sermon* 198.2 and 198.4). The problem with this practice, according to Augustine, is that such private reciprocity is born out of personal interest, and thus is at odds with true Christian charity. Similarly problematic are the banqueting and drunkenness on this day, as well as the gambling – all for personal gain, not for Christian charity.

---

[13] Ibid., 198.3.

[14] Cameron, *The Last Pagans*, 790, makes this argument.

[15] Graf, "Fights about Festivals," 175–186, suggests that these sermons are a reaction to the imperial law.

To a pagan, however, these practices were part of a shared society, a "collective rite of social integration" in the words of one scholar.[16]

In his discussion of the games on the New Year, Augustine alludes three times to sacrifice.[17] John Scheid has proposed that these Augustinian references can be understood in the light of the late fourth-century description of New Year festivities in Antioch provided by the rhetorician Libanius; in a rhetorical exercise, Libanius noted a sacrifice, offered on the first day of the year, by a horse trainer and the people, who asked the gods for victory at the upcoming New Year games.[18] The first day of January, the Kalends, was also the traditional day for swearing in the new consuls and for sacrificing to Jupiter.[19] Though Augustine is silent about such public ceremonies in his sermon of 1 January 404, Scheid argues that we can still use Libanius's text to clarify Augustine's sermon because so many of the other rites are similar to those noted by Augustine.[20] Indeed, these late antique New Year rites are widely attested. Scheid sees the Augustinian references as alluding not only to public rites but also to private rites that were traditionally celebrated on the morning of New Year's day, including the making of auspices and predictions about the future. Indeed, private auguries continued to be performed into the later fifth century, as Maximus of Turin (*Sermon* 98.2–3) and Caesarius (*Sermons* 192, 193) attest. Such private rites of divination were harder for the Christians to control, but by Augustine's time there were no longer public sacrifices, even though some might have wished for them; as he says: "It was their [the pagans'] very priests who used to turn to the idols and offer them victims for their congregation and would still like to do so now" (*Sermon* 198.16).

Augustine devotes the bulk of his New Year's Day sermon (17–24) to arguments against the worship of idols, specifically Neptune, Tellus, Juno, Vulcan, and Mercury. These were well-known deities, but since these deities have no particular association with the New Year,

---

[16] Scheid, "Les réjouissances des calends," 358.

[17] Augustine, *Sermon* 198.3, 193.13, and 193.16.

[18] Libanius, *Progymnasmata*, 5.7–8, trans. Charles Gibson, in *Libanius's Progymnasmata: Model Exercises in Greek Prose Composition and Rhetoric* (Atlanta, 2008) 438–441, here 439. See also Libanius's *Oration IX: On the Kalends*, in the translation by Mark J. B. Wright, "Appendix: Libanios *Oration IX*," *Archiv für Religionsgeschichte* 13 (2012) 205–209. See Scheid, "Les réjouissances des calends," 356–358.

[19] The definitive study of the New Year remains Michel Meslin, *La fête des calends de janvier sous l'Empire romain*, Collection Latomus 115 (Brussels, 1970).

[20] Scheid, "Les réjouissances des calends," 357–358.

their enumeration has led to speculation about the activities on this day. Scheid has compared these passages in Augustine with the New Year *Sermons* of the bishop of Ravenna, Peter Chrysologus, who in the 430s described processions of idols parading through the streets:

> The days are now coming, the days that mark the new year are coming, and the demons arrive with all their pomp, a full fledged worship of idols is set up, and the new year is consecrated with age-old sacrilege. They fashion Saturn, they make Jupiter, they form Hercules, they exhibit Diana with her young servants, they lead Vulcan around roaring out tales of his obscenities, and there are even those whose names must be left unmentioned, since they are hideous monsters. . . . Moreover, human beings are dressed as beasts. . . . These are not amusements, no they are not; they are sins. A human being is changed into an idol; and if it is a sin to go to idols, what do you think it is to be an idol?[21]

As Alan Cameron has observed, this procession of demons was not the traditional procession (*pompa circensis*) that took part at the *ludi Romani*, the Roman games, but a procession of Romans, many of whom were wearing the masks representing the gods; some were pretending to be animals, particularly stags, in what appears a late antique variation of the festivities of this day.[22] But there were also statues of the gods being paraded, at least according to another sermon of Peter Chrysologus (*Sermon* 155.1), in which the bishop decries the pulling and dragging of images of the gods in public. The physical presence of these idols – and of people dressed up as idols – fueled Augustine's lengthy attack on idol worship.

Peter Chrysologus, like Augustine, focuses on the actions of private individuals on the New Year. As he talks of Christians welcoming such idols into their own homes (*Sermon* 155A.2), Peter is particularly concerned about the domestic lives of his congregants. Such private practices seem as well to be the object of attack in the sermons of the bishop Caesarius in Arles; people looking for *auguria* – auguries – that they will prosper in the New Year were doing so in private, and were

---

[21] Peter Chrysologus, *Sermon* 155A. Translation here by William B. Palardy, *Saint Peter Chrysologus, Selected Sermons* (Washington, D.C., 2005) 264–266.

[22] Cameron, *The Last Pagans*, 787–788.

not engaged in any public auspices undertaken by the state, as had once been the case.[23] Indeed, in a very interesting late fourth-century case, the orator and senator Symmachus details the kind of public auspices that had been given over to prominent citizens to undertake on their own.[24] Such privatization seems likely, and as noted above, private rites were much harder to control. Individuals taking the auspices to ensure a prosperous New Year disturbed Caesarius, precisely because they were beyond the reach of the church.

Thus we see that as religious leaders tried to make their communities "Christian," they widened their definition of problematic pagan practices. They focused increasingly on private rites associated with popular activities that they considered demonic. Their ire was provoked by the New Year's exchange of gifts and the staging of private auspices, as well as the public processions of the gods, or of men and women dressed like the pagan gods, as described above. It would be easy for modern scholars to label such New Year activities as mere customs, devoid of religious meaning. But that is certainly not the way that Augustine and many of his fellow bishops saw these rites, and some pagans also viewed these rites as having religious meanings, as the testimony of the rhetorican Libanius and the unnamed pagans in the sermons (discussed above) attest.[25] The view that predominates is that they were a religious practice.

PAGAN REACTIONS TO THE SACK OF ROME IN 410 IN THE SERMONS OF AUGUSTINE

The success of Christianity and imperial actions against pagan rites makes it difficult to hear alternative viewpoints in the fifth century. Hence, to discern how pagans reacted to the sack of Rome in 410, I turn in this section to a hostile witness, Augustine, who describes their responses in sermons directed to the Christians of the empire. The 408–409 sieges that led to Alaric's 410 sack of Rome challenged the religious faith of many Romans; how could a Christian god allow

[23] Caesarius, *Sermons*, 192; trans. Mary M. Mueller, Fathers of the Church 31 (Grand Rapids, Mich., 1956) 193.

[24] Michele Renee Salzman, "The End of Public Sacrifice: Changing Definitions of Sacrifice in Post-Constantinian Rome and Italy," in *Ancient Mediterranean Sacrifice*, ed. Jennifer Wright Knust and Zsuzsanna Várhelyi (Oxford, 2011) 167–186.

[25] See note 17 above, and Libanius, *Oration* 9.6, also discussed by Graf, "Fights about Festivals," 175–177.

for the sacking of the capital for the first time in eight hundred years? In the immediate aftermath of these events, in the face of a number of refugees from the city of Rome, Augustine tried to answer the doubts raised by these events for his North African congregants in some eight sermons delivered in the fall of 410 and through 411.[26]

Sermon 296, delivered late in 411, vividly presents an unnamed pagan who challenges Christians in the light of the 410 devastation. Augustine models a Christian response to this pagan, in part because, as he indicates, there were those in his audience who, though Christian, shared the pagans' perspective. Some pagans, according to Augustine, claimed that the sack was the direct result of the end of sacrifices and a sign of divine wrath.[27] This line of argumentation and this view of divine anger is in keeping with pagan notions of divinity, but it was clearly making an impression on the Christians in Augustine's audience as well, which is why Augustine counsels his congregants to cut short their conversations with such pagans: "For the time being, give him [the pagan] a very short answer, to get rid of him. You, however, should have quite other thoughts. You weren't called to embrace the earth, but to obtain heaven."[28] Augustine denigrates the pagan interlocutor as a "lover of worldly felicity and grumbler against the living God, who prefers to serve demons and sticks and stones."[29] And though he urges his congregants to stop talking to these "insulting" pagans, he describes at length their arguments. According to Augustine, pagans complain that the present disaster is worse than past ones and that, even more, the Christian god had not protected his followers, a view that accords well with common expectations of reciprocity between worshiper and divinity. It is the strength of this criticism that leads Augustine to assert that it was the distinctive mark of the Christian to endure temporal evils so as to "hope for everlasting goods." The promise of eternal rewards cannot satisfy the pagan, who desires earthly satisfactions, and

---

[26] Augustine, Sermon 33a (= Sermon 23, CCSL 41.417–22); Sermon 15A (= Sermon 21, CCSL 41.202–11); Sermon 25 (CCSL 41.334–39); Sermon 113A 9 (= Sermon 24, Miscellanea Agostiniana [Rome, 1930–1931] 1:141–55; Sermon 81 (PL 38.499–506); Sermon 296 (= Sermon 1, 133–138; Miscellanea Agostiniana, 1:401–412); Sermon 105 (PL 38.618–625); Sermon on the Destruction of the City of Rome (De excidio urbis Romae, CCSL 46.243–62). For these sermons studied as a unit, see especially Theodore S. de Bruyn, "Ambivalence within a Totalizing Discourse: Augustine's Sermons on the Sack of Rome," Journal of Early Christian Studies 1.4 (1993) 405–441.

[27] Augustine, Sermon 296.9.

[28] Ibid.

[29] Ibid.

indeed, Augustine's pagan interlocutor goes on to bemoan all the catastrophes that have befallen the Roman Empire under the Christian god.[30]

The pagans who question the power of the Christian god to help human worshipers continued to vex Augustine; the same doubt lies at the heart of *Sermon* 105, preached in 111, likely in Carthage, soon after *Sermon* 296.[31] Again, the destruction of Rome looms large, taking up five of the thirteen sections of this sermon (secs. 9–13). Now Augustine claims that pagans are attacking him for his explanation for the sack of Rome:

> "But he shouldn't say these things about Rome," people have been saying about me. "Oh, if only he would shut up about Rome!" As though I were hurling taunts, and not rather interceding with the Lord, and in whatever way I can be encouraging you. Far be it from me to hurl taunts. . . . So what am I saying, when I don't shut up about Rome, other than what they say about our Christ is false, that it's he that has ruined Rome, that gods of stone and wood used to protect Rome? Add the value of bronze; add more, that of silver and gold. . . . There you have the sort of guardians to whom learned men [*docti homines*] have entrusted Rome, having eyes and unable to see. Or if they were able to save Rome, why did they themselves perish before?[32]

The "learned men" to whom Augustine refers must, in the context of this speech, be the pagans who have placed their trust in idols,[33] and who trace the cause of the ruin of Rome to the displacement of these idols and their associated rituals and "on account of these adversities blaspheme our Christ."[34]

A key argument that pagans used, as Augustine and others attest, was that the disregard for cult statues had angered the gods and had

---

[30] Ibid., 296.10.

[31] Othmar Perler with Jean-Louis Maier, *Les voyages de saint Augustin* (Paris, 1969) 397–405, for this date. Augustine mentions Carthage in *Sermon* 105.12.

[32] Augustine, *Sermon* 105.12.

[33] Some scholars have attributed these remarks to Christians, but in the light of the criticism of Christ, pagans seem the only possible source. For diverse opinions on this, see De Bruyn, "Ambivalence," 415.

[34] Augustine, *Sermon* 105.11–105.12.

led to the barbarian invasions that destroyed Rome.[35] In *Sermon* 105, Augustine turns to recent history to counter this criticism. The Gothic king Radagaisus, a pagan, had threatened Rome in 405, and Romans claimed that the loss of their traditional gods and rites had brought this danger upon Rome. According to Augustine, however, the event should be read differently: Radagaisus's defeat at the hands of Christian soldiers in 405 proved, rather, the power of the Christian god.[36]

In the immediate aftermath of 410, pagans and Christians tried to understand these events by finding solace in the same text as their pagan peers: *Aeneid* 1.278–279, in which Jupiter predicts that the empire of the Romans would be "without end." Pagans cited this text as upholding the traditional notion that the eternity of Rome and its empire depended on Jupiter; abandonment of the state cult and failure to sacrifice would thus threaten the survival of the state. Such arguments for preserving tradition moved pagans, and even Christians. It is somewhat surprising to find Augustine also using this text to put forth his case, but he gives it an important twist, subjecting it to an allegorical interpretation; the empire "without end" promised to the Romans is that of the heavenly kingdom, not the earthly Roman one. These lines were widely disseminated. A late fourth- or early fifth-century inscription discovered near the Scala Santa in St. John Lateran reproduces this passage from Vergil, with its prophesy of an empire without end (1.278).[37] That these lines were thus preserved shows the enduring appeal of traditional literature and ideals like that of *Roma Aeterna*, Eternal Rome – and explains why Augustine took up this text.[38]

In another sermon, Augustine calls pagans who ridicule the faithful "impious" (*impii*) and "infidels."[39] He tries to shore up his congregation's faith, while complaints surface that there are "many misfortunes in Christian times" and that Christianity is to blame.[40] That

---

[35] See, for example, Zosimus, *Historia nova*, 4.59 and 5.41, trans. with commentary Ronald T. Ridley, *New History* (Canberra, 1982).

[36] Augustine, *Sermon* 105.13. According to Orosius, *History against the Pagans*, 7.37.5–9, Radagaisus's assault led the pagans in Rome to reconsider sacrifice and the "city seethed with blasphemy." Augustine returns to this set of ideas in *City of God*, 5.23.

[37] Silvio Panciera, "His ego nec metas rerum nec tempora pono: Virgilio in un'inedita iscrizione romana," in *Epigrafi, epigrafia, epigrafisti: Scritti vari editi e inediti (1956–2005) con note complementari e indici* (Rome, 2006) 333–343, originally published in *Studi Tardoantichi* 2 (1986) 191–210.

[38] On the idea of Eternal Rome, see François Paschoud, *Roma Aeterna: Études sur le patriotisme romain dans l'Occident latin à l'époque des grandes invasions* (Rome, 1967).

[39] Augustine, *Sermon* 113A.1.

[40] Ibid., 113A.11.

the complainers are pagans seems very likely, for directly after criticizing the attacks of the *impii*, Augustine points to the amphitheater
in Hippo Diarrhtys and mocks the kind of piety it teaches: "Brothers
you see the amphitheater which now falls. Extravagance built that. You
think that piety built it? It was built by none other than the extravagance of godless men. Don't you wish that what extravagance built
will someday fall down, and that what piety builds will rise?"[41] The
theater, as we saw, was one object of the Christian attack on New Year
festivities.

As noted, according to Augustine, pagans responded to 410 by
blaming the Christians for disregarding the gods and their images; they
pointed to the city's destruction, and argued on the basis of history and
poetry, notably Vergil. But in another sermon, *On the Destruction of the
City of Rome*, Augustine indicates that some pagans had taken to criticizing the Christian god, on the basis of biblical texts.[42] This lengthy
sermon summarizes Augustine's view of pagans and Christians talking
about the sack of Rome in 410, and for that reason, suggests a date
late in 411, though the exact place and time of this sermon's delivery
is unknown. The text at issue is Abraham's intercession with God on
behalf of Sodom (Gen. 18:16–33). If God would have saved Sodom
for the sake of at least ten righteous individuals, they asked, why he
did not save Rome? The question is posed by those whom Augustine
says "impiously attack our Scriptures, not those who search them with
reverence." The impious, presumably the pagans, have the attention
of his congregation when they ask such "vehement and formidable
questions":[43] "In such a great number of the faithful, in such a great
number of chaste men and women dedicated to God, in such a great
number of servants and handmaids of God, was it impossible to find
fifty just people, or forty, or thirty, or twenty, or even ten?"[44] It takes
Augustine the remainder of this sermon to explain that though there are
people in Rome who are viewed as righteous by commonly accepted
standards, by God's standards one cannot claim them to be wholly righteous. Moreover, God did spare Rome, he claims, for a city is more than

[41] Ibid., 113A.13.

[42] Augustine, *On the Destruction of the City of Rome* (*De excidio urbis Romae*) was once
doubted as an authentic sermon, but those doubts have been put to rest by Marie
M. O'Reilly, *Sancti Aurelii Augustini De excidio urbis Romae sermo* (Washington, D.C.,
1955). See, too, de Bruyn, "Ambivalence," 405–441.

[43] Augustine, *On the Destruction of the City of Rome*, 2 (2), modified from the translation
of O'Reilly, 57.

[44] Ibid.

its houses, and its inhabitants have survived.[45] This important distinction between the physical city (*urbs*) and community or commonwealth (*civitas*) will lie at the heart of Augustine's later *magnum opus*, *City of God*. But for now, Augustine concludes with the optimistic note, Rome is "chastised not lost."[46]

CONCLUSION

The vehemence with which Augustine depicts pagans as impious and insulting was certainly a useful rhetorical tool for a preacher. Nonetheless, such rhetoric would not work if the arguments and attitudes did not resonate with contemporaries. That recently converted Christians might share some of the doubts of their pagan neighbors lends urgency to Augustine's sermons on the New Year and on the the sack of Rome in 410. Though the antipagan rhetoric of Augustine's sermons are imperfect indicators of the survival of paganism in a world in which animal sacrifice and state funding – the earmarks of classical traditional paganism – were gone, yet the private rites and long-standing pagan attitudes and explanations persisted into the fifth-century Christian empire. His sermons, and the antipagan attacks in the sermons of bishops across the empire, were important factors in defining and ultimately undermining what remained of traditional pagan religion in the fifth-century Roman empire.

[45] Ibid., 6 (6), trans. O'Reilly, 67.
[46] Ibid., 8 (7), trans. O'Reilly, 71.

20: MEDITERRANEAN JEWS IN A CHRISTIANIZING EMPIRE

Joseph E. Sanzo and Ra'anan Boustan

One hallmark of the Christianization of the Roman Empire in Late Antiquity was a preoccupation with dividing people into discrete categories.[1] Primarily motivated by concerns over the porous boundaries that imperfectly separated various religious communities from one another in social reality,[2] this drive to define "self" and "other" represented a potent means for managing – while never homogenizing or eliminating – difference.[3] Indeed, this period saw the rapid crystallization of the ideological desire *and* institutional capacity of both church and state to classify, manage, and, in some cases, subject to targeted acts of violence various dissident religious groupings with whom Christians might feel themselves to be in conflict, Jews among them.[4]

Jewish historians and scholars of rabbinic Judaism have persuasively stressed the formative impact that the Christianization of the Roman Empire had on the nature of Jewishness as a social category, as well as on the forms and structures of Jewish culture and society from the late fourth to early sixth century.[5] Yet, at the same time, it has been rightly

[1] Averil Cameron, "Ascetic Closure and the End of Antiquity," in *Asceticism*, ed. Vincent L. Wimbush and Richard Valanstasis (New York, 1995) 147–161, esp. 156.

[2] Jonathan Z. Smith, "What a Difference a Difference Makes," in *"To See Ourselves as Others See Us": Christians, Jews, "Others" in Late Antiquity*, ed. Jacob Neusner and Ernest S. Frerichs (Chico, Calif., 1985) 3–48.

[3] Andrew S. Jacobs, *Christ Circumcised: A Study in Early Christian History and Difference* (Philadelphia, 2012).

[4] Fergus Millar, *A Greek Roman Empire: Power and Belief under Theodosius II, 408–450* (Berkeley, 2006) 116–129.

[5] Seth Schwartz, *Imperialism and Jewish Society, 200 B.C.E. to 640 C.E.* (Princeton, N.J., 2001); Daniel Boyarin, *Border Lines: The Partition of Judaeo-Christianity* (Philadelphia,

observed that, to a significant degree, the Jewish populations of the Roman Empire remained fully integrated in the venerable structures of Mediterranean life well into the sixth century.[6] What, then, are we to make of this puzzling juxtaposition between the far-reaching impact of Christianization on Jews and Judaism, on the one hand, and the broad continuities in the fabric of Mediterranean society, on the other?

This chapter explores the impact of Christianization on Mediterranean Jewish life during the "long fifth century," from Theodosius I (r. 379–395) to Anastasius (r. 491–518). We begin by proposing a model of Christianization that gives due consideration to the intense competition, shifting allegiances, and even bitter invective that existed within and across imperial and ecclesiastical domains. Not only did church and empire only occasionally align but, more important, they often fought openly about Jewish populations and their institutions. We then turn to three episodes of Christian violence against Jews in the late fourth and early fifth century. We argue that the complex relationship between ecclesiastical and imperial institutions disclosed in these episodes provides insight into the anatomy of Christianization, as this process unfolded both locally and empire-wide, and, accordingly, helps explain both the continuities and the changes in Jewish life throughout Late Antiquity.

In emphasizing moments of conflict and violence between Jews and Christians, we do not intend to downplay either the ongoing daily interactions among these groups or the generative impact of Christian idioms and institutional forms on Jewish literary and material culture. Rather, we believe that these episodes will allow us to move beyond the grand narratives of this period to consider the variegated conditions of Jewish communal life at the conjunction of church and empire.

CHRISTIANIZATION AND THE SHIFTING CONJUNCTIONS OF CHURCH AND EMPIRE

The concept of "Christianization" requires us to take great care, especially as it relates to the transformation of Jewish life in Late Antiquity. In fact, there is powerful explanatory value in treating "church"

2004); Peter Schäfer, *The Jewish Jesus: How Christianity and Judaism Shaped Each Other* (Princeton, N.J., 2012).

[6] Paula Fredriksen, *Augustine and the Jews: A Christian Defense of Jews and Judaism* (New York, 2008).

and "empire" as distinct analytical categories, so that the historian can trace how these institutional forces intersected at times and diverged at others.[7] In this regard, applying the label "Christian" to the Roman Empire from Constantine onward can be misleading. Imperial privilege was not extended to a single and continuous group of "orthodox" Christians. The specific Christians that received imperial support – that is, those designated as orthodox – frequently shifted according to the sympathies and practical concerns of the emperors and their officials.[8] In other words, Christianization should not be conceptualized in overly general terms as a uniform, empire-wide process in which the "Christian" empire replaced its "pagan" forerunner. Rather, this notion must be nuanced to account for the complex processes of appropriation through which ecclesiastical and imperial elites Christianized traditional Roman forms of knowledge and educational institutions.[9]

In light of the imperial–ecclesiastical situation, it should come as no surprise that late antique Christians held divergent views about the proper relationship between church and empire and also about the extent to which the empire could genuinely be understood as Christian. Robert Markus has demonstrated that there were different perspectives on the relationship between empire and church, both immediately before and immediately after the sack of Rome in 410.[10] At one end of the spectrum, Eusebius viewed the empire under Constantine as the eschatological culmination of Christian salvation history.[11] At the other end, Augustine divided the church and the empire into separate categories (or "cities"), the latter encompassing all earthly rule (not just the Roman Empire) and only occasionally and inscrutably intersecting with the former.[12]

---

[7] Millar, *Greek Roman Empire*, 140–148. For critique of overly general or uniform models of Christianization, see Edward D. Hunt, "Christianising the Roman Empire: The Evidence of the Code," in *The Theodosian Code*, ed. Jill Harries and Ian Wood (Ithaca, N.Y., 1993) 143–158.

[8] Millar, *Greek Roman Empire*, 168–191.

[9] Hervé Ingelbert, *Interpretatio christiana: Les mutations des savoirs, cosmographie, géographie, histoire, dans l'antiquité chrétienne, 30–630 après J.-C.* (Paris, 2001).

[10] Robert A. Markus, "The Roman Empire in Early Christian Historiography," *Downside Review* 81 (1963) 340–354.

[11] E.g., *Praeparatio evangelica*, 1.4; *Historia ecclesiastica*, 10.1.3–6; *Oratio de Laudibus Constantini*, 1.6; 3.5–6; 18.12; *Vita Constantini*, passim. See also, Prudentius, *Contra Symmachum*, 1.587–590.

[12] *De civitate Dei*, 28.53.1–2; 20.11. In Markus's words, "In Augustine's hands the Roman Empire has lost its religious dimension.... [T]he Empire is no longer

In addition, certain believers in Jesus, who suffered real or perceived persecution under this self-proclaimed Christian empire, questioned the extent to which the empire was truly Christian at all.[13] In the early fifth century, the so-called Donatists of North Africa grew increasingly alienated from imperial institutions and ultimately suffered state-sponsored repression and violence.[14] Christian hesitation about – or even direct criticism of – the Roman Empire did not abate with the tighter embrace of "orthodoxy" under Theodosius II. On the contrary, the later fifth and sixth centuries saw the deep and lasting rupture between the imperially sponsored Chalcedonian churches and the anti-Chalcedonian opposition. Thus, Stephen, the anti-Chalcedonian bishop of Herakleopolis Magna, deploys the stark language of the Apocalypse of John to describe his Chalcedonian opponents, including the emperor Justinian, who rigorously promoted and defended the Chalcedonian faith: "I saw, said John in his Apocalypse, a star that had fallen from heaven. The pit of the abyss was opened. Smoke of a great fire went up. The sun and the air became dark through the smoke of the pit, the pit of the impiety which the rulers had gathered up who had come together to Chalcedon. This very pit of the abyss was opened again in the days of the Emperor Justinian."[15] Even as the relationship between church and empire hardened in imperial discourse, voices such as Stephen's offer us important perspective on the "Christian empire" from those Christians whose theological commitments were out of step with the imperially sponsored form of Christianity.[16] For Stephen and other anti-Chalcedonians, imperial support for the Chalcedonian faith meant that there was a rupture between the empire and the "true" church.[17] Thus, rather than a "Christian empire," anti-Chalcedonians

God's chosen instrument for the salvation of men, no longer is it indispensible for the unfolding of his plan in history" ("Roman Empire in Early Christian Historiography," 347).

[13] Averil Cameron, "The Violence of Orthodoxy," in *Heresy and Identity in Late Antiquity*, ed. Eduard Iricinschi and Holger M. Zellentin (Tübingen, 2008) 102–114; Garth Fowden, *Empire to Commonwealth: Consequences of Monotheism in Late Antiquity* (Princeton, N.J., 1993) 125–127.

[14] On this intra-Christian conflict, see Brent D. Shaw, *Sacred Violence: African Christians and Sectarian Hatred in the Age of Augustine* (Cambridge, 2011).

[15] Karl Heinz Kuhn, ed. and trans., *A Panegyric on Apollo, Archimandrite of the Monastery of Isaac, by Stephen Archbishop of Heracleopolis Magna*, 2 vols. (Louvain, 1978) 2: 10–11.

[16] For the date of the *Panegyric on Apollo*, see Kuhn, *Panegyric on Apollo*, 1: xii.

[17] David W. Johnson, "Anti-Chalcedonian Polemics in Coptic Texts, 451–641," in *The Roots of Egyptian Christianity*, ed. Birger A. Pearson and James E. Goehring

and other marginalized Christian groups saw themselves as confronting a "heretical empire."[18]

These diverse perspectives should remind us that the portrait of a single, unified Christian empire was largely a construct of the powerful and so runs the risk of obfuscating the spectrum of opinions on church-empire relations as well as the shifting configurations of church and empire throughout Late Antiquity.[19] We suggest, therefore, that the Christianization of the empire between the late fourth and early sixth centuries is best seen as an uneven process that unfolded, without strict coordination, at various social, institutional, and symbolic registers.

This complex relationship between church and empire is especially significant for our purposes since Mediterranean Jewish life during the long fifth century was increasingly shaped at the intersection of imperial and ecclesiastical forces. As we shall see, imperial protection of Jews, their property, and their communal institutions was largely dependent upon the ability of the empire to restrain the more extreme elements of the church. Yet, the dynamic and shifting nature of the interaction between church and empire meant that the precise impact of these forces on Jewish life could vary tremendously from context to context.

Mediterranean Jews at the Intersection of Church and Empire

Although imperial legislation in the post-Constantinian period typically treated "heretics" as outlaws, it took a more nuanced approach to the relationship between Jews, the empire, and various other groups and institutional interests in society, including the church.[20] In fact, beginning in the late fourth century, Jews enjoyed the official protection of the empire specifically against Christian violence.[21] Two laws

---

(Philadelphia, 1986) 216–234; Tito Orlandi, "Patristic Texts in Coptic," in *Patrology: The Eastern Fathers from the Council of Chalcedon (451) to John of Damascus († 750)*, ed. Angelo di Berardino (Cambridge, 2006) 491–570, esp. 555–565.

[18] Markus, "Roman Empire in Early Christian Historiography," 345.

[19] Peter Brown, "Christianization and Religious Conflict," in *The Cambridge Ancient History*, vol. 13: *The Late Empire, A.D. 337–425*, ed. Averil Cameron and Peter Garnsey (Cambridge, 1998) 632–664.

[20] Millar, *Greek Roman Empire*, 149–157.

[21] Edward D. Hunt, "St. Stephen in Minorca: An Episode in Jewish–Christian Relations in the Early Fifth Century AD," *Journal of Theological Studies* n.s. 33 (1982) 106–123, here 117.

issued by Arcadius (with Honorius) on 17 June 397 exemplify this protection. The first law (*Codex Theodosianus*, 16.8.12) requires a meeting
of governors to ensure their knowledge of the necessity "to repel the
assaults of those who attack Jews, and that their synagogues should
remain in their accustomed peace."[22] The second law (*CTh* 9.45.2)
prohibited Jews from feigning Christian conversion in order to avoid
paying debts owed. The latter law was a significant blow to Christian proselytization to the Jews, which relied heavily on the appeal of
asylum.[23]

This legal imperative to protect the Jews and their synagogues from
acts of violence occasionally angered certain Christians. For instance,
the Syriac *Life of Simeon Stylites* records a letter that Simeon wrote to
Theodosius II containing a stark prediction of divine retribution against
the emperor for his wrong-headed support of the Jews:

> Now that your heart is exalted and you have disregarded the
> Lord your God who gave you the glorious diadem and the
> royal throne, now that you have become a friend and com-
> panion and protector to unbelieving Jews, behold suddenly
> the righteous judgment of God will overtake you and all
> who are of the same mind as you in this matter. You will lift
> up your hands to heaven and say in your affliction, "Truly
> this anger has come on me because I broke faith with the
> Lord God."[24]

These ominous words — whether they are Simeon's or merely the
work of his anonymous biographer — stress that imperial support of
the Jews will provoke God to punish not only the emperor but his
entire empire. More important, this testimony epitomizes the pressures
exerted on the emperors during this period to achieve balance between

---

[22] Translated in Amnon Linder, *The Jews in Imperial Roman Legislation* (Detroit, 1987)
198. All translations of *Codex Theodosianus* are taken from Linder's book.

[23] Linder, *Jews in Roman Imperial Legislation*, 199. An additional law, dating to
24 September 416, allowed Jews who had converted to Christianity in order to
escape financial obligations to return to Judaism (*CTh* 16.8.23). Conversely, imperial
legislation also placed significant restrictions on Jewish proselytization of Christians
(e.g., *CTh* 3.1.5).

[24] *Life of Simeon Stylites*, 121–123, trans. Millar, *Greek Roman Empire*, 128. The *vita*
was probably written shortly after the death of Simeon in 459; see Frederick Lent,
trans., *The Life of Saint Simeon Stylites: A Translation of the Syriac Text in Bedjan's Acta
Martyrum et Sanctorum* (Merchantville, N.J., 2009) ix.

administrating a successful empire and appeasing the convictions of certain Christians.[25]

This balance did not always tip in favor of Jewish interests in legislative action. Increasingly during the fifth century, many imperial laws were issued that placed heavy restrictions on the Jews, especially in instances in which the Jews and their customs were perceived to threaten Christian hegemony or imperial stability.[26] One notable area of legislation surrounds the future construction of synagogues. Although imperial law continued to protect synagogues from being destroyed, various laws prohibited the construction of new synagogues. For example, *CTh* 16.8.27 states, "What we legislated recently concerning the Jews and their synagogues shall remain in force, namely, that they shall never be permitted to build new synagogues, neither shall they dread that the old ones shall be seized from them."[27]

Yet, despite such laws against the construction of synagogues, it is precisely in the late fourth and fifth century that we find a proliferation in the building of synagogues.[28] The tension between law and reality reflects problems that premodern empires faced more generally, both in terms of the sheer limitations of enforcement and the general ideology of governance.[29] Even more, the synagogue emerged during this period as the preeminent institution of Jewish life, as Jews in Palestine and elsewhere engaged with – and actively appropriated – newly hegemonic forms of Christian piety, ritual practice, and notions of sacred space. For instance, local Jewish communities commissioned the first figural mosaics for synagogue floors and began to place chancel

---

[25] Millar, *Greek Roman Empire*, 128.

[26] See especially the following laws from the *Codex Theodosianus* or transmitted in later witnesses to it: *CTh* 3.1.5 (preserved in the *Breviarium Alaricianum* 3.1.5); 16.2.31 together with 16.5.46 (cf. *Constitutiones Sirmondianae* 14); 16.5.44; 16.8.6 (cf. 16.9.2); 16.8.7 (received by *Brev.* 16.3.2 and *Codex Justinianus* 1.7.1); 16.8.18 (received by *Cod. Just.* 1.9.11); 16.8.19; 16.8.22, 25, 27. In a law dating to 438, Theodosius II barred Jews from political or military service on the grounds that incorrect belief may lead to treachery (*Novellae Theodosianae* 3.2).

[27] The earlier legislation alluded to here probably refers to *CTh* 16.8.25, dating to 15 February 423 (Linder, *The Jews in Roman Imperial Legislation*, 290). This law instructs that "no synagogue shall be constructed from now on, and the old ones shall remain in their state." See also *CTh* 16.8.27 and *Cod. Just.* 1.9.8.

[28] Jodi Magness, *The Archaeology of the Holy Land from the Destruction of Solomon's Temple to the Muslim Conquest* (New York, 2012) 309–319.

[29] Clifford Ando, *Imperial Ideology and Provincial Loyalty in the Roman Empire* (Berkeley, 2000).

screens in front of the Torah shrine at that same time that comparable artistic and architectural forms came to characterize church buildings throughout the Mediterranean.[30] And these synagogues served as the performative locus for a novel form of Hebrew liturgical poetry (*piyyut*) with significant poetic, prosodic, and thematic affinities to contemporary genres of Christian hymnology in Syriac, Greek, and other languages.[31] These expressions of Jewish piety would continue to develop and flourish – in tandem with their Christian counterparts – over the subsequent several centuries. Thus, not only was repressive legislation more often honored in the breach than in the observance, but Christianization forged cultural resources that proved generative for Jewish religious expression. As Hayim Lapin has written, one facet of Christianization was "the emergence of Jews as a particular kind of subject, governed by specific rules that neither prohibited their existence or practices – as Roman law attempted for Christian heresies and for pagans – nor fully incorporated them without religion- or ethnos-specific limitations."[32]

These imperial laws also reveal that Jewish life within the Christianizing Roman Empire varied according to the religious and political conditions on the ground. Indeed, Christianization did not look the same at all times and in all places. Not only did the particular group or belief-structure that was considered "Christian" from the vantage point of the empire frequently change, but limits were placed by the empire on what Christians could or could not do to the Jews. It should be highlighted that this distinction between the institutions of church and empire should not imply that "religion" and "politics" were separate categories in antiquity.[33] We now turn to consider three examples that demonstrate some of the diverse configurations of

---

[30] Lee I. Levine, *The Ancient Synagogue: The First Thousand Years*, 2nd ed. (New Haven, 2005) 210–249, 466–498, 519–529; Joan R. Branham, "Sacred Space under Erasure in Ancient Synagogues and Early Churches," *Art Bulletin* 74 (1992) 375–394.

[31] Ophir Münz-Manor, "Liturgical Poetry in the Late Antique Near East: A Comparative Approach," *Journal of Ancient Judaism* 1 (2010) 336–361.

[32] Hayim Lapin, *Rabbis as Romans: The Rabbinic Movement in Palestine, 100–400 CE* (Oxford, 2012) 17; see also the succinct formulation in Brown, "Christianization and Religious Conflict," 642–643.

[33] On the problem associated with "religion" as a discrete category in antiquity, see now Brent Nongbri, "Dislodging 'Embedded' Religion: A Brief Note on a Scholarly Trope," *Numen* 55 (2008) 440–460; Nongbri, *Before Religion: A History of a Modern Concept* (New Haven, Conn., 2013).

imperial and Christian forces, and their impact on Jewish life in the fifth century.

JEWISH COMMUNITIES AT THE INTERSECTION OF LOCAL AND GLOBAL FORCES: THREE TEST CASES

Jewish life within the Christianizing Roman Empire of Late Antiquity depended largely on the particular interaction of three microforces: the local Jewish community, the local Christian community, and the local presence of imperial representatives. These localized factors were further influenced by empire-wide dynamics of church and empire. In some cases, church and empire, as Mediterranean-wide structures, were absent in interactions between local Jews and Christians, while, in other cases, Jewish–Christian interactions were ultimately shaped by these "global" forces. In this sense, we believe it more useful to approach examples of anti-Jewish violence not as chapters in a single, empire-wide story of Jewish–Christian relations, but rather as punctuated moments in which the ever-shifting relationship between church and empire crystallized at the local level.

Based on what can be reconstructed from the fragmentary literary, documentary, and archaeological record, relations between Jews and Christians during the fifth century varied considerably across the Roman Empire. Sometimes relations were peaceful or at least not marked by physical violence.[34] For instance, in 402 Christians in Tripolitania consulted with Jewish scholars concerning the proper translation of the Hebrew Bible after a riot erupted over Jerome's new Latin translation.[35] John Chrysostom also alludes to close relations between Jews and Christians in Antioch – albeit much to his chagrin. He writes: "If, then, the Jews fail to know the Father, if they crucified the Son, if they thrust off the help of the Spirit, who should not make bold to declare plainly that the synagogue is a dwelling of demons? God is not worshipped there. Heaven forbid! From now on it remains a

---

[34] For "peaceful coexistence" between Jews and Christians, see Leonard Victor Rutgers, "Archaeological Evidence for the Interaction of Jews and Non-Jews in Late Antiquity," *American Journal of Archaeology* 96 (1992) 101–118; John S. Crawford, "Jews, Christians, and Polytheists in Late-Antique Sardis," in *Jews, Christians, and Polytheists in the Ancient Synagogue: Cultural Interaction during the Greco-Roman Period*, ed. Steven Fine (London, 1999) 190–200.

[35] Augustine, *Ep.* 71.3.5; Shaw, *Sacred Violence*, 284.

place of idolatry. But still some people pay it honor as a holy place."[36] Chrysostom here expresses his concern that some of the Christians within his flock did not have sufficient theological or social reservations about visiting synagogues or turning to Jewish ritual experts for blessings.

The pluralistic posture adopted by some Christians well reflects the function of synagogues within local communities. As several scholars have noted, synagogues served as local municipal buildings that facilitated quotidian interactions between Jews, Christians, and other local residents, ranging from business and civic matters to more mundane contacts.[37] Of course, synagogues served a unique and special function for Jews as a marker of religious identity and difference. Paula Fredriksen captures the social function of the synagogues in the late antique city when she argues that synagogues were exclusive for Jews, but inclusive for outsiders.[38] In many – if not most – places in the "Christian empire," Jews and Christians interacted on a regular basis without tension and certainly without the overt threat of verbal confrontation or physical violence.

Nevertheless, interactions between Jews and Christians occasionally turned violent. We have already seen the various imperial laws issued to protect Jews and synagogues from Christian aggression and expropriation. These laws indicate that there were instances of Christian violence against Jews and their synagogues.[39] In addition to evidence implicit within imperial legislation, we possess literary sources documenting specific instances of Christian violence against Jews and their institutions. As a general pattern, the literary record suggests that such violent outbreaks tended to take place in contexts in which imperial presence was absent, thin, or overshadowed by ecclesiastical forces, thus leaving Jews vulnerable to the more extreme factions of the local church and its bishop.

---

[36] *Adversus Judaeos*, 1.3.3. Translation from Paul W. Harkins, trans., *John Chrysostom, Discourses against Judaizing Christians* (Washington, D.C., 1979) 11.

[37] See, e.g., Paula Fredriksen, "What Parting of the Ways? Jews and Gentiles in the Ancient Mediterranean City," in *The Ways that Never Parted: Jews and Christians in Late Antiquity and the Early Middle Ages*, ed. Adam H. Becker and Annette Yoshiko Reed (Tübingen, 2003) 35–63.

[38] Ibid., 52.

[39] For the classic analyses that emphasize conflict between Jews and Christians, see Jean Juster, *Les juifs dans l'empire romain*, 2 vols. (Paris, 1914); Michael Avi-Yonah, *The Jews of Palestine: A Political History from the Bar-Kokhba War to the Arab Conquest* (Oxford, 1976).

Bishops at the edges of the empire could take advantage of the weak imperial presence in their cities and, under the right circumstances, could enact violence against local Jews. A good example of how a bishop could exploit a gap in imperial power is found in the coerced conversion of the Jews on the Balearic island of Minorca off the coast of Spain. We learn from an encyclical letter written by Bishop Severus of the Minorcan city of Jamona (*Epistula Severi*) that the recently "discovered" relics of the proto-martyr Stephen (Acts 6:8–8:1) were brought by "a certain priest, conspicuous for his sanctity" to a church in another Minorcan city (Magona) in 416.[40] According to Severus, the presence of Stephen's bones so moved Christians that they were compelled to confront local Jews, with whom they had previously enjoyed friendly relations (*Ep. Sev.* 5.1–2). In Severus's words, "In every public place, we battled against the Jews over the Law; in every household, we fought for the faith" (*Ep. Sev.* 5.2). In reality, however, the power of these relics was channeled into anti-Jewish sentiment through the preaching of Severus for over a year and a half.[41] In early February 418, Severus led an energized mob of Christians from Jamona to Magona and together they gained control over the synagogue and set it ablaze (*Ep. Sev.* 13.3–14.1).[42] Eventually – so legend has it – the entire Jewish community of Magona converted to Christianity and was forced to pay for a basilica to be built on the site of the former synagogue.

While Severus's account contains many far-fetched details, it is unlikely that it is pseudonymous or that it is a complete fabrication.[43] As Scott Bradbury has observed, not only does Severus demonstrate correct calendrical knowledge of the year 418, but the mass conversion of Jews in Minorca is also attested in other near contemporary sources, especially a letter written by Consentius to Augustine (ca. 419).[44] More recently, Ross Kraemer has supplemented Bradbury's argument for its

---

[40] Scott Bradbury, ed. and trans., *Severus of Minorca, Letter on the Conversion of the Jews* (Oxford, 1996). All translations are taken from Bradbury's book.

[41] Fredriksen, *Augustine and the Jews*, 359.

[42] While Severus fails to mention who started the fire, it seems clear that Christians were involved since they had control over it.

[43] For a rejection of the authenticity and historical reliability of *Ep. Sev.*, see especially Bernhard Blumenkranz, *Die Judenpredigt Augustins: Ein Beitrag zur Geschichte der jüdisch-christlichen Beziehungen in den ersten Jahrhunderten* (Basel, 1946) 57–58. Blumenkranz's objections, here and elsewhere, to the authenticity and historicity of *Ep. Sev.* are treated at length in Bradbury, *Severus of Minorca*, 10–15.

[44] For discussion of Consentius's letter and other contemporaneous sources, see Bradbury, *Severus of Minorca*, 9–15. This letter (plus another) was discovered with

authenticity and general historicity by pointing to the rather restrained anti-Jewish invective of the letter, which stands in marked contrast to the more vituperative anti-Jewish tractates of episcopal authors like Chrysostom.[45]

The balance between church and empire in the Minorcan affair swung heavily in favor of the church. Although *Epistula Severi* is dated in reference to the reign of Emperor Honorius and to the (second) consulship of Constantius (*Ep. Sev.* 31.1), the account gives the impression that the imperial presence in Magona was limited to two Jews with the title *defensor*, Theodorus (*Ep. Sev.* 6) and Caecilianus (*Ep. Sev.* 19.6–8).[46] Despite Severus's focus on Theodorus, Caecilianus was in fact the senior civic magistrate in Magona in 418.[47] As *defensores*, Theodorus and Caecilianus would have been charged with protecting the weak in Magona from abuse at the hands of its powerful citizens.[48] There is also a passing reference to Litorius, father of Meletius's wife Artemisia, who is said to have been a *comes* (*Ep. Sev.* 24.2). The letter's presentation of a Jewish *comes*, however, must be met with considerable skepticism since it was during the early fifth century that the empire began limiting the number of court positions for Jews.[49] Moreover, the traditional associations with Artemisia's name (e.g., water and honey) and their correspondence to her conversion narrative in *Epistula Severi* (she converts when her servant brings her water that smells and tastes like honey [24.3–11]) raise serious questions about the historicity of this episode and, hence, makes it even more improbable that she had a Jewish father who was a *comes*.[50] In the end, whatever imperial representatives were present in Magona, they were unable to stop the mob

---

manuscripts of Augustine's letters and published as Epistle 12* by Johannes Divjak, *Oeuvres des Saint Augustin* (Paris, 1987).

[45] Ross S. Kraemer, "Jewish Women's Resistance to Christianity in the Early Fifth Century: The Account of Severus, Bishop of Minorca," *Journal of Early Christian Studies* 17 (2009) 635–665, here 644.

[46] On the office of *defensor civitatis*, see Robert M. Frakes, "Late Roman Social Justice and Origin of the *Defensor Civitatis*," *Classical Journal* 89 (1994) 337–348. A law issued in 409 states that *defensores* were required to be Christian (*Cod. Just.* 1.55.8), although it was not until 438 that Jews were specifically prohibited from holding the office (*Nov. Theod.* 3.2). The need for such a law suggests that Minorca was not unique in having a Jewish *defensor*.

[47] Bradbury, *Severus of Minorca*, 38.

[48] A. H. M. Jones, *The Later Roman Empire, 284–602: A Social Economic and Administrative Survey* (Oxford, 1964) 145.

[49] Hunt, "St. Stephen in Minorca," 121.

[50] Kraemer, "Jewish Women's Resistance," 655–656.

of Christians from destroying the synagogue despite imperial legislation already in place to prevent this very kind of violence.[51] In fact,
Severus and his followers could deploy a combination of physical violence, threats, and intimidation to compel the Jews to convert and to
do so without facing any interference from imperial authorities.[52]

This incident on Minorca also illustrates how local and global
Christian traditions could intersect in highly specific ways, sometimes
with devastating results for Jews. That Stephen's relics were used as
a pretext for the persecution of Jews is hardly surprising, given the
emphasis on Jewish guilt for the stoning of Stephen in Acts 6:8–8:1.[53]
And, indeed, there is some evidence that incidents of anti-Jewish violence linked to the arrival of Stephen's relics occurred elsewhere as
well.[54] Yet, in each case where we hear of anti-Jewish violence or the
expropriation of Jewish communal property triggered by the relics of
Stephen, we find highly specific local conditions in which an episcopal
figure is in a position to capitalize on the absence of empire.[55] This
event – or perhaps cluster of events – demonstrates how local religious
and political dynamics gave concrete expression to Christian traditions
and objects that circulated throughout the Mediterranean; it was only
under certain conditions that these sacred objects exerted their powerful
impact on Jewish life.

Violence against Jews was not limited to tiny islands at the edges
of the empire; it could also occur in traditional imperial strongholds.
In 388, Christians, at the instigation of the town's bishop, burned a

---

[51] Theodorus is said to have converted to Christianity, seemingly under coercion (*Ep. Sev.* 16.16, 18.18). For imperial legislation prior to 416 that protected Jews and synagogues from Christian violence, see *CTh* 16.8.9; 16.8.12; 6.8.20, together with 2.8.26 and 8.8.8. For discussion, see Linder, *Jews in Roman Imperial Legislation*, 262–267.

[52] Kraemer, "Jewish Women's Resistance," 649; see also Carlo Ginzburg, "The Con-version of Minorcan Jews (417–418): An Experiment in the History of Histori-ography," in *Christendom and Its Discontents: Exclusion, Persecution, and Rebellion, 1000–1500*, ed. Scott L. Waugh and Peter D. Diehl (Cambridge, 1996) 207–19.

[53] On the anti-Jewish dimensions of the "martyrdom" of Stephen in the book of Acts, see Shelly Matthews, *Perfect Martyr: The Stoning of Stephen and the Construction of Christian Identity* (Oxford, 2010).

[54] It has been suggested that the arrival of Stephen's relics in the Syrian city of Edessa provided its bishop, Rabbula, a pretext for the conversion of a synagogue into a church dedicated to Saint Stephen, much like what occurred in Minorca; see Hans J. W. Drijvers, "The Protonike Legend, the *Doctrina Addai*, and Bishop Rabbula of Edessa," *Vigiliae Christianae* 51 (1997) 298–315.

[55] Bradbury, *Severus of Minorca*, 23.

synagogue in Callinicum, a city on the Euphrates known for its strong defense and vibrant trade.[56] Upon hearing of this event from the eastern count (*comes orientis militarium partium*), Theodosius I (347–395) ordered that the synagogue be rebuilt at the expense of the church and that the monks responsible receive due punishment.[57]

Word of the Callinicum affair and Theodosius's reaction to it quickly reached Ambrose of Milan, who was then in Aquileia in northern Italy (*Epistula* 41.1). In response, Ambrose wrote a chastising letter to the emperor, condemning him for requiring the bishop to pay for the rebuilding of the synagogue (*Ep.* 40). From Ambrose's perspective, by asking the bishop to pay for the synagogue, Theodosius was in fact demanding that the bishop either follow orders, whereby he would betray his Christian faith, or reject the imperial imperative and run the risk of becoming a martyr (*Ep.* 40.7). Further complicating matters, Ambrose's earlier intervention had already prompted Theodosius to exempt the bishop of Callinicum from paying for the rebuilding of the synagogue.[58] Nevertheless, at least from Ambrose's perspective, this exemption was insufficient, as Theodosius had simply transferred the financial – and theological – burden to the *comes orientis* (*Ep.* 40.9).[59] Ambrose confronted the emperor directly in a sermon delivered in his presence (*Ep.* 41.2–26).[60] Theodosius finally consented to drop all compulsory retribution when Ambrose refused to allow him to receive the Eucharist until he had withdrawn all previous orders concerning Callinicum.

The despoliation of the synagogue at Callinicum offers important insight into the shifting conjunction of Christianity and the Roman Empire and its impact on the empire's Jews.[61] Like the case of Minorca, the event provides a clear example of the kinds of violent actions that were possible when and where the local imperial presence was overshadowed by (or embodied in) the town's bishop. Indeed, the immediate imperial action taken was at the intermediary level (the eastern count)

---

[56] The primary source for the destruction of the synagogue at Callinicum is Ambrose, *Eps.* 40 and 41, on which see Neil McLynn, *Ambrose of Milan: Church and Court in a Christian Capital* (Berkeley, 1994) 301.

[57] On the title *comes orientis militarium partium* in Ambrose's letter, see McLynn, *Ambrose of Milan*, 298 n. 26.

[58] Ibid., 300.

[59] Ibid., 300–301.

[60] On Ambrose's rhetoric of violence, see Thomas Sizgorich, *Violence and Belief in Late Antiquity: Militant Devotion in Christianity and Islam* (Philadelphia, 2009) 81–107.

[61] For other possible motives, see McLynn, *Ambrose of Milan*, 302.

and in the form of a letter subsequently written to the emperor. What is more, the count's motivations for involving the emperor in this affair are unclear. Was his intention to demand justice on behalf of the Jews or to assuage imperial wrath against the local Christians?[62] In either case, what is clear is that the Jews of Callinicum were very much at the mercy of the city's bishop, with little immediate support from external imperial forces.

At an empire-wide level, the destruction of the synagogue at Callinicum and the events that ensued epitomize the tenuous position of the Jews in the dynamic relationship between the global institutions of church and empire. While Theodosius's initial stance was to demand restitution from Christians on behalf of the Jews for the destruction of their synagogue, he was forced by a powerful bishop from a different region to rescind his order, thus momentarily aligning church and empire to powerful effect. But Theodosius's approach to the empire's role in Jewish–Christian disputes was to change yet again. In a law issued just five years after the despoliation of the synagogue at Callinicum, the same Theodosius – perhaps with the experience of Callinicum in mind – ordered that "those who presume to commit illegal deeds under the name of the Christian religion and attempt to destroy and despoil synagogues" ought to be punished (*CTh* 16.8.9). Thus, over the course of only half a decade and under the rule of a single emperor, the legislative and administrative map for the conjunction of empire, Judaism, and Christianity was drawn in multiple – and, at times, contradictory – ways.

The relationship of a local Jewish community to imperial and ecclesiastical forces took on yet a different configuration in the great urban center of Alexandria in the early fifth century. In 415, Cyril, bishop of Alexandria expelled the Jews from the city against the wishes of the augustal prefect, Orestes.[63] That Cyril removed *all* Jews from the city has been appropriately questioned, given the apparent size of the Jewish population in Alexandria and their centrality in local industry and trade.[64] It is unlikely, however, that Socrates invented out of whole

---

[62] Ibid., 299 n. 27.

[63] Socrates Scholasticus, *Historia ecclesiastica*, 7.13.15. Cf. John of Nikiu, *Chron.* 84.89–99. See Robert L. Wilken, *Judaism and the Early Christian Mind: A Study of Cyril of Alexandria's Exegesis and Theology* (New Haven, 1971) 54–68; Christopher Haas, *Alexandria in Late Antiquity: Topography and Social Conflict* (Baltimore, 1997) 295–316; Victor Tcherikover and Alexander Fuks, eds., *Corpus Papyrorum Judaicarum*, 3 vols. (Cambridge, Mass., 1957–1963) 1: 98–101.

[64] E.g., Wilken, *Judaism and the Early Christian Mind*, 57. See also *CTh* 13.5.18.

cloth Cyril's act of violence against the Alexandrian Jews. This conflict between Cyril and Orestes was a reflex of the broader power struggle in Alexandria between bishops and imperial authorities. As Socrates notes, "Now Orestes had long regarded with jealousy the growing power of the bishops, because they encroached on the jurisdiction of the authorities appointed by the emperor."[65]

Although it is difficult to reconstruct from the highly partisan sources the underlying causes for the expulsion of the Jews from Alexandria, Robert Wilken has plausibly suggested that Cyril's actions were precipitated by his anti-Jewish reading of the Bible.[66] What is abundantly clear is that Orestes' influence over Alexandrian life was limited insofar as he could not curb the anti-Jewish inclinations of the Alexandrian bishop.[67] Christopher Haas sums up the situation: "Given the instability of imperial administration during 414 and the strong line taken against dissenters by 415, it is not surprising that Cyril should have acted confidently in his dealings with Alexandria's Jews and pagans. This also goes a long way toward explaining the ineffectiveness of the augustal prefect, Orestes."[68] The "instability" in the imperial administration of the city may explain why there was apparently no imperial response to the letters written by either Orestes or Cyril.[69] In this case, the fate of the Jews depended entirely on a local struggle between the imperial and ecclesiastical forces on the ground in Alexandria. Unfortunately for the Jews, the latter prevailed and many were probably expelled from the city. The expulsion of the Jews from Alexandria during the bishopric of Cyril thus demonstrates that, even in regions with traditionally strong ties to the empire, bishops could exploit momentary weaknesses in the central imperial administration to circumvent local authorities and to enact punishments against the Jews.

---

[65] Soc. *Hist. eccl.* 7.13. Translation from Andrew C. Zenos, trans., *Socrates Scholasticus, Ecclesiastical History*, Nicene and Post-Nicene Fathers 2.2 (Grand Rapids, Mich., 1957) 159.

[66] Wilken, *Judaism and the Early Christian Mind*, 61; see also Haas, *Alexandria in Late Antiquity*, 300–301.

[67] Haas, *Alexandria in Late Antiquity*, 302; Tcherikover and Fuks, *Corpus papyrorum Judaicarum*, 98. Cyril's political shrewdness can also be seen in his subsequent dealings with the emperor over the Nestorian controversy; see Susan Wessel, *Cyril of Alexandria and the Nestorian Controversy: The Making of a Saint and of a Heretic* (Oxford, 2004) 74–111.

[68] Haas, *Alexandria in Late Antiquity*, 302.

[69] Soc. *Hist. eccl.* 7.13.18–19. On the lack of imperial response to these letters, see Millar, *Greek Roman Empire*, 127.

CONCLUSION

Certain patterns emerge from these instances of Christian aggression or violence against Jews in the Roman Empire of Late Antiquity. In each case, local bishops were the primary players in inflicting violence against the Jewish community with which they were in contact. Whether they were constrained by imperial authorities (Stephen of Minorca and the bishop of Callinicum) or had to square off against local officials (Cyril of Alexandria), bishops could reshape the relationship of Jews to their immediate urban context as well as to the larger structures of empire. Yet even Jews who lived in cities with traditional and significant ties to the empire could not depend on the protection of local imperial institutions. The most powerful bishops, such as Ambrose or Cyril, could even compel emperors to change course on violence against Jews – albeit temporarily – or expel the Jews against the wishes of the local imperial representative.

The circumstances at Minorca, Callinicum, and Alexandria conform to the basic pattern presented in legal texts of imperial protection of Jews against Christian violence. Despite the occasional restrictive law, the empire offered a great deal of protection to the Jews against those Christians bent on confrontation. The reason behind this largely positive approach to the Jews is not clear. The assessment offered by Bernard Bachrach remains the most plausible: "An anti-Jewish policy was not pursued during the first century and a half following the Edict of Toleration because the imperial government had a sound understanding of political realities. It saw the potential cost, in terms of social dislocation, economic decline, and military conflict, that the Jewish *gens* could impose if it were attacked."[70] But the empire's capacity to manage the confrontational impulses within Christian communities was not the same everywhere and at all times. The power of the empire was limited or overshadowed by the church in many regions, particularly at the "edges" of the empire, where local bishops exerted considerable formal and persuasive power. Indeed, Stephen and his episcopal impresario had little in their way when they impelled a group of Christians to march against the Jewish community of Magona in a corner of the Mediterranean world.

---

[70] Bernard S. Bachrach, "The Jewish Community of the Later Roman Empire as Seen in the *Codex Theodosianus*," in Neusner and Frerichs, *"To See Ourselves as Others See Us,"* 399–421, here 421.

These case studies make clear how much the ever-shifting negotiations of church and state could reframe the conditions of Jewish life
in the Roman Empire. Yet, at the same time, these moments of conflict
tell only a small part of the story of Christianization, which simultaneously constrained and stimulated Jewish cultural expression. These
emergent forms would gradually reshape Judaism in the Mediterranean
world, as the transitional period of the fifth century gave way to the
more assertively governed empire and more sharply delineated society
of the Age of Justinian.

21: ORDERING INTELLECTUAL
LIFE

Edward Watts

Education in the Roman Empire was traditionally a decentralized and lightly regulated affair. Hellenistic educational centers like Athens and Alexandria remained important, but the imperial period saw other cities across the empire emerge and grow into important centers of teaching.[1] Some, like Smyrna and Byzantium, even managed to establish themselves as temporary rivals to the old centers.[2] Students could study where they wanted, generally for as long as their teacher would have them. The wealthiest took advantage of this and collected a long list of intellectual mentors.[3] Teachers organized their cohorts of students as they wished and sometimes jumped from city to city in search of better, more lucrative posts.[4] Emperors regularly offered the honor of composing imperial letters to individual teachers they favored and they named other teachers to the membership of the Alexandrian Mouseion, but generally they remained aloof from the actual operation of schools.[5]

---

[1] See, for example, Eumenius's *For the Restoration of the Schools*, a discussion of the schools of third-century Autun; and Ausonius, *Professores*, for a profile of Gallic schools more widely during the late third and fourth centuries.

[2] Philostratus, *Vitae Sophistarum*, 511, 515, 531 on Smyrna; Phil. *VS* 591 on Byzantium.

[3] Herodes Atticus is the most notable of these collectors. He claimed intellectual descent from Favorinus (Phil. *VS* 490), Polemo (*VS* 538), and a host of others (*VS* 564).

[4] E.g., Scopelian (Phil. *VS* 516) and Philiscus (*VS* 621).

[5] Naphtali Lewis, "The Non-Scholar Members of the Alexandrian Museum," *Mnemosyne* 16 (1963) 257–261; and Naphtali Lewis, "*Literati* in the service of Roman Emperors: Politics before culture," in *Coins, Culture and History in the Ancient World: Numismatic and Other Studies in Honor of Bluma L. Trell*, ed. Lionel Casson and Martin Price (Detroit, 1981) 149–166.

The last decades of the fourth century and the first few of the fifth saw a remarkable shift in the way that education was administered. The period saw a high level of imperial investment in educational infrastructure. Alexandria and possibly Constantinople saw the construction of huge new auditorium complexes. Other publicly owned spaces (like the Athenian Metroon) seem to have been remodeled to serve as lecture halls.[6] An unprecedented level of imperial scrutiny accompanied this investment. From the 360s until the 420s, emperors issued laws requiring the registration of all teachers in the empire,[7] restricting the places in which publicly funded teachers could give instruction,[8] and regulating the salaries of all publicly funded teachers.[9] They also mandated the amount of time a student could be in school, the amount of time he could spend watching shows, and the punishments to be inflicted if he misbehaved.[10] One law of Valentinian and Valens even established a registry that monitored the progress and performance of students.[11]

The intellectual diversity that had once characterized philosophical instruction also melted away as the fifth century dawned. Instead of the Stoics and Aristotelians who once wandered the landscape, fifth-century philosophers were mostly ecumenical Platonists who drew liberally upon Aristotle (and less liberally upon Stoicism) and increasingly taught from a standard curriculum. For much of the age of Attila, the wealthy, privately funded Athenian Neoplatonic school served as the intellectual home of this new Platonism. It trained the most influential teachers, generated exciting new ideas, and attracted substantial donations from benefactors.[12] Medical and legal training saw a similar

---

[6] On the Metroon, see Grzegor Majcherek, "The Late Roman Auditoria: An Archeological Overview," in *Journal of Juristic Papyrology*, suppl. 8: *Alexandria Auditoria of Kôm el-Dikka and Late Antique Education*, ed. Tomasz Derda, Tomasz Markiewicz, and Ewa Wipszycka (Warsaw, 2007) 11–50, here 42–43.

[7] For the registry of teachers, see *Codex Theodosianus*, 13.3.5, and the discussion of Edward Watts, *City and School in Late Antique Athens and Alexandria* (Berkeley, 2006) 68–70.

[8] *CTh* 14.9.3.

[9] E.g., *CTh* 13.3.11

[10] *CTh* 14.9.1. These laws specifically target male students because the emperors were interested in future civil servants, none of whom would be women. The rest of this essay concerns the intersection of this male-dominated institution with the educational system and, as a result, the experience of female students falls beyond its purview.

[11] *CTh* 14.9.1.

[12] On the prominence of the Athenian school of Plutarch, see Watts, *City and School*, 79–142.

standardization in their curricula. Although neither medicine nor law had a center with quite the gravitational force of the Athenian Platonic school, Alexandrian doctors and the lawyers teaching in Rome, Constantinople, and Berytus shaped the training given students in ways that would be difficult to imagine in an earlier period.

By the 530s, however, this empire-wide system of education had come apart. The great centers of learning of the West had disappeared and many of those in the East were diminished. Philosophical and medical education was no longer centered in the great Greek cities of Athens and Alexandria as their teaching found its way into Syriac and Latin monastic settings. Only legal instruction remained effectively centralized, though the combination of political change, natural disaster, and Justinian's reforms meant that law was taught in fewer places in 540 than it had been in 360. And yet, as the intellectual world of the early fifth century contracted and fragmented, its remnants bore the unmistakable mark of this process of centralization. Even if the institutions the state created had largely disappeared, they exerted a profound effect on what intellectual culture and education would be like in the early medieval period.

This chapter will explain the creation, development, and disappearance of this relatively centralized system of education in the long fifth century. It will begin by considering why later Roman emperors decided to take such an interest in the education of young men and what steps they took to ensure that it was done in ways that the empire considered useful. The next section will consider the emergence of dominant centers of philosophy and medical teaching as well as the increasing standardization of the philosophical, medical, and legal curricula. It will conclude by examining the factors that led to the breakdown of these centralized intellectual institutions and the curricular elements that survived this process.

EMPERORS AND THE SCHOOLS

Imperial interest in education was a delayed effect of the administrative revolution that reshaped the Roman world in the later third and early fourth century.[13] Beginning with the reign of Diocletian and continuing

---

[13] For an interesting recent assessment of this topic, see John N. Dillon, *The Justice of Constantine: Law, Communication, and Control* (Ann Arbor, 2012).

through that of Constantine and his sons, the Roman state dramatically expanded the size and scope of its administrative infrastructure. The number of provinces increased, the staffs of their governors grew, and above them stood a steeper, multilayered imperial hierarchy.[14]

Emperors came to depend upon the educational system to identify capable and well-trained candidates who could effectively serve in these capacities. As the fourth century dawned, teachers became one of the prime resources upon which imperial officials relied to find this new bureaucratic talent. Libanius, for example, frequently wrote to officials to recommend that his best students be given positions in imperial administration.[15] His letters show that capable students from the best families pursued governorships or other relatively high-ranking positions, while less capable or ambitious students aimed lower, perhaps for positions on a governor's staff or as advocates with privileges that allowed them to argue in court.[16] But the key challenge for both aspirant and emperor was that of connecting the able and energetic with those in a position to employ them.

As the fourth century progressed, emperors came to recognize that the educational system, while an imperfect tool, offered the best chance of efficiently making these matches. This led them to get more involved in its operation. In 370, Valentinian and Valens ordered the office of tax assessment to compile an annual list of the city's students and "dispatch it to the bureaus of Our Clemency in order that we may learn the merits and education of the various students and may judge whether they may ever be necessary to Us."[17] This was undoubtedly a way to get around the time-consuming task of discerning the true potential of students amidst the empty praises that populated the standard letters of reference. It also reflected a new reality in which the state depended upon schools to efficiently and effectively identify the men who would enable it to keep functioning.

This occurred at the same time that the empire became increasingly interested in ensuring that students were educated in a good

---

[14] Peter J. Heather, "New Men for New Constantines? Creating an Imperial Elite in the Eastern Mediterranean," in *New Constantines: The Rhythm of Imperial Renewal in Byzantium, 4th–13th Centuries*, ed. Paul Magdalino (London, 1994) 11–33.

[15] For this process, see the discussion of Raffaela Cribiore, *The School of Libanius in Late Antique Antioch* (Princeton, 2007) 198–200.

[16] Note, for example, Libanius's letters from 360 on behalf of the well-placed Miccalus (*Epistolae*, 97–99) and those he wrote for the less well-positioned Bassus (*Ep. 175*).

[17] *CTh* 14.9.1.

environment. The first move in this direction was Julian's law mandating that teachers register with the emperor so that their moral character could be verified.[18] That law, of course, formed part of the existing legal basis upon which Julian built his prohibition of Christians teaching, but its mandate that teachers register with the emperor remained in force even after the ban on Christians teaching was rescinded.[19]

Emperors did more than monitor the moral probity of teachers. The fifth century saw emperors and cities invest resources in centralizing and improving the spaces in which instruction took place. In the fourth century, teachers taught where they could. Libanius for example taught in his house, in a spot next to the marketplace, and, at times, a room in the Antiochene city hall.[20] In Athens, both Julianus and Prohaeresius taught in a private home despite the fact that each apparently held an imperially funded chair of rhetoric.[21]

By the 420s, the situation for public teachers in certain cities had begun to change. The famous law of 425 establishing what was once called the "University of Constantinople" shows a new imperial interest in regulating the spaces in which instruction occurred.[22] It permits teachers accustomed to teaching in private homes to continue to do so but prohibits "those who are established within the auditorium of the Capitol . . . from teaching such studies in private homes" and punishes violators with the loss of their public stipends.[23] The law's second segment then specifies that the school should have "three orators and ten grammarians" for Latin instruction, "five sophists and ten grammarians" for Greek, a professor of philosophy, and two "who explain the formulas and statutes of the law." Each of them was also to be given "a specifically designated place" in which he was to teach.[24]

---

[18] CTh 13.3.5, discussed above.
[19] CTh 13.3.6, which eliminates Julian's prohibition of Christians teaching but does nothing to end the practice of registering teachers.
[20] Libanius, Orationes, 1.101–102. The broader Antiochene setting is described in Libanius, Or. 22.31; Or. 5.45–52; cf. Cribiore, School of Libanius, 44.
[21] Eunapius, Vitae Sophistarum, 483.
[22] CTh 14.9.3. For the anachronistic "University of Constantinople" see the interesting discussion of Henri-Irénée Marrou, Histoire de l'éducation dans l'Antiquité (Paris, 1956) 411–412.
[23] CTh 14.9.3.
[24] CTh 14.9.3.1 (trans. Clyde Pharr et al., The Theodosian Code and Novels and the Sirmondian Constitutions [Princeton, 1952], modified).

Emperors had not always been so ready to privilege teachers of grammar and rhetoric over professors of philosophy.[25] In the second century, Marcus Aurelius had famously endowed five chairs in Athens with four of these to be occupied by philosophers, one by a rhetorician, and none by grammarians.[26] Imperial priorities had shifted for comprehensible reasons. Grammar and rhetoric attracted the most students both because they were lower-level studies of letters and because nearly all of the civilian officials an emperor would employ were expected to have rhetorical training. The emperors evidently determined that these more popular and more useful subjects merited the most imperial support.

Another consideration that distinguished these imperial appointments in Constantinople from, say, the Athenian chairs of the second century was the increased regulation of where and when the appointed professors could teach. The preface of Theodosius II's law emphasizes that public professors in Constantinople were not to teach privately.[27] This was an important change. Into the fourth century, teachers receiving public funds continued to regularly offer instruction in their homes.[28] Constantinopolitan public teachers, however, were now either to use public spaces alone or give up their public positions.

The most puzzling piece of this law, however, concerns the nature of these spaces. Each teacher was to be given his own, unshared classroom in something called the "auditorium of the Capitol," evidently a spatially defined and deliberately constructed university district.[29] No trace of such a district has been found in Constantinople,[30] but at roughly the same time that this Constantinopolitan law was issued, perhaps as many as twenty-five lecture halls were constructed across at least two city blocks on a vacant piece of land in the very center of

---

[25] A similar emphasis upon Greek and Latin grammar and rhetoric is found in Gratian's law about teaching in Trier (CTh 13.3.11).

[26] These were in addition to an existing Athenian civic chair in rhetoric. For discussion see Watts, City and School, 33–34.

[27] The real goal was an elimination of the practice of public teachers requiring students to pay for additional private instruction off site.

[28] Eunap. Vit. Soph. 483.

[29] "capitolii auditorium," CTh 14.9.3.

[30] The baths of Zeuxippus are one possible site for the Constantinopolitan auditorium (Cribiore, School of Libanius, 44 n. 9). For similar auditoria in Berytus in the fourth century, see Expositio totius mundi et gentium, 25, and the discussion of Linda Jones Hall, Roman Berytus: Beirut in Late Antiquity (London, 2004) 66–67.

Alexandria.[31] They seem to have been part of a larger, deliberately constructed scholastic quarter in the city that included a public theater, a colonnaded portico, and an open space or park in which people could congregate.[32] The complex abutted a bathhouse (which could have conceivably contained a library) and a public latrine to the northeast and the city's famous Tychaion to the northwest, but the classrooms were otherwise spatially set apart from the rest of the city.[33]

No law establishing or regulating this complex survives, but a number of surviving texts give indications of how it may have been used. In the 480s, Zacharias Scholasticus describes a space in which grammarians, rhetoricians, philosophers, and doctors are all known to have taught.[34] Each professor used the lecture room for a scheduled period of time and, when his classes concluded, another professor and group of students would take the room over from him.[35] Professors only turned up on the days that they taught. In contrast to Constantinople, some philosophers appear to have given extra, informal instruction in their homes on days when they were not scheduled to use the lecture halls.[36]

Alexandria also provides the one known fifth-century instance of the imperial government directly intervening in the content of teaching. Following a riot that involved Alexandrian teachers, students, monks, and church officials, an imperial commission was sent to investigate the city's teachers.[37] Its investigation came to focus upon a group of pagan philosophers who taught in the city's complex of lecture halls. As it progressed, the public salaries of the philosophers were suspended and the teachers were denied access to the city's classrooms.[38] It concluded only when Nicomedes, the official leading the investigation, extracted a commitment from Ammonius, the holder of an Alexandrian chair of

---

[31] The remains are described and analyzed in detail by Majcherek, "The Late Roman Auditoria," 11–50.

[32] This open space may well be the "temenos of the Muses" described by Zacharias Scholasticus (*Ammonius*, lines 361–369).

[33] A city street lay to their west and the remains of a small building containing an apse and a larger public latrine to their south.

[34] For grammarians and philosophers, see the in-depth discussions in Zacharias's *Life of Severus*. The physician Gessius is described in Zacharias's *Ammonius*. For rhetoric, see the profile of the schools presented in the *Life of Isidore* by Damascius.

[35] Zach. *Vit. Sev.* 23.

[36] Ibid.

[37] On this riot and its aftermath see Edward Watts, *Riot in Alexandria* (Berkeley, 2010).

[38] Damasc. *Vit. Isid.* 117A–C.

philosophy, to eliminate some elements of his teaching that Christians found objectionable.[39]

CURRICULAR HEGEMONY

Nicomedes' investigation shows the particular ways in which the centralization of financial resources and teaching facilities could create new types of pressures on fifth-century teachers. Those who taught privately faced fewer of these direct pressures in the fifth century, but even teaching circles that neither used a publicly provided classroom nor centered around a publicly salaried professor became much less intellectually diverse. Perhaps nothing better illustrates this trend than the recentralization of Platonic teaching in the city of Athens. Athens had long been the city to which Greek philosophers looked for definitive teaching. For Platonists, this relationship was a formal one for as long as the Academy founded by Plato survived. After the Academy disintegrated in the aftermath of the Sullan sack of Athens in 91 BCE, the city retained a sort of informal intellectual primacy even as Platonic centers grew up around the Roman world.[40] By the end of the third century, however, the rise of innovative and exciting Platonic teaching in non-Athenian circles such as those headed by Ammonius Saccas and Plotinus combined with the post-Herulian devastation of city to push Athens out of this traditional role. Athenian teachers such as Longinus were seen as old-fashioned and, for most of the fourth century, influential Platonists like Iamblichus and his followers established and maintained schools in such cities as Apamea and Ephesus.[41] Athens had become a backwater to which ideas traveled only after they had been hashed out elsewhere.

The revitalization of Athenian philosophy began around 400. The central figure in this was an Athenian named Plutarch, the son and grandson of two Athenians who had become familiar with the

---

[39] Richard Sorabji, "Divine Names and Sordid Deals in Ammonius' Alexandria," in *The Philosopher and Society in Late Antiquity*, ed. Andrew Smith (Swansea, U.K., 2005) 203–214.

[40] For the demise of the Academy in the first century BCE, see John Glucker, *Antiochus and the Late Academy* (Göttingen, 1978).

[41] On Longinus, see Porphyry, *Vita Plotini*, 14. The vibrancy of the early and mid-fourth-century circles in Syria and Asia Minor is described at length in Eunapius's *Lives of the Sophists*.

teachings of Iamblichus through the nephew of one of his students.[42] Plutarch's teaching incorporated these ideas and, by the first decade of the fifth century, his school had begun to draw students from across the Mediterranean.[43] By the 440s, Plutarch's successors, Syrianus and Proclus, transformed his school into the center at which the eastern empire's most acclaimed philosophers trained.[44]

A combination of factors enabled the Athenian Platonic school to develop such prominence. The most important, of course, was the succession of philosophers who headed the institution. The Athenian scholarchs Plutarch, Syrianus, Proclus, and Damascius all ranked as the best philosophical minds of their respective generations. Each was also a staunch, open supporter of traditional religion in ways that the confessional politics of the age made nearly impossible in cities like Constantinople and Alexandria. They also proved adept at creating networks of powerful and wealthy supporters, with Plutarch and Proclus showing particular skill in appealing to the empire's pagan elite.[45] Collectively, the scholarchs showed themselves to be expert fundraisers. The school always remained in private hands and, by the time of Proclus's death, its endowment yielded 1,000 *solidi* annually "as pious lovers of learning at the times of their death bequeathed to the philosophers the requisite means . . . for the philosophical life."[46] Publicly funded Alexandrian contemporaries could only look on enviously at their richer, more comfortably supported Athenian colleagues.[47]

These were not Athens's only advantages in the fifth century. The educational changes of the long fifth century opened new types of opportunities for a privately administered, niche institution like the Athenian Neoplatonic school. The correlation between grammatical and rhetorical study and positions in imperial administration meant that many students were unlikely to continue their studies through to philosophy. Many fifth-century students on this professional track dabbled in introductory-level philosophy (which mainly would have consisted of the study of Aristotle), but their numbers were small enough

---

[42] Watts, *City and School*, 87–96.

[43] Synesius, *Epistula* 136.

[44] Those trained in Athens included, among many others, Hermeias, Ammonius, Isidore, and Asclepiodotus of Alexandria.

[45] Among the influential figures courted were the prefect Herculius (*Inscriptiones Graecae* 2–3.2 4224), a senator named Rufinus (Marinus, *Vita Procli*, 23) and the senator Theagenes (Damasc. *Vit. Isid.* 100A–B).

[46] Damasc. *Vit. Isid.* 102.

[47] Olympiodorus, *In Alcibiadem*, 140–141.

and their interests limited enough that few philosophers could subsist solely on income from philosophical teaching.[48] Philosophers including Julian's friend Chrysanthius, the Alexandrian Mouseion member Horapollon, and the Christian John Philoponus seem primarily to have taught grammar.[49] Even Syrianus, the Athenian successor of Plutarch, once authored a commentary on Hermogenes. By the time of Proclus, however, the financial resources of the Athenian Platonic schools seems to have freed its professors from the obligation to teach anything but philosophy and supporting disciplines such as math and astronomy.[50] Instead of shepherding future bureaucrats through grammatical instruction, the Athenian philosophers were able to concentrate their energies on what Damascius called the "leisure and tranquility of the philosophical life."[51]

When he wrote this, Damascius described not just the teaching of philosophy but the creation of a scholastic environment that encouraged students to behave in particular ways.[52] This had long been the purpose of a philosophical circle, but the practical realities of fifth-century education meant that many students who sat through a philosophy course in Constantinople or Alexandria had no interest in making the personal and emotional commitments that full-fledged membership in a philosophical circle usually entailed.[53] For many, the Aristotelian *Organon* (the collection of six Aristotelian works on logic) was a mere intellectual way station before they moved on to law school, medical school, or a career at court. A different sort of student traveled to Athens. They were men such as Marinus or Damascius, who saw their embrace of philosophy as a conversion and understood their training in it to be

---

[48] Among the fifth-century students who took a small amount of philosophy before moving on to something different were the future lawyer and bishop Zacharias Scholasticus, the physician Gessius, and Aeneas of Gaza. Technically speaking, it was considered bad form for philosophers to charge their students fees. Most, though, expected regular "gifts" from students (e.g., Olympiodorus, *In Gorgiam*, 43.2; Olymp. *In Alc.* 140.15–22).

[49] Chrysanthius: Eunap. *Vit. Soph.* 502; Horapollon: *Vit. Sev.* 15; Philoponus: Simplicius, *De Caelo*, 119.7, a title Simplicius elsewhere indicates that Philoponus used for himself.

[50] This is a natural implication of the situation described by Damascius in *Vit. Isid.* 102.

[51] Ibid.

[52] Edward Watts, "Doctrine, Anecdote, and Action: Reconsidering the Social History of the Last Platonists (ca. 430–ca. 550 CE)," *Classical Philology* 106 (2011) 226–244.

[53] See Watts, "Doctrine, Anecdote, and Action," 231–234, for discussion of students of this type.

preparation for a lifestyle guided by divine reason.[54] Some men with this level of devotion did attend Alexandrian or Aphrodisian schools, but even these usually spent some time in Athens as a culmination of their education.[55]

This status gave Athenian Platonists a great deal of influence upon the shape of fifth-century philosophical instruction. They trained the majority of the most prominent philosophers of the fifth and early sixth centuries. Because of this, the curriculum used by most Mediterranean teachers in the later fifth and early sixth centuries grew out of that established in Athens. This provided a comprehensive training in philosophical virtue that consisted of the sequential study of a cycle of texts. Students worked through one text at a time, a process that took about fifty days per work.[56] The first two years of instruction focused primarily upon Aristotle's *Organon* and treated logic, ethics, physics, mathematics, and theology.[57] Students then advanced to the study of Plato and read a set sequence of ten dialogues designed to help them develop political, purifying, theoretical, and theological virtues. These dialogues were arranged hierarchically according to the scale of virtues created by Plotinus, systematized by Porphyry, and first integrated into a teaching curriculum by Iamblichus.[58]

Although elements of the teaching differed from teacher to teacher and school to school, the relative uniformity of later fifth-century philosophical teaching contrasted markedly with the situation in the last decade of the fourth century.[59] In the 390s, Themistius taught philosophy in Constantinople in a way that clearly privileged Aristotle over

---

[54] For the conversions of Marinus and Damascius see *Vit. Isid.* 97A (Marinus) and 137A–D (Damascius). On the broader idea of late antique philosophical communities defined by philosophical actions, see Watts, "Doctrine, Anecdote, and Action," 237–241.

[55] Examples of Alexandrian students traveling to Athens include Proclus, Hermeias, Ammonius, Asclepiodotus, Isidore, and Simplicius.

[56] Leendert G. Westerink, *Commentaries on the Phaedo* I (Amsterdam, 1976) 26.

[57] Marin. *Vit. Proc.* 9.

[58] Dominic O'Meara, *Pythagoras Revived: Mathematics and Philosophy in Late Antiquity* (Oxford, 1989) 97–99, and Jean Pépin, *Théologie cosmique et théologie chrétienne* (Paris, 1964) 380–386.

[59] For differences between teachers, see, for example, the profound difference of opinion between Proclus and Damascius about the proper ways to read Iamblichus (Polymnia Athanassiadi, "The Oecumenism of Iamblichus: Latent Knowledge and Its Awakening," *Journal of Roman Studies* 85 [1995] 244–250).

Plato.[60] At the same time, Hypatia, a Platonist who evidently had little interest in Iamblichus and his teaching, stood out as the most influential Alexandrian teacher.[61] While this was not the Antonine age, in which different chairs were necessary for representatives of each of the major philosophical systems, the fourth century still permitted enough intellectual diversity that figures such as Themistius and Hypatia attracted significant followings. This was not true of the later fifth and sixth centuries, a period when the Athenian curriculum became the basis for the instruction given by Alexandrian teachers as diverse as Ammonius, Olympiodorus, and the author of the later sixth-century *Anonymous Prolegomena to Platonic Philosophy*.[62]

A similar (but less clearly illustrated) process unfolded with medical education. A range of competing centers thrived in the fourth century, most notably the school of Zeno of Cyprus, which produced Julian's celebrated physician Oribasius of Pergamum, among others.[63] While Zeno's student Magnus of Nisibis did teach in a public classroom in Alexandria, Eunapius mentions intellectual descendants of Zeno who were active in places as diverse as Asia Minor and Gaul.[64] Like fourth-century philosophy, fourth-century medicine had no clear and unquestioned center.

This had changed by the later fifth century. Alexandria not only came to produce the period's most celebrated physicians but, like Athens, it enjoyed such a dominant position that it came to shape the way that medicine was taught.[65] Like the Athenian philosophical curriculum, the Alexandrian medical curriculum consisted of eleven works of Hippocrates and fifteen or sixteen treatises of Galen, read in a

---

[60] Themistius (*Orationes*, 20.234–236) describes the teaching of his father as part of an ecumenical system that drew upon Plato, Socrates, and Epicurus, but in which Aristotle was always central. This may give some sense of his own priorities.

[61] On her teaching, see Watts, *City and School*, 192–193.

[62] For the *Anonymous Prolegomena*, see Leendert G. Westerink, ed., *Prolégomènes à la philosophie de Platon* (Paris, 1990).

[63] For the intellectual family of Zeno, see Eunap. *Vit. Soph.* 497–500. For Oribasius in particular, see ibid., 498–99; Eunapius, *Historia*, fr. 8; Philostorgius, *Historia Ecclesiastica*, 7.15; Julian, *Epistolae*, 14.

[64] Eunapius (*Vit. Soph.* 498) calls Magnus's Alexandrian facility a *koinon didaskalion*, probably an individual meeting space. Other descendants of Zeno include Oribasius, Ionicus of Sardis, and Theon (who settled in Gaul).

[65] John Duffy, "Byzantine Medicine in the Sixth and Seventh Centuries: Aspects of Teaching and Practice," *Dumbarton Oaks Papers* 38 (1984) 21–27.

specific order.[66] And, in much the same way that Platonic works were matched to specific philosophical virtues, each of these medical works was chosen to correspond to a particular area of medical instruction like anatomy or physiology.[67] Lecture notes taken by late antique Alexandrian medical students even suggest that the students were taught a particular "Alexandrian mode of exegesis" that systematically approached the texts of Hippocrates in much the same that philosophy students were taught to analyze a work of Plato or Aristotle.[68] It may not be coincidental that the increasing dominance of this "textual" approach to medical education seems to coincide both with the emergence of the term iatrosophist and with a series of critical literary profiles of medical inefficacy.[69]

Legal instruction perhaps best demonstrates how the long fifth century's unique combination of imperial administrative attention and curricular hegemony reshaped teaching. In the Republic and early empire, law was taught somewhat informally. Latin schoolboys famously memorized the Twelve Tables and could receive informal instruction from jurists, but it was not until the reign of Tiberius that any jurist began systematic instruction or charged fees.[70] Paid, systematized legal instruction eventually spread throughout the empire. Between the fourth and sixth centuries, law schools of some sort existed in

---

[66] Ibid., 21–22. The syllabus has been reconstructed by Leendert G. Westerink in appendix 2 of his unpublished paper "Academic Practice about 500: Alexandria," cited by Duffy.

[67] Duffy, "Byzantine Medicine," 22.

[68] For the overlap between methods used in philosophical and medical classrooms see Leendert G. Westerink, "Philosophy and Medicine in Late Antiquity," *Janus* 51 (1964) 169–177. Note, however, the cautions of Mossman Roueché, "Did Medical Students Study Philosophy in Alexandria?," *Bulletin of the Institute of Classical Studies* 43 (1999) 153–169.

[69] Though the term "iatrosophist" is commonly applied to earlier figures like Oribasius and appears in the headings of manuscripts of the physicians Severus (first century CE) and Cassius (second–third centuries CE), the first figure referred to as an iatrosophist by contemporaries is the later fifth-century Alexandrian physician Gessius (Zach. *Ammon.* 1.6; Damasc. *Vit. Isid.* 128). For criticism of iatrosophists, see, for example, Sophronius, *Narratio miraculorum sanctorum Cyri et Joannis*, miracle 30.

[70] Justinian, *Digesta Iustiniani Augusti*, 1.2.49, in *Corpus iuris civilis*, ed. Paul Krueger, Theodor Mommsen, et al. (Berlin, 1872), vol. 1. For discussion of the evolution of Roman legal education see Clyde Pharr, "Roman Legal Education," *Classical Journal* 39 (1939) 257–270. For Late Antiquity in particular note the concise but extremely helpful discussion of Caroline Humfress, "Law Schools," in *Late Antiquity: A Guide to the Post-Classical World*, ed. Glen W. Bowersock et al. (Cambridge, Mass., 1999) 540–541.

Alexandria, Antioch, Autun, Caesarea, Carthage, Marseilles, Narbonne, and Toulouse as well Berytus, Constantinople and Rome, the three major centers of late Roman legal education.[71] The spread of legal education in this period had much to do with the promise of positions in imperial administration that awaited many graduates.[72]

Although legal education spread widely there is evidence that nearly all of the intellectual and textual diversity once included in the informal curriculum of the early imperial period had disappeared. Before Justinian's great reform of the curriculum in 533, students used six out of the "two thousand books" that existed and read approximately sixty thousand of the three million lines of text written by jurists across a four-year course of study.[73] As in the medical and philosophical schools, the selections of material and the order in which it was presented was apparently standardized and taught in the same sequence throughout the empire.[74] Unlike the medical and philosophical schools, however, the number of law schools, teachers, and publicly funded positions grew even as diversity within the curriculum declined.[75] In this case, the standardization of the curriculum seems to have been a product of quickly growing demand for trained lawyers.

CENTRIFUGAL FORCES AND THE END OF ANCIENT EDUCATION

For most of antiquity, a desire to enter into and function within high society had driven the pursuit of literary education. The *paideia* that educated men possessed established the rules for elite interaction. *Paideia* could secure one an invitation to a dinner party, an offer of hospitality when visiting a new city, or a productive literary relationship. While it served as antiquity's most important social currency, a literary education was difficult to monetize and did not lead to secure

---

[71] For this list see Humfress, "Law Schools," 541. One should add Antioch to it on the basis of Libanius, *Ep.* 433.

[72] Justinian, *Institutiones Justiniani*, praef. 7, in Krueger and Mommsen, *Corpus iuris civilis*, vol. 1. This passage will be discussed further below.

[73] Justinian, *Constitutio omnem*, 1 (trans. Alan Watson, ed., *The Digest of Justinian* [Philadelphia, 2009]).

[74] Ibid.

[75] Libanius (*Or.* 48.22), for example, complained about the rapid growth of legal education in the fourth century. In 533, Justinian felt compelled to close all law schools aside from those in Rome, Constantinople, and Berytus (*Const. omnem* 7).

employment.[76] This changed with the dramatic government expansion of the fourth century. As imperial officials superintended the opening of administrative positions to members of the vast provincial elite, the empire's grammarians and sophists became important gatekeepers. This new reality distorted Roman education. With increased imperial attention came greater regulation, more resources to build and fund large intellectual centers like those in Alexandria and Constantinople, and a set of incentives that increased demand for the more popular disciplines like grammar, rhetoric, and law. The decreased emphasis upon philosophical and medical teaching in major centers like Constantinople opened the door for places such as Athens or Alexandria to position themselves as leading centers for the study of less popular disciplines.

Each of these realities, however, depended greatly upon the cultural and political integrity of the Roman Empire. The twenty-five classrooms of Alexandria could comfortably seat perhaps thirty students each, the large theater on the site could seat hundreds more, and, because teachers and students took turns using these spaces, the entire complex could probably effectively educate well more than a thousand students at a time. Alexandria was a large city, but a paying student population of this size included many, many students who came from elsewhere in the empire.[77] Other prominent centers saw similar influxes of non-native students. As the case of Augustine shows, even the schools of medium-sized cities like Thagaste needed to serve ambitious students who hoped to move on to somewhere bigger and better.

The centrifugal forces that pulled at the Mediterranean world in the later fifth century disrupted much of the social and political infrastructure that supported this educational edifice. Within the eastern empire, the bureaucracy continued to pull students from the schools into imperial service, a practice that, under Justinian, led to even more imperial interest in the functioning of schools. In fact, Justinian wrote that one of the impulses behind the creation of the legal curriculum outlined in the *Institutes* was his hope that when students "have completed [their] course of study, covering the whole field of law, [they] may be able to govern the portions of our empire which are entrusted to

---

[76] On the social significance of *paideia* in late antiquity see Peter R. L. Brown, *Power and Persuasion in Late Antiquity* (Madison, 1992) 35–36.

[77] In the 470s alone, we know of Alexandrian students who traveled to the city from Syria, Palestine, Asia Minor, and Italy.

[them]."[78] The *Institutes* thus aimed primarily to make law students better civil servants.[79] Although they did not attract the same level of direct imperial intervention, rhetorical and grammatical teaching continued to thrive in the East well into the sixth century.[80]

As the Roman world lost control of increasing amounts of territory in the West, however, the people living in those areas were cut off from the imperial system and the explicit rewards it tied to schooling. The law schools operating in Autun and Narbonne during the time of Ausonius certainly closed in the fifth century, as did the rhetorical school at which Ausonius once worked. So, presumably, did the medical school where Ausonius's father once taught.[81] Once Gaul passed from Roman control, both the imperial funds supporting the teachers and the imperial opportunities awaiting their students went away. Most of the schools likely did too.

In Italy, one sees a slightly different phenomenon. The political separation of Italy from the East in the later fifth and early sixth century led to a cultural separation as well. In the fourth century, Italians had strongly developed intellectual ties with teachers in the Greek East. Libanius and Symmachus appear to have corresponded sporadically,[82] and the Roman senator (and urban prefect) Praetextatus appears to have had quick access to contemporary Greek philosophical paraphrases written by Themistius.[83] These sorts of interactions continued into the fifth century. Italian intellectuals connected to eastern Platonic circles turn up in Damascius's *Life of Isidore* as important members of the larger Mediterranean philosophical social world.[84] By the 520s, however, this moment had clearly passed. The new reality was one in which Boethius felt compelled to create a fully translated philosophical curriculum that could be accessed textually without direct interaction with a philosophical master.[85] The nature of his project reflects a remarkable pessimism

---

[78] Just. *Inst.* praef. 7.

[79] One should, however, note that, even with this attention, the competence of civil servants was far from uniform. For discussion see Cribiore, *School of Libanius*, 197–199.

[80] The rhetorical school of Choricius in Gaza is a particularly notable example.

[81] Ausonius, *Parentalia*, 1.

[82] Liban. *Ep.* 1004.

[83] For Praetextatus's translations, see Alan Cameron, *The Last Pagans of Rome* (New York, 2011) 542–544.

[84] For discussion, see Watts, "Doctrine, Anecdote, and Action," 240–241.

[85] On the initial plans for translations of these works see Boethius, *2 In de Interpretatione*, 79.9–80.9; and John Marenbon, *Boethius* (Oxford, 2003) 17–42.

about Italy's philosophical vitality in a world where intellectual contact with the East is greatly restricted. It did, however, preserve the Aristotelian elements of the philosophical curriculum the age of Attila helped create.

Intellectual life in the sixth-century eastern empire was largely unaffected by political fragmentation, but different forces combined to destabilize the philosophical and medical institutions that had dominated in the long fifth century. Some of these are well-known. The emperor Justinian famously shut the Athenian Platonic school in 529, apparently as a response to the school's religious teaching.[86] Philosophy's center of gravity then shifted to Alexandria, but even that city's cultural dominance had begun to falter in the sixth century. The late 520s and early 530s saw the beginnings of a move to translate key elements of the medical and philosophical curricula into Syriac. Sergius of Reshaina, the Alexandrian-trained physician at the heart of this project, had a far more optimistic view about the future of high-level instruction than did Boethius.[87] His students would still read Aristotle in the original Greek, but the commentaries they used and the instruction that a professor gave them were both to be in Syriac. The effect of this on Alexandria was likely negligible at first, but Syria and Palestine had long been places that regularly sent students to Alexandria. Sergius's program was the first step in a longer process through which medical and philosophical training moved into Syriac centers of learning in Nisibis and Qenneshre.[88] This shift drew students away from Alexandria and separated the city from an area that had once looked to it for cultural leadership. However, as in Italy, when these Syriac-speaking scholars moved out of the Alexandrian cultural orbit, they carried with them curricula and interpretative frameworks that took shape during the long fifth century.

The period between the death of Constantius II and the accession of Justinian saw the needs of a growing Roman bureaucracy catalyze

---

[86] Malalas, *Chronicle*, 18.47; cf. Watts, *City and School*, 128–138.

[87] On Sergius, see Henri Hugonnard-Roche, *La logique d'Aristote du grec au syriaque*, Textes et Traditions 9 (Paris, 2004) 23–37; and John Watt, "Commentary and Translation in Syriac Aristotelian Scholarship: Sergius to Baghdad," *Journal of Late Antique Religion and Culture*, forthcoming.

[88] For Nisibis, see Adam Becker, *Fear of God and the Beginnings of Wisdom: The School of Nisibis and the Development of Scholastic Culture in Late Antique Mesopotamia* (Philadelphia, 2006). For Qenneshre, see John Watt, "A Portrait of John Bar Aphthonia, Founder of the Monastery of Qenneshre," in *Portraits of Spiritual Authority*, ed. Jan W. Drijvers and John Watt (Leiden, 1999) 155–169.

a remaking of educational life in the Mediterranean. The significance of literary education became less clear as students pursued it both for its cultural value and as a possible avenue through which to secure imperial appointments. Imperial interest in, funding for, and regulation of teachers and their students also changed the dynamics of a cultural world in which teaching had previously been primarily a local affair. The fifth century also saw the leveling out of the diversity of texts and curricula taught in the empire. Perversely, these paired processes of centralization and systematization made it easier for the core contents of these curricula to survive the centrifugal forces that buffeted the Mediterranean. As such, the long fifth century helped prepare Roman intellectual culture for survival in a post-Roman world.

22: REAL AND IMAGINED GEOGRAPHY

Scott F. Johnson

In the year 363, following Julian's disastrous eastern campaign, the new emperor Jovian ceded the northern Mesopotamian city of Nisibis to the Persians. The Syriac poet Ephrem was one of the Roman subjects forced to abandon the city and move westward, inside the redrawn border of the Roman Empire, to the city of Edessa (modern Urfa in southeastern Turkey).[1] There is no evidence that the poet ever traveled beyond these two cities. However, when Ephrem's sixth-century Syriac biographer composed his *Life*, he introduced a wide range of travels to his career, saying that Ephrem traveled to the Council of Nicaea, to Egypt to meet with Apa Bishoi, and to Cappadocia to meet with Basil of Caesarea.[2] The long fifth century – between Ephrem's death and the reimagined Ephrem in the *Life* – was a formative period for the geographical imagination of Christian writers. In both the East and the West, a heightened interest in physical movement and travel in the Mediterranean developed between the fourth and sixth centuries. This interest formed a component of how Late Antiquity incorporated the familiar Mediterranean *oikoumene*, or known world, into a universal Christian vision of the cosmos. As geographical awareness became more prominent during this period two things happened: the number of texts

---

[1] On the capitulation of Nisibis, see Ammianus Marcellinus, *Rerum gestarum libri*, 25.9 ed. and trans. John C. Rolfe Cambridge, 1935. Jan Willem Drijvers ("Ammianus, Jovian, and the Syriac Julian Romance," *Journal of Late Antiquity* 4 [2011] 280–297) provides a comparison of Ammianus's account with that of the (very different) Syriac *Julian Romance*.

[2] Joseph P. Amar, ed. and trans., *The Syriac Vita Tradition of Ephrem the Syrian*, 2 vols. (Leuven, 2011).

dealing with travel increased;[3] and, importantly, the shape of the physical world became a fundamental literary metaphor for the organization of knowledge itself.

A natural tendency might be to attempt to link this rise in geographical awareness in literature to the advent of Christian pilgrimage and on-the-ground tourism in the Holy Land. However, a remarkable fact about this period is that not a single pilgrimage text in any Christian language (Latin, Greek, Syriac, Coptic, Armenian) survives specifically from the fifth century. Thus there is a curious gap in the survival of pilgrimage narratives *exactly when we expect such texts to be in vogue*. This gap requires some interpretation. What we find is that geography, both real and imagined, shows up in a diverse array of other genres and that it permeated the thought and writing of the period. So, while it proves impossible to trace the history of pilgrimage literature in the fifth century, there may be other avenues open for discussing the emergence of a grand vision of Christian geography, clearly in effect at the end of our period.

LETTERS

One of the genres that stands in for pilgrimage during the fifth century is the letter. Right at the beginning of the fifth century come two of the most celebrated letters of Late Antiquity, both describing journeys made in the eastern Mediterranean. These letters show flourishes of literary skill, as well as an acquaintance with the tools of novelistic writing, and are examples of how geography could be used in a highly literary fashion. One of the letters was by Synesius of Cyrene, in Greek to his brother, describing a perilous sea voyage from Alexandria to Cyrene (*Ep.* 5), and the other is Jerome's letter in Latin to Eustochium, on the occasion of her mother Paula's death (*Ep.* 108; *Epitaphium Paulae*). Synesius wrote his letter in the year 401,[4] and Jerome wrote to Eustochium in 404.

Synesius's letter is an example of how geography could conjure certain emotions and images, contrary to (even in place of) description

---

[3] Of course, we have only a sample, perhaps not representative, of what was originally written.

[4] Jacqueline Long, "Dating an Ill-Fated Journey: Synesius, *Ep.* 5," *Transactions of the American Philological Association* 122 (1992) 351–380.

of the physical world and the experience of late antique travel. Synesius is indebted to the image of sea travel portrayed in the Greek novels from the early empire but he was also skilled in the artistic description (*ekphrasis*) of natural phenomena.[5] The dramatic narrative setting of perilous sea travel, from Alexandria to Cyrene dominates *Epistula* 5,[6] even as the precise route of the voyage remains somewhat unclear.[7] A relatively short trip in reality (as Synesius himself comments elsewhere, in *Ep.* 53), this long, mock-epic letter is embroidered with numerous quotations from Homer. He even mentions the emotional impact that reading the *Odyssey* had on him as a schoolboy. The crew is clearly meant to resemble a band of pirates, except with the twist that they are predominantly Jews and choose to observe the Sabbath in the middle of a storm. In this point, at least, one might think the litterateur yields to the social realities of his own day, but even then the narrative seems to parody both the story of Jonah and of Jesus' calming of the Sea of Galilee (see Matt. 8:23–27). Finally, in closing this letter to his brother Euoptius, Synesius comments that his story is more enjoyable for retaining both tragic and comic elements, thereby highlighting his literary self-awareness (and causing us to question whether any of it really happened). The typical "happily ever after" aura of his micro-novel's conclusion is punctuated by a tongue-in-cheek imperative to avoid sea travel at all costs.

Jerome's *Epistula* 108 to Eustochium is bound up with Jerome's own biography and status as Roman inhabitant of the Holy Land.[8] In this way perhaps, Jerome's letter differs from Synesius's, given that the historicity of the events is a prominent theme, not least in constructing the close friendship between himself and Paula, which lasted for over twenty years. Jerome recounts the pilgrimage-inspired travels that Eustochium, Paula, and he made together to and within the Holy

---

[5] Xaver Simeon, "Untersuchungen zu den Briefen des Bischofs Synesios von Kyrene," *Rhetorische Studien* 18 (1933) 62–78. He may have had expertise in ship building as well: see Lionel Casson, "Bishop Synesius' Voyage to Cyrene," *American Neptune* 12 (1952) 294–296; Fik J. Meijer, "The Ship of Bishop Synesius," *International Journal of Nautical Archaeology* 15 (1986) 67–69; and Casson, "Comment on 'The Ship of Bishop Synesius' (*IJNA* 15:67–9)," *IJNA* 16 (1987) 67.

[6] Antonio Garzya, ed., *Synesii Cyrenensis epistulae* (Rome, 1979).

[7] For an attempt to trace it, see Yaacov Kahanov, "The Voyage of Synesius," *Journal of Navigation* 59 (2006) 435–444.

[8] For what follows, see esp. Andrew Cain, "Jerome's *Epitaphium Paulae*: Hagiography, Pilgrimage, and the Cult of Saint Paula," *Journal of Early Christian Studies* 18 (2010) 105–139.

Land during Eustochium's youth. Jerome also says explicitly that he is not going to write a comprehensive travel narrative but only mention places named in Holy Scripture.[9] The three arrived in Jerusalem, by two separate routes, in 385 (just a year or two after Egeria). Within three years they had built at Bethlehem several buildings probably financed by Paula: a monastery for Jerome and the monks; a nearby convent, including a chapel; and a hostel for pilgrims.[10] In an earlier letter from 403, Jerome says that he and Paula were receiving crowds of monks from "India, Persia, and Ethiopia."[11] One goal of *Ep.* 108 seems to have been to cement the significance of Bethlehem over and against Jerusalem. There is for Paula an even greater sense of "going native" than for Egeria: whereas Egeria merely notes the presence of Greek, Syriac, and Latin in the Holy Week liturgy in Jerusalem,[12] Paula actually learns enough Hebrew from Jerome to chant the Psalms without an accent.[13]

Of course, the values Paula possesses in this letter are precisely the values Jerome espoused: scholarship, asceticism, orthodoxy. She also demonstrates a tactile approach to holy sites that is bold for the age: Paula fervently kisses the place where Jesus' body was laid, "as when a parched man, having waited a long while, at last comes to water."[14] This has been called evidence of a "sacramental imagination,"[15] but one might also think of it as a spatiotemporal imagination, or a metonymic imagination, making a specific place, the tomb, stand in for Jesus Christ himself. In a striking example of such metonymy, Paula is buried in the grotto adjoining the cave where Jesus was born, explicitly signaling

[9] Jerome, *Epistula* 108.8.1, in *Sancti Eusebii Hieronymi epistulae*, ed. Isidor Hilberg and Margit Kamptner (Vienna, 1996).

[10] *Ep.* 108.14.3–4, ed. Hilberg and Kamptner; Cain, "*Epitaphium Paulae*," 111–112.

[11] *Ep.* 107.2, ed. Hilberg and Kamptner; Cain, "*Epitaphium Paulae*," 112.

[12] Egeria, *Itinerarium*, 47.3–4, in *Égérie, Journal de voyage: Itinéraire*, ed. Pierre Maraval (Paris, 2002).

[13] *Ep.* 108.26, ed. Hilberg and Kamptner; Cain, "*Epitaphium Paulae*," 122. On Jerome and Hebrew, see Adam Kamesar, *Jerome, Greek Scholarship, and the Hebrew Bible: A Study of the "Quaestiones Hebraicae in Genesim"* (Oxford, 1993); Stefan Rebenich, "Jerome: The '*Vir Trilinguis*' and the 'Hebraica Veritas,'" *Vigiliae Christianae* 47 (1993) 50–77; Michael Graves, *Jerome's Hebrew Philology: A Study Based on His Commentary on Jeremiah* (Leiden, 2007); Gorge K. Hasselhoff, "Revising the Vulgate: Jerome and His Jewish Interlocutors," *Zeitschrift für Religions und Geistesgeschichte* 64 (2012) 209–221.

[14] *Ep.* 108.9.2, ed. Hilberg and Kamptner; Cain, "*Epitaphium Paulae*," 118. Cf. John 4:14, Rev. 21:6.

[15] Francine Cardman, "The Rhetoric of Holy Places: Palestine in the Fourth Century," *Studia Patristica* 17 (1982) 23, cited by Cain, "*Epitaphium Paulae*," 119.

that her resurrection is linked to the life of Christ (cf. Phil. 3:10–11). The attitudes of wealthy western Christians to the sites of Jesus' life seem somewhat more cavalier in the fifth century than in the fourth: Paula and Jerome's shared confidence in their role as benefactors and guardians of a holy site lends a cultic significance to Paula's own memory.

ENCYCLOPEDIC TOPOGRAPHY

To understand such letters in their literary context, the reader must have some awareness of the boom in Christian pilgrimage to the Holy Land that occurred during and immediately following the reign of Constantine the Great (306–337).[16] The *Bordeaux Pilgrim* from 333 is the first surviving account of such a pilgrimage, a text that follows the Roman *itinerarium* genre closely, while incorporating numerous sites of Christian devotion, mostly stemming from the Old Testament.[17] Egeria's famous pilgrimage to the Holy Land comes from the latter half of the century, likely in 381–384.[18] Depending on how representative she was of her own time, Egeria's invaluable narrative testifies to the emergence of a much larger pilgrimage circuit, now including Sinai and Egypt, as well as Edessa in Mesopotamia, Seleukeia-on-the-Kalakadnos in Isauria, and Constantinople.[19] She was also clearly enmeshed in

---

[16] Edward D. Hunt, *Holy Land Pilgrimage in the Later Roman Empire, AD 312–460* (Oxford, 1982); Kenneth G. Holum, "Hadrian and St. Helena: Imperial Travel and the Origins of Christian Holy Land Pilgrimage," in *The Blessings of Pilgrimage*, ed. Robert G. Ousterhout (Urbana, 1990) 66–81; John Wilkinson, "Jewish Holy Places and the Origins of Christian Pilgrimage," in ibid., 41–53; Pierre Maraval, "The Earliest Phase of Christian Pilgrimage in the Near East (before the 7th Century)," *Dumbarton Oaks Papers* 56 (2002) 63–74.

[17] The standard edition of the *Bordeaux Pilgrim* can be found in Paul Geyer and Otto Cuntz, *Itineraria et alia geographica* (Turnhout, 1965). See Jaś Elsner, "The *Itinerarium Burdigalense*: Politics and Salvation in the Geography of Constantine's Empire," *Journal of Roman Studies* 90 (2000) 181–195; and on the Old Testament sites, Wilkinson, "Jewish Holy Places."

[18] Paul Devos, "La date du Voyage d'Égérie," *Analecta Bollandiana* 85 (1967) 165–194.

[19] Scott F. Johnson, "Reviving the Memory of the Apostles: Apocryphal Tradition and Travel Literature in Late Antiquity," in *Revival and Resurgence in Christian History*, ed. Kate Cooper and Jeremy Gregory (Woodbridge, 2008) 10–20; Benet Salway, "Travel, *Itineraria*, and *Tabellaria*," in *Travel and Geography in the Roman Empire*, ed. Colin Adams and Ray Laurence (London, 2001) 22–66.

the rise of monastic foundations during this period, though perhaps not a nun herself.[20] Both of these pilgrims engaged in a pattern of geographical writing that was deeply indebted to Roman models but which became flexible enough to form a completely new genre, and one that is subsequently represented in Latin by numerous texts through the whole medieval period.[21] Nevertheless, despite this surge in Holy Land pilgrimage and in Christian itineraries, the genre of written pilgrimage following Egeria does not reemerge until the much more developed work of the *Piacenza Pilgrim* in 570.

What does appear in the fifth century are Holy Land topographical registers, not pilgrimage narratives but instead catalogs of sites and relics. These correspond, in form at least, to the secular *notitiae* ("accountings") and *laterculi* ("land registers") that seem to stem from an obsessive desire in the Roman provincial administration of the fifth century to catalog the topography of the various regions and cities of the empire. This rich literary tradition includes the *Notitia dignitatum* (Accounting of Offices; East, ca. 394–395 and West, ca. 420–430),[22] the *Notitia Galliarum* (Accounting of [the regions of] Gaul; ca. 400),[23] the *Libellus de regionibus urbis Romae* (Handbook to the Quarters of the City of Rome; late fourth cent.),[24] the *Notitia urbis Alexandrinae* (Accounting of the City of Alexandria),[25] the *Notitia urbis Constantinopolitanae* (Accounting of the City of Constantinople; ca. 425–430),[26] and the *Laterculus Polemii Silvii* (Land Register of Polemius Silvius; 448–449).[27] These

---

[20] Hagith Sivan, "Who Was Egeria? Piety and Pilgrimage in the Age of Gratian," *Harvard Theological Review* 81 (1988) 59–72; Hagith Sivan, "Holy Land Pilgrimage and Western Audiences: Some Reflections on Egeria and Her Circle," *Classical Quarterly* 38 (1988) 528–535.

[21] Scott F. Johnson, "Travel, Cartography, and Cosmology," in *The Oxford Handbook of Late Antiquity*, ed. Scott F. Johnson (Oxford, 2012) 578–579.

[22] In Otto Seeck, ed., *Notitia dignitatum: Accedunt notitia urbis Constantinopolitanae et Laterculi provinciarum* (Berlin, 1876) 1–102 and 103–225 (East and West).

[23] In Seeck, *Notitia dignitatum*, 261–274.

[24] In Arvast Nordh, ed., *Libellus de regionibus urbis Romae* (Lund, 1949).

[25] Michael the Syrian, *Chronicle*, 5.3 (ed. Jean-Baptiste Chabot, *Chronique de Michel le Syrien, patriarche Jacobite d'Antioche [1166–1199]*, 4 vols. [Paris 1899–1924] 1.114–115 [lower text] and 1.72–73); see Peter M. Fraser, "A Syriac '*Notitia Urbis Alexandrinae*,'" *JEA* 37 (1951) 103–108.

[26] In Seeck, *Notitia dignitatum*, 229–243; trans. John Matthews as "The *Notitia Urbis Constantinopolitanae*," in *Two Romes: Rome and Constantinople in Late Antiquity*, ed. Lucy Grig and Gavin Kelly (Oxford, 2012) 81–115.

[27] Ed. Theodor Mommsen, in MGH AA 9.1: 511–551; Seeck, *Notitia dignitatum*, 254–260.

secular texts all show that geography served as a primary organizing principle for various types of content. The Christian analogs to the *notitiae* are thus topographical mini-encyclopedias of specific regions of Jerusalem and its environs in the fifth century. (The form of such texts was soon copied and applied to other sites of Christian tourism, notably Rome.)[28]

The Latin text known as the *Breviarius of Jerusalem* in its original version dates to about 400, but was enlarged at least twice around 500.[29] At heart it is a short, focused work centered on the Church of the Anastasis and the shrine of the True Cross. It includes mentions of well-known New Testament themes of pilgrim interest, such as the stone with which Stephen was stoned and the pinnacle on which Satan placed Jesus to tempt him, but it also includes Old Testament objects, such as the horn with which David was anointed. In this mode of "stacking" or "doubling" famous motifs or objects from all biblical periods onto one geographical location, it resembles closely Egeria's pilgrimage narrative from the 380s, as well as the later *Piacenza Pilgrim* from 570.[30] Whereas in its short form the text could easily have served as a hand list of relics, to be posted or distributed on site, the longer versions show an expected literary tendency to embellish and add layers of detail, suggesting perhaps the process of combining multiple textual sources into a single, authoritative, and significantly longer list. That this embellishment occurred between 400 and 500 indicates the interest in pilgrimage which continued to grow.

In the middle of the century another Latin topography appears in the form of a letter addressed to a "Faustus," which is usually attributed to Eucherius, bishop of Lyon (ca. 430–ca. 450).[31] This letter was known to authors in the seventh and eighth centuries, such as Adomnán and Bede. It quotes Jerome's *Ep.* 129 to Dardanus, which is a survey of the Judean landscape, as well as Jerome's translation of Eusebius's *Onomasticon*, the *Liber locorum*.[32] It also demonstrates a knowledge of Hegesippus, through his Latin translation of Josephus, and, possibly, certain classical

---

[28] See the texts in Geyer and Cuntz, *Itineraria et alia geographica*, 1.281–343.

[29] Ibid., 1.109–112.

[30] Scott F. Johnson, "Apostolic Geography: The Origins and Continuity of an Hagiographic Habit," *DOP* 64 (2010) 13–14.

[31] In Geyer and Cuntz, *Itineraria et alia geographica*, 1.237–243.

[32] On the *Liber locorum*, see R. Steven Notley and Ze'ev Safrai, Eusebius, *Onomasticon: The Place Names of Divine Scripture, Including the Latin Edition of Jerome* (Boston, 2005). On Jerome's geographical imagination, see Susan Weingarten, *The Saint's Saint: Hagiography and Geography in Jerome* (Leiden, 2005).

Latin authors such as Pomponius Mela and Tacitus.[33] Eucherius is very specific about distances, though he never discusses way stations, hostels, or similar travelers' facilities. His view of Judea and Palestine is centered on Jerusalem, and all the spokes of the wheel of his vision are described from that hub. He shares with pilgrim narratives an interest not just in holy relics and sites from the Bible but also in living holy men and women and the monasteries that housed them. The combination of these contemporary observations on the emergent late antique Holy Land – with a bookishness that encompassed all the important early Christian scholarly writings on geography – is typical of this transitional period when the Christian biblical past was being integrated with the Christian imperial present.[34] Later, particularly after the Arab conquest, this united vision of Christian past and present became formative for writers in the West, such as Adomnán on Iona (Scotland) and Bede in Northumbria, who never set foot in the Holy Land.

Finally, at the beginning of the sixth century, around 518, comes Theodosius's *Topography of the Holy Land*, which provides a litmus test between Egeria (381–384) and the *Piacenza Pilgrim* (570) for just how developed the local industry of touristic pilgrimage had become during the fifth century.[35] The first part of this text is organized around various short itineraries out from Jerusalem in one-way journeys (i.e., not circuits). These spokes often overlap, especially in the north in Galilee. There is no thematic organization: New Testament and Old Testament sites are randomly juxtaposed, and numerous errors of both topography/onomastics and biblical citation are made. Theodosius notes that there were twenty-four churches on the Mount of Olives alone, which (if true in his time) shows just how far the Christian monumentalization of Jerusalem had come in less than two hundred years: the *Bordeaux Pilgrim* (333) mentions only four churches in the whole region (including Mamre), all built by Constantine. When Theodosius turns to the chief holy sites of Jesus' passion the scale gets much smaller – he begins measuring in paces rather than miles. This has a focalizing effect that is

---

[33] Pomponius Mela's *Chorographia* seems to have been used by the collator of the *Antonine Itinerary* at the end of the third century: Salway, "Travel, *Itineraria*, and *Tabellaria*," 184–185. It was the dominant literary text in Latin for regional description during the Roman Empire: for editions see Alain Silberman, ed., *Pomponius Mela: Chorographie* (Paris, 1988); also Kai Brodersen, ed., *Pomponius Mela: Kreuzfahrt durch die alte Welt* (Darmstadt, 1994); Frank E. Romer, trans., *Pomponius Mela's Description of the World* (Ann Arbor, 1998).

[34] Compare Elsner, "*Itinerarium Burdigalense*," for the earlier period.

[35] Geyer and Cuntz, *Itineraria et alia geographica*, 1.115–125.

not employed at this granular a level in earlier texts. There is, however, no linear organization to his collection of lists. In the end it is a jumble of information culled from various sources. This motley presentation is exemplified by the second half of the text: after its focused discussion of the Golgotha/Anastasis area, the text inexplicably jumps from Jerusalem to the Black Sea, then down to Memphis in Egypt, up to Cappadocia, back to Jerusalem, then to "Arabia," then to "Armenia," then to Ephesus, then to Sinai, then to Mesopotamia and Persia, then back to a section on Asia Minor wherein it compiles a random assortment of cities and distances between them. In the middle of all of this zigzagging come interesting digressions, but they are completely irrelevant to the topographical organization: a notice on the monument to Jesus' baptism in the Jordan, a story criticizing the career of the *cubicularius* Urbicius (personal attaché to the emperor; fl. 470–490),[36] and a mention of the feast of the Finding of the True Cross. Theodosius thus exemplifies certain aspects of the geographical literary tradition and not others: his emphasis on touristic sites and the presence of monks and churches is in line with what one reads in, for instance, the earlier *Life of Melania the Younger* (in Greek and Latin), the contemporary *Life of Peter the Iberian* (in Syriac), and, later, the *Piacenza Pilgrim* (in Latin), but the notional organization is less clear in Theodosius than in those texts and is notably less route-oriented than the *Bordeaux Pilgrim* or Egeria.

The link between travel, infrastructure, and the accumulation of information on the page is demonstrated above all during this period in the famous Peutinger Table, a secular document not at all connected with pilgrimage and the Holy Land. The Peutinger Table is the only world map to survive from Greco-Roman civilization and dates (at least, on the traditional date) to the fifth century, extant today in a medieval copy from about 1200.[37] Just how typical this map was of Roman mapping techniques, the mind of the late antique geographer,

---

[36] *Prosopography of the Later Roman Empire*, 2.1188 "Urbicius 1."

[37] On the date of the surviving copy, see Richard Talbert, *Rome's World: The Peutinger Map Reconsidered* (Cambridge, 2010) 83–84. For images of the map, see the edition in Ekkehard Weber, *Tabula Peutingeriana: Codex Vindobonensis 324, Vollst. Faks-Ausg. im Originalformat* (Graz, 1976); along with digital color photographs taken in 2000 and presented at http://www.cambridge.org/us/talbert/. Emily Albu has argued for a Carolingian date for the original Peutinger Table: see Emily Albu, "Imperial Geography and the Medieval Peutinger Map," *Imago Mundi* 57 (2005) 136–148; and Emily Albu, "Rethinking the Peutinger Map," in *Cartography in Antiquity and the Middle Ages: Fresh Perspectives, New Methods*, ed. Richard Talbert and Richard W. Unger (Leiden, 2008) 111–119.

or of a secular versus Christian worldview, are all fundamental yet contested topics. Two scholars who have recently studied the map in detail, Richard Talbert and Benet Salway, both conclude that the map is more likely to have been ornamental than functional (contrary to traditional thinking that the map was rolled up like a scroll and used for travel in the field).[38] Talbert has argued that, while certain physical details of the map are surprisingly accurate,[39] the map was designed "for the accomplishment of primarily noncartographic ends."[40] It creates, in his words, "an arresting impression," particularly in its amassing of detail and in its "exquisite compactness."[41] Moreover, contrary to the strictly itinerary-oriented view of the Peutinger Table advocated by, for example, Kai Brodersen – who would like to read this complex map as merely an *itinerarium pictum*, "an illustrated itinerary"[42] – Benet Salway has explored how "a certain level of spatial awareness in more than one dimension is often inherent in the structure of these texts," despite being structured as mere lists.[43] The networks of routes – not just the

---

[38] Talbert, in the most thorough modern study of the Peutinger Table to date (*Rome's World*), argues that the map should be placed at least a century earlier than normally thought – back to the Tetrarchic period around 300 – and that it was possibly set up in the apse of an imperial reception hall (*aula*) as a symbol of the reach of Roman authority in the *oikoumene* (ibid., 144–145). A critical summary of the functionalist view can be found at ibid., 5. See also Richard Talbert, "Konrad Miller, Roman Cartography, and the Lost Western End of the Peutinger Map," in *Historische Geographie der alten Welt: Grundlagen, Erträge, Perspektiven*, ed. Ulrich Fellmeth, Peter Guyot, and Holger Sonnabend (Hildesheim, 2007) 353–366; Richard Talbert, "Peutinger's Roman Map: The Physical Landscape Framework," in *Wahrnehmung und Erfassung geographischer Räume in der Antike*, ed. Michael Rathmann (Mainz am Rhein, 2007) 220–230; Richard Talbert, "Rome's Marble Plan and Peutinger's Map: Continuity in Cartographic Design," *Althistorisch-Epigraphische Studien (Österreichischen Gesellschaft für Archäologie)* 5 (2005) 627–634; Richard Talbert, "Cartography and Taste in Peutinger's Roman Map," in *Space in the Roman World: Its Perception and Presentation*, ed. Richard Talbert and Kai Brodersen (Münster, 2004) 113–141.

[39] Talbert, "Peutinger's Roman Map," 224–226, esp. 224.

[40] Talbert, *Rome's World*, 122.

[41] Ibid., 154.

[42] For linear (or "hodological") thinking, see Pietro Janni, *La mappa e il periplo: Cartografia antica e spazio odologico* (Rome, 1984); Brodersen, *Pomponius Mela*, 59–68, 268–285; Kai Brodersen, "Review Article: Mapping (In) the Ancient World," *JRS* 94 (2004) 183–190; and, for Christian texts, Blake Leyerle, "Landscape as Cartography in Early Christian Pilgrimage Narratives," *Journal of the American Academy of Religion* 64 (1999) 119–143.

[43] B. Salway, "The Nature and Genesis of the Peutinger Map," *Imago Mundi* 57 (2005) 119–135; Salway, "Travel, *Itineraria*, and *Tabellaria*"; Benet Salway, "Sea and River Travel in the Roman Itinerary Literature," in Talbert and Brodersen, *Space in the*

routes themselves – that are visualized on the Peutinger Table may thus offer a clue as to how late Roman travelers, Christian or not, thought about the relationship between regions and directionality. This comes into focus especially as the artistry of such geographical compilations is acknowledged as a starting point.

POETRY, TRANSLATION, AND EDUCATION

The fifth century is framed by two Latin translations of the most famous Greek verse geographical work from the early empire, the *Periegesis* (lit. "leading around" or "description") of Dionysius Periegetes. These translations (both also in verse) were written by Avienus in the late fourth century, and by Priscian Caesariensis (the grammarian) in early sixth-century Constantinople.[44] Avienus also wrote his own geographical work, influenced not by pilgrimage texts but by the time-honored Greek *periplous* (lit. "sailing around") genre, called the *Ora maritima* (Coastlines).[45] Related in topic, though not in content or style, is the slightly earlier *Expositio totius mundi et gentium* (A Description of the Whole World and Its Nations), seemingly a very empire-focused work – at least, in its goal of cataloging the merits of each Roman province – though, curiously, it begins in the mythical Far East with peoples and countries who often dwelled at or beyond the boundaries of Roman geographical knowledge.[46] In fact, this combination of workmanlike data with imaginative reconstruction proves to have

Roman World, 43–96; Benet Salway, "The Perception and Description of Space in Roman Itineraries," in *Wahrnehmung und Erfassung geographischer Räume in der Antike*, ed. M. Rathmann (Mainz am Rhein, 2007) 181–209; Benet Salway, "Putting the World in Order: Mapping in Roman Texts," in *Ancient Perspectives: Maps and Their Place in Mesopotamia, Egypt, Greece, and Rome*, ed. Richard Talbert (Chicago, 2012) 193–234; Benet Salway, "There but Not There: Constantinople in the *Itinerarium Burdigalense*," in Grig and Kelly, *Two Romes*, 293–324.

44 Avienus: Paul van de Woestijne, ed., *La Descriptio orbis terrae d'Avienus* (Bruges, 1961). Priscian: Paul Van de Woestijne, ed., *La Périégèse de Priscien* (Bruges, 1953).

45 In Dietrich Stichtenoth, ed., *Rufus Festus Avienus: Ora maritima* (Darmstadt, 1968); John P. Murphy, trans., *Rufus Festus Avienus: Ora maritima, A Description of the Seacoast from Brittany Round to Massilia* (Chicago, 1977).

46 In Jean Rougé, ed., *Expositio totius mundi et gentium* (Paris, 1966); A. A. Vasiliev, trans., "*Expositio totius mundi*: An Anonymous Geographic Treatise of the Fourth Century A.D.," *Seminarium Kondakovianum* 8 (1936) 1–39. On the borders of the ancient *oikoumene*, see James Romm, *The Edges of the Earth in Ancient Thought: Geography, Exploration, and Fiction* (Princeton, 1992).

been habitual among geographical thinkers in this period and after, perhaps deriving some impetus from the popularity of novelistic literature about Alexander the Great. For instance, we see the resonance of Alexander combined with these aesthetic traits in the Peutinger Table, which at its far eastern end includes the caption, "Hic Alexander responsum accepit usq[ue] quo Alexander" ("Here Alexander was given the [oracular] reply: 'How far, Alexander?'"), emphasizing the link made in Late Antiquity between Alexander's legendary conquests and the limits of geographical knowledge of the East.[47] Avienus also made a Latin translation of the most famous cosmological poem in Greek from the Hellenistic world, the *Phaenomena* (Celestial Bodies) of Aratus. In translating the *Phaenomena*, Avienus stood in an illustrious tradition: as Lactantius notes, both Cicero and Germanicus had done the same.[48]

It is important to emphasize that the connection between geography and cosmology in late antique literature is not simply a vague legacy of Ptolemy's astronomical writings: rather, it stems directly from the educational curriculum of Late Antiquity.[49] In fact, Aratus's *Phaenomena*, whether in its original Greek or in Latin translation, appears in numerous pedagogical contexts in the period. Taking Aratus (and other classical authors like Manilius) as models, many authors of Late Antiquity, in both prose and verse, make no sharp distinction between geographical and cosmological thought. Moreover, they often use geography and cosmology as a organizational framework or container for holding various types of information. Of course, in the sixth century, the standout example is Cosmas Indicopleustes' *Christian Topography*, which comprises ten books of elaborate, polemical, biblicist cosmology – with specific attacks on his fellow Alexandrian John Philoponus – and an evocative eleventh book that includes a natural history of the

---

[47] See also, for the high empire, Grant Parker, *The Making of Roman India: Greek Culture in the Roman World* (Cambridge, 2008).

[48] Lactantius, *Institutiones divinae*, 1.21.38; Cicero, *De oratore*, 1.16. See Gustav Sieg, *De Cicerone, Germanico, Avieno, Arati interpretibus* (Halle an der Saale, 1886). For Aratus: Douglas A. Kidd, ed., *Aratus: Phaenomena* (Cambridge, 1997). For Avienus's translation of Aratus: Jean Soubrian, ed., *Aviénus: Les Phénomènes d'Aratos* (Paris, 1981). For a surviving Latin version of Aratus attributed to Germanicus, see André Le Boeuffle, ed., *Les Phénomènes d'Aratos* (Paris, 1975); a translation can be found in David B. Gain, *The Aratus Ascribed to Germanicus Caesar* (London, 1976). See also the study of Mark D. Possanza, *Translating the Heavens: Aratus, Germanicus, and the Poetics of Latin Translation* (New York, 2004).

[49] See further in Johnson, "Travel, Cartography, and Cosmology."

flora and fauna up and down the Red Sea coast and an account of his purported visit to Taprobane (Sri Lanka) and southern India.[50] Despite its patent idiosyncrasy, the *Christian Topography* is a rich compendium of geographical, cosmological, and natural historical observation.[51] Such texts were not unique to the sixth century: although not as boldly anti-classical or biblicist as Cosmas, the fifth-century authors still show signs of experimentation and the creative organization of real and imagined knowledge.

Perhaps due to the widespread use of Latin translations of Aratus and Dionysius, the literary interest in geography was especially prominent among secular Latin authors of the fifth century. It is notable that both Macrobius and Martianus Capella, though not Christians themselves, had a tremendous impact on medieval Christian worldviews. In prose, Macrobius's *Commentary on the Dream of Scipio* (ca. 430) represents an early example of the trend toward encyclopedic education through a geographical and cosmological framework.[52] The work is presented as a commentary on the conclusion of Cicero's *De republica*, in which Scipio Africanus is taken to heaven to meet his grandfather, who shows Scipio the celestial spheres. The beauty, magnificence, and order of the spheres is designed to teach the younger Scipio that he should value the eternal soul and the divinely ordained universe over physical and temporal things on earth. As regards its geographical section, the *Commentary* is famous for presenting the clearest ancient account of the *klimata* ("climates"; terrestrial zones of latitude), and its medieval exemplars from the ninth century onward often include maps of these zones purportedly reproducing the map Macrobius himself attached to his text (*Commentary* 2.9.7).[53]

---

[50] Wanda Wolska-Conus, ed., *Cosmas Indicopleustès: "Topographie chrétienne,"* 3 vols. (Paris, 1968).

[51] See Wanda Wolska-Conus, *La Topographie chrétienne de Cosmas Indicopleustes: Théologie et science au VIe siècle* (Paris, 1962); Maja Kominko, "The Map of Cosmas, the Albi Map, and the Tradition of Ancient Geography," *Mediterranean Historical Review* 20 (2005) 163–186; Maja Kominko, "New Perspectives on Paradise: The Levels of Reality in Byzantine and Medieval Maps," in *Cartography in Antiquity and the Middle Ages: Fresh Perspectives, New Methods*, ed. Richard Talbert and Richard W. Unger (Leiden, 2008) 139–153.

[52] James Willis, ed., *Macrobius, Saturnalia: Apparatu critico instruxit, In Somnium Scipionis commentarios selecta varietate lectionis* (Stuttgart, 1994); William H. Stahl, trans., *Macrobius: Commentary on the Dream of Scipio* (New York, 1990).

[53] William H. Stahl, "Astronomy and Geography in Macrobius," *TAPhA* 73 (1942) 249–258; Oswald A. W. Dilke, *Greek and Roman Maps* (Baltimore, 1998) 174.

Similar in encyclopedic scope, though unique in terms of genre, is Martianus Capella's *Marriage of Philology and Mercury* (ca. 470).[54] Much about the late antique divisions and categorizations of knowledge can be gleaned from this work, the medieval popularity of which has been well studied.[55] Martianus Capella treats geography in his discussion of geometry. In fact, the personified *Geometria* is, for Martianus, literally the description of the spherical earth, not the mathematical principles deduced from such a study (as it would be defined today). Late antique geographical thought was intimately connected with models of the celestial sphere and the organization of the natural and supernatural worlds. Thus, Martianus Capella's introduction of the subject: "First, I must explain my name [*Geometria*], to counteract any impression of a grimy itinerant coming into this gilded senate chamber of the gods and soiling this gem-bedecked floor with dirt collected on earth. I am called Geometry because I have often traversed and measured out the earth, and I could offer calculations and proofs for its shape, size, positions, regions, and dimensions. There is no portion of the earth's surface that I could not describe from memory."[56] Martianus offers the reader models of celestial movement, but these models are not goals in themselves. Instead, they frame a long discussion of natural wonders and the order of peoples inhabiting the *oikoumene*. Thus "the earth's surface" in the quotation above does not mean geometrical "surface" as we might mathematically conceive it today, but rather all that lives and moves on the literal surface of the earth. Geometry's special pleading about the dirt on her feet gives

---

[54] James Willis, ed., *Martianus Capella* (Leipzig, 1983); William H. Stahl and Richard Johnson, trans., *Martianus Capella: The Marriage of Philology and Mercury* (New York, 1977). See also Danuta Shanzer, *A Philosophical and Literary Commentary on Martianus Capella's* De nuptiis Philologiae et Mercurii, *Book 1* (Berkeley, 1986); William H. Stahl and Richard Johnson, *The Quadrivium of Martianus Capella: Latin Traditions in the Mathematical Sciences, 50 B.C–A.D. 1250* (New York, 1991); Mariken Teeuwen and Sinead O'Sullivan, eds., *Carolingian Scholarship and Martianus Capella* (Turnhout, 2011); Andrew Hicks, "Martianus Capella and the Liberal Arts," in *The Oxford Handbook of Medieval Latin Literature*, ed. Ralph J. Hexter and David Townsend (Oxford, 2012) 307–334.

[55] Muriel Bovey, *Disciplinae Cyclicae: L'organisation du savoir dans l'oeuvre de Martianus Capella* (Trieste, 2003); Brigitte Englisch, *Die Artes liberals im frühen Mittelalter (5.–9. Jh.): Das Quadrivium und der Komputus als Indikatoren für Kontinuität und Erneuerung der exakten Wissenschaften zwischen Antike und Mittelalter* (Stuttgart, 1994).

[56] Martianus Capella 588, in James Willis, ed., *Martianus Capella* (Leipzig, 1983); Stahl and Johnson, *Martianus Capella: The Marriage*, 220.

her away as a "grimy itinerant" naturalist instead of a sterile, detached mathematician.

Thus, it is worth noting that there was a distinction, recognized in the time, between mathematical or geometrical astronomy (Ptolemy) and what has been called "the astronomy of the liberal arts," into which category we might place Macrobius and Martianus Capella, as well as Chalcidius, the fourth-century translator of Plato's *Timaeus*.[57] These three secular or non-Christian Latin writers were all well aware of the geometrical basis of the relationship between geography and astronomy, as it was then practiced, but mathematics for them seems to have been less about what *caused* celestial motion but, rather, evidence of the perfection of celestial and terrestrial creation.[58] For these scholars of the "liberal arts," mathematics (particularly in Ptolemy's *Almagest* and *Geography*) proved above all the harmony of the divine order, and was read alongside Plato, Aristotle, and even Pliny the Elder under the guiding assumption that all of these classical *auctores* were ultimately trying to describe the manifest glory of a Creator.

To take this point further, whatever mathematical knowledge the fifth-century scholars of the Latin liberal arts may have come by, it did not lead them in the direction of observation of planetary and astral events, neither in terms of predictive astrology nor in terms of the practical uses of terrestrial astronomy for specifically Christian purposes, such as the *computus* for Easter or the regulation of the daily office of prayer.[59] Although *computus* is a development in late antique monastic

---

[57] Stephen C. McCluskey, "Martianus and the Traditions of Early Medieval Astronomies," in *Carolingian Scholarship and Martianus Capella*, ed. Mariken Teeuwen and Sinead O'Sullivan (Turnhout, 2011) 221–244, esp. 230. See also, more generally, Stephen C. McCluskey, *Astronomies and Cultures in Early Medieval Europe* (Cambridge, 1998); and Daniela Dueck, *Geography in Classical Antiquity* (Cambridge, 2012) chaps. 2 and 3. On Chalcidius, see McCluskey, *Astronomies and Cultures*, 119–120; Jan H. Waszink, *Studien zum Timaioskommentar des Calcidiu* (Leiden, 1964); and Jan H. Waszink, ed., *Timaeus, a Calcidio translatus commentarioque instructus*, 2nd ed. (London, 1977).

[58] McCluskey, "Martianus," 231. Natalia Lozovsky, *The Earth Is Our Book: Geographical Knowledge in the Latin West c. 400–1000* (Ann Arbor, 2000) 145: "Sharing the Platonic skepticism about knowledge gained through the senses, 'geographers' valued an intellectual cognition of the world over an empirical one."

[59] On *computus*, see Alden A. Mosshammer, *The Easter Computus and the Origins of the Christian Era* (Oxford, 2008); McCluskey, *Astronomies and Cultures*, 77–96. On calculating the hours of prayer, see Stephen C. McCluskey, "Gregory of Tours, Monastic Timekeeping, and Early Christian Attitudes to Astronomy," *Isis* 81 (1990) 8–22; McCluskey, *Astronomies and Cultures*, 97–113.

culture contemporary to the encyclopedic texts discussed here, the two genres (*computus* and encyclopedia or natural history) only cross paths later – around the time of Bede (673–735 CE) – when the qualitative elements of these encyclopedic texts were used to adorn the strict quantitative *computus* tables.[60]

Although writing in a secular tradition, both Macrobius and Martianus Capella were enormously influential on later Christian thinking about the shape and organization of the world, and it is not insignificant that both texts were valued for their perpetuation of received habits of reading and education. They provided models not just for geographical content but for how a scholar should go about organizing and publishing that content. The *Marriage of Philology and Mercury* in particular was well known by succeeding generations of scholars and was fundamental for the two-tiered *quadrivium* and *trivium* system of higher education from the Carolingian period on.[61] In the sixth century, both Fulgentius and Boethius knew the work (the latter only vaguely), and it underwent critical revision in Rome in 534; Cassiodorus knew of the book's good reputation but was unable to lay his hands on it; and Gregory of Tours speaks generally about its value for higher education (*Hist. Franc.* 10.31).[62]

CONCLUSION: THE CASE OF INDIA

It is well known that late antique and medieval writers often meant very different things when invoking the land they called "India."[63]

---

[60] McCluskey, "Martianus," 233. See also, for the early evidence of insular *computus*, Alden A. Mosshammer, "The Computus of 455 and the Laterculus of Augustalis, with an Appendix on the Fractional Method of Agriustia," in *The Easter Controversy of Late Antiquity and the Early Middle Ages: Its Manuscripts, Texts, and Tables*, ed. Immo Warntjes and Daibhí Ó Cróinín (Turnhout, 2011) 21–47.

[61] Teeuwen and O'Sullivan, *Carolingian Scholarship*.

[62] Danuta Shanzer, "Review Article. Felix Capella: *Minus Sensus Quam Nominis Pecudalis*; *De nuptiis Philologiae et Mercurii* by James Willis," *Classical Philology* 81 (1986) 62–63; Lozovsky, *Earth Is Our Book*, 25–26. It is not certain if any surviving texts on astronomy or geography should be ascribed to Boethius, though it is clear that he wrote on these subjects: see David Pingree, "Boethius' Geometry and Astronomy," in *Boethius: His Life, Thought, and Influence*, ed. Margaret T. Gibson (Oxford, 1981) 155–161.

[63] The classic article on the subject is Albrecht Dihle, "The Conception of India in Hellenistic and Roman Literature," *Cambridge Classical Journal* n. s. 10 (1964) 15–23. For the following two paragraphs, see Philip Mayerson, "A Confusion of Indias:

Most often, it seems, what was meant was either the southern Arabian peninsula along the Red Sea (Arabia Felix = Himyar = Yemen), or Ethiopia, particularly the kingdom of Axum and its port city of Adulis.[64] Less frequently, it would seem, did they mean the actual Indian subcontinent. These divergent meanings speak precisely to the intersection of real and imagined geography in Late Antiquity. Indeed, some of the principal sources of confusion were the inherited traditions of where the apostles (and later missionary successors) had been sent in their commission to bring the gospel to the whole world (Matt. 28:18–20). The apostle Matthew was said to have gone to "Ethiopia"; Bartholomew was said to have gone to "India"; and sometime later the teacher of Clement of Alexandria, Pantaenus, arrived in "India" to find the "Indians" reading Matthew's gospel in Hebrew, given to them by Bartholomew (Eusebius, *HE* 5.10.2; Jerome, *De vir. ill.* 36)! Obviously conversant with a similar story kernel, the "Arian" historian Philostorgius says that the emperor Constantius II sent a "Theophilus" to India, where he encountered Bartholomew's disciples.[65]

In situating the history of Frumentius's famous fourth-century mission to "India" within these inherited tales of the apostles, the fifth-century historians Rufinus, Socrates Scholasticus, and Gelasius of Cyzicus all use different modifiers when talking about where Frumentius actually went. Rufinus calls it "further India" (*ulterior India*); Socrates calls it "inner India" (*Indōn tōn endoterō*); and Gelasius calls it "innermost India" (*endotatēn Indian*). According to tradition it was Athanasius of Alexandria who commissioned Frumentius's endeavor, sending him to Axum and converting the king Aizanas ('Ezana) in around 357. Thus, if tradition holds, the "India" of Frumentius was the Axumite kingdom of Ethiopia.[66] In other words, it would appear that none of these

---

Asian India and African India in the Byzantine Sources," *Journal of the American Oriental Society* 113 (1993) 169–174.

[64] On the Red Sea during Late Antiquity, see Christian Robin, "Arabia and Ethiopia," in *The Oxford Handbook of Late Antiquity*, ed. Scott F. Johnson (Oxford, 2012), 247–332; Glen W. Bowersock, *Empires in Collision in Late Antiquity* (Waltham, Mass., 2012); and Glen W. Bowersock, *The Throne of Adulis: Red Sea Wars on the Eve of Islam* (Oxford, 2013).

[65] Mayerson, "Confusion of Indias," 172.

[66] See Bowersock, *Empires in Collision*, 8–11, and the references at nn. 8–9; for the chronology, see Robin, "Arabia and Ethiopia," 274–275; and for the "conversion" of Ethiopia, see Zeev Rubin, "Greek and Ge'ez in the Propaganda of King 'Ezana of Axum: Religion and Diplomacy in Late Antiquity," *Semitica et Classica* 5 (2012) 139–150; and Glen W. Bowersock, "Helena's Bridle and the Chariot of Ethiopia,"

historians are referring (in reality) to a place anywhere near the Indian subcontinent.

Moreover, Rufinus refers to another India, "nearer India" (*citerior India*), which is the place, according to him, that had been assigned to the apostle Bartholomew. This distinction between "further India" and "nearer India" in Rufinus can be matched up with a later source – expanding on Eusebius and Jerome – that claims that Pantaenus, upon finding disciples of Bartholomew, "preached to the Indians who are called 'fortunate.'"[67] It is therefore likely that we are perceiving some shred of early tradition behind all of these references, a tradition which claimed that Bartholomew, and after him Pantaenus, were missionaries to Arabia Felix ("Arabia the Fortunate or Pleasant"). What these writers may have perceived in their mind is a different matter, of course, and perhaps even inaccessible today. Suffice it to say that the nomenclature for "India" in the fourth and fifth centuries was clearly unstandardized, and, since all of these church historians were borrowing from one another and basing their geographical assumptions on inherited models from early Christian apocrypha and from Eusebius, the opportunities abounded for citing authoritative sources without questioning the sources' own geographical assumptions. In other words, there was no late antique attempt to get back to first principles when it came to defining "India." In fact, from the literary evidence alone, it would seem that when it is asserted by ancient authors that Roman ports on the Red Sea (e.g., Clysma) were trading with "India" this label nearly always refers to Ethiopia or south Arabia.[68]

Another text referring to India, and perhaps with more legitimacy, is the Greek work commonly known as *On the Peoples of India and the Brahmans*, attributed to the bishop and monastic historian Palladius of

in *Antiquity in Antiquity: Jewish and Christian Pasts in the Greco-Roman World*, ed. Gregg Gardner and Kevin L. Osterloh (Tübingen, 2008) 383–393.

[67] The source, a "Sophronius," is dated to after the sixth century but the geographical title in Greek is known from earlier sources, *Indois tois kaloumenois Eudaimosin* (presumably translating the Roman provincial name in Latin): see Mayerson, "Confusion of Indias," 171–172.

[68] Mayerson, "Confusion of Indias," 174. However, that does not mean that the kingdoms of Himyar and Axum did not trade with the Indian subcontinent nor that Romans had no knowledge of that trade: see Stuart Munro-Hay, "The Foreign Trade of the Aksumite Port of Adulis," *Azania: Archaeological Research in Africa* 17 (1982) 107–125; and Timothy Power, *The Red Sea from Byzantium to the Caliphate: AD 500–1000* (Cairo, 2012).

Helenopolis and dating (probably) to sometime in the fifth century.[69] The book is in two parts: the first brief fifteen chapters represent a late antique Christian account of a journey to India via Axum; the last four chapters comprise an interpolated and possibly epitomated work on the Brahmans that Palladius attributes to the historian Arrian.[70] In the first part Palladius acknowledges that he himself never made a journey to India. Instead, the journey is recounted in the form of a letter from a *scholastikos* (or lawyer) of Egyptian Thebes whom Palladius met in Adulis before the *scholastikos* set out for India. Palladius clearly uses "India" to refer to different regions: when he is discussing his own travels, "India" often means Ethiopia or south Arabia; but, when relating the travels of the *scholastikos*, he describes Taprobane as a land where "the great king of the Indians rules." Thus, it seems in Palladius's case that he applies the metonym "India" differently according to the perspective of the narrator, a fact which should, at the least, alert historians to the slippery nature of geographical description in Late Antiquity.

Through this test case of India, and in the numerous texts of various genres surviving from the period, the fifth century appears to be a time when the geographical imaginations of antiquity and early Christianity were being combined and resynthesized. Sometimes this led to confusion about real terrestrial geography. However, it may be that the most significant change was in the function of geographical knowledge,

---

[69] Editions in John D. M. Derrett, "The History of 'Palladius' on the Races of India and the Brahmans," *Classica and Mediaevalia* 21 (1960) 64–135; also in Wilhelm Berghoff, *Palladius: De gentibus Indiae et Bragmanibus* (Meisenheim am Glan, 1967). Dating and attribution are contested: Mayerson, "Confusion of Indias," 170; Jehan Desanges, "D'Axoum à l'Assam, aux portes de la Chine: Le voyage du 'Scholasticus de Thèbes' (entre 360 et 500 après J.-C.)," *Historia* 18 (1969) 627–639; Derrett, "*On the Races of India and the Brahmans*"; Günther C. Hansen, "Alexander und die Brahmanen," *Klio* 43–45 (1965) 351–386. Derrett favors dating this work to Julian's reign, 361–363, on the basis of reports of fears by the Indians that Rome would attack them (e.g., Amm. *Res Gest.* 22.7.10). Because of this early dating, Derrett is forced to abjure the traditional attribution to Palladius of Helenopolis. Desanges and Berghoff both argue for Palladius's authorship in the early fifth century.

[70] This second section, quite apart from its use by Palladius, appears separately in the earliest manuscript of the Greek *Alexander Romance* (manuscript Par. Gr. 1711, 11th cent.) and may contain some authentic recollection of Alexander's interaction with the Brahmans, although distorted by its appropriation of Cynic diatribe. It certainly seems as if "Arrian" represents an accurate rendering of Megasthenes' accounts of Alexander's conversations with the Brahmans/gymnosophists at Taxila, particularly on the points of vegetarianism and suicide by fire: see Richard Stoneman, "Who Are the Brahmans? Indian Lore and Cynic Doctrine in Palladius' *De Bragmanibus* and Its Models," *Classical Quarterly* 44 (1994) 500–510.

rather than the content. Far from being focused solely on the remit of Roman power, or deriving authority exclusively from the mathematicians of Alexandria, geography in the fifth century served as both a metaphor and an encyclopedia. Between the real Ephrem and the one drawn by a Syriac hagiographer of the sixth century lay the transformation of Egypt and Cappadocia into sites of authoritative memory: the titular founders of Coptic and Greek monasticism, Apa Bishoi and Basil of Caesarea, became metonymies for real, authoritative traditions which could be accessed and appropriated through imagined journeys that embroidered the saint. Likewise, the *oikoumene* was a container for all of knowledge and human endeavor, especially Roman endeavor (or post-Alexander endeavor), painted vividly onto the Peutinger Table, and enumerated ad nauseam in multiple *notitiae* and topographies of individual cities and regions throughout the known world. Sometimes these fifth-century archives of microregions were expressed through narrative journeys, as in the topographical literature relating to the Holy Land. However, there is no true fifth-century "there-and-back-again" story that survives, at least not one in the style of the fourth-century pilgrimages of the *Bordeaux Pilgrim* and Egeria. Christian travel is certainly occurring in the fifth century – expanding, even – but our access to it comes from different sources. The fact that these sources suggest, on the one hand, a burgeoning, generalized geographical imagination and, on the other, a literary or aesthetic movement not based primarily on genre or form, bespeaks a lively engagement with geography as a mode of communication and knowledge, and one which served for centuries as a venerable model in both the West and the East.

23: SELECTED ANCIENT SOURCES

Maya Maskarinec

AMMIANUS MARCELLINUS (ca. 330–after 392): the most important historian for the fourth century. An aristocrat from Antioch, Ammianus was a military officer who traveled widely during and after his campaigns. He incorporated his observations into his Latin history, the *Res Gestae*, which, by his account, covered the period from 96 to 378; the surviving parts cover from 358 to 378, concluding with the battle of Adrianople and its aftermath. A "classicizing" historian, following the model of Tacitus, Ammianus was a pagan who celebrates Julian, but nevertheless also provides commentary on Christian affairs. His history is characterized by geographic and ethnographic excurses that survey the situation in the empire, while his narrative provides a gloomy outlook on the future.

Ammianus Marcellinus, ed. and trans. John C. Rolfe, 3 vols. (London, 1935–1939).

AUGUSTINE (354–430): an extremely influential theologian and bishop of Hippo. His major works, written in Latin, include the autobiographical *Confessions* and the *City of God*, a reflection on the meaning of human society in the aftermath of the Gothic sack of Rome by Alaric's troops in 410. Numerous sermons, letters, and treatises also survive, addressing doctrinal and practical concerns.

The City of God against the Pagans, trans. Robert. W. Dyson (Cambridge, 1998); and *City of God*, trans. Henry Bettenson (London, 2003); *Confessions*, trans. Henry Chadwick (Oxford, 1991).

AVESTA: the sacred texts of Zoroastrianism, orally transmitted for about approximately 1,500 years before being redacted in writing in the late Sasanian era, ca. 500–636.

Partial trans. in Prods O. Skjaervø, *The Spirit of Zoroastrianism* (New Haven, 2012). Martin L. West, *The Hymns of Zoroaster* (London, 2010).

BEISHI: THE HISTORY OF THE NORTH, written by Li Dashi in the middle of the seventh century, describes the history of the various dynasties of northern China from the end of the fourth century to the beginning of the Tang dynasty (618). The book's descriptions of events in Central Asia in the fifth and early sixth centuries provide some evidence regarding the Hunnic past in Central Asia. Not translated into a western language.

CHRONICON PASCHALE = EASTER CHRONICLE. Written in Constantinople, probably in the 630s, this anonymous Greek universal chronicle is named for the methods it presents for calculating the date of Easter. It covers the period from Adam to 628, but is especially useful for the sixth and early seventh centuries.

Chronicon Paschale, 284–628 A.D., trans. Michael Whitby and Mary Whitby (Liverpool, 1989).

CORIPPUS, FLAVIUS CRESCONIUS (d. after 567): a Latin poet in Africa, who was in Constantinople by ca. 566. His epic poem, *Johannis*, probably delivered ca. 549 in Carthage, is an eight-book account of the Byzantine campaign against the Berbers in North Africa. Despite its rhetorical style and decidedly imperial perspective, this work is an important source on North Africa. In ca. 566, he also composed a poem in honor of the emperor Justin II's accession to the throne in Constantinople.

In laudem Iustini Augusti minoris, libri IV, ed. and trans. Averil Cameron (London, 1976). *The Iohannes or De bellis Libycis of Flavius Cresconius Corippus*, intro. and trans. George W. Shea (Lewiston, NY, 1998).

EVAGRIUS SCHOLASTICUS (d. after 594): a lawyer and government official from Antioch. His six-book *Church History* comprises ecclesiastical and secular events, with a focus on Antioch, from 431 to 594. He was a strong proponent of Chalcedonian theology.

The Ecclesiastical History of Evagrius Scholasticus, trans. Michael Whitby (Liverpool, 2000).

FIRDAWSI: the author of the *Shahnameh*, or *Book of Kings*, a poetic epic composed in New Persian ca. 1000 C.E. The text relates the mythical history of the rulers of Iran from the primordial kings of the earth to the last Sasanian, Yazdgird III. Firdawsi creatively adapted oral and written sources from the Sasanian era to compose the work, which constitutes a major repository, alongside the history of al-Ṭabari, of Sasanian historiographical traditions.

Partial trans. in Dick Davis, *The Shahnameh* (New York, 2007).

FAUSTUS OF BYZANTIUM (P 'avstos Buzand): Armenian historian of the end of the fourth to fifth century, who wrote a history of Armenia especially concerned with the role played by the Mamikonian family in the wars with Iran. Parts of the history are still extant for the fourth century and mention Persian conflict with a Hunnic group.

Trans. in Nina Garsoïan, *The Epic Histories Attributed to P'awstos Buzand (Buzandaran patmut'iwnk')* (Cambridge, Mass., 1989).

THE GALLIC CHRONICLE OF 452: an anonymous Latin Chronicle, beginning in 379, which continues Jerome's chronicle. It focuses on events in Gaul and concludes with Attila's invasion of Italy in 452.

Trans. in Alexander Murray, *From Roman to Merovingian Gaul: A Reader* (Peterborough, Ont., 2000) 76–85.

GREGORY OF TOURS (ca. 540–593/594): the most important historian of Merovingian France. Gregory was an aristocrat, bishop of Tours, and an advisor to Merovingian kings. His Latin *Histories in Ten Books* (also known as the *History of the Franks*) covers the period from the creation of the world to Gregory's own time, with particular focus on the late sixth century. It traces the rise of the Franks within the framework of Christian history. His *Glory of the Martyrs* documents the miraculous powers of notable saints. He was also the author of numerous other works, of which only fragments survive.

History of the Franks, trans. Ormonde M. Dalton (Oxford, 1927). *Glory of the Martyrs*, ed. and trans. Raymond Van Dam (Liverpool, 2004).

HYDATIUS LEMICENSIS (ca. 395–ca. 470): Spanish bishop who traveled to the East as a youth. His Latin *Chronicle*, a continuation of Jerome's chronicle, covers the period 379–469 and is an important source for the history of Spain in the fifth century, which he regards with pessimism.

Trans. in Alexander Murray, *From Roman to Merovingian Gaul: A Reader* (Peterborough, ONnt., 2000) 85–98, and Richard W. Burgess, *The Chronicle of Hydatius and the Consularia Constantinopolitana* (Oxford, 1993).

JEROME (d. 420): a biblical exegete and translator who spent his life in both East and West. A devout Christian deeply steeped in classical culture, he was the spiritual advisor to wealthy elites in Rome, but he also spent time as an ascetic in the Syrian desert. Among his many works was a translation of the Bible into Latin (the Vulgate); *On Famous Men*, a series of biographies of preeminent Christians; diatribes against certain theological positions (Arianism, Origenism, and Pelagianism); letters; and a Latin translation and expansion of Eusebius's *Chronicle* (a history of the world from Abraham to 325). This *Chronicle*, which ends in 379, would be continued in subsequent centuries (e.g., *Gallic Chronicle of 452* [after 452] and chronicles by Prosper of Aquitaine [ca. 390–460], Hydatius [ca. 395–ca. 470], and Marcellinus Comes [early sixth century]).

For *Chronicle*, Malcolm D. Donalson, *A Translation of Jerome's Chronicon with Historical Commentary* (Lewiston, N.Y., 1996). For *Dialogue against the Pelagians*, John H. Hritzu, *Dogmatic and Polemical Work* (Washington, D.C., 1965). *Letters*, trans. William H. Fremantle, George Lewis, and William G. Martley (New York, 1893). *Saint Jerome: On Illustrious Men*, trans. Thomas P. Halton (Washington, D.C., 1999).

JORDANES (died ca. 552): most important source of the early history of the Goths. A notary of professed Gothic origins based in Constantinople, Jordanes wrote Latin histories that were influenced by both the Gothic and Byzantine worlds of which he was part. His *Romana* traces Roman history from Romulus to 550/551. His *Getica* (whose precise relationship to Cassiodorus's earlier *Getica* is much disputed) is a history of the Goths from their origins to 551. It includes legends and customs of the Goths, as well as a noteworthy account of Attila. He concludes the work expressing the hope that the Romans and Goths may be reconciled.

The Gothic History of Jordanes, trans. Charles C. Mierow (Princeton, 1915; repr. New York, 1960).

LEO I (d. 461): bishop of Rome. He famously led an embassy to Attila, convincing him to withdraw his troops from Italy. His writings promote Rome's primacy and Roman doctrines as orthodox, but also reflect his close ties with the Emperor Valentinian III in Constantinople. His sermons often address the practical concerns of his urban congregations.

Trans. in Philipp Jaffé, *Leo the Great, Gregory the Great* (New York, 1895).

LIANGSHU: THE BOOK OF LIANG was written by Yao Silian and submitted to the Chinese imperial throne in 629. It describes the history of the southern Chinese Liang dynasty (502–557) and mentions the activities of certain groups of Huns in Central Asia. Not translated into a western language.

LIBANIUS (d. 393): a rhetorician and teacher who belonged to the landowning elite of Antioch. Although deeply steeped in classical culture and an adamant pagan who admired the pagan emperor Julian, Libanius was also associated with prominent Christians. Many of his speeches, including an autobiography, and letters survive.

Selected Works, ed. and trans. Albert F. Norman, 3 vols. (London, 1969–1977). *Oration IX: On the Kalends*, trans. Mark J. B. Wright, "Appendix: Libanios *Oration IX*," *Archiv für Religionsgeschichte* 13 (2012) 205–209. *Libanius's Progymnasmata: Model Exercises in Greek Prose Composition and Rhetoric*, trans. Charles Gibson (Atlanta, 2008).

LIBER PONTIFICALIS = THE BOOK OF THE POPES: a collection of papal biographies first compiled in the sixth or early seventh century, based on earlier sources. Entries include information about each pope (name, parentage, origin) and significant events of their reigns, often focusing on papal munificence.

The Book of the Popes, trans. Louis R. Loomis (New York, 1916).

JOHN MALALAS (ca. 490–570s): author of the first Byzantine universal chronicle. Malalas was educated in Antioch before becoming a bureaucrat in Constantinople. His eighteen-book *Chronicle* covers the period from Creation to the time of Justinian I (d. 565), with special focus on Antioch. It is characterized by a straightforward style, while the later books draw on oral sources and his first-hand observations. Although the only surviving Greek manuscript breaks off in 565, the text exerted great influence on later chroniclers.

The Chronicle of John Malalas, trans. Elizabeth Jeffreys, Michael Jeffreys, and Roger Scott (Melbourne, 1986).

MALCHUS OF PHILADELPHIA (fifth and sixth centuries): Constantinopolitan sophist and author of a lost history, the *Byzantiaka*. Its contents are uncertain, but according to Photius (ca. 810–893), it covered the period from the death of Leo I (473 or 474) to the death of the western emperor Julius Nepos (480). The surviving fragments focus on events in the East.

Trans. in Roger C. Blockley, ed., *The Fragmentary Classicising Historians of the Later Roman Empire: Eunapius, Olympiodorus, Priscus, and Malchus* (Liverpool, 1983) 2: 402–462.

MARCELLINUS COMES (early sixth century): an Illyrian who became an official in Constantinople under Justinian. He received many official honors, including the rank of *comes*. His Latin *Chronicle*, a continuation of Jerome's, covers the period from 379 to 534. It focuses on Constantinople and the East and often incorporates first-hand observations and public documents.

The Chronicle of Marcellinus: A Translation and Commentary, Brian Croke (Sydney, 1995).

OLYMPIODORUS OF THEBES (early fifth century): a pagan historian and poet whose extensive travels with his talking parrot included an embassy to Donatus, king of the Huns. His Greek history, dedicated to the emperor Theodosius II, covers the period 407–422 and gives particular attention to military and administrative affairs. Only fragments of his history survive, but it was a source for his contemporary Sozomen and later Zosimus.

Trans. in Roger C. Blockley, ed., *The Fragmentary Classicising Historians of the Later Roman Empire: Eunapius, Olympiodorus, Priscus, and Malchus* (Liverpool, 1983) 2: 151–220.

PRISCUS OF PANIUM (410s–after 472): a rhetorician in Constantinople. Although his history of the Roman Empire only survives in fragments, Priscus is an essential source on the Huns, as he provides an eyewitness account of his visit to the court of Attila in 449 as part of an embassy from Constantinople. Especially noteworthy is Priscus's debate with a Greek who had defected to the Huns concerning life in the two cultures. He also described his travels to Rome and Egypt. Priscus's history was influential in the Byzantine Empire.

Trans. in Roger C. Blockley, ed., *The Fragmentary Classicising Historians of the Later Roman Empire: Eunapius, Olympiodorus, Priscus, and Malchus* (Liverpool, 1983) 2: 222–400.

PROCOPIUS OF CAESAREA (ca.500 – ca. 565): the most important historian for the reign of Justinian. Although based in Constantinople, Procopius participated in the Byzantine campaigns to Persia and the West and incorporated his observations into his works, which were written in Greek. His *Wars* (eight books) describes the imperial campaigns in Persia, North Africa, and Italy, as well as the fifth-century circumstances that brought them about; the *Buildings* is a panegyric on Justinian's building program; the *Secret History* or *Anecdota* is an invective against the emperor and his court. Procopius's style and content are strongly influenced by models of "classical" historiography, especially Thucydides. His works are noteworthy for their detailed narratives of events and descriptions of peoples and places.

Works, ed. and trans. Henry B. Dewing, 7 vols. (Cambridge, Mass., 1914–1940).

PROSPER OF AQUITAINE (ca. 390–460): a theologian from southwest France who also spent time in Rome working for Pope Leo. He wrote a Latin *Chronicle*, a continuation of Jerome's, which covers the period to 455 and includes his first-hand accounts of events in the early fifth century, in particular the theological controversies in which he was engaged. His many other works include a commentary on the psalms, as well as poetry.

Partial trans. in Alexander Murray, *From Roman to Merovingian Gaul: A Reader* (Peterborough, Ont., 2000), 62–76.

QUODVULTDEUS OF CARTHAGE (d. 439): bishop of Carthage in the 430s during the Vandal invasion of North Africa and correspondent of Augustine of Hippo. His sermons lament the situation, interpreted as God's punishment, and urge for the perseverance of the Nicene Christians against the Arian Vandals.

Trans. in Richard George Kalkmann, "Two Sermons: 'De Tempore Barbarico' Attributed to St. Quodvultdeus, Bishop of Carthage: A Study of the Text and Attribution with Translation," Ph.D. diss., Catholic University of America, 1963.

SALVIAN OF MARSEILLES (fifth century): a priest who composed many ecclesiastical treaties in Latin. His most famous work, *Governance of God*, critiques contemporary society, contrasting Roman corruption and decadence with barbarian virtue. He is a valuable source on urban life and the end of Roman administration in fifth-century Gaul.

The Writings of Salvian, the Presbyter, trans. Jeremiah F. O'Sullivan (Washington, D.C., 1947; repr. 1977).

SIDONIUS, GAIUS APOLLINARIS (ca. 431–ca. 490): a wealthy aristocrat born in Lyons. Sidonius was a classically educated Christian who was deeply involved in politics. In 467, he traveled to the emperor Anthemius in Rome to plead for the defense of Gaul against the Visigoths, and later he later became bishop of Auvergne.

A prolific writer, his works include poems, panegyrics (addressed to western emperors, as well as to a Visigothic king), and approximately 150 letters. These provide much material on the dissolution of the Roman state in Gaul.

Sidonius Poems and Letters: In Two Volumes, ed. and trans. William B. Anderson, 2 vols. (Cambridge, Mass., 1935–1965).

SOCRATES SCHOLASTICUS (ca. 380–439): a lawyer and ecclesiastical historian in Constantinople. His seven-book *Church History* in Greek, a continuation of Eusebius's chronicle, covers the period 305–439 (each book is equivalent to an eastern emperor's reign). It emphasizes events in Constantinople and is noteworthy for its detail and use of documentary sources. It was an influential source for later historians, such as Sozomen.

Ecclesiastical History, trans. Andrew C. Zenos (New York, 1890; repr. Grand Rapids, Mich., 1952).

SOZOMEN SCHOLASTICUS (fifth century): a lawyer and ecclesiastical historian, who was born near Gaza, but moved to Constantinople. His *Church History* (in Greek) is a continuation of Eusebius's, and covers the period 324–425. A contemporary of Olympiodorus, Sozomen likewise dedicated his history to Theodosius II. He is an important source on Christianization among the Armenians, Saracens, and Goths, as well as on the persecution of Christians in Persia.

The Ecclesiastical History of Sozomen, trans. Chester D. Hartranft (New York, 1890; repr. Grand Rapids, Mich., 1952); *Ecclesiastical History*, trans. Edward Walford (London, 1855).

STEPHANOS ORBELIAN: an Armenian metropolitan from the reigning family of Syunik, who wrote a history of his family and region at the very end of the thirteenth century, making use of numerous lost sources.

Histoire de la Siounie par Stephannos Orbelian, trans. Marie-Félicité Brosset (St. Petersburg, 1864–1866).

SYNESIUS OF CYRENE (late fourth/early fifth century): a wealthy aristocrat who was actively involved in public service. He became bishop of Ptolemais, despite his philosophic doubts. His prolific writings, in verse and prose, frequently defend classical culture and criticize the ineffectiveness of contemporary emperors.

The Essays and Hymns of Synesius of Cyrene, trans. Augustine Fitzgerald, 2 vols. (London, 1930). *The Letters of Synesius of Cyrene*, trans. Augustine Fitzgerald (London, 1926).

TAISHO TRIPITAKA : a modern edition (Chinese and Japanese, 1934) in one hundred volumes of all the known texts of the Chinese Buddhist canon. It contains, in passing, the oldest known reference to the Huns (Zhu Fahu, *Taisho Tripitaka*, 11.310, 3.186). Partial trans. at http://www.bdkamerica.org/default.aspx?MPID=31&series=0.

THEMISTIUS (ca. 317–ca. 388): a successful pagan rhetorician writing in Greek. Based in Constantinople, where he was appointed prefect by Theodosius I, Themistius also traveled widely on official business. Thirty-four of his speeches survive, addressed to many fourth-century emperors (e.g., Constantius II, Valentinian I, Gratian, Theodosius). He was also the author of philosophic essays advocating Neo-platonic ideals.

Partial trans. in Peter J. Heather and John Matthews, *The Goths in the Fourth Century* (Liverpool, 1991); Peter Heather and David Moncur, *Politics, Philosophy and Empire in the Fourth Century: Themistius' Select Orations* (Liverpool, 2001).

THEODORET OF CYRRHUS (ca. 393–ca. 466): theologian and bishop. Born and classically educated in Antioch. As bishop of Cyrrhus he took part in many theological disputes (i.e., Nestorianism). His many writings (in Greek) include the *Religious History*; biographies of monks, which provide insight into Syrian monasticism; the *Church History*, covering the period 323–428, which narrates the "Orthodox" victory over Arianism; and more than two hundred letters, which provide insights into daily life.

The Ecclesiastical History, Dialogues and Letters of Theodoret, trans. B. Jackson (New York 1892; repr. Grand Rapids, Mich., 1953). *A History of the Monks of Syria*, trans. Richard M. Price (Kalamazoo, Mich., 1985).

THEODOSIAN CODE (*Codex Theodosianus*): Latin law book published in 438. The emperors Theodosius II and Valentinian III had all imperial constitutions (as well as appropriate writings by jurists) from the time of Constantine I onward gathered into a corpus. The result was sixteen books of more than 2,500 constitutions, ordered into titles by topic and sorted chronologically. It provides a wealth of material for social historians, as well as insight into the trends toward increasing legal codification.

The Theodosian Code and Novels and the Sirmondian Constitutions, trans. Clyde Pharr et al. (Princeton, 1952; repr. 1970).

THEOPHANES THE CONFESSOR (ca. 760–817): an aristocrat born in Constantinople, who attained a high rank at the court of

Leo IV and then became a monk. His Greek *Chronographia* is a continuation of George the Synkellos's and covers 285–813. Its unnamed sources are much disputed.

The Chronicle of Theophanes Confessor: Byzantine and Near Eastern history, AD 284–813, trans. Cyril Mango and Roger Scott (Oxford, 1997).

VICTOR OF VITA (late fifth century): an important source for the history of North Africa and the Vandals. Victor was bishop of Vita and an ecclesiastical historian. As a Nicene Christian and an opponent of the Vandals, his Latin *History of the Vandal Persecutions*, published ca. 486, focused on the religious persecutions suffered by Nicene Christians under the Arian Vandal kings Geiseric (439–477) and Huneric (477–484). Although biased and exaggerated, the work draws on official documents.

Victor of Vita: History of the Vandal Persecution, trans. John Moorhead (Liverpool, 1992).

WEISHU: THE BOOK OF WEI, written in the middle of the sixth century by Wei Shou, describes the history from 386 to 550 of the Northern Wei, a dynasty originating from the steppe world that dominated northern China. The chapters of the *Weishu* regarding China's western neighbors (although a later reconstruction of the original text) are key to understanding the history of the Huns in Central Asia. Not translated into a western language.

ZOSIMUS (fifth/sixth century): the last pagan historian. A lawyer and official, Zosimus was highly critical of Christianity and contemporary affairs. His *New History*, written in Greek ca. 501, survives in a single manuscript, which breaks off in 410. Zosimus views history in terms of the decline of the Roman Empire, as caused by its Christianization, providing a markedly different perspective than contemporaneous historians.

New History, trans. Ronald T. Ridley (Melbourne, 1982).

BIBLIOGRAPHY

ANCIENT SOURCES

Al-Dīnawarī. *Kitāb al-akhbār al-ṭiwāl*. Ed. ʿAbd al-Munʿim ʿĀmir. Cairo, 1960.

Al-Ṭabarī. *Taʾrīkh al-rusul waʾl mulūk*. Ed. Michael de Goeje. Leiden, 1879–1901. Trans. Clifford Bosworth, *The History of al-Ṭabarī*, vol. 5: *The Sāsānids, the Byzantines, the Lakhmids, and Yemen*. Albany, 1999.

Ambrosius. *Epistulae et acta*. 4 vols. Ed. Otto Faller and Michaela Zelser. CSEL 82. Vienna, 1968–1990.

———. *Expositio evangelii secundum Lucam*. Ed. Marcus Adriaen and Paolo A. Ballerini. CCSL 14. Turnhout, 1957.

Ammianus Marcellinus. *Res gestae*. Ed. and trans. John C. Rolfe, *Ammiani Marcellini: Rerum gestarum libri qui supersunt*. 3 vols. Cambridge, Mass., 1935–1939.

Ananias Širakacʿi. *Ašxarhacʿoycʿ*. Trans. Robert Hewsen, *The Geography of Ananias of Širak*. Wiesbaden, 1992.

Anthologia Latina. Ed. D. R. Shackleton Bailey. Stuttgart, 1982.

Anthologia Palatina. Ed. William Roger Paton. *The Greek Anthology*, vol. 1. London, 1920.

Aratus. *Phaenomena*. Ed. Douglas Kidd, *Aratus: Phaenomena*. Cambridge, 1997. Also ed. Jean Soubiran, ed., *Aviénus: Les Phénomènes d'Aratos,* Paris, 1981. Also ed. André Le Boeuffle, *Les Phénomènes d'Aratos,* Paris, 1975. Trans. David B. Gain, *The Aratus Ascribed to Germanicus Caesar,* London, 1976.

Asterius. *Homilies 1–44 of Saint Asterius of Amaseia*. Ed. Cornelis Datema. Leiden, 1970.

Augustine. *Against the Academics: Sancti Aurelii Augustini Contra academicos libri tres*. Ed. Pius Knöll. CSEL 63. Vienna, 1922.

———. *Commentary on Psalms: Sancti Aurelii Augustini Enarrationes in Psalmos*. Ed. Eligius Dekkers and Johannes Fraipont. CCSL 38–40. Turnhout, 1956.

———. *Confessions: Sancti Aurelii Augustini Confessionum libri XIII*. Ed. Pius Knöll. CSEL 33. Prague, 1900.

———. *De civitate Dei*. Ed. Bernhard Dombart and Aernhard Kalb. CCSL 47–48. Turnhout, 1955. Trans. Henry Bettenson, *City of God*, London, 2003.

———. *Epistles: Sancti Aurelii Augustini Epistulae*. Ed. J.-P. Migne. PL 33, 38–39. Paris, 1865.

———. *Epistolae ex duobus codicibus nuper in lucem prolatae*. CSEL 88. Ed. Johannes Divjak. CSEL 88. Vienna, 1981. Trans. Edmund Hill, *Letters 211—270, 1–29: The Works of Saint Augustine: A Translation for the 21st Century*, vol. 2, part 4, New York, 2005.

———. *In Iohannis evangelium tractatus CXXIV*. Ed. Radbodus Willems. CCSL 36. Turnhout, 1954.

————. *Sermo Morin Guelferbytanus*. PL Supplementum. 2 vols. Ed. Adalbert Hamman. Paris, 1960.

————. *Sermons*. Ed. Edmund Hill, *The Works of St. Augustine: A Translation for the 21st Century, Sermons*, vol. 3, part 8. New York, 1997. Also ed. François Dolbeau, "Nouveaux sermons de saint Augustin pour la conversion des païens et des donatistes IV," *Recherches Augustiniennes* 26 (1992) 69–141, repr. François Dolbeau, ed., *Augustin d'Hippone: Vingt-six sermons au peuple d'Afrique*, Collection des Études Augustiniennes, Antiquité 137 (Paris, 1996) 345–417.

————. *Tractates on the Gospel of John*. 3 vols. Trans. John W. Rettig. Fathers of the Church 78, 79, 88. Washington, D.C., 1988–1995.

Avesta. Partial trans. in Prods O. Skjaervø, *The Spirit of Zoroastrianismn* (New Haven, 2012), and Martin L. West, *The Hymns of Zoroaster* (London, 2010).

Avienus. *Descriptio orbis terrae*. Ed. Paul van de Woestijne, *La Descriptio orbis terrae d'Avienus*. Bruges, 1961.

Avitus of Vienne. *In ordinatione episcopi*. Ed. Rudolf Peiper, *Alcimi Ecdicii Aviti Viennenensis episcopi Opera quae supersunt*. MGH AA, 6, 2. Berlin, 1883.

Caesarius of Arles. *Sermons*. Trans. Mary M. Mueller. 3 vols. Fathers of the Church 31, 47, 56. Grand Rapids, Mich., 1956–1973.

Cassian, John. *De incarnatione Domini contra Nestorium*. PL 514. Ed. Michael Petschenig and Gottfried Kreuz. PL 514. CSEL 17, Vienna, 2004. Trans. Marie-Anne Vannier, *De incarnatione: Jean Cassien, Traité de l'Incarnation contre Nestorius*, Sagesses Chrétiennes, Paris, 1999.

Cassiodorus. *Cassiodori Senatoris Variae*. Ed. Theodor Mommsen. MGH AA 13. Berlin, 1894.

————. *Magni Aurelii Cassiodori Variarum libri XII*. Ed. Åke J. Fridh. CCSL 96. Turnhout, 1973.

Cassius Dio. *Historiae romanae*, 2nd ed. Ed. Ursul Philip Boissevain. 5 vols. Berlin, 1955–1969. Trans. Earnest Cary. *Roman History*, 9 vols. Loeb Classical Library 32, 37, 53, 66, 82, 83, 175–177, Cambridge, Mass., 1914–1927; repr. 1961–1984.

Chronicon Paschale. Ed. Ludwig Dindorf. *Chronicon Paschale*. CSHB 4. Bonn, 1832. Trans. Michael Whitby and Mary Whitby, *Chronicon Paschale, 284–628 A.D.*, Translated Texts for Historians 7, Liverpool, 1989.

Claudius Claudianus. Ed. and trans. Maurice Platnauer, *Claudian*. 2 vols. London, 1922.

Codex Iustinianus. See Justinian.

Codex Theodosianus. See Theodosius.

Constantine VII Porphyrogenitus. *De Administrando Imperio*. Ed. Gyula Moravcsik, trans. Romilly Jenkins, *Constantine Porphyrogenitus: De Administrando Imperio*. 2nd ed. Washington, D.C., 1967.

Constantius of Lyon. *Vita Germani*. Ed. René Borius, *Vie de saint Germain d'Auxerre*. SC 112. Paris, 1965.

Corippus, Flavius Cresconius. *In laudem Iustini Augusti minoris, libri IV*. Ed. and trans. Averil Cameron. London, 1976.

————. *The Iohannis or De bellis Libycis of Flavius Cresconius Corippus*. Intro. and trans. George W. Shea. Lewiston, N.Y.: 1998.

Cyprian of Carthage, *Epistulae*. In Gerard Diercks, ed., *Sancti Cypriani episcopi epistularium*. CCSL 3B–C. Turnhout, 1994–1996.

Dexippus, Publius Herennius. Ed. Felix Jacoby, *Die Fragmente der griechischen Historiker*, Leiden, 1926.

Dracontius of Carthage. *Dracontius: Œuvres*. 4 vols. Eds. Claude Moussy, Colette Camus, Jean Bouquet, and Étienne Wolff. Paris, 1985–1996.

Ełiše. *History of the Armenians*. Trans. Robert W. Thomson, *The History of Łazar P'arpec'i*. Atlanta, 1991.

———. *History of Vardan and the Armenian War*. Trans. Robert W. Thomson. London, 1982.

———. *Vasn Vardanants' ew Hayoc' Paterazmin*. Ed. Ervand Ter-Minasean. Yerevan, Armenia, 1957.

Ennodius of Pavia. *Panegyricus Dictus.Clementissimo Rege Theodorico*. Ed. W. A. Hartel, *Magni Felicis Ennodii Opera Omnia*. Vienna, 1882.

———. *Vita S. Epiphanii*. Trans. Roy J. Deferrari, *Early Christian Biographies*. Washington, D.C., 1952.

Ērānšahr, *Šahrestānīhā ī*. Ed. and trans. Touraj Daryaee, *Šahrestānīhā ī Ērānšahr: A Middle Persian Text on Late Antique Geography, Epic, and History*. Costa Mesa, Calif., 2002.

Eugippius. *Vita sancti Severini*. Ed. Pius Knoell, *Evgippii Vita Sancti Severini*. CSEL 9.2. Vienna, 1885. Trans. Ludwig Bieler, with Ludmilla Krestan, *The Life of Saint Severin*, Fathers of the Church 55, Washington, D.C., 1965.

Eunapius of Sardis. Ed. and trans. Roger C. Blockley. *The Fragmentary Classicising Historians of the Later Roman Empire: Eunapius, Olympiodorus, Priscus and Malchus*. Vol. 2. Liverpool, 1983.

Eusebius of Caesarea. *Onomasticon: the place names of divine scripture*. Trans. R. Steven Notley and Ze'ev Safrai. Boston, 2005.

Evagrius Scholasticus. Trans. Michael Whitby, *The Ecclesiastical History of Evagrius Scholasticus*. Liverpool, 2000.

Expositio totius mundi et gentium. Ed. Jean Rougé. Paris, 1969. Trans. A. A. Vasiliev, "*Expositio totius mundi*: An Anonymous Geographic Treatise of the Fourth Century A.D.," *Seminarium Kondakovianum* 8 (1936) 1–39.

Faustus of Byzantium. *Patmut'iwn Hayoc'*. Ed. and trans. Nina Garsoïan, *The Epic Histories Attributed to P'awstos Buzand (Buzandaran patmut'iwnk')*. Cambridge, Mass., 1989.

Firdawsī. *Šāhnāmeh*. Vol. 7. Ed. Djalal Khaleghi-Motlagh. New York, 2007. Partial trans. in Dick Davis, *The Shahnameh*, New York, 2007.

Fontes iuris romani antejustiniani. Ed. Salvatore Riccobono. Florence, 1941.

Fredegarius Scholasticus. *Chronicon*. Ed. Bruno Krusch, *Fredegarii et aliorum chronica*. MGH SSRM 2. Hannover, 1888.

The Gallic Chronicle of 452. Ed. Theodor Mommsen. MGH AA 9. Berlin, 1892. Also Richard Burgess. "The Gallic Chronicle of 452: A New Critical Edition with a Brief Introduction." In *Society and Culture in Late Antique Gaul: Revisiting the Sources*, ed. Ralph Mathisen and Danuta Shanzer, 52–84, Aldershot, 2001. Trans. Alexander Murray, *From Roman to Merovingian Gaul: A Reader*, 76–85, Peterborough, Ont., 2000.

Fulgentius Ferrandus. *Vita S. Fulgentii episcopi Ruspensis*. Ed. Gabriel G. Lapeyre, *Vie de Saint Fulgence de Ruspe*, Paris, 1929. Trans. Robert B. Eno, *Fulgentii, Selected Works*, Fathers of the Church 95, Washington, D.C., 1997.

Gelasius I. *Epistolae*. Ed. Andreas Thiel, *Epistolae Romanorum pontificum genuinae et quae ad eos scriptae sunt a S. Hilario usque ad Pelagium II*. Braunsberg, 1868.

Gennadius. *De viris illustribus*. Ed. Ernest C. Richardson. In *Texte und Untersuchungen zur Geschichte der altchristlichen Literatur* 14.1 (1896). Repr., Turnhout, 2010.

Gerontius. *Vita Melaniae Junioris*. Trans. Elizabeth A. Clark, *The Life of Melania, the Younger: Introduction, Translation, and Commentary*. New York, 1984.

Gesta Senatus Romani de Theodosiano publicando. See Theodosius.

Gregory of Tours. *Historia*. Eds. Bruno Krusch and Wilhelm Levison, *Gregorii Episcopi Turonensis Libri historiarum X*. MGH SRM 1. Hannover, 1965.

History of Karka d-Beit Slok. Ed. Paul Bedjan, *Acta martyrum et sanctorum*. Vol. 2. Paris, 1891.

Hydatius Lemicensis. *Chronicon*. Ed. and trans. Richard W. Burgess, *The Chronicle of Hydatius and the Consularia Constantinopolitana*. Oxford, 1993.

Isidore of Seville. *Chronica Maiora*. Ed. Theodor Mommsen. MGH AA 11. Berlin, 1894. Trans. Guido Donini and Gordon Ford, *Isidore of Seville's History of the the Kings of the Goths, Vandals and Sueves*, 2nd ed., Leiden, 1970.

Jerome. *Dialogus adversus Pelagianos*. Ed. Claudio Moreschini. CCSL 80. Turnhout, 1990. Trans. John H. Hritzu. *Dogmatic and Polemical Works*, Fathers of the Church 53, Washington, D.C., 1965.

———. *Epistulae*. Ed. Isidor Hilberg, *Sancti Eusebii Hieronymi Epistvlae*. CSEL 54–56. Vienna, 1910–1918. Trans. William H. Fremantle, George Lewis, and William G. Martley, *Letters*, NPNF, 2nd ser., 6, New York, 1893.

John Cassian. See Cassian, John

John of Antioch. *Fragmenta*. Ed. and trans. Sergei Mariev, *Iohannis Antiocheni Fragmenta quae supersunt omnia*. CFHB, Series Berolinensis 47. Berlin, 2008.

———. *Ioannis Antiocheni Fragmenta ex Historia Chronica*. Ed. Umberto Roberto, *Introduzione, edizione critica e traduzione*. Texte und Untersuchungen zur Geschichte der altchristlichen Literatur 154. Berlin, 2005.

John Lydus. *De Magistratibus*. Ed. and trans. Anastasius Bandy, *Ioannes Lydus on Powers or the Magistracies of the Roman State*. Philadelphia, 1983.

John Malalas. *Chronicon*. Ed. Hans Thurn. CFHB 35. Berlin, 2000. Trans. Elizabeth Jeffreys, Michael Jeffreys, and Roger Scott, *The Chronicle of John Malalas*, Byzantina Australiensia 7, Melbourne, 1986.

Jordanes. *Romana et Getica*. Ed. Theodor Mommsen. MGH AA 5.1. Berlin, 1882.

Justinian. *Corpus iuris civilis*. Eds. Paul Krueger, Theodor Mommsen, Rudolf Schoell, and Wilhelm Kroll. 3 vols. Vol. 1: *Institutiones, Digesta*; vol. 2: *Codex Iustinianus*; vol. 3: *Novellae*. Berlin, 1872–1895, repr. 1963–1965. Trans. Peter Birks and Grant McLeod, *Justinian's Institutes*, Ithaca, N.Y., 1987. Also trans. in Alan Watson, ed., *The Digest of Justinian*, rev. English-language ed., 2 vols., Philadelphia, 1998; repr. 2009.

Łazar P'arpec'i. *Patmut'iwn Hayoc'*. Ed. Galust Ter-Mkrtchean. Tbilisi, Georgia, 1904. Trans. Robert W. Thomson, *History of the Armenians: The History of Łazar P'arpec'i*. Atlanta, 1991.

Leges Burgundionum. Ed. Ludwig Rudolf von Salis, MGH LNG, 2, 1. Hannover, 1892.

Leo. *Epistles*. Ed. Philipp Jaffé, *Regesta Pontificum Romanorum ab condita ecclesia ad annum post Christum natum*. Leipzig, 1885.

———. *Sermons*. Ed. Antoine Chavasse, *Sancti Leonis Magni Romani pontificis tractatus septem et nonaginta*. CCSL 138–138a. Turnhout, 1973.

Libanius. *Orationes*. Eds. Richard Foerster and Eberhard Richsteig. *Opera Libanii*. 12 vols. Leipzig, 1903–1927. Also *Oration IX: On the Kalends*, trans. Mark J. B. Wright, "Appendix: Libanios *Oration* IX," *Archiv für Religionsgeschichte* 13 (2012) 205–209.

————. *Progymnasmata*. Ed. Richard Foerster. Vol. 8 of *Opera Libanii*. Repr., Hildesheim, 1963. Trans. Charles Gibson, *Libanius's Progymnasmata: Model Exercises in Greek Prose Composition and Rhetoric*, Atlanta, 2008.

Malchus of Philadelphia. *Fragmenta*. Ed. and trans. Blockley, *FCH*.

Marcellinus Comes. *Chronicon*. Ed. Theodor Mommsen. MGH AA 11. Berlin, 1894. Also ed. and trans. Brian Croke, *The Chronicle of Marcellinus: A Translation and Commentary*, Byzantina Australiensia 7, Sydney, 1995.

Mark the Deacon. *Vita Porphyrii Episcopi Gazensis*. Eds. Henri Grégoire and Marc-Antoine Kugener. *Vie de Porphire évéque de Gaza*, Paris, 1930. Also Claudia Rapp, "Mark the Deacon," In *Medieval Hagiography: An Anthology*, ed. Thomas Head, 53–75, New York 2000.

Menander Protector. *Historia*. Ed. and trans. Roger C. Blockley, *The History of Menander the Guardsman*. Liverpool, 1985.

Movsês Daskhurants'i [Kałankatvats'i]. *The History of the Caucasian Albanians by Movses Dasxuranci*. Trans. Charles J. F. Dowsett. Oxford, 1961.

Nestorius. *Liber Heraclidis*. Ed. Paul Bedjan, *Le livre d'Héraclide de Damas*. Paris,1910.

Nilus of Ancyra. *De voluntaria paupertate*. PG 79.968C–1060D.

Novellae Theodosii. See Theodosius.

Novellae Valentiniani. See Theodosius.

Olympiodorus of Thebes. *Fragmenta*. Ed. and trans. Blockley, *FCH*.

Orosius. *Historiae adversum paganos*. Ed. Karl Zangemeister, Leipzig, 1889. Trans. Andrew T. Fear, *Seven Books of History against the Pagans*, Translated Texts for Historians 54, Liverpool, 2010.

Pachomius. *Regula*. Ed. Amand Boon, *Pachomiana latina: Règle et épitres de S. Pachome, épitre de S. Théodore et "Liber" de S. Orsiesius—texte latin de S. Jérôme*. Louvain, 1932.

Palladius. *Historia Lausiaca*. Ed. Cuthbert Butler, *The Lausiac History of Palladius*. 2 vols. Nendeln, Liechtenstein, 1967.

Papyri *Ravenna*. Jan-Olof Tjäder, ed., *Die nichtliterarischen lateinischen Papyri Italien aus der Zeit 445–700*. Lund, Sweden, 1955–1982.

Papyrus *Nessana 3*. Casper J. Kraemer, ed., *Excavations at Nessana III: The Non-Literary Papyri*. Cambridge, Mass., 1958.

Papyrus *Petra 3*. Antti Arjava, Matias Buchholz, and Traianos Gagos, eds., *The Petra Papyri III*. Amman, 2007.

Papyrus *PFlor*. Girolamo Vitelli and Domenico Comparetti, eds. *Papiri greco-egizii, Papiri Fiorentini: Supplementi Filologico-Storici ai Monumenti Antichi*. Milan, 1906–1915.

Papyrus *PGiess*. Otto Eger, Ernst Kornemann, and Paul M. Meyer, eds. *Griechische Papyri im Museum des oberhessischen Geschichtsvereins zu Giessen*. Leipzig, 1910–1912.

Papyrus *POxy*. Bernard P. Grenfell, Arthur S. Hunt, et al., eds. *The Oxyrhynchus Papyri*. London, 1898–2010.

Parthemius. *Rescriptum ad Sigisteum*. Ed. Adalbert G. Hamman. PL, Supplementa 3. Paris, 1963.

Patrick (Patricius). *Epistula ad milites Corotici*. Ed. and trans. Richard P. C. Hanson. SC 249. Paris, 1978.

Pelagius, *Epistulae*. In Samuel Loewenfeld, ed., *Epistolae pontificum Romanorum ineditae*. Leipzig, 1854; repr. Graz, 1959.

Peter Chrysologus, *Sermons*. Trans. George E. Ganss, *Selected Sermons and Saint Valerian, Homilies*. Fathers of the Church 17. New York, 1953. Also trans. William B. Palardy,

Saint Peter Chrysologus, Selected Sermons, Fathers of the Church 3, Washington, D.C., 2005.

Philostorgius. *Historia ecclesiastica.* Ed. and trans. Philip R. Amidon. Leiden, 2007.

Pomponius Mela. *Chorographia.* Ed. Alain Silberman, *Pomponius Mela: Chorographie,* Paris, 1988. Also ed. Kai Brodersen, *Pomponius Mela: Kreuzfahrt durch die alte Welt,* Darmstadt, 1994. Trans. Frank E. Romer, *Pomponius Mela's Description of the World,* Ann Arbor, 1998.

Possidius. *Vita Augustini.* Ed. Michele Pellegrino, *Vita di S. Agostino.* Verba Seniorum 4, Alba, Italy, 1955. Trans. Audrey Fellowes, *The Life of Saint Augustine by Possidius Bishop of Calama,* Villanova, Pa., 1988.

Priscian. *Periegetes.* Ed. Paul Van de Woestijne, *La Périégèse de Priscien.* Bruges, 1953.

Priscus of Panium. *Fragmenta.* Ed. and trans. Blockley, *FCH,* vol. 2. Also ed. Pia Carolla, *Priscus Panita, Excerpta et Fragmenta,* Berlin, 2008.

Procopius of Caesarea. *Works.* Ed. and trans. Henry B. Dewing. 5 vols. Cambridge, Mass., 1914–1940.

Prosper of Aquitaine. *Chronicon.* Ed. Theodor Mommsen, *Prosperi Tironis epitoma chronicon.* MGH AA 9. Berlin, 1892. Partial trans. in Alexander C. Murray, *From Roman to Merovingian Gaul: A Reader,* Peterborough, Ont., 2000.

———. *De vera humilitate.* Ed. Mary K. C. Krabbe, *Epistula ad Demetriadem de vera humilitate.* Washington, D.C., 1956.

Quodvultdeus of Carthage. *De tempore barbarico.* Ed. Rene Braun. CCSL 60. Turnhout, 1976. Trans. Richard George Kalkmann, "Two Sermons : 'De Tempore Barbarico' Attributed to St. Quodvultdeus, Bishop of Carthage: A Study of the Text and Attribution with Translation." Ph.D. diss., Catholic University of America, 1963.

Regula Quattuor Patrum. Ed. Adalbert de Vogüé, *Régles des saints pères.* 2 vols. SC 277, 297–298. Paris, 1977, 1982.

Šahrestānīhā ī Ērānšahr. Ed. and trans. Touraj Daryaee, *Šahrestānīhā ī Ērānšahr: A Middle Persian Text on Late Antique Geography, Epic, and History.* Costa Mesa, Calif., 2002.

Salvian of Marseille. *Ad ecclesiam sive Adversus avaritiam.* Trans. Jeremiah O'Sullivan, *The Writings of Salvian, the Presbyter.* Fathers of the Church 3. New York, 1947.

———. *De gubernatione Dei.* Ed. Georges Lagarrigue. Paris, 1975. Trans. Jeremiah F. O'Sullivan, *On the Government of God.* In *The Writings of Salvian, the Presbyter,* Fathers of the Church 3, New York, 1947; repr. 1977.

———. *Epistulae.* Ed. Karl Halm. MGH AA 1.1. Berlin, 1877.

———. *Oeuvres,* vol. 1: *Les lettres, les livres de Timothée à l'Église.* Ed. Georges Lagarrigue. Sources Chrétiennes 176. Paris, 1971.

Sententiae Syriace. Ed. Walter Selb. Vienna, 1990.

Severus of Antioch. *Liber contra impium Grammaticum.* Ed. J. Lebon, *Severi Antiocheni liber contra impium Grammaticum.* CSCO 111–112. Louvain, 1929–1952.

Severus of Minorca. *Epistula Severi.* Ed. and trans. Scott Bradbury, *Letter on the Conversion of the Jews.* Oxford, 1996.

Shenoute. *Besa: The Life of Shenoute.* Ed. John Leipoldt and E. Walter Crum. CSCO SC 2.2. Leuven, 1906.

———. *Canon 7.* Ed. and trans. Stephen Emmel, *Shenoute's Literary Corpus.* Louvain, 2004.

———. *De Aethiopum invasionibus.* Ed. John Leipoldt and E. Walter Crum. CSCO SC 2.4. Leuven, 1908.

Sidonius, Gaius Apollinaris. *Epistulae*. Ed. and trans. William B. Anderson, *Sidonius Poems and Letters: In Two Volumes*. Cambridge, Mass., 1936–1965.

Širakacʻi, Ananias. *Ašxarhacʻoycʻ*. Trans. Robert Hewsen, *The Geography of Ananias of Širak*. Wiesbaden, 1992.

Socrates Scholasticus. *Historia ecclesiastica*. Ed. Robert Hussey, *Socratis scholastici Ecclesiastica historia*, 3 vols. Oxford, 1853. Trans. Andrew C. Zenos, *Church Histories*, NPNF, 2nd ser., 2, New York, 1890; repr. Grand Rapids, Mich., 1952.

Sozomen Scholasticus. *Historia ecclesiastica*. Ed. Joseph Bidez and Günther Christian Hansen, *Sozomenus Kirchengeschichte*. GCS 50. Berlin, 1960. Trans. Edward Walford, *Ecclesiastical History*, London, 1855.

Stephanos Orbelian. Trans. Marie-Félicité Brosset, *Histoire de la Siounie par Stephannos Orbelian*. St. Petersburg, 1864–1866.

Sulpicius Severus. *Vita Martini*. Ed. Carolus Halm, *Sulpicii Severi Vita Sancti Martini, Sulpicii Severi Opera quae supersunt*. Vol. 1. CSEL 1. Vienna, 1866.

Symmachus. *Relationes*. Ed. Otto Seeck, *Aurelii Symmachi quae supersunt*. MGH AA 6.1. Berlin, 1883.

Synesius of Cyrene. *Epistulae*. Ed. J.-P. Migne. PG 66. Paris, 1859. Trans. Augustine Fitzgerald, "Concerning Dreams." In *The Essays and Hymns of Synesius of Cyrene*. Vol. 2. London, 1926.

———. *Oratio de regno*. Ed. J.-P. Migne. PG 66. Paris, 1859.

Theodoret of Cyrrhus. *Epistolae*. Ed. Yvan Azéma. 4 vols. Paris, 1955–1998.

———. *Historia Religiosa*. Trans. Richard M. Price, *A History of the Monks of Syria*, Cistercian Studies Series 88, Kalamazoo, Mich., 1985.

Theodosius. *Codex Theodosianus*. Ed. Theodor Mommsen and Paul M. Meyer, *Theodosiani liri XVI cum constitutionibus Sirmondianis*. 2 vols. Berlin, 1905, repr. 1971. Trans. Clyde Pharr et al., *The Theodosian Code and Novels and the Sirmondian Constitutions*, Princeton, 1952; repr. 1970.

———. *Novellae*. See Theodosius, *Codex Theodosianus*, vol. 2.

Theophanes the Confessor. *Chronographia*. Ed. Carl de Boor. Leipzig, 1883. Trans. Cyril Mango and Roger Scott, *The Chronicle of Theophanes Confessor: Byzantine and Near Eastern History, AD 284–813*, Oxford, 1997.

Theophylactus Simocatta. Trans. Michael Whitby and Mary Whitby, *The History of Theophylact Simocatta: An English Translation with Introduction and Notes*. Oxford, 1986.

Valentinian III. See Theodosius, *Codex Theodosianus*.

Vegetius. *Epitoma rei militaris*. Ed. Michael D. Reeve. Oxford, 2004. Trans. N. P. Milner, *Epitome of Military Science*, 2nd ed., Translated Texts for Historians 16, Liverpool, 1996.

Victor of Tonnuna. *Chronicon*. Ed. Carmen Cardelle de Hartmann, *Victoris Tunnunensis Chronicon cum reliquiis ex Consularibus Caesaraugustanis et Johannis Biclarensis Chronicon*. CCSL 173A. Turnhout, 2001.

Victor of Vita. *Historia persecutionis*. Ed. Michael Petschenig, CSEL 7. Vienna, 1881. Trans. John Moorhead, *Victor of Vita: History of the Vandal Persecution*, Translated Texts for Historians 10, Liverpool, 1992. Also, ed., trans., and comm. Serge Lancel, *Histoire de la persécution vandale en Afrique suivie de La passion des sept martyrs, Registre des provinces et des cités d'Afrique*, Paris, 2002.

Visigothic Pizzarras. Ed. Isabel Velázquez Soriano, *Documentos de época visigoda escritos en pizarra (sigl. vi–viii)*. Turnhout, 2000.

Vita Alexandris Akoimeti. Ed. and trans. E. de Stoop, *La Vie d'Alexandre l'Acémète: Texte grec et traduction francaise.* PO 6.5. Paris, 1911.

Vita Hypatii. Ed. Société des Bollandistes. Bibliotheca Hagiographica Graeca 760. Brussels, 1909. Ed. and French trans. Gerard J. M. Bartelink, *Callinicos: Vie d'Hypatios,* Paris, 1971.

Vita Matronae. Ed. Société des Bollandistes. Bibliotheca Hagiographica Graeca 1221. Bruxelles, 1909.

Vita Olympiades. Ed. François Halkin. 3rd ed. Bibliotheca Hagiographica Graeca 1375. Brussels, 1957. Also ed. Hippolyte Delehaye, "Vita Sanctae Olympiadis," *Analecta Bollandiana* 15 (1896) 409–423. Trans. Elizabeth Clark, *Jerome, Chrysostom, and Friends,* New York, 1982.

Vita S. Danielis Stylitae. Trans. Elizabeth Dawes and Norman H. Baynes, *Three Byzantine Saints.* London, 1977.

Vitae Patrum Iurensium. Trans. Tim Vivian, Kim Vivian, and Jeffrey Burton Russell, *The Life of the Jura Fathers: The Life and Rule of the Holy Fathers Romanus, Lupicinus, and Eugendus, Abbots of the Monasteries in the Jura Mountains.* Spencer, Mass., 1999.

Zamyād Yašt. Ed. and trans. Almut Hintze, *Zamyād Yašt: Introduction, Avestan Text, Translation.* Wiesbaden, 1994.

Zarērān. Ayādgār ī. Ed. and trans. Davoud Monchi-Zadeh, *Die Geschichte Zarēr's.* Acta Universitatis Upsaliensis. Uppsala, Sweden, 1981.

Zosimus. *Historia nova.* Ed. François Paschoud. 3 vols. Paris, 1971–1989. Trans. Ronald T. Ridley, *New History,* Sydney, 1982. Also, *Neue Geschichte,* trans. Otto Veh, Stuttgart, 1990.

Secondary Sources

Adams, Robert. *Heartland of Cities: Surveys of Ancient Settlement and Land Use on the Central Floodplain of the Euphrates.* Chicago, 1981.

Albu, Emily. "Imperial Geography and the Medieval Peutinger Map." *IM* 57 (2005) 136–148.

———. "Rethinking the Peutinger Map." In *Cartography in Antiquity and the Middle Ages: Fresh Perspectives, New Methods,* ed. Richard Talbert and Richard W. Unger, 111–119. Leiden, 2008.

Alciati, Roberto and Mariachiara Giorda. "Possessions and Asceticism: Melania the Younger and Her Slow Way to Jerusalem." *ZAC* 14 no. 2 (2010) 425–444.

Alemany, Agustí. *Sources on the Alans: A Critical Compilation.* Leiden, 2000.

Aliev, Askar A., Murtazali S. Gadjiev, M. Gaye Gaither, et al. "The Ghilghilchay Defensive Long Wall: New Investigations." *AWE* 5 (2006) 143–177.

Alizadeh, Karim. "Ultan Qalasi: A Fortified Site in the Sasanian Borderlands (Mughan Steppe, Iranian Azerbaijan)." *Iran* 49 (2011) 55–77.

Alram, Michael and Matthias Pfisterer. "Alkhan and Hephthalite Coinage." In *Coins, Art and Chronology, vol. 2: The First Millenium C.E. in the Indo-Iranian Borderlands,* ed. Michael Alram et. al., 13–38. Vienna, 2010.

Amar, Joseph P. *The Syriac Vita tradition of Ephrem the Syrian.* Leuven, 2011.

Amory, Patrick. *People and Identity in Ostrogothic Italy, 489–554.* Cambridge, 1997.

Anderson, Edward Runni. *Alexander's Gate, Gog and Magog, and the Inclosed Nations.* Cambridge, Mass., 1932.

Ando, Clifford. *Imperial Ideology and Provincial Loyalty in the Roman Empire.* Berkeley, 2000.

Anke, Bodo. *Studien zur reiternomadischen Kultur des 4. bis 5. Jahrhunderts.* 2 vols. Weissbach, 1988.

Asutay-Effenberger, Neslihan. *Die Landmauer von Konstantinopel-Istanbul: Historisch-topographische und baugeschichtliche Untersuchungen.* Berlin, 2007.

Athanassiadi, Polymnia. "The Oecumenism of Iamblichus: Latent Knowledge and Its Awakening." *JRS* 85 (1995) 244–250.

Atzeri, Lorena. *Gesta Senatus de Theodosiano publicando: Il Codice Teodosiano e la sua diffusione ufficiale in Occidente.* Berlin, 2008.

Avi-Yonah, Michael. *The Jews of Palestine: A Political History from the Bar-Kokhba War to the Arab Conquest.* Oxford, 1976.

Bachrach, Bernard. *A History of the Alans in the West: From Their First Appearance in the Sources of Classical Antiquity through the Early Middle Ages.* Minneapolis, 1973.

———. "The Jewish Community of the Later Roman Empire as Seen in the Codex Theodosianus." In *"To See Ourselves as Others See Us": Christians, Jews, and "Others" in Late Antiquity,* ed. Jacob Neusner and Ernest S. Frerichs, 399–421. Chico, Calif., 1985.

———. "Fifth-Century Metz: Late Roman Christian Urbs or Ghost Town?" Antiquité Tardive 10 (2002) 361–383.

Badewien, Jan. *Geschichtstheologie und Sozialkritik im Werke Salvians von Marseilles.* Göttingen, 1980.

Bagnall, Roger S. "Landholding in Late Roman Egypt: The Distribution of Wealth." *JRS* 82 (1992) 128–149.

Bagnall, Roger S., Alan Cameron, Seth R. Schwartz, and Klaas A. Worp. *Consuls of the Later Roman Empire.* Atlanta, 1987.

Bagnall, Roger S. and Bruce W. Frier. *The Demography of Roman Egypt.* Cambridge Studies in Population, Economy and Society in Past Time 23. Cambridge, 1994.

Bailey, Harold. "Harahuna." In *Asiatica: Festschrift für Friedrich Weller zum 65. Geburtstag,* 12–21. Leipzig, 1954.

Bailey, Lisa. *Christianity's Quiet Success: The Eusebius Gallicanus Sermon Collection and the Power of the Church in Late Antique Gaul.* Notre Dame, Ind., 2010.

Baldwin, Barry. "Priscus of Panium." *Byzantion* 50 (1980) 18–61.

Banaji, Jairus. *Agrarian Change in Late Antiquity: Gold, Labour, and Aristocratic Dominance.* Oxford 2001, 2007.

———. "Aristocracies, Peasantries and the Framing of the Early Middle Ages." *JOAC* 9 (2009) 59–91.

Barford, Paul M. "Silent Centuries: The Society and Economy of the Northwestern Slavs." In *East Central and Eastern Europe in the Early Middle Ages,* ed. Florin Curta, 60–99. Ann Arbor, 2005.

Barnes, Timothy. "Foregrounding the Theodosian Code." *JRA* 14 (2001) 671–685.

———. "Synesius in Constantinople." *GRBS* 27 (1986) 93–112.

Barnish, Sam. "Transformation and Survival in the Western Senatorial Aristocracy, c. AD 400–700." *PBSR* 66 (1988) 120–155.

Barnish, Sam, A. D. Lee, and Michael Whitby. "Government and Administration." In *The Cambridge Ancient History,* vol. 14: *Late Antiquity: Empire and Successors,* A.D.

425–600, ed. Averil Cameron, Bryan Ward-Perkins, and Michael Whitby, 165–206. Cambridge, 2001.

Barnwell, Paul S. *Emperors, Prefects and Kings*. London, 1992.

Barth, Fredrik, ed. *Ethnic Groups and Boundaries: The Social Organisation of Ethnic Difference*. Boston, 1969.

Batty, Roger. *Rome and the Nomads: The Pontic and Danubian Realm in Antiquity*. Oxford, 2007.

Baumer, Christoph. *The History of Central Asia: The Age of the Steppe Warriors*. London, 2012.

Bäuml, Franz H. and Marianna D. Birnbaum, eds. *Attila: The Man and His Image*. Budapest,1993.

Beaucamp, Joëlle. "Byzantine Egypt and Imperial Law." In *Egypt in the Byzantine World, 300–700*, ed. Roger S. Bagnall, 271–287. Cambridge, 2007.

Becker, Adam. *Fear of God and the Beginnings of Wisdom: The School of Nisibis and the Development of Scholastic Culture in Late Antique Mesopotamia*. Philadelphia, 2006.

Beeley, Christopher. *The Unity of Christ: Continuity and Conflict in Patristic Tradition*. New Haven, 2012.

Bell, Peter. *Social Conflict in the Age of Justinian*. Oxford, 2013.

Bemmann, Jan. "Hinweise auf Kontakte zwischen dem hunnischen Herrschaftsbereich in Südosteuropa und dem Nordem." In *Attila und die Hunnen*, ed. Bodo Anke, Historisches Museum der Pfalz, Speyer. 176–183. Stuttgart, 2007.

Benjamin, Walter. "Critique of Violence." In *Walter Benjamin: Selected Writings*, vol. 11: *1913–1926*, ed. and trans. Marcus Bullock and Michael W. Jennings. Cambridge, Mass., 2004.

Benton, Lauren. *Law and Colonial Cultures*. Cambridge 2002.

Berghoff, Wilhelm, ed. *Palladius: De gentibus Indiae et Bragmanibus*. Beiträge zur klassischen Philologie 24. Meisenheim am Glan, 1967.

Berkowitz, Beth A. "The Limits of 'Their Laws': Ancient Rabbinic Controversies about Jewishness (and Non-Jewishness)." *Jewish Quarterly Review* 99.1 (2009) 121–157.

Berndt, Guido M. *Konflikt und Anpassung: Studien zu Migration und Ethnogenese der Vandalen*. Historische Studien, 489. Husum, Germany, 2007.

Bishop, M. C. and J. C. Coulston. *Roman Military Equipment*. Oxford, 2006.

Blockley, Roger C. "Dexippus and Priscus and the Thucydidean Account of the Siege of Plataea." *Phoenix* 26 (1972) 18–27.

_____. *East Roman Foreign Policy: Formation and Conduct from Diocletian to Anastasius*. Leeds, 1992.

_____. *The Fragmentary Classicising Historians of the Later Roman Empire: Eunapius, Olympiodorus, Priscus and Malchus*. 2 vols. Liverpool, vol. 1, 1981; vol. 2, 1983.

_____. "Roman-Barbarian Marriages in the Late Empire." *Florilegium* 4 (1982) 63–79.

_____. "Subsidies and Diplomacy: Rome and Persia in Late Antiquity." *Phoenix* 39 (1985) 62–74.

_____. "The Division of Armenia between the Romans and the Persians at the End of the Fourth Century A.D." *Historia* 36 (1987) 222–234.

Blumenkranz, Bernhard. *Die Judenpredigt Augustins: Ein Beitrag zur Geschichte der jüdischchristlichen Beziehungen in den ersten Jahrhunderten*. Basel, 1946.

Bøe, Sverre. *Gog and Magog: Ezekiel 38–39 as Pre-text for Revelation 19, 17–21 and 20, 7–10*. Tübingen, 2001.

Bóna, István. *Das Hunnenreich*. Budapest, 1991.

Börm, Henning. "Das Königtum der Sasaniden—Strukturen und Probleme. Bemerkungen aus althistorischer Sicht." *Klio* 90 (2008) 423–443.

————. "'Es war allerdings nicht so, dass sie im Sinne eines Tributes erhielten, wie vielemeinten...': Anlässe und Funktion der persischen Geldforderungen an die Römer (3. bis 6. Jh.)." *Historia* 57 (2008) 327–346.

————. "Herrscher und Eliten." In *Commutatio et Contentio: Studies in the Late Roman, Sasanian, and Early Islamic Near East*, ed. H. Börm and Josef Wiesehöfer, 159–198. Düsseldorf, 2010.

Bovey, Muriel. *Disciplinae Cyclicae: L'organisation du savoir dans l'oeuvre de Martianus Capella*. Trieste, 2003.

Bowersock, Glen W. "Helena's Bridle and the Chariot of Ethiopia." In *Antiquity in Antiquity: Jewish and Christian Pasts in the Greco-Roman World*, ed. Gregg Gardner and Kevin L. Osterloh, 383–393. Tübingen, 2008.

————. *Empires in Collision in Late Antiquity*. Menahem Stern Jerusalem Lectures. Waltham, Mass., 2012.

————. *The Throne of Adulis: Red Sea Wars on the Eve of Islam*. Oxford, 2013.

Bowman, Alan K. "Landholding in the Hermopolite Nome in the Fourth Century A.D." *JRS* 75 (1985) 137–163.

————. *The Town Councils of Roman Egypt*. Toronto, 1971.

Boyarin, Daniel. *Border Lines: The Partition of Judaeo-Christianity*. Philadelphia, 2004.

Bradbury, Scott. *Severus of Minorca, Letter on the Conversion of the Jews*. Oxford, 1996.

Brakke, David. "The Making of Monastic Demonology: Three Ascetic Teachers on Withdrawal, and Resistance." *CH* 70 (2001) 19–48.

————. "Shenoute, Weber, and the Monastic Prophet: Ancient and Modern Articulations of Ascetic Authority." In *Foundations of Power and Conflicts of Authority in Late Antique Monasticism*, ed. Alberto Camplani and Giovanni Filoramo, 47–73. Louvain, 2007.

Branham, Joan R. "Sacred Space under Erasure in Ancient Synagogues and Early Churches." *ABull* 74 (1992) 375–94.

Brennan, Peter. "The Notitia Dignitatum." In *Les literatures techniques dans l'antiquité romaine*, ed. Fondation Hardt pour l'étude de l'Antiquité classique, 147–178. Geneva, 1995.

————. "The Last of the Romans: Roman Identity and the Roman Army in the Late Roman Near East." *MedArch* 11 (1998) 191–203.

Brock, Sebastian P. "Greek and Syriac in Late Antique Syria." In *Literacy and Power in the Ancient World*, ed. Alan K. Bowman and Greg Woolf, 149–161. Cambridge, 1994.

Brodersen, Kai, ed. *Pomponius Mela: Kreuzfahrt durch die alte Welt*. Darmstadt, 1994.

————. *Terra Cognita: Studien zur römischen Raumerfassung*. Hildesheim, 1995.

————. "Review Article: Mapping (in) the Ancient World." *JRS* 94 (2004) 183–190.

Brooks, James. *Captives and Cousins: Slavery, Kinship, and Community in the Southwest Borderlands*. Chapel Hill, N.C., 2002.

Brosseder, Ursula and Bryan K. Miller, eds. *Xiongnu Archaeology: Multidisciplinary Perspectives of the First Steppe Empire in Inner Asia*. Bonn, 2011.

Brown, Peter R. L. *Augustine of Hippo: A Biography*. 2nd ed. Berkeley, 2000.

————. "Christianity and Local Culture in Late Roman Africa." *JRS* 58 (1968) 85–95.

————. "Christianization and Religious Conflict." In *The Cambridge Ancient History*, vol. 13: *The Late Empire, A.D. 337–425*, ed. Averil Cameron and Peter Garnsey, 632–666. Cambridge, 1998.

————. *Poverty and Leadership in the Later Roman Empire*. Hanover, N.H., 2002.

————. *Power and Persuasion in Late Antiquity*. Madison, 1992.

————. *The Making of Late Antiquity*. Cambridge, Mass., 1978.

————. *The Rise of Western Christendom: Triumph and Diversity, A.D. 200–1000*. 2nd ed. Cambridge, Mass., 2003.

————. *The World of Late Antiquity*. London, 1971.

————. *Through the Eye of a Needle: Wealth, the Fall of Rome, and the Making of Christianity in the West 350–550 AD*. Princeton, 2012.

Bülow, Gerda von. "The Fort of Iatrus in Moesia Secunda: Observations on the Late Roman Defensive System on the Lower Danube (Fourth–Sixth Centuries AD)." In *The Transition to Late Antiquity: On the Danube and Beyond*, ed. Andrew G. Poulter, 459–478. Oxford, 2007.

Burgess, Richard. "A New Reading for Hydatius' Chronicle 177 and the Defeat of the Huns in Italy." *Phoenix* 42 (1988) 357–363.

Burgess, Richard, et al. "Urbicius' *Epitedeuma*: An Edition, Translation and Commentary." *ByzZ* 98 (2005) 35–74.

————. "The Accession of Marcian in the light of Chalcedonian Apologetic and Monophysite Polemic." *ByzZ* 86 no. 1 (1994) 47–68.

Burkitt, Francis. *Euphemia and the Goth*. London, 1913.

Burns, Thomas S. "The Settlement of 418." In *Fifth-Century Gaul: A Crisis of Identity*, ed. John F. Drinkwater and Hugh Elton, 53–63. Cambridge, 1992.

Burrus, Virginia. *The Making of a Heretic: Gender, Authority, and the Priscillianist Controversy*. Berkeley, 1995.

Bury, John B. "Justa Grata Honoria." *JRS* 9 (1919) 1–13.

Butcher, Kevin. *Roman Syria and the Near East*. Los Angeles, 2003.

Cain, Andrew. "Jerome's Epitaphium Paulae: Hagiography, Pilgrimage, and the Cult of Saint Paula." *JECS* 18 (2010) 105–139.

Caldwell III, Craig H. "The Balkans." In *The Oxford Handbook of Late Antiquity*, ed. Scott F. Johnson, 92–111. Oxford, 2012.

Cameron, Alan. "The Empress and the Poet: Paganism and Politics at the Court of Theodosius II." *YCIS* 27 (1982) 258–263.

————. *The Last Pagans of Rome*. New York, 2011.

————. Jacqueline Long, and Lee Sherry. *Barbarians and Politics at the Court of Arcadius*. Vol. 19. Berkeley, 1993.

Cameron, Averil. "Ascetic Closure and the End of Antiquity." In *Asceticism*, ed. Vincent L. Wimbush and Richard Valanstasis, 147–161. New York, 1995.

————. "Vandal and Byzantine Africa." *The Cambridge Ancient History*, vol. 14: *Late Antiquity: Empire and Successors, A.D. 425–600*, ed. Averil Cameron, Bryan Ward-Perkins, and Michael Whitby, 552–569. Cambridge, 2001.

————. "The Violence of Orthodoxy." In *Heresy and Identity in Late Antiquity*, ed. Eduard Iricinschi and Holger M. Zellentin, 102–114. Tübingen, 2008.

————. *The Later Roman Empire*. Cambridge, Mass., 1993.

————. *The Mediterranean World in Late Antiquity, AD 395–700*. Abingdon, U.K., 2012.

Canepa, Matthew P. *The Two Eyes of the Earth: Art and Ritual of Kingship between Rome and Sasanian Iran*. Berkeley, 2009.

Caner, Daniel. *Wandering, Begging Monks: Spiritual Authority and the Promotion of Monasticism in Late Antiquity*. Berkeley, 2002.

———. "Toward a Miraculous Economy: Christian Gifts and Material 'Blessings' in Late Antiquity." *JECS* 14 (2006) 329–77.

Cardman, Francine. "The Rhetoric of Holy Places: Palestine in the Fourth Century." *SP* 17 (1982) 18–25.

Carlà, Filippo. *L'oro nella tarda antichità: Aspetti economici e sociali*. Turin, 2009.

Casson, Lionel. "Bishop Synesius' Voyage to Cyrene." *AN* 12 (1952) 1.294–296.

———. "Comment on 'The Ship of Bishop Synesius' (*IJNA* 15:67–69)." *IJNA* 16 (1987) 67.

Cecconi, Giovanni A. "Conscience de la crise, groupements de pression, idéologie du beneficium: L'État impérial tardif pouvait-il se réformer?" *AnTard* 13 no. 1 (2005) 281–304.

Cereti, Carlo. "Xiiaona and Xyôn in Zoroastrian Texts." In *Coins, Art and Chronology, vol. 2: The First Millennium C.E. in the Indo-Iranian Borderlands*, ed. Michael Alram et al., 59–72. Vienna, 2010.

Chabot, Jean-Baptiste, ed. *Chronique de Michel le Syrien, Patriarche jacobite d'Antioche (1166–1199)*. Paris, 1899–1924.

Chadwick, Henry. *Boethius: The Consolations of Music, Logic, Theology, and Philosophy*. Oxford, 1990.

———. *The Church in Ancient Society: From Galilee to Gregory the Great*. Oxford, 2003.

Chanock, Martin. *Law, Custom and Social Order: The Colonial Experience in Malawi and Zambia*. Cambridge, 1984.

Chapman Stacey, Robin. *Dark Speech: The Performance of Law in Early Ireland*. Philadelphia, 2007.

Charles, Michael. *Vegetius in Context*. Stuttgart, 2007.

Chastagnol, André. *Le sénat romain sous le règne d'Odoacre*. Bonn, 1966.

———. *L'album municipal de Timgad*. Bonn, 1978.

Christensen, Artur. *L'Iran sous les Sassanides*. Copenhagen, 1936.

Christie, Neil. *From Constantine to Charlemagne: An Archaeology of Italy, AD 300–800*. Aldershot, 2006.

Clark, Elizabeth. *The Origenist Controversy: The Cultural Construction of an Early Christian Debate*. Princeton, 1992.

Clover, Frank M. "The Family and Early Career of Anicius Olybrius." *Historia* 27 (1978) 169–196.

Cohen, Robin. *Global Diasporas: An Introduction*. 2nd ed. Cambridge, 2008.

———. *The Cambridge Survey of World Migration*. Cambridge, 2010.

Colditz, Iris. "Altorientalische und Avesta-Traditionen in der Herrschertitulatur des vorislamischen Iran." In *Religious Themes and Texts of pre-Islamic Iran and Central Asia: Studies in Honour of Professor Gherardo Gnoli*, ed. Carlo Cereti et al., 61–78. Wiesbaden, 2003.

Collins, Roger. "Law and Ethnic Identity in the Western Kingdoms in the Fifth and Sixth Centuries." In *Medieval Europeans: Studies in Ethnic Identity and National Perspectives in Medieval Europe*, ed. Alfred P. Smyth, 1–23. London, 1998.

———. *Visigothic Spain, 409–711*. London, 2004.

Conant, Jonathan. *Staying Roman: Conquest and Identity in Africa and the Mediterranean, 439–700*. Cambridge, 2012.

Connolly, Serena. "Roman Ransomers." *AHB* 20 (2006) 115–131.

Cooper, Kate. *The Fall of the Roman Household*. Cambridge, 2007.

Corcoran, Simon. "Observations on the Sasanian Law-Book in the Light of Roman Legal Writing." In *Law, Custom and Justice in Late Antiquity and the Early Middle Ages*, ed. Alice Rio, 77–114. London, 2011.

Courtois, Christian. *Les Vandales et l'Afrique*. Paris, 1955.

————. *Victor de Vita et son œuvre*. Algiers, 1954.

Crawford, John S. "Jews, Christians, and Polytheists in Late-Antique Sardis." In *Jews, Christians, and Polytheists in the Ancient Synagogue: Cultural Interaction during the Greco-Roman Period*, ed. Steven Fine, 190–200. London, 1999.

Cribb, Joe. "The Kidarites, the Numismatic Evidence." In *Coins, Art and Chronology*, vol. 2: *The First Millennium C.E. in the Indo-Iranian Borderlands*, ed. Michael Alram, 91–146. Vienna, 2010.

Cribiore, Raffaela. *The School of Libanius in Late Antique Antioch*. Princeton, 2007.

Croke, Brian. "Evidence for the Hun Invasion of Thrace in AD 422." *GRBS* 18 (1977) 347–367. Reprint in *Christian Chronicles and Byzantine History, 5th–6th Centuries*, no. 12. Aldershot, 1992.

————. "Anatolius and Nomus: Envoys to Attila." *Byzantinoslavica* 42 (1981) 159–170. Reprint in *Christian Chronicles and Byzantine History, 5th–6th Centuries*, no. 13. Aldershot, 1992.

————. "Two Early Byzantine Earthquakes and Their Liturgical Commemoration." *Byzantion* 51 (1981) 122–147. Reprint in *Christian Chronicles and Byzantine History, 5th–6th Centuries*, no. 9. Aldershot, 1992.

————. "The Context and Date of Priscus Fragment 6." *CPh* 78 (1983) 297–308. Reprint in *Christian Chronicles and Byzantine History, 5th–6th Centuries*, no. 14. Aldershot, 1992.

————. "Basiliscus the Boy Emperor." *GRBS* 24 (1983) 81–91. Reprint in *Christian Chronicles and Byzantine History, 5th–6th Centuries*, no. X. Aldershot, 1992.

————. *Count Marcellinus and His Chronicle*. Oxford, 2001.

————. "Dynasty and Ethnicity: Emperor Leo I and the Eclipse of Aspar." *Chiron* 34 (2005) 147–203.

————. "Reinventing Constantinople: Theodosius I's Imprint on the Imperial City." In *From the Tetrarchs to the Theodosians*, ed. Scott McGill, Cristiana Sogno, and Edward Watts, 241–264. New York, 2010.

Curta, Florin. *Southeastern Europe in the Middle Ages, 500–1250*. Cambridge, 2006.

————. *The Making of the Slavs: History and Archaeology of the Lower Danube Region, c. 500–700*. Cambridge, 2001.

Daffinà, Paolo. "Chih-chih Shan-Yü." *RSO* 44, no. 33 (1969) 199–232.

Dagron, Gilbert. "Les moines et la ville: Le monachisme à Constantinople jusqu'au concile de Chalcédoine (451)." *T&MBYZ* 4 (1970) 229–76.

————. *Naissance d'une capitale: Constantinople et ses institutions de 330 à 451*. Paris, 1974.

————. "Constantinople, la primauté après Rome." In *Politica retorica e simbolismo del primato: Roma e Costantinopli (secoli IV–VII)*, ed. Rosario Soraci and Elia Febronia, 23–38. Catania, 2002.

————. *Emperor and Priest*. Cambridge, 2003.

Daryaee, Touraj. "History, Epic, and Numismatics: On the Title of Yazdgerd I (rāmšahr)." *AJN* 15 (2002) 89–95.

————. "Sasanians and Their Ancestors." In *Proceedings of the 5th Conference of the Societas Iranologica Europaea*, ed. Antonio Panaino and Andrea Piras, 387–393. Milan, 2006.

de Bruyn, Theodore S. "Ambivalence within a Totalizing Discourse: Augustine's Sermons on the Sack of Rome." *JECS* 1.4 (1993) 405–441.

de Ste Croix, Geoffrey. *The Class Struggle in the Ancient Greek World.* London, 1983.

de Vogüé, Adalbert. *Les règles des saints pères.* Editions du Cerf 297. Paris, 1982.

Delbrueck, Richard. *Dittici consolari tardoantichi.* Ed. Marilena Abbatepaolo. Bari, 2008.

Delmaire, Roland. "Les dignitaires laics au Concile de Chalcedoine: Notes sur la hiérarchie et les présénces au milieu du Ve siècIe." *Byzantion* 54 (1984) 141–75.

Demandt, Alexander. *Der Fall Roms: Die Auflösung des römischen Reiches im Urteil der Nachwelt.* Munich, 1984.

———. "Der spätrömische Militäradel." *Chiron* 10 (1980) 609–636.

———. *Die Spätantike.* 2nd. ed. Munich, 2007.

Dennis, George. *Maurice's Strategikon.* Philadelphia, 1984.

Dennis, George and Ernst Gamillscheg. *Das Strategikon des Maurikios.* Vienna, 1981.

Derrett, J. D. M. "The History of 'Palladius' on the Races of India and the Brahmans." *C&M* 21(1960) 64–135.

———. "The Theban Scholasticus and Malabar in c. 355–60." *JAOS* 82 (1962) 21–31.

Desanges, Jehan. "D'Axoum à l'Assam, aux portes de la Chine: Le voyage du 'Scholasticus de Thèbes' (entre 360 et 500 après J.-C.)." *Historia* 18 (1969) 627–639.

Devos, Paul. "La date du voyage d'Égérie." *AB* 85 (1967) 165–194.

Di Cosmo, Nicola. "Ethnogenesis, Coevolution and Political Morphology of the Earliest Steppe Empire: The Xiongnu Question Revisited." In *Xiongnu Archaeology: Multidisciplinary Perspectives of the First Steppe Empire in Inner Asia*, ed. Ursula Brosseder and Bryan K. Miller, 35–48. Bonn, 2011.

———. *Ancient China and Its Enemies.* Cambridge, 2002.

Di Cosmo, Nicola and Michael Maas, *Eurasian Empires in Late Antiquity: Rome, China, Iran, and the Steppe ca. 250–650.* Cambridge, Forthcoming.

Diefenbach, Steffen. "Zwischen Liturgie und Civilitas: Konstantinopel im 5. Jhd. und die Etablierung eines städtischen Kaisertums." In *Bildlichkeit und Bildort von Liturgie: Schauplätze in Spätantike, Byzanz und Mittelalter*, ed. Rainer Warland, 21–47. Wiesbaden, 2002.

Dietz, Maribel. *Wandering Monks, Virgins, and Pilgrims. Ascetic Travel in the Mediterranean World, AD 300–800.* University Park, Pa., 2005.

Dignas, Beate, and Engelbert Winter. *Rome and Persia in Late Antiquity.* Cambridge, 2008.

Dihle, Albrecht. "The Conception of India in Hellenistic and Roman Literature." *Cambridge Classical Journal* n.s. 10 (1964) 15–23.

Dilke, Oswald Ashton Wentworth. *Greek and Roman Maps.* Baltimore, 1998.

Dillon, John N. *The Justice of Constantine: Law, Communication, and Control.* Ann Arbor, 2012.

Divjak, Johannes. *Oeuvres des Saint Augustin.* Paris, 1987.

Dodds, Eric R. *Pagan and Christian in an Age of Anxiety.* Cambridge, 1965.

Dossey, Leslie. *Peasant and Empire in Christian North Africa.* Berkeley, 2010.

Drijvers, Han J. W. "The Protonike Legend, the *Doctrina Addai,* and Bishop Rabbula of Edessa." *VChr* 51 (1997) 298–315.

Drijvers, Jan Willem. "Ammianus, Jovian, and the Syriac Julian Romance." *JLA* 4 (2011) 280–297.

Drinkwater, John F. "Bacaudae of Fifth-Century Gaul." In *Fifth-Century Gaul: A Crisis of Identity?*, ed. John F. Drinkwater and Hugh Elton, 208–217. Cambridge, 1992.

————. *The Alamanni and Rome 213–496 (Caracalla to Clovis)*. Oxford, 2007.

Drinkwater, John F., and Hugh Elton, eds. *Fifth-Century Gaul: A Crisis of Identity?* Cambridge, 1992.

Dueck, Daniela, and Kai Brodersen. *Geography in Classical Antiquity*. Cambridge, 2012.

Duffy, John. "Byzantine Medicine in the Sixth and Seventh Centuries: Aspects of Teaching and Practice." *DOP* 38 (1984) 21–27.

Dunbabin, Katherine M. D. *The Roman Banquet: Images of Conviviality*. Cambridge, 2003.

Durliat, Jean. *De la ville antique à la ville byzantine: Le problème des subsistances*. Collection de l'Ecole française de Rome 136. Paris, 1990.

Elsner, Jaś. "The Itinerarium Burdigalense: Politics and Salvation in the Geography of Constantine's Empire." *JRS* 90 (2000) 181–195.

————. "Inventing Christian Rome: The Role of Early Christian Rome." In *Rome the Cosmopolis*, ed. Catharine Edwards and Greg Woolf, 71–99. Cambridge, 2003.

Elm, Susanna. *Virgins of God: The Making of Asceticism in Late Antiquity*. Oxford, 1994.

————. *Sons of Hellenism, Fathers of the Church: Emperor Julian, Gregory of Nazianzus, and the Vision of Rome*. Berkeley, 2012.

Elton, Hugh. *Warfare in Roman Europe, AD 350–425*. Oxford, 1996.

————. "Defense in Fifth-Century Gaul." In *Fifth-Century Gaul: A Crisis of Identity?*, ed. John F. Drinkwater and Hugh Elton, 167–176. Cambridge, 1992.

————. "Cavalry in Late Roman Warfare." In *The Late Roman Army in the Near East from Diocletian to the Arab Conquest*, ed. Ariel Lewin and Pietrina Pellegrini, 377–381. BAR S1717. Oxford, 2007.

————. "Imperial Politics at the Court of Theodosius II." In *The Power of Religion in Late Antiquity*, ed. Andrew Cain and Noel Lenski, 133–142. Aldershot, 2009.

Emmel, Stephen. *Shenoute's Literary Corpus*. 2 vols. CSCO 599–600, subsidia 111–112. Louvain, 1994.

————. "The Historical Circumstances of Shenoute's Sermon God Is Blessed." In *Themelia: Spätantike und koptologische Studien Peter Grossmann zum 65. Geburtstag*, ed. Peter Grossman, Martin Krause, and Sofia Schaten, 81–96. Wiesbaden, 1998.

————. "From the Other Side of the Nile: Shenoute and Panopolis." In *Perspectives on Panopolis: An Egyptian Town from Alexander the Great to the Arab Conquest*, ed. Arno Egberts, Brian Paul Muhs, and Joep van der Vliet, 95–113. Leiden, 2002.

————. "Shenoute the Monk: The Early Monastic Career of Shenoute the Archimandrite." In *Il monachesimo tra eredità e aperture: Atti del simposio "Testi e temi nella tradizione del monachesimo cristiano" per il 500 anniversario dell'Istituto Monastico di Sant'Anselmo, Roma, 28 maggio–10 giugno 2002*, ed. Maciej Bielawsi and Daniël Hombergen, 151–174. Rome, 2004.

————. "Shenoute of Atripe and the Christian Destruction of Temples in Egypt." In *From Temple to Church*, ed. Johannes Hahn, Stephen Emmel, and Ulrich Gotter, 161–201. Leiden, 2008.

Englisch, Brigitte. *Die Artes liberales im frühen Mittelalter (5.–9. Jh.): Das Quadrivium und der Komputus als Indikatoren für Kontinuität und Erneuerung der exakten Wissenschaften zwischen Antike und Mittelalter*. Stuttgart, 1994.

Enoki, Kazuo. "On the Date of the Kidarites (I)." *MRDTB* 27 (1969) 1–26.

Erdy, Miklòs. "An Overview of the Xiongnu Type Cauldron Finds of Eurasia in Three Media, With Historical Observations." In *The Archaeology of the Steppes*, ed. Bruno Genito, 379–438. Naples, 1994.

Esders, Stefan. "Grenzen und Grenzüberschreitungen: Religion, Ethnizität und politische Integration am Rande des oströmischen Imperiums (4.–7.Jh.)." In *Gestiftete Zukunft im mittelalterlichen Europa*, ed. Wolfgang Huschner and Frank Rexroth, 3–28. Berlin, 2008.

Esmonde Cleary, A. S. *The Roman West, AD 200–500: An Archaeological Study.* Cambridge, 2013.

Feissel, Denis. "Les actes de l'État imperial dans l'épigraphie tardive (324–610): Prolégomènes à un inventaire." In *Selbstdarstellung und Kommunikation: Die Veröffentlichung staatlicher Urkunden auf Stein und Bronze in der römischen Welt*, ed. Rudolf Haensch, 97–128. Munich, 2009.

Feissel, Denis, and Klaas A. Worp. "La requête d'Appion, évêque de Syene, à Théodose II: P. Leid. Z révisé." *Oudheidkundige Mededelingen* 68 (1988) 97–111.

Ferguson, John. "Aspects of Early Christianity in North Africa." In *Africa in Classical Antiquity. Nine Studies*, ed. Lloyd A. Thompson and John Ferguson, 182–191. Ibadan, Nigeria, 1969.

Filippo, Carlà. *L'oro nella tarda antichità: Aspetti economici e sociali.* Turin, 2009.

Fischer, Hubert. *Die Schrift des Salvian von Marseille "An die Kirche."* Frankfurt, 1976.

Fisher, Greg. *Between Empires: Arabs, Romans, and Sasanians in Late Antiquity.* Oxford, 2011.

Foss, Clive. "Syria in Transition, A.D. 550–750: An Archaeological Approach." *DOP* 51 (1997) 189–269.

Fournet, Jean-Luc, and Jean Gascou. "Liste des pétitions sur papyrus des Ve–VIIe siècles." In *La pétition à Byzance*, ed. Denis Feissel and Jean Gascou, 141–196. Paris, 2004.

Fowden, Elizabeth Key. *The Barbarian Plain: Saint Sergius between Rome and Iran.* Berkeley, 1999.

Fowden, Garth. *Empire to Commonwealth: Consequences of Monotheism in Late Antiquity.* Princeton, 1993.

Frakes, Robert M. "Late Roman Social Justice and Origin of the Defensor Civitatis." *CJ* 89 (1994) 337–348.

Francovich Onesti, Nicoletta. *I Vandali: Lingua e storia.* Rome, 2002.

Fraser, Peter M. "A Syriac 'Notitia Urbis Alexandrinae.'" *JEA* 37 (1951) 103–108.

Fredriksen, Paula. "What Parting of the Ways? Jews and Gentiles in the Ancient Mediterranean City." In *The Ways That Never Parted: Jews and Christians in Late Antiquity and the Early Middle Ages*, ed. Adam H. Becker and Annette Yoshiko Reed, 35–63. Tübingen, 2003.

———. *Augustine and the Jews: A Christian Defense of Jews and Judaism.* New York, 2008.

Friedman, Lawrence M. "Legal Culture and Social Development." *Law and Society Review* 4 (1969) 29–44.

Frier, Bruce. W. "Demography." In *The Cambridge Ancient History*, vol. 11: *The High Empire, A.D. 70–192*, ed. Alan K. Bowman, Peter Garnsey, and Domonic Rathbone, 787–816. 2nd ed. Cambridge, 2000.

Frye, Richard N. *The Heritage of Central Asia: From Antiquity to the Turkish Expansion.* Princeton, 1998.

Galanter, Marc. "Justice in Many Rooms: Courts, Private Ordering, and Indigenous Law." *Journal of Legal Pluralism and Unofficial Law* 19 (1981) 1–48.

Garnsey, Peter. *Famine and Food Supply in the Graeco-Roman World*. Cambridge, 1989.

———. "Roman Citizenship and Roman Law in the Late Empire." In *Approaching Late Antiquity*, ed. Simon Swain and Mark Edwards, 133–155. Oxford, 2004.

Garsoïan, Nina. "Byzantium and the Sasanians." In *The Cambridge History of Iran*, vol. 3, pt. 1: *The Seleucid, Parthian, and Sasanian Periods*, ed. Ehsan Yarshater, 568–592. Cambridge, 1983.

———. "La politique arménienne des sassanides." In *Trésors d'Orient: Mélanges offerts Rika Gyselen*, ed. Philippe Gignoux et al., 67–79. Paris, 2009.

———. *The Epic Histories Attributed to P'awstos Buzand (Buzandaran Patmut'iwnk)*. Cambridge, Mass., 1989.

———. "Une coïncidence supplémentaire entre les sources arméniennes et perses: Le cas du grand vizir Mihr Narseh." *REArm* 27 (1998–2000) 311–320.

Garzya, Antonio, ed. *Synesii Cyrenensis epistulae*. Rome, 1979.

Geary, Patrick. *The Myth of Nations: The Medieval Origins of Europe*. Princeton, 2002.

———. "Using Genetic Data to Revolutionalize Understanding of Migration History." *Institute for Advanced Study eNews, Spring 2013*, http://www.ias.edu/about/publications/ias-letter/articles/2013-spring/geary-history-genetics, accessed 17 July 2013.

Geyer, Paul, and Otto Cuntz, eds. *Itineraria et alia geographica*. 2 vols. CCSL 175–176. Turnhout, 1965.

Gibson, Margaret, ed. *Boethius: His Life, Thought, and Influence*. Oxford, 1981.

Gignoux, Philippe. "Les inscriptions en moyen-perse de Bandiān." *StIr* 27 (1998) 251–258.

Gil Egea, María Elvira. *África en tiempos de los vándalos: Continuidad y mutaciones de las estructuras sociopolíticas romanas*. Alcalá de Henares, 1998.

Gillett, Andrew. "Ethnogenesis: A Contested Model of Early Medieval Europe." *History Compass* 4.2 (2006) 241–260.

———. "Rome, Ravenna, and the Emperors." *PBSR* 69 (2001) 131–167.

———. *Envoys and Political Communication in the Late Antique West, 411–533*. Cambridge, 2003.

Ginzburg, Carlo. "The Conversion of Minorcan Jews (417–418): An Experiment in the History of Historiography." In *Christendom and its Discontents: Exclusion, Persecution, and Rebellion, 1000–1500*, ed. Scott L. Waugh and Peter D. Diehl, 207–219. Cambridge, 1996.

Glucker, John. *Antiochus and the Late Academy*. Göttingen, 1978.

Gnoli, Gherardo. *The Idea of Iran: An Essay on Its Origin*. Rome, 1989.

Godłowski, Kasimierz. "Das Aufhören der Germanischen Kulturen an der Mittleren Donau und das Problem des Vordringens der Slawen." In *Die Völker an der mittleren und unteren Donau im fünften und sechsten Jahrhundert*, ed. Herwig Wolfram and Falko Daim, 225–232. Denkschriften der Österreichischen Akademie der Wissenschaften, phil.-hist. Kl. Vienna, 1980.

Goetz, Hans-Werner, Jörg Jarnut, and Walter Pohl, eds. *Regna and Gentes: The Relationship between Late Antique and Early Medieval Peoples and Kingdoms in the Transformation of the Roman World*. The Transformation of the Roman World 13. Leiden, 2003.

Goffart, Walter A. *Barbarians and Romans, AD 418–584: The Techniques of Accommodation.* Princeton, 1980.

———. *The Narrators of Barbarian History (AD 550–800): Jordanes, Gregory of Tours, Bede, and Paul the Deacon.* Princeton, 1988.

———. *Barbarian Tides: The Migration Age and the Later Roman Empire.* Philadelphia, 2006.

———. "The Technique of Barbarian Settlement in the Fifth Century: A Personal, Streamlined Account with Ten Additional Comments." *JLA* 3 (2010) 65–98.

Golden, Peter. *An Introduction to the History of the Turkic Peoples.* Wiesbaden, 1992.

———. *Central Asia in World History.* Oxford, 2011.

———. "The Peoples of the South Russian Steppes." In *The Cambridge History of Early Inner Asia*, ed. Denis Sinor, 256–284. Cambridge, 1990.

Goodrich, Richard. *Contextualizing Cassian: Aristocrats, Ascetics, and Reformation in Fifth-Century Gaul.* Oxford, 2007.

Gracanin, Hrvoje. "The Huns and South Pannonia." *ByzSlav* 64 (2006) 29–76.

Gray, Patrick T. R. "The Legacy of Chalcedon: Christological Problems and Their Significance." In *The Cambridge Companion to the Age of Justinian*, ed. Michael Maas, 215–238. Cambridge, 2005.

Graf, Fritz. "Fights about Festivals: Libanius and John Chrysostom on the Kalendae Ianuariae in Antioch." *Archiv für Religionsgeschichte* 13 (2012) 175–186.

Graves, Michael. *Jerome's Hebrew Philology: A Study Based on His Commentary on Jeremiah.* Supplements to *VChr* 90. Leiden, 2007.

Greatrex, Geoffrey. "Byzantium and the East in the Sixth Century." In *The Cambridge Companion to the Age of Justinian*, ed. Michael Maas, 477–509. Cambridge, 2005.

———. "Justin I and the Arians." *SP* 34 (2001) 72–81.

———. "La du sortoj de la romia Imperio." *Aktoj de la IKU, 66a sesio.* Rotterdam, forthcoming.

———. *Rome and Persia at War, 502–532.* Leeds, 1998.

———. "Roman Identity in the Sixth Century." In *Ethnicity and Culture in Late Antiquity*, ed. Stephen Mitchell and Geoffrey Greatrex, 267–292. London, 2000.

———. "The Two Fifth-Century Wars between Rome and Persia." *Florilegium* 12 (1993) 1–14.

Greatrex, Geoffrey, Hugh Elton, and Richard Burgess. "Urbicius' *Epitedeuma*: An edition, translation and commentary." *ByzZ* 98 no 1 (2005) 35–74.

Greatrex, Geoffrey, and Samuel N. C. Lieu. *The Roman Eastern Frontier and the Persian Wars, part 2: AD 363–630: A Narrative Sourcebook.* London, 2002.

Green, Dennis. "Linguistic Evidence for the Early Migrations of the Goths." In *The Visigoths from the Migration Period to the Seventh Century: An Ethnographic Perspective*, ed. Peter Heather, 11–42. Woodbridge, U.K., 1999.

Grenet, Frantz. "Crise et sortie de crise en Bactriane-Sogdiane aux IVe–Ve siècles: De l'héritage antique à l'adoption de modèles sassanides." In *La Persia e l'Asia Centrale da Alessandro al X Secolo*, ed. W. Belardi et al., 367–390. Rome, 1996.

———. "Découverte d'un relief sassanide dans le nord de l'Afghanistan." *CRAI* 1 (2005) 115–134.

———. "Regional Interaction in Central Asia and Northwest India in the Kidarite and Hephthalite Periods." In *Indo-Iranian Languages and Peoples*, ed. Nicholas Sims-Williams, 203–224. Oxford, 2002.

Grey, Cam. *Constructing Communities in the Late Roman Countryside.* Cambridge, 2011.

————. "Salvian, the Ideal Christian Community and the Fate of the Poor." In *Poverty in the Roman World*, ed. Margaret Atkin and Robin Osborne, 168–182. Cambridge, 2007.

Griffe, Élie. *La Gaule Chrétienne a l'époque Romaine*, vol. 2: *L'Église des Gaules au Ve siècle*. Paris, 1966.

Griffith, Sidney H. "Ephraem, the Deacon of Edessa, and the Church of the Empire." In *Diakonia*, ed. Thomas Halton and Joseph P. Williman, 22–52. Washington, D.C., 1986.

Grig, Lucy. "Portraits, Pontiffs and the Christianization of Fourth-Century Rome." *PBSR* 72 (2004) 203–230.

Grig, Lucy, and Gavin Kelly, eds. *Two Romes: Rome and Constantinople in Late Antiquity*. Oxford, 2012.

Grossmann, Peter. *Christliche Architektur in Ägypten*. Handbook of Oriental Studies 62. Leiden, 2002.

Grubbs, Judith Evans. *Women and the Law in the Roman Empire*. London, 2002.

Guy, J.-C. *Jean Cassien: Institutions cénobitiques*. SC 109. Paris, 1965.

Gwynne, David M. "Episcopal Leadership." In *The Oxford Handbook of Late Antiquity*, ed. Scott F. Johnson, 876–915. Oxford, 2012.

Gyselen, Rika. *Great-Commander (wuzurg-framadār) and Court Counsellor (dar-andarzbed) in the Sasanian Empire (224–651): The Sigillographic Evidence*. Rome, 2008.

————. "New Evidence for Sasanian Numismatics: The Collection of Ahmad Saeedi." In *Contributions à l'histoire et la géographie historique de l'empire sassanide*, ed. Rika Gyselen, 49–140. Bures-sur-Yvette, 2004.

————. "Primary Sources and Historiography of the Sasanian Empire." *StIr* 38 (2009) 163–190.

Haarer, Fiona. *Anastasius I: Politics and Empire in the Late Roman World*. Cambridge, 2006.

Haas, Christopher. *Alexandria in Late Antiquity: Topography and Social Conflict*. Baltimore, 1997.

Haldon, John. *Warfare, State and Society in the Byzantine World, 565–1204*. London, 1999.

Hallebeek, Jan. "The Roman Pontiff as Direct Judge of Appeal and the Identity of the Latin Church." In *Religious Identity and the Problem of Historical Foundation: The Foundational Character of Authoritative Sources in the History of Christianity and Judaism*, ed. Judith Frishman, Willemien Otten, and Gerard Rouwhorst, 387–404. Leiden, 2004.

Halleux, André de. "Le décret Chalcédonien sur les prérogatives de la nouvelle Rome." *ETL* 64 (1988) 288–323.

Halsall, Guy. *Barbarian Migrations and the Roman West, 376–568*. Cambridge, 2007.

————. *Early Medieval Cemeteries: An Introduction to Burial Archaeology in the Post-Roman West*. Skelmorlie, U.K., 1995.

————. *Settlement and Social Organization: The Merovingian Region of Metz*. Cambridge, 1995.

————. "Social Identities and Social Relationships in Early Merovingian Gaul." In *Franks and Alamanni in the Merovingian Period: An Ethnographic Perspective*, ed. Ian Wood, 141–175. Woodbridge, U.K., 1998.

————. "The Technique of Barbarian Settlement in the Fifth Century: A Reply to Walter Goffart." *JLA* 3 (2010) 99–112.

Hansen, Günther Christian. "Alexander und die Brahmanen." *Klio* 43, no. 45 (1965) 351–380.

Harper, Kyle."Slave Prices in Late Antiquity (and in the Very Long Term)." *Historia* 59 (2010) 206–238.

_____. *Slavery in the Late Roman World, AD 275–425: An Economic, Social, and Institutional Study*. Cambridge, 2011.

_____. "The Greek Census Inscriptions of Late Antiquity." *JRS* 98 (2008) 83–119.

Harries, Jill. "Not the Theodosian Code: Euric's Law and Late Fifth-Century Gaul." In *Society and Culture in Late Antique Gaul: Revisiting the Sources*, ed. Ralph Mathisen and Danuta Shanzer, 39–51. Aldershot, 2001.

_____. *Sidonius Apollinaris and the Fall of Rome, AD 407–485*. Oxford, 1994.

_____. "The Roman Imperial Quaestor from Constantine to Theodosius II." *JRS* 78 (1988) 148–172.

Hasselhoff, Görge K. "Revising the Vulgate: Jerome and His Jewish Interlocutors." *ZRGG* 64 no. 3 (2012) 209–221.

Hatlie, Peter. *The Monks and Monasteries of Constantinople, ca. 350–850*. Cambridge, 2007.

Hayashi, Toshio. "Hunnic Cauldrons." In *Studies on Ancient Cauldrons: Cultic or Daily Vessels in the Eurasian Steppes*. Tokyo, 2011.

Hays, Gregory. "'Romuleis Libicisque Litteris': Fulgentius and the 'Vandal Renaissance.'" In *Vandals, Romans, and Berbers*, ed. Andy Merrills, 101–132. Aldershot, 2004.

Heather, Peter J. "Cassiodorus and the Rise of the Amals: Genealogy and the Goths under Hun Domination." *JRS* 79 (1989) 103–28.

_____. *Empires and Barbarians: The Fall of Rome and the Birth of Europe*. London, 2009.

_____. "Ethnicity, Group Identity, and Social Status in the Migration Period." In *Franks, Northmen, and Slavs: Identities and State Formation in Early Medieval Europe*, ed. Ildar H. Garipzanov et al., 17–50. Turnhout, 2008.

_____. *Goths and Romans, 332–489*. Oxford, 1991.

_____. "Law and Society in the Burgundian Kingdom." In *Law, Custom and Justice in Late Antiquity and the Early Middle Ages*, ed. Alice Rio, 115–154. London, 2011.

_____. "New Men for New Constantines? Creating an Imperial Elite in the Eastern Mediterranean." In *New Constantines: The Rhythm of Imperial Renewal in Byzantium, 4th–13th Centuries*, ed. Paul Magdalino, 11–33. London, 1994.

_____. "Senators and Senates." *Cambridge Ancient History*, vol. 13: *The Late Empire, A.D. 337–425*, ed. Averil Cameron and Peter Garnsey, 184–210. Cambridge, 1997.

_____. "The Anti-Scythian Tirade of Synesius' *De Regno*." *Phoenix* 42 (1988) 152–172.

_____. *The Fall of the Roman Empire: A New History*. London, 2005.

_____. *The Goths*. Oxford, 1996.

_____. "The Huns and the End of the Roman Empire in Western Europe." *EHR* 110 (1995) 4–41.

_____. "Why Did the Barbarian Cross the Rhine?" *JLA* 2.1 (2009) 3–29.

Heather, Peter J., and John Matthews. *The Goths in the Fourth Century*. 2nd ed. Liverpool, 2004.

Hedeager, Lotte. "Empire, Frontier and the Barbarian Hinterland: Rome and Northern Europe from ad 1–400." In *Centre and Periphery in the Ancient World*, ed. Michael Rowlands, Mogens Larsen, and Kristian Kristiansen, 125–140. Cambridge, 1987.

Heichelheim, Fritz M. "The Text of the *Constitutio Antoniniana*." *JEA* 26 (1941) 10–22.

Heinzelmann, Martin. *Bischofsherrschaft in Gallien: Zur Kontinuität römischer Führungsschichten von 4. bis 7. Jahrhundert: Soziale, prosopographische und bildungsgeschichtliche Aspekte.* Zurich, 1976.

———. "The 'Affair' of Hilary of Arles (445) and Gallo-Roman Identity in the Fifth Century." In *Fifth-Century Gaul: A Crisis of Identity?*, ed. John F. Drinkwater and Hugh Elton, 239–251. Cambridge, 1992.

Hen, Yitzhak. *Roman Barbarians, The Royal Court and Culture in the Early Medieval West.* London, 2007.

Hendy, Michael. *Studies in the Byzantine Monetary Economy c. 300–1450.* Cambridge, 1985.

Henning, Walter B. "The Date of the Sogdian Ancient Letters." *BSOAS* 12.3–4 (1948) 601–615.

Heucke, Clemens. "Die Herrschaft des oströmischen Kaisers Zenon: Ein Beispiel für Integration?" In *Migration und Integration: Aufnahme und Eingliederung im historischen Wandel*, ed. Mathias Beer, Martin Kintzinger, and Marita Krauss, 45–54. Stuttgart, 1997.

Hicks, Andrew. "Martianus Capella and the Liberal Arts." In *The Oxford Handbook of Medieval Latin Literature*, ed. Ralph J. Hexter and David Townsend, 307–334. Oxford, 2012.

Hillner, Julia. "Clerics, Property, and Patronage: The Case of the Roman Titular Churches." *AnTard* 14 (2006) 59–68.

———. "Domus, Family, and Inheritance: The Senatorial Family House in Late Antique Rome." *JRS* 93 (2003) 129–145.

———. "Families, Patronage and the Titular Churches of Rome." In *Religion, Dynasty, and Patronage in Early Christian Rome, 400–800*, ed. Kate Cooper and Julia Hillner, 190–224. Cambridge, 2007.

Hirschfeld, Yitzhak. "Farms and Villages in Byzantine Palestine." *DOP* 51 (1997) 31–71.

Hohlfelder, Robert L. "Marcian's Gamble: A Reassessment of Eastern Imperial Policy toward Attila, AD 450–453." *AJAH* 9 (1984) 54–69.

Holum, Kenneth G. "Hadrian and St. Helena: Imperial Travel and the Origins of Christian Holy Land Pilgrimage." In *The Blessings of Pilgrimage*, ed. Robert G. Ousterhout, 66–81. Urbana, Ill., 1990.

———. "In the Blinking of an Eye: The Christianizing of Classical Cities in the Levant." In *Religion and Politics in the Ancient Near East*, ed. Adele Berlin, 131–150. Bethesda, Md., 1996.

———. *Theodosian Empresses: Women and Imperial Dominion in Late Antiquity.* Berkeley, 1982.

Honoré, Tony. *Law in the Crisis of Empire, 379–455 AD: The Theodosian Dynasty and Its Quaestors with a Palingenesia of Laws of the Dynasty.* Oxford, 1998.

Hopkins, Keith. "Taxes and Trade in the Roman Empire 200 B.C.–A.D. 400." *JRS* 70 (1980) 101–125.

Horden, Peregrine, and Nicholas Purcell. *The Corrupting Sea: A Study of Mediterranean History.* Vol. 1. Oxford, 2000.

Horedt, Kurt. *Siebenburgen im Frühmittelalter.* Bonn, 1986.

Howard-Johnston, James. "The Late Sasanian Army." In *Late Antiquity: Eastern Perspectives*, ed. Teresa Bernheimer and Adam Silverstein, 87–127. Oxford, 2012.

———. "The Sasanians' Strategic Dilemma." In *Commutatio et Contentio: Studies in the Late Roman, Sasanian, and Early Islamic Near East*, ed. Henning Börm and Josef Wiesehöfer, 37–70. Düsseldorf, 2010.

———. "The Two Great Powers in Late Antiquity: A Comparison." In *The Byzantine and Early Islamic Near East*, vol. 3: *States, Resources and Armies*, ed. Averil Cameron, 157–226. Studies in Late Antiquity and Early Islam 1. Princeton, 1995.

Howe, Tankred. *Vandalen, Barbaren, und Arianer bei Victor von Vita*. Frankfurt am Main, 2007.

Hugonnard-Roche, Henri. *La logique d'Aristote du grec au syriaque*. Textes et Traditions 9. Paris, 2004.

Humfress, Caroline. "Law Schools." In *Late Antiquity: A Guide to the Post-Classical World*, ed. Glen W. Bowersock et al., 540–541. Cambridge, Mass., 1999.

Humphries, Mark. "'Gog Is the Goth': Biblical Barbarians in Ambrose of Milan's De fide." In *Unclassical Traditions*, vol. 1, ed. Christopher Kelly, Richard Flower, and Michael Stuart Williams, 45–57. *Cambridge Classical Journal* suppl. 34. Cambridge, 2010.

———. "International Relations." In *Cambridge History of Greek and Roman Warfare*, ed. Philip Sabin, Michael Whitby, and Hans van Wees, 235–269. Cambridge, 2007.

———. "Valentinian III and the City of Rome (A.D. 425–55): Patronage, Politics, and Power." In *Two Romes: Rome and Constantinople in Late Antiquity*, ed. Lucy Grig and Gavin Kelly, 161–182. Oxford 2012.

Hunt, David. "Christianising the Roman Empire: The Evidence of the Code." In *The Theodosian Code*, ed. Jill Harries and Ian Wood, 143–158. Ithaca, N.Y., 1993.

———. *Holy Land Pilgrimage in the Later Roman Empire, AD 312–460*. Oxford, 1982.

———. "St. Stephen in Minorca: An Episode in Jewish-Christian Relations in the Early Fifth Century AD." *JTS* 33 (1982) 106–123.

Hunter, David G. *Marriage, Celibacy, and Heresy in Ancient Christianity: The Jovinianist Controversy*. Oxford, 2007.

Huyse, Philip. "Die königliche Erbfolge bei den Sasaniden." In *Trésors d'Orient: Mélanges offerts à Rika Gyselen*, ed. Philippe Gignoux et al, 145–157. Paris, 2009.

Ingelbert, Hervé. *Interpretatio christiana: Les mutations des savoirs, cosmographie, géographie, histoire, dans l'antiquité chrétienne, 30–630 après J.-C.* Paris, 2001.

Innes, Matthew. *Introduction to Early Medieval Europe, 300–900*. Milton Park, U.K., 2007.

———. "Land, Freedom and the Making of the Medieval West." *TRHS* 16 (2006) 39–74.

Iricinschi, Eduard, and Zellentin, Holger M., eds. *Heresy and Identity in Late Antiquity*. Tübingen, 2008.

Jacobs, Andrew S. *Christ Circumcised: A Study in Early Christian History and Difference*. Philadelphia, 2012.

Jalland, Trevor. *The Life and Times of St. Leo the Great*. New York, 1941.

James, Norman W. "Leo the Great and Prosper of Aquitaine: A Pope and His Adviser." *JTS* 44 (1993) 554–584.

Janni, Pietro. *La mappa e il periplo: Cartografia antica e spazio odologico*. Rome, 1984.

Jenal, Georg. *Italia ascetica atque monastica: Das Asketen-und Mönchtum in Italien von den Anfängen bis zur Zeit de Langobarden (ca. 150/250–604)*. 2 vols. Stuttgart, 1995.

Johnson, David W. "Anti-Chalcedonian Polemics in Coptic Texts, 451–641." In *The Roots of Egyptian Christianity*, ed. Birger A. Pearson and James E. Goehring, 216–234. Philadelphia, 1986.

Johnson, Scott F. "Apostolic Geography: The Origins and Continuity of a Hagiographic Habit." *DOP* 64 (2010) 5–25.

———. "Reviving the Memory of the Apostles: Apocryphal Tradition and Travel Literature in Late Antiquity." In *Revival and Resurgence in Christian History*, eds. Kate Cooper and Jeremy Gregory, 10–20. Woodbridge, U.K., 2008.

———. "Travel, Cartography, and Cosmology." In *The Oxford Handbook of Late Antiquity*, ed. Scott F. Johnson, 562–594. Oxford, 2012.

Jones, A. H. M. *The Greek City from Alexander to Justinian*. Oxford, 1940.

———. *The Later Roman Empire, 284–602: A Social, Economic, and Administrative Survey*. 3 vols. Oxford, 1964.

Jones, A. H. M., John Martindale, and John Morris, eds. *The Prosopography of the Later Roman Empire, 260–395*. 3 vols. Cambridge, 1971–1992.

Jones Hall, Linda. *Roman Berytus: Beirut in Late Antiquity*. London, 2004.

Juster, Jean. *Les juifs dans l'empire romain*. 2 vols. Paris, 1914.

Kadra, Fatima. *Les Djedars: Monuments funéraires Berbères de la région de Frenda*. Algiers, 1983.

Kaegi, Walter Emil. *Byzantium and the Decline of Rome*. Princeton, 1968.

Kageyama, Etsuko. "The Winged Crown and the Triple-Crescent Crown in the Sogdian Funerary Monuments from China: Their Relation to the Hephthalite Occupation of Central Asia." *JIAA* 2 (2007) 11–23.

Kahanov, Yaacov. "The Voyage of Synesius." *Journal of Navigation* 59 (2006) 435–444.

Kaim, Barbara. "Où adorer les dieux? Un spectaculaire temple de feu d'époque sassanide." *DA* 317 (2006) 66–71.

Kaiser, Reinhold. *Die Burgunder*. Stuttgart, 2004.

Kaldellis, Anthony. *Hellenism in Byzantium*. Cambridge, 2007; repr. 2009.

Kamesar, Adam. *Jerome, Greek Scholarship, and the Hebrew Bible: A Study of the Quaestiones Hebraicae in Genesim*. Oxford, 1993.

Kazanski, Michel. "Les Goths et les Huns: À propos des relations entre les barbares sédentaires et les nomades." *AM* 22 (1992) 191–221.

Kazanski, Michel, and Anna Mastykova. *Les peuples du Caucase du Nord*. Paris, 2003.

Kelly, Christopher. *Attila the Hun: Barbarian Terror and the Fall of the Roman Empire*. London, 2008. = *The End of Empire: Attila the Hun and the Fall of Rome*. New York, 2009.

———. "Emperors, Government and Bureaucracy." In *The Cambridge Ancient History*, vol. 13: *The Late Empire, A.D. 337–425*, ed. Averil Cameron and Peter Garnsey, 138–183. Cambridge, 1998.

———. *Ruling the Later Roman Empire*. Cambridge, Mass., 2004.

Kahlos, Maijastina. *Debate and Dialogue: Pagan and Christian Cultures, c. 360–430*. Aldershot, 2007.

Kidd, Douglas, ed. *Aratus: Phaenomena*. Cambridge Classical Texts and Commentaries 34. Cambridge, 1997.

Kim, Hyun Jin. *The Huns, Rome and the Birth of Europe*. Cambridge, 2013.

Kingsley, Charles. *The Roman and the Teuton*. London, 1890.

Kitchen, T. E. "Contemporary Perceptions of the Roman Empire in the Later Fifth and Sixth Centuries." Ph.D. diss., Cambridge University, 2008.

Klingshirn, William E. *Caesarius of Arles*. Cambridge, 1994.

———. "Charity and Power: Caesarius of Arles and the Ransoming of Captives in Sub-Roman Gaul." *JRS* 75 (1985) 183–203.

Kohl, Philip L. *The Making of Bronze Age Eurasia*. Cambridge, 2007.

Kolb, Frank. *Herrscherideologie in der Spätantike*. Berlin, 2001.

Kolesnikov, A. I. "Dopolnitelnie Istochniki po Istorii Rannesrednovekovovo Irana i Evo Vostochnikh Sosedei." In *Tsentralnaya Aziya ot Akhemenidov do Timuridov: Arkheologiya, Istoriya, Etnologiya, Kultura*, ed. V. P. Nikonorov, 112–115. St. Petersburg, 2005.

Kominko, Maja. "New Perspectives on Paradise: The Levels of Reality in Byzantine and Medieval Maps." In *Cartography in Antiquity and the Middle Ages: Fresh Perspectives, New Methods*. ed. Richard Talbert and Richard W. Unger, 139–153. Technology and Change in History 10. Leiden, 2008.

———. "The Map of Cosmas, the Albi Map, and the Tradition of Ancient Geography." *MHR* 20 (2005) 163–186.

Kos, Marjeta S. "The Family of Romulus Augustulus." In *Antike Lebenswelten: Konstanz—Wandel—Wirkungsmacht: Festschrift für Ingomar Weiler zum 70. Geburtstag*, ed. Peter Mauritsch et al., 439–449. Wiesbaden, 2008.

Krabbe, Mary K. C. *Epistula ad Demetriadem de vera humilitate*. Washington, D.C., 1956.

Kraemer, Ross S. "Jewish Women's Resistance to Christianity in the Early Fifth Century: The Account of Severus, Bishop of Minorca." *JECS* 17 (2009) 635–665.

Krannich, Torsten. *Von Leporius bis zu Leo dem Grossen: Studien zur lateinischsprachigen Christologie im fünften Jahrhundert nach Christus*. Studien und Texte zu Antike und Christentum 32. Tubingen, 2005.

Krautheimer, Richard. *Three Christian Capitals: Topography and Politics*. Berkeley, 1983.

Krawiec, Rebecca. *Shenoute and the Women of the White Monastery: Egyptian Monasticism in Late Antiquity*. Oxford, 2002.

Kuhn, Karl Heinz, ed. and trans. *A Panegyric on Apollo, Archimandrite of the Monastery of Isaac, by Stephen Archbishop of Heracleopolis Magna*. 2 vols. Louvain, 1978.

Kulikowski, Michael. *Late Roman Spain and Its Cities*. Baltimore, 2004.

———. "Nation versus Army: a Necessary Contrast?" In *On Barbarian Identity: Critical Approaches to Ethnicity in the Early Middle Ages*, ed. Andrew Gillett, 69–84. Turnhout, 2002.

———. *Rome's Gothic Wars*. Cambridge, 2007.

———. "The *Notitia Dignitatum* as a Historical Source." *Historia* 49 (2000) 358–377.

———. "The Western Kingdoms." In *The Oxford Handbook of Late Antiquity*, ed. Scott F. Johnson, 31–59. Oxford, 2012.

Kunsthistorisches Museum Wien. "Gemme: Siegelstein Alarichs II., König der Westgoten." Kunsthistorisches Museum Wien, Bilddatenbank, http://bilddatenbank.khm.at/viewArtefact?id=71108, accessed July 16 2013.

La Vaissière, Etienne de. "Central Asia and the Silk Road." In *The Oxford Handbook of Late Antiquity*, ed. Scott F. Johnson, 142–169. Oxford, 2012.

———. "Huns et Xiongnu." *CAJ* 49–1 (2005) 3–26.

———. "Is There a 'Nationality of the Hephthalites'?" *BAI* 17 (2003) 119–132.

———. *Sogdian Traders: A History*. Leiden, 2005.

Lafferty, Maura K. "Translating Faith from Greek to Latin: Romanitas and Christianitas in Late Fourth-Century Rome and Milan." *JECS* 11 (2003) 21–62.

Lafferty, Sean D. W. *Law and Society in the Age of Theoderic the Great: A Study of the Edictum Theoderici*. Cambridge, 2013.

Lagarrigue, Georges. *Salvien de Marseille: Oeuvres*. 2 vols. SC 176 and 220. Paris, 1971, 1976.

Lambert, David. "The Use of Decay: History in Salvian's *De Gubernatione Dei*." *AugStud* 30 (1999) 115–130.

Laniado, Avshalom. *Recherches sur les notables municipaux dans l'Empire Protobyzantin*. Paris, 2002.

Lapin, Hayim. *Rabbis as Romans: The Rabbinic Movement in Palestine, 100–400 CE*. Oxford, 2012.

Laporte, Jean-Pierre. "Les djedars, monuments funéraires berbères de la region de Frenda et de Tiaret." In *Identités et culture dans l'Algérie Antique*, ed. Claude Briand-Ponsart, 321–406. Rouen, 2005.

Latour, Bruno. *The Making of Law: An Ethnography of the Conseil d'Etat*. Trans. Marina Brilman. Cambridge, 2009.

Layton, Bentley. "Social Structure and Food Consumption in an Early Monastery: The Evidence of Shenoute's Canons and the White Monastery Federation AD 385–465." *Muséon* 115 (2002) 25–55.

Lee, A. D. "The Army." *The Cambridge Ancient History*, vol. 13: *The Late Empire, A.D. 337–425*, ed. Averil Cameron and Peter Garnsey, 211–237. Cambridge, 1998.

———. "The Eastern Empire: Theodosius to Anastasius." *The Cambridge Ancient History*, vol. 14: *Late Antiquity: Empire and Successors, A.D. 425–600*, ed. Averil Cameron, Bryan Ward-Perkins, and Michael Whitby, 33–62. Cambridge, 2001.

———. *War in Late Antiquity: A Social History*. London, 2007.

Lenski, Noel. "Captivity and Romano-Barbarian Interchange." In *Romans, Barbarians and the Transformation of the Roman World*, ed. Ralph W. Mathisen and Danuta Shanzer, 185–198. Farnham, U.K., 2011.

———. "Captivity and Slavery among the Saracens in Late Antiquity (ca. 250–630 CE)." *AnTard* 19 (2011) 237–266.

———. "Captivity, Slavery, and Cultural Exchange between Rome and the Germans from the First to the Seventh Century CE." In *Invisible Citizens: Captives and Their Consequences*, ed. Catherine Cameron, 80–109. Salt Lake City, 2008.

———. *Failure of Empire: Valens and the Roman State in the Fourth Century AD*. Berkeley, 2002.

———. "Schiavi armati e formazione di eserciti privati nel mondo tardoantico." In *Ordine e sovversione nel mondo greco e romano*, ed. Gianpaolo Urso, 145–175. Pisa, 2009.

———. "The Gothic Civil War and the Date of the Gothic Conversion." *Greek Roman and Byzantine Studies* 36 (1995) 51–87.

———. "Valens and the Monks: Cudgeling and Conscription as a Means of Social Control." *DOP* 58 (2004) 93–117.

Lent, Frederick, trans. *The Life of Saint Simeon Stylites: A Translation of the Syriac Text in Bedjan's Acta Martyrum et Sanctorum*. Merchantville, N.J., 2009.

Leone, Anna. *Changing Townscapes in North Africa from Late Antiquity to the Arab Conquest*. Bari, Italy, 2007.

Lepelley, Claude. *Les cités de l'Afrique romaine au Bas-Empire*. 2 vols. Paris, 1981.

———. "Quelques aspects de l'administration des provinces romaines d'Afrique avant la conquête vandale." *AnTard* 10 (2002) 61–72.

Lerner, Judith A., and Nicholas Sims-Williams. *Seals, Sealings, and Tokens from Bactria to Gandhara (4th to 8th Century CE).* Vienna, 2011.

Levine, Lee I. *The Ancient Synagogue: The First Thousand Years.* 2nd ed. New Haven, 2005.

Levy, Ernst. "The Reception of Highly Developed Legal Systems by Peoples of Different Cultures." *Washington Law Review* 25 (1950) 233–245.

Lévy, Sylvain. "Notes chinoises sur l'Inde, V: Quelques documents sur le bouddhisme indien dans l'Asie centrale." *BEFEO* 5 (1905) 253–305.

Lewis, Naphtali. "Literati in the Service of Roman Emperors: Politics before Culture." In *Coins, Culture and History in the Ancient World: Numismatic and Other Studies in Honor of Bluma L. Trell,* ed. Lionel Casson and Martin Price, 149–166. Detroit, 1981.

———. "The Non-Scholar Members of the Alexandrian Museum." *Mnemosyne* 16 (1963) 257–261.

Leyerle, Blake. "Landscape as Cartography in Early Christian Pilgrimage Narratives." *JAAR* 64 (1996) 119–143.

Leyser, Conrad. *Authority and Asceticism from Augustine to Gregory the Great.* Oxford, 2000.

Liebeschuetz, J. H. W. G. "Alaric's Goths: Nation or Army?" In *Fifth-Century Gaul: A Crisis of Identity?,* ed. John F. Drinkwater and Hugh Elton, 75–83. Cambridge, 1992.

———. *Antioch: City and Imperial Administration in the Later Roman Empire.* Oxford, 1972.

———. *Barbarians and Bishops.* Oxford, 1990.

———. "*Gens* into *regnum*: The Vandals." In *Regna et Gentes: The Relationship between Late Antique and Early Medieval Peoples and Kingdoms in the Transformation of the Roman World,* ed. Hans-Werner Goetz, Jörg Jarnut, and Walter Pohl, 55–83. Leiden, 2003.

———. *The Decline and Fall of the Roman City.* Oxford, 2001.

Liebs, Detlef. *Die Jurisprudenz im spätantiken Italien (260–640 n. Chr.).* Berlin, 1987.

———. "Roman Vulgar Law in Late Antiquity." In *Aspects of Law in Late Antiquity: Dedicated to A. M. Honoré on the Occasion of His Sixtieth Year of Teaching in Oxford,* ed. A. J. Boudewijn Sirks, 35–53. Oxford, 2008.

———. *Römische Jurisprudenz in Gallien (2 bis 8 Jahrhundert).* Berlin, 2002.

Lim, Richard. "Augustine and Roman Public Spectacles." In *A Companion to Augustine,* ed. Mark Vessey. Chichester, 2012.

———. "Christian Triumph and Controversy." In *Late Antiquity: A Guide to the Postclassical World,* ed. Glen W. Bowersock, Peter Brown, and Oleg Grabar, 196–218. Cambridge, Mass., 1999.

Lincoln, Bruce. "Human Unity and Diversity in Zoroastrian Mythology." *HR* 50 (2010) 7–20.

Linder, Amnon. *The Jews in Roman Imperial Legislation.* Detroit, 1987.

Lindner, Rudi. "Nomadism, Horses and Huns." *P&P* 92 (1981) 3–19.

Liu, Xinriu. *The Silk Road in World History.* Oxford, 2010.

Loening, Edgar. *Geschichte des deutschen Kirchenrechts, vol. 1: Das Kirchenrecht in Gallien von Constantin bis Chlodovech.* Strassburg, 1878.

Long, Jaqueline. "Dating an Ill-Fated Journey: Synesius, Ep. 5." *TAPhA* 122 (1992) 351–380.

López, Ariel G. *Shenoute of Atripe and the Uses of Poverty: Rural Patronage, Religious Conflict and Monasticism in Late Antique Egypt.* Berkeley, 2013.

Lozovsky, Natalia. *The Earth Is Our Book: Geographical Knowledge in the Latin West c. 400–1000.* Ann Arbor, 2000.

Luttwak, Edward. *The Grand Strategy of the Byzantine Empire.* Cambridge, Mass., 2009.

Maas, Michael. "Barbarians: Problems and Approaches." In *The Oxford Handbook of Late Antiquity,* ed. Scott F. Johnson, 60–91. Oxford, 2012.

————. "Ethnicity, Orthodoxy and Community in Salvian of Marseilles." In *Fifth-Century Gaul: A Crisis of Identity?,* ed. John F. Drinkwater and Hugh Elton, 275–284. Cambridge, 1992.

————. "Fugitives and Ethnography in Priscus of Panium." *BMGS* 19 (1995) 146–160.

————. "Mores et Moenia: Ethnography and the Decline of Urban Constitutional Autonomy in Late Antiquity." In *Integration and Authority in the Early Middle Ages,* ed. Walter Pohl and Max Diesenberger, 25–35. Vienna, 2002.

————, ed. *The Cambridge Companion to the Age of Justinian.* Cambridge, 2005.

————. "The Equality of Empires: Procopius on Adoption and Guardianship across Imperial Borders." In *Motions of Late Antiquity: Religion, Politics, and Society from Constantine to Charlemagne. Essays in Honor Peter Brown,* ed. Jamie Kreiner and Helmut Reimitz. Turnhout, 2015.

MacCormack, Sabine. *Art and Ceremony in Late Antiquity.* Berkeley, 1981.

MacGeorge, Penny. *Late Roman Warlords.* Oxford, 2002.

Madden, Mary Daniel. *The Pagan Divinities and Their Worship as Depicted in the Works of Saint Augustine Exclusive of the "City of God."* Washington, D.C., 1930.

Maenchen-Helfen, Otto. "Pseudo-Huns." *CAJ* 1 (1955) 101–106.

————. "The Ethnic Name Hun." In *Studia Serica Bernhard Karlgren Dedicata,* ed. Soren Egerod, 223–238. Copenhagen, 1959.

————. "The Legend of the Origin of the Huns." *Byzantion* 17 (1945) 244–251.

————. *The World of the Huns: Studies in Their History and Culture.* Ed. Max Knight. Berkeley, 1973.

Magness, Jodi. *The Archaeology of the Holy Land from the Destruction of Solomon's Temple to the Muslim Conquest.* New York, 2012.

Majcherek, Grzegorz. "The Late Roman Auditoria: An Archeological Overview." *Journal of Juristic Papyrology,* suppl. 8, *Alexandria Auditoria of Kôm el-Dikka and Late Antique Education.* Ed. Tomasz Derda, Tomasz Markiewicz, and Ewa Wipszycka, 11–50. Warsaw, 2007.

Mango, Cyril. *Le développement urbain de Constantinople, IVe–VIIe siècles.* 2nd ed. T&MBYZ 2. Paris, 2004.

————. "The Shoreline of Constantinople in the Fourth Century." In *Byzantine Constantinople,* ed. Nevra Necipoğlu, 17–28. Leiden, 2001.

Mann, John. "Power, Force and the Frontiers of the Empire." *JRS* 69 (1979) 175–183.

Mapwar, Bashuth. "La résistance de l'Église catholique à la foi arienne en Afrique du Nord: Un exemple d'une église locale inculturée?" In *Cristianesimo e specificità regionali nel Mediterraneo latino (sec IV–VI),* 189–213. Rome, 1994.

Maraval, Pierre, ed. *Egérie, Journal de voyage: Itinéraire.* 2nd ed. SC. Paris, 2002.

————. "The Earliest Phase of Christian Pilgrimage in the Near East (before the 7th Century)." *DOP* 56 (2002) 63–74.

Marazzi, F. I. *"Patrimonia Sanctae Romanae Ecclesia" nel Lazio (secoli IV–X).* Strutture amministrative e prassi gestionale. Rome, 1998.

————. "Rome in Transition: Economic and Political Change in the Fourth and Fifth Centuries." In *Early Medieval Rome and the Christian West*, ed. Julia Smith, 21–41. Leiden, 2000.

Marcone, Arnaldo. "Late Roman Social Relations." *The Cambridge Ancient History*, vol. 13: *The Late Empire, A.D. 337–425*, ed. Averil Cameron and Peter Garnsey, 338–370. Cambridge, 1998.

Marenbon, John. *Boethius*. Oxford, 2003.

Markus, Robert A. *The End of Ancient Christianity*. Cambridge, 1990.

————. "The Roman Empire in Early Christian Historiography." *Downside Review* 81 (1963) 340–354.

Marrou, Henri-Irénée. *Histoire de l'éducation dans l'antiquité*. Paris, 1965.

Marshak, Boris. "K Voprosu o Vostochnykh Protivnikakh Irana." *Strany i Narody Vostoka* 10 (1971) 58–66.

Martin, Jochen. "Das Kaisertum in der Spätantike." In *Usurpationen in der Spätantike*, ed. François Paschoud and Joachim Szidat, 47–62. Stuttgart, 1997.

Mathisen, Ralph W. "Adnotatio and Petitio: The Emperor's Favour and Special Exceptions in Early Byzantine Law." In *La pétition à Byzance*, ed. Denis Feissel and Jean Gascou, 25–34. Paris, 2004.

————. *Ecclesiastical Factionalism and Religious Controversy in Fifth-Century Gaul*. Washington, D.C., 1989.

————. "Hilarius, Germanus and Lupus: The Aristocratic Background of the Chelidonius Affair." *Phoenix* 33 (1979) 160–169.

————. "Patricians as Diplomats in Late Antiquity." *ByzZ* 79 (1986) 35–49.

————. "Peregrini, Barbari, and Cives Romani: Concepts of Citizenship and the Legal Identity of Barbarians in the Later Roman Empire." *AHR* 111 (2006) 1011–1040.

————. *Roman Aristocrats in Barbarian Gaul*. Austin, Tex., 1993.

Matthews, John. "Anicius Manlius Severinus Boethius." In *Boethius: His Life, Thought, and Influence*, ed. Margaret Gibson, 73–89. Oxford, 1981.

————. *Laying Down the Law: A Study of the Theodosian Code*. New Haven, 2000.

————. "Roman Law and Barbarian Identity in the Late Roman West." In *Ethnicity and Culture in Late Antiquity*, ed. Stephen Mitchell and Geoffrey Greatrex, 31–45. London, 2000.

————. "The Notitia Urbis Constantinopolitanae." In *Two Romes: Rome and Constantinople in Late Antiquity*, ed. Lucy Grig and Gavin Kelly, 81–115. Oxford, 2012.

————. *The Roman Empire of Ammianus*. Baltimore, 1989.

————. *Western Aristocracies and Imperial Court, A.D. 364–425*. Oxford, 1975; repr. 1998.

Matthews, Shelly. *Perfect Martyr: The Stoning of Stephen and the Construction of Christian Identity*. Oxford, 2010.

Maxwell, Jaclyn. "Paganism and Christianization." In *The Oxford Handbook of Late Antiquity*, ed. Scott F. Johnson, 849–875. Oxford, 2012.

Mayerson, Philip. "A Confusion of Indias: Asian India and African India in the Byzantine Sources." *JAOS* (1993) 169–174.

Mazza, Roberta. "Tra oriente e occidente: La gestione del patrimonium Petri in Italia meridionale." In *Paessagi e insediamenti rurali in Italia meridionale fra tardoantica e altomedioevo*, ed. Giuliano Volpe and Maria Turchiano, 703–714. Bari, 2006.

McCluskey, Stephen C. *Astronomies and Cultures in Early Medieval Europe*. Cambridge, 1998.

———. "Gregory of Tours, Monastic Timekeeping, and Early Christian Attitudes to Astronomy." *Isis* 81 (1990) 8–22.

———. "Martianus and the Traditions of Early Medieval Astronomies." In *Carolingian Scholarship and Martianus Capella: Cultural Encounters in Late Antiquity and the Middle Ages 12*, ed. Mariken Teeuwen and Sinead O'Sullivan, 221–244. Turnhout, 2011.

McCormick, Michael. "Emperor and Court." In *Cambridge Ancient History*, vol. 14: *Late Antiquity: Empire and Successors, A.D. 425–600*, ed. Averil Cameron, Bryan Ward-Perkins, and Michael Whitby, 135–163. Cambridge, 2001.

———. *Eternal Victory: Triumphal Rulership in Late Antiquity, Byzantium and the Early Medieval West*. Cambridge, 1990.

McDonough, Scott. "A Question of Faith? Persecution and Political Centralization in the Sasanian Empire of Yazdgard II (438–457 C.E.)." In *Violence in Late Antiquity: Perceptions and Practices*, ed. Harold A. Drake, 69–81. Aldershot, 2007.

———. "Bishops or Bureaucrats?: Christian Clergy and the State in the Middle Sasanian Period." In *Current Research in Sasanian Archaeology, Art, and History*, ed. Derek Kennett and Paul Luft, 87–92. Oxford, 2008.

McEvoy, Meaghan. "Rome and the Transformation of the Imperial Office in the Late Fourth–Mid-Fifth Centuries AD." *PBSR* 78 (2010) 151–192.

McLynn, Neil. *Ambrose of Milan: Church and Court in a Christian Capital*. Berkeley, 1994.

———. "From Palladius to Maximinus: Passing the Arian Torch." *JECS* 4 (1996) 477–493.

Meijer, Fik J. "The Ship of Bishop Synesius." *IJNA* 15, no. 1 (1986) 67–68.

Merkelbach, Reinhold, and J. Trumpff. *Die Quellen des griechischen Alexanderromans*. Zetemeta 9. Munich, 1977.

Merrills, Andy. "The Perils of Panegyric: The Lost Poem of Dracontius and Its Consequences." In *Vandals, Romans, and Berbers*, ed. Andy Merrills, 145–162. Aldershot, 2004.

———. "The Secret of My Succession: Dynasty and Crisis in Vandal North Africa." *EMedE* 18.2 (2010) 135–159.

Merrills, Andy, and Richard Miles. *The Vandals*. Chichester, 2010.

Meslin, Michel. *La fête des calends de janvier sous l'Empire romain*. Collection Latomus 11. Brussels, 1970.

———. *Les Ariens d'occident, 335–430*. Paris, 1967.

Meyer-Plath, Bruno, and Alfons Schneider. *Die Landmauer von Konstantinopel*. Berlin, 1943.

Miles, Richard. "The Anthologia Latina and the Creation of Secular Space in Vandal North Africa." *AnTard* 13 (2005) 305–320.

Millar, Fergus. *A Greek Roman Empire: Power and Belief under Theodosius II, 408–450*. Berkeley, 2006.

———. "Ethnic Identity in the Roman Near East, 325–450: Language, Religion, and Culture." *MedArch* 11 (1998) 159–176.

Mitchell, Stephen. *A History of the Later Roman Empire*. Oxford, 2007.

Mitteis, Ludwig. *Griechische Urkunden der Papyrussammlung zu Leipzig*. Leipzig, 1906.

Modéran, Yves. "L'établissement territorial des Vandales en Afrique." *AnTard* 10 (2002) 87–122.

————. *Les Maures et l'Afrique Romaine (IVe–VIe siècle)*. Bibliothèque des Écoles françaises d'Athènes et de Rome 314. Rome, 2003.

————. "Une guerre de religion: Les deux Églises d'Afrique à l'époque vandale." *AnTard* 11 (2003) 21–44.

Mommaerts, T. Stanford, and David H. Kelley. "The Anicii of Gaul and Rome." In *Fifth-Century Gaul: A Crisis of Identity*, ed. John F. Drinkwater and Hugh Elton, 111–121. Cambridge, 1992.

Monnickendam, Yifat. "The Kiss and the Earnest: Early Roman Influences on Syriac Matrimonial Law." *Le Muséon* 125 (2012) 307–334.

Moorhead, John. *Theoderic in Italy*. Oxford, 1992.

————. *The Roman Empire Divided, 400–700*. Harlow, U.K., 2001.

Moshkova, Marina G. "A Brief Review of the History of the Sauromatian and Sarmatian Tribes." In *Nomads of the Eurasian Steppes in the Early Iron Age*, ed. Jeannine Davis-Kimball, Vladimir A. Bashilov, and Leonid T. Yablonsky, 85–95. Berkeley, 1995.

Mosig-Walburg, Karin. "Königtum und Adel in der Regierungs Zeit Ardashirs II., Shapurs III., und Wahrams IV." In *Commutatio et Contentio: Studies in the Late Roman, Sasanian, and Early Islamic Near East*, eds. Henning Börm and Josef Wiesehöfer, 159–198. Düsseldorf, 2010.

Mosshammer, Alden A. "The Computus of 455 and the Laterculus of Augustalis, with an Appendix on the Fractional Method of Agriustia." In *The Easter Controversy of Late Antiquity and the Early Middle Ages: Its Manuscripts, Texts, and Tables*, ed. Immo Warntjes and Daibhí Ó Crónín, 21–47. Studia Traditionis Theologiae 10. Turnhout, 2011.

————. *The Easter Computus and the Origins of the Christian Era*. Oxford, 2008.

Munro-Hay, Stuart. "The Foreign Trade of the Aksumite Port of Adulis." *Azania: Archaeological Research in Africa* 17 (1982) 107–125.

Münz-Manor, Ophir. "Liturgical Poetry in the Late Antique Near East: A Comparative Approach." *JAJ* 1 (2010) 336–361.

Murphy, John P. *Rufus Festus Avienus, Ora Maritima: A Description of the Seacoast from Brittany round to Massilia*. Chicago, 1977.

Nechaeva, Ekaterina. *Embassies, Negotiations, Gifts: Systems of East Roman Diplomacy in Late Antiquity*. Stuttgart, 2014.

————. "The 'Runaway' Avars and Late Antique Diplomacy." In *Romans, Barbarians, and the Transformation of the Roman World*, ed. Ralph W. Mathisen and Danuta Schanzer, 175–184. Burlington, Vt., 2011.

Neil, Bronwen. "Blessed are the Rich: Leo the Great and the Roman Poor." *SP* 44 (2010) 533–548.

————. "Leo I on Poverty." In *Preaching Poverty in Late Antiquity*, ed. Pauline Allen, Bronwen Neil, and Wendy Mayer, 171–203. Leipzig, 2009.

Nelken, David. "Using Legal Culture: Purposes and Problems." In *Using Legal Culture*, ed. David Nelken, 1–51. London, 2012.

Nicasie, Martijn. *Twilight of Empire*. Amsterdam, 1998.

Nöldeke, Theodor. *Das iranische Nationalepos*. Berlin, 1920.

————. "'Der beste der arischen Pfeilschützen' im Awestâ und im Tabarî." *ZDMG* 35 (1881) 445–447.

Nongbri, Brent. *Before Religion: A History of a Modern Concept*. New Haven, 2013.

———. "Dislodging 'Embedded' Religion: A Brief Note on a Scholarly Trope." *Numen* 55 (2008) 440–460.

Nordh, Arvast, ed. *Libellus de regionibus urbis Romae*. Lund, Sweden, 1949.

Nutton, Vivian. "The Beneficial Ideology." In *Imperialism in the Ancient World*, ed. Peter D. A. Garnsey and C. Richard Whittaker, 209–222. Cambridge, 1978.

O'Flynn, John M. "A Greek on the Roman Throne: The Fate of Anthemius." *Historia* 41 (1991) 122–128.

O'Meara, Dominic J. *Pythagoras Revived: Mathematics and Philosophy in Late Antiquity*. Oxford, 1989.

O'Reilly, Marie. *V. Sancti Aurelii Augustini De excidio urbis Romae Sermo: A Critical Text and Translation with Introduction and Commentary*. Washington, D.C., 1955.

Ocker, Christopher. "Augustine, Episcopal Interests, and the Papacy in Late Roman Africa." *JEH* 42 (1991) 179–201.

Oost, Stewart Irvin. "Aëtius and Majorian." *CPh* 59.1 (1964) 23–29.

———. *Galla Placidia Augusta: A Biographical Essay*. Chicago, 1968.

Orlandi, Silvia. *Epigrafia anfiteatrale dell'occidente romano*, vol. 6: *Roma*. Rome, 2004.

Orlandi, Tito. "Patristic Texts in Coptic." In *Patrology: The Eastern Fathers from the Council of Chalcedon (451) to John of Damascus († 750)*, ed. Angelo di Berardino, 491–570. Cambridge, 2006.

Ortman, Scott G. *Genes, Language, and Culture in Tewa Ethnogenesis, AD 1150–1400*. Tempe, Ariz., 2009.

Pack, Roger. "Folklore and Superstition in the Writings of Synesius." *Classical Weekly* 43 (1949) 51–56.

Palme, Bernhard. "Law and Courts in Late Antique Egypt." In *Aspects of Law in Late Antiquity: Dedicated to A. M. Honoré on the Occasion of His Sixtieth Year of Teaching in Oxford*, ed. A. J. Boudewijn Sirks, 55–76. Oxford, 2008.

———. "The Imperial Presence: Government and Army." In *Egypt in the Byzantine World, 300–700*, ed. Roger S. Bagnall, 244–270. Cambridge, 2007.

Panciera, Silvio. "His ego nec metas rerum nec tempora pono: Virgilio in un'inedita iscrizione romana." In *Epigrafi, epigrafia, epigrafisti: Scritti vari editi e inediti (1956–2005) connote complementari e indici, 333–343*. Rome, 2006. Originally published in *Studi Tardoantichi* 2 [1986] 191–210.

Pany, Doris, and Karin Wiltschke-Schrotta. "Artificial Cranial Deformation in a Migration Period Burial of Schwarzenbach, Lower Austria." *Viavias* 2 (2008) 18–23.

Papadogiannakis, Yannis. *Christianity and Hellenism in the Fifth-Century Greek East*. Washington, D.C., 2012.

Parker, Grant. *The Making of Roman India: Greek Culture in the Roman World*. Cambridge, 2008.

Parlato, Sandra. "Successo euroasiatico dell'etnico 'Unni.'" In *La Persia e l'Asia Centrale da Alessandro al X secolo, 555–566*. Rome, 1996.

Paschoud, François. *Roma Aeterna: Études sur le patriotisme romain dans l'Occident latin à l'époque des grandes invasions*. Rome, 1967.

Patlagean, E. *Pauvreté économique et pauvreté social à Byzance, 4–7ème siècles*. Paris, 1977.

Patterson, Orlando. "Slavery, Gender and Work in the Pre-Modern World and Early Greece." In *Slave Systems, Ancient and Modern*, ed. Enrico Dal Lago and Constantina Katsari, 32–69. Cambridge, 2008.

Pépin, Jean. *Théologie cosmique et théologie chrétienne*. Paris, 1964.

Perler, Othmar, with Jean-Louis Maier. *Les voyages de saint Augustin*. Paris, 1969.

Pharr, Clyde. "Roman Legal Education." *CJ* 39 (1939) 257–270.

Pichéry, Eugène. *Jean Cassien: Conférences.* 3 vols. SC 42, 54, 64. Paris, 1955, 1958, 1959.

Pingree, David. "Boethius' Geometry and Astronomy." In *Boethius: His Life, Thought, and Influence,* ed. Margaret T. Gibson, 155–161. Oxford, 1981.

Pohl, Walter. *Die Awaren: Ein Steppenvolk in Mitteleuropa, 567–822.* Munich, 1988.

———. "Die Gepiden und die Gentes an der mittleren Donau nach dem Zerfall des Attilareiches." In *Die Völker an der mittleren und unteren Donau im fünften und sechsten Jahrhundert,* ed. Herwig Wolfram and Falko Daim, 239–305. Denkschriften der Österreichischen Akademie der Wissenschaften, phil.-hist. Kl. 145. Vienna, 1980.

———. *Die Völkerwanderung.* 2nd ed. Stuttgart, 2005.

———. "Huns, Avars, Hungarians: Comparative Perspectives Based on Written Evidence." In *The Complexity of Interaction along the Eurasian Steppe Zone in the First Millennium AD,* ed. Jürgen Bemmann and Michael Schmauder. Forthcoming.

———. "Introduction: Christian and Barbarian Identities in the Early Medieval West." In *Post-Roman Transitions: Christian and Barbarian Identities in the Early Medieval West,* ed. Walter Pohl and Gerda Heydemann. Turnhout, 2013.

———. "Introduction: Ethnicity, Religion and Empire." In *Visions of Community in the Post-Roman World: The West, Byzantium and the Islamic World, 300–1100,* ed. Walter Pohl, Clemens Gantner, and Richard Payne, 1–23. Farnham, U.K., 2012.

———. "Introduction: Strategies of Identification. A methodological profile." In *Strategies of Identification: Ethnicity and Religion in Early Medieval Europe,* ed. Walter Pohl and Gerda Heydemann, 1–64. Turnhout, 2013.

———, ed. *Kingdoms of the Empire: The Integration of Barbarians in Late Antiquity.* The Transformation of the Roman World 1. Leiden, 1997.

———. "Pistis e potere: Coesione etnica negli eserciti barbarici nel periodo delle migrazioni." In *Archeologia e storia delle migrazioni: Europa, Italia, Mediterraneo fra tarda età romana e alto medioevo,* ed. Carlo Ebanista and Marcello Rotili, 55–64. Cimitile, 2011.

———. "Rome and the Barbarians in the Fifth Century." *AnTard* 16 (2008) 93–101.

———. "Telling the Difference: Signs of Ethnic Identity." In *Strategies of Distinction: The Construction of Ethnic Communities, 300–800,* ed. Walter Pohl and Helmut Reimitz, 17–69. Leiden, 1998.

Possanza, D. Mark. *Translating the Heavens: Aratus, Germanicus, and the Poetics of Latin Translation.* New York, 2004.

Possekel, Ute. *Evidence of Greek Philosophical Concepts in the Writings of Ephrem the Syrian.* CSCO Subsidia 580.102. Leuven, 1999.

Potter, David S. "The Unity of the Roman Empire." In *From the Tetrarchs to the Theodosians: Later Roman History and Culture, 284–450 C.E.,* ed. Christiana Sogno, Scott McGill, and Edward Watts, 13–32. Cambridge, 2010.

Poulter, Andrew G. *Nicopolis ad Istrum: A Roman, Late Roman, and Early Byzantine City. Excavations 1985–1992.* London, 1995.

———. "The Use and Abuse of Urbanism in the Danubian Provinces During the Later Roman Empire." In *The City in Late Antiquity,* ed. John Rich, 99–135. London, 1992.

Pourshariati, Parvaneh. *Decline and Fall of the Sasanian Empire: The Sasanian-Parthian Confederacy and the Arab Conquest of Iran.* London, 2009.

Power, Timothy. *The Red Sea from Byzantium to the Caliphate, AD 500–1000.* Cairo, 2012.

Price, Richard, and Michael Gaddis. *The Acts of the Council of Chalcedon.* Vol. 3. Liverpool, 2005.

Prinz, Friedrich. *Frühes Mönchtum im Frankenreich.* Munich, 1965.

Pritsak, Omelian. "From the Säbirs to the Hungarians." In *Hungaro-Turcica: Studies in Honour of Julius Németh,* ed. Gyula Káldy-Nagy, 17–30. Budapest, 1976.

Pryor, John and Elizabeth Jeffreys. *The Age of the Dromon: The Byzantine Navy ca. 500–1204.* Leiden, 2006.

Rance, Philip. "*Drungus*, ΔΡΟΥΓΓΟΣ, and ΔΡΟΥΓΓΙΣΤΙ: A Gallicism and Continuity in Late Roman Cavalry Tactics." *Phoenix* 58 (2004) 96–130.

———. "Simulacra pugnae: The Literary and Historical Tradition of Mock Battles in the Roman Army." *GRBS* 41 (2000) 223–275.

———. "The Fulcum, the Late Roman and Byzantine Testudo: The Germanization of late Roman Tactics?" *GRBS* 44 (2004) 265–326.

Rapp, Claudia. "Hagiography and Monastic Literature between Greek East and Latin West in Late Antiquity." In *Cristianità d'occidente e cristianità d'oriente (secoli VI–IX)* 2: 1221–1280. Spoleto, 2004.

———. *Holy Bishops in Late Antiquity. The Nature of Christian Leadership in an Age of Transition.* Berkeley, 2005.

Ravegnani, Elisabetta. *Consoli e dittici consolari nella tarda antichità.* Rome, 2006.

Rebenich, Stefan. "Jerome: The '*vir trilinguis*' and the '*hebraica veritas.*'" *VChr* (1993) 50–77.

Reimitz, Helmut. *Writing for the Future: History, Identity, and Ethnicity in the Merovingian and Carolingian Kingdoms, 6th to 9th Centuries.* Forthcoming.

Rekavandi, Hamid Omrani. "Sasanian Walls, Hinterland Fortresses, and Abandoned Ancient Irrigated Landscapes: The 2007 Season on the Great Wall of Gurgan and the Wall of Tammishe." *Iran* 46 (2008) 151–178.

Rekavandi, Hamid Omrani, Eberhard W. Sauer, Tony Wilkinson, et al. "An Imperial Frontier of the Sasanian Empire: Further Fieldwork at the Great Wall of Gurgan." *Iran* 45 (2007) 95–136.

Renfrew, Colin, and Peter Bahn. *Archaeology: Theories, Methods and Practice.* 5th ed. London, 2008.

Richardot, Philippe. *La fin de l'armée romaine (284–476).* Paris, 1998.

Robin, Christian J. "Arabia and Ethiopia." In *The Oxford Handbook of Late Antiquity,* ed. Scott F. Johnson, 247–332. Oxford, 2012.

Romer, Frank E. *Pomponius Mela's Description of the World.* Ann Arbor, 1998.

Romm, James. *The Edges of the Earth in Ancient Thought: Geography, Exploration, and Fiction.* Princeton, 1992.

Rougé, Jean, ed. *Expositio totius mundi et gentium.* SC 124. Paris, 1966.

Roueché, Charlotte. "Acclamations in the Later Roman Empire." *JRS* 74 (1984) 181–199.

———. *Performers and Partisans at Aphrodisias in the Roman and Late Roman Periods.* London, 1993.

Roueché, Mossman. "Did Medical Students Study Philosophy in Alexandria?" *BICS* 43.1(1999) 153–169.

Rousseau, Philip. *Ascetics, Authority and the Church in the Age of Jerome and Cassian.* 2nd ed. Notre Dame, Ind., 2010.

Rubenson, Samuel. "Argument and Authority in Early Monastic Correspondence." In *Foundations of Power and Conflicts of Authority in Late-Antique Monasticism: Proceedings of the International Seminar Turin, December 2–4, 2004*, ed. Alberto Camplani and Giovanni Filoramo, 75–87. Orientalia Lovaniensia Analecta. Dudley, Mass., 2007.

Rubin, Zeev. "Greek and Geʿez in the Propaganda of King ʿEzana of Axum: Religion and Diplomacy in Late Antiquity." *SemClas* 5 (2012) 139–150.

———. "Nobility, Monarchy, and Legitimation under the Later Sasanians." In *The Byzantine and Early Islamic Near East*, vol. 6: *Elites Old and New in the Byzantine and Early Islamic Near East*, ed. John Haldon and Lawrence Conrad, 235–273. Princeton, 2004.

———. "The Mediterranean and the Dilemma of the Roman Empire in Late Antiquity." *MHR* 1 (1986) 13–62.

———. "The Sassanid Monarchy." In *The Cambridge Ancient History*, vol. 14: *Late Antiquity: Empire and Successors, A.D. 425–600*, ed. Averil Cameron, Bryan Ward-Perkins, and Michael Whitby, 638–661. Cambridge, 2001.

Ruggini, L. Cracco. "La Sicilia e la fine del mondo antico (IV–VI secolo)." In *La Sicilia antica*, vol. 2.2: *La Sicilia Romana, 483–524*. Naples, 1980.

Rummel, Philipp von. *Habitus barbarus: Kleidung und Repräsentation spätantiker Eliten im 4. und 5. Jahrhundert*. Berlin, 2007.

Russell, Josiah C. *Late Ancient and Medieval Population*. Transactions of the American Philosophical Society 48.3. Philadelphia, 1958.

Russell, Paul S. "Nisibis as the Background to the Life of Ephrem the Syrian." *Hugoye: Journal of Syriac Studies* 8 (2005) 179–235.

Rutgers, Leonard V. "Archaeological Evidence for the Interaction of Jews and Non-Jews in Late Antiquity." *AJA* 96 (1992) 101–118.

Sabin, Phil, Michael Whitby, and Hans van Wees, eds. *The Cambridge History of Greek and Roman Warfare*. Cambridge, 2007.

Salway, Benet. "Putting the World in Order: Mapping in Roman Texts." In *Ancient Perspectives: Maps and Their Place in Mesopotamia, Egypt, Greece, and Rome*, ed. Richard Talbert, 193–234. Chicago, 2012.

———. "Sea and River Travel in the Roman Itinerary Literature." In *Space in the Roman World: Its Perception and Presentation*, ed. Richard Talbert and Kai Brodersen, 43–96. Münster, 2004.

———. "The Nature and Genesis of the Peutinger Map." *IM* 57 (2005) 119–135.

———. "The Perception and Description of Space in Roman Itineraries." In *Wahrnehmung und Erfassung geographischer Räume in der Antike*, ed. Michael Rathmann, 181–209. Mainz am Rhein, 2007.

———. "There But Not There: Constantinople in the Itinerarium Burdigalense." In *Two Romes: Rome and Constantinople in Late Antiquity*, ed. Lucy Grig and Gavin Kelly, 293–324. Oxford, 2012.

———. "Travel, Itineraria, and Tabellaria." In *Travel and Geography in the Roman Empire*, ed. Colin Adams and Ray Laurence, 22–66. London, 2001.

Salzman, Michele Renee. "Competing Claims to 'Nobilitas' in the Western Empire of the Fourth and Fifth Centuries." *JECS* 9.3 (2001) 359–385.

———. "Leo in Rome: The Evolution of Episcopal Authority in Fifth-Century Rome." In *Istituzioni, carismi ed esercizio del potere (IV–VI secolo d.C.)*, ed. Giorgio Bonamente and Rita Lizzi Testa, 343–356. Bari, 2010.

———, "Leo the Great: Response to Crisis and the Shaping of a Christian *Cosmopolis*." In *The Transformation of City and Citizenship in the Classical World: From the Fifth*

Century BCE to the Fifth Century CE, ed. Harold Drake and Claudia Rapp, 183–201. Cambridge, 2014.

_____. "The End of Public Sacrifice: Changing Definitions of Sacrifice in Post-Constantinian Rome and Italy." In *Ancient Mediterranean Sacrificed*, ed. Jennifer Wright Knust and Zsuzsanna Várhelyi, 167–186. Oxford, 2011.

_____. *The Making of a Christian Aristocracy: Social and Religious Change in the Western Empire*. Cambridge, 2002.

Sandwell, Isabella. *Religious Identity in Late Antiquity: Greeks, Jews, and Christians in Antioch*. Cambridge, 2007.

Sarnowski, Tadeusz. "Die Principia von Novae im späten 4. und frühen 5. Jh." In *Der Limes ander unteren Donau von Diokletian bis Heraklios*, ed. Gerda von Bülow and Aleksandra Dimitrova-Milčeva, 56–63. Sofia, 1999.

Sarris, Peter. "Aristocrats, Peasants and the State in the Later Roman Empire." In *Der wiederkehrende Leviathan: Staatlichkeit und Staatswerdung in Spätantike und Früher Neuzeit*, ed. Peter Eich, Sebastian Schmidt-Hofner, and Christian Wieland, 377–394. Heidelberg, 2011.

_____. *Economy and Society in the Reign of Justinian*. Cambridge, 2006.

_____. *Empires of Faith: The Fall of Rome to the Rise of Islam, 500–700*. Oxford, 2011.

_____. "The Early Byzantine Economy in Context: Aristocratic Property and Economic Growth Reconsidered." *EMedE* 19.3 (2011) 255–284.

_____. "The Origins of the Manorial Economy: New Insights from Late Antiquity." *EHR* 99 (2004) 279–311.

Schäfer, Peter. *The Jewish Jesus: How Christianity and Judaism Shaped Each Other*. Princeton, 2012.

Scorpan, Constantin. *Limes Scythiae: Topographical and Stratigraphical Research on the Late Roman Fortifications on the Lower Danube*. Oxford, 1980.

Scheid, John. "Les réjouissances des calends de janvier d'après le sermon Dolbeau 26: Nouvelles lumières sur une fête mal connue." In *Augustin prédicateur (395–411)*, ed. Goulven Madec, 353–365. Paris, 1998.

Scheidel, Walter. "Demography." In *The Cambridge Economic History of the Greco-Roman World*, ed. Walter Scheidel, Ian Morris, and Richard Saller, 38–86. Cambridge, 2007.

Schindel, Nikolaus. *Sylloge Nummorum Sasanidarum Israel: The Sasanian and Sasanian-Type Coins in the Collections of the Hebrew University*. Vienna, 2009.

_____. *Sylloge Nummorum Sasanidarum Paris-Berlin-Wien*, vol. 3: *Shapur II.–Kawad I.* Vienna, 2004.

Schlumberger, Daniel. "La nécropole de Shakh tépé près de Qunduz." *Comptes-rendus desséances de l'année: Académie des inscriptions et belles-lettres* 108.2 (1964) 207–211.

Schroeder, Caroline. "Child Sacrifice in Egyptian Monastic Culture: From Familial Renunciation to Jephthah's Lost Daughter." *JECS* 20 (2012) 269–302.

_____. *Monastic Bodies: Discipline and Salvation in Shenoute of Atripe*. Philadelphia, 2007.

_____. "Prophecy and *Porneia* in Shenoute's Letters: The Rhetoric of Sexuality in a Late Antique Egyptian Monastery." *Journal of Near Eastern Studies* 65 (2006) 81–97.

Schlütz, Frank, and Frank Lehmkuhl. "Climatic Change in the Russian Altai, Southern Siberia, Based on Palynological and Geomorphological Results, with Implications for Climatic Teleconnections and Human History since the Middle Holocene." *Vegetation History and Archaeobotany* 16 (2007) 101–118.

Schmidt, Ludwig. *Geschichte der Wandalen*. Leipzig, 1901.

Schwarcz, Andreas. "Relations between Ostrogoths and Visigoths in the Fifth and Sixth Centuries and the Question of Visigothic Settlement in Aquitaine and Spain." In *Integration and Authority in the Early Middle Ages*, ed. Walter Pohl and Max Diesenberger, 217–226. Vienna, 2002.

Schwartz, Seth. *Imperialism and Jewish Society, 200 B.C.E. to 640 C.E.* Princeton, 2001.

Ščukin, Mark, Michel Kazanski, and Oleg Sharev. *Des les Goths aux Huns: Le nord de la Mer Noire au Bas-empire et a l'époque des grandes migrations.* Oxford, 2006.

Seeck, Otto, ed. *Notitia dignitatum: Accedunt notitia urbis Constantinopolitanae et Laterculi provinciarum.* Berlin, 1876.

Sessa, Kristina. *The Formation of Papal Authority in Late Antique Italy.* Cambridge, 2012.

———. "Ursa's Return: Captivity, Remarriage, and the Domestic Authority of Roman Bishops in Fifth-Century Italy." *JECS* 19 (2011) 401–432.

Sguaitamatti, Lorenzo. *Der spätantike Konsulat.* Fribourg, 2012.

Shahîd, Irfan. *Byzantium and the Arabs in the Fifth Century.* Washington, D.C., 1989.

Shanzer, Danuta. *A Philosophical and Literary Commentary on Martianus Capella's De nuptiis Philologiae et Mercurii, Book 1.* Classical Studies 32. Berkeley, 1986.

———. "Review Article. *Felix Capella: Minus Sensus Quam Nominis Pecudalis (Martianus Capella: 'De nuptiis Philologiae et Mercurii,'* edited by James Willis)." *CPh* 81 (1986) 62–81.

Shaw, Brent. *Sacred Violence: African Christians and Sectarian Hatred in the Age of Augustine.* Cambridge, 2011.

Shayegan, M. Rahim. *Arsacids and Sasanians: Political Ideology in Post-Hellenistic and Late Antique Persia.* Cambridge, 2011.

Silbey, Susan S. "After Legal Consciousness." *Annual Review of Law and Social Sciences* 1 (2005) 323–368.

Sieg, Gustav. "De Cicerone, Germanico, Avieno, Arati interpretibus." Ph.D. diss., Martin-Luther Universität Halle-Wittenberg. Halle an der Saale, 1886.

Simeon, Xaver. *Untersuchungen zu den Briefen des Bischofs Synesios von Kyrene.* Rhetorische Studien 18. Paderborn, 1933.

Sims-Williams, Nicholas. *Bactrian Documents from Northern Afghanistan,* vol. 1: *Legal and Economic Documents.* Oxford, 2000.

———. "The Sasanians in the East: A Bactrian Archive from Northern Afghanistan." In *The Sasanian Era: The Idea of Iran,* vol. 3, ed. Vesta Sarkhosh Curtis and Sarah Stewart, 88–102. London, 2008.

Sims-Williams, Nicholas, and Frantz Grenet. "The Historical Context of the Sogdian Ancient Letters." In *Transition Periods in Iranian History,* ed. Philippe Gignoux, 101–122. Paris, 1987.

Sinor, Denis. "Horse and Pasture in Inner Asian History." *Oriens extremus* 19 (1972) 171–183. Reprint in *Inner Asia and Its Contacts with Medieval Europe,* no. 2. London, 1977.

———, ed. *The Cambridge History of Early Inner Asia.* Cambridge, 1990.

———. "The Hun Period." In *Cambridge History of Early Inner Asia,* ed. Denis Sinor, 177–205. Cambridge, 1990

Sirks, A. J. Boudewijn. *Food for Rome: The Legal Structure of the Transportation and Processing of Supplies for the Imperial Distributions in Rome and Constantinople.* Amsterdam, 1991.

———. *The Theodosian Code: A Study.* Norderstedt, Germany, 2007.

Sivan, Hagith. "Holy Land Pilgrimage and Western Audiences: Some Reflections on Egeria and Her Circle." *CQ* 38 (1988) 528–535.

———. "On Foederati, Hospitalitas, and the Settlement of the Goths in A.D. 418." *AJP* 108 (1987) 759–772.

———. "Who Was Egeria? Piety and Pilgrimage in the Age of Gratian." *HTR* 81 (1988) 59–72.

Sizgorich, Thomas. "Intentions and Audiences: History, Hagiography, Martyrdom and Confession in Victor of Vita's Historia Persecutionis." In *Vandals, Romans and Berbers: New Perspectives on Late Antique North Africa*, ed. Andy Merrills, 271–290. London, 2004.

———. *Violence and Belief in Late Antiquity: Militant Devotion in Christianity and Islam.* Philadelphia, 2009.

Smith, Jonathan Z. "What a Difference a Difference Makes." In *"To See Ourselves as Others See Us": Christians, Jews, "Others" in Late Antiquity*, ed. Jacob Neusner and Ernest S. Frerichs, 3–48. Chico, Calif., 1985.

Snee, Rochelle. "Gregory Nazianzen's Anastasia Church: Arianism, the Goths, and Hagiography." *DOP* 52 (1998) 157–186.

Sogno, Cristiana. "Roman Matchmaking." In *From the Tetrarchs to the Theodosians: Later Roman History and Culture, 284–450 CE*, ed. Scott McGill, Cristiana Sogno, and Edward Watts, 55–72. Cambridge 2010.

Sorabji, Richard. "Divine Names and Sordid Deals in Ammonius' Alexandria." In *The Philosopher and Society in Late Antiquity*, ed. Andrew Smith, 203–214. Swansea, U.K., 2005.

Sotinel, Claire. "Les évêques italiens dans la société de l'Antiquité tardive: L'emergence d'une nouvelle élite?" In *Le trasformazioni delle "elites" in età tardoantica*, ed. Rita Lizzi Testa, 377–404. Saggi di storia antica 25. Rome, 2006.

Soubiran, Jean, ed. *Aviénus: Les Phénomènes d'Aratos.* Paris, 1981.

Stahl, William Harris. "Astronomy and Geography in Macrobius." In *TAPhA* (1942) 232–258.

———. *Macrobius: Commentary on the Dream of Scipio.* New York, 1990.

Stahl, William Harris, with Evan L. Burge. *Martianus Capella and the Seven Liberal Arts, vol. 2: The Marriage of Philology and Mercury.* New York, 1977.

Stahl, William Harris, with Richard Johnson and Evan L. Burge. *Martianus Capella and the Seven Liberal Arts, vol. 1: The Quadrivium of Martianus Capella: Latin Traditions in the Mathematical Sciences, 50 B.C.–A.D. 1250.* New York, 1991.

Steinacher, Roland. *Die Vandalen: Aufstieg und Fall römischer Barbaren.* Stuttgart, forthcoming.

Stichtenoth, Dietrich, ed. *Rufus Festus Avienus: Ora maritime.* Darmstadt, 1968.

Stickler, Timo. *Aëtius.* Munich, 2002.

———. "The Foederati." In *A Companion to the Roman Army*, ed. Paul Erdkamp, 495–514. Oxford, 2007.

Stoneman, Richard. "Who Are the Brahmans? Indian Lore and Cynic Doctrine in Palladius' *De Bragmanibus* and Its Models." *CQ* 44 (1994) 500–510.

Stroheker, Karl Friedrich. *Der senatorische Adel im spätantiken Gallien.* Tubingen, 1948.

Syvänne, Ilkka. *The Age of Hippotoxotai: Art of War in Roman Military Revival and Disaster (491–636).* Tampere, Finland, 2004.

Szádeczky-Kardoss, Samuel. "The Avars." In *The Cambridge History of Early Inner Asia*, ed. Dennis Sinor, 206–228. Cambridge, 1990.

Täckholm, Ulf. "Aetius and the Battle on the Catalaunian Fields." *Opuscula Romana* 7 (1969) 259–276.

Talbert, Richard, ed. *Ancient Perspectives: Maps and Their Place in Mesopotamia, Egypt, Greece, and Rome.* Chicago, 2012.

————. "Cartography and Taste in Peutinger's Roman Map." In *Space in the Roman World: Its Perception and Presentation*, ed. Richard Talbert and Kai Brodersen, 113–141. Münster, 2004.

————. "Konrad Miller, Roman Cartography, and the Lost Western End of the Peutinger Map." In *Historische Geographie der alten Welt: Grundlagen, Erträge, Perspektiven; Festgabe für Eckart Olshausen aus Anlass seiner Emeritierung*, ed. Ulrich Fellmeth, Peter Guyot, and Holger Sonnabend, 353–366. Hildesheim, 2007.

————. "Peutinger's Roman Map: The Physical Landscape Framework." In *Wahrnehmung und Erfassung geographischer Räume in der Antike*, ed. Michael Rathmann, 220–230. Mainz am Rhein, 2007.

————. "Rome's Marble Plan and Peutinger's Map: Continuity in Cartographic Design." *Althistorisch-Epigraphische Studien* (Österreichischen Gesellschaft für Archäologie) 5 (2005) 627–634.

————. *Rome's World: The Peutinger Map Reconsidered.* Cambridge, 2010.

————. "Urbs Roma to Orbis Romanus: Roman Mapmaking on a Grand Scale." In *Ancient Perspectives: Maps and Their Place in Mesopotamia, Egypt, Greece, and Rome*, ed. Richard Talbert, 163–192. Chicago, 2012.

Talbert, Richard, and Kai Brodersen, eds. *Space in the Roman World: Its Perception and Presentation.* Münster, 2004.

Talbert, Richard, and Richard W. Unger, eds. *Cartography in Antiquity and the Middle Ages: Fresh Perspectives, New Methods.* Leiden, 2008.

Tate, Georges. *Les campagnes de la Syrie du Nord du IIe au VIIe siècle: Un exemple d'expansion démographique et économique à la fin de l'antiquité.* Institut français d'archéologie du Proche Orient, Bibliothèque archéologique et historique 133. Paris, 1992.

Taylor, David G. K. "Bilingualism and Diglossia in Late Antique Syria and Mesopotamia." In *Bilingualism in Ancient Society*, ed. J. N. Adams, Mark Janse, and Simon Swain, 298–331. Oxford, 2002.

Tcherikover, Victor, and Alexander Fuks, ed. *Corpus Papyrorum Judaicarum.* 3 vols. Cambridge, Mass., 1957–1963.

Teeuwen, Mariken. "Writing between the Lines: Reflections of Scholarly Debate in a Carolingian Commentary Tradition." In *Carolingian Scholarship and Martianus Capella*, ed. M. Teeuwen and Sinead O'Sullivan, 11–34. Turnhout, 2011.

Teeuwen, Mariken, and Sinead O'Sullivan, eds. *Carolingian Scholarship and Martianus Capella.* Turnhout, 2011.

Teja, Ramón. "Il cerimoniale imperiale." In *Storia di Roma, vol. 3.1: L'età tardoantico*, ed. A. Carandini et al., 613–642. Turin, 1993.

Thébert, Yvon. "Private Life and Domestic Architecture in Roman Africa." In *A History of Private Life, vol. 1: From Pagan Rome to Byzantium*, ed. Paul Veyne, trans. Arthur Goldhammer, 313–410. Cambridge, Mass., 1987.

Thomson, Robert. "Armenian Ideology and the Persians." In *La Persia e Bisanzio*, ed. Antonio Carile, 373–389. Rome, 2004.

Thompson, Edward A. "The Foreign Policies of Theodosius II and Marcian." *Hermathena* 76 (1950) 58–75.

————. *The Huns*. Oxford, 1948; repr., 1996.

————. "The Settlement of the Barbarians in Southern Gaul." *JRS* 46 (1956) 65–75.

Thonemann, Peter. *The Maeander Valley: A Historical Geography from Antiquity to Byzantium*. Cambridge, 2011.

Toubert, Pierre. "'Scrinium' et 'Palatium'": La formation de la bureaucratie romano-pontificale aux VIII–IX siècles." In *Roma nell'alto medioevo*, 57–119. Spoleto, 2001.

Traina, Giusto. *428 AD: An Ordinary Year at the End of the Roman Empire*. Princeton, 2009.

Treadgold, Warren. *Byzantium and Its Army, 284–1081*. Stanford, 1995.

Trombley, Frank R. *Hellenic Religion and Christianization c. 370–529*. 2 vols. Leiden, 1993.

Tsafrir, Yoram, and Gideon Foerster. "Urbanism at Scythopolis-Bet Shean in the Fourth to Seventh Centuries." *DOP* 51 (1997) 85–146.

Tsuda, Takeyuki, and Brenda Baker, eds. *Migration and Disruptions: Unifying Themes in Studies of Ancient and Contemporary Migrations*. Forthcoming.

Tumolesi, Patrizia Sabbatini, Silvia Orlandi, and Marco Buonocore. *Epigrafia anfiteatrale dell'occidente romano: Alpes Maritimae, Gallia Narboneneis, Tres Galliae, Germaniae, Britannia*. Vol. 6. Rome, 2005.

Twyman, Briggs L. "Aetius and the Aristocracy." *Historia* 19 (1970) 480–503.

Ullmann, Walter. "Leo I and the Theme of Papal Primacy." *JTS* 11 (1960) 25–51.

ur-Rahman, Aman, Frantz Grenet, and Nicholas Sims-Williams. "A Hunnish Kushan-shah." *JIAA* 1 (2006) 125–131.

Urbańczyk, Przemysław. "Foreign Leaders in Early Slavic Societies." In *Integration and Authority in the Early Middle Ages*, ed. Walter Pohl and Max Diesenberger, 257–267. Vienna, 2002.

Van Dam, Raymond. "Bishops and Clerics: Numbers and Their Implications." In *Episcopal Elections in Late Antiquity*, ed. Johan Leemans, P. Van Nuffelen, S. W. J. Keough, and C. Nicolaye, 217–242. Arbeiten zur Kirchengeschichte 119. Berlin, 2011.

————. "Imagining an Eastern Roman Empire: A Riot at Antioch in 387 C.E." In *The Sculptural Environment of the Roman Near East: Reflections on Culture, Ideology, and Power*, ed. Yaron Z. Eliav, Elise A. Friedland, and Sharon C. Herbert, 451–481. Leuven, 2008.

————. *Leadership and Community in Late Antique Gaul*. Berkeley, 1985.

————. "Merovingian Gaul and the Frankish Conquests." In *The New Cambridge Medieval History*, vol. 1. ed. Paul Fouracre, 193–231. Cambridge, 2005.

————. *Rome and Constantinople: Rewriting Roman History During Late Antiquity*. Waco, Tex., 2010.

————. *The Roman Revolution of Constantine*. Cambridge, 2007.

van Donzel, Emeri, and Andrea Schmidt. *Gog and Magog in Early Eastern Christian and Islamic Sources: L Sallam's Quest for Alexander's Wall*. Leiden, 2010.

Vasiliev, A. A. "*Expositio totius mundi*: An Anonymous Geographic Treatise of the Fourth Century A.D." *Seminarium Kondakovianum* 8 (1936) 1–39.

Veilleux, Armand. *Pachomian Koinonia*. 3 vols. Kalamazoo, Mich., 1980–1982.

Vondrovec, Klaus. *The Coinage of the Iranian Huns and their Successors from Bactria to Gandhara (4th to 8th century CE)*. Vienna, forthcoming.

Walker, Joel. "From Nisibis to Xi'an: The Church of the East in Late Antique Eurasia." In *The Oxford Handbook of Late Antiquity*, ed. Scott F. Johnson, 994–1052. Oxford, 2012.

Ward-Perkins, Bryan. "Land, Labour and Settlement." In *The Cambridge Ancient History*, vol 14: *Late Antiquity: Empire and Successors, A.D. 425–600*, ed. Averil Cameron, Bryan Ward-Perkins, and Michael Whitby, 315–345. Cambridge, 2000.

———. "The Cities." In *The Cambridge Ancient History*, vol. 13: *The Late Empire, A.D. 337–425*, eds. Averil Cameron and Peter Garnsey, 371–410. Cambridge, 1998.

———. *The Fall of Rome and the End of Civilization*. Oxford, 2005.

Waszink, Jan H. *Studien zum Timaioskommentar des Calcidius*. Philosophia antiqua 12. Leiden, 1964.

———, ed. *Timaeus, a Calcidio translatus commentarioque instructus*. London, 1977.

Watt, John. "A Portrait of John Bar Aphthonia, Founder of the Monastery of Qenneshre." In *Portraits of Spiritual Authority*, ed. Jan W. Drijvers and John Watt, 155–169. Leiden, 1999.

———. "Commentary and Translation in Syriac Aristotelian Scholarship: Sergius to Baghdad." *Journal of Late Antique Religion and Culture*. Forthcoming.

Watts, Edward. *City and School in Late Antique Athens and Alexandria*. Berkeley, 2006.

———. "Doctrine, Anecdote, and Action: Reconsidering the Social History of the Last Platonists (c. 430–c. 550 CE)." *CPh* 106 (2011) 226–244.

———. *Riot in Alexandria*. Berkeley, 2010.

Weber, Ekkehard, ed. *Tabula Peutingeriana: Codex Vindobonensis 324*. Vollst. Faks.-Ausg. Im Originalformat. Graz, 1976.

Weingarten, Susan. *The Saint's Saints: Hagiography and Geography in Jerome*. Leiden, 2005.

Wells, Peter S. *The Barbarians Speak: How the Conquered Peoples Shaped Roman Europe*. Princeton, 1999.

Wessel, Hendrik. *Das Recht der Tablettes Albertini*. Berlin, 2003.

Wessel, Susan. *Cyril of Alexandria and the Nestorian Controversy: The Making of a Saint and of a Heretic*. Oxford, 2004.

———. *Leo the Great and the Spiritual Rebuilding of a Universal Rome*. Leiden, 2008.

Westerink, Leendert G. *Commentaries on the Phaedo I*. Amsterdam, 1976.

———. "Philosophy and Medicine in Late Antiquity." *Janus* 51 (1964) 169–177.

———. *Prolégomenes à la philosophie de Platon*. Paris, 1990.

Wharton, Annabel J. *Refiguring the Classical City: Dura Europos, Jerash, Jerusalem and Ravenna*. Cambridge, 1995.

Whitby, Mary. "The St Polyeuktos Epigram (AP 1.10): A Literary Perspective." In *Greek Literature in Late Antiquity*, ed. Scott F. Johnson, 159–188. Aldershot, 2006.

Whitby, Michael. "Army and Society in the Late Roman World: A Context for Decline?" In *A Companion to the Roman Army*, ed. Paul Erdkamp, 515–531. Oxford, 2007.

———. "Recruitment in Roman Armies from Justinian to Heraclius (ca. 565–615)." In *The Byzantine and Early Islamic Near East*, vol. 3: *States, Resources and Armies*, ed. Averil Cameron, 41–124. Princeton, 1995.

———. "The Army c. 420–602." In *The Cambridge Ancient History*, vol. 14: *Late Antiquity: Empire and Successors, A.D. 425–600*, ed. Averil Cameron, Bryan Ward-Perkins, and Michael Whitby, 286–314. Cambridge, 2001.

———. "The Balkans and Greece 420–602." In *The Cambridge Ancient History,* vol. 14: *Late Antiquity: Empire and Successors,* A.D. *425–600,* ed. Averil Cameron, Bryan Ward-Perkins, and Michael Whitby, 701–730. Cambridge, 2001.

Whitby, Michael, and Mary Whitby, ed. and trans. *The History of Theophylact Simocatta: An English Translation with Introduction and Notes.* Oxford, 1986.

Whittaker, C. R. *Frontiers of the Roman Empire: A Social and Economic Study.* Baltimore, 1994.

———. "Mental Maps: Seeing Like a Roman." In *Thinking Like a Lawyer: Essays on Legal History and General History for John Crook on His Eightieth Birthday,* ed. Paul McKechnie, 81–112. Leiden, 2002.

Whittaker, C. R., and Garnsey, Peter. "Rural Life in the Later Roman Empire." In *The Cambridge Ancient History, vol. 13: The Late Empire,* A.D. *337–425,* ed. Averil Cameron and Peter Garnsey, 277–311. Cambridge, 1998.

Whittow, Mark. "Geographical Survey." In *The Oxford Handbook of Byzantine Studies,* ed. Elizabeth Jeffreys, John Haldon, and Robin Cormack, 219–231. Oxford, 2008.

Wickham, Chris. *Framing the Early Middle Ages: Europe and the Mediterranean, 400–800.* Oxford, 2005.

Wightman, Edith M. *Gallia Belgica.* Berkeley, 1985.

Wilken, Robert L. *Judaism and the Early Christian Mind: A Study of Cyril of Alexandria's Exegesis and Theology.* New Haven, 1971.

Wilkinson, John. *Jerusalem Pilgrims before the Crusades.* Warminster, 2002.

———. "Jewish Holy Places and the Origins of Christian Pilgrimage." In *The Blessings of Pilgrimage,* ed. Robert G. Ousterhout, 41–53. Urbana, Ill., 1990.

Williams, Rhys H. "Politicized Evangelicalism and Secular Elites: Creating a Moral Other." In *Evangelicals and Democracy in America,* vol. 2: *Religion and Politics,* ed. Steven Brint and Jean Reith Schroedel, 143–178. New York, 2009.

Willis, James, ed. *Macrobius, Saturnalia: Apparatu critico instruxit, In Somnium Scipionis-commentarios selecta varietate lectionis.* Stuttgart, 1994.

———, ed. *Martianus Capella.* Leipzig, 1983.

Wipszycka, Ewa. "Les formes institutionelles et les formes d'activité économique du monachisme égyptien." In *Foundations of Power Foundations of Power and Conflicts of Authority in Late-Antique Monasticism: Proceedings of the International Seminar Turin, December 2–4, 2004,* ed. Alberto Camplani and Giovanni Filoramo, 109–154. Orientalia Lovaniensia Analecta. Dudley, Mass., 2007.

Woestijne, P. van de, ed. *La Descriptio orbis terrae d'Avienus.* Bruges, 1961.

———, ed. *La Périégèse de Priscien.* Bruges, 1953.

Wolfram, Herwig. *History of the Goths.* Berkeley, 1988.

———. *Intitulatio I: Lateinische Königs- und Fürstentitel bis zum Ende des 8. Jahrhunderts.* Graz, 1967.

———. *The Roman Empire and Its Germanic Peoples.* Berkeley, 1997.

Wolska-Conus, Wanda, ed. *Cosmas Indicopleustès: Topographie chrétienne.* SC 141, 159, 197. 3 vols. Paris, 1968.

———. *La Topographie Chrétienne de Cosmas Indicopleustes: Théologie et science au VIe siècle.* Paris, 1962.

Wood, Ian. "Ethnicity and the Ethnogenesis of the Burgundians." In *Typen der Ethnogenese unter besonderer Berücksichtigung der Bayern* 1, ed. Herwig Wolfram and Walter Pohl, 53–69. Vienna, 1990.

_____. "Report: The European Science Foundation's Programme on the Transformation of the Roman World and Emergence of Early Medieval Europe." *EMedE* 6 (1997) 217–227.

_____. "The Frontiers of Western Europe: Developments East of the Rhine in the Sixth Century." In *The Sixth Century. Production, Distribution and Demand*, ed. Richard Hodges and William Bowden, 231–253. Leiden, 1998.

_____. *The Merovingian Kingdom, 450–751*. London, 1994.

_____. *The Modern Origins of the Early Middle Ages*. Oxford, 2013.

Wood, Philip. "Syriac and the 'Syrians.'" In *The Oxford Handbook of Late Antiquity*, ed. Scott F. Johnson, 170–194. Oxford, 2012.

Woolf, Greg. *Becoming Roman*. Cambridge, 1999.

_____. *Tales of the Barbarians*. Chichester, 2011.

Wormald, Patrick. "The Leges Barbarorum: Law and Ethnicity in the Post-Roman West." In *Regna and Gentes: The Relationship between Late Antique and Early Medieval Peoples and Kingdoms in the Transformation of the Roman World*, ed. Hans-Werner Goetz, Jörg Jarnut, and Walter Pohl, 21–53. London, 2003.

Yarshater, Ehsan. "The Iranian National History." In *The Cambridge History of Iran*, vol. 3.1: *The Seleucid, Parthian and Sasanian Periods*, ed. W. William Bayne Fisher, Peter Avery, Gavin R. G. Hambly, and Charles Melville, 359–477. Cambridge, 1983.

Yuzbashian, K. N. *Armyanskaya Epopeya v Veka: Ot Avarairskoi Bitvi k Soglasheniyu v Nuarsake*. Moscow, 2001.

Zecchini, Giuseppe. *Aezio: L'ultima difesa dell'Occidente romano*. Rome, 1983.

Ziche, Hartmut G. "Administrer la propriéte de l'église: L'évêque comme clerc et comme entrepreneur." *AnTard* 14 (2006) 69–78.

Zuckerman, Constantin. "L'empire d'Orient et les Huns: Notes sur Priscus." *T&MBYZ* 12 (1994) 159–182.

Zürcher, Emil. *The Buddhist Conquest of China*. Leiden, 1972.

INDEX

Lightning Source UK Ltd.
Milton Keynes UK
UKHW05f0251250718
326238UK00011B/87/P